Lecture Notes in Computer Scie

Commenced Publication in 1973
Founding and Former Series Editors:
Gerhard Goos, Juris Hartmanis, and Jan van Leeuwen

Thomas Schwentick   Dan Suciu (Eds.)

Database Theory – ICDT 2007

11th International Conference
Barcelona, Spain, January 10-12, 2007
Proceedings

 Springer

Volume Editors

Thomas Schwentick
University of Dortmund
44221 Dortmund, Germany
E-mail: thomas.schwentick@udo.edu

Dan Suciu
University of Washington
Computer Science & Engineering
Seattle, WA 98195-2350, USA
E-mail: suciu@cs.washington.edu

Library of Congress Control Number: 2006938752

CR Subject Classification (1998): H.2, F.1.3, F.4.1, I.2.1, H.4, F.2, H.3

LNCS Sublibrary: SL 3 – Information Systems and Application, incl. Internet/Web and HCI

ISSN   0302-9743
ISBN-10   3-540-69269-X Springer Berlin Heidelberg New York
ISBN-13   978-3-540-69269-0 Springer Berlin Heidelberg New York

Springer is a part of Springer Science+Business Media

springer.com

© Springer-Verlag Berlin Heidelberg 2006
Printed in Germany

Typesetting: Camera-ready by author, data conversion by Scientific Publishing Services, Chennai, India
Printed on acid-free paper   SPIN: 11965893   06/3142   5 4 3 2 1 0

Preface

This volume collects the papers presented at the 11th International Conference on Database Theory, ICDT 2007, held during January 10–12, 2007, in Barcelona, Spain.

ICDT (http://alpha.luc.ac.be/~lucp1080/icdt/) now has a long tradition of international conferences, providing a biennial scientific forum for the communication of high-quality and innovative research results on theoretical aspects of all forms of data management systems and database technology. The conference usually takes place in Europe, and previous conferences were held in Rome (1986), Bruges (1988), Paris (1990), Berlin (1992), Prague (1995), Delphi (1997), Jerusalem (1999), London (2001), Siena (2003) and Edinburgh (2005). ICDT has merged with the Symposium on Mathematical Fundamentals of Database Systems (MFDBS), initiated in Dresden in 1987, and continued in Visegrad in 1989 and Rostock in 1991.

This year ICDT received 111 paper submissions (after 138 titles and abstracts were first announced). Two of the papers were later withdrawn and one was rejected as it was 24 pages long (instead of 15). From the remaining 108 submissions, the ICDT Program Committee selected 25 papers for presentation at the conference. Most of these papers were "extended abstracts" and preliminary reports on work in progress. It is anticipated that most of these papers will appear in a more polished form in scientific journals. The proceedings also contain three invited papers by Jan Chomicki, Cynthia Dwork, and Laura Haas. The Best Newcomer Award, for the best submission written solely by authors who had never published in earlier ICDT proceedings, was given by the Program Committee to Piotr Wieczorek for his paper "Complexity of Typechecking XML Views of Relational Databases."

We would like to thank a number of people who made ICDT 2007 a successful event. First of all, the authors who submitted papers, the members of the Program Committee for their efforts in reviewing and selecting the papers, the external referees for their help, and, importantly, Andrei Voronkov for supplying his marvelous conference management system EasyChair. A great thanks is owed to Albert Atserias and his Organizing Committee for hosting the conference and for running the conference website. We are also deeply indebted to Wim Martens for preparing the proceedings. Last but not least, we are very grateful to the sponsors, Departament d'Universitats Recerca i Societat de la Informació de la Generalitat de Catalunya; Universitat Politècnica de Catalunya; and Grup de recerca ALBCOM.

January 2007   Thomas Schwentick and Dan Suciu

Organization

Program Co-chairs

Thomas Schwentick   University of Dortmund
Dan Suciu   University of Washington

Program Committee

Marcelo Arenas	PUC Chile
Albert Atserias	UPC Barcelona
Michael Benedikt	Bell Laboratories
Diego Calvanese	Free University of Bozen-Bolzano
Alin Deutsch	UC San Diego
Amr El Abbadi	UC Santa Barbara
Wenfei Fan	University of Edinburgh
Floris Geerts	University of Edinburgh
Carlos Hurtado	Universidad de Chile
Gyula O.H. Katona	Hungarian Academy of Sciences
Hans-Joachim Klein	Christian Albrechts University of Kiel
Phokion Kolaitis	IBM Almaden
Gabriel Kuper	University of Trento
Kim S. Larsen	University of Southern Denmark
Chen Li	UC Irvine
Maarten Marx	University of Amsterdam
Kobbi Nissim	Ben Gurion University
Stijn Vansummeren	Hasselt University
Gottfried Vossen	University of Münster

Local Organization

Albert Atserias (Co-chair)
Jaume Baixeries
Jos Luis Balczar (Co-chair)
Ricard Gavald

External Reviewers

Loredana Afanasiev	Shyam Antony	Leo Bertossi
Foto Afrati	Ziv Bar-Yosef	Leopoldo Bertossi
Rasmus Andersen	Pablo Barcelo	Henrik Björklund

Joan Boyar
Loreto Bravo
Andrea Calì
Rada Chirkova
Giovanni Conforti
Laszlo Csirmaz
René dePont Christensen
Mayur Deshpande
Rolf Fagerberg
Ronald Fagin
Lene Favrholdt
Bernd Freisleben
Hannes Frey
Ariel Fuxman
Sorabh Gandhi
Giuseppe De Giacomo
Torsten Grust
Claudio Gutierrez
Stephan Hagemann
Stephen Hegner
Bijit Hore
Carlos Hurtado
Dmitri V. Kalashnikov
Attila Kiss
Christoph Koch
Bart Kuijpers

Martha Larson
Georg Lausen
Iosif Lazaridis
Jens Lechtenboerger
Domenico Lembo
Maurizio Lenzerini
Carolin Letz
Chen Li
Leonid Libkin
Andrei Lopatenko
Carsten Lutz
Jim Lynch
Wim Martens
Davide Martinenghi
Maarten Marx
Klaus Meer
Ahmed Metwally
Gilad Mishne
Prasenjit Mitra
Frank Neven
Kobbi Nissim
Werner Nutt
Dan Olteanu
Rodrigo Paredes
Stacy Patterson
Vassia Pavlaki

Jorge Perez
Benny Pinkas
Riccardo Rosati
Arsany Sawires
Nicole Schweikardt
Luc Segoufin
Houtan Shirani-Mehr
Helmut Seidl
Michal Shmueli-Scheuer
Prasad Sriram
Utkarsh Srivastava
Jianwen Su
Dan Suciu
Wang-Chiew Tan
Balder ten Cate
Sergio Tessaris
Alejandro Vaisman
Rares Vernica
Thomas Wilke
Marcel Worring
Ping Wu
Dawit Yimam Seid
Xingbo Yu
Marcin Zukowski

Sponsoring Institutions

Departament d'Universitats Recerca i Societat de la Informació de la Generalitat de Catalunya

Universitat Politècnica de Catalunya

Grup de recerca ALBCOM

Table of Contents

Incompleteness, Inconsistency, and Uncertainty

XML Schemas and Typechecking

Stream Processing and Sequential Query Processing

Ranking

XML Update and Query

Query Containment

Consistent Query Answering: Five Easy Pieces*

Jan Chomicki

Dept. of Computer Science and Engineering
University at Buffalo
Buffalo, NY 14260-2000
chomicki@cse.buffalo.edu

Abstract. Consistent query answering (CQA) is an approach to querying inconsistent databases without repairing them first. This invited talk introduces the basics of CQA, and discusses selected issues in this area. The talk concludes with a summary of other relevant work and an outline of potential future research topics.

1   Introduction

The notion of *inconsistency* has been extensively studied in many contexts. In classical logic, an inconsistent set of formulas implies every formula (*triviality*). In databases, a database instance is inconsistent if it does not satisfy integrity constraints (*constraint violation*). Those two kinds of inconsistency are closely related: an inconsistent database instance, together with the integrity constraints, may be represented as an inconsistent set of formulas. However, triviality is not a problem in the database context because the semantics of query answers does not take integrity constraints into account.

Nowadays more and more database applications have to rely on multiple, often autonomous sources of data. Even if the sources are separately consistent, inconsistency may arise when they are integrated together. For example, different data sources may record different salaries or addresses of the same employee. At the same time, the application may require that the integrated, global database contain a single, correct salary or address. Similarly, different sensors may register inconsistent readings of the same quantity that need to be resolved.

In order to deal with inconsistency in a flexible manner, database research and practice have developed different approaches that we will illustrate using a simple example.

Example 1. Consider a database schema consisting of two unary relations P_1 and P_2, and the denial integrity constraint $\forall x.\ (\neg P_1(x) \lor \neg P_2(x))$. Assume a database instance consists of the following facts: $\{P_1(a), P_1(b), P_2(a)\}$. Under *prevention* (usual constraint enforcement), such instance could not arise: only one of $P_1(a)$ and $P_2(a)$ could be inserted into the database. Under *ignorance* (constraint non-enforcement), no distinction is made between $P_1(a)$ and $P_1(b)$,

---

* Research supported by NSF grant IIS-0119186.

T. Schwentick and D. Suciu (Eds.): ICDT 2007, LNCS 4353, pp. 1–17, 2007.

despite that the latter, not being involved in a constraint violation, appears to represent more reliable information. Under *isolation* [18], both $P_1(a)$ and $P_2(a)$ are dropped (or ignored in query answering). Under *weakening* [6,49], $P_1(a)$ and $P_2(a)$ are replaced by $P_1(a) \lor P_2(a)$. Allowing *exceptions* [15] means that the constraint is weakened to $\forall x. (\neg P_1(x) \lor \neg P_2(x) \lor x = a)$, but query answering is not affected.

A seperate class of responses to inconsistency is based on the notion of *repair*: a consistent instance minimally different from the original one, in this case $\{P_1(a), P_1(b)\}$ or $\{P_2(a), P_1(b)\}$. Such repairs can be *materialized* [30] or *virtual*. *Virtual repairing*, which is usually called *consistent query answering* [3], does not change the database but rather returns query answers true in all repairs (*consistent* query answers). So the query asking for all such consistent x that $P_1(x)$ is true, returns only $x = b$.

Example 2. Consider the following instance of a relation *Location*, which records the current location of employees. Such a relation may be built from active-badge sensor readings, employee calendars, and other data sources.

Name	Campus	Building
Mary	North	Bell
Mary	North	Knox
John	South	Hayes

and the functional dependency *Name → Campus Building*. Note that for both employees the database contains a single campus, while two different buildings are recorded for Mary, violating the functional dependency.

There are two (minimal) repairs: one is obtained by removing the first tuple, the other by removing the second tuple. (Removing more tuples violates repair minimality.) The consistent answer to the query Q_1:

```
SELECT * FROM Location
```

is just the tuple (John,South,Hayes), because neither of the first two tuples appears in the result of the query in both repairs. On the other hand, the query Q_2:

```
SELECT Name, Campus FROM Location
```

has two consistent answers: (Mary,North) and (John,South), because Q_2 returns those two tuples in both repairs. Using Q_2 the user can extract reliable information about the *campus* location of both employees, despite the fact that the information about the *building* where Mary is located is inconsistent.

Consistent query answering was first proposed by Arenas et al. [3]. That paper was followed by numerous further papers that explored several different dimensions of consistent query answering:

- different notions of repair minimality (leading to different semantics for consistent query answers);
- different classes of queries and integrity constraints;
- different methods of computing consistent query answers.

What follows is a collection of short essays about consistent query answering (CQA). They address the following topics: the basic concepts and results of Arenas et al. [3] (Section 2), computational complexity of CQA (Section 3), referential integrity (Section 4), and improving the informativeness of CQA in the presence of aggregation or probabilistic information (Section 5). The last essay (Section 6) briefly summarizes other research on CQA and outlines some directions for future work. The essay topics were chosen to introduce the central concepts of CQA and illustrate the breadth of the area. By no means is this article a comprehensive survey of CQA research; such surveys are already available elsewhere [8,11,25].

2   The Basics

We use the standard setting of relational databases. We assume the existence of a database schema R, which is a finite set of relation names and the associated arities. Database instances are mappings from the database schema to finite sets of tuples of the appropriate arity. We also assume that relation columns can be labelled by attributes and typed by associating with them one of the two domains: uninterpreted constants or rational numbers.

Given a database schema R and the built-in predicates over the numeric domain $(=, \neq, <, >, \leq, \geq)$, we define the *first-order language* $\mathcal{L}_R$ in the standard way. Database instances can be viewed as first-order structures over $\mathcal{L}_R$. The built-in predicates have infinite, fixed extensions.

2.1   Integrity Constraints

Integrity constraints are closed first-order $\mathcal{L}_R$-formulas. In the sequel we will denote: relation symbols by $P, P_1, \ldots, P_m$, atomic formulas by $A_1, \ldots, A_n$, tuples of variables and constants by $\bar{t}, \bar{x}, \ldots$, and quantifier-free formulas referring to built-in predicates by φ.

In this paper we consider the following basic classes of integrity constraints:

1. *Universal integrity constraints*: $\forall^*. A_1 \vee \cdots \vee A_n \vee \neg A_{n+1} \vee \cdots \vee \neg A_m \vee \varphi$.
2. *Denial constraints*: $\forall^*. \neg A_1 \vee \cdots \vee \neg A_m \vee \varphi$.
3. *Binary constraints*: universal constraints with at most two occurrences of database literals.
4. *Functional dependencies (FDs)*: $\forall \bar{x}, \bar{y}, \bar{z}, \bar{y}', \bar{z}'. (\neg P(\bar{x}, \bar{y}, \bar{z}) \vee \neg P(\bar{x}, \bar{y}', \bar{z}') \vee \bar{y} = \bar{y}')$. A more familiar formulation of the above FD is $X \to Y$ where X is

the set of attributes of P corresponding to $\bar{x}$ and Y the set of attributes of P corresponding to $\bar{y}$ (and $\bar{y}'$).

5. *Referential integrity constraints*, known as *inclusion dependencies (INDs)*: $\forall \bar{x}, \bar{y}.\, \exists \bar{z}.\, (\neg P_2(\bar{x}, \bar{y}) \lor P_1(\bar{y}, \bar{z}))$. Again, this is often written as $P_2[Y_2] \subseteq P_1[Y_1]$ where Y_1 (resp. Y_2) is the set of attributes of P_1 (resp. P_2) corresponding to $\bar{y}$.

Given a set of FDs and INDs IC and a relation P_1 with attributes U, a *key* of P_1 is a minimal set of attributes X of P_1 such that IC entails the FD $X \to U$. In that case, we say that each FD $X \to Y \in IC$ is a *key* dependency and each IND $P_2[Y] \subseteq P_1[X] \in IC$ is a *foreign key constraint*. If, additionally, X is the only key of P_1, then both kinds of dependencies are termed *primary*.

Definition 1. *Given an instance I of a database schema R and a set of integrity constraints IC, we say that I is* consistent *if $I \models IC$ in the standard model-theoretic sense;* inconsistent *otherwise.*

Queries are formulas over the same language $\mathcal{L}_R$ as the integrity constraints. *Conjunctive queries* [23,1] are queries of the form $\exists^*.\, A_1 \land \cdots \land A_n \land \varphi$ where φ is a conjunction of built-in atomic formulas.

Definition 2. *A tuple $\bar{t}$ is an* answer *to a query $Q(\bar{x})$ in an instance I iff $I \models Q(\bar{t})$.*

2.2   Repairs and Consistent Query Answers

We introduce now the framework of Arenas et al. [3]. It is based on two fundamental notions: *repair* and *consistent query answer*. The symmetric difference Δ is used to capture the distance between two instances I and I': $\Delta(I, I') = (I - I') \cup (I' - I)$.[1]

We assume that we are dealing with *satisfiable* sets of integrity constraints.

Definition 3. *Given a set of integrity constraints IC and database instances I and I', we say that I' is a* repair *of I w.r.t. IC if $I' \models IC$ and there is no instance I'' such that $I'' \models IC$ and $\Delta(I, I'') \subset \Delta(I, I')$.*

We denote by $Repairs_{IC}(I)$ the set of repairs of I w.r.t. IC. This set is nonempty for satisfiable sets of constraints.

Given a query $Q(\bar{x})$ to a database instance I, we want as *consistent* answers those result tuples that are unaffected by the violations of IC, even when I violates IC.

Definition 4. *A tuple $\bar{t}$ is a* consistent answer *to a query $Q(\bar{x})$ in a database instance I w.r.t. a set of integrity constraints IC iff $\bar{t}$ is an answer to the query $Q(\bar{x})$ in every repair I' of I w.r.t. IC. We can define* true *being a consistent answer to a Boolean query in a similar way.*

---

[1] The difference is defined component-wise for every relation symbol in the schema.

Note: If the set of integrity constraints IC is clear from the context, we omit it for simplicity.

The notion of consistent query answer corresponds to the notion of *certain* answer, developed in the context of incomplete databases by Lipski and Imieliński [45,42], because repairs can be viewed as *possible worlds*. In some cases, as in Example 1, one can represent the set of repairs w.r.t FDs as a disjunctive database or a table with OR-objects [43]: disjunctive information is used to model resolved conflicts. The correspondence in the other direction breaks down, however, already in very simple cases [5].

2.3   Query Rewriting

Arenas et al. [3] propose a method to compute consistent query answers based on *query rewriting*. Given a set of integrity constraints IC, a query Q is rewritten into a query Q^{IC} such that for every instance I the set of answers to Q^{IC} in I is equal to the set of consistent answers to Q in I. Typically, we expect Q and Q^{IC} to belong to the same class of queries, for example first-order queries or SQL. In such a case, the computation of consistent query answers can be done using the same query engine.

The method proposed in [3] is relatively simple and draws on earlier work in semantic query optimization [22]. The rewriting applies to and produces first-order queries. When a literal in the query can be resolved with an integrity constraint the resolvent forms a *residue*. All such residues are then conjoined with the literal to form its expanded version. If a literal that has been expanded appears in a residue, the residue has to be further expanded until no more changes occur. For denial constraints, however, only a single expansion is necessary.

Example 3. Consider Example 2, the FD $f_1 : Name \rightarrow Building$ and the query $Location(x, y, z)$. The rewritten query Q^{f_1}:

$$Q^{f_1} \equiv Location(x, y, z) \land \forall y', z'. \left(Location(x, y', z') \Rightarrow z = z' \right).$$

Clearly, the rewritten query can be formulated in SQL.

2.4   Limitations

The notion of repair (Definition 3) has been revisited many times since the publication of [3]. For instance, one can minimize the *cardinality* of the set of changes [50], as opposed to minimizing the *set* of changes under set inclusion, as in Definition 3. Moreover, attribute-based changes were considered in [14,58,59] (this issue is discussed further in Section 6). Surprisingly, the notion of consistent query answer (Definition 4) has been almost universally adopted in the recent literature of the subject (but see Section 5).

The scope of the query rewriting method detailed above (and further developed in [21]) is quite limited. It applies to first-order queries without disjunction or quantification, and binary universal integrity constraints. So, for example, the query Q_2 from Example 2 cannot be handled. A rewriting method that can handle a rather large subset of conjunctive queries at the price of limiting integrity constraints to primary key FDs was recently proposed by Fuxman and Miller [38]. This method, which can handle Q_2 from Example 2, is discussed in more detail in the next section. Adding quantification *and* disjunction has proved to be much harder: the approach of [38] has been extended in that direction by Lembo et al. [47]. The paper [38] was further generalized to include *exclusion dependencies* by Grieco et al. [41].

3   Computational Complexity

We note first that already in the presence of a single *primary key dependency* there are inconsistent relation instances with exponentially many repairs [5]. Thus Definition 4 does not yield a practical method for computing consistent query answers. Below, we show a number of cases in which the latter problem can be solved in polynomial time, and later we characterize the intractable cases in detail. We limit ourselves to *universal* constraints here; inclusion dependencies are discussed in Section 4. We consider two basic decision problems:

- *repair checking*: Is a database instance a repair of another instance w.r.t. the integrity constraints?
- *consistent query answering (CQA)*: Is a tuple a consistent query answer to a query in a database instance w.r.t. the integrity constraints?

The motivation to study repair checking, in addition to CQA, comes from *data cleaning* where a single, consistent database instance needs to be constructed. The repair-checking algorithms can typically be adapted to yield such an instance.

We adopt here the *data complexity* assumption [1,46,57], which measures the complexity of the problem as a function of the number of tuples in a database instance. The query and the integrity constraints are considered fixed.

3.1   Tractable Cases

It is easy to see that for denial constraints repair checking can be done in polynomial time: check whether a potential repair I' is a subset of the database instance I and satisfies the integrity constraints, and whether adding any other tuple from $I - I'$ to I' leads to a constraint violation.

Query rewriting approaches that produce first-order queries provide polynomial-time algorithms for CQA: rewrite the query and evaluate the rewritten query on the original database. Note that the rewriting of the query is done independently of the database instance, and therefore does not affect data complexity.

However, the original query rewriting approach of [3] was applicable only to very restricted classes of queries and constraints (see the previous section).

Recently, that approach was generalized by Fuxman and Miller [38] to allow restricted existential quantification in queries in the context of primary key FDs. The rewriting method of [38] applies to a class of conjunctive queries C_{forest}, defined using the notion of the join graph of a query. The vertices of the join graph are the query literals; an edge runs from a literal A_i to a different literal A_j if there is an existentially-quantified variable which occurs in a nonkey attribute of A_i and any attribute of A_j. The class C_{forest} consists of those conjunctive queries that have a join graph which is a forest, and which have no repeated relation symbols or built-in predicate symbols.

Example 4. Consider the following query Q:

$$Q \equiv \exists x, y, z. P_1(x, y) \wedge P_2(y, z).$$

Assume that the first attributes of both P_1 and P_2 are primary keys. Then Q expresses a *foreign-key*[2] join and belongs to C_{forest}. Then the rewritten query Q' is:

$$Q' \equiv \exists x, y, z. P_1(x, y) \wedge P_2(y, z) \wedge \forall y'. \big(P_1(x, y') \Rightarrow \exists z'. P_2(y', z') \big).$$

Another way to obtain tractability is through the notion of *conflict graph*[5,26]. The vertices of the conflict graph are the tuples in the database; an edge connects two vertices if they violate together an integrity constraint (we assume binary constraints for the moment). A conflict graph is a compact, polynomial-size representation of the set of all repairs of the database: the repairs correspond to maximal independent sets of the graph. The conflict graph can be used to compute consistent answers to queries. Chomicki and Marcinkowski [26] describe a polynomial-time algorithm for CQA that is applicable to quantifier-free queries and denial integrity constraints[3]. The algorithm enumerates repairs, trying to show that a tuple is not a consistent answer. The crucial observation is that only fixed-size fragments of repairs need to be considered.

3.2   Intractable Cases

Computational complexity analysis helps to delineate the boundary between the tractable and the intractable cases. We start the discussion of the relevant complexity results by recalling one of the fundamental results in this area.

Theorem 1. *For conjunctive queries and primary key FDs, CQA is co-NP-complete.*

---

[2] Note that while the variable y plays here the role of a foreign key, the corresponding *foreign-key constraint* is not taken into account in CQA. We discuss such constraints in Section 4.

[3] To deal with denial constraints, conflict graphs are generalized to *conflict hypergraphs*.

Proof. We describe here the proof of [26] because it is the simplest and was – to our knowledge – chronologically the first. A different proof appears in [19].

The proof is by reduction from MONOTONE 3-SAT. Let $\beta = \phi_1 \wedge \ldots \phi_m \wedge \psi_{m+1} \ldots \wedge \psi_l$ be a conjunction of propositional clauses, such that all occurrences of variables in ϕ_i are positive and all occurrences of variables in ψ_i are negative. To encode such formulas, we use two binary relation schemas P_1 and P_2, each with two attributes of which the first is the key. We build a database instance I such that $I(P_1)$ contains the tuple (i, p) if the variable p occurs in the clause ϕ_i, and $I(P_2)$ contains the tuple (i, p) if the variable p occurs in the clause ψ_i. The query $Q \equiv \exists x, y, z. \big(P_1(x, y) \wedge P_2(z, y)\big)$. Now there is an assignment which satisfies β iff there exists a repair of I in which Q is false.

In the above proof, the query Q does not belong to C_{forest} because it contains a join between nonkey attributes, which produces a cycle in the join graph. In the full version of [38], Fuxman and Miller show that several other natural relaxations of the C_{forest} property also lead to co-NP-completeness of CQA. For a class C^* of conjunctive queries, they prove a *dichotomy* result: CQA for each query in C^* is in P iff the join graph of the query does not contain a cycle.

For universal constraints, repair checking is co-NP-complete and CQA Π_2^p-complete in most cases, as recently shown by Staworko et al. [53]. The computational complexity of consistent query answering is summarized in Figure 1. For the purpose of exposition, we refer there to subsets of relational algebra instead of sublanguages of first-order logic. For each result, we cite the primary source, except for those that follow from the definitions or other results.

	Primary keys	Arbirary keys	Denial	Universal
$\sigma, \times, -$	P	P[3]	P	Π_2^p-complete[53] P(binary)[3]
$\sigma, \times, -, \cup$	P	P	P[26]	Π_2^p-complete
σ, π	P[26]	co-NPC[26]	co-NPC	Π_2^p-complete[53]
$\sigma, \pi, \times$	co-NPC[26] P(C_{forest})[38]	co-NPC	co-NPC	Π_2^p-complete
$\sigma, \pi, \times, -, \cup$	co-NPC	co-NPC	co-NPC	Π_2^p-complete

Fig. 1. Complexity of CQA: relational algebra

Proving co-NP-completeness of CQA for a class of first-order queries C is sufficient to show that unless P=NP there is no query rewriting method that (a) returns first-order queries, and (b) is applicable to all queries in C.

4   Referential Integrity Constraints

For denial constraints, integrity violations can only be removed by *deleting* tuples, so all the repairs are subsets of the given database instance. The picture changes when we consider general universal or referential integrity constraints. Violations of such constraints can also be removed by *adding* tuples.

Example 5. Consider a database schema with two relations $P_1(AB)$ and $P_2(C)$, the inclusion dependency $P_1[B] \subseteq P_2[C]$, and the key dependency $A \rightarrow B$. Consider I' such that $I'(P_1) = \{(a, b), (a, c)\}$ and $I'(P_2) = \{b\}$. Then we have the following repairs:

$$I'_1(P_1) = \{(a, b)\}, I'_1(P_2) = \{b\}$$
$$I'_2(P_1) = \{(a, c)\}, I'_2(P_2) = \{b, c\}$$

Allowing repairs constructed using insertions makes sense if the information in the database may be incomplete[4]. The latter is common in data integration applications where the data is pulled from multiple sources, typically without any guarantees on its completeness. On the other hand, if we know that the data in the database is complete but possibly incorrect, as in data warehousing applications, it is natural to consider only repairs constructed using deletions. Current language standards like SQL:1999 [51] allow only deletions in their repertoire of referential integrity actions.

The above considerations have lead to the definition of two new, more restricted classes of repairs:

 - *D-repairs*, constructed using a minimal set of deletions [26] (I'_1 in Example 5),
 - *I-repairs*, constructed using a minimal set of deletions and some, not necessarily minimal set of insertions [19] (in Example 5, this includes I'_1 and I'_2, as well as any consistent supersets of those).

Each of those classes of repairs leads to a different notion of consistent query answer. We consider first D-repairs. Note the following properties of this class of repairs:

1. Every database instance has a single D-repair w.r.t. any set of INDs, which is obtained by deleting the tuples violating the constraints.
2. Given a set of primary key FDs F and a set of foreign-key constraints IN, every repair of a database instance w.r.t. $F \cup IN$ may be obtained as a repair of the single D-repair of the instance w.r.t. IN (this is because repairing w.r.t. F does not lead to any new violations of IN).

---

[4] *Incompleteness* here does not mean that the database contains *indefinite information* in the form of nulls or disjunctions [56]. Rather, it means that the *Open World Assumption* is adopted, i.e., the facts missing from the database are not assumed to be false.

The second property implies that one can adapt any polynomial-time method for CQA w.r.t. primary key constraints, for example [38], to compute consistent query answers w.r.t. any set of primary key and foreign-key constraints in polynomial time. However, if one goes beyond this simple setting, the interactions between FDs and INDs get complex, and both repair checking and CQA become quickly intractable [26]. Ultimately, for arbitrary FDs and INDs repair checking is co-NP-complete and CQA Π_2^P-complete. (All of those results hold under the definition of CQA in which D-repairs are substituted for repairs.)

We consider now I-repairs. Calì et al. [19] show that for such repairs in the presence of primary key FDs and arbitrary INDs CQA becomes undecidable. This is shown by a reduction from the implication problem for those constraints which is known to be undecidable [1]. Calì et al. [19] define a class of INDs, called *non-key-conflicting*, for which the interaction between FDs and INDs is limited and consequently CQA is co-NP-complete. Technically, they relate CQA to *conjunctive query containment* under integrity constraints [44]. Calì et al. [19] also analyze repairs (in the sense of Definition 3) in the same setting, obtaining undecidability of CQA in the general case and Π_2^P-completeness of CQA for non-key-conflicting INDs.

5   More Informative Consistent Query Answers

In the previous section we considered varying the notion of repair. Here we keep the original notion of repair but slightly adjust the notion of consistent query answer. The motivation comes from aggregate queries and probabilistic databases.

Example 6. Consider the following instance of the relation $Emp(Name, Salary)$ with the key $Name$:

Name	Salary
John	50K
John	60K
Mary	55K

Now the query

```
SELECT MAX(Salary) FROM Emp
```

returns 55K in one repair and 60K in the the other. So there is no consistent answer in the sense of Definition 4.

To provide more informative query answers to aggregation queries, Arenas et al. [4] propose to return the *minimal interval* containing the set of the values of the aggregate function obtained in some repair. In Example 6, the interval [55K,60K] is returned. The paper [4] contains a detailed analysis of the data

	$\|F\| = 1$	$\|F\| \geq 2$
MIN(A),MAX(A),SUM(A),AVG(A),COUNT(*)	P	NP-complete
COUNT(A)	NP-complete	NP-complete

Fig. 2. Complexity of scalar aggregation queries

complexity of computing interval answers in the presence of FDs, and showed the influence of the cardinality $|F|$ of the given set of FDs F. The results are summarized in Figure 2.

The tractable cases are typically obtained by query rewriting. The exception is AVG(A), which is computed by an iterative algorithm.

Example 7. The query

```
SELECT MAX(Salary) FROM Emp
```

is rewritten as

```
SELECT SUM(P.MinS), SUM(P.MaxS)
FROM (SELECT MIN(Salary) AS MinS, MAX(Salary) AS MaxS
      FROM Emp GROUP BY Name) P
```

Fuxman and Miller [37] develop a comprehensive framework for rewriting SQL queries with aggregation by combining the methods of [38] and [4]. The framework also allows grouping constructs in queries.

The notion of repair and consistent query answer has been generalized to the context of *probabilistic databases* by Andritsos et al. [2]. In such databases probabilities are associated with individual tuples. Assume the presence of a primary key FD. Then the probabilities of the conflicting tuples sum up to one. A repair also has an associated probability, which is the product of the probabilities of the tuples belonging to the repair. There is a natural way to compute the probability of an answer: sum up the probabilities of the repairs in which the answer appears in the query result. Such answers, with the associated probabilities, are called *clean answers* [2]. Clearly, consistent answers are those clean answers that have probability one. Andritsos et al. [2] present a way to compute clean answers through query rewriting. Their method applies to a class of conjunctive queries closely related to C_{forest} (see Section 3).

Example 8. Figure 3a contains a probabilistic version of the relation *Emp* with the key *Name*. The clean answers to the query

```
SELECT Name FROM Emp WHERE Salary > 52K
```

are shown in Figure 3b. The rewritten query that computes the clean answers is

```
SELECT Name, SUM(Probability) FROM Emp WHERE Salary > 52K
GROUP BY Name
```

Name	Salary	Probability
John	50K	0.6
John	60K	0.4
Mary	55K	1

(a)

Name	Probability
John	0.4
Mary	1

(b)

Fig. 3. (a) *Emp* with probabilities; (b) Clean answers

6   Other and Future Work

A major line of work on CQA involves capturing repairs as *answer sets* of logic programs with negation and disjunction [4,39]. Such approaches are quite general, being able to handle arbitrary universal constraints and first-order queries. Determining whether an atom is a member of all answer sets of such a logic program is Π_2^p-complete [28]. Therefore, a direct implementation of CQA using a disjunctive logic programming system like dlv [48] or smodels [52] is practical only for very small databases. Recently, special optimization techniques in this area have been developed by Eiter et al. [29]. Answer-set-based techniques have been particularly effective in addressing the semantic problems of data integration, where the main issue is how to reconcile repairing the violations of integrity constraints with satisfying the rules describing the mappings between different databases. This issue was addressed in the context of LAV-mappings by Bravo and Bertossi [16,9], and in the context of peer-to-peer mappings by Calvanese et al. [20].

It is natural to consider *preferences* or *priorities* in repairing. For example, if a database violates an FD because of conflicting data coming from different sources such conflicts may be resolved if the sources have different reliability. Similarly, new information may be preferred to old information. In a data cleaning process, preferences are typically encoded using conflict resolution rules. In CQA, more declarative approaches have been pursued. Staworko et al. [55] consider priority relations defined on atoms and discuss various ways in which such relations could be lifted to the level of repairs, yielding *preferred repairs*. Typically, optimization with respect to an additional criterion, represented by the priority, increases the complexity of repair checking and CQA. Flesca et al. [40] define preferred repairs directly, using a numeric utility function.

Repairs in the sense of Definition 3 have been criticised as *too coarse-grained*: deleting a tuple to remove an integrity violation potentially eliminates useful information in that tuple. More fine-grained methods seek to define repairs by minimizing *attribute modifications* [10,14,58]. In particular, Bertossi et al. [10] and Bohannon et al. [14] use various notions of numerical distance between tuples. In both cases the existence of a repair within a given distance of the original database instance turns out to be NP-complete. To achieve tractability, Bertossi et al. [10] propose approximation, and Bohannon et al. [14], heuristics.

Wijsen [59] has recently shown how to combine tuple- and attribute-based repairs in a single framework. To achieve the effect of attribute-based repairing, his approach decomposes an inconsistent relation using a lossless-join decomposition and subsequently joins the obtained projections [5]. PJ-repairs are defined to be the repairs (in the sense of Definition 3) of the resulting relation. Thus, query evaluation methods of Section 3 can be readily applied in that framework.

Another direction is *repairs with nulls*. A repair with nulls can represent a *set* of ground repairs. This is particularly useful when dealing with INDs.

Example 9. Consider a slightly modified database schema from Example 5, consisting now of two relations $P_1(AB)$ and $P_2(CD)$, and an inclusion dependency $P_1[B] \subseteq P_2[C]$. Assume an instance I is as follows: $I(P_1) = \{(a,b)\}$ and $I(P_2) = \emptyset$. This instance has a repair I_1 where $I_1(P_1) = \emptyset, I_1(P_2) = \emptyset$. However, there are also infinitely many repairs I' of the form $I'(P_1) = \{(a,b)\}, I'(P_2) = \{b,\alpha\}$ where α is a constant. All such repairs can be represented as a single repair I_{null} where $I_{null}(P_1) = \{(a,b)\}, I_{null}(P_2) = \{(b,null)\}$

Notice that nulls can also be used to represent a resolved version of an inconsistency associated with an FD, as in Example 2: there would be a single repair consisting of the tuples (Mary,North,null) and (John,South,Hayes). Since the formal semantics of nulls [56] is based on possible worlds that are closely related to repairs, it should be feasible to incorporate repairs with nulls into the CQA framework, using a common semantic basis. This has not been done yet, however. Bravo and Bertossi [17] take a different, more syntactic approach that simulates *SQL nulls* (whose semantic problems are well known [56]) within a logic programming approach to repair specification.

For the CQA framework to be applicable to XML databases, the basic notions of repair and consistent query answer need to be redefined. This is done for DTDs only in [54] and DTDs with functional dependencies in [34]. Staworko et al. [54] propose to base repair minimality on *tree edit distance* [13], while Flesca et al. [34] use an approach more akin to that of [3]. More expressive integrity constraint languages for XML, for example [32], should be considered next.

There are now several prototype CQA systems: CONQUER [37] (based on query rewriting), HIPPO [27] (based on conflict hypergraphs), and INFOMIX [29] (based on answer set programming). Those systems are capable of handling databases with several million tuples.

Considering the number of researchers, projects, and publications involved, consistent query answering seems to be enjoying significant interest as a research topic. Below we identify some of the current and future challenges in this area (in addition to those mentioned earlier):

Coping with semantic heterogeneity. The number of different repair semantics proposed so far, particularly when one considers variations involving nulls and priorities, may overwhelm a potential user. The ways need to be found to provide guidance which semantics are appropriate for specific applications. Also, methods

---

[5] For a consistent relation such transformation is an identity but for an inconsistent one this is usually not the case.

that unify various approaches within a single framework, as for example [59], should be studied.

Integration with other tools. Ultimately, repairing and CQA should become tools in data integration toolboxes. We have already mentioned incorporating CQA in several data integration frameworks [16,9,20] but still more work is needed in the context of data exchange [31]. Also, integration of CQA with data cleaning seems to be in order. CQA is unnecessarily conservative in the presence of data errors and duplicates. Moreover, integrity violations in an integrated database are often due to structural or semantic discrepancies between the sources, and thus the quality of schema matching/mapping clearly influences the usefulness of CQA [24]. In a broader sense, CQA fits within the framework of *data quality management* [7].

Applications. Very few real-life applications of repairing and consistent query answering have been reported so far. Franconi et al. [36] summarize an application of attribute-based repairing in the area of census data. Flesca et al. [35,33] describe a tool for acquiring and repairing balance-sheet data. That work is notable for its use of *aggregation constraints*. Generally, it seems that most potential applications find repairing more useful than CQA. In many cases, the data in the database is relatively *static*, so it makes sense to invest a considerable effort into its cleaning and repairing. Such data can then be repeatedly used. CQA appears to be more suitable to *dynamic* environments, particularly those that require real-time decisions based on the available data.

Acknowledgments

The collaboration and the interaction with the following people are gratefully acknowledged: Marcelo Arenas, Leopoldo Bertossi, Wenfei Fan, Jerzy Marcinkowski, Sławomir Staworko, and Jef Wijsen.

References

1. S. Abiteboul, R. Hull, and V. Vianu. *Foundations of Databases.* Addison-Wesley, 1995.
2. P. Andritsos, A. Fuxman, and R. Miller. Clean Answers over Dirty Databases. In *IEEE International Conference on Data Engineering (ICDE)*, 2006.
3. M. Arenas, L. Bertossi, and J. Chomicki. Consistent Query Answers in Inconsistent Databases. In *ACM Symposium on Principles of Database Systems (PODS)*, pages 68–79, 1999.
4. M. Arenas, L. Bertossi, and J. Chomicki. Answer Sets for Consistent Query Answering in Inconsistent Databases. *Theory and Practice of Logic Programming*, 3(4–5):393–424, 2003.
5. M. Arenas, L. Bertossi, J. Chomicki, X. He, V. Raghavan, and J. Spinrad. Scalar Aggregation in Inconsistent Databases. *Theoretical Computer Science*, 296(3): 405–434, 2003.
6. C. Baral, S. Kraus, J. Minker, and V. S. Subrahmanian. Combining Knowledge Bases Consisting of First-Order Theories. *Computational Intelligence*, 8:45–71, 1992.

7. C. Batini and M. Scannapieco. *Data Quality: Concepts, Methodologies and Techniques*. Springer, 2006.
8. L. Bertossi. Consistent Query Answering in Databases. *SIGMOD Record*, 35(2), June 2006.
9. L. Bertossi and L. Bravo. Consistent Query Answers in Virtual Data Integration Systems. In Bertossi et al. [12], pages 42–83.
10. L. Bertossi, L. Bravo, E. Franconi, and A. Lopatenko. Complexity and Approximation of Fixing Numerical Attributes in Databases Under Integrity Constraints. In *International Workshop on Database Programming Languages*, pages 262–278. Springer, LNCS 3774, 2005.
11. L. Bertossi and J. Chomicki. Query Answering in Inconsistent Databases. In J. Chomicki, R. van der Meyden, and G. Saake, editors, *Logics for Emerging Applications of Databases*, pages 43–83. Springer-Verlag, 2003.
12. L. Bertossi, A. Hunter, and T. Schaub, editors. *Inconsistency Tolerance*. Springer-Verlag, 2004.
13. P. Bille. A Survey on Tree Edit Distance and Related Problems. *Theoretical Computer Science*, 337(1-3):217–239, 2003.
14. P. Bohannon, M. Flaster, W. Fan, and R. Rastogi. A Cost-Based Model and Effective Heuristic for Repairing Constraints by Value Modification. In *ACM SIGMOD International Conference on Management of Data*, pages 143–154, 2005.
15. A. Borgida. Language Features for Flexible Handling of Exceptions in Information Systems. *ACM Transactions on Database Systems*, 10(4):565–603, 1985.
16. L. Bravo and L. Bertossi. Logic Programs for Consistently Querying Data Integration Systems. In *International Joint Conference on Artificial Intelligence (IJCAI)*, pages 10–15, 2003.
17. L. Bravo and L. Bertossi. Semantically Correct Query Answers in the Presence of Null Values. In *EDBT Workshops (IIDB)*. Springer, 2006.
18. F. Bry. Query Answering in Information Systems with Integrity Constraints. In *IFIP WG 11.5 Working Conference on Integrity and Control in Information Systems*, pages 113–130. Chapman &Hall, 1997.
19. A. Calì, D. Lembo, and R. Rosati. On the Decidability and Complexity of Query Answering over Inconsistent and Incomplete Databases. In *ACM Symposium on Principles of Database Systems (PODS)*, pages 260–271, 2003.
20. D. Calvanese, G. De Giacomo, D. Lembo, M. Lenzerini, and R. Rosati. Inconsistency Tolerance in P2P Data Integration: An Epistemic Logic Approach. In *International Workshop on Database Programming Languages*, pages 90–105. Springer, LNCS 3774, 2005.
21. A. Celle and L. Bertossi. Querying Inconsistent Databases: Algorithms and Implementation. In *International Conference on Computational Logic*, pages 942–956. Springer-Verlag, LNCS 1861, 2000.
22. U. S. Chakravarthy, J. Grant, and J. Minker. Logic-Based Approach to Semantic Query Optimization. *ACM Transactions on Database Systems*, 15(2):162–207, 1990.
23. A. Chandra and P. Merlin. Optimal Implementation of Conjunctive Queries in Relational Databases. In *ACM SIGACT Symposium on the Theory of Computing (STOC)*, pages 77–90, 1977.
24. J. Chomicki. Consistent Query Answering: Opportunities and Limitations. In *DEXA Workshops (LAAIC)*, pages 527–531. IEEE Computer Society Press, 2006.
25. J. Chomicki and J. Marcinkowski. On the Computational Complexity of Minimal-Change Integrity Maintenance in Relational Databases. In Bertossi et al. [12], pages 119–150.

26. J. Chomicki and J. Marcinkowski. Minimal-Change Integrity Maintenance Using Tuple Deletions. *Information and Computation*, 197(1-2):90–121, 2005.
27. J. Chomicki, J. Marcinkowski, and S. Staworko. Computing Consistent Query Answers Using Conflict Hypergraphs. In *International Conference on Information and Knowledge Management (CIKM)*, pages 417–426. ACM Press, 2004.
28. E. Dantsin, T. Eiter, G. Gottlob, and A. Voronkov. Complexity and Expressive Power of Logic Programming. *ACM Computing Surveys*, 33(3):374–425, 2001.
29. T. Eiter, M. Fink, G. Greco, and D. Lembo. Efficient Evaluation of Logic Programs for Querying Data Integration Systems. In *International Conference on Logic Programming (ICLP)*, pages 163–177, 2003.
30. S. M. Embury, S. M. Brandt, J. S. Robinson, I. Sutherland, F. A. Bisby, W. A. Gray, A. C. Jones, and R. J. White. Adapting Integrity Enforcement Techniques for Data Reconciliation. *Information Systems*, 26(8):657–689, 2001.
31. R. Fagin, P. G. Kolaitis, R. J. Miller, and L. Popa. Data Exchange: Semantics and Query Answering. *Theoretical Computer Science*, 336(1):89–124, 2005.
32. W. Fan and J. Simeon. Integrity Constraints for XML. *Journal of Computer and System Sciences*, 66(1):254–201, 2003.
33. B. Fazzinga, S. Flesca, F. Furfaro, and F. Parisi. DART: a Data Acquisition and Repairing Tool. In *EDBT Workshops (IIDB)*. Springer, 2006.
34. S. Flesca, F. Furfaro, S. Greco, and E. Zumpano. Querying and Repairing Inconsistent XML Data. In *Web Information Systems Engineering*, pages 175–188. Springer, LNCS 3806, 2005.
35. S. Flesca, F. Furfaro, and F. Parisi. Consistent Query Answers on Numerical Databases under Aggregate Constraints. In *International Workshop on Database Programming Languages*, pages 279–294. Springer, LNCS 3774, 2005.
36. E. Franconi, A. L. Palma, N. Leone, S. Perri, and F. Scarcello. Census Data Repair: a Challenging Application of Disjunctive Logic Programming. In *International Conference on Logic for Programming, Artificial Intelligence, and Reasoning (LPAR)*, pages 561–578. Springer-Verlag, LNCS 2250, 2002.
37. A. Fuxman and R. J. Miller. ConQuer: Efficient Management of Inconsistent Databases. In *ACM SIGMOD International Conference on Management of Data*, pages 155–166, 2005.
38. A. Fuxman and R. J. Miller. First-Order Query Rewriting for Inconsistent Databases. In *International Conference on Database Theory (ICDT)*, pages 337–351. Springer, LNCS 3363, 2005. Full version to appear in JCSS.
39. G. Greco, S. Greco, and E. Zumpano. A Logical Framework for Querying and Repairing Inconsistent Databases. *IEEE Transactions on Knowledge and Data Engineering*, 15(6):1389–1408, 2003.
40. S. Greco, C. Sirangelo, I. Trubitsyna, and E. Zumpano. Preferred Repairs for Inconsistent Databases. In *International Conference on Database and Expert Systems Applications (DEXA)*, pages 44–55, 2004.
41. L. Grieco, D. Lembo, R. Rosati, and M. Ruzzi. Consistent Query Answering under Keys and Exclusion Dependencies: Algorithms and Experiments. In *International Conference on Information and Knowledge Management (CIKM)*, pages 792–799. ACM Press, 2005.
42. T. Imieliński and W. Lipski. Incomplete Information in Relational Databases. *Journal of the ACM*, 31(4):761–791, 1984.
43. T. Imieliński, S. Naqvi, and K. Vadaparty. Incomplete Objects - A Data Model for Design and Planning Applications. In *ACM SIGMOD International Conference on Management of Data*, pages 288–297, Denver, Colorado, May 1991.

44. D. S. Johnson and A. Klug. Testing Containment of Conjunctive Queries under Functional and Inclusion Dependencies. *Journal of Computer and System Sciences*, 28(1):167–189, 1984.
45. W. Lipski Jr. On Semantic Issues Connected with Incomplete Information Databases. *ACM Transactions on Database Systems*, 4(3):262–296, 1979.
46. P. C. Kanellakis. Elements of Relational Database Theory. In Jan van Leeuwen, editor, *Handbook of Theoretical Computer Science*, volume B, chapter 17, pages 1073–1158. Elsevier/MIT Press, 1990.
47. D. Lembo, R. Rosati, and M. Ruzzi. On the First-Order Reducibility of Unions of Conjunctive Queries over Inconsistent Databases. In *EDBT Workshops (IIDB)*, 2006.
48. N. Leone, G. Pfeifer, W. Faber, T. Eiter, G. Gottlob, S. Perri, and F. Scarcello. The DLV System for Knowledge Representation and Reasoning. *ACM Transactions on Computational Logic*, 2006. To appear.
49. J. Lin and A. O. Mendelzon. Merging Databases under Constraints. *International Journal of Cooperative Information Systems*, 7(1):55–76, 1996.
50. A. Lopatenko and L. Bertossi. Complexity of Consistent Query Answering in Databases under Cardinality-Based and Incremental Repair Semantics. In *International Conference on Database Theory (ICDT)*, 2007. To appear.
51. Jim Melton and Alan R. Simon. *SQL:1999 Understanding Relational Language Components*. Morgan Kaufmann, 2002.
52. P. Simons, I. Niemelä, and T. Soininen. Extending and Implementing the Stable Model Semantics. *Artificial Intelligence*, 138(1-2):181–234, June 2002.
53. S. Staworko and J. Chomicki. Consistent Query Answers in the Presence of Universal Constraints. Manuscript, October 2006.
54. S. Staworko and J. Chomicki. Validity-Sensitive Querying of XML Databases. In *EDBT Workshops (dataX)*. Springer, 2006.
55. S. Staworko, J. Chomicki, and J. Marcinkowski. Priority-Based Conflict Resolution in Inconsistent Relational Databases. In *EDBT Workshops (IIDB)*. Springer, 2006.
56. R. van der Meyden. Logical Approaches to Incomplete Information: A Survey. In J. Chomicki and G. Saake, editors, *Logics for Databases and Information Systems*, chapter 10, pages 307–356. Kluwer Academic Publishers, Boston, 1998.
57. M. Y. Vardi. The Complexity of Relational Query Languages. In *ACM Symposium on Theory of Computing (STOC)*, pages 137–146, 1982.
58. J. Wijsen. Database Repairing Using Updates. *ACM Transactions on Database Systems*, 30(3):722–768, 2005.
59. J. Wijsen. Project-Join Repair: An Approach to Consistent Query Answering Under Functional Dependencies. In *International Conference on Flexible Query Answering Systems (FQAS)*, 2006.

Ask a Better Question, Get a Better Answer
A New Approach to Private Data Analysis

Cynthia Dwork

Microsoft Research
dwork@microsoft.com

Abstract. Cryptographic techniques for reasoning about information leakage have recently been brought to bear on the classical problem of *statistical disclosure control* – revealing accurate statistics about a population while preserving the privacy of individuals. This new perspective has been invaluable in guiding the development of a powerful approach to private data analysis, founded on precise mathematical definitions, and yielding algorithms with provable, meaningful, privacy guarantees.

1 Introduction

The problem of *statistical disclosure control* – revealing accurate statistics about a population while preserving the privacy of individuals – has a venerable history. An extensive literature spans multiple disciplines: statistics, theoretical computer science, security, and databases. In recent years the problem has been revisited, bringing to the discussion techniques from the cryptographic community for defining and reasoning about information leakage. This new perspective has been invaluable in guiding the development of a powerful approach to private data analysis, founded on precise mathematical definitions, and yielding algorithms with provable, meaningful, privacy guarantees and, frequently, excellent accuracy.

Statistical databases may be of two types: non-interactive (the traditional model) and interactive. In the former, a *sanitization* of the data is published. All statistical analysis is carried out on the published, sanitized, data. Sanitization is a broad concept, and can include summaries, histograms, and even synthetic databases generated from a model learned from the actual data. The principal aspect here is the "one-shot" nature of the non-interactive approach: once the sanitization has been published the original data have no further use; they could even be destroyed. In contrast, in the interactive model a privacy mechanism sits between the data and the user. The user interacts with the privacy mechanism, which may modify the actual query or the query outcome, in order to preserve privacy.

The division between the models is somewhat artificial; nevertheless, separation results exist, and it is now clear that the interactive setting is much more powerful; for example, to obtain statistically meaningful information in the non-interactive case can provably require a huge database (exponential in the number

T. Schwentick and D. Suciu (Eds.): ICDT 2007, LNCS 4353, pp. 18–27, 2007.

of attributes) [12], which is simply not the case for interactive mechanisms. We may use the term *privacy mechanism* for either type of mechanism.

Dinur and Nissim [7] initiated a rigorous study of the interactive model; in particular, they focused on a class of techniques that Adam and Wortmann, in their encyclopedic 1989 survey of statistical disclosure control methods, call *output perturbation* [1]. Roughly speaking, this means that noise is added to the output of the query, so a true answer of, say, 4,286, may be reported as 4,266 or 4,300. The degree of distortion, that is, the expected magnitude of the noise, is an important measure of the utility of the statistical database. Dinur and Nissim investigated the question of how large the magnitude of the noise must be when the number of queries is large.

They began with a very simplistic and abstract setting, in which the database consists of a single Boolean attribute. That is, each row of the database is either zero or one. A *query* is a subset of the rows, and the defined true answer to the query is the sum of the rows in the subset (equivalently, the number of ones in the specified set of rows). It is helpful to think of the query as a vector $x \in \{0,1\}^n$, where n is the number of rows in the database, henceforth denoted DB. The true answer to the query is $x \cdot DB$. An output perturbation mechanism adds noise to the true answer, and returns this sum as the response to the query. We use the terms *true answer* to denote the real number of ones in the rows specified by the query, and *response* to denote the output of the privacy mechanism.

Dinur and Nissim did not initially explicitly define privacy. Instead they defined what we will call *blatant non-privacy*: the ability to reconstruct, say, 99.99%, or, more precisely, $n - o(n)$, entries of a database of n rows (the adversary will not necessarily know which of the reconstructed entries are the correct ones). They showed that to prevent blatant non-privacy, the magnitude of the noise added in each response cannot always be small:

1. The magnitude of the noise cannot always be $o(n)$ if the adversary can make 2^n queries to the database (in fact, if the error is always within a bound E then the database can be approximated by a candidate of Hamming distance at most $O(E)$ from the real database);
2. If the adversary is polynomial time bounded and makes only $O(n \log^2 n)$ randomly chosen queries, the magnitude of the noise cannot always be $o(\sqrt{n})$.

These results are independent of the distribution of the noise.

The first result uses brute force to rule out databases that are too far from the actual database. The second uses linear programming to accomplish the same task; the result holds with all but negligible probability over the choice of queries.

The Dinur-Nissim setting, while at first blush simplistic, is in fact sufficiently rich to capture many natural questions. For example, the rows of the database may be quite complex, but the adversary-user may know enough information about an individual in the database to uniquely identify his row. In this case the goal is to prevent the learning of any *additional* bit of information about the individual. Of course, even knowing enough to identify a single individual does not give the adversary the power to identify everyone in the database. However, careful use of hash functions can handle the "row-naming problem." Thus, we may have a scenario in which an adversary reconstructs a close approximation to the database, in which each row is identified with a set of hash values, and a "secret bit" is learned for many rows. If the adversary knows (or later learns) enough about an individual to identify, directly or through elimination, his row in the database, then the adversary can learn the individual's secret bit.

"Just Give Me a Noisy Table". Research statisticians like to "look at the data." Indeed, conversations with experts in this field frequently involve pleas for a "noisy table" that will permit significantly accurate answers to be derived for computations that are not specified at the outset. The Dinur-Nissim results say that no "noisy table" can provide very accurate answers to all questions; otherwise the table could be used to simulate the interactive mechanism, and a Dinur-Nissim style attack could be mounted against the table. But what about a table that yields reasonably accurate answers to "most" questions, permitting some questions to have wildly inaccurate answers? We will see in Section 2 that this relaxation is of little help in protecting privacy. We therefore advocate switching to an interactive strategy using the techniques of Section 3.

1.1   When n Is Very Large

Dinur and Nissim obtained their negative results while we were thinking about privacy for enormous databases, in particular, the Hotmail user database of over $n = 100,000,000$ users. In such a setting, asking $n \log^2 n$ queries is simply unreasonable. This suggests the following natural question: suppose the number of queries is limited, so the attacks above cannot be carried out. For example, suppose the number of queries is sub-linear in n. Can privacy be preserved by noise that is, say, always of magnitude $o(\sqrt{n})$? Since the sampling error for a property that occurs in a constant fraction of the population is on the order of $\Theta(\sqrt{n})$, this would mean that the noise added for protecting privacy is smaller than the sampling error.

More generally, let T be an upper bound on the number of queries to be tolerated. What magnitude noise is sufficient to ensure privacy against T queries? As we will see, the answer to this question is very satisfactory. In particular, the magnitude of the noise will depend only on T, and not on n.

To answer our question we must pose it precisely, which means that we must define privacy, preferably in a way that makes sense for arbitrary databases, and not just n-bit vector databases. Of course, when the databases are arbitrary the queries may be more complex than a simple inner product – which may not even make sense, depending on the data type.

Organization of This Paper. The rest of this paper is organized as follows. Section 2 summarizes some recent extensions of the Dinur-Nissim results. Section 3.1 describes a natural definition of a privacy-preserving statistical database, held as a desideratum for 29 years, and gives some intuition for why it cannot be achieved. However, just as the negative results of [7] yielded insight into how to permit accuracy while ensuring privacy by focusing our attention on "reasonable" numbers of queries, the counter-example to the natural definition exhibited flaws in the definition – the wrong question was being asked! The deeper understanding resulted in a new concept, *differential privacy*. This is described in Section 3.2. Finally, a concrete privacy mechanism achieving differential privacy is presented in Section 3.3, and our question about the magnitude of noise sufficient to maintain privacy against T queries is answered.

2   Strengthening the Impossibility Results

We[1] have recently extended the Dinur-Nissim results in several ways summarized in Theorem 1. The proof of Part 1 is the "right" version of Dinur-Nissim: it specifies an explicit set of exactly n queries that always yields blatant non-privacy. Parts 2-4 consider the case in which there may be some small errors but also a constant fraction of the errors may be *unbounded*. The case of unbounded errors with zero small errors is similar to the situation with error-correcting codes, when a symbol is either correct (zero error) or incorrect (no assumptions). We have one result of this type, and several with "mixed" errors.

Theorem 1. *In each case below a query is defined by an n-dimensional vector x, the database is an n-dimensional vector DB, and the true answer is $x \cdot DB$. The response is the true answer plus noise. All the results will hold independent of how the noise is generated, and even if the privacy mechanism knows all questions in advance.*

1. *If the noise is restricted to $o(\sqrt{n})$ in every response, then the system is blatantly non-private against a polynomial time bounded adversary asking exactly n queries $x \in \{\pm 1\}^n$. More generally, a noise bound of α translates to reconstruction of $n - 9\alpha^2$ entries. The attack uses Fourier analysis in a straightforward way.*
2. *Let ρ be any constant less than 0.239. If the noise is unbounded on up to a ρ fraction of the responses and restricted to $o(\sqrt{n})$ on the remaining $(1 - \rho)$ fraction, then the system is blatantly non-private against a polynomial time bounded adversary asking $\Theta(n)$ queries in $\mathcal{N}(0,1)^n$, that is, each query is a vector of standard normals. More generally, a bound of α on the small noise yields reconstruction in $n - \Theta(\alpha^2)$ entries.*
3. *For any fixed $\delta > 0$, if the noise is unbounded on a $(1/2 - \delta)$ fraction of the queries and restricted to $o(\sqrt{n})$ on the remaining $(1/2 + \delta)$ fraction, then the system is blatantly non-private against*
   (a) an exponential-time adversary asking only $O(n)$ queries
   (b) a polynomial time adversary against a non-interactive solution (eg, a noisy table) asking only $O(n)$ questions, where the break is in the list-decoding sense; that is, the adversary can produce a constant-sized list

---

[1] These results were obtained jointly with Frank McSherry, Kunal Talwar, and Sergey Yekhanin.

>   of candidate databases containing at least one that agrees with the true
>   database in at least $n - o(n)$ entries.
>   The queries for both parts of this result are randomly chosen vectors $x \in \{\pm 1\}^n$ and the attack works with overwhelming probability over the choice
>   of queries.

4. *If the noise is unbounded on up to $1/2 - \delta$ of the responses, but is* zero *in the remaining $1/2 + \delta$, then the system is blatantly non-private against a polynomial time bounded adversary making $O(n)$ queries with integer coefficients in the interval $[-c, c]$, where $c = c(\delta)$ is a constant that goes to infinity as δ approaches 0. The attack uses algebraic geometry codes.*

In all but Part 4, if the database has $\Omega(n)$ ones, then $x \cdot DB$ has expected magnitude close to $\sqrt{n}$. Thus, even on the queries on which the system gives "small" error $o(\sqrt{n})$, the magnitude of the error is close to the magnitude of the answer. And still the system is blatantly non-private.

The attack in Theorem 1.2 is inspired by recent results of Donoho [8, 9] and Candes, Rudelson, Tao, and Vershynin [4], in which linear programming is used for compressed sensing and decoding in the presence of errors. Indeed, our query matrices are exactly the ones studied in [4]. Our result is stronger in two ways: we tolerate small noise everywhere, and our proof is more direct, yielding a better decoding bound and a sharp threshold even in the zero small noise case[2].

3   Differential Privacy

3.1   Motivation for the Definition

Development of the notion of differential privacy was guided by a different type of impossibility result than those discussed so far. A classical desideratum for statistical databases was articulated in [5]:

> (Dalenius, 1977) Access to a statistical database should not enable one to learn anything about an individual that could not be learned without access[3].

This goal cannot be achieved when the database has any utility [10]:

> "The obstacle is in *auxiliary information*, that is, information available to the adversary other than from access to the statistical database, and the intuition behind the proof of impossibility is captured by the following example. Suppose one's exact height were considered a highly

---

[2] In an alternate version of Theorem 1.2 the queries may be randomly chosen vectors in $\{\pm 1\}^n$. Unlike the case with Gaussian queries, this alternate version does not necessarily return the exact database when size of the "small" errors is set to 0 (instead of $o(\sqrt{n})$).

[3] This is analogous to Goldwasser and Micali's definition of *semantic security* against an eavesdropper, which says, roughly, that nothing can be learned about a plaintext from the ciphertext that could not be learned without seeing the ciphertext [15].

sensitive piece of information, and that revealing the exact height of an individual were a privacy breach. Assume that the database yields the average heights of women of different nationalities. An adversary who has access to the statistical database and the auxiliary information "Terry Gross is two inches shorter than the average Lithuanian woman" learns Terry Gross' height, while anyone learning only the auxiliary information, without access to the average heights, learns relatively little."

As further noted in [10], the impossibility result applies regardless of whether or not Terry Gross is in the database. This led to the following, alternative notion [10, 12]:

> *Differential Privacy:* Access to a statistical database should not enable one to learn anything about an individual *given that her data are in the database* than can be learned when her data are *not* in the database.

While differential privacy does not rule out a bad disclosure, it assures the individual that it will not be the inclusion of her data in the database that causes it, nor could the disclosure be avoided through any action or inaction on the part of the user of the database.

3.2   Formal Definition

The privacy mechanism is a randomized algorithm that takes the database as input and produces an output.

Definition 1. *A randomized function $\mathcal{K}$ gives ϵ-differential privacy if for all data sets D_1 and D_2 differing on at most one element, and all $S \subseteq Range(\mathcal{K})$,*

$$\Pr[\mathcal{K}(D_1) \in S] \leq \exp(\epsilon) \times \Pr[\mathcal{K}(D_2) \in S] \tag{1}$$

A mechanism $\mathcal{K}$ satisfying this definition ensures a participant that even if she removed her data from the data set, no outputs (and thus consequences of outputs) would become significantly more or less likely. For example, if the database were to be consulted by an insurance provider before deciding whether or not to insure Terry Gross, then the presence or absence of Terry Gross in the database will not significantly affect her chance of receiving coverage.

This definition naturally extends to group privacy as well. If the definition is satisfied as written, then the inclusion/exclusion of the data of any c participants yields a factor of $\exp(\epsilon c)$ (instead of $\exp(\epsilon)$), which may be tolerable for small c. Since the *sine qua non* of a statistical database is to teach information about the population as a whole, it is natural, indeed essential, that the privacy bounds deteriorate as group size increases.

3.3   Achieving Differential Privacy

We now describe a concrete interactive privacy mechanism achieving ϵ-differential privacy (see [12] for a full treatment). The mechanism works by adding appropriately chosen random noise to the true answer $a = f(X)$, where f is the *query function* and X is the database. A helpful example to keep in mind is (a vector of d) queries of the form "How many rows in the database satisfy predicate P?" where the true answer is a vector of d integers (one per query). It is noteworthy that "counting" queries of this type are a very powerful privacy-preserving interface to the database. For example, it is shown in [3] that many popular datamining tasks, including principal component analysis, association rules, k-means clustering, and the ID3 decision tree creation, can be carried out with excellent accuracy while only using a small number of counting queries.

The magnitude of the noise is chosen as a function of the largest change a single participant could have on the output to the query function; we refer to this quantity as the *sensitivity* of the function.

Definition 2. *For $f : \mathcal{D} \to R^d$, the $L1$-sensitivity of f is*

$$\Delta f = \max_{D_1, D_2} \| f(D_1) - f(D_2) \|_1 \tag{2}$$

for all D_1, D_2 differing in at most one element.

Note that sensitivity is a property of the function alone, and is independent of the database. So we may assume that sensitivity is known to the user. For many types of queries Δf will be quite small. In particular, the counting queries "How many rows have property P?" have $\Delta f = 1$. Our techniques will introduce the least noise when Δf is small.

The privacy mechanism, denoted $\mathcal{K}_f$ for a query function f, computes $f(X)$ and independently adds noise with a scaled symmetric exponential distribution with variance σ^2 (to be determined in Theorem 2) in each component. This distribution is described by the density function

$$\Pr[\mathcal{K}_f(X) = a] \propto \exp(-\| f(X) - a \|_1 / \sigma) \tag{3}$$

and the mechanism simply adds, to each coordinate of $f(X)$, independently generated samples of this distribution.

Theorem 2. *[10, 12] For $f : \mathcal{D} \to R^d$, $\mathcal{K}_f$ gives $(\Delta f / \sigma)$-differential privacy.*

Proof. Starting from (3), we apply the triangle inequality within the exponent, yielding for all possible responses r

$$\Pr[\mathcal{K}_f(D_1) = r] \leq \Pr[\mathcal{K}_f(D_2) = r] \times \exp(\| f(D_1) - f(D_2) \|_1 / \sigma) . \tag{4}$$

The second term in this product is bounded by $\exp(\Delta f / \sigma)$. Thus (1) holds for singleton sets $S = \{a\}$, and the theorem follows by a union bound.

Theorem 2 describes a relationship between Δf, σ, and the privacy differential. To achieve ϵ-differential privacy, it suffices to choose $\sigma \geq \epsilon / \Delta f$. Significantly, the theorem holds regardless of any auxiliary information that may be available to the adversary, and is independent of the computational power of the adversary. Moreover, composition is simple: to handle T adaptively chosen queries of respective sensitivities $\Delta f_1, \ldots, \Delta f_T$ it suffices to replace Δf with $\sum_{i=1}^{T} \Delta f_i$ in the noise generation procedure[4].

We may now answer our earlier question: What magnitude noise is sufficient to ensure privacy against T queries? The sensitivity of each query in Theorems 1.1, 1.3, and the ± 1 variant of 1.2, is $\Delta f = 1$ (and the sensitivity of a query in Theorem 1.4 is c). The sensitivity of any sequence of T such queries is thus at most $T\Delta f = T$ (or $Tc = O(T)$ for the case of Theorem 1.4), so the answer in all these cases is $O(T/\epsilon)$.

The situation for Theorem 1.2 is a bit different: there is no upper bound on $|\mathcal{N}(0,1)|$, and a sanitizer that rejects Gaussian queries if they exceed any fixed constant in even one coordinate would be unreasonable. A simple-minded approach would be to take $\log^2 n$ to be an upper bound on Δ (and reject any query vector with L_∞ norm exceeding this amount), which yields $T \log^2 n$ as an upper bound on the sensitivity of any sequence of T queries. This yields noise magnitude $O(T \log^2 n/\epsilon)$. However, we can design a solution that does better. We do this for the pedagogic value of exhibiting the tightness of the tradeoff between accuracy (smallness of noise) and privacy.

A series of T queries implicitly defines a $T \times n$ matrix A, where each row of the matrix corresponds to a single inner product query, and the output is the $T \times 1$ matrix given by $A \cdot DB$. To put things in context, Theorem 1.2 discusses blatant non-privacy when $T = \Omega(n)$ and the matrix A is drawn from $\mathcal{N}(0,1)^{T \times n}$; we are now looking at smaller values of T.

The privacy mechanism will use noise calibrated to sensitivity $\Delta = 2T$. It will also impose a sensitivity *budget* of $2T$ on each row of the database, as we now explain. Let x be a query vector. For each $1 \le i \le n$ the budget for row i is charged $|x_i|$. More generally, the cost of A to the budget for row i of the database is the L_1 norm of the ith column of A. The privacy mechanism will answer a query unless is would break the budget of even one row in the database, in which case the mechanism will answer no further questions. Note that the budget and the charges against it are all public and are independent of the database, so this stopping condition reveals nothing about the data.

Since the noise is calibrated for sensitivity $2T$ and no sensitivity budget of $2T$ is exceeded, differential privacy is ensured. We claim that for $T \ge \text{polylog}(n)$, with overwhelming probability over choice of A, the privacy mechanism will answer all T questions before shutting down. Note that A contains nT standard normals, and so with overwhelming probability the maximum magnitude of any entry will not exceed, say, $\log^2 nT$. In the sequel we assume we are in this high probability case.

Consider random variables $X_1, \ldots, X_T$, each in $[0, \log^2 nT]$. Let $S = \sum_{i=1}^{T} X_i$. Hoeffding's inequality says that

$$\Pr[S - E[S] \ge tT] \le \exp\left(-\frac{2T^2 t}{\sum_{i=1}^{T} \log^4 nT}\right)$$

---

[4] There are compelling examples in which it is possible to do much better. The interested reader is referred to [12].

We may use this as follows. Since a_{ij} is distributed according to a standard normal, its expected magnitude is $\sqrt{2/\pi}$. Consider a column j of A, and let $X_i = |a_{ij}|$ for $I = 1, \ldots, T$. By linearity of expectation, $E[S] = TE[|\mathcal{N}(0,1)|]$. So Hoeffding's bound says that

$$\Pr[S - T(\sqrt{2/\pi}) \geq tT] \leq \exp\left(-\frac{2T^2 t}{\sum_{i=1}^{T} \log^4 nT}\right) = \exp\left(-\frac{2Tt}{\log^4 nT}\right)$$

In particular when $T \geq \log^6(Tn)$ this is negligible for all $t \in \Omega(1)$. By a union bound we see that, as desired, the probability that even one of the n per-row budgets is exceeded is negligible in n.

The bottom line is that, even in the setting of Theorem 1.2, noise of magnitude $O(T/\epsilon)$ is sufficient to ensure privacy against T queries.

We remark that a "better" answer appears in the literature [7, 13, 3]. This is obtained using a slightly weaker, but also reasonable, definition of privacy, in which, roughly speaking, the mechanism is permitted to fail to deliver full ϵ-differential privacy with some small probability δ. Under this relaxed definition one may employ Gaussian noise rather than symmetric exponential noise. This leads to noise of magnitude $\Omega((\sqrt{\log 1/\delta})\sqrt{T}/\epsilon)$. We prefer the exponential noise because it "behaves better" under composition and because the guarantee is absolute ($\delta = 0$).

4 Final Remarks

A Trusted Center. Throughout this paper we have assumed that the data collector and the privacy mechanism are trustworthy. Thus, we are making the problem as easy as possible, yielding stronger lower bounds and impossibility results. The literature also studies the setting in which the data contributors do not trust the data collector to maintain privacy and so first randomize their own data [14, 2]. Of course, since randomized response is a non-interactive mechanism it is subject to the negative conciseness result of [12] mentioned in the Introduction.

"Our Data, Ourselves". A different tack was taken in [11], where, using cryptographic techniques for *secure function evaluation*, the data collector/protector is replaced by a distributed privacy mechanism.

When Noise Makes no Sense. McSherry and Talwar have initiated an exciting investigation of differential privacy in cases in which adding noise may not make sense; for example, the output of a "query," or in general of any operation on a set of private inputs, may not be a number. Given an input vector x (playing the role of a database) and a possible outcome y, assume there is a real-valued *utility* function $u(x,y)$ that evaluates the outcome y for the input set x. As an example, x could be bids for a digital good, y could be a price, and $u(x,y)$ could be the resulting revenue. This has resulted in the design of approximately-truthful and collusion-resistant mechanisms with near-optimal revenue. More generally, y can be a classifer, an expert, or a heuristic.

References

[1] N. R. Adam and J. C. Wortmann, Security-Control Methods for Statistical Databases: A Comparative Study, *ACM Computing Surveys* 21(4): 515-556 (1989).

[2] R. Agrawal, R. Srikant, D. Thomas. Privacy Preserving OLAP. *Proceedings of SIGMOD 2005.*

[3] A. Blum, C. Dwork, F. McSherry, and K. Nissim. Practical privacy: The SuLQ framework. In *Proceedings of the 24th ACM SIGMOD-SIGACT-SIGART Symposium on Principles of Database Systems*, pages 128–138, 2005.

[4] E. J. Candes, M. Rudelson, T. Tao, and R. Vershynin, Error Correction via Linear Programming. In *Proceedings of the 46th IEEE Annual Symposium on Foundations of Computer Science*, 2005.

[5] T. Dalenius, Towards a methodology for statistical disclosure control. *Statistik Tidskrift 15*, pp. 429–222, 1977.

[6] D. E. Denning, *Secure statistical databases with random sample queries*, ACM Transactions on Database Systems, 5(3):291–315, September 1980.

[7] I. Dinur and K. Nissim. Revealing information while preserving privacy. In *Proceedings of the 22nd ACM SIGMOD-SIGACT-SIGART Symposium on Principles of Database Systems*, pages 202–210, 2003.

[8] D. Donoho. For Most Large Underdetermined Systems of Linear Equations, the minimal l1-norm solution is also the sparsest solution. *Manuscript*, 2004. Available at http://stat.stanford.edu/~donoho/reports.html

[9] D. Donoho. For Most Large Underdetermined Systems of Linear Equations, the minimal l1-norm near-solution approximates the sparsest near-solution. *Manuscript*, 2004. Available at http://stat.stanford.edu/~donoho/reports.html

[10] C. Dwork. Differential Privacy. *Invited Paper; Proceedings of ICALP 2006.*

[11] C. Dwork, K. Kenthapadi, F. McSherry , I. Mironov and M. Naor. Our Data, Ourselves: Privacy via Distributed Noise Generation. *Proceedings of Eurocrypt 2006*

[12] C. Dwork, F. McSherry, K. Nissim, and A. Smith. Calibrating noise to sensitivity in private data analysis. In *Proceedings of the 3rd Theory of Cryptography Conference*, pages 265–284, 2006.

[13] C. Dwork and K. Nissim. Privacy-preserving datamining on vertically partitioned databases. In *Advances in Cryptology: Proceedings of Crypto*, pages 528–544, 2004.

[14] A. Evfimievski, J. Gehrke, and R. Srikant. Limiting privacy breaches in privacy preserving data mining. In *Proceedings of the 22nd ACM SIGMOD-SIGACT-SIGART Symposium on Principles of Database Systems*, pages 211–222, June 2003.

[15] S. Goldwasser and S. Micali, Probabilistic encryption. *Journal of Computer and System Sciences 28*, pp. 270–299, 1984; prelminary version appeared in *Proceedings 14th Annual ACM Symposium on Theory of Computing*, 1982.

Beauty and the Beast: The Theory and Practice of Information Integration

Laura Haas

IBM Almaden Research Center, 650 Harry Road, San Jose, CA 95120
laura@almaden.ibm.com

Abstract. Information integration is becoming a critical problem for businesses and individuals alike. Data volumes are sky-rocketing, and new sources and types of information are proliferating. This paper briefly reviews some of the key research accomplishments in information integration (theory and systems), then describes the current state-of-the-art in commercial practice, and the challenges (still) faced by CIOs and application developers. One critical challenge is choosing the right combination of tools and technologies to do the integration. Although each has been studied separately, we lack a unified (and certainly, a unifying) understanding of these various approaches to integration. Experience with a variety of integration projects suggests that we need a broader framework, perhaps even a theory, which explicitly takes into account requirements on the result of the integration, and considers the entire end-to-end integration process.

Keywords: Information integration, data integration, data exchange, data cleansing, federation, extract/transform/load.

1 Introduction

"For us…growth is a way of life. So we'll continue to grow"[1]. Nearly two thirds of CEOs surveyed recently said that growth is the key priority, requiring quick delivery of new products and services in response to rapidly changing market conditions [2]. Yet only 13% felt that their business was well-positioned to react quickly [2]. They stressed the need to capture and understand all available information to make rapid business decisions, but today that is not such an easy task. In fact, 68% of the CEOs listed the integration of disparate applications and infrastructure as a key issue for their business, one that slows them down and stops the flow of information [2]. Meanwhile, customers tell us that 30% of their people's time is spent just looking for the information they need to do their jobs.

Why is information so hard to find? Partly, this is due to the increasing volumes of information available on line. But there is a second, deeper problem, and that is the fragmentation of information, and the proliferation of information sources. Even

---

[1] Mukesh Ambani, chairman and managing director of Reliance Industries, India's largest private sector company, as quoted in [1].

T. Schwentick and D. Suciu (Eds.): ICDT 2007, LNCS 4353, pp. 28–43, 2007.
© Springer-Verlag Berlin Heidelberg 2007

within a relatively controlled environment such as an enterprise Information Technology (IT) organization, customers report many database instances, often hidden behind applications, not to mention document repositories and other sources of unstructured information. For example, analysts report [3] that 79% of companies (of all sizes) have more than two document stores, while 25% have more than fifteen. Information is not only hard to find, but further complications such as overlapping, conflicting and incomplete information are inevitable. Almost any business with multiple business units has multiple sources of customer information, for example – often with conflicting information for the same customers.

Information integration is the database community's answer to these problems. The goal of information integration is to enable rapid development of new applications requiring information from multiple sources. This simple goal hides many challenges, from identifying the best data sources to use, to creating an appropriate interface to (or schema for) the integrated data. Much research has focused on how best to do the integration itself, for example, how to query diverse sources with differing capabilities and how to optimize queries or execution plans. Other issues concern how to cleanse information to get a consistent view, how to deal with uncertainty and trace data lineage, and how to identify the same object in different data sources (a problem known by various names, including entity resolution). There has been a lot of progress on individual challenges, but information integration remains a difficult task. We believe that one reason for that is that these challenges are inter-related, part of the overall process of integration, and yet have been largely considered in isolation. Thus, the separate solutions do not always work well together. Perhaps more importantly, the solutions that are relevant to a particular integration task depend heavily on the application requirements regarding data qualities (*e.g.*, currency, consistency, completeness) and quality of service (*e.g.*, response time, availability, resources consumed). We lack a clear view of information integration that positions the various technologies relative to each other and relative to the application requirements for the integration problem that must be solved.

The rest of this paper is structured as follows. Section 2 elaborates on the overall information integration challenge, and presents an extended example of a real integration problem to motivate our suggestions for future work. In Section 3, we briefly survey the research underpinnings of information integration, showing how the research applies to our example, while Section 4 reviews the state of the art in the industry today, showing what products are available for use. Section 5 comes back to the issue of unification and the end-to-end information integration problem. We pose a new challenge to the research community with both theoretical and systems implications, and explore several possible approaches. Finally, the paper concludes in section 6.

2 Information Integration Illustrated

There is no one integration problem; the challenges vary depending on the environment. In this paper, we focus on information integration within an enterprise. This environment typically includes a broad mix of sources, many structured (*e.g.*, relational or other databases), but increasingly many unstructured (*e.g.*, document repositories, web pages, email). The uses for the integrated data are likely to vary greatly, from mission-critical applications to exploratory queries and everything in between. A broad range of technologies is used to handle this range of needs. In this section, we first provide an overview of the integration process in the enterprise context, and then illustrate it through an extended example.

2.1 The Information Integration Process

Research on information integration has focused on particular aspects of integration, such as schema mapping or replication, individually. But for businesses, information integration is really a process, with four major tasks: *understanding, standardization, specification* and *execution*.

Understanding. The first task in information integration is to understand the data. This may include discovering relevant information (including keys, constraints, data types, and so on) and analysing it to assess quality and to determine statistical properties (for example, data distributions, frequent values, inconsistent values). During this task the integrator may look for relationships among data elements (such as foreign keys, or redundant columns) and possibly (for unstructured data) meaning. Metadata is central to this phase, though used in all. Both tools and end users leverage it to find and understand the data to be integrated. It is also produced as the output of analysis, to be exploited by later tasks in the process.

Standardization. This task typically leverages the work of the previous task to determine the best way to represent the integrated information. This includes designing the "target" or integrated schema, deciding at the field level what the standard representation should be (*e.g.*, will full names be represented as first name followed by last name, or last name comma first name?), and even defining the terminology and abbreviations to use ("str" vs. "st" for "street"). In addition to these rules on how data is represented, other rules that specify how to cleanse or repair data may be provided. Issues here include how to handle inconsistent or incomplete data (for example, if we find multiple phone numbers for the same person, should we keep all of them, or only the most recent?) and how to identify data that refers to the same objects (for example, is John Q Public the same person as John Public?).

Specification. In this step, the artifacts that will control the actual execution are produced. As a result, the techniques and technologies used for specification are intimately linked to the choice of execution engine(s). For example, mapping tools specify the relationship between source(s) and target(s), and then typically can generate a query or other executable artifact (*e.g.*, XSLT) that would produce data in the desired target form. Often, however, the specification is part of actually configuring an integration engine to do the desired integration. Thus, determining the execution engine should be thought of as part of specification.

Execution. This is where the integration actually happens. Integration can be accomplished via materialization, federation and/or indexing. *Materialization* creates and stores the integrated data set; this may be thought of as eager integration. There are many techniques for materialization. *Extract/Transform/Load (ETL)* jobs extract data from one or more data sources, transform them as indicated in the job script, and then store the result in another data source. *Replication* makes and maintains a copy of data, often differentially by reading database log files. *Caching* captures query results for future reuse. **Federation** creates a virtual representation of the integrated set, only materializing selected portions as needed; it can be thought of as lazy integration. Federation is a form of **mediation**; in general, mediation refers to an integration technique in which requests are sent to a "mediator" process which does routing and translation of requests. **Search** takes a different approach, creating a single index over the data being integrated. This is commonly used for unstructured data, and represents a partial materialization, since typically the index identifies relevant documents, which will be fetched dynamically at the user's request.

Note that these tasks are interdependent, and existing tools often support (pieces of) several of these tasks. They may be overlapped in practice; for instance, it is not necessary to have a complete understanding before starting to standardize. Likewise, a particular integration may not require all of the subtasks for any task, and in really simple cases, some tasks may seem to vanish altogether.

The integration process is iterative, and never-ending. Change is constant; there is always another source to deal with, a new application with new requirements, an update to some schema, or just new data that requires analysis.

2.2 An Extended Example

Consider a typical integration problem. A major company, Grande, acquires a small company, Chico, with less than fifty employees. Chico has three products, several "databases" per product (ranging from design docs scattered about the file system to requirements docs in a document management system to relational databases tracking line items and owners, and so on), two orders databases (one for mail orders, one for the web), a defect tracking database for support, and other information sources. Several Chico IT staff members quit in the transition, so knowledge about the data is lost.

The combined enterprise needs to ensure that Chico continues to do business during the transition (so their sales, support and development databases and processes must continue to operate). But the duplication of databases, processes and IT staff is costly, so they also need to consolidate their operations reasonably quickly. In the meantime, they have immediate needs to correlate information across the old and new systems. For example, Chico's customers overlap with Grande's. The new, bigger Grande wants to send mail to all existing customers who might be interested in Chico's products, but not to those who already have them. They may want to quickly get to a single phone number for support across the combined product set.

For our example, we'll focus on this latter scenario. The support representative answering the phone needs to be able to check customer entitlement quickly, *i.e.*, he must be able to look up a customer and discover the level of service for which the customer has paid. Ideally, this would be solved by providing the support person with a single list of customers, duplicates removed, information merged, or the equivalent. But that is not so easy, as customer information for Chico is scattered across multiple tables; there is no single customer list, even for Chico alone. Further, Chico checked entitlement by looking up the product registration number in the orders database(s) to

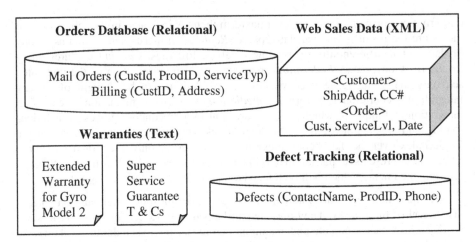

Fig. 1. Chico's customer-related data is spread over multiple data sources, in multiple formats. Only partial schemas are shown; the real data would have many more tables, and columns, as well as richer XML document types. Gathering full information on customer entitlement requires detailed knowledge of the sources, a complex join and understanding the service types.

see if the customer bought support, and if so, at what level. Grande was more focused on customer accounts, with a certain level of service for a customer based on overall sales (*e.g.*, Gold vs. Platinum customers). So not only is the information about customers organized differently, but the semantics of customer entitlement are also different for the two companies. Eventually, the combined company will want to settle on a single scheme, but in the short term, they just want to continue to support both customer sets, smoothly.

Janet Lee, a Grande IT architect, is asked to set up this combined customer support system. Janet is not familiar with the Chico systems, of course, and because of the loss of Chico staff, she will not have the benefit of their expertise. She needs first to *understand* what information is available to her. She will need to find the Chico customer information and information on what types of support exist. This information is spread over order, billing and defect tables in multiple databases and in the document management system that tracks contracts (Figure 1). She will probably need to talk to someone in sales to understand the Chico support semantics, and she will likely want to inspect or analyze the relational data so that she knows what she is up against in terms of *standardization*. For that task, she will need to specify how to represent various data, such as address (Chico doesn't store state, and the address is all in a single field, where Grande has state, city and zip all in separate fields). She will design a merged representation, and define the rules that determine what happens when there is disagreement (for example, when the same customer appears in both databases with different information)[2]. She may also need to write rules to determine when data refers to the same customer. Janet then needs to *specify* how to do the

---

[2] Note that the order of these may vary a bit, for example, some tools would allow Janet to write these "cleansing" rules as part of specifying the integration.

integration. Although there are some tools that will support an abstract, nonprocedural way of doing this, for example, mapping tools, even these today tend to be associated with a particular integration engine.

So Janet now faces the question of how to *execute* the actual integration. She could, for example, choose to materialize the combined customer list. To do that, she'll need to define an Extract/Transform/Load (ETL) job, deciding how often it needs to run, or whether it can be run once, and then refreshed incrementally at regular intervals. A differential refresh might be better handled using a replication product – and if the transformations needed are simple enough, the replication engine might be *all* that is needed. In any case, she will need to set up one or both products and configure them to reach the actual data sources, and to run her job or jobs. Alternatively, she could choose to federate the various data sources, providing a single (virtual) view of the combined data. In this case, she will need to set up and configure the federation software to reach the data sources, and then define appropriate views over the data. In a customer support environment, a good search capability is typically critical. It is possible that Janet could return the information needed by the support representative just via search. She will want to evaluate that possibility, and possibly set up search software, configuring crawlers, getting an index built, and so on. Of course, a combination of these various integration engines may be the best approach – materializing critical information for the first, fast check, keeping it up-to-date via replication, using federation to "drill down" if the customer has further questions about their account, and using search as a way to retrieve details of the relevant service plans.

How will Janet decide? To make her decision, she must take a number of factors into account. She will think about the requirements of the task: how quickly must the information be returned, how many end users will be using the system simultaneously, whether it will be needed 24x7, and so on. Other requirements apply to the data quality: how current must the data be, how complete, how accurate. Janet will also think about the physical constraints on the solution, for example, how much storage space is available, the processing power at her disposal, a limit on total cost, perhaps. Finally, the policies Grande has in place for security or to comply with relevant industry regulations will also affect the solution. For purposes of this paper, we will refer to these varied types of requirements – qualities of service, qualities of data, physical constraints and policies – as the *solution desiderata*. These desiderata are critical to determining the best techniques to use for a particular scenario; however, only Janet's experience allows her to make the decision – there are no studies or formal guidance on what desiderata require which integration techniques.

To summarize, in order to integrate enough data for this one critical but simple scenario, Janet must go through quite a complex process. She will need to develop an understanding of the data and its semantics. She will need to assess the quality and degree of overlap of the data, identifying common customers and merging and standardizing their information while dealing with any inconsistencies. She will need to design the integrated view or target schema. Finally, she will need to choose one or more integration engines to deploy, configure them to reach the various data sources, and create the instructions needed (the ETL script, view, or program) for them to instantiate the target schema. In our simple example, Janet is dealing with primarily relational data. If some of the data is unstructured, her task is harder still. Fortunately, the research and development communities have made great strides towards tools to address these challenges. In the next two sections, we examine some of the highlights of this work.

3   Research in Information Integration

There are thousands of papers relevant to information integration. Many focus on some aspect of one of the stages of the process described above, *e.g.*, discovering primary keys (one piece of understanding the data). Others propose broader solutions for specific environments, for example, querying deep web data sources. It is beyond the scope of this paper to survey the literature (see [4] for an excellent introduction). Instead, we categorize the work into four broad areas, one for each step in the integration process, and provide a few pointers to work in each category, to give a feeling for the accomplishments to date. Not all of the literature is amenable to this crude categorization, as we also briefly illustrate. Despite the weighty body of literature, the information integration challenge is far from solved, especially in the enterprise context.

In the area of understanding the data and data sources, there has been much recent cross-disciplinary work (spanning data management, information retrieval, statistics and machine learning). Key areas of focus include structure discovery [5], which aims to determine the schema for data automatically, data summarization and analysis [6, 7], to determine characteristics such as value distributions and dependencies, text analytics [8], which tries to find specific concepts in text, and source selection [9, 10], which chooses the best data source(s) to answer a particular query.

Research on standardization has focused around several aspects of reconciling different data sets [11, 12]. A key challenge is *entity resolution* (often known as semantic resolution or deduplication), the problem of determining when two data objects refer to the same real-world entity [13]. Other aspects under study include dealing with inconsistent data [14, 15], and how to measure quality and incorporate it in systems [16]. In general, if data can be inconsistent, there can be uncertainty, sparking a renewed surge of interest in probabilistic databases [17].

In specification, the major topics of interest have been schema mapping and schema matching [18, 19]; although work on dataflow systems [20] and workflow [21] is also relevant, these technologies have not typically been applied to information integration by the research community (though they are used in enterprises). Model management [22] takes a broad view of managing and manipulating schemas. Schema mapping tools such as Clio [23] help the user align a target schema with (potentially multiple) source schemas, allowing a nonprocedural specification and typically generating the runtime artifacts needed to populate the target schema from the source(s). Dataflow programming could be used as a more procedural way to specify how to create the target data; workflow tools are similarly procedural, but centered on the operations rather than the data.

There are many ways to integrate information. As described in our example, materialization, federation, search, as well as "application integration" techniques (workflow or business process integration, hard-wired code, composing Enterprise

Java Beans, and so on) all may apply to the execution step. Initially, the research community focused on integration via materialization, with emphasis on data transformation [24], and replication [25, 26]. In the early 1980's, attention shifted to querying across distributed databases [27, 28], and more recently, to mediation [29, 30, 31] approaches. The Garlic project [32] explored a form of mediation now known as federation, which extended a relational query processor [33], and thus fit easily into enterprise environments. Database theory has made strong contributions in this area, both formalizing and extending these basic techniques [4, 34, 35]. While search [36] was initially conceived of as a way to find unstructured information, it has rapidly become a means of information integration [37], though with radically different properties than either materialization or federation. While those integration techniques allow for precise queries spanning data from multiple sources with structured results composed of data from multiple sources, search poses an imprecise query to one or more sources, and returns a ranked list of results, each typically from a single source. This form of integration is "good enough" for some integration scenarios, requires much less work for the initial three integration tasks in our process, and may also be used as an aid to understanding the data.

Of course, not all work fits nicely into one of these categories. For example, many papers are now focusing on integration in the context of the world-wide web [38]. These papers often tackle multiple steps, but in this narrower context. Likewise, much research has been done on integration in the context of bioinformatics [39]. Specialized integration languages [40] and the use of domain ontologies [41] have gained some traction in this community.

This discussion is far from comprehensive, but gives a flavor for both the broad range of problems and the types of approaches that have been taken. The results have led to great progress in the tools available to the industry, as we show in the following section. However, while research has solved subsets of the overall problem, there is little today in the way of complete and unified solutions.

4 The State of Information Integration in Practice

Out in the marketplace, tools for integrating information are proliferating. Many smaller companies sell products addressing one or more of the integration steps we have enumerated. Meanwhile, larger companies, most notably IBM and Informatica, are consolidating tools for the various steps into powerful platforms for information integration and access [42, 43]. Rather than trying to cover all the products on the market, we will instead describe in some detail the present market leader, namely, IBM Information Server [44].

IBM Information Server (IIS) is a platform for information integration. It consists of a suite of products (Figure 2) that together cover all the integration tasks. There are multiple products for any task. For example, IIS includes three products, each aimed at a different level of understanding of the data. WebSphere Information Analyzer analyzes source data, discovering schema elements such as primary and foreign keys, and checking adherence to integration and quality rules defined by the user; it supports understanding the physical data. It provides detailed profiling of the data in each column (cardinality, nullability, range, scale, length, precision, etc.). WebSphere

Understand:
- WebSphere Information Analyzer
- WebSphere Business Glossary
- Rational Data Architect

Standardize:
- Rational Data Architect
- WebSphere QualityStage

Specify:
- Rational Data Architect
- Each execution engine

Execute:
- WebSphere DataStage
- WebSphere Federation Server
- WebSphere Replication Server
- WebSphere Data Event Publisher

Operational platform:
- Connectors to databases, applications, and web sources
- WebSphere Metadata Server and Metadata Workbench
- WebSphere Information Services Director

Fig. 2. Individual products comprising IBM Information Server, listed by the integration task they support. Additional products in the suite provide a common platform for the products listed to run on. That platform includes connectivity to a broad range of sources, shared metadata, and the ability to invoke the various products as services, from a range of different programming environments.

Business Glossary lets the user define and manage a vocabulary for their enterprise, and link the terms to the underlying data (providing business-level understanding). It is designed for business users and subject-matter experts to define data standards and record business terminology definitions, rules and taxonomies. It is useful both for understanding and standardization in our framework.

IBM Rational Data Architect (RDA) is a full-function data modeling tool that can be used with any database management system. RDA supports understanding of data at the logical level. It allows the design and exploration of logical schemas, including relationship discovery (*i.e.*, finding foreign keys), and production of physical schemas. RDA also incorporates the Clio [23] mapping capabilities, which are useful in conjunction with an integration project. Thus, RDA also spans our understanding and standardization tasks. In fact, from a mapping, RDA can generate out the artifacts needed by the federation engine, hence it handles specification for federation as well.[3]

IIS includes WebSphere Metadata Server to capture the insight gained (and standardization decisions made) in using these products and to make that knowledge available to the other tools in the suite. Metadata Server provides a unified repository

---

[3] In fact, it handles specification for any integration that can be done by an SQL engine today. Incorporating additional Clio capabilities would give it the ability to also handle XML to SQL, SQL to XML and XML to XML transformations.

for metadata access and analysis. It provides import and export to twenty common modeling and business intelligence tools, as well as being leveraged by the products of the IIS suite.

A key component of standardization is data cleansing, provided for IIS by WebSphere QualityStage. QualityStage allows the user to set the formats for data records, examine, correct and enrich data fields, and match and link records that may represent the same object. The user can specify rules to determine which values should "survive" merging of similar records. A graphic interface allows the user to set up the rules for this cleansing in a dataflow design metaphor, and to tune the rules by observing their impact on a dataset. The dataflow design metaphor of QualityStage is also exploited by WebSphere DataStage, one of several products in the suite aimed at execution. The same graphic interface allows the user to design complex transformation logic visually, exploiting a large library of transforms (shared with QualityStage). DataStage is used for materialization. It can be invoked in batch or real-time, and can extract, transform and load vast volumes of information.

IIS also includes other integration engines, most notably WebSphere Federation Server, which allows query access to heterogeneous data sources as if all the data were in a single (virtual) database. Federation Server supports full SQL and SQL/XML [45] access, with optimized query plans and materialized query tables for caching data. It can be configured graphically using Rational Data Architect, or using a Wizard in its own control center. Other integration engines include several replication products, which allow synchronization of multiple copies of data. Each product addresses a specific set of requirements. For example, one product focuses on flexible scheduling, SQL-based transformation, and support for a variety of configurations to handle typical business intelligence and application integration scenarios, while another focuses on high throughput, low latency replication, for high availability or workload distribution. The suite also provides event-publishing capabilities (allowing database changes to be captured as XML messages and put on a queue for an application to interpret). Event publishing is often used as a way of integrating applications (by sending messages between them), and also as a way to feed information to ETL engines to trigger a job. For example, using WebSphere Event Publisher with WebSphere DataStage allows DataStage ETL jobs to be fed a stream of data values to transform and load, so that it can integrate information in real-time, driven by changes to the data, as opposed to batch processing.

This is a wide range of products, but even IIS is not sufficient for all integration needs. In particular, while several of the products deal with both structured and unstructured data, as a whole they offer more features to deal with structured datasets. Hence, the various engines are increasingly interoperating with related IBM products for content federation [46] and enterprise search and text analysis [47, 48].

This brief description is offered as an example of the types of products that exist today. For each product mentioned, there are many competitive products that could be substituted. Each typically has its own unique strengths. Further, a particular function (*e.g.*, finding relationships among data records) may be present in many products. Different vendors will package functionality differently, depending on the strengths of their products and the market niche they expect to address with them.

Looking back to the extended example from Section 2.2, Janet's pain becomes more concrete. Which products should she use for which steps in the integration? Will

Rational Data Architect and WebSphere Federation Edition provide better results than WebSphere QualityStage and DataStage? How can she know that the products she chooses will meet the application desiderata?

5 The "Big I" Challenge

Despite the many products available today, there are still many opportunities for research in each of the basic functions needed. We don't have an ultimate answer on how to tell that two pieces of data refer to the same object, for example. We are still learning how to automate schema integration. The wealth of research pointed to in Section 3 shows how rich an area integration is for new discoveries.

However, in working with customers such as Janet over the last few years, we have come to believe that there is a more global problem that needs to be addressed. The issue that we see is that there is no theoretical – nor much practical – guidance for the many Janets of the world on how to make these choices. This is problematic, because the wrong choice can lead to bad results: orders of magnitude difference in performance, lack of flexibility to accommodate changes in the company's processes, or just difficult, time-wasting implementations.

More concretely, what is wrong with today's products, from the consumer standpoint? There are too many, with too much functional overlap. (We have described a relatively simple situation, in which they were all IBM products. In general, the poor customer would be choosing from many products from many different companies, much less compatible with each other than the IBM suite). Once an integration approach is chosen, it is hard to switch; for example, the work done to use federation today would have to be largely redone to move to a materialization approach, as might be desired if the data were really massive or response time were critical, for example. This is too bad, as federation is much better for rapid prototyping to show the benefits of integration than materialization, which typically requires months (and sometimes years) of effort before the benefits are visible. When you consider that integration is an ongoing effort (new sources and new requirements for information arrive constantly), flexibility becomes a major issue.

The products are also too hard to use together to support a complete integration scenario. Most of the industrial-strength integration products available today have many knobs that must be set to configure them to meet a particular set of requirements. They are typically too focused on their own functionality and not on smooth interoperability with other tools needed in the integration process. Hence, they may be difficult or expensive to use in combination. The emergence of product suites such as IIS as described above is a start at addressing this problem, but there is still progress needed, especially when dealing with products from multiple vendors.

Ultimately, the time until the customer realizes value from the integration project (and her investment in the tools) is too long, and the costs are too high. Because of the complexity of these decisions, even for a simple case such as that in our example, consulting engagements are frequently needed in even the best-staffed IT departments in order to deliver a successful integration. Bringing in a specialist makes the project more likely to succeed, but with high associated cost. It also adds another step to the process – finding the right expert.

We need enormous advances in integration technology to get beyond these issues. In an ideal world, integration would happen almost automatically. In this world, the user would specify what information he wants, what he wants the result to look like, and what properties he needs the result to have, and the system would "do it" (though probably with user involvement at various points to verify key decisions, etc). This is hardly a new vision. We are basically arguing for nonprocedural information access. In a simpler time, relational databases were the answer to the same quest. The difference is that in today's world, the information needed for a new application is likely to come from multiple heterogeneous sources.

More concretely, we would like to see the various integration execution engines converge, so that, to the user, there is no visible difference between an ETL engine, a replication engine, federation or even search in terms of the first three steps of the integration process. Understanding, standardization and specification should be done the same way, regardless. The execution will just happen, based on the solution desiderata: the qualities of service desired, the constraints, and so on. The user might be blissfully unaware of what execution engine (or engines) does the actual integration under the covers.

To reach this information integration "nirvana", a number of advances in technology are needed. We must raise the level of abstraction significantly above where it is today, where characteristics of individual products become primary concerns for the integrator. A critical challenge is to represent *all* the information needed for the task. Today, an important component of that information is found only in the user's head, or, in a well-disciplined IT department, perhaps in one or more requirement documents. This is the information on the solution desiderata. Because it is not available in a machine interpretable format, we have no way for an integration tool to consider those requirements and hence, automate integration.

The level of abstraction needs to rise in other ways, as well. For example, it must support logical or even business-level descriptions of what information is needed, as opposed to concrete physically-linked descriptions such as column and table names, or existing view definitions. Janet should be able to say she wants customer information and the system should find and deliver it. That will require much richer metadata than we have today, much of which will need to be derived automatically. To support the rising level of abstraction, more sophisticated techniques are needed to automate the various parts of the process, from discovery to entity resolution to configuration and tuning.

There are challenges here for both the theoretical and the more systems-oriented research communities. From the theoretical perspective, we lack a deep understanding of what fundamental operations are needed to integrate information. While Bernstein [22] has suggested a set of operations, we do not know if they are complete, nor do we have precise semantics for them. Is there a unifying theory of integration that subsumes the separate problems of data integration and data exchange? We have posited that achieving our goal requires being able to represent the solution desiderata. What role do these properties or characteristics of the result play, what aspects can be represented and how? We need a model of these desiderata, and how they relate to the integration task. We have wished for fully automatic integration. How close to our goal can we possibly get?

From a systems research perspective, there are several approaches one might take to this challenge. Perhaps the simplest is to start by building an "Integration Advisor", on the model of today's physical design advisors [49, 50]. This tool would lead the user through the various integration steps, asking for input on the desiderata, and then recommend the appropriate engines, and perhaps even generate the configuration information needed. This would simplify the integration process greatly. However, there are still many issues to be addressed in creating this tool, such as what input must the user provide, what really are the tradeoffs among the different integration approaches, which desiderata matter, and so on. Another approach would be to start with a language to express the integration desired (covering data plus desiderata), and then build a system to interpret (or compile) that request against the tools and engines on hand today. In other words, this approach would treat the current set of integration engines as given, and the result of compilation would be a script that invoked one or more of them to accomplish the integration. Alternatively, the system could compile to a new engine with a complete set of operators for integration. In this last case, we are returned to the questions of what is the model of information and what are the basic operations that we posed above to the theory community, as presumably this system would be the interpreter of some subset of those operations.

These are big challenges, and they hide a raft of further interesting problems. How can we deal with uncertainty in a general way within the integration context? How can we exploit the results of the discovery algorithms that are being developed to tell us more about the data? Can we extend our theories of integration to include uncertainty and newly produced knowledge? How much can we model, and how much must we just make informed engineering choices?

We have focused in this paper on an information-centric view of integration. But in fact, the most common form of integration today is still enterprise application integration (EAI). Confronted with a myriad of choices of tools and techniques, many customers fall back on the most popular alternative: writing a special-purpose application, possibly exploiting some workflow or other process support tools. We call this application-level, procedural style of integration *process integration*. Integration at the application level is unfortunate, for several reasons. First, it is not clear that writing a special-purpose application will be simpler even for an easy first project as in our example. All of the initial hard work to understand the data and standardize on an integrated representation will need to be done anyway, and an integration approach chosen, *i.e.,* whether to materialize, federate and/or search. Without the use of at least some information integration tools, a lot of code will be written to accomplish the integration [51]. Second, when the code for the integration is in the application, it can only be optimized by the programmer, so performance will be only as good as the programmer [52]. Third, it may be harder to reuse the work done for this application when the next application over the same data or data sources comes along.

We will never be able to stop programmers from writing code to do integration if they want to do it. But we can ask how far we can and should go in terms of simplification. What if we could not only relieve customers from deciding whether ETL or federation was the answer, but also unify many of the basic tools that are used in the application for integration (for example, business process integration, message queuing, and so on)? Can we replace all the process integration and information integration techniques with a single integration engine? This is what we refer to as the "Big I" vision: a single engine for all integration needs, which takes a nonprocedural specification of those needs and automatically chooses the right approach or combination of approaches.

6 Conclusion

In this paper, we have presented a snapshot of the world of information integration as it stands today. We have made great progress in both the theoretical foundations of information integration and in the algorithms and tools that support it. Still, information integration remains a daunting task. There are many improvements needed: to the basic integration engines themselves, to the tools for understanding, standardizing and specifying what is needed, and to the theory behind them. These improvements will simplify certain aspects of the task, but they will not, by themselves, eliminate the many choices that must be made by a talented expert today. We therefore posed a challenge to the research community: can we move beyond the individual techniques for integration to a fundamental understanding of what integration is, and armed with that understanding, can we build a single integration engine that automatically uses the right techniques for the right situation? We hypothesized that the key to achieving this goal may lie in being able to represent and reason about the full set of desiderata for the integrated system.

There is plenty of work to do, and many areas we could not touch on in this paper. We focused on the problem of integration within the enterprise. In recent years, much research has focused on the exciting world of data outside the enterprise, on the worldwide web. Much of this work is applicable within the enterprise, though it typically requires significant adaptation to work effectively with the constraints and issues of that environment. More recently, research is emerging (again) on integration of personal information, for example the information on your laptop [52]. New challenges and techniques will doubtless be found in this environment as well.

Acknowledgments. I am grateful to my colleagues who have worked with me on integration and related issues over the years at the IBM Almaden Research Center (IBMers and visitors both), and to my many colleagues in IBM's Information Management division who introduced me to the real-world challenges. In particular, I would like to thank Lee Scheffler and Mike Beckerle for many deep and stimulating discussions on our shared vision of a simpler world of integration, which Lee christened "the Big I". Finally, I'd like to thank Phokion Kolaitis, Ron Fagin, and Mike Beckerle for reading and improving earlier drafts of this work.

References

1. Jacob, K.J.: Betting on Brain Power. The Week. Feb 2, 2003. Available at http://www.the-week.com/23feb02/biz2.htm
2. IBM Business Consulting Services: Your Turn, The Global CEO Study 2004. Available from http://www.bitpipe.com/detail/RES/1129048329_469.html
3. Moore, C., Markham, R.: The Future of Content in the Enterprise. Forrester Report (2003)

4. Lenzerini, M.: Data Integration: A Theoretical Perspective. PODS (2002) 233-246
5. IEEE Data Eng. Bull. Special Issue on Structure Discovery, 26:3 (2003)
6. Barbará, D., DuMouchel W., Faloutsos, C., Haas, P. J., Hellerstein, J. M., Ioannidis, Y. E., Jagadish, H. V., Johnson, T., Ng, R. T., Poosala, V., Ross, K. A., Sevcik, K. C.: The New Jersey Data Reduction Report. IEEE Data Eng. Bull. 20:4 (1997) 3-45
7. Ilyas, I. F., Markl, V., Haas, P. J., Brown, P., Aboulnaga, A.: CORDS: Automatic Discovery of Correlations and Soft Functional Dependencies. SIGMOD (2004) 647-658
8. Doan, A., Ramakrishnan, R., Vaithyanathan, S.: Managing information extraction: state of the art and research directions. SIGMOD (2006) 799-800
9. Gravano, L., García-Molina, H., Tomasic, A.: GlOSS: text-source discovery over the Internet. ACM Transactions on Database Systems (TODS) 24:2 (1999) 229-264
10. Powell, A. L., French, J. C., Callan, J., Connell, M., Viles, C. L.: The impact of database selection on distributed searching. SIGIR (2000) 232-239
11. Hernández, M. A., Stolfo, S. J.: Real-world Data is Dirty: Data Cleansing and The Merge/Purge Problem. Data Min. Knowl. Discov. 2:1 (1998) 9-37
12. Johnson, T., Dasu, T.: Exploratory Data Mining and Data Cleaning. John Wiley (2003)
13. Koudas, N., Sarawagi, S., Srivastava, D.: Record Linkage: Similarity Measures and Algorithms. SIGMOD (2006) 802-803
14. Lembo, D., Lenzerini, M., Rosati, R.: Source inconsistency and incompleteness in data integration. KRDB (2002)
15. Bertossi, L. E., Chomicki, J.: Query Answering in Inconsistent Databases. Logics for Emerging Applications of Databases (2003) 43-83
16. Naumann, F., Gertz, M., Madnick, S. E.: Proc. Information Quality (MIT IQ Conference), Sponsored by Lockheed Martin, MIT, Cambridge, MA, USA (2005)
17. IEEE Data Eng. Bull. Special Issue on Probabilistic Data Management, 29:1 (2006)
18. Miller, R. J., Haas, L. M., Hernández, M. A.: Schema Mapping as Query Discovery. VLDB (2000) 77-88
19. Rahm, E., Bernstein, P. A.: A survey of approaches to automatic schema matching. VLDB J. 10:4 (2001) 334-350
20. Johnston, W. M., Hanna, J. P., Millar, R. J. Advances in dataflow programming languages. ACM Comput. Surv. 36:1 (2004) 1-34
21. Rinderle, S., Reichert, M., Dadam, P.: Flexible Support of Team Processes by Adaptive Workflow Systems. Distributed and Parallel Databases 16:1 (2004) 91-116
22. Bernstein, P.A.: Applying Model Management to Classical Meta Data Problems. Proc. CIDR (2003) 209-220
23. Haas, L. M., Hernández, M. A., Ho, H., Popa, L., Roth, M.: Clio grows up: from research prototype to industrial tool. SIGMOD (2005) 805-810
24. Shu, N. C., Housel, B. C., Taylor, R. W., Ghosh, S. P., Lum, V. Y.: EXPRESS: A Data EXtraction, Processing, amd REStructuring System. ACM Trans. Database Syst. 2:2 (1977) 134-174
25. Breitbart, Y., Komondoor, R., Rastogi, R., Seshadri, S., Silberschatz, A.: Update Propagation Protocols For Replicated Databases. SIGMOD (1999) 97-108
26. Kemme, B., Alonso, G.: A new approach to developing and implementing eager database replication protocols. ACM Trans. Database Syst. 25:3(2000) 333-379
27. Dayal, U., Hwang, H.-Y.: View Definition and Generalization for Database Integration in a Multidatabase System. IEEE Trans. Software Eng. 10:6 (1984) 628-645
28. Lohman, G. M., Daniels, D., Haas, L. M., Kistler, R., Selinger, P. G.: Optimization of Nested Queries in a Distributed Relational Database. VLDB (1984) 403-415

29. Wiederhold, G. Mediators in the architecture of future information systems. IEEE Computer 25:3 (1992) 38-49

30. Papakonstantinou, Y., Gupta, A., Haas, L. M.: Capabilities-Based Query Rewriting in Mediator Systems. PDIS (1996) 170-181

31. Levy, A. Y., Rajaraman, A., Ordille, J. J.: Querying Heterogeneous Information Sources Using Source Descriptions. VLDB (1996) 251-262

32. Roth, M. T., Schwarz, P. M., Haas, L. M.: An Architecture for Transparent Access to Diverse Data Sources. In Dittrich, K. R., Geppert, A. (eds.): Component Database Systems. Morgan Kaufmann Publishers (2001)175-206

33. Haas, L. M., Kossmann, D., Wimmers, E. L., Yang, J.: Optimizing Queries Across Diverse Data Sources. VLDB (1997) 276-285

34. Fagin, R., Kolaitis, P. G., Miller, R. J., Popa, L.: Data exchange: semantics and query answering. Theor. Comput. Sci. 336:1 (2005) 89-124

35. Kolaitis, P. G.: Schema mappings, data exchange, and metadata management. PODS (2005) 61-75

36. Zobel, J., Moffat, A.: Inverted files for text search engines. ACM Comput. Surv. 38:2 (2006)

37. Meng, W., Yu, C., Liu, K.: Building efficient and effective metasearch engines. ACM Comput. Surv. 34:1 (2002) 48-89

38. Chang, K. C.-C., Cho, J.: Accessing the web: from search to integration. SIGMOD (2006) 804-805

39. Leser, U., Naumann, F., Eckman, B. A.: Data Integration in the Life Sciences (DILS 2006). Lecture Notes in Computer Science, Vol. 4075. Springer-Verlag, Berlin Heidelberg New York (2006)

40. Buneman, P., Davidson, S. B., Hart, K., Overton, G. C., Wong, L.: A Data Transformation System for Biological Data Sources. VLDB (1995) 158-169

41. Blake, J. A., Bult, C. J.: Beyond the data deluge: Data integration and bio-ontologies. Journal of Biomedical Informatics 39:3 (2006) 314-320

42. http://www-306.ibm.com/software/data/integration/

43. http://www.informatica.com/

44. http://www-306.ibm.com/software/data/integration/info_server/overview.html

45. ISO/IEC 9075-14:2003 Information technology -- Database languages -- SQL -- Part 14: XML-Related Specifications (SQL/XML). International Organization for Standardization (2003)

46. http://www-306.ibm.com/software/data/integration/db2ii/editions_content.html

47. http://www-306.ibm.com/software/data/integration/db2ii/editions_womnifind.html

48. Ferrucci, D., Lally, A.: UIMA: an architectural approach to unstructured information processing in the corporate research environment. Natural Language Engineering 10:3-4 Cambridge University Press, New York (2004) 327-348

49. Zilio, D. C., Rao, J., Lightstone, S., Lohman, G. M., Storm, A., Garcia-Arellano, C., Fadden, S.: DB2 Design Advisor: Integrated Automatic Physical Database Design. VLDB (2004) 1087-1097

50. Agrawal, S., Chaudhuri, S., Kollár, L., Marathe, A. P., Narasayya, V. R., Syamala, M.: Database Tuning Advisor for Microsoft SQL Server 2005. VLDB (2004) 1110-1121

51. Saracco, C., Englert S., Gebert, I.: Using DB2 Information Integrator for J2EE Development: A Cost/Benefit Analysis. May 2003. On IBM Developerworks, available at www.ibm.com/developerworks/db2/library/techarticle/0305saracco1/0305saracco1.html

52. Halevy, A. Y., Franklin, M. J., Maier, D.: Principles of dataspace systems. PODS (2006) 1-9

Approximate Data Exchange

Michel de Rougemont[1,*] and Adrien Vieilleribière[2]

[1] University Paris II & LRI CNRS
mdr@lri.fr
[2] University Paris-Sud & LRI CNRS
vieille@lri.fr

Abstract. We introduce *approximate data exchange*, by relaxing classical data exchange problems such as Consistency and Typechecking to their approximate versions based on Property Testing. It provides a natural framework for consistency and safety questions, which first considers approximate solutions and then exact solutions obtained with a Corrector.

We consider a model based on transducers of words and trees, and study ε-Consistency, i.e., the problem of deciding whether a given source instance I is ϵ-close to a source I', whose image by a transducer is also ε-close to a target schema. We prove that ε-Consistency has an ε-tester, i.e. can be solved by looking at a constant fraction of the input I. We also show that ε-Typechecking on words can be solved in polynomial time, whereas the exact problem is PSPACE-complete. Moreover, data exchange settings can be composed when they are close.

1 Introduction

Data exchange considers the situation when a source send information to a target and respects a target schema and specific constraints which link the source and the target structures. Fagin et al. [7] consider relational structures with a source schema, a target schema, constraints associated with tuple-generated-dependencies, and define the *Existence-of-Solution* problem. Arenas and Libkin [3] extend the framework to ordered and unordered trees where schemas are regular properties, and constraints are Source to Target dependencies.

We introduce *approximate data exchange* which applies to classical data-exchange but also to the situation where sources may be imperfect. Let Source-consistency be the decision problem, where given a data-exchange setting and an input structure I, we decide if there is a solution J in the target schema. We define the ε-Source-consistency problem by relaxing the source instance I to an I' close to I and a solution J' for I' close to the schema. We consider the special case when a transducer provides the solution and show that this problem is simpler than its exact version. Given an instance source I in the source schema K_S, we also find in linear time a target instance J in the target schema, using a Corrector. If the Source is imperfect because of noise, we still provide

---

* Work supported by ACI *Vera* of the French ministry of research.

T. Schwentick and D. Suciu (Eds.): ICDT 2007, LNCS 4353, pp. 44–58, 2007.
© Springer-Verlag Berlin Heidelberg 2007

a solution which maybe approximate or exact. The ranking of Web data, i.e. to determine if XML documents are close or far from predefined DTDs, is a typical application of this problem. The Transducer may provide a translation from tags in foreign languages into english tags used by the DTDs, and we determine if each document is ε-Source-consistent to the setting defined by the Transducer and a DTD.

Property Testing is a framework for approximate decision problems, which considers classes of finite structures with a distance between structures. Given a parameter $0 \leq \varepsilon \leq 1$, an ε-tester [15,11] for a property P decides if a structure satisfies the property P or if it is ε-far from satisfying the property P. A property is *testable* if for all ε, there exists an ε-tester whose time complexity is independent of the size of the structure and only depends on ε. When the structure is ε-close to the property, a *corrector* finds in linear time a structure which satisfies the property and which is ε-close to the initial structure. Although we use an approximate version of data-exchange, we may provide an exact target structure (the Target-search problem) in linear time, when the source is ε-consistent.

The main results of the paper use the *Edit Distance with Moves* on words and trees, and a transducer model to link source and target instances. Under these hypotheses, we show that many approximate data exchange problems can be efficiently solved.

- ε-Source-consistency on words and trees, i.e. the problem to decide if a given source instance I is ε-close to a source I' such that its image by the transducer is ε-close to the target schema, has a tester, i.e. can be solved by looking at a constant fraction of the input I.

- ε-Target composition on words and trees can be solved in linear time, for ε-composable settings, i.e. when the target schema of the first setting is closed to the source schema of the second setting.

These results are based on the testers and correctors for words (resp. trees) introduced in [12] for regular words (resp. regular trees) and depend on this specific *Edit Distance with Moves*. We also use the embedding of words and trees into statistical vectors introduced in [9] which yields natural testers to decide Equality, Membership of a regular language and a polynomial time algorithm to decide if two non-deterministic automata are ε-equivalent. A corrector for XML along this theory presented in [4], is also used for ε-Target search and ε-composition.

Although the main motivation is on trees, we first study these problems on words, as unranked trees are coded as binary trees with the Rabin encoding, and then coded as data words. The statistical representation of a tree is the statistical embedding of its encoded data word.

In section 2, we review the basic data exchange models, and define approximate data exchange problems. We study some of these problems on words in section 3, and on trees in section 4, in the special case when the data exchange setting uses transducers.

2   Preliminaries

2.1   Data Exchange

Let $\mathbf{K}$ be a class of finite structures, $\mathbf{K_S}, \mathbf{K_T} \subseteq \mathbf{K}$ two subclasses, and a binary relations $\mathcal{T}$ between structures $I \in K_S$ and $J \in K_T$. A pair of structures (I, J) satisfies a *data exchange setting* $\Delta = (\mathbf{K_S}, \mathcal{T}, \mathbf{K_T})$ if $I \in \mathbf{K_S}$, $J \in \mathbf{K_T}$ and $(I, J) \in \mathcal{T}$. The motivation is to view a source instance I as a finite model of a schema $\mathbf{K_S}$ and study which possible target instances J can be found such that they are models of a target schema $\mathbf{K_T}$ and satisfy a relation $\mathcal{T}$ between the two schemas. Such possible target instances are called solution for I with respect to the data exchange setting and are written $Sol_\Delta(I)$.

Fagin and al. [7] studied the relational case and defined several decision problems, given a *data exchange setting* $\Delta = (\mathbf{K_S}, \mathcal{T}, \mathbf{K_T})$ where $\mathbf{K_S}$ is a source schema, $\mathbf{K_T}$ the target schema and $\mathcal{T}$ is specified by formulae Ψ called tuple-dependencies. Arenas and Libkin [3] studied the case of trees when the schemas are regular tree languages and $\mathcal{T}$ is specified by source-to-target dependencies. In both cases the relation $\mathcal{T}$ is defined as the set of pairs (I, J) such that $(I, J) \models \wedge_{\Psi \in \mathcal{T}} \Psi$.

Given a finite alphabet Σ and a finite set A of attributes, we consider a class $\mathbf{K_{\Sigma, A}}$ of (Σ, A) labeled tree structures I which can be ordered or unordered. They have two domains: D is the set of nodes, and Str the set of attribute values.

- On unordered trees, $I = (D, Str, \text{Child}, r, L, \lambda)\}$
- On ordered trees, $I = (D, Str, \text{Firstchild}, \text{Nextsibling}, r, L, \lambda)\}$

where r is the root of the tree, $L : D \rightarrow \Sigma$ defines the node label, and $\lambda : D \times A \rightarrow Str$ is a partial function which defines the attributes values of a node, when they exist. On unordered trees Child is the edge relation of an unranked tree, whereas on ordered trees Firstchild defines the first child of a node and Nextsibling defines the successor along the siblings. Target schemas $\mathbf{K_{\Sigma, A}}$ may have their value set $Str_T = Str \cup V$ for $V \subseteq Var$ and Var is a fixed infinite set of values distinct from Str, called nulls.

Example 1. Strings, Relations and Trees as $\mathbf{K_{\Sigma, A}}$ classes.

(a) Let $\Sigma = \{0, 1\}$, $A = \emptyset$, $D = \{1, ..., n\}$, $Str = \emptyset$, $\mathbf{K_1} = \{I = (D, Str, \text{Child}, r, L, \lambda)\}$ where Child in the natural successor over D and $L : D \rightarrow \{0, 1\}$. This class represents binary words of length n. If $A' = \{A_1, A_2\}$, $Str = \{a, c\}$, we have binary words with two attributes, and values in Str.
    For example $1.0_{[A_1=a]} \cdot 1_{[A_1=c, A_2=c]} \cdot 0_{[A_1=a]} \cdot 1.0_{[A_1=a]}$ is a word where certain letters have attribute values. For example $L(2) = 0$ and $\lambda(2, A_1) = a$.
(b) Let $\Sigma = \emptyset$, $A = \{A_1, A_2, A_3\}$, $D = \{1, ..., n\}$, and Str an arbitrary set of string values, $\mathbf{K_2} = \{I = (D, Str, \text{Child}, r, L, \lambda)\}$, such that Child is the edge relation of an unranked tree of depth 1 whose leaves have attributes A_1, A_2, A_3 and values in Str. This class represents ternary relations with $n - 1$ tuples having values in Str.
(c) Let $\Sigma = \{0, 1\}$, $D = \{d_1, ..., d_n\}$, $A = \emptyset$, $Str = \emptyset$. The class of unranked ordered trees with n nodes without attributes is given by
$$\mathbf{K_3} = \{I = (D, Str, \text{Firstchild}, \text{Nextsibling}, L, \lambda)\}$$

2.2   Transformations

Two main approaches can be used to specify transformations between a source instance and possible target instances. Let $\mathcal{T}$ be a binary relation defined by some pairs of structures (I, J) where $I \in \mathbf{K_S}$ and $J \in \mathbf{K_T}$ for a target schema $\mathbf{K_T}$. The transformation $\mathcal{T}$ can be defined by regular transductions or by logical formulas linking source and target structures. In the first case, a deterministic transducer without null transitions associates a unique J, whereas in the second case there may be infinitely many J.

Transducers. A transduction transforms a source structure I into a target structure J in the language of the target. It does not change the basic structure of I but transforms the tags from the source language to tags of the target language. There is a large literature on tree transducers and our model is close to the top-down tree transducers of [13], but also handles attributes values.

Let $\mathbf{K_S}$ be a set of (Σ_S, A_S) trees and $\mathbf{K_T}$ be a set of (Σ_T, A_T) trees. A transducer associates in a top-down manner with a node v with label in Σ_S and attribute values along attributes in $A_S = \{A^1, ..., A^k\}$, a local new finite (Σ_T, A_T) subtree and new attribute values for each node of that tree. In particular, a node v with attribute values $A_1 = a$ can generate a child node with label A_1 and data-value a, and conversely. This setting is motivated by the XSLT language where this feature is standard.

Let H_{Σ_T, A_T} be the set of finite sequences of *finite trees* (hedges) with attributes in A_T and values in $Str \cup Var$. Let $H_{\Sigma_T, A_T}[Q]$ be the set of finite sequences of finite trees where one leaf of each tree is a distinguished element labelled by a sequence of states in Q, which is possibly empty.

The transducer is defined by three functions. The function δ defines the local tree transformation at each node, the function h defines the transformation of attribute values (into possibly null values) and the *partial* function μ defines the positions of the new attribute values in the new finite tree t introduced by δ.

Definition 1. *A tree transducer between (Σ_S, A_S) trees and (Σ_T, A_T) trees is defined by (Q, q_0, δ, h, μ) where:*

- $\delta : \Sigma_S \times Q \to H_{\Sigma_T, A_T}[Q]$
- $h : \Sigma_S \times Q \times A_S \to \{1\} \cup Var$,
- $\mu : \Sigma_S \times Q \times A_T \times D_T \to \{1, 2, ...k\}$, *where D_T is the set of nodes of the sequence of trees (hedge) defined by δ.*

The function h extends to a function $h' : \Sigma_S \times Q \times Str \to Str \cup Var$ as follows. For label $l \in L_S$, state $q \in Q$, if $h(l, q, A_S^i) = 1$ then $h'(l, q, x_i) = x_i$. If $h(l, q, A_i) = V \in Var$ then $h'(l, q, x_i) = V$. Notice that this model is precisely what XSLT allows, but some attribute values may be kept in some state, i.e. when $h(l, q, A_S^i) = 1$, and assigned Null values in some other states.

A top-down run starts with the root node in state q_0 and transforms each node in a top-down manner. A node v with label $l \in L_S$, state q, attributes in A_S and attribute values in Str is replaced by a finite subtree with labels in L_T, attributes in A_T and attribute values in $Str \cup Var$, through the transformation $\mathcal{T}(l, q)$ defined by:

- $\delta(l, q) = (t_1, t_2, ..t_s)$ a set of finite trees with a distinguished leaf element labelled by a sequence of states. The trees t_i are inserted below the node v as siblings, as defined in [13], where duplications and deletions are allowed.
- Let v a node with attribute values $x_1, ..., x_k \in Str$. The function h extends to a function h' which determines if the value is kept or assigned to a Null value.
- If $\mu(l, q, A_T^1, w) = i$ then the value of the first attribute of node $w \in D_T$ is the value $h'(x_i)$. The function sets the value of the attribute of w as the image through h', defined by h of the $i - th$ value of the node v.

Notice the μ is a finite object as it only depends on finite trees and finitely many attributes. The set Str is not finite as it depends on arbitrary trees but the set Var of Null values is finite and determined by the labels and states. At each node, we apply the transformation $T(l, q)$ for label l and state q and we obtain a tree T' with labels in Σ_T, attributes in A_T, and attribute values in $Str \cup Var$. In the case of strings, if each $\delta(a, p) = u[q]$ where u is a finite word, we obtain the classical transducer which replaces in state p a letter a with the word u and goes to state q. The transducer is *linear* when no duplication is allowed.

Example 2. Linear transduction on strings with attributes. Let $\Sigma_S = \{0, 1\}$, $A_S = \{N, M\}$, $D = \{1, ..., n\}$, $\mathbf{K_S} = \{I = (D, Str, \text{Child}, r, L, \lambda)\}$ where Child in the natural successor over D and $L : D \to \{0, 1\}$, as in example 1 of binary words. Let $\Sigma_T = \{a, b, c\}$, $A_T = \{P\}$, and the corresponding $\mathbf{K_T}$, defined by the transducer (Q, q, δ, h, μ):

- $Q = \{q\}$, $\delta(0, q) = c.d[q]$, $\delta(1, q) = b.d[q]$, i.e. words with only one successor,
- for all l, q, $h(l, q, M) = 1$, $h(l, q, N) = V_1$. Hence $h'(l, q, a) = a$, $h'(l, q, c) = V_1 \in Var$,
- μ sets the value of the attribute M on the node c of the word $c.d$ with the value @M of the attribute M.

The image of the word on the label set $\{0, 1\}$, with attributes N, M defined by $1.0_{[N=a]}.1_{[N=c, M=c]}.0_{[M=c]}.1.0_{[N=a]}$ is a word on the label set $\{a, b, c\}$ with attribute P and attribute values in $Str \cup Var$, i.e. $b.d.c_{[P=a]}.d.b.d.c_{[P=V_1]}.b.d.c.d$

In practice, the transducer is deterministic and defined by an XSLT program π.

Example 3. Consider the following Source and Target XML structures associated with an XSLT transducer.

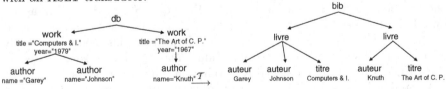

The transducer takes the *db* tree as input and produces the *bib* tree as output.

Logic based transformations. For a source instance I and a target instance J, a logical specification of source to target dependencies (tgd) is typically given by formulae Ψ where a notion of satisfaction for $(I, J) \models \Psi$ is defined. In this model, $\mathcal{T}_{STD}(I) = Sol_\Delta(I)$ is understood as $\{J : \quad (I, J) \models \Psi_i, \quad \forall \Psi_i \in T\}$ A Data Exchange setting $\Delta = (\mathbf{K_S}, \mathcal{T}, \mathbf{K_T})$ is specified by a Source schema $\mathbf{K_S}$, a Target Schema $\mathbf{K_S}$, and the relation $\mathcal{T}$.

A *Tree pattern formula* [3] is a formula $\varphi_S(x, y) \rightarrow \psi_T(x, z)$ defined by a conjunctive formula $\varphi_S(x, y)$ in the language of $\mathbf{K_S}$ with free variables for attribute values and a conjunctive formula $\psi_T(x, z)$ in the language of $\mathbf{K_T}$ with free variables for attribute values. Define $(I, J) \models \varphi_S(x, y) \rightarrow \psi_T(x, z)$ if a node v in I is such that $I, v \models \varphi_S(x, y)$ there exists a node v' in J such that $J, v' \models \psi_T(x, z)$. Such formulas Ψ_i are called STDs for Source to Target Dependencies.

Example 4. Some STDs lead to transducers. On a relational setting: $R(x, x, y) \rightarrow T(x, y)$. On an XML setting: $bd[book(@title = x[author(@name = y)]] \rightarrow bib[livre(@auteur = y, @titre = x)]$

In this approach, the settings do not compose, if we strictly rely on first-order formulas [8]. The search for minimal target structures may lead to structures much smaller then the sources, using optimization techniques, and therefore which may be far from target structures obtained by transductions.

Main Data Exchange problems. Let Δ be a data exchange setting where the relation $\mathcal{T}$ is arbitrary and I a source instance.

- *Source-consistency* decides if a source instance I given as input is such that there is $J \in \mathcal{T}(I)$ satisfying $J \in \mathbf{K_T}$.
- *Target-search* takes a source instance I given as input and produces a target structure J as output such that $(I, J) \in \mathcal{T}$ and $J \in \mathbf{K_T}$.
- *Typechecking* or *Safeness* decides if a data exchange Δ given as input is such that for all $I \in \mathbf{K_S}$, $\mathcal{T}(I) \subseteq \mathbf{K_T}$.
- *Boolean Query Answering* decides if an instance I is such that all J such that $(I, J) \in \mathcal{T}$ satisfy a boolean query, i.e. a subclass $\mathbf{K_T^Q}$ on the target structures.

The *Source-consistency, Target-search* become simple (linear time) for deterministic transducers, regular words and regular trees, as we only check if $\mathcal{T}(I) \in \mathbf{K_T}$. The typechecking problem is PSPACE complete on words and NEXPTIME complete on trees, as a function of the size of the regular expression or of the DTD [16]. For two settings $\Delta_1 = (\mathbf{K_S^1}, \mathcal{T}^1, \mathbf{K_T^1})$ and $\Delta_2 = (\mathbf{K_S^2}, \mathcal{T}^2, \mathbf{K_T^2})$, we wish to compose the Target-search problems and find a new setting $\Delta = (\mathbf{K_S}, \mathcal{T}, \mathbf{K_T})$ such that $Sol_\Delta(I) = \{ J : \exists J', J' \in Sol_{\Delta_1}(I) \wedge J \in Sol_{\Delta_2}(J')\}$.

2.3 Property Testing and Approximation

Property Testing has been initially defined in [15] and studied for graph properties in [11]. It has been successfully extended to various classes of finite structures, such as words where regular languages are proved testable [2,1] for the Hamming distance, and trees where regular tree languages are proved testable

[12] for the Edit Distance with Moves. A tester decides if an input structure satisfies a property or is far from this property by looking at a constant fraction of the input, independent of the global size of the input.

We say that two unary structures $U_n, V_m \in \mathbf{K}$ such as words and trees, whose domains are respectively of size n and m, are ε-close if their distance $\mathsf{dist}(U_n, V_m)$ is less than $\varepsilon \times \max(n, m)$. They are ε-far if they are not ε-close. The distance of a structure U_n to a class $\mathbf{K}$ is $\mathsf{dist}(U_n, \mathbf{K}) = Min_{V \in \mathbf{K}}\{\mathsf{dist}(U_n, V)\}$. In this paper, we consider this notion of closeness for words and trees since the representation of their structure is of linear size. For other classes, such as binary structures or graphs, one may define the closeness relatively to the representation size (e.g. $\varepsilon . n^2$ for graphs) instead of the domain size.

Definition 2. *Let $\varepsilon \geq 0$ be a real. An ε-tester for a class $\mathbf{K}_0 \subseteq \mathbf{K}$ is a randomized algorithm A such that:*
(1) If $U \in \mathbf{K}_0$, A always accepts;
(2) If U is ε-far from $\mathbf{K}_0$, then $\Pr[A \text{ rejects}] \geq 2/3$.

The *query complexity* is the number of boolean queries to the structure U of $\mathbf{K}$. The *time complexity* is the usual time complexity where the complexity of a query is one and the time complexity of an arithmetic operation is also one. A class $\mathbf{K}_0 \subseteq \mathbf{K}$ is *testable* if for every sufficiently small $\varepsilon > 0$, there exists an ε-tester whose time complexity depends only on ε.

Definition 3. *An ε-corrector for a class $\mathbf{K}_0 \subseteq \mathbf{K}$ is a (randomized) algorithm A which takes as input a structure I which is ε-close to $\mathbf{K}_0$ and outputs (with high probability) a structure $I' \in \mathbf{K}_0$, such that I' is ε-close to I.*

Let the *Edit distance with moves* between two strings w and w', written $\mathsf{dist}(w, w')$, the minimal number of elementary operations on w to obtain w', divided by $max\{|w|, |w'|\}$. An *elementary operation* on a word w is either an *insertion, a deletion* of a letter, a *modification* of a letter or of an attribute value, or a *move* of a subword of w into another position.

Let the *Edit distance with moves* between two ordered unranked trees T and T', written $\mathsf{dist}(T, T')$, the minimal number of elementary operations on T to obtain T', divided by $max\{|T|, |T'|\}$. An *elementary operation* on a tree T is either an *insertion, a deletion* of a node or of an edge, a *modification* of a letter (tag) or of an attribute value, or a *move* of an entire subtree of T into another position. When an XML file is given by its DOM representation, these operations take unit costs.

Approximate Schemas. We first consider classes of structures on the same language $\mathcal{L}$, i.e. with the same alphabet Σ and attibutes A.

Definition 4. *Let $\varepsilon \geq 0$. Let $\mathbf{K}_1, \mathbf{K}_2$ be two classes of structures. We say that $\mathbf{K}_1$ is ε-contained in $\mathbf{K}_2$, if all but finitely many words of $\mathbf{K}_1$ are ε-close to $\mathbf{K}_2$. $\mathbf{K}_1$ is ε-equivalent, written $\equiv_\varepsilon$, to $\mathbf{K}_2$, if both $\mathbf{K}_1$ is ε-contained in $\mathbf{K}_2$ and $\mathbf{K}_2$ is ε-contained in $\mathbf{K}_1$.*

Example 5. Let $\mathbf{K}_1 = O^*1^*$ and $\mathbf{K}_2 = c(ab)^*ca^*$ be two regular expressions. There is a transducer with one state which replaces the letter 0 by ab and the letter 1 by a. The transducer $\mathcal{T}$ is specified by $0|ab$ and $1|a$. The image of O^*1^* by $\mathcal{T}$ is $\mathcal{T}(O^*1^*) = (ab)^*a^*$, which is ε-close to $c(ab)^*ca^*$ for any ε. Any word $w \in (ab)^*a^*$ of length n is at distance $2/n$ from a word of $c(ab)^*ca^*$, as two insertions of c are required.

A Statistical Embedding on Strings and Trees. For a finite alphabet Σ and a given ε, let $k = \frac{1}{\varepsilon}$. Let the $\mathrm{dist}(w, w')$ be the *Edit distance with moves* and the embedding of a word in a vector of k-*statistics*, describing the number of occurrences of all subwords of length k in w. Let w be a word of length n, let $\#u$ be the number of occurrences of u of length k in w and:

$$\mathsf{ustat}(w)[u] \stackrel{\mathrm{def}}{=} \frac{\#u}{n-k+1}$$

The vector $\mathsf{ustat}(w)$ is of dimension $|\Sigma|^k$ is also the *probability distribution* that a uniform random subword of size k of w be a specific u, i.e.

$$\mathsf{ustat}(w)[u] = \Pr_{j=1,\ldots,n-k+1}[w[j]w[j+1]\ldots w[j+k-1] = u]$$

This embedding is a generalized Parikh mapping [14] and is also related to [5], where the subwords of length k were called *shingles*. The statistical embedding of [9] associates a statistics vector $\mathsf{ustat}(w)$ of fixed dimension with a string w and a union of polytopes H in the same space to a regular expression r, such that the distance between two vectors (for the L_1 norm) is approximately $\mathrm{dist}(w, w')$ and the distance between a vector and a union of polytopes is approximately $\mathrm{dist}(w, L(r))$. Other embeddings on words [6] and trees [10] depend on the size of the structures.

Example 6. For a lexicographic enumeration of the length 2 binary words, $w = 000111$, $r_1 = 0^*1^*$, $r_2 = (001)^*1^*$, $k = 2$,

$$\mathsf{ustat}(w) = \begin{pmatrix} 2/5 \\ 1/5 \\ 0 \\ 2/5 \end{pmatrix}. Let\ \ s_0 = \begin{pmatrix} 1 \\ 0 \\ 0 \\ 0 \end{pmatrix}, s_1 = \begin{pmatrix} 0 \\ 0 \\ 0 \\ 1 \end{pmatrix}, s_2 = \begin{pmatrix} 1/3 \\ 1/3 \\ 1/3 \\ 0 \end{pmatrix}$$

$H_1 = \mathrm{Convex - Hull}(s_0, s_1)$ is the polytope associated with r_1 and $H_2 = \mathrm{Convex - Hull}(s_1, s_2)$ the polytope associated with r_2.

These techniques yield the simple testers of [9] for:

- Equality tester between two words w and w' of approximately the same length. Sample the words with at least $N \in O(\frac{(\ln|\Sigma|)|\Sigma|^{2/\varepsilon}}{\varepsilon^3})$ samples, define $\widehat{\mathsf{ustat}}(w)$ and $\widehat{\mathsf{ustat}}(w')$ as the ustat of the samples. Reject if $|\widehat{\mathsf{ustat}}(w) - \widehat{\mathsf{ustat}}(w')|_1 \geq \varepsilon$.
- Membership tester between a word and a regular expressions r. Compute $\widehat{\mathsf{ustat}}(w)$ as before and the polytope H associated with r in the same space. Reject if the geometrical distance from the point $\widehat{\mathsf{ustat}}(w)$ to the polytope H is greater then ε.

– Equivalence tester between two regular expressions r_1 and r_2. Associate the polytopes H_1 and H_2 in the same space as $\mathsf{ustat}(w)$, represented by the nodes $H_{1,\varepsilon}$ and $H_{2,\varepsilon}$ on a grid of step ε. If $H_{1,\varepsilon} \neq H_{2,\varepsilon}$ then r_1 and r_2 are ε far.

The membership tester is polynomial in the size of the regular expression (or non-deterministic automaton) whereas it was exponential in this parameter in [12]. In this paper, we use the Membership tester and the Equivalence tester.

Unranked trees can be coded as binary trees with the Rabin encoding, i.e. ordered trees of degrees at most 2. We define the k-compression of a tree T, as in figure 1. We remove every node whose subtree has size $\leq k = 1/\varepsilon$, and encode the removed subtrees into the labels of their ancestor nodes. The resulting tree has at most $\varepsilon.n$ nodes with two successors, as most of the nodes have only one successor. Using at most $\varepsilon.n$ moves, we end up with a word with labels $w(T)$ that encodes T such that $\mathsf{ustat}(w(T))$ can be approximately sampled from samples on T. The previous results on words are extended to trees trough this encoding.

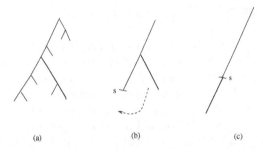

(a)   (b)   (c)

Fig. 1. Binary tree in (a), its k-compressed form in (b) and its word embedding in (c)

Approximate Data Exchange. Consider a distance dist between structures of a class **K**. We can consider the ε-approximate version of the classical data exchange problems. Let Δ be a data exchange setting, I a source instance and a parameter ε.

– ε-*Source-consistency* decides if a source instance I given as input is ε-close to a source I' such that there exists J' ε-close to $\mathbf{K_T}$ and $(I', J') \in \mathcal{T}$.
– ε-*Target search* computes, given a source instance I as input, a target instance $J \in \mathbf{K_T}$ which is ε-close to $\mathcal{T}(I)$.
– ε-*Typechecking* or ε-*Safeness* decides if a data exchange Δ given as input is such that for all $I \in \mathbf{K_S}$, $\mathcal{T}(I)$ is ε-close to $\mathbf{K_T}$.
– ε-*Boolean Query Answering* decides if an instance I is ε-close to a source I' such that all J' such that $(I', J') \in \mathcal{T}$ are ε-close to a subclass $\mathbf{K_T^Q}$ on the target structures.

We took the most liberal definitions where we allow approximations on the source instance I and on the solution J. We could restrict these definitions and allow asymetric approximations. We consider the *special case of Transducers*, as a first step, and show that ε-*Source-consistency* can be decided in $O(1)$, whereas the exact version is decided in $O(n)$. We give a condition to compose such data exchange settings, based on similar approximations: only close schemas can be composed.

Definition 5. *Let* $\varepsilon \geq 0$. *Two settings* $\Delta^1 = (\mathbf{K_S^1}, \mathcal{T}^1, \mathbf{K_T^1})$ *and* $\Delta^2 = (\mathbf{K_S^2}, \mathcal{T}^2, \mathbf{K_T^2})$, *are* ε-*composable is they are* ε-*safe and if* $\mathbf{K_T^1}$ *is* ε-*close to* $\mathbf{K_S^2}$.

We will show how to compose settings, using correctors. We will nest the transducers with the correctors and obtain an ε-composition.

3 Approximate Data Exchange on Strings

In this section a data exchange setting is defined with a deterministic transducer and we consider the approximate Data Exchange problems when Schemas are regular.

3.1 ε-Source-Consistency

We present an ε-Tester for ε-Source-consistency, first for the case of a transducer with one state, and generalize it in a second step.

Example 7. Let Δ^1 be defined as in example 3. The setting Δ^1 is not consistent as $\mathcal{T}^1$ does not output the character c. For a given instance such as 0001111, $\mathcal{T}^1(I) = ababab.aaaa$ is at distance $\frac{1}{5}$ from the target schema $c(ab)^*ca^*$. A corrector for $\mathbf{K_T}$ will transform $ababab.aaaa$ into $c.ababab.c.aaaa$ in linear time.

Notice that we cannot apply a direct approach where we would test if I is ε-close to $\mathcal{T}^{-1}(\mathbf{K_T}) \cap \mathbf{K_s}$, as the distances are not kept by the inverse transformation. The Tester follows a simple *sampling approach*. It samples I to obtain a random subword u and estimate $\mathsf{ustat}(I)$. We then look at $\mathcal{T}(u)$ and obtain a subword v of $\mathcal{T}(I)$, which we will sample with specific probabilities. As the transducer produces words of different lengths, we have to adjust the sampling probabilities to guarantee a uniform distribution on $\mathcal{T}(I)$.

Transducer with One State. Let $k = 1/\varepsilon$, $\alpha = \min_{a \in \Sigma_s} |\mathcal{T}(a)| > 0$, $\beta = LCM_{a \in \Sigma_s} |\mathcal{T}(a)|$, i.e. the Least Common Multiplier of the lengths $\mathcal{T}(a)$.

Tester$_1(w, k, N)$:
1. Repeat until N outputs are generated.
  { Choose $i \in_r \{1, ..., n\}$ uniformly, let $a = w[i]$ and $\gamma = |\mathcal{T}(a)|$,
    choose $b \in_r \{0, 1\}$ whith $Prob(b = 1) = \frac{\gamma}{\beta}$,
    If (b=1) { Choose $j \in_r \{0, ..., \gamma - 1\}$ uniformly and
        output the subword of length k begining at position j in $\mathcal{T}(a)$ and
        continuing with k letters on the right side }
  }.
2. If the geometrical distance between $\widehat{ustat}$ and $H(\mathbf{K_T})$ is greater than ε
then reject else accept.

Let $N_0 = O(\beta \ln(1/\varepsilon) \ln(|\Sigma_T|)/(\alpha \varepsilon^3))$.

Lemma 1. *For any data exchange setting Δ, $\varepsilon > 0$ and $N \geq N_0$, $Tester_1(w, k, N)$ is an ε-tester which decides if a source word w is ε-Source consistent with respect to Δ.*

General Transducer. Let $\mathcal{A}$ be a deterministic transducer with m states. We generalize the previous tester, and sample subwords u of w which yield subwords of $\mathcal{T}(w)$. We do not know however the state q in which the transducer is, on sample u. We will consider all the possible states $S_u \subseteq Q$ but need to make sure that the possible states of the samples, i.e. $S_{u_1}, ... S_{u_N}$ are compatible, i.e. can be obtained by paths which meet only a set Π of connected components of the automaton. We will enumerate all possible such Π in the acyclic graph defined by the connected components, and apply a Tester which tests if w is close to a word w' such that a run on w' starting in some state of Π meets only the connected components of Π.

A connected component of $\mathcal{A}$ is a set S of states such that for each pair (s, s') of states of S there is a path from s to s' in $\mathcal{A}$. Let $\mathcal{G}$ be the directed acyclic graph (DAG) associated with the connected components of $\mathcal{A}$, i.e. a node is a connected component C_i and there is an edge from C_i to C_j if there is a path in $\mathcal{A}$ from a state $s \in C_i$ to a state $s' \in C_j$

Definition 6. *A set Π of connected components is admissible for $\mathcal{A}$ if there exists a word x and a state q in one of the connected components of Π such that the run from q on x meets exactly the connected components of Π. Such a word x is called Π-compatible from q.*

A word w is ε-source consistent along Π, if there is an ε-close w' which is Π-compatible from the initial state q_0 such that $\mathcal{T}(w')$ is ε-close to $\mathbf{K}$. Let H_Π be the polytope associated to the automaton reduced to Π.

Tester$_2(w, k, N, \Pi)$:
Generate $u_1...u_N$ words of length k in w.
Estimate $\widehat{ustat}(w)$: if it is ε-far from H_Π, reject.
If it is ε-close to H_Π, associate a set of states S_{u_i} with each u_i from which u_i is Π-compatible.
Apply Tester$_1(w, k, N)$ for each possible states of S_{u_i}, as $\mathcal{T}(u_i)$ is well defined.
Accept if there is choice of states such that Tester$_1(w, k, N)$ accepts, else reject.

Let $N_0 = O(\beta \ln(1/\varepsilon) \ln(|\Sigma_T|)/(\alpha \varepsilon^3))$.

Lemma 2. *For $N \geq N_0$, $\varepsilon > 0$, $Tester_2(w, k, N, \Pi)$ is an ε-tester which decides if a source word w is ε-source consistent along Π.*

Tester$_3(w, k, N)$:
Generate all Π and apply Tester$_2(w, k, N, \Pi)$.
If there is a Π such that Tester$_2(w, k, N, \Pi)$ accepts, then accept, else reject.

Theorem 1. *If* $N \geq \beta \ln(1/\varepsilon) \ln(|\Sigma_T|)/(\alpha\varepsilon^3)$, $\varepsilon > 0$, $Tester_3(w, k, N)$ *is an* ε-*tester which decides if a source word* w *is* ε-*Source-consistent.*

Intrepretation with the Word Embedding. Let $\mathsf{ustat}(w)$ be the statistics vector of dimension $|\Sigma_S|^k$, associated with w. There are two tasks to perform: find a w' close to w readable by T and find the image $T(w')$ close to $\mathbf{K_T}$. Let H_T be the target union of polytopes associated with $\mathbf{K_T}$ by the embedding. Consider the automaton associated with T where all states accept, when we ignore the output. Let G_T be the union of polytopes associated with the language accepted by this automaton. Each polytope corresponds to a Π.

All the polytopes of G_T which are ε-close to $\mathsf{ustat}(w)$ indicate a possible w' given by its statistics vector $\mathsf{ustat}(w')[u]$ along a fixed Π. Define the image $\mathsf{ustat}(T(w'))$ relative to Π as the set of statistics vector $\mathsf{ustat}[v]$ of dimension $|\Sigma_T|^k$ which are possible images of w' by T. This set is defined as the convex-hull C of the $\mathsf{ustat}[v]$ *limit* vectors such that there exist states $s_1.....s_p$ in Π such that for some i $T(s_i, u_i) = v_j$, and $\mathsf{ustat}[v_j] = \mathsf{ustat}(w')[u_i]$ if $|v_j| = k$. If $|v_j| > k$,then the weight of $\mathsf{ustat}(w')[u_i]$ is uniformly distributed over all subwords v of length k of v_j. The set of i for which there is no s_i must be of density less than ε. The Tester is simply: If C is ε-close to H_T, then Accept, else Reject.

3.2 ε-Typechecking

The Typechecking (or Safety) problem is hard in general, as it involves the comparison of schemas, a PSPACE problem for regular schemas on strings, but an undecidable problem on context-free schemas. In [9], it is shown that ε-equivalence and ε-containment are PTIME for regular schemas and EXPTIME for context-free schemas. We then obtain:

Theorem 2. *Given* $\epsilon > 0$, *a transducer* T *and regular schemas* $\mathbf{K_S}$ *and* $\mathbf{K_T}$, *there exists an* ε-*tester which decides* ϵ-*safety of* $(\mathbf{K_S}, T, \mathbf{K_T})$, *in Polynomial time.*

3.3 ε-Composition

Let $\Delta^1 = (\mathbf{K_S^1}, T^1, \mathbf{K_T^1})$ and $\Delta^2 = (\mathbf{K_S^2}, T^2, \mathbf{K_T^2})$ be two settings. Let $\Delta^{2\circ1} = (\mathbf{K_S^1}, T^{2\circ1}, \mathbf{K_T^2})$ such that $T^{2\circ1} = \mathcal{C}_T^2 \circ T^2 \circ \mathcal{C}_S^2 \circ \mathcal{C}_T^1 \circ T^1$ where $\mathcal{C}_X^i$ is a corrector for $\mathbf{K_X^i}$. Recall that a corrector for a regular schema $\mathbf{K_X^i}$ is a deterministic linear time program wich takes a word w ε-close to $\mathbf{K_X^i}$ as input and produces a word $w' \in \mathbf{K_X^i}$ which is ε-close to w. An ε-**solution** of $I \in \mathbf{K_S^1}$ with respect to $\Delta^{2\circ1}$ is an instance $J_{2\circ1} \in \mathbf{K_T^2}$ such that $\exists J_T^1 \in \mathbf{K_T^1}, I_S^2 \in \mathbf{K_S^2}, \varepsilon_1, \varepsilon_2, \varepsilon_3, \ \varepsilon_1 + \varepsilon_2 + \varepsilon_3 \leq \varepsilon$ such that:

$$\mathsf{dist}(T^1(I), J_T^1) \leq \varepsilon_1 \wedge \mathsf{dist}(J_T^1, I_S^2) \leq \varepsilon_2 \wedge \mathsf{dist}(T^2(I_S^2), J_{2\circ1}) \leq \varepsilon_3$$

Theorem 3. *Let* Δ_1 *and* Δ_2 *be two* ε-*composable settings. Then* $J = T_{2\circ1}(I)$ *is an* ε-*solution for* I *with respect to* $\Delta^{2\circ1}$.

Proof. Let $J_1 = T^1(I)$. There is a $J_T^1 \in \mathbf{K_T^1}$ which is ε_1-close to J_1. There is a $J_S^2 \in \mathbf{K_S^2}$ which is ε_3-close to J_T^1. Let $J_2 = T^2(J_S^2)$. There is a $J^{2\circ1} \in \mathbf{K_T^2}$ which is ε_2-close to J_2. Using the triangular inequality, we conclude that $J^{2\circ1}$ a ε-Solution for I with respect to $\Delta^{2\circ1}$.

Example 8. Let Δ^1 be defined as in example 3(a) and let $\Delta^2 = (\mathbf{K_S^2}, T^2, \mathbf{K_T^2})$ such that $\mathbf{K_S^2} = a^*d(ab)^*$, $\mathbf{K_T^2} = 0^+(022)^*3$ and $T^2 : a|0, b|22, d|3$. Let us apply the transformations:

$$I = 00011 \xrightarrow{T^1} ababababaa \xrightarrow{C_T^1} cababababcaa \xrightarrow{C_S^2} aadababababab \quad (1)$$
$$\xrightarrow{T^2} 003022022022 \xrightarrow{C_T^2} 000220220223 = J_{2\circ1}$$

The second corrector C_S^2 makes one move (aa moves to the end) and two deletions (c are removed) and C_T^2 makes one move ("3" moves to the end). Δ^1 and Δ^2 are ϵ-composable and therefore this sequence of operations guarantees that the result is in the target shema and is obtained by few corrections.

4   Approximate Data Exchange on Trees

The basic results on approximate data exchange on words generalize to unranked ordered trees via a coding of a tree T as binary tree $e(T)$. Consider the classical (Rabin) encoding, where each node v of the unranked tree is a node v in the binary encoding, the left successor of v in the binary tree is its first successor in the unranked tree, the right successor of v in the binary tree is its first sibling in the unranked tree. New nodes with labels $\perp$ are added to complete the binary tree when there are no successor or no sibling in the unranked tree. If we remove the leaves labelled with $\perp$, we consider trees with degree at most 2, where nodes may only have a left or a right successor and call these structures *extended* 2-ranked trees. The Edit distance with moves on unranked trees is equivalent to the same distance on these extended 2-ranked trees, on which we apply the k-compression and obtain a word $w(T)$.

4.1 ε-Source-Consistency Via the Tree Embedding

Let $\mathsf{ustat}(T)$ be the statistical vector of T defined by the tree embedding, i.e. the statistics vector of the word $w(T)$, obtained in the compression described in section 2.

From the $\mathsf{ustat}(T)$ vector, we have to find a close $\mathsf{ustat}'(T)$ vector whose image by the transducer has a statistics vector close to the polytope H_T of the target schema $\mathbf{K_T}$ defined by the embedding. Consider a grid of step ε on each dimension, and the set I_ε of $\mathsf{ustat}'(T)$ points on the grid which are ε-close to $\mathsf{ustat}(T)$ and to some polytope of H_T as in the case of words.

For each of the points of I_ε, construct its image C by T with set of connected component Π, determined with one of the polytopes of H_T. C is the convex-hull of the $\mathsf{ustat}[v]$ *limit* vectors in the target space, such that there exist states $s_1.....s_{|\Sigma_S|^k}$ in Π such that: (i) for most i, $\mathcal{T}(s_i, u_i) = v_j$, and ustat$[v_j]$ = ustat$(w')[u_i]$ if $|v_j| = k$. If $|v_j| > k$,then the weight of ustat$(w')[u_i]$ is uniformly distributed over all subwords v of length k of v_j. (ii) the fraction of i for which there is no such s_i is of density less than ε, i.e. $\sum_i$ ustat$[u_i] \le \varepsilon$.

Given a point ustat $\in I_\varepsilon$ the test is: If C is ε-close to H_T, then Accept, else Reject this point. We need the following lemmas:

Lemma 3. *If there is a point in I_ε such that its C is ε close to H_T, there exists a T' ε-close to T such that its image is ε-close to $\mathbf{K_T}$.*

Lemma 4. *If C is ε far to H_T for all points of I_ε, T is not ε-close to a T' whose image is ε-close to $\mathbf{K_T}$.*

Tree Consistency Tester(T, k) :
Generate all points of I_ε.
  {For each point I_ε and compatible Π, compute C.
  If C is close to H_T accept,}
Else reject.

Theorem 4. *For all $\varepsilon, k = 1/\varepsilon$, Tree Consistency Tester(T, k) is an ε-tester for the ε-Source consistency problem on trees.*

4.2 ε-Source-Consistency Via Sampling

The Tester follows an approach, similar to the one presented for strings and uses the Membership ε-Tester presented in [12]. It samples I to obtain a random subtree t with a uniform distribution. We look at $\mathcal{T}(t)$ and obtain a subtree t' of $\mathcal{T}(I)$. As the transducer produces trees of different sizes, we have to adjust the sampling probabilities to guarantee the near-uniform distribution of t'. A random subtree of size k in an unranked tree is defined through the encoding of an unranked tree as as an extended 2-ranked tree.

Theorem 5. *For any data exchange setting Δ, and $\varepsilon > 0$, there is an ε-tester which decides if a source tree T is ε-Source consistent with respect to Δ.*

4.3 ε-Typechecking ε-Composition

The image of a regular by a transducer is regular for linear transducers but not in general. In this case, we generalize the methods introduced in section 3.

Theorem 6. *For any data exchange setting Δ with a linear transducer, and $\varepsilon > 0$, ε-Safety with respect to Δ can be decided in time exponential in the representation.*

Theorem 7. *Let Δ_1 and Δ_2 be ε-composable settings $J = \mathcal{T}_{2\circ1}(I)$ is an ε-Solution for I with respect to $\Delta^{2\circ1} = (\mathbf{K_S^1}, \mathcal{T}^{2\circ1}, \mathbf{K_T^2})$.*

5   Conclusion

We introduced a framework for approximate data exchange and considered the ε-Source-consistency, ε-Typechecking and ε-Composition problems in the special case of deterministic transducers.

We showed that for the *Edit distance with Moves*, ε-Source-consistency is testable on words and trees, and that ε-Typechecking is polynomial on words.

We need to generalize this approach to transformations which may generate an infinite set of solutions, for example with transducers with null transitions and more generally with Logic-based transformations.

References

1. N. Alon, E. Fischer, M. Krivelevich, and M. Szegedy. Efficient testing of large graphs. *Combinatorica*, 20:451–476, 2000.
2. N. Alon, M. Krivelich, I. Newman, and M. Szegedy. Regular languages are testable with a constant number of queries. *SIAM Journal on Computing*, 30(6), 2000.
3. M. Arenas and Leonid Libkin. Xml data exchange: Consistency and query answering. In *ACM Principles on Databases Systems*, 2005.
4. U. Boobna and M. de Rougemont. Correctors for XML data. In *XML Database Symposium*, pages 97–111, 2004.
5. A. Broder. On the resemblance and containment of documents. In *Compression and Complexity of Sequences*, pages 21–29, 1997.
6. G. Cormode and S. Muthukrishnan. The string edit distance matching problem with moves. In *Symposium on Discrete Algorithms*, pages 667–676. Society for Industrial and Applied Mathematics, 2002.
7. R. Fagin, P. G. Kolaitis, R. J. Miller, and Lucian Popa. Data exchange: Semantics and query answering. In *International Conference on Database Theory*, pages 207–224, 2002.
8. R. Fagin, P. G. Kolaitis, L. Popa, and W. C. Tan. Composing schema mappings: Second-order dependencies to the rescue. In *ACM Principles on Databases Systems*, pages 83–94, 2004.
9. E. Fischer, F. Magniez, and M. de Rougemont. Approximate satisfiability and equivalence. In *Proceedings of 21st IEEE Symposium on Logic in Computer Science*, 2006.
10. M. Garofalakis and A. Kumar. Xml stream processing using tree-edit distance embeddings. *ACM Transactions on Database Systems*, 30(1):279–332, 2005.
11. O. Goldreich, S. Goldwasser, and D. Ron. Property testing and its connection to learning and approximation. *Journal of the ACM*, 45(4):653–750, 1998.
12. F. Magniez and M. de Rougemont. Property testing of regular tree languages. In *International Colloquium on Automata Languages and Programming*, pages 932–944, 2004.
13. W. Martens and F. Neven. Frontiers of tractability for typechecking simple XML transformations. In *ACM Principles on Databases Systems*, pages 23–34, 2004.
14. R. J. Parikh. On context-free languages. *Journal of the ACM*, 13(4):570–581, 1966.
15. R. Rubinfeld and M. Sudan. Robust characterizations of polynomials with applications to program testing. *SIAM Journal on Computing*, 25(2):23–32, 1996.
16. L. J. Stockmeyer and A. R. Meyer. Word problems requiring exponential time (preliminary report). In *ACM Symposium on Theory of Computing*, pages 1–9, 1973.

Determinacy and Rewriting of Conjunctive Queries Using Views: A Progress Report

Alan Nash[1], Luc Segoufin[2], and Victor Vianu[1,*]

[1] UC San Diego
[2] INRIA and Univ. Paris 11

Abstract. Suppose we are given a set of exact conjunctive views $\mathbf{V}$ and a conjunctive query Q. Suppose we wish to answer Q using $\mathbf{V}$, but the classical test for the existence of a conjunctive rewriting of Q using $\mathbf{V}$ answers negatively. What can we conclude: (i) there is no way Q can be answered using $\mathbf{V}$, or (ii) a more powerful rewriting language may be needed. This has been an open question, with conventional wisdom favoring (i). Surprisingly, we show that the right answer is actually (ii). That is, even if $\mathbf{V}$ provides enough information to answer Q, it may not be possible to rewrite Q in terms of $\mathbf{V}$ using just conjunctive queries – in fact, no monotonic language is sufficiently powerful. We also exhibit several well-behaved classes of conjunctive views and queries for which conjunctive rewritings remain sufficient. This continues a previous investigation of rewriting and its connection to semantic determinacy, for various query and view languages.

1 Introduction

The question of whether a given set $\mathbf{V}$ of views on a database can be used to answer another query Q arises in many different contexts. For instance, it is a central issue in data integration, semantic caching, security and privacy. The question can be formulated at several levels. The most general definition is information theoretic: $\mathbf{V}$ *determines* Q (which we denote $\mathbf{V} \twoheadrightarrow Q$) iff $\mathbf{V}(D_1) = \mathbf{V}(D_2) \rightarrow Q(D_1) = Q(D_2)$, for all database instances D_1 and D_2. Intuitively, determinacy says that $\mathbf{V}$ provides enough information to uniquely determine the answer to Q. However, it does not say that this can be done effectively, or using a particular query language. The next formulation is language specific: a query Q can be *rewritten* in terms of $\mathbf{V}$ using a rewriting language $\mathcal{R}$ iff there exists some query $R \in \mathcal{R}$ such that $Q(D) = R(\mathbf{V}(D))$ for all databases D.

What is the relationship between determinacy and rewriting? Suppose $\mathcal{R}$ is a rewriting language. Clearly, if Q can be rewritten in terms of $\mathbf{V}$ using some query $R \in \mathcal{R}$, then $\mathbf{V} \twoheadrightarrow Q$. The converse is generally not true. Given a view language $\mathcal{V}$ and query language $\mathcal{Q}$, if $\mathcal{R}$ can be used to rewrite a query Q in $\mathcal{Q}$ in terms of a set of views $\mathbf{V}$ in $\mathcal{V}$ whenever $\mathbf{V} \twoheadrightarrow Q$, we say that $\mathcal{R}$ is *complete* for $\mathcal{V}$-to-$\mathcal{Q}$ rewritings.

---

* Work supported in part by the NSF under grant number INT-0334764.

T. Schwentick and D. Suciu (Eds.): ICDT 2007, LNCS 4353, pp. 59–73, 2007.

Query rewriting using views has been investigated in the context of data integration for some query languages, primarily conjunctive queries (CQs). However, the connection between rewriting and the semantic notion of determinacy has received little attention. For example, a classical algorithm allows to test whether a CQ query has a CQ rewriting using a set of exact CQ views. Suppose the algorithm says there is no such rewriting. Does this mean that the view does not determine the query, or could it be that CQs are just not powerful enough to rewrite Q in terms of $\mathbf{V}$? If so, what is the language needed for the rewriting?

In [14], a subset of the authors undertook a systematic investigation of these issues. They considered view languages $\mathcal{V}$ and query languages $\mathcal{Q}$ ranging from first-order logic (FO) to CQ and studied two main questions:

(i) is it decidable whether $\mathbf{V}\twoheadrightarrow Q$ for $\mathbf{V}$ in $\mathcal{V}$ and Q in $\mathcal{Q}$?
(ii) is $\mathcal{Q}$ complete for $\mathcal{V}$-to-$\mathcal{Q}$ rewritings? If not, how must $\mathcal{Q}$ be extended in order to express such rewritings?

As usual, all definitions and results come in two flavors: in the *unrestricted* case, databases can be finite or infinite. In the *finite* case, databases are assumed to be finite. The results of [14] concern languages ranging from FO to CQ, in both the unrestricted and finite cases. However, the main questions remained open for CQ, the simplest and most common language for defining views and queries. In the present paper we report some progress on this front. First, we settle in the negative the question of whether CQ is complete for CQ-to-CQ rewriting. In fact, no monotonic language can be complete for CQ-to-CQ rewriting. We then provide several classes of CQ views and queries for which CQ remains complete for rewriting, and for which determinacy is decidable. One such class consists of monadic CQ views and arbitrary CQ queries. Beyond monadic views, CQ can only remain complete for very limited classes of views. Indeed, we show that non-monotonic rewrite languages are required even for very simple CQ views whose patterns are trees, and that differ from simple paths by a single edge. We show that CQ remains complete for binary views consisting of a simple path.

Related work.   Answering queries using views arises in numerous contexts including data integration [15], query optimization and semantic caching [8], data warehousing, support of physical data independence by describing storage schemas as views [9], etc. The problem comes in several flavors, depending on assumptions on the views and their use. Mainly, the different settings vary along these dimensions:

(i) assumptions on the views: these may be *exact* (i.e. contain precisely the set of tuples in their definitions), or just *sound* (they provide only a subset of the tuples in the answer).
(ii) how the views are used: *query rewriting* requires reformulating the query in terms of the views, using some query language. One may require an *equivalent* rewriting, or just a *maximally contained* one. Another use of views is called *query answering*. This consists of finding all *certain* answers to a query given an instance of the view [1].

In our investigation, we focus on exact view definitions, and equivalent query rewritings, with the accompanying information-theoretic notion of determinacy. Results on equivalent query rewriting using exact views have focused primarily on CQs and UCQs (unions of CQs). It is shown in [12] that it is NP-complete whether a given (U)CQ query has an equivalent (U)CQ rewriting in terms of given (U)CQ views. Several polynomial-time special cases are identified for CQs in [7]. Answering queries using views in the presence of binding patterns is considered in [13]. Views and queries defined by CQs with arithmetic comparisons over dense orders are considered in [3], where it is shown that the existence of an equivalent rewriting using Datalog with comparisons is decidable.

The relation of rewriting to the information-theoretic notion of determinacy has received little attention. In [10,11], Grumbach and Tininini consider the problem of computing an aggregate function using a given set of aggregate functions including count, average, sum, product, maximum. In particular, [11] introduces the notion of *subsumption* of a query by a view, which is identical to our notion of determinacy. Using this, they define completeness of a rewriting algorithm, and produce such an algorithm for simple aggregate functions on a single relation. Despite the similarity in flavor, none of the results transfer to the setting we consider.

In [5], the authors consider the notion of *lossless* view with respect to a query, in the context of regular path queries on semi-structured data. Losslessness is considered under the exact view assumption and under the sound view assumption. In the first case, losslessness is equivalent to determinacy and it remains open whether losslessness is decidable for regular path views and queries. In the second case, losslessness is shown to be decidable using automata-theoretic techniques. Again, these results have no bearing upon ours because of the differences in the settings and because we consider exact views.

Bancilhon and Spyratos [4] defined the notion of determinacy in the context of their investigation of view updates. In particular, they defined the notion of *view complement*. The complement of a view is another view so that together they uniquely determine the underlying database. Thus, a view and its complement determine the identity query on the database.

This paper is a direct follow-up of [14]. We briefly summarize the results of [14] for some key combinations of query and view languages. In the unrestricted case, FO turns out to be complete for FO-to-FO rewritings, as a consequence of Craig's Interpolation theorem [6]. Unfortunately this does not extend to the finite case: FO is no longer complete for FO-to-FO rewritings. In fact, any language complete for FO-to-FO rewritings must express all computable queries.

For views expressed in weaker languages, less powerful rewriting languages are needed. If views are expressed in $\exists$FO (existential FO), FO is still not complete for $\exists$FO-to-FO rewritings. However, both $\exists$SO and $\forall$SO (existential and universal second-order logic formulas) are complete for such rewritings. In fact $\exists$SO $\cap$ $\forall$SO is a lower bound, even if views are restricted to UCQs.

Consider UCQ views and queries. Similarly (but for different reasons), UCQ is not complete for UCQ-to-UCQ rewritings, nor are much more powerful languages such as Datalog $^{\neq}$. This also turns out to hold for CQ$^{\neq}$-to-CQ rewritings.

The results on determinacy are mostly negative: it is shown that determinacy is undecidable even for UCQ views and queries. The question is left open for CQs (although completeness of CQ and, as a corollary, decidability of determinacy, are erroneously claimed for CQs in the unrestricted case, as discussed below).

Organization. After recalling some basic concepts and notation in Section 2, we show in Section 3 that CQs are not complete for CQ-to-CQ rewriting. For the unrestricted case, we exhibit an effective FO rewriting of Q in terms of $\mathbf{V}$, whenever $\mathbf{V}$ determines Q. For the finite case, the upper bound of $\exists SO \cap \forall SO$ shown in [14] remains the best available. In Section 4 we consider special cases of CQs for which determinacy is decidable and CQ remains complete as a rewriting language.

2   Basic Concepts and Notation

We begin with some basic definitions and notation. A database schema σ is a finite set of relation symbols with associated non-negative arities. A relation with arity zero is referred to as a *proposition*. A database instance D over σ associates a relation $D(R)$ of appropriate arity with values from some fixed infinite domain **dom** to each relation symbol R in σ (true/false for propositions). The domain of an instance D consists of the set of elements in **dom** occurring in D and is denoted $dom(D)$. The set of all instances over σ is denoted by $\mathcal{I}(\sigma)$. By default, all instances are assumed to be finite unless otherwise specified. Queries are defined as usual, as computable mappings from instances of an input schema to instances of an output schema that are generic, i.e. commute with isomorphisms of **dom** (e.g., see [2]). We assume familiarity with the query languages first-order logic (FO) and conjunctive queries (CQ).

Let σ and $\sigma_{\mathbf{V}}$ be database schemas. A *view* $\mathbf{V}$ from $\mathcal{I}(\sigma)$ to $\mathcal{I}(\sigma_{\mathbf{V}})$ is a set consisting of one query $Q_V : \mathcal{I}(\sigma) \to \mathcal{I}(V)$ for each $V \in \sigma_{\mathbf{V}}$. We refer to σ and $\sigma_{\mathbf{V}}$ as the input and output schemas of $\mathbf{V}$, respectively.

Consider a query Q over schema σ and a view $\mathbf{V}$ with input schema σ and output schema $\sigma_{\mathbf{V}}$. We say that $\mathbf{V}$ *determines* Q, denoted $\mathbf{V} \twoheadrightarrow Q$, iff for all $D_1, D_2 \in \mathcal{I}(\sigma)$, if $\mathbf{V}(D_1) = \mathbf{V}(D_2)$ then $Q(D_1) = Q(D_2)$. Suppose $\mathbf{V} \twoheadrightarrow Q$ and let R be a query over $\mathcal{I}(\sigma_{\mathbf{V}})$. We say that Q can be *rewritten* in terms of $\mathbf{V}$ using R iff for each $D \in \mathcal{I}(\sigma)$, $Q(D) = R(\mathbf{V}(D))$. In other words, $Q = R \circ \mathbf{V}$. This is denoted by $Q \Rightarrow_{\mathbf{V}} R$. Note that several R's may satisfy this property, since such R's may behave differently on instances in $\mathcal{I}(\sigma_{\mathbf{V}})$ that are not in the image of $\mathbf{V}$.

Let $\mathcal{Q}$ be a query language and $\mathcal{V}$ a view language. A query language $\mathcal{R}$ is *complete* for $\mathcal{Q}$-to-$\mathcal{V}$ rewritings iff for every $Q \in \mathcal{Q}$ and $\mathbf{V} \in \mathcal{V}$ for which $\mathbf{V} \twoheadrightarrow Q$, there exists $R \in \mathcal{R}$ such that $Q \Rightarrow_{\mathbf{V}} R$.

In the unrestricted case, where database instances may be infinite, we will denote by $\mathbf{V} \overset{\infty}{\twoheadrightarrow} Q$ and by $Q \overset{\infty}{\Rrightarrow}_\mathbf{V} R$ the fact that $\mathbf{V}$ determines Q and that R is a rewriting of Q using $\mathbf{V}$. Note that $\overset{\infty}{\twoheadrightarrow}$ implies $\twoheadrightarrow$ and $\overset{\infty}{\Rrightarrow}$ implies $\Rightarrow$ but that the converse does not generally hold [14].

3 CQ Is Not Complete for CQ-to-CQ Rewriting

In this section, we show that CQ is not complete for CQ-to-CQ rewriting. In fact, no monotonic language can be complete for CQ-to-CQ rewriting. We exhibit effective FO rewritings of CQ queries in terms of CQ views, whenever the views determine the query in the unrestricted case.

Before stating the main result of the section, we recall a test for checking whether a CQ query has a CQ rewriting in terms of a given set of CQ views. The test is based on the chase.

Let σ be a database schema and $Q(\bar{x})$ a CQ over σ with free variables $\bar{x}$. The *frozen body of Q*, denoted $[Q]$, is the instance over σ such that $(x_1, \ldots, x_k) \in R$ iff $R(x_1, \ldots, x_k)$ is an atom in Q. For a set $\mathbf{V}$ of CQs, $[\mathbf{V}]$ is the union of the $[Q]$'s for all $Q \in \mathbf{V}$. For a mapping α from variables to variables and constants, we denote by $\alpha([Q])$ the instance obtained by applying α to all variables in $[Q]$.

Recall that a tuple $\bar{c}$ is in $Q(D)$ iff there exists a homomorphism $h_{\bar{c}}$ from $[Q]$ to D such that $h_{\bar{c}}(\bar{x}) = \bar{c}$. In this case we say that $h_{\bar{c}}$ *witnesses* $\bar{c} \in Q(D)$, or that $\bar{c} \in Q(D)$ via $h_{\bar{c}}$.

Let $\mathbf{V}$ be a CQ view from $\mathcal{I}(\sigma)$ to $\mathcal{I}(\sigma_\mathbf{V})$. Let S be a database instance over $\mathcal{I}(\sigma_\mathbf{V})$ and C a set of elements. We define the $\mathbf{V}$-inverse of S relative to a domain C, denoted $\mathbf{V}_C^{-1}(S)$, as the instance D over σ defined as follows. Let V be a relation in $\sigma_\mathbf{V}$, with corresponding query $Q_V(\bar{x})$. For every tuple $\bar{c}$ belonging to V in S, we include in D the tuples of $\alpha_{\bar{c}}([Q_V])$ where $\alpha_{\bar{c}}(\bar{x}) = \bar{c}$ and $\alpha_{\bar{c}}$ maps every variable of $[Q_V]$ not in $\bar{x}$ to some new distinct value not in $dom(S) \cup C$. Thus, $\mathbf{V}_C^{-1}(S)$ is obtained as a *chase* of S in which all values introduced as witnesses are outside $dom(S)$ and C. To simplify, we usually assume that C consists of the entire domain of the instance when $\mathbf{V}^{-1}$ is applied, and omit specifying it explicitly. Thus, all witnesses introduced by an application of $\mathbf{V}^{-1}$ are new elements.

The following key facts are observed in [9] and [14]:

Proposition 1. *Let $Q(\bar{x})$ be a CQ and $S = \mathbf{V}([Q])$. Let $Q_\mathbf{V}(\bar{x})$ be the CQ over $\sigma_\mathbf{V}$ for which $[Q_\mathbf{V}] = S$. We have the following:*

(i) $Q_\mathbf{V} \circ \mathbf{V}$ is equivalent to the CQ whose frozen body is $\mathbf{V}^{-1}(S)$;
(ii) $Q \subseteq Q_\mathbf{V} \circ \mathbf{V}$;
(iii) If $\bar{x} \in Q(\mathbf{V}^{-1}(S))$ then $Q = Q_\mathbf{V} \circ \mathbf{V}$. In particular, $\mathbf{V} \twoheadrightarrow Q$.
(iv) If Q has a CQ rewriting in terms of $\mathbf{V}$, then $Q_\mathbf{V}$ is such a rewriting.

Note that Proposition 1 applies both to the finite and unrestricted cases. We can now show the following.

Theorem 1. *CQ is not complete for CQ-to-CQ rewriting.*

Proof. We exhibit a set of CQ views **V** and a CQ Q such that $\mathbf{V} \twoheadrightarrow Q$ but $\bar{x} \notin Q(\mathbf{V}^{-1}(S))$, where $S = \mathbf{V}([Q])$. By Proposition 1, this shows that Q has no CQ rewriting in terms of **V**.

Let the database schema consist of a single binary relation R. Consider the set **V** consisting of the following three views (with corresponding graphical representations):

$$V_1(x, y) = \exists \alpha \exists \beta [R(\alpha, x) \wedge R(\alpha, \beta) \wedge R(\beta, y)] \qquad x \leftarrow \alpha \rightarrow \beta \rightarrow y$$
$$V_2(x, y) = \exists \alpha [R(x, \alpha) \wedge R(\alpha, y)] \qquad x \rightarrow \alpha \rightarrow y$$
$$V_3(x, y) = \exists \alpha \exists \beta [R(x, \alpha) \wedge R(\alpha, \beta) \wedge R(\beta, y)] \qquad x \rightarrow \alpha \rightarrow \beta \rightarrow y$$

Let $\quad Q(x, y) = \exists a \exists b \exists c [R(a, x) \wedge R(a, b) \wedge R(b, c) \wedge R(c, y)]$.
We first show that $\mathbf{V} \twoheadrightarrow Q$. To do so, we prove that the formula

$$\varphi(x, y): \quad \exists d[V_1(x, d) \wedge \forall e(V_2(e, d) \rightarrow V_3(e, y))]$$

is a rewriting of Q using **V**. In other words, for each database D over σ and $u, v \in dom(D)$, $\langle u, v \rangle \in Q(D)$ iff $\varphi(u, v)$ holds on the instance $V(D)$.

Suppose $\langle u, v \rangle \in Q(D)$ via a homomorphism h. Note that we also have $\langle x, c \rangle \in V_1([Q])$, via a homomorphism h'. It follows that $h \circ h'$ is a homomorphism from $[V_1]$ to D mapping $\langle x, c \rangle$ to $\langle u, h(c) \rangle$. We let $d = h(c)$ and from the above we have $\langle u, d \rangle \in V_1(D)$. Now because there is an edge $\langle c, y \rangle$ in $[Q]$ we have an edge $\langle h(c), v \rangle$ in D. Therefore for every e such that $\langle e, d \rangle \in V_2(D)$, $\langle e, v \rangle \in V_3(D)$. Thus, $\varphi(u, v)$ holds on $V(D)$. Conversely, suppose $\varphi(u, v)$ holds on $V(D)$. Then there exists d such that $\langle u, d \rangle \in V_1(D)$, so by definition of V_1 there exist α, β such that $R(\alpha, u) \wedge R(\alpha, \beta) \wedge R(\beta, d)$ holds in D. But then $\langle \alpha, d \rangle \in V_2(D)$ so by definition of φ, $\langle \alpha, v \rangle \in V_3(D)$. It follows that there exist b', c' such that $R(\alpha, b') \wedge R(b', c') \wedge R(c', v)$ holds in D. This together with the fact that $R(\alpha, u)$ holds in D, implies that $\langle u, v \rangle \in Q(D)$. Thus, $\varphi(x, y)$ is a rewriting of Q using **V**, so $\mathbf{V} \twoheadrightarrow Q$.

In view of Proposition 1, it remains to show that $\langle x, y \rangle \notin Q(\mathbf{V}^{-1}(S))$, where $S = \mathbf{V}([Q])$. Clearly, $S = \mathbf{V}([Q])$ is the instance:

V_1	V_2	V_3
x c	a c	a y
b c	b y	
c y		

and $\mathbf{V}^{-1}(S)$ is depicted in Figure 1.

It is easily checked that $\langle x, y \rangle$ does not belong to Q applied to the above instance. Thus, Q has no CQ rewriting in terms of **V**. $\square$

Remark 1. Note that Theorem 1 holds in the finite as well as the unrestricted case. This shows that Theorem 3.3 in [14], claiming that CQ is complete for CQ-to-CQ rewriting in the unrestricted case, is erroneous. Also, Theorem 3.7, claiming decidability of determinacy in the unrestricted case as a corollary, remains unproven. The source of the problem is Proposition 3.6, which is unfortunately false (the views and queries used in the above proof are a counterexample).

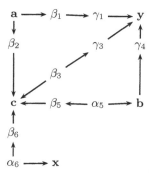

Fig. 1. The graph of $\mathbf{V}^{-1}(S)$ (elements in $dom(S)$ are in boldface)

As a consequence of the proof of Theorem 1 we have:

Corollary 1. *No monotonic language is complete for CQ-to-CQ rewriting.*

Proof. Consider the set of CQ views $\mathbf{V}$ and the query Q used in the proof of Theorem 1. It was shown that $\mathbf{V} \twoheadrightarrow Q$. Consider the database instances $D_1 = [Q]$ and $D_2 = R$ where R is the relation depicted in figure 1. By construction, $\mathbf{V}(D_1) \subset \mathbf{V}(D_2)$. However, $\langle x, y \rangle \in Q(D_1)$ but $\langle x, y \rangle \notin Q(D_2)$, so $Q(D_1) \not\subseteq Q(D_2)$. Thus the mapping $Q_{\mathbf{V}}$ is non-monotonic. □

FO rewriting in the unrestricted case. For the set of views $\mathbf{V}$ and query Q above, we showed that Q has a simple FO rewriting in terms of $\mathbf{V}$. We next exhibit general FO rewritings of CQ queries in terms of CQ views, when these determine the query in the unrestricted case. First, we recall a characterization of determinacy in the unrestricted case, based on the chase. Let $\mathbf{V}$ be a set of CQ views and $Q(\bar{x})$ a CQ over the same database schema σ. We construct two infinite instances D_∞ and D'_∞ such that $\mathbf{V}(D_\infty) = \mathbf{V}(D'_\infty)$ as follows. We first define inductively a sequence of instances $\{D_k, S_k, V_k, V'_k, S'_k, D'_k\}_{k \geq 0}$, constructed by a chase procedure. Specifically, D_k, D'_k are instances over the database schema σ, and S_k, V_k, V'_k, S'_k are instances over the view schema $\sigma_{\mathbf{V}}$. We will define $D_\infty = \bigcup_k D_k$ and $D'_\infty = \bigcup_k D'_k$. For the basis, $D_0 = [Q]$, $S_0 = V_0 = \mathbf{V}([Q])$, $S'_0 = V'_0 = \emptyset$, and $D'_0 = \mathbf{V}^{-1}(S_0)$. Inductively, $V'_{k+1} = \mathbf{V}(D'_k)$, $S'_{k+1} = V'_{k+1} - V_k$, $D_{k+1} = D_k \cup \mathbf{V}^{-1}(S'_{k+1})$, $V_{k+1} = \mathbf{V}(D_{k+1})$, $S_{k+1} = V_{k+1} - V'_{k+1}$, and $D'_{k+1} = D'_k \cup \mathbf{V}^{-1}(S_{k+1})$ (recall that new witnesses are introduced at every application of $\mathbf{V}^{-1}$).

Referring to the proof of Theorem 1, note that the instance depicted in Figure 1 coincides with D'_0.

The following properties are easily checked.

Proposition 2. *Let D_∞ and D'_∞ be constructed as above. The following hold:*

1. $\mathbf{V}(D_\infty) = \mathbf{V}(D'_\infty)$.
2. *There exist homomorphisms from D_∞ into $[Q]$ and from D'_∞ into $[Q]$ that are the identity on $dom([Q])$.*

3. *For every pair of database instances I, I' such that $\mathbf{V}(I) = \mathbf{V}(I')$ and $\bar{a} \in Q(I)$, there exists a homomorphism from D'_∞ into I' mapping the free variables $\bar{x}$ of Q to $\bar{a}$.*

As a consequence of the above we have the following.

Proposition 3. *Let $\mathbf{V}$ be a set of CQ views and $Q(\bar{x})$ a CQ over the same database schema, where $\bar{x}$ are the free variables of Q. Then $\mathbf{V} \stackrel{\infty}{\rightarrow} Q$ iff $\bar{x} \in Q(D'_\infty)$.*

Proof. Suppose $\mathbf{V} \stackrel{\infty}{\rightarrow} Q$. By (1) of Proposition 2, $\mathbf{V}(D_\infty) = \mathbf{V}(D'_\infty)$. It follows that $Q(D_\infty) = Q(D'_\infty)$. But $[Q] = D_0 \subset D_\infty$, so $\bar{x} \in Q(D_\infty)$. It follows that $\bar{x} \in Q(D'_\infty)$. Conversely, suppose that $\bar{x} \in Q(D'_\infty)$. Let I, I' be database instances such that $\mathbf{V}(I) = \mathbf{V}(I')$. We have to show that $Q(I) = Q(I')$. By symmetry, it is enough to show that $Q(I) \subseteq Q(J)$. Let $\bar{a} \in Q(I)$. By (3) of Proposition 2, there exists a homomorphism from D'_∞ into I' mapping $\bar{x}$ to $\bar{a}$. It follows by (2) of Proposition 2 that there is a homomorphism from Q into I' mapping $\bar{x}$ to $\bar{a}$, so $\bar{a} \in Q(I')$. □

We are now ready to show that FO is complete for CQ-to-CQ rewriting in the unrestricted case. Let $\mathbf{V}$ be a set of CQ views and $Q(\bar{x})$ be a CQ with free variables $\bar{x}$, both over database schema σ. Recall the sequence $\{D_k, S_k, V_k, V'_k, S'_k, D'_k\}_{k \geq 0}$ defined above for each $\mathbf{V}$ and Q. For each finite instance S over $\sigma_{\mathbf{V}}$, let ϕ_S be the conjunction of the literals $R(t)$ such that $R \in \sigma_{\mathbf{V}}$ and $t \in S(R)$. Let $k > 0$ be fixed. We define a sequence of formulas $\{\varphi_i^k\}_{i=0}^k$ by induction on i, backward from k. First, let

$$\varphi_k^k = \exists \bar{\alpha}_k \phi_{S_k},$$

where $\bar{\alpha}_k$ are the elements in $dom(S_k) - dom(V'_k)$.
For $0 \leq i < k$ let

$$\varphi_i^k = \exists \bar{\alpha}_i [\phi_{S_i} \wedge \forall \bar{\alpha}'_{i+1}(\phi_{S'_{i+1}} \rightarrow \varphi_{i+1}^k)]$$

where $\bar{\alpha}_i$ are the elements in $dom(S_i) - dom(V'_i)$, and $\bar{\alpha}'_{i+1}$ are the elements in $dom(S'_{i+1}) - dom(V_i)$.
We can now show the following (proof omitted).

Theorem 2. *Let $\mathbf{V}$ be a set of CQ views and Q be a CQ, both over database schema σ. If $\mathbf{V} \stackrel{\infty}{\rightarrow} Q$, then there exists $k \geq 0$ such that $Q \stackrel{\infty}{\Rightarrow}_{\mathbf{V}} \varphi_0^k$.*

Remark. In [14] we showed, using Craig's Interpolation Theorem, that for any set $\mathbf{V}$ of FO views and FO query Q such that $\mathbf{V} \stackrel{\infty}{\rightarrow} Q$ there exists an FO rewriting of Q using $\mathbf{V}$. However, this result is not constructive, as the interpolation theorem itself is not constructive. On the other hand, Theorem 2 provides a constructive algorithm to obtain the rewriting formula. Indeed, assume that $\mathbf{V} \stackrel{\infty}{\rightarrow} Q$ and $\mathbf{V}$ and Q are CQs. Then we know that there is a k such that $\bar{x} \in Q(D'_k)$. Therefore, k can be computed by generating the D'_i until $\bar{x} \in Q(D'_i)$. Once we have k, the formula φ_0^k is easy to compute. Note that Theorem 2 works only for CQ views and queries, while the interpolation argument applies to all FO views and queries.   □

Note that the complexity of the formula φ_0^k provided by Theorem 2 for rewriting Q in terms of $\mathbf{V}$ when $\mathbf{V} \overset{\infty}{\twoheadrightarrow} Q$ is intimately related to the minimum k for which $\bar{x} \in Q(D_k')$. Indeed, φ_0^k has exactly k quantifier alternations. It is therefore of interest to know whether there might be a constant bound on k. In addition to yielding a simpler rewriting with a fixed number of quantifier alternations, this would also provide a decision procedure for unrestricted determinacy: just test that $\bar{x} \in Q(D_k')$. Recall that it remains open whether determinacy is decidable. Unfortunately, there is no constant bound on k. This is shown below by a generalization of the example used in the proof of Theorem 2.

Example 1. The following shows that for each $k > 0$ there exists a set of CQ views $\mathbf{V}$ and a CQ query $Q(\bar{x})$ such that $\bar{x} \in Q(D_k')$ but $\bar{x} \notin Q(D_i')$ for $i < k$.
    Let $P_n(x, y)$ be the CQ on a binary relation R stating that there is a path of length n from x to y in R. Consider the set $\mathbf{V}$ of views consisting of

$$
\begin{aligned}
V_1(x, y) &= \exists \alpha [R(\alpha, x) \wedge P_{k+1}(\alpha, y)], \\
V_2(x, y) &= P_{k+1}(x, y), \\
V_3(x, y) &= P_{k+2}(x, y).
\end{aligned}
$$

Let $Q(x, y) = \exists a [R(a, x) \wedge P_{2k+1}(a, y)]$.
    It can be shown that $\langle x, y \rangle \in Q(D_k')$, but $\langle x, y \rangle \notin Q(D_i')$ for $i < k$. Note that the example in the proof of Theorem 1 is a special case of the above with $k = 1$.

4   Well-Behaved Classes of CQ Views and Queries

We next consider restricted classes of views and queries for which CQ remains complete for rewriting. As a consequence, determinacy for these classes is decidable.

4.1   Monadic Views

In this section we consider the special case when the views are monadic. A *monadic* conjunctive query (MCQ) is a CQ whose result is unary. We show the following.

Theorem 3. *(i) CQ is complete for MCQ-to-CQ rewriting.*
(ii) Determinacy is decidable for MCQ views and CQ queries.

Note that (ii) is an immediate consequence of (i), in view of Proposition 1.
    Towards proving (i), we first note that it is enough to consider monadic queries. Indeed, we show that for MCQ views, determinacy of arbitrary CQ queries can be reduced to determinacy of MCQ queries.

Proposition 4. *Let* **V** *be a set of MCQ views and* $Q(x_1, \ldots, x_k)$ *a CQ query with free variables* $x_1, \ldots, x_k$, *over the same database schema* σ. *Let* $Q_i(x_i)$ *be the MCQ with free variable* x_i, *obtained by quantifying existentially in* Q *all* x_j *for* $j \neq i$.

(i) if **V**$\twoheadrightarrow$*Q then Q is equivalent to* $\bigwedge Q_i(x_i)$;
(ii) if $Q = \bigwedge Q_i(x_i)$ *then* **V**$\twoheadrightarrow$*Q iff* **V**$\twoheadrightarrow$*Q_i(x_i) for* $1 \leq i \leq k$.

Proof. Consider (i). Suppose **V**$\twoheadrightarrow$*Q* and consider $[Q]$. We show that for $i \neq j$, no tuple t_i of $[Q]$ containing x_i is connected to a tuple t_j of $[Q]$ containing x_j in the Gaifman graph of $[Q]$. This clearly proves (i).

Consider instances A and B over σ defined as follows. Let D consist of k elements $\{a_1, \ldots, a_k\}$. Let $A = \{R(a, \ldots, a) \mid R \in \sigma, a \in D\}$, and let B contain, for each $R \in \sigma$ of arity r, the cross-product D^r. Clearly, $\mathbf{V}(A) = \mathbf{V}(B)$ (all views return D in both cases), so $Q(A) = Q(B)$. But $Q(B) = D^k$, so $Q(A) = D^k$. In particular, $\langle a_1, \ldots, a_k \rangle \in Q(A)$. This is only possible if there is no path in the Gaifman graph of $[Q]$ from a tuple containing x_i to one containing x_j for $i \neq j$. Part (ii) is obvious. □

In view of Proposition 4, it is enough to prove that CQ is complete for MCQ-to-MCQ rewriting. As a warm-up, let us consider first the case when **V** consists of a single view $V(x)$, and the database schema is one binary relation. Let $Q(x)$ be an MCQ, and suppose that $V\twoheadrightarrow Q$. We show that Q is equivalent to V. Since Q_V is a query, $Q \subseteq V$ (Q cannot introduce domain elements not in V). It remains to show that $V \subseteq Q$. If $Q(D) \neq \emptyset$ it follows by genericity of Q_V that $V(D) \subseteq Q(D)$; however, it is conceivable that $Q(D) = \emptyset$ but $V(D) \neq \emptyset$. Let $A = [V]$ and $B = \{(v, v) \mid v \in V([V])\}$. Clearly, $V(A) = V(B)$. It follows that $Q(A) = Q(B)$. Clearly, $x \in Q(B)$, since $x \in V([V])$ and $(x, x) \in B$. But then $x \in Q(A) = Q([V])$, so there exists a homomorphism from $[Q]$ to $[V]$ fixing x. It follows that $V \subseteq Q$, which completes the proof.

Unfortunately, the above approach for single views does not easily extend to multiple monadic views. Indeed, suppose we have two views V_1, V_2. The stumbling block in extending the proof is the construction of two instances A and B such that $V_1(A) = V_1(B)$ *and* $V_2(A) = V_2(B)$, and forcing the existence of a homomorphism showing that Q can be rewritten using V_1, V_2. As we shall see, the multiple views case requires a more involved construction.

Given two instances D and D' over the same schema, we say that D' *retracts* to D if $D \subseteq D'$ and there is a homomorphism from D' to D fixing the domain of D.

Let **V** be a set of MCQ views and $Q(x)$ an MCQ query with free variable x, both over database schema σ, such that **V**$\twoheadrightarrow$*Q*. We wish to show that Q has a CQ rewriting in terms of **V**. The idea of the proof is the following. Recall, from Proposition 1 (iii), that Q has a CQ rewriting in terms of **V** iff Q_V is such a rewriting, where Q_V is the CQ over σ_V whose body is $\mathbf{V}([Q])$. This in turn holds iff there is a homomorphism from $[Q]$ into $\mathbf{V}^{-1}(\mathbf{V}([Q]))$ fixing x. To show that this is the case, consider $A_0 = [Q]$ and $B_0 = \mathbf{V}^{-1}(\mathbf{V}([Q]))$.

We show the following key lemma.

Lemma 1. *There exist finite instances A and B over σ such that A retracts to A_0, B retracts to B_0, and $\mathbf{V}(A) = \mathbf{V}(B)$.*

Note that the lemma suffices to conclude the proof of Part (i) of Theorem 3. Indeed, $\mathbf{V}(A) = \mathbf{V}(B)$ implies that $Q(A) = Q(B)$. But $x \in Q(A)$ (since A contains $[Q]$) so $x \in Q(B)$. Since B retracts to B_0 and $x \in dom(B_0)$, this implies that $x \in Q(B_0)$ so there is a homomorphism fixing x from $[Q]$ to $B_0 = \mathbf{V}^{-1}(\mathbf{V}([Q]))$. This establishes (i) of Theorem 3.

Let us fix $\mathbf{V} = \{V_1, \ldots, V_k\}$ where the V_i are MCQs over database schema σ. Consider an instance D over the schema $\sigma_{\mathbf{V}}$ of the image of $\mathbf{V}$. For each element a in the domain of D, we denote its *type* in $\mathbf{V}(D)$ as the set $\tau(D, a) = \{i \mid a \in V_i(D)\}$. More precisely, a *type* S of $\sigma_{\mathbf{V}}$ is a subset of $[k] = \{1, \ldots, k\}$. A type S is *realized* in D if $\tau(D, c) = S$ for some $c \in dom(D)$. A type S is *realizable* if it is realized in some D. We also denote by $\#(S, D)$ the number of elements $c \in dom(D)$ for which $\tau(D, c) = S$. Note that two instances over $\sigma_{\mathbf{V}}$ are isomorphic iff for all types S, the number of elements of type S in the two instances is the same. Also, if we construct instances A and B over σ such that $\mathbf{V}(A)$ and $\mathbf{V}(B)$ are isomorphic and x has the same type in $\mathbf{V}(A)$ and $\mathbf{V}(B)$, then there are instances A' and B' isomorphic to A and B by isomorphisms preserving x, such that $\mathbf{V}(A') = \mathbf{V}(B')$. Thus, to establish Lemma 1, it is enough to prove the following variant.

Lemma 2. *There exist finite instances A and B over σ such that A retracts to A_0, B retracts to B_0, x has the same type in $\mathbf{V}(A)$ and $\mathbf{V}(B)$, and for each type S, the number of elements of type S in $\mathbf{V}(A)$ is the same as the number of elements of type S in $\mathbf{V}(B)$.*

The proof of the lemma requires some technical development, to which the rest of the section is dedicated. For conciseness, we introduce the following notation. Let A and B be structures, with $a \in dom(A)$ and $b \in dom(B)$. We write $A \to B$ to mean that there is a homomorphism h from A to B, and $Aa \circ\!\!\to Bb$ if furthermore $h(a) = b$. We also write $Aa \leftarrow\!\!\circ\!\!\to Bb$ if $Aa \circ\!\!\to Bb$ and $Bb \circ\!\!\to Aa$.

We assume wlog that for all i, V_i is minimized, and that no two V_i are equivalent. We also use the following notation. For each type S, let V_S be the minimized body of the query $\bigwedge_{i \in S} V_i(x_S)$, where x_S is a fresh variable. For technical reasons, we enforce that the V_S for distinct S's have disjoint domains. By slight abuse of notation, we use V_S to denote both the query $\bigwedge_{i \in S} V_i(x_S)$ and its body, as needed.

We construct instances A and B satisfying the requirements of Lemma 2. Consider first A_0 and B_0. Recall that, by construction, B_0 retracts to A_0 and for all $V \in \mathbf{V}$, $V(B_0)$ and $V(A_0)$ agree on $dom(A_0)$. In particular, all elements in A_0, including x, have the same type in $\mathbf{V}(A_0)$ and $\mathbf{V}(B_0)$. Note that, if A retracts to A_0 and B retracts to B_0, then x also has the same type in $\mathbf{V}(A)$ and $\mathbf{V}(B)$.

Observe that we can assume wlog that the body of each view V_i is connected. Otherwise, let W_i be the MCQ whose body is the connected component of V_i containing x_i. Suppose A retracts to A_0 and B retracts to B_0. Recall that B_0

retracts to A_0. If it is not the case that $V_i \rightarrow A_0$ then $V_i(A) = V_i(B) = \emptyset$, and for each S such that $i \in S$, $\#(S, A) = \#(S, B) = 0$. Thus, V_i can be eliminated from $\mathbf{V}$ in our construction. Otherwise, $V_i \rightarrow A_0$, so $V_i(A) = W_i(A)$ and $V_i(B) = W_i(B)$. Thus, V_i can be replaced by W_i. In view of the above, we henceforth assume that all views in $\mathbf{V}$ have connected bodies.

To construct A and B satisfying the requirements of the lemma, we augment A_0 and B_0 with special instances that we call *bricks*. Let Δ be the set of realizable types S in $[k]$ for which $\#(S, A_0) \neq \#(S, B_0)$, and let $\Delta = \{S_1, \ldots, S_r\}$. For each $i \in [r]$ and $n_i > 0$, let $V_{S_i}^{n_i}$ be the instance constructed from V_{S_i} by replacing x_{S_i} with $n_i + 1$ copies (x_{S_i}, m) of x_{S_i}, $0 \leq m \leq n_i$, connected to the other elements in V_{S_i} in the same way as x_{S_i}. Clearly, $V_{S_i} x_{S_i} \longleftrightarrow V_{S_i}^{n_i}(x_{S_i}, m)$ for $0 \leq m \leq n_i$. A brick Z consists of the disjoint union of the $V_{S_i}^{n_i}$, $1 \leq i \leq r$ for some choice of the n_i. Furthermore, we ensure that $dom(Z)$ is disjoint from $dom(A_0)$ and $dom(B_0)$. Let Z_0 denote the brick where each $n_i = 0$, i.e. Z_0 is isomorphic to $V_{S_1} \cup \ldots \cup V_{S_r}$.

Lemma 3. *Let $\Delta = \{S_1, \ldots, S_r\}$ and Z be a brick. Then for each $i \in [r]$, $\tau(Z, (x_{S_i}, m)) = S_i$, $0 \leq m \leq n_i$. In particular, $\#(S_i, Z) = \#(S_i, Z_0) + n_i$, $1 \leq i \leq r$.*

Proof. Consider $i \in [r]$, and fix m, $0 \leq m \leq n_i$. Clearly, $(x_{S_i}, m) \in V_{S_i}(Z)$, so $S_i \subseteq \tau(Z, (x_{S_i}, m))$. Suppose $j \in \tau(Z, (x_{S_i}, m))$. Then $(x_{S_i}, m) \in V_j(Z)$. Since V_j is connected and $V_{S_i}^{n_i}$ is disjoint from the rest of Z, $(x_{S_i}, m) \in V_j(V_{S_i}^{n_i})$. As noted earlier, $V_{S_i}^{n_i}(x_{S_i}, m) \circ\!\!\longrightarrow V_{S_i} x_{S_i}$. Thus, $x_{S_i} \in V_j(V_{S_i})$, so $V_{S_i} \subseteq V_j$. Since S_i is realizable, this implies that $j \in S_i$. Thus, $\tau(Z, (x_{S_i}, m)) = S_i$. Also, it is easily seen that for each $v \in dom(V_{S_i})$ where $v \neq x_{S_i}$, $\tau(v, Z_0) = \tau(v, Z)$. As a consequence, $\#(S_i, Z) = \#(S_i, Z_0) + n_i$. □

For each $S_i \in \Delta$ let $\alpha_i = \#(S_i, A_0)$ and $\beta_i = \#(S_i, B_0)$. Let Z_A be the brick for which $n_j = \beta_j$, $1 \leq j \leq r$, and Z_B be the brick for which $n_j = \alpha_j$, $1 \leq j \leq r$. Then the following holds.

Lemma 4. *Let $\Delta = \{S_1, \ldots, S_r\}$. Let Z_A and Z_B be the bricks constructed as above, $A = A_0 \cup Z_A$, and $B = B_0 \cup Z_B$. The following hold:*

(i) A retracts to A_0 and B retracts to B_0;
(ii) $\#(S, A) = \#(S, B)$ for all realizable types in $[k]$.

Proof. Consider (i). Let $i \in [r]$. Since $\#(S_i, A_0) \neq \#(S_i, B_0)$, $V_{S_i} \rightarrow A_0$ or $V_{S_i} \rightarrow B_0$, so $V_{S_i} \rightarrow A_0$. Since $V_{S_i}^{n_1} \rightarrow V_{S_i}$, it follows that $V_{S_i}^{n_i} \rightarrow A_0$ for all $i \in [r]$. It follows that $Z_A \rightarrow A_0$ so A retracts to A_0. Similarly, since $V_{S_i} \rightarrow A_0$, $a \in V_{S_i}(A_0)$ for some $a \in dom(A_0)$. By construction, $a \in V_{S_i}(B_0)$, so $V_{S_i} \rightarrow B_0$ for all $i \in [r]$. Similarly to the above, $Z_B \rightarrow B_0$ so B retracts to B_0.

Next consider (ii). Since A retracts to A_0, $\tau(A, a) = \tau(A_0, a)$ for every $a \in dom(A_0)$. Since A_0 and Z_A are disjoint and all view bodies are connected, $\tau(A, a) = \tau(Z_A, a)$ for every $a \in dom(Z_A)$. Thus, $\#(S, A) = \#(S, A_0) + \#(S, Z_A)$ for every type S. Similarly, $\#(S, B) = \#(S, B_0) + \#(S, Z_B)$ for every type S. Let

S be a realizable type. Suppose first $S \notin \Delta$, so $\#(S, A_0) = \#(S, B_0)$. It remains to show that $\#(S, Z_A) = \#(S, Z_B)$. By Lemma 3, $\tau(Z_A, (x_i, m)) = S_i$ for each $S_i \in \Delta$. It follows that $\{a \mid a \in Z_A, \tau(Z_A, a) = S\} = \{a \mid a \in Z_0, \tau(Z_0, a) = S\}$. Thus, $\#(S, Z_A) = \#(S, Z_0)$. Similarly, $\#(S, Z_B) = \#(S, Z_0)$. Thus, $\#(S, Z_A) = \#(S, Z_B)$ so $\#(S, A) = \#(S, B)$.

If $S_i \in \Delta$, let $z_i = \#(S_i, Z_0)$. Recall that $\alpha_i = \#(S_i, A_0)$ and $\beta_i = \#(S_i, B_0)$. By the above, $\#(S_i, A) = \#(S_i, A_0) + \#(S, Z_A)$. By Lemma 3, $\#(S_i, Z_A) = \#(S_i, Z_0) + n_i = z_i + \beta_i$, so $\#(S_i, A) = \alpha_i + z_i + \beta_i$. Similarly, $\#(S_i, B) = \#(S_i, B_0) + \#(S_i, Z_B) = \beta_i + z_i + \alpha_i$. It follows that $\#(S_i, A) = \#(S_i, B)$, proving (ii).

This concludes the proof of Lemma 2 and that of Theorem 3.

4.2 Path Views

We have seen above that CQ is complete for MCQ-to-CQ rewriting. Unfortunately, extending this result beyond monadic views is possible only in a very limited way. Recall the example used in the proof of Theorem 1. It shows that even very simple binary views render CQ incomplete. Indeed, the views used there are trees, and differ from simple paths by just a single edge. In this section we show that CQ is complete (and therefore determinacy is decidable) in the case where the database schema is a binary relation R, and $\mathbf{V}$ consists of a single view

$$P_k(x, y) = \exists x_1 \ldots \exists x_{k-1} R(x, x_1) \wedge R(x_1, x_2) \wedge \ldots \wedge R(x_{k-1}, y)$$

where $k \geq 2$, providing the nodes connected by a path of length k. Note that the case where the view in a path of length 1 is trivial since then the view provides the entire database.

We show the following.

Theorem 4. *Let Q be a CQ query over R and $k \geq 2$.*
(i) If $P_k \twoheadrightarrow Q$ then Q has a CQ rewriting in terms of P_k.
(ii) Given a CQ query Q, it is decidable whether $P_k \twoheadrightarrow Q$.

Proof. In view of (iv) of Proposition 1, the existence of a CQ rewriting is decidable, so (ii) follows from (i).

Consider (i). Let Q be a CQ and suppose $P_k \twoheadrightarrow Q$. We show that there is a CQ rewriting of Q using P_k. To this end, we construct two finite instances I and J such that $P_k(I) = P_k(J)$, J consists of several disjoint copies of D_0', and $\bar{x} \in Q(I)$. This implies that $\bar{x} \in Q(D_0')$ and (i) follows from Proposition 1. The construction of I and J is done using a careful modification of the chase procedure.

Consider the beginning of the chase sequence as defined in Section 3. Let $D_0 = [Q]$, $S_0 = V(D_0)$, $D_0' = V^{-1}(S_0)$, $V_1' = V(D_0')$, and $S_1' = V_1' - S_0$.

Lemma 5. S_0 *and* S_1' *have disjoint domains.*

Proof. Suppose that $\langle a, b \rangle \in P_k(D_0')$ for some $a \in dom(S_0)$ (the case when $b \in dom(S_0)$ is similar). We show that b cannot be in $dom(D_0') - dom(S_0)$. Since $\langle a, b \rangle \in P_k(D_0')$, there is a path of length k from a to b. Note that D_0' has no cycles of length less than k. It follows that either $a = b$ or $d(a, b) = k$. In the first case we are done. If $d(a, b) = k$, by construction of D_0', b can only be in $dom(S_0)$. □

Next, let us construct a special binary relation M as follows. The domain of M consists of $dom(S_1')$ and, for each $\alpha \in dom(S_1')$, new distinct elements $x_1^\alpha, \ldots, x_{k-1}^\alpha$. M has the following edges:

$$\text{for each } \alpha \in dom(S_1'), \text{ the edges} \quad \alpha \to x_1^\alpha \to \ldots \to x_{k-1}^\alpha;$$

$$\text{and for each } \langle \alpha, \beta \rangle \in S_1', \text{ an edge} \quad x_{k-1}^\alpha \to \beta.$$

The following is easily shown by construction of M.

Lemma 6. *Let* M *be constructed as above. Then* $P_k(M)$ *consists of* k *disjoint copies of* S_1'. *Specifically,* $\langle \alpha, \beta \rangle \in S_1'$ *iff* $\langle \alpha, \beta \rangle \in P_k(M)$ *and* $\langle x_i^\alpha, x_i^\beta \rangle \in P_k(M)$ *for* $1 \leq i \leq k - 1$.

We now use M to construct our desired instances I and J. Let I consist of k disjoint copies of $[Q]$ together with M, and J consist of k disjoint copies of D_0'. Then by Lemma 5, respectively Lemma 6, $P_k(J)$ and $P_k(I)$ both consist of k disjoint copies of S_0 and k disjoint copies of S_1'. By appropriately renaming elements as needed, we obtain $P_k(I) = P_k(J)$. Since $P_k \twoheadrightarrow Q$, $Q(I) = Q(J)$. But $\bar{x} \in Q(I)$ since I contains $[Q]$. It follows that $\bar{x} \in Q(J)$. Since J retracts to D_0' it follows that $\bar{x} \in Q(D_0')$ so by Proposition 1, Q has a CQ rewriting in terms of P_k. This completes the proof of Theorem 4. □

5   Conclusion

Several important questions remain unresolved for conjunctive queries. First, decidability of determinacy remains open in both the finite and unrestricted cases. In fact, it remains open whether unrestricted and finite determinacy coincide. Note that if the latter holds, this implies decidability of determinacy. Indeed, then determinacy would be r.e. (using the chase procedure) and co-r.e. (because failure of finite determinacy is witnessed by finite instances).

If it turns out that finite and infinite determinacy are distinct for CQs, then it may be the case that unrestricted determinacy is decidable, while finite determinacy is not. Also, we can obtain FO rewritings whenever **V** determines Q in the unrestricted case, while the best complete language in the finite case remains $\exists$SO $\cap$ $\forall$SO. Since unrestricted determinacy implies finite determinacy, an algorithm for testing unrestricted determinacy could be used in practice as a sound but incomplete algorithm for testing finite determinacy: all positive answers would imply finite determinacy, but the algorithm could return false negatives. When the algorithm accepts, we would also have a guaranteed FO rewriting. Thus, the unrestricted case may turn out to be of practical interest if finite determinacy is undecidable, or to obtain FO rewritings.

While we exibited some classes of CQ views for which CQ remains complete as a rewriting language, we do not yet have a complete characterization of such well-behaved classes. Note that a slight increase in the power of the rewrite language, such as using UCQ or $CQ^{\neq}$ instead of CQ, does not help. Indeed, a consequence of our results here and in [14] is that there is gap, in the following sense: if CQ is not sufficient to rewrite Q in terms of $\mathbf{V}$, then a non-monotonic language is needed for the rewriting.

Acknowledgments. The authors would like to thank Alin Deutsch and Sergey Melnik for useful discussions related to the material of this paper.

References

1. S. Abiteboul and O. Duschka. Complexity of answering queries using materialized views. PODS 1998, 254-263.
2. S. Abiteboul, R. Hull, and V. Vianu. *Foundations of Databases.* Addison Wesley, 1995.
3. F. Afrati, C. Li, and P. Mitra. Answering queries using views with arithmetic comparisons. PODS 2002, 209-220.
4. F. Bancilhon and N. Spyratos. Update semantics of relational views. *ACM Trans. Database Syst.* 6(4): 557-575, 1981.
5. D. Calvanese, G. De Giacomo, M. Lenzerini, and M.Y. Vardi. Lossless regular views. PODS 2002, 247-258.
6. C. C. Chang and H. J. Keisler. *Model Theory.* North-Holland, 1977.
7. C. Chekuri and A. Rajaraman. Conjunctive query containment revisited. ICDT 1997, 56-70.
8. S. Dar, M.J. Franklin, B. Jonsson, D. Srivastava and M. Tan. Semantic data caching and replacement. VLDB 1996, 330-341.
9. A. Deutsch, L. Popa, and V. Tannen. Physical data independence, constraints and optimization with universal plans. VLDB 1999, 459-470.
10. S. Grumbach, M. Rafanelli, and L. Tininini. Querying aggregate data. PODS 1999, 174-184.
11. S. Grumbach and L. Tininini. On the content of materialized aggregate views. PODS 2000, 47-57.
12. Alon Y. Levy, Alberto O. Mendelzon, Yehoshua Sagiv, and Divesh Srivastava. Answering queries using views. PODS 1995, 95-104.
13. A. Rajaraman, Y. Sagiv, and J.D. Ullman. Answering queries using templates with binding patterns. PODS 1995, 105-112.
14. L. Segoufin and V. Vianu. Views and queries: determinacy and rewriting. PODS 2005, 49-60.
15. J.D. Ullman. Information integration using logical views. ICDT 1997, 19-40.

Compact Samples for Data Dissemination*

Tova Milo, Assaf Sagi, and Elad Verbin

School of Computer Science
Tel Aviv University
{milo,sagiassa,eladv}@post.tau.ac.il

Abstract. We consider data dissemination in a peer-to-peer network, where each user wishes to obtain some subset of the available information objects. In most of the modern algorithms for such data dissemination, the users periodically obtain samples of peer IDs (possibly with some summary of their content). They then use the samples for connecting to other peers and downloading data pieces from them. For a set O of information objects, we call a sample of peers, containing at least k possible providers for each object $o \in O$, a *k-sample*.

In order to balance the load, the k-samples should be *fair*, in the sense that for every object, its providers should appear in the sample with equal probability. Also, since most algorithms send fresh samples frequently, the size of the k-samples should be *as small as possible*, to minimize communication overhead. We describe in this paper two novel techniques for generating fair and small k-samples in a P2P setting. The first is based on a particular usage of uniform sampling and has the advantage that it allows to build on standard P2P uniform sampling tools. The second is based on non-uniform sampling and requires more particular care, but is guaranteed to generate the smallest possible fair k-sample. The two algorithms exploit available dependencies between information objects to reduce the sample size, and are proved, both theoretically and experimentally, to be extremely effective.

1   Introduction

We consider in this paper data dissemination in a peer-to-peer network, where each user wishes to obtain some subset of the available information objects. In most of the modern algorithms for such data dissemination, the users periodically obtain samples of peer IDs, (possibly with some summary of the peers' content). They then use the samples for connecting to other peers and downloading data pieces from them. It is desirable that the peer samples (1) contain enough providers for each requested object, so that users have a sufficient choice of data sources, (2) are 'fair', so that the requests for objects are spread evenly over their providers, and (3) are as small as possible, so that the communication overhead is minimized when samples are sent frequently. The goal of this paper

---

* The research has been partially supported by the European Union Project EDOS and by the Israel Science Foundation.

is to devise peer-sampling algorithms that achieve the above three goals. Our algorithms take advantage of "correlations" between data objects to improve performance. To motivate the study of this problem, let us briefly describe its practical origin and explain how a good solution to the problem can contribute to better performance of data dissemination platforms.

Motivation. In a data dissemination scenario, various information objects are to be disseminated to peers in the network. The original distributors of the objects are one or more *source* peers who initially hold the data. The other peers are interested in obtaining some subset of the available objects. When the number of peers to which the data is to be disseminated is large, it is practically impossible to have all peers downloading the data directly from the original sources. Indeed, most data dissemination platforms are based on peer cooperation, where each peer provides to other needing peers the objects (or parts thereof) which she has already acquired [3].[1] In such a setting, all peers serve essentially both as information consumers *and* information providers - a peer interested in obtaining a certain object serves also as a provider for it.

In order for a peer to connect with peers that may assist her in obtaining a certain object, she needs to obtain information about other peers in the system holding it. For this end, data dissemination algorithms typically supply the requesting peer with information about a set of k peers (for some constant k), chosen randomly from the set of all peers in the system that hold the object [14]. The peer then chooses a subset that is most beneficial to her, e.g. in terms of bandwidths or available object pieces, and connects to those peers to obtain the data. New peer samples may be supplied periodically (or upon request) to the peers to allow them to acquire new, possibly more suitable, data sources. Depending on the particular data dissemination algorithm being used, the details of which object pieces are available at each of the sample peers may be either encoded as summary information given in the sample or, alternatively, may be obtained by querying the given peer [18]. To abstract this and ignore the specific implementation details, we assume the existence of a function $objects(n)$ that, given a network peer n, tells which (pieces of) objects may be provided by n.

The sampling domain for an object o may consist of those peers that actually hold (pieces of) of o, or of the peers that declared their wish to obtain that object. The rationale for the latter is that such peers, being interested in o, are likely to have already obtained some of its pieces (or will soon manage to). Most algorithms take the latter approach as it guarantees the sampling domain to be fairly stable (it is determined once the peers declare their wishes) [5]. This is also what we assume here. In order not to overload certain peers, the samples are required to be *fair*, in the sense that for every object o the peers (potentially) providing o should appear in the sample with equal probability [8]. Also, since most algorithms send fresh samples *frequently* it is desirable that their size be as small as possible, to minimize communication overhead. Finally, to be able

---

[1] Data objects are typically fragmented into *blocks*. A peer who shares an object might not have yet completed its download and hence shares only the blocks downloaded thus far.

to guarantee that a certain number of samples can be sent within a *fixed* time period, the dissemination algorithms need to know the *bound* on the samples' size. To put this in terms of the problem mentioned at the beginning of the section, *one would like the samples sent to a given peer to contain at least k providers for each of the objects that she requested, be fair, and have the worst-case bound on their size be as small as possible.*

For a set of objects O, we call a fair sample of the network peers, containing at least k providers for each object $o \in O$, a *k-sample* (the formal definition is given in sec. 2). Our goal is to devise sampling algorithms that minimize the worst-case bound on the k-samples' size. Before presenting our results, let us consider a simple example.

Example. Consider a peer-to-peer network consisting of a set N of peers and holding a set $\mathcal{O}$ of distinct information objects. Let n be some network peer that is interested in obtaining a set of objects $O \subseteq \mathcal{O}$. For simplicity, assume a simple network architecture where some *coordinating* peer is informed of the peer's request and is in charge of providing her with corresponding k-samples. (In more general architectures the task may be distributed among several peers). Consider first a simple method that the coordinator peer can use for generating k-samples for O: For each $o \in O$, sample (uniformly) k peers among the providers for o (we will see in the following section standard techniques to perform such sampling). The k-sample then consists of the union of the sampled sets. Clearly its size is bounded by $k|O|$. Interestingly, although rather naïve, the bound obtained by this simple algorithm is in fact the tightest we could find in the existing literature since current systems treat the dissemination of distinct information objects separately (see more on that in Section 5). So the question motivating the present work is can one do better?

It turns out that the answer is often positive. The key observation is that, in practice, one can typically detect *correlations* between object requests, which can be used to significantly reduce the k-sample size. As a simple example, consider three objects A, B and C. The naïve sampling algorithm described above yields for them a k-sample of size $3k$. Now, assume that the coordinator knows that every peer interested in obtaining B also wants A (implying that the set of potential providers of B is included in that of A). If the two sets of providers happen to be identical then clearly a k-sample of size $2k$ suffices: the same set of k peers sampled for A can also be used for B. Even if the B's are not provided by all the A-peers but only by say, 75% of them, a k-sample of size $2\frac{1}{3}k$ still suffices: a sample of $1\frac{1}{3}k$ A-peers contains on the average k B-peers.

Our results. Based on the above observation, we present in this paper two classes of algorithms for generating compact k-samples. The first employs uniform peer sampling. Its main advantage is that it allows to build on standard P2P uniform sampling tools e.g.[16,13]. The sampling procedure here amounts to (1) grouping the requested objects, based on the correlations between their providers, and (2) uniformly sampling providers for each object group. The crux is to determine the optimal objects' grouping, i.e. the one that minimizes the resulting samples' size. We show the problem to be NP-hard but provide a linear time, constant-factor *approximation algorithm* for it. Furthermore, we show, experimentally, that our approximation algorithm yields in practice results much better than its worse case bound - indeed, the generated k-samples are of size very close to the minimal possible. We next consider non-uniform sampling. We first show that for k-samples generated using non-uniform sampling, the size of the minimal possible k-sample can be determined in linear time. We then propose a new simple distributed sampling technique that allows to generate such minimal k-samples in a decentralized P2P environment. To illustrate the benefit that our new sampling techniques can bring to existing data dissemination platforms, we tested experimentally the performance improvement that can be obtained by incorporating them in the popular BitTorrent[2], showing significant gain.

The paper is organized as follows. Section 2 introduces the basic formalisms used throughout the paper. Section 3 studies the generation of compact k-samples via uniform sampling. Non-uniform sampling is considered in Section 4. We conclude in Section 5 considering related work. The full proofs of the results as well as a detailed description of the experiments can be found in the full version of the paper [17].

2   Preliminaries

We introduce here the basic formalisms used throughout the paper, including our abstraction of the P2P network as an objects-providers bipartite graph, and the notions of k-samples and uniform peer sampling.

Objects-Providers graph. As mentioned in the Introduction, peer requests serve as a good indication for the availability of objects on the given peers. The rationale is that peers that are interested in a given object are likely to quickly obtain (at least some pieces of) the object and be able to provide them to other peers. Consequently we consider from now on each network peer n that requested a certain object o as a provider of o. Consider a peer-to-peer network consisting of a set N of peers and holding a set $\mathcal{O}$ of distinct information objects. The availability of the objects in the network peers can be represented as a bipartite graph consisting of two sets of nodes, one representing the objects and the other representing peers, with edges connecting each peer node to the nodes of the objects that it provides. Overloading notation, we will use $\mathcal{O}$ for both the objects and the nodes representing them. Peers that provide the same set of objects are grouped together and represented in the graph by a single node. We associate with each such node a *weight* that reflects the number of peers that it represents (as a fraction of the overall number of all peers). More formally,

Definition 1. *An* objects-providers *graph* $g = (\mathcal{O}, P, E, w)$ *is a weighted bipartite graph where* $\mathcal{O}$ *and* P *are two disjoint sets of nodes called the* object nodes *and the* provider nodes, *resp.;* $E \subseteq \mathcal{O} \times P$ *is the set of edges of the graph; and* $w : P \to [0, 1]$ *is a* weight *function, associating to each provider node* $p \in P$ *some weight* $w(p)$, *s.t.* $\Sigma_{p \in P} w(p) = 1$.

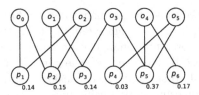

Fig. 1. An objects-providers graph

We will use below $o, o_1, \ldots$ to denote object nodes as well as the information objects that they represent. We use $p, p_1, \ldots$ to denote provider nodes and $n, n_1, \ldots$ to denote the actual network peers. We use v to denote an arbitrary graph node. Consider the objects-providers graph in Fig. 1, which will serve as a running example throughout this paper. $\mathcal{O}$ here consists of six information objects $o_0 \ldots o_5$ which are provided by six types of providers. Here, the peers represented by the node p_2 provide the objects o_0, o_1 and o_2 and form 15% of the overall set of peers providing objects in $\mathcal{O}$.

For a set of nodes s in the graph g, we denote by $N(s)$ the set of nodes in g that are *neighbors* of some node in s. When s is a singleton set consisting of a single node v, we use $N(v)$ as a shorthand for $N(\{v\})$. Observe that for any information object $o \in \mathcal{O}$, the nodes in $N(o)$ represent the set of peers that provide o. Indeed, the sum of the neighbors' weight, $\sum_{p \in N(o)} w(p)$, describes precisely the number of o's providers (as a fraction of the overall number of the providers of $\mathcal{O}$). We refer to this sum as the *popularity of o* (in g). To continue with our running example, the popularity of o_4 is $w(p_5) + w(p_6) = 0.54$.

The objects-providers graph for a given network may be constructed in different ways, depending on the particular application setting: for instance by considering the full set of peers' requests (e.g. in a centralized setting or when the number of peers is not too big); by drawing a random sample of the network peers as representatives for the requests distribution (e.g. in a distributed setting with a large number of peers); using logs and history information (in environments where peers tend to repeatedly request similar data); using known dependencies between information objects (when such dependencies are available); or by some combination of the above.

In the remainder of this paper we assume that we are given an objects-providers graph, and ignore the particular method used for its construction. We will return to this topic in Section 3.3, showing that the algorithms that we propose *do not require in practice to actually build the objects-providers graph but use only a very partial knowledge of its shape, which can be easily obtained in a distributed manner by simple uniform sampling.*

k-samples. Consider a network peer that is interested in obtaining a set of objects $O \subseteq \mathcal{O}$. A *k-sample* for O is a fair sample of the network peers containing at least k providers for each object $o \in O$. More precisely,

Definition 2. *A k-sample (for a set O of information objects) is a randomly generated entity consisting of a subset $K \subseteq N$ of the network peers and*

supporting a function PROVIDERS(*o*) *which returns, for each object o ∈ O, a subset $K_o \subseteq K$ of providers for o, where the following two properties hold:*

1. *(sufficient number of providers) For each object o ∈ O, the expected size of* PROVIDERS(*o*) *is at least k, i.e. $E[\|K_o\|] \geq k$;*
2. *(fairness) For each object o ∈ O, each of o's providers has an equal probability of appearing in* PROVIDERS(*o*).

Our goal here is to design sampling algorithms that - given as input, an objects-providers graph *g* describing the availability of objects in the network peers, a request for a set of objects *O* and a number *k* - generate small k-samples (for *O*). When measuring the quality of a sampling algorithm, we look at the maximal size of *K* in the samples generated for the given input. *We are interested in devising sampling algorithms where for any g, O, and k, the worst-case bound on the size of K is minimal.*

Uniform sampling. For the generation of k-samples, we naturally need a method to sample the network peers. We present in the following sections some particular sampling techniques aimed at minimizing the sampled set's size. But before doing so, let us consider some of the standard methods used nowadays for peer sampling in P2P networks. Peer sampling has received much attention in recent research on P2P networks and is used in various applications for data dissemination, gossip-based communications and querying (see e.g. [11,15,9]). Much of the work has focused on *uniform sampling* of network peers, proposing various techniques that vary in their resilience to failures, communication over-head, etc. [16,13]. Ignoring the particular algorithmic details, a uniform peer sampling technique can be viewed as a function *GetProvidersSample(R, l)*, where *R* is a Boolean predicate on peers and *l* is the size of the required sample. *GetProvidersSample(R, l)* returns *l* peers, drawn with uniform probability, from the set of all network peers that satisfy the predicate *R*. In our context we are interested in sampling peers that provide a certain set of objects. For a set of information objects *O*, R_O will denote the predicate that is true for those peers that provide some object in *O*. Namely, for a network peer *n*, $R_O(n) = True$ iff $O \cap objects(n) \neq \emptyset$.

3   Uniform k-Sampling

Given an objects-providers graph *g* and a set of objects *O* in *g*, our goal is to generate the smallest possible k-samples for *O*. Namely k-samples where the maximal size of the set *K* of peer IDs (in any of the random instances) is minimal. The first sampling method that we present is based on uniform sampling. It has the advantage that it can employ any of the standard P2P sampling techniques mentioned in the previous section (hence enjoy whatever benefits they bring, such as resilience to failures, communication efficiency, etc.). To get some intuition, let us first describe two simple (not necessarily optimal) ways to use uniform sampling for the generation of a k-sample. Our novel sampling method is presented next (first intuitively and then formally). In all the examples below we assume that we are given the objects-providers graph of Figure 1 and we want to generate a k-sample for the set of objects $O = \{o_1, o_2, o_3, o_4\}$.

Method 1: Individual sample for each object. The naïve sampling algorithm, described in the introduction, samples k providers for each object $o \in O$, by running $GetProvidersSample(R_{\{o\}}, k)$. The set K of the k-sample then consists of the union of the sampled sets, with the function PROVIDERS(o) returning o's sample. Clearly the size of the k-sample here is bounded by $k|O|$. In our running example, for $k = 3$ the size is bounded by $3 \cdot 4 = 12$.

Implementation wise, the K peers are transmitted in an array, containing essentially a concatenation of the individual object samples. PROVIDERS(o) returns for each object o the corresponding array fragment. It is important to note that a simplistic implementation of PROVIDERS(o) that simply returns *all* the peers in K that provide o would be inadequate as it may violate the *fairness* of the k-sample. To see this, consider the following simple example. Assume that the set O contains two objects, o_u, an unpopular object provided by a very small fraction of the peers, and o_p, a very popular object provided by most peers. Consider a peer n that happens to provide both objects. n has a high probability of being sampled for o_u (hence of appearing in K), a higher probability than any of the other providers of o_p. To guarantee the fairness of PROVIDERS(o_p), it is essential to restrict its answer to those peers sampled (uniformly) for o_p, ignoring those other peers in K (like n) which happen to also provide o_p.

Method 2: One sample for all objects. An alternative method is to run only one sampling instance, $GetProvidersSample(R_O, l)$, drawing a single sample of size l (for some constant l, to be defined below), from the set of *all the providers* of objects in O. The set K here consists of all the peers in this sample, with the function PROVIDERS(o) returning the network peers $n \in K$ for which $o \in objects(n)$. The use of uniform sampling guarantees that requirement 2 (fair sample) holds. To satisfy requirement 1 (at least k providers for each object), the size l of the sample should be large enough to contain k providers even for non-popular objects (i.e. objects provided only by few peers). Clearly if the least popular object $o \in O$ is provided by β of the providers of O, to assure an expectancy of k providers for o, the sample size should be at least $l = \left\lceil k \cdot \frac{1}{\beta} \right\rceil$.

In our running example, the least popular objects o_1 and o_2 are each provided by 0.29 of the providers of O. Consequently, the size of the required sample (hence also the bound on size of the k-sample) is $\left\lceil 3 \cdot \frac{1}{0.29} \right\rceil = 11$, a bit smaller than the one obtained with the previous naïve construction.

In general this method beats the naïve construction whenever $|O| > \frac{1}{\beta}$, β being the relative popularity of the least popular object in O. It performs particularly well when there are no "very unpopular" objects. For instance, in the extreme case where all objects are provided by all providers, $\beta = 1$ and a k-sample of size k suffices. The naïve construction, on the other hand, is superior when some objects are provided by only a very small fraction of the peers.

Method 3: Object Partitioning. The new method that we propose in this paper combines the advantages of the two previous ones. It partitions the objects into several sets $s_1, \ldots, s_m$. A sample is then drawn for each set s_i, from the set of all the providers of objects in s_i. The size of the sample for s_i is dictated, as above, by the popularity of the least popular object in s_i. The set K of the k-sample consists of the union of the s_i samples. Finally, for any object $o \in s_i$, the function PROVIDERS(o) returns the peers, in s_i's sample, which provide o.[2] Observe that the previous two methods are in fact special cases of this new method: In the first naïve sampling we have $|O|$ singleton sets, one per each object in O; in the second method there is a single set s_1 consisting of all the objects in O. If the least popular object in a set of objects s_i is provided by β_{s_i} of the providers of s_i, then a call to $GetProvidersSample(R_{s_i}, \left\lceil k \cdot \frac{1}{\beta_{s_i}} \right\rceil)$ will draw a sample with an expectancy of at least k providers for each object $o \in s_i$. The maximal size of the obtained k-sample is thus $\sum_{s_i} \left\lceil k \cdot \frac{1}{\beta_{s_i}} \right\rceil$. The challenge is *to find the optimal partitioning of objects into sets so as to minimize this sum.*

Consider again our running example and assume that we partition the objects in O into two sets, $s_1 = \{o_1, o_2\}$ and $s_2 = \{o_3, o_4\}$. The providers of objects in s_1 (represented in the graph by p_1, p_2 and p_3) form 0.43 of the overall set of peers. o_1 and o_2 are each provided by 0.67 of these providers, hence the required size of s_1, for $k = 3$, is $\left\lceil 3 \cdot \frac{1}{0.67} \right\rceil = 5$. Similarly, the providers of objects in s_2 (represented by $p_3, \ldots, p_6$) form 0.61 of the overall set of peers. o_3 and o_4 are each provided by 0.76 of these providers, hence the required size of s_2 is $\left\lceil 3 \cdot \frac{1}{0.76} \right\rceil = 4$. Thus, the size of the k-sample here is bounded by $5 + 4 = 9$, smaller than in any of the previous two methods. In this example this is also the optimal partitioning.

Observe that the reduction in size here, relative to the previous two methods, is not too big because our running example contains, for simplicity, only very few information objects. In practice, results on real-life scenarios demonstrate significant size reduction [17].

3.1   Formal Problem Statement

Consider a partitioning of the objects in O into (not necessarily disjoint) sets $s_1, \ldots, s_m$. As explained above, the size of the k-sample generated for such a partitioning is bounded by $\sum_{s_i} \left\lceil k \cdot \frac{1}{\beta_{s_i}} \right\rceil$, where β_{s_i} is the fraction of peers, among the providers of s_i, providing the least popular object o in s_i. To make this more precise we use the following notations.

Given an objects-providers graph g and a set s of information objects in g, the *popularity of the set s* (in g), denoted $SPop(s)$, is the fraction of peers, among all providers, that provide some object in s. Putting this in terms of the graph g,

---

[2] Implementation wise, the sent k-sample is an array containing the concatenation of the samples drawn for the s_i sets. Given the partitioning details (the object sets and their samples' size), PROVIDERS(o) returns for each $o \in s_i$, the peers n in the s_i fragment of the array s.t. $o \in objects(n)$.

$SPop(s)$ is the sum of the weights of the provider nodes in g that are neighbors to the object nodes in s. Namely, $SPop(s) = \sum_{p \in N(s)} w(p)$.

Observe that when s contains a single object o, the set's popularity is precisely the popularity of o, as defined in Section 2, namely the fraction of peers, among all providers, that provide o. The *relative-popularity of o w.r.t s*, denoted $relPop(o, s)$, is the fraction of peers, among the providers of s, that provide o. Namely, $relPop(o, s) = \frac{SPop(\{o\})}{SPop(s)}$.

Going back to the generation of our k-sample, the sample size for a set s_i is dictated by the object $o \in s_i$ with the least relative-popularity. Namely, the sample size for s_i should be at least $\left\lceil k \cdot \frac{1}{min_{o \in s_i} relPop(o, s_i)} \right\rceil$. Consequently, for a partitioning S of the objects in O to sets, the overall size of the k-sample is bounded by

$$(*) \quad \sum_{s_i \in S} \left\lceil k \cdot \frac{1}{min_{o \in s_i} relPop(o, s_i)} \right\rceil = \sum_{s_i \in S} \left\lceil \frac{k \cdot SPop(s_i)}{min_{o \in s_i} SPop(\{o\})} \right\rceil$$

The value of $(*)$ naturally depends on the particular partitioning of objects to sets. We denote by $size^{\lceil\rceil}(S)$ the value of $(*)$ for a given partitioning S. For an objects-providers graph g, a set of objects O in g, and an integer k, we refer to the problem of finding a partitioning S of the objects in O for which $size^{\lceil\rceil}(S)$ is minimal as the *Object Partitioning Problem* (denoted $OPP^{\lceil\rceil}$). We will call such a partitioning S an *optimal* solution (for g, O, and k) and denote the value of $size^{\lceil\rceil}(S)$ for it by $opt^{\lceil\rceil}$.

We will also define a variant of this problem, denoted OPP (with no ceiling), where the objective is to minimize the value of

$$(**) \quad size(S) = \sum_{s_i \in S} \frac{k \cdot SPop(s_i)}{min_{o \in s_i} SPop(\{o\})}$$

The size of an optimal solution for OPP is denoted by opt. For some purposes, such as to prove NP-Hardness of $OPP^{\lceil\rceil}$, we will go through OPP first.

3.2   Observations

We provide next some observations about the possible structure of an optimal solution. These will be useful later for studying the complexity of the problem and for proposing algorithms to solve it.

Provider contribution. Consider some objects-providers graph g, a set of objects O, and a partitioning S of the objects of O into sets. Let $s_i \in S$ be some objects set and let $o_i \in S_i$ be the least popular object in s_i. Looking at the formula $(*)$ from the previous subsection, it is easy to see that for every object $o \in s_i$, each of its providers p (neighbor nodes in the graph g) contributes to $size^{\lceil\rceil}(S)$ a value $\frac{k \cdot w(p)}{SPop(\{o_i\})}$ (not yet regarding the ceiling we have to take). If a provider provides objects that belong to different sets, then the provider will contribute to $size^{\lceil\rceil}(S)$ such a value for each of these sets. We can therefore see that a provider's contribution to the value of $size^{\lceil\rceil}(S)$ depends on the number of sets that the objects that it provides participate in, and on the popularity of the least popular object in each of these sets.

Looking at things from the provider's view point, the partitioning of the objects into groups can be viewed as *labeling* each provider with labels that identify the sets to which the objects that it provides belong. Each label placed on a provider induces a cost that he has to pay, and all providers who provide a given object must have at least one label common to all of them (describing the set(s) that contain the object). Our problem can thus be described as a labeling problem: *we want to find an optimal labeling for the providers, namely one that minimizes their overall contribution to $size^{\sqcap}(S)$*. This alternative description of the problem will prove useful later on in the various proofs.

"Nice" partitioning. Given an objects-providers graph g and a set of objects O, a partitioning S for the objects in O is called a *nice partitioning* if (1) all the sets $s \in S$ are pairwise disjoint and (2) there are no two distinct sets s, s' in S whose least popular objects are equally unpopular. Namely for all $s, s' \in S, s \neq s' \rightarrow min_{o \in s} SPop(\{o\}) \neq min_{o' \in s'} SPop(\{o'\})$.

The following lemma shows that when searching for an optimal solution for $OPP^{\sqcap}$ (resp., OPP) it is sufficient to look at nice partitioning.

Lemma 1. *For every objects-providers graph g, a set of objects O in g, and an integer k, there always exists a nice partitioning for the objects in O which is an optimal solution for $OPP^{\sqcap}$ (resp., for OPP).*

Proof. We prove the lemma for $OPP^{\sqcap}$. The proof for OPP follows exactly the same lines. Let us look at some optimal solution S for $OPP^{\sqcap}$. Consider the nice partitioning S' obtained from S by removing redundant objects and unifying sets with equal least object popularity. It is easy to see from formula (∗) that $size^{\sqcap}(S') \leq size^{\sqcap}(S)$. Since S is an optimal solution it must be the case that $size^{\sqcap}(S') = size^{\sqcap}(S)$, hence S' is an optimal solution as well.

The above lemma is interesting since it allows to reduce the search space when searching for an optimal solution. Specifically, in every nice partitioning the number of sets is bounded by the number of the distinct popularity values for objects in O. We will use this extensively in our analysis of the problem.

3.3   Algorithms and Complexity

We will see below that both $OPP^{\sqcap}$ and OPP are NP-Hard and will propose linear and polynomial approximation algorithms for them. But before we do that, let us first consider a restricted case that can be solved in polynomial time and can shed some light on the structure of optimal solutions.

Consider an objects-providers graph g and a set O of information objects in g, where the objects in O each have one of two possible popularity values. This is for instance the case in our running example, where objects in O have popularity 0.29 or 0.54. Indeed, the popularities of $\{o_1, o_2, o_3, o_4\}$ are respectively $\{0.29, 0.29, 0.54, 0.54\}$.

By Lemma 1 we know that in this case there exists a nice optimal partitioning for O consisting of (at most) two sets, s_1 and s_2, such that all the less popular objects belong to s_1 while the more popular objects may be spread between s_1 and s_2. To find the optimal partitioning we only need to to determine which popular objects belong to s_1 and which to s_2. We show next that this can be determined in PTime. We first consider OPP and then OPP$^{\sqcap}$.

Theorem 1. OPP *can be solved in polynomial time when the information objects in O each have one of two possible popularity values.*

Proof. (sketch) We provide here an intuition for the polynomial algorithm. The full algorithm and its correctness proof appear in the full version of the paper [17]. The algorithm works as follows. First, given the objects-providers graph g and a set of objects O, we construct a new weighted bipartite graph G. For every provider node $p \in g$ that provides some object in O, the graph G contains two nodes, v_p^1 and v_p^2. The node v_p^i, $i = 1, 2$ will be used to represent the case where none of the O objects provided by p belongs to the set s_i (The graph edges and the weights of the nodes are described later on).

Next, we find a maximum-weight independent set[3] W for G (known to be polynomially solvable for bipartite graphs [12]). Finally, we use W to determine the partitioning of objects of O into the sets s_1, s_2: For every provider node p s.t. $v_p^1 \in W$, all the objects in O provided by p are placed in s_2. For every provider p s.t. $v_p^2 \in W$, all the objects in O provided by p are placed in s_1. The remaining objects are placed arbitrarily.

Theorem 2. *The same algorithm is an approximation algorithm for OPP$^{\sqcap}$ that gives a solution whose value is at most $opt^{\sqcap} + 1$, where $opt^{\sqcap}$ is the size of an optimal solution.*

Proof. Let $opt^{\sqcap}$ be the optimal value of OPP$^{\sqcap}$ for an objects-providers graph g and a set of objects O in g. Let S be the solution produced by the above algorithm. Let opt be the optimal value of OPP on the same instance. We have shown that $opt = size(S)$. We wish to prove that $size^{\sqcap}(S) \leq opt^{\sqcap} + 1$. Obviously, $opt \leq opt^{\sqcap}$. On the other hand, $size^{\sqcap}(S) < opt + 2$, because the only change in the objective function is the ceiling sign added to each of the two summands. Therefore, $size^{\sqcap}(S) < opt^{\sqcap} + 2$. Since both expressions here are integral, it follows that $size^{\sqcap}(S) \leq opt^{\sqcap} + 1$.

It is open whether OPP$^{\sqcap}$ has an exact polynomial solution in the case of two object popularities. We can show however that as soon as objects have more than two distinct popularities, both OPP and OPP$^{\sqcap}$ become NP-Hard. The proof appears in [17].

Theorem 3. OPP$^{\sqcap}$ *and OPP are both NP-Hard, even for objects-providers graphs where the object nodes have only three popularity values and all the weights of the provider nodes are equal.*

---

[3] An *independent set* is defined as a subset W of the nodes in the graph G such that no pair of nodes in W is connected by an edge in G.

Proof. (sketch) We prove that the problems are NP-Hard by reduction from the problem of minimum unweighted 3-multiway cut (3MC) (also referred to in the literature as 3-Terminal cut or 3-multiterminal cut), known to be NP-Hard [6]. In the 3MC problem a graph G and three distinguished nodes v_1, v_2, v_3 are given. The objective is to find a partitioning of the nodes in G into three sets V_1, V_2, V_3 s.t. for $i = 1, 2, 3$ node v_i is in partition V_i, so as to minimize the number of edges going between different partitions. The full reduction is given in [17].

Clearly an optimal solution can be found in exponential time by enumerating all possible solutions. As this is too expensive, we propose next two simple algorithms that approximate the optimal solution up to a constant factor.

The PartitionByPopularity algorithm. Our first approximation algorithm partitions the information objects into sets based on their popularity. It has several advantages: (1) It is simple and runs in linear time. (2) It does not require knowing the exact structure of the objects-providers graph but only the popularity of the objects.[4] (3) It is *on-line* for the objects, namely if a new object is added then the partitioning of already-existing objects does not change.

To describe the algorithm we use the following notation. For two numbers $c > 1$ and $x > 0$, let $IPower_c(x) = c^{\lfloor \log_c x \rfloor}$. That is, $IPower_c(x)$ is the integral power of c smaller than x and closest to it. Given a constant number c, the algorithm PartitionByPopularity(c) partitions the objects in O into sets based on the value of $IPower_c(SPop(\{o\}))$. Formally, we define $s_i = \{o : IPower_c(SPop(\{o\})) = c^i\}$, and the solution S is simply the collection of all non-empty s_i's.

Theorem 4. PartitionByPopularity(c) *is a* $\frac{c^2}{c-1}$*-approximation algorithm for* OPP *for any* $c > 1$. *Namely, it gives a solution whose value is at most* $\frac{c^2}{c-1} \cdot opt$, *where opt is the size of an optimal solution.*

Corollary 1. *(Optimizing on the value of c)* PartitionByPopularity(2) *is a 4-approximation algorithm for* OPP.

The proof is omitted for space constraints. We have a slightly weaker bound for OPP$^{\sqcap}$.

Theorem 5. PartitionByPopularity(c) *is a* $\frac{2c^2}{c-1}$*-approximation algo. for* OPP$^{\sqcap}$ *for any* $c > 1$.

Corollary 2. *(Optimizing on the value of c)* PartitionByPopularity(2) *is an 8-approximation algorithm for* OPP$^{\sqcap}$.

We conclude with a remark about the tightness of the approximation factor of PartitionByPopularity(2). We provide in [17] a particular example of inputs to OPP for which the algorithm indeed produces a result 4 times the value of

---

[4] This can be easily obtained in a distributed manner by a simple uniform peers sampling.

the optimal solution (it is open whether the 8 factor for OPP$^\sqcap$ is indeed tight). Our experiments[17] show however that this algorithm yields in practice results much better than its worst case bound.

The OrderByPopularity algorithm. Our second approximation algorithm is of polynomial time complexity. While its worst-case constant factor is the same as that of PARTITIONBYPOPULARITY, it yields in practice even better results. The algorithm first sorts the information objects according to their popularity, and puts them (in sorted order) into an array. To partition the objects it splits the array into non-overlapping intervals. Each partition contains the objects in the corresponding interval. To find the optimal splitting it employs standard dynamic programming. The overall complexity of the dynamic programming phase here is $o(|g| \cdot |O|^2)$: There are $o(|O|^2)$ possible intervals (i.e. partitions) to check, and the contribution of each partition to the overall length of the k-samples can be computed in time linear in g.

It is easy to see that partitions obtained by Methods 1 and 2 described previously, as well as by PARTITIONBYPOPULARITY, all belong to the search space of this algo.: in all these algorithms, each partition, when sorted internally by object popularity, forms a continuous interval of the overall popularity order of objects. The k-samples constructed by ORDERBYPOPULARITY are thus assured to be at least as compact as those generated by the previous algos.

4 Non-uniform Sampling

The sampling methods described in the previous section build on standard P2P uniform sampling tools. An alternative approach, based on non-uniform sampling, is considered briefly next. We first show that, given an objects-providers graph g and a set O of requested objects, the minimal bound on the size of the k-samples (for O) can be determined in time linear in g. Next we describe a non-uniform sampling method achieving this bound.

Size. Consider a P2P network with a set N of peers providing some object in O. Let p be some provider node in the object-providers graph g. We denote by o_p the least popular object in O that p provides. Note that for any object $o \in O$, $SPop(\{o\}) \cdot |N|$ is the absolute number of nodes that provide o (for definition of $SPop$ see Sec. 3). Define $\bar{X}_p = \frac{k \cdot w(p)}{SPop(\{o_p\})}$. Denote $\bar{l} = \sum_{p \in g} \bar{X}_p$, and $l = \lceil \bar{l} \rceil$. We claim that l is the minimal possible bound on the size of the k-sample for O. A proof to the claim is in [17].

Sampling. To generate a sample of this size, we sample the network peers, non-uniformly: For every provider node p in the graph g, each of the nodes n that it represents is selected with probability $X_n = \frac{k}{SPop(\{o_p\}) \cdot |N|}$. In [17] we describe a simple distributed P2P algorithm to perform such sampling. The algorithm is an adjustment of an existing P2P uniform-sampling method (RanSub [16]) to non-uniform sampling. Let K be the set of sampled peers. To complete the k-sample's definition, we define what subset of peers ($K_0 \subseteq K$) is returned by PROVIDERS(o) for every object $o \in O$. To ensure fairness, PROVIDERS(o) samples peers from K as follows: Each peer $n \in K$ that provides o is chosen to be in K_o with probability $\frac{k}{SPop(\{o\}) \cdot |N|}/X_n$ [5]. We prove in [17] that the sampling is fair and that $E[|K_o|] \geq k$.

5   Related Work and Conclusion

We studied in this paper the problem of peer sampling for the dissemination of data in a peer-to-peer network. We introduced the notion of k-samples - fair samples that contain a sufficient number of providers for each requested object. We then proposed algorithms with varying complexity for the generation of compact k-samples. To illustrate the benefit that our new sampling techniques can bring to existing data dissemination platforms, we tested experimentally the performance improvement that can be obtained by incorporating them in the popular BitTorrent[2] platform, showing significant gain. The experimental result are reported in[17]. Two questions that remain open are the existence of an exact polynomial solution for OPP$^\sqcap$ in the case of two object popularities, and the tightness of the 8 factor in the approximation algorithm for OPP$^\sqcap$.

Peer sampling is used extensively in epidemic/gossip-based methods for disseminating information between network nodes. Such data dissemination is the basis of a wide range of application, including replicated databases [1], content distribution [11], failure detection [20] and probabilistic multicast [9]. Those methods depend on nodes acquiring information about other nodes in the network, or a *sample* in large networks. Peer sampling is also used in a variety of P2P systems (e.g. [4]) and for load balancing [7]. The compact samples generated by our algorithms may help to reduce the communication overhead in such applications. There has been an extensive previous work on uniform peer sampling in P2P networks, ranging from dedicated techniques developed for a particular system or protocol (e.g. [8]), to general-purpose sampling algorithms (e.g. [16,13]). All these methods sample each requested object separately, yielding, for a set O of requested objects, samples of size bounded by $k|O|$. To our knowledge the present work is the first attempt to use correlations between object requests to reduce the sample size. Non-uniform sampling has received relatively little attention. An algorithm in which a probability for each node to appear in the sample may be defined, is given for instance in [21]. Our non-uniform k-sampling method from Section 4 can be built on top of such an algorithm.

We are currently incorporating our k-sampling algorithms in the Information Dissemination Platform (IDiP) developed in Tel Aviv University. More generally we believe them to be useful in the general context of publish/subscribe systems [10,19], where users inherently have heterogeneous needs.

---

[5] This probability is ≤ 1 because $\frac{k}{SPop(\{o\}) \cdot |N|}/X_n = \frac{SPop(\{o_p\})}{SPop(\{o\})}$ and we assumed that $SPop(\{o_p\}) \leq SPop(\{o\})$.

References

1. D. Agrawal, A. El Abbadi, and R. C. Steinke. Epidemic algorithms in replicated databases. *PODS'97*.
2. Bittorrent. `http://bittorrent.com`.
3. J. W. Byers, J. Considine, M. Mitzenmacher, and S. Rost. Informed content delivery across adaptive overlay networks. *SIGCOMM'02*.
4. M. Castro, P. Druschel, A.M. Kermarrec, and A. Rowstron. SCRIBE: A large-scale and decentralized application-level multicast infrastructure. *IEEE JSAC, 20(8)*, October 2002.
5. B. Cohen. Incentives build robustness in BitTorrent. *In Proc. of the Workshop on the Economics of P2P Systems, Berkeley, CA*, 2003.
6. E. Dahlhaus, D. S. Johnson, C. H. Papadimitriou, P. D. Seymour, and M. Yannakakis. The complexity of multiterminal cuts. *SIAM*, 23(4):864–894, 1994.
7. M. Dahlin. Interpreting stale load information. *The 19th IEEE Int. Conf. on Distributed Computing Systems (ICDCS)*, May 1999.
8. P. Eugster, S. Handurukande, R. Guerraoui, A. Kermarrec, and P. Kuznetsov. Lightweight probabilistic broadcast. *In Proc. of The Int. Conf. on Dependable Systems and Networks (DSN 2001)*, July 2001.
9. P. T. Eugster and R. Guerraoui. Probabilistic multicast. *In Proc. of the Int. Conf. on Dependable Systems and Networks (DSN'02)*, June 2002.
10. F. Fabret, H.-A. Jacobsen, F. Llirbat, J. Pereira, K. Ross, and D. Shasha. Filtering algorithms and implementation for very fast publish/subscribe systems. *In Proc. of ACM SIGMOD'01*.
11. M. J. Freedman, E. Freudenthal, and D. Maziéres. Democratizing content publication with Coral. *In Proc. 1st USENIX/ACM Symp. on Networked Systems Design and Implementation (NSDI '04)*, 2004.
12. M. R. Garey and D. S. Johnson. *Computers and Intractability, A Guide to the Theory of NP-Completeness*. W.H. Freeman and Company, 1979.
13. C. Gkantsidis, M. Mihail, and A. Saberi. Random walks in peer-to-peer networks. *INFOCOM'04*.
14. M. Jelasity, R. Guerraoui, A. Kermarrec, and M. van Steen. The peer sampling service: Experimental evaluation of unstructured gossip-based implementations. *5th Int. Middleware Conference, Toronto*, October 2004.
15. D. Kostic, R. Braud, C. Killian, E. Vandekieft, J. W. Anderson, A. C. Snoeren, and A. Vahdat. Maintaining high bandwidth under dynamic network conditions. *USENIX*, 2005.
16. D. Kostic, A. Rodriguez, J. Albrecht, A. Bhirud, and A. Vahdat. Using random subsets to build scalable network services. *In Proc. of USITS'03*, 2003.
17. T. Milo, A. Sagi, and E. Verbin. Compact samples for data dissemination (full version). Tech. Report. `http://www.cs.tau.ac.il/ milo/work/Samples.pdf`.
18. Y. Minsky, A. Trachtenberg, and R. Zippel. Set reconciliation with nearly optimal communication complexity. *Int. Symp. on Information Theory*, June 2001.
19. M. Petrovic, H. Liu, and H. Jacobsen. CMS-ToPSS: efficient dissemination of RSS documents. *VLDB'05*.
20. S. Ranganathan, A. D. George, R. W. Todd, and M. C. Chidester. Gossip-style failure detection for scalable heterogeneous clusters. *Cluster Computing*, 4(3):197–209, July 2001.
21. M. Zhong, K. Shen, and J. Seiferas. Non-uniform random membership management in peer-to-peer networks. *INFOCOM'05*.

Privacy in GLAV Information Integration

Alan Nash[1,*] and Alin Deutsch[2,**]

[1] IBM Almaden Research Lab
anash@us.ibm.com
[2] University of California San Diego
deutsch@cs.ucsd.edu

Abstract. We define and study formal privacy guarantees for information integration systems, where sources are related to a public schema by mappings given by source-to-target dependencies which express inclusion of unions of conjunctive queries with equality. This generalizes previous privacy work in the global-as-view publishing scenario and covers local-as-view as well as combinations of the two.

We concentrate on *logical* security, where malicious users have the same level of access as legitimate users: they can issue queries against the global schema which are answered under "certain answers" semantics and then use unlimited computational power and external knowledge on the results of the queries to guess the result of a secret query ("the secret") on one or more of the sources, which are not directly accessible. We do not address issues of *physical* security, which include how to prevent users from gaining unauthorized access to the data.

We define both absolute guarantees: how safe is the secret? and relative guarantees: how much of the secret is additionally disclosed when the mapping is extended, for example to allow new data sources or new relationships between an existing data source and the global schema? We provide algorithms for checking whether these guarantees hold and undecidability results for related, stronger guarantees.

1   Introduction

We define and analyze formal privacy guarantees for information integration systems. Such guarantees have been recently studied for the case of *database publishing* where views of the underlying sources are exposed to users (see Related Work). This corresponds to the global-as-view closed-world scenario. Here we extend this study to include the case of *database integration*.

We study the case where sources are related to a public schema by mappings given by source-to-target dependencies which express inclusion of unions of conjunctive queries with equality. Such framework is also known as *global-local-as-view (GLAV)* and was introduced in [12] and studied in [4,5,15,11] as a generalization of *global-as-view (GAV)* and *local-as-view (LAV)* integration [22,14,16]. Users may issue queries against the public schema for which the information integration system returns the certain answers [22,14,16].

---

* Work performed while the author was at the University of California, San Diego.
** Funded by an Alfred P. Sloan fellowship and by NSF CAREER award IIS-0347968.

T. Schwentick and D. Suciu (Eds.): ICDT 2007, LNCS 4353, pp. 89–103, 2007.

We consider the case where the attacker is a malicious user who has no further access to the sources than any other user. All the attacker can do is issue queries against the integration system and apply arbitrary computational power on the answers to these queries together with external knowledge to obtain some information ("the secret") which the defender wishes to conceal. We do not address such security issues as how to prevent unauthorized access to the data sources.

The goal of the defender is to determine to what extent the information system is vulnerable to attacks of this kind. The defender specifies the secret as a query against one or several data sources. The objective of the attacker is to obtain the answer to or at least partial information on the answer to the secret on the data sources which the defender wants to conceal.

Database Publishing versus Data Integration. Prior work on privacy in databases has not addressed the data integration setting, but has focused on database *publishing*, in which materialized views of the underlying source are exposed, thus corresponding to a global-as-view, closed-world integration scenario [14]. In database publishing, the attacker can access the full extent of any view V by simply issuing the identity query SELECT * FROM V. Therefore every attack strategy considered in the literature assumes the availability of all view extents. This assumption no longer holds in a data integration setting, where there is no materialized view instance and queries posed by the attacker are answered under so-called *certain answers* semantics [16]. Consequently, the intuitive attack based on the identity query is in general ineffective.

Example 1. Assume there is one source S in the system over a private schema consisting of the single binary relation $PA(patient, ailment)$, recording what ailment each patient is treated for. The information integration system exports the public schema which consists of two binary relations $PD(patient, doctor)$ and $DA(doctor, ailment)$, connecting patients to doctors they see and doctors to ailments they treat. The source S is registered via the single source-to-target constraint $\phi: \forall p, a\, PA(p, a) \rightarrow \exists d\, PD(p, d) \wedge DA(d, a)$. This registration is a standard source-to-target embedded dependency [11], and it is an equivalent way to capture the local-as-view registration [14] using the conjunctive query view $PA(p, a) :\!- PD(p, d), DA(d, a)$. The registration basically means that the private database owner cannot provide doctor information, but states that each patient is treated by some doctor for the ailment.

Now consider an attack modeled after the classic privacy breach strategy in database publishing. It would start by issuing the queries $Q_{PD}(p, d) :\!- PD(p, d)$ and $Q_{DA}(d, a) :\!- DA(d, a)$, in an attempt to find the patient-doctor and doctor-ailment associations in order to subsequently join them and to thus reduce the possible patient-ailment combinations to guess among [18,8].

However, the certain answers to Q_{PD}—which are the tuples in $Q_{PD}(T)$ for *every* target instance T satisfying constraint ϕ—give precisely the empty set, regardless of the extent of source instance S. To see why, notice that the doctor name is not specified, so for each particular name constant, there is at least one possible T which does not contain it. A similar argument shows that Q_{DA} has no certain answers either.

Therefore our first task in studying the defense strategies in data integration is to identify what queries the attacker should pose to gain the most insight into the secret. For Example 1 above, it turns out that one well-chosen query suffices.

Example 2. In the setting of Example 1, all the attacker needs to do to reveal the source completely is to issue the query $Q_\phi(p, a) :- PD(p, d), DA(d, a)$. Under certain answer semantics, the result is precisely the extent of source table PA. Therefore, the query Q_ϕ is optimal for the attacker, since after obtaining the extent of PA she may compute *any* secret query on PA.

In general however, determining the "optimal" queries to start the attack with is challenging. It is a priori not even clear that there exists one single set of queries leading to the highest privacy breach. Even if this were the case, it is not clear that such a set would be finite; an infinite series of queries (each possibly depending on the answer to its predecessors) could potentially outperform any finite series of queries.

Contributions. We study privacy in the context of information integration systems, which introduces substantial new aspects over data publishing. To the best of our knowledge, this is the first such study. Our specific contributions include the following.

(a) We identify optimal attack (and therefore defense) strategies. In particular, we show that there is a finite set of unions of conjunctive queries which the attacker can issue that are optimal in the sense that no further information is gained by issuing additional queries. The required queries are very different in LAV and GAV integration scenarios, but our approach unifies the attack strategy extending it to a GLAV setting.

(b) We define absolute and relative privacy guarantees, dependent on the source S_0, and provide corresponding algorithms to check them against the optimal attack strategy. The absolute guarantees depend only on the current state of the information integration system, while the relative ones relate the state of the information integration system before and after a change in the mapping between the data sources and the public schema. Such a change may arise for example as a result of introducing new data sources, or if a source owner decides to publish additional proprietary data. The guarantees (formalized in Section 4) are:

1. The source is not completely exposed (i.e. the attacker cannot infer its exact extent without resorting to external knowledge).
2. The secret is not completely exposed.
3. The secret has not been further exposed (i.e. nothing new can be learned about it) by extending the source-target mapping to export further information.
4. The source has not been further exposed by extending the source-target mapping.

Note that Guarantee 1 does not depend on the secret; if the source is completely exposed, the attacker may compute the result of any query whatsoever against it. Furthermore, we identify Guarantee 4 as the natural adaptation to data integration of the notion of *perfect privacy* introduced in data publishing [18].

(c) While in general the complexity of our algorithms ranges from **NP** to Π_2^P in the size of the source instance, we identify a practically relevant PTIME case.

(d) We define additional guarantees corresponding to the ones above, but defined in terms of *all possible sources*. These guarantee flavors are of significant interest as they do not require re-checking after each update on the sources. We show however that all but one of them are undecidable (we do not know whether the latter is decidable or not). These results establish the source-dependent guarantees as the best we can hope for in the trade-off between strength of guarantees and their decidability.

Paper Outline. The remainder of this paper is organized as follows. In Section 2 we introduce the required notation. In Section 3, we model the general strategy the attacker follows and in Section 4 we present the guarantees that the defender can provide. In Section 5 we provide algorithms to check the guarantees and our theoretical results, which include correctness and complexity of the algorithms. We discuss related work in Section 6 and conclude in Section 7. The proofs are shown in the extended version of this paper [19].

2 Preliminaries

Queries. Unless otherwise specified, all our queries are $UCQ^=$ queries; that is, unions of conjunctive queries with equalities (we also allow constants). We only consider safe queries (i.e. with all head variables appearing in their body). Given a query Q and a database D, $Q(D)$ is the answer to Q on D.

Constraints. A *constraint* is a boolean query. We denote sets of constraints with capital Greek letters and individual constraints with lowercase Greek letters. We consider constraints of the form $\forall \bar{x}(P(\bar{x}) \rightarrow Q(\bar{y}))$, where $\{\bar{y}\} \subseteq \{\bar{x}\}$, where $\{\bar{x}\}$ is the set of free variables in the *premise* P, where $\{\bar{y}\}$ is the set of free variables in the *conclusion* Q, and where P and Q are $UCQ^=$ queries. In constraints, we allow Q to be unsafe; intuitively, the safety of the constraint comes from the safety of P. Such constraints are similar to and generalize *embedded dependencies* [1] by allowing disjunctions; we call them $IC(UCQ^=)$ constraints because they express containment of $UCQ^=$ queries. Unless otherwise specified, all our constraints are of this kind. We write $D \models \Sigma$ if the database D satisfies the set of constraints Σ.

Information Integration Systems. As in [16], we define an *information integration system* to consist of four parts $(\sigma_S, \sigma_T, \Sigma, S)$: σ_S is the *source* or *private* schema, σ_T is the *target* or *public* schema, Σ is a finite set of constraints over the joint schema $\sigma_S \cup \sigma_T$ specifying how the sources relate to the targets, and S is the source. We assume that σ_S and σ_T are disjoint. We say that T is a *possible target* of S under Σ if $(S,T) \models \Sigma$. That is, if the database obtained from putting S and T together satisfies Σ. We define the *certain answers* to a query Q over σ_T under the constraints Σ on source S to be $\text{cert}_\Sigma^Q(S) := \bigcap_{(S,T) \models \Sigma} Q(T)$. That is, $\text{cert}_\Sigma^Q(S)$ is the set of tuples which appear in $Q(T)$ for every possible target T of S. This corresponds to what is known as the *open world assumption*. We say that Σ is *source-to-target* if every constraint in Σ contains only relation symbols from σ_S in the premise and relation symbols from σ_T in the conclusion. All our information systems are given by source-to-target mappings, in the spirit of the Clio system [11].

GAV, LAV and GLAV Integration. This setting generalizes two very important particular cases occurring frequently in practice and in the literature [14,16]. In Global-As-View (GAV) integration systems, the conclusion of each constraint in Σ is a *single* relational atom, with all variables appearing in the premise (see Example 4 below). In

Local-As-View (LAV) integration, the premise is a single relational atom, with all variables appearing in the conclusion (as seen in Example 1). The general case is therefore also known as Global-Local-As-View (GLAV).

3   Modeling Attacks Against the Integration System

Recall that we consider the scenario where each of the user's queries Q is processed by the information integration system $\mathcal{I} := (\sigma_S, \sigma_T, \Sigma, S_0)$ and the certain answers $\text{cert}_\Sigma^Q(S_0)$ are returned to the user. The user has no other access to the source S_0.

The attacker is a malicious user whose objective is to obtain the answer to or at least partial information on secret, specified as the answer to a query Q_Z against the source S_0. The attacker has no further access to the sources than ordinary users.

However, we consider that all users know the source schema and how it relates to the target schema using source-to-target constraints. It has been argued before even in the context of database publishing [18] that assuming otherwise would be naive. After all, the only way of communicating to users the meaning of data contributed by a source is via a source schema (be it the real one, or an abstract, conceptual one) and its relationship to the target schema. For instance, even if users do not know the names of the hospital database tables and their attributes, they understand enough about the application domain to assume that these include patients, doctors, ailments, and they can easily observe whether patient names and ailments are hidden or not. It is therefore prudent to assume that in most applications, attackers can reverse-engineer a source schema, or an abstraction thereof which is equivalent with respect to information capacity. The attack against privacy can then be conducted using the real or the reverse-engineered schema.

Since the attacker understands the semantics of the source schema, she will have no trouble formulating the query Q_Z which specifies the secret.[1] The only obstacle in her way is the integration system's rejection of queries which are not formulated against its target schema. Instead, the attacker may issue several queries against the integration system, then apply arbitrary computational power on the answers in order to obtain information about the secret $Q_Z(S_0)$.

Possible sources and secrets. Note that the attacker cannot distinguish among sources that lead to the same answers for the queries she issued. She thus reduces the set of possible sources/secrets to those which are indistinguishable w.r.t. the issued queries, applying external knowledge to distinguish among the reduced set. Clearly, the optimal outcome for the attacker is to reduce the set of sources/secrets to guess from as much as possible by posing the "right" queries. To state our guarantees, we formalize the notions of "possible sources" and "possible secrets." Intuitively, possible sources and possible secrets are those which cannot be distinguished, respectively, from the source S_0 and the secret $Q_Z(S_0)$ exclusively by issuing queries to $\mathcal{I}$; discriminating among them requires the attacker to use external knowledge.

We say that S is a *possible source* if the certain answers to *any* query Q for $(\sigma_S, \sigma_T, \Sigma, S)$ are exactly the same as the certain answers to Q for $(\sigma_S, \sigma_T, \Sigma, S_0)$. That is,

---

[1] For brevity, we refer to Q_Z as the "secret query", though we assume that only its answer is secret, not its definition.

for all queries Q, $\mathrm{cert}^Q_\Sigma(S) = \mathrm{cert}^Q_\Sigma(S_0)$. We say that Z is a *possible secret* if it is the result $Q_Z(S)$ of the secret query Q_Z on some possible source S. In particular, the source S_0 is a possible source and the secret $Q_Z(S_0)$ is a possible secret. Clearly, any source which has the same possible targets as S_0 is a possible source.

The attacker wishes to obtain a set of secrets/sources which approximates as best as possible the set of possible secrets/sources. She will then distinguish among these using external knowledge and, if necessary, randomly guess among the secrets/sources which remain indistinguishable even by external knowledge.

Attacker's external knowledge. The attacker's external knowledge has been modeled in the literature as additional constraints on the secrets or on the sources, or as a probability distribution on them [18,8]. Here, we abstract away from the particular representation, modeling it with two "black box" oracles PICKSOURCE and PICKSECRET. These represent any means of reducing the input possibilities based on external knowledge, followed by a random pick from the reduced set (if it is not a singleton).

PICKSECRET accepts as input a finite description of a set $\mathcal{Z}$ which is an approximation of the set of possible answers to the query Q_Z, and picks one secret from $\mathcal{Z}$. The following is a general strategy for the attacker in case PICKSECRET is available:

Procedure ATTACKSECRET

1. Issue several queries $Q_1, \ldots, Q_k$ against $\mathcal{I}$ to obtain $A_1, \ldots, A_k$ where $A_i := \mathrm{cert}^{Q_i}_\Sigma(S_0)$.
2. Using $A_1, \ldots, A_k$, compute a finite description $\Sigma_{\mathcal{Z}}$ which approximates as well as possible the set $\mathcal{Z}$ of possible secrets (that is, the set of answers to $Q_Z(S)$ for those sources S which satisfy $A_i = \mathrm{cert}^{Q_i}_\Sigma(S)$).
3. Return PICKSECRET($\Sigma_{\mathcal{Z}}$)

Similarly, PICKSOURCE accepts as input a finite description Σ_S of a set which approximates the possible sources and picks one of them. The following is a general strategy for the attacker in case only PICKSECRET is available:

Procedure ATTACKSOURCE

1. Issue several queries $Q_1, \ldots, Q_k$ against $\mathcal{I}$ to obtain $A_1, \ldots, A_k$ where $A_i := \mathrm{cert}^{Q_i}_\Sigma(S_0)$.
2. Using $A_1, \ldots, A_k$, compute a finite description Σ_S which approximates as well as possible the set S of possible sources S (that is, those which satisfy $A_i = \mathrm{cert}^{Q_i}_\Sigma(S)$).
3. Set $S := $ PICKSOURCE(Σ_S)
4. Return $Q_Z(S)$.

The attacker's access to PICKSECRET, but not to PICKSOURCE models the case when she has no external knowledge about the possible sources, but may have sufficient independent knowledge to form an opinion about the possible secrets. We assume that PICKSOURCE may use PICKSECRET as a subroutine whenever both are available and that the attacker chooses to use PICKSOURCE whenever it is available.

4   Privacy Guarantees

The goal of the defender is to determine to what extent the information system $\mathcal{I} = (\sigma_S, \sigma_T, \Sigma, S_0)$ is vulnerable to attacks of the kind outlined in Section 3. The defender specifies the secret as a query Q_Z over σ_S. We analyze what kinds of guarantees the defender can provide and how he can verify whether they hold. We consider both *absolute* guarantees, pertaining to how private the secret is for $\mathcal{I}$ and *relative* guarantees, pertaining to whether the secret has been exposed further in going from $\mathcal{I}$ to a new system $\mathcal{I}'$.

Our privacy guarantees focus on the crucial steps 1 and 2 in the general attack strategies. In these, the attacker attempts to facilitate the task of the oracle as much as possible by restricting the set of options to guess from. The fewer options are obtained, the less external knowledge is needed to guess the secret.

In Section 5, we investigate how good an approximation of possible secrets and sources the attacker can obtain. We obtain there the following surprising result:

Corollary 1 (of Theorem 1 in Section 5). *There exists a finite set of queries whose certain answers can be used to construct a finite axiomatization of the sets of possible sources and secrets.*

A conservative defender must therefore assume that any attacker is able, by posing a carefully chosen set of queries, to obtain a *precise* description of the sets of possible sources and secrets. This is why we focus our guarantees on these sets.

Absolute Guarantees. We now introduce two minimal guarantees guarding against full disclosure of the source, respectively secret. The worst case for the defender is when the certain answers to some finite set of queries $\mathcal{Q}$ are sufficient to determine the source S_0 exactly. In this case, the attacker may obtain not only the secret $Q_Z(S_0)$, but any information she wishes of the source under our assumptions.

Guarantee 1. *The source S_0 is not completely exposed by the information system $\mathcal{I}$. That is, there are at least two possible sources.*

Even if the source is not completely exposed, the secret might be. That is, there is more than one possible source, but the result of the secret query on all of them is the same (in short, there is only one possible secret). In this case the attacker may not know the source S_0, but she may learn the secret $Q_Z(S_0)$.

Guarantee 2. *The secret $Q_Z(S_0)$ is not completely exposed by the information system $\mathcal{I}$. That is, there are at least two possible secrets.*

Relative Guarantees. Guarantees 1 and 2 only avoid a complete privacy breach in which source, respectively secret are fully exposed. This is of course the weakest guarantee one could provide. Ideally, we would like the guarantee that nothing can be "learned" about the secret given the information system. The following example however shows that such a guarantee is unreasonably strong and is violated by most systems, which is why we need to set our sights on more relaxed guarantees.

Example 3. Consider an information system whose only source relation contains tuples associating the patient with the ailment he suffered from and the doctor who treated him: $PDA(patient,doctor,ailment)$. The secret, as in Example 1, is the association between patients and their ailment: $Q_Z(p,a) :- PDA(p,d,a)$. The source registration only exports the projection of this source relation on its doctor attribute: $\forall p, d, a \ PDA(p, d, a) \rightarrow D(d)$ (where D is the target schema). Since neither patients nor ailments are registered, this registration is seemingly safe. However, an attacker can still learn from it some (small amount of) information about the secret. Indeed, if the registered list of doctors is empty, then the source relation must be empty as well, so no patient can suffer from any ailment. If however there is even one doctor in the registered list, then there is a non-zero probability of a certain patient suffering from some disease. Clearly, the attacker has "learned" something about the secret upon observing the list of doctors, and the idealized guarantee is violated. At the same time, ruling out this registration boils down to asking the source owner to not register any data, even if it avoids the attributes involved in the secret query.

Since the absolute Guarantees 1 and 2 are too weak and the idealized guarantee considered above is too strong, we consider a more pragmatic class of *relative* guarantees. These assume that the data owner is willing to live with the current exposure of the secret or source, but wants to make sure that changing the constraints of the information system will not lead to further exposure.

There are two strong relative guarantees the defender can provide. The first applies in case the defender knows that the attacker has no external knowledge about possible sources (but may have external knowledge about possible secrets):

Guarantee 3. If the attacker has no external knowledge about the possible sources, then secret $Q_Z(S_0)$ has not been further exposed in going from the information system $\mathcal{I} := (\sigma_S, \sigma_T, \Sigma, S_0)$ to the information system $\mathcal{I}' := (\sigma_S, \sigma_T, \Sigma', S_0)$. That is, the set of possible secrets under Σ is the same as the set of possible secrets under Σ'.

The second guarantee applies when the defender cannot safely assume that the attacker will not distinguish among sources.

Guarantee 4. The secret $Q_Z(S_0)$ has not been further exposed in going from the information system $\mathcal{I} := (\sigma_S, \sigma_T, \Sigma, S_0)$ to the information system $\mathcal{I}' := (\sigma_S, \sigma_T, \Sigma', S_0)$. That is, the set of possible sources under Σ is the same as the set of possible sources under Σ'.

Example 2 in the introduction illustrates a case when Guarantee 1 fails, as there is a client query which fully reveals the source. Therefore, for any secret query Q_Z, Guarantee 2 fails as well, since the attacker can retrieve the full secret by running Q_Z on the exposed source. There are cases when the underlying source is not fully exposed (Guarantee 1 holds), but the secret is (Guarantee 2 fails). For lack of space, we illustrate such a scenario in the extended version [19], where we also show a scenario where Guarantee 3 holds but Guarantee 4 fails.

Source-independent guarantees. Guarantees 1, 2, 3, and 4 are all given in terms of a specific source S_0. For each such Guarantee i, we can define a corresponding Guarantee i' which has the same statement, but instead of referring to *some* source S_0, is quantified over *all* sources. These source-independent guarantee flavors are of significant interest as they do not require re-checking after each update on the sources.

5   Algorithms

In this section we outline algorithms for checking Guarantees 1 through 4. These algorithms are based on reduction to the problem of checking implication of constraints.

The implication problem for constraints is to determine whether, given a set of constraints Σ and a constraint ϕ, Σ implies ϕ, written $\Sigma \models \phi$. $\Sigma \models \phi$ holds if every database that satisfies Σ also satisfies ϕ. In general, checking implication of IC(UCQ$^=$) constraints is undecidable, as this class includes functional and inclusion dependencies, for which the implication problem is undecidable [1]. However, our reduction yields constraints which we call *convergent* for which checking implication and equivalence of two sets of constraints is in $\mathbf{\Pi_2^P}$ (Theorem 2). Checking whether $\Sigma \models \phi$ holds for convergent constraints can be done by a well-known procedure known as the *chase* [1]. We do not describe this procedure here; instead we assume we have a procedure IMPLIES to check whether $\Sigma \models \phi$ holds. We say that Σ and Σ' are equivalent (which we write $\Sigma \equiv \Sigma'$) in case Σ implies every constraint in Σ' and conversely.

We now reduce the problem of checking guarantees to the implication problem. For instance, to check Guarantee 1 and Guarantee 2, the idea is to find a set of constraints Δ_1 which axiomatize the possible sources (respectively, possible secrets) and a set of constraints Δ_2 which axiomatize the actual source (respectively, the actual secret) and to check whether Δ_1 implies Δ_2. Guarantee 1 (respectively, Guarantee 2) holds if and only iff $\Delta_1 \not\models \Delta_2$. Since as it turns out Δ_1 and Δ_2 are convergent sets, the latter implication is decidable.

The constraints are obtained by the following procedures: AXINSTANCE(D) returns constraints which axiomatize the database D. That is, $D' \models$ AXINSTANCE(D) iff $D = D'$. AXSOURCES yields constraints which axiomatize the possible sources. AXSECRETS returns constraints which axiomatize the possible secrets. Before detailing the procedures, we show how they yield an algorithm for checking the various guarantees. The algorithm is inspired by the following corollary of Theorem 1 below.

Corollary 2 (of Theorem 1)

1. *Guarantee 1 holds iff* AXSOURCES($\mathcal{I}$) $\not\models$ AXINSTANCE(S_0).
2. *Guarantee 2 holds iff* AXSECRETS($\mathcal{I}, Q_Z$) $\not\models$ AXINSTANCE($Q_Z(S_0)$).
3. *Guarantee 3 holds iff* AXSECRETS($\mathcal{I}, Q_Z$) $\equiv$ AXSECRETS($\mathcal{I}', Q_Z$).
4. *Guarantee 4 holds iff* AXSOURCES($\mathcal{I}$) $\equiv$ AXSOURCES($\mathcal{I}'$).

For instance by Corollary 2 we can use the procedures IMPLIES, AXINSTANCE and AXSOURCES to check Guarantee 1 as follows (Guarantees 2 through 4 are checked similarly):

Procedure GUARANTEEONEHOLDS($\mathcal{I}$)
Set $\Delta_1 :=$ AXSOURCES($\mathcal{I}$). Set $\Delta_2 :=$ AXINSTANCE(S_0). Return not IMPLIES(Δ_1, Δ_2).

We define our procedures next.

In Algorithm 1, R^D denotes the extent of relation R in database D, and $\bar{c} \in R^D$ ranges over all tuples in R^D. In Algorithm 2, given a constraint $\phi \in$ IC(UCQ$^=$) we define Q_ϕ to be the UCQ$^=$ query whose body is the conclusion of ϕ and whose head is $Q_\phi(\bar{x})$ where $\bar{x}$ are the free variables in the conclusion of ϕ. We define P_ϕ similarly as the query obtained from the premise of ϕ.

Notice that the procedure which issues queries against the integration system is AXSOURCES, and that these queries are precisely those corresponding to the conclusions of the source-to-target constraints. The auxiliary procedure AXONE used within AXSOURCES gives constraints which are satisfied precisely by the sources that agree with

Algorithm 1. AxINSTANCE(D)

returns constraints which are satisfied precisely by database D.
That is, $D' \models$ AxINSTANCE(D) iff $D = D'$.
1: **for** every relation R in the signature $\sigma(D)$ of D **do**
2:    Set $\delta_R^1 := R(\bar{x}) \rightarrow \bigvee_{\bar{c} \in R^D} \bar{x} = \bar{c}$.
3:    Set $\delta_R^2 := R(\bar{x}) \leftarrow \bigvee_{\bar{c} \in R^D} \bar{x} = \bar{c}$.
4: **end for**
5: **return** $\{\delta_R^i : R \in \sigma(D), i \in \{1,2\}\}$.

Algorithm 2. AxSOURCES($\mathcal{I}$)

returns constraints axiomatizing the possible sources.
That is, $S \models$ AxSOURCES($\mathcal{I}$) iff S is a possible source.
1: **for** every $\phi \in \Sigma$ **do**
2:    Issue the query Q_ϕ against $\mathcal{I}$ to obtain $A_{Q_\phi} := \text{cert}_\Sigma^{Q_\phi}(S_0)$.
3: **end for**
4: **return** $\bigcup_{\phi \in \Sigma}$ AxONE($\Sigma, Q_\phi, A_{Q_\phi}$).

Algorithm 3. AxONE($\Sigma, Q_\phi, A_{Q_\phi}$)

returns constraints which are satisfied precisely by the sources which agree with S_0 on the
result A_{Q_ϕ} of query Q_ϕ (which is the conclusion of constraint ϕ).
1: Set $R_\phi :=$ REWRITE(Σ, Q_ϕ).
  // Set Σ_ϕ^r to the set of constraints over schema $\sigma_S \cup \{Q_\phi\}$ which capture R_ϕ:
2: let R_ϕ be the UCQ$^=$ query $R_\phi(\bar{x}) :- \bigvee_i B_i(\bar{x})$
  Set $\Sigma_\phi^r = \{\forall \bar{x} \bigvee_i B_i(\bar{x}) \rightarrow Q_\phi(\bar{x}), \forall \bar{x} Q_\phi(\bar{x}) \rightarrow \bigvee_i B_i(\bar{x})\}$
3: Set $\Sigma_\phi^e :=$ AxINSTANCE(A_{Q_ϕ})
4: Set $\Sigma_\phi := \Sigma_\phi^r \cup \Sigma_\phi^e$.
5: **return** Σ_ϕ.

Algorithm 4. AxSECRETS($\mathcal{I}, Q_Z$)

returns constraints which axiomatize the possible secrets.
1: Set $\Phi_1 :=$ AxSOURCES($\mathcal{I}$).
  // Set Φ_2 to the set of constraints over schema $\sigma_S \cup \{Q_Z\}$ which capture Q_Z:
2: Let Q_Z be the UCQ$^=$ query $Q_Z(\bar{x}) :- \bigvee_i B_i(\bar{x})$
  Set $\Phi_2 = \{\forall \bar{x} \bigvee_i B_i(\bar{x}) \rightarrow Q_Z(\bar{x}), \forall \bar{x} Q_Z(\bar{x}) \rightarrow \bigvee_i B_i(\bar{x})\}$
3: **return** $\Phi_1 \cup \Phi_2$.

S_0 on the query Q_ϕ (the conclusion of constraint ϕ). AxONE employs the auxiliary
procedure REWRITE(Σ, Q) which produces a rewriting R of Q in terms σ_S satisfying
$R(S) = \text{cert}_\Sigma^Q(S)$ for any S. Such an algorithm was provided in [9] for the case where
Q is a Datalog program and $\Sigma \subseteq \text{IC}(\text{UCQ}^=)$ gives a local-as-view mapping. The
extension to source-to-target constraints $\Sigma \subseteq \text{IC}(\text{UCQ}^=)$ is straightforward (see e.g.,
[23]). For the purposes of procedure AxSOURCES defined below, it is sufficient to have
R axiomatizable by $\text{IC}(\text{UCQ}^=)$. However, to ensure decidability of implication on the
result of AxSOURCES, we need R to be a UCQ$^=$ query. It is known from [9] that when
Σ is source-to-target R is a UCQ$^=$ query.

Due to space limitations, we leave a detailed illustration of the algorithm for the extended version [19]. Here we only remark that in Example 1, the identity queries against the target schema turned out to be useless to the attacker, in contrast to the case of database publishing where the identity queries are the first step required to reveal the extent of the views. This is now explainable by our results: the identity queries are not the conclusions of the source-target constraints. On the other hand, query Q_ϕ in Example 2 constitutes the optimal attack. Our results also imply that when the integration system conforms to a global-as-view case, identity queries against the relations in the target schema lead to optimal attack strategies. We illustrate such an attack in Example 4 below (more examples can be found in [19]).

Example 4. Source S now conforms to schema $\{H(ssn, patient, doctor, ailment)\}$ where H is a history relation listing the social security number and name of patients, as well as the doctor who treated them for an ailment. The registration is given by constraint $\phi_1 = \forall s, p, d, a\ H(s, p, d, a) \rightarrow PD(p, d)$ which exports the projection of H on patient and doctor into PD. Note that this specification corresponds to the standard global-as-view registration given by view $PD(p, d) :- H(s, p, d, a)$. Since the projection of H is all that the source exports, the best an attacker can hope for is to retrieve its exact extent. But how should she query the system to this end? It is easy to show that the projection of H on patients and doctors coincides with the certain answers $\mathrm{cert}_\Sigma^{Q_{\phi_1}}(S)$ to the identity query Q_{ϕ_1} on table PD ($Q_{\phi_1}(p, d) :- PD(p, d)$). This is precisely the conclusion of ϕ_1.

5.1 Correctness

In this section we show (in Theorem 1) that $\mathrm{AXSOURCES}(\mathcal{I})$ axiomatizes precisely the set of possible sources (indistinguishable modulo *all* queries) and that $\mathrm{AXSECRETS}(\mathcal{I})$ axiomatizes precisely the set of possible secrets for an information integration system $\mathcal{I} := (\sigma_S, \sigma_T, \Sigma, S_0)$. In particular, the finite set $\mathcal{Q}_0$ of UCQ$^=$ queries issued by procedure $\mathrm{AXSOURCES}$ and consisting of the conclusions of all constraints in Σ suffices to obtain as much information about the source and about the secret as is possible to obtain by querying $\mathcal{I}$. Therefore, among the attacks following the general strategy outlined in Section 3, the optimal algorithms $\mathrm{OPTATTACKSOURCE}$ and $\mathrm{OPTATTACKSECRET}$ are obtained from $\mathrm{ATTACKSOURCE}$ and $\mathrm{ATTACKSECRET}$ by replacing lines 1 and 2 with calls to respectively, $\mathrm{AXSOURCES}$ and $\mathrm{AXSECRETS}$.

We define the *equivalence class* of S under the mapping given by Σ to be $[S]_\Sigma := \{S' : \forall T\ (S, T) \models \Sigma \text{ iff } (S', T) \models \Sigma\}$. That is, $[S]_\Sigma$ is the set of all sources which have the same possible targets as S. Clearly, given $\mathcal{I} := (\sigma_S, \sigma_T, \Sigma, S_0)$, the members of $[S_0]_\Sigma$ cannot be distinguished from the actual source S_0 or from each other by querying $\mathcal{I}$. Indeed, for any query Q and any $S \in [S_0]_\Sigma$, $\mathrm{cert}_\Sigma^Q(S) = \bigcap_{(S,T)\models\Sigma} Q(T) = \bigcap_{(S_0,T)\models\Sigma} Q(T) = \mathrm{cert}_\Sigma^Q(S_0)$. The following theorem shows that $\mathrm{AXSOURCES}(\mathcal{I})$ axiomatizes $[S_0]_\Sigma$ which is hence precisely the set of possible sources. It also shows that $\{Q_Z(S) : S \in [S_0]_\Sigma\}$ is the set of possible secrets, axiomatized by $\mathrm{AXSECRETS}(\mathcal{I}, Q_Z)$.

Theorem 1. *Given an information system $\mathcal{I} := (\sigma_S, \sigma_T, \Sigma, S_0)$:*

1. *The equivalence class $[S_0]_\Sigma$ is axiomatized by* AxSOURCES$(\mathcal{I})$ *and* AxSOURCES$(\mathcal{I}) \subseteq$ IC(UCQ$^=$).
2. *For any secret query Q_Z, the set $\{Q_Z(S) : S \in [S_0]_\Sigma)\}$ is axiomatized by* AxSECRETS$(\mathcal{I}, Q_Z)$ *and* AxSECRETS$(\mathcal{I}, Q_Z) \subseteq$ IC(UCQ$^=$).

This fundamental theorem allows us to (a) state the guarantees independently of the class of queries which the attacker is allowed to issue (we assume that the attacker can issue at least conjunctive queries), (b) outline an optimal attack strategy, and (c) provide algorithms for checking the guarantees.

As an immediate implication of Theorem 1, we obtain some interesting results for pure LAV and pure GAV integration, prefigurated by the discussion preceding Section 5.1: The source is always completely exposed in LAV information integration systems, since the optimal query is the view definition itself, for which the certain answers are exactly the tuples in the source. That is, Guarantee 1 always fails. Moreover, in this case the identity queries are useless, since they always return the empty set if the view registration contains at least one existential variable. The only queries required by an optimal attack against a GAV information integration system are the identity queries.

5.2 Complexity

We call a finite set of constraints Σ *convergent* if there exists a polynomial p such that for every $Q \in$ UCQ$^=$, the result Q^Σ of chasing Q with Σ is the union of conjunctive queries $Q_1, \ldots, Q_k \in$ CQ$^=$ satisfying $|Q_i| \le p(|Q|)$ for $i \in \{1, \ldots, k\}$.

Theorem 2. *If $\Sigma, \Sigma' \subseteq$ IC(UCQ$^=$) are finite sets of convergent constraints and $\phi \in$ IC(UCQ$^=$), then checking whether $\Sigma \not\models \phi$ is decidable in Π_2^P in the combined size of Σ and ϕ and checking whether $\Sigma \models \Sigma'$ or $\Sigma \equiv \Sigma'$ is decidable in Π_2^P in the combined size of Σ and Σ'. Furthermore, if ϕ or Σ' have a single model, then the complexity is* coNP.

Theorem 3. AxSOURCES$(\mathcal{I})$ *and* AxSECRETS$(\mathcal{I}, Q_Z)$ *each yield a set of convergent constraints, in time polynomial in the combined size of S_0 and of* REWRITE(Σ, Q_ϕ) *for every $\phi \in \Sigma$.*

Corollary 3. *Checking whether Guarantees 1 and 2 hold is in* **NP** *in the combined size of S_0,* REWRITE(Σ, Q_ϕ) *for every $\phi \in \Sigma$, and in the case of Guarantee 2, Q_Z.*

Corollary 4. *Checking whether Guarantees 3 and 4 hold is Π_2^P in the combined size of S_0,* REWRITE(Σ, Q_ϕ) *for every $\phi \in \Sigma$,* REWRITE(Σ', Q_ϕ) *for every $\phi \in \Sigma'$, and in the case of Guarantee 3, Q_Z.*

5.3 An Important Tractable Case

Our algorithms for checking guarantees are in general prohibitively expensive, as the **NP** and Π_2^P upper bounds (in Corollaries 3 and 4) include the size of the instance S_0. In this section we show that a practically relevant integration setting, which we call *tagged-union* integration, admits polynomial-time guarantee checking.

Definition 1. An integration is said to have *tagged-unions* if each target relation R has some attribute a such for each constraint $\phi \in \Sigma$ and each R-atom occurring in the conclusion Q_ϕ, a constant c_ϕ occurs in the attribute a such that $c_\phi \neq c'_\phi$ for all distinct $\phi, \phi' \in \Sigma$. No constant is needed if R appears in only one constraint.

All of our examples have tagged-union, since relation names are not shared across conclusions. The tagged-union restriction is quite realistic. While in a car dealership portal there will be many local dealers exporting their car ads into the same target ad relation, each dealer would likely tag the ad with the dealership name, address or phone number. Similarly for scenarios integrating any large community of vendors. Even for our medical example, one would expect various wards or hospitals to tag the published patient or doctor names with their affiliation. For example, consider a Honda and a Toyota dealer who integrate their private data into a brokerage portal (of target schema *deals*), using the tagged-union constraints ϕ_H, respectively ϕ_T:

$(\phi_H) \forall \bar{x}\, myhondas(\bar{x}) \rightarrow deals(\text{"Honda"}, \bar{x})$ $(\phi_T) \forall \bar{x}\, mytoyotas(\bar{x}) \rightarrow deals(\text{"Toyota"}, \bar{x})$.

Theorem 4. *In tagged-union integration systems, Guarantees 1 through 4 are decidable in polynomial time in the size of the source instance S_0.*

The **NP** and Π_2^P upper bounds of Corollaries 3 and 4 are now confined to the combined size of the constraints in Σ and the size of each REWRITE result, but these are data-independent.

5.4   Undecidability of Source-Independent Guarantees

We use the following undecidability results in our proofs below. A view V determines a query Q iff for all databases D_1, D_2, if $V(D_1) = V(D_2)$, then $Q(D_1) = Q(D_2)$. Checking whether V determines Q when $V, Q \in \text{UCQ}$ is undecidable ([21]).

Theorem 5. *Checking Guarantee 2' is undecidable.*

Theorem 6. *Checking Guarantee 4' is undecidable.*

Since Guarantee 4' is a particular case of Guarantee 3' (for Q_Z the identity query over σ_S), we obtain the following corollary:

Corollary 5. *Checking Guarantee 3' is undecidable.*

The decidability of Guarantee 1' remains an open problem.

6   Related Work

One line of prior research focused on implementing access control in data publishing, i.e. allowing clients to see only those published views which they are authorized to. The techniques are based on cryptographically encoding the data (see [17] and references within). Our work is orthogonal to work on access control, as it helps data owners design the views (and more generally, mappings) such that attackers cannot breach privacy using only *authorized* accesses.

[2] introduces c-tables, a compact formalism for finitely representing large (and potentially infinite) sets of possible worlds, and shows Π_2^P-complete data complexity for

checking that the sets of possible sources represented by two c-tables are the same. c-tables are not sufficiently expressive to model the set of possible sources corresponding to a materialized view instance. [13] introduces *database templates* to this end and shows how to compute them using the chase, but does not address the comparison of the sets of possible sources. We describe possible sources by a different formalism, namely a finite axiomatization.

[10] focuses on limiting privacy breaches in a scenario in which the aggregation of a set of private client data items is computed at the server. [3] takes aggregation into account and shows that exposing the result of counting queries allows the retrieval of an isomorphic copy of the structure of the database.

[20] takes a dual approach to ours (though in a closed world). While we use queries to specify the secret, [20] uses conjunctive query views to specify what may be seen by outsiders. In this setting, conjunctive client queries asked against the proprietary database are answered only if they have a rewriting using the allowable views.

Perfect Privacy. [18] addresses privacy in database publishing, i.e. in a closed-world, GAV scenario. The work pioneers the idea of specifying the secret as a conjunctive query over the base schema and checking the so-called *perfect privacy* guarantee. This consists in checking that a newly exported view does not modify the attacker's a priori belief about the secret. The attacker's belief is modeled as a probability distribution on the set of possible sources, with the simplifying assumption that the tuples in the secret answer are *independent events*. [8] adopts the notion of perfect privacy from [18] (still in a publishing, not integration scenario), but provides a more general formalization of attacker's beliefs by lifting the independence assumption on secret tuples. With this formalization, perfect privacy is shown in [8] to reduce to the preservation of the set of possible sources. Consequently, Guarantee 4 in this paper is the natural adaptation of perfect privacy from data publishing (in the flavor of [8]) to a data integration scenario.

Probabilistic Databases. One could envision quantitative privacy guarantees, e.g. by requiring a particular secret tuple to appear in no more than a fraction of the possible sources. Such approaches face the challenge of the set of possible sources being potentially infinite, in which case "counting" it must be defined carefully (see [6,7] for pioneering work in this direction, though in a database publishing setting).

7   Discussion

Privacy-preserving Updates. We can express guarantees corresponding to Guarantees 3 and 4, in which the mapping does not change (that is, $\Sigma = \Sigma'$), but the extent of the source does (S_0 is replaced by S_0'). The new guarantees would check that the possible sources, respectively secrets, do not change when S_0 is updated.

Conceptually, we can straightforwardly adapt our algorithms for checking Guarantees 3 and 4 to this new situation. All we need to do is call AXSOURCES (AXSECRETS) on the information system before and after the update (in the case of AXSECRETS, using the same Q_Z). Then we check that the obtained source (secret) axiomatizations imply each other. However, as such a test would have to be performed at run time, further work on efficient run-time algorithms is required towards a practical tool.

Target Constraints. We have modularized our privacy algorithms to work in the presence of arbitrary constraints on the target schema, provided that (i) the integration system can return the certain answers in this case, and (ii) there exists an algorithm REWRITE(Σ, Q) which produces a rewriting of Q in terms of σ_S returning the certain answers of Q on any source, and (iii) REWRITE(Σ, Q) returns a UCQ$^=$ query. It is known from [9] that when there are no target constraints, REWRITE(Σ, Q) returns a UCQ$^=$ query, but returns a recursive Datalog program when the target constraints are full dependencies. In this case, Theorem 1 still holds but the obtained constraints are not convergent and therefore Theorem 3 does not apply so we can not make any claims on the complexity of checking these guarantees. [9] provides no rewriting for more general target constraints.

References

1. S. Abiteboul, R. Hull, and V. Vianu. *Foundations of Databases*. Addison-Wesley, 1995.
2. S. Abiteboul, P. Kanellakis, and G. Grahne. On the representation and querying of sets of possible worlds. *Theoretical Computer Science*, 78:159–187, 1991.
3. M. Bielecki and J. V. den Bussche. Database interrogation using conjunctive queries. In *ICDT*, pages 259–269, 2003.
4. A. Cali, D. Calvanese, G. D. Giacomo, and M. Lenzerini. Data integration under integrity constraints. In *CAiSE*, 2002.
5. A. Cali, G. D. Giacomo, and M. Lenzerini. Models of information integration: Turning local-as-view into global-as-view. In *FMII*, 2001.
6. N. N. Dalvi, G. Miklau, and D. Suciu. Asymptotic conditional probabilities for conjunctive queries. In *ICDT*, 2005.
7. N. Dalvi, D. Suciu. Answering queries from statistics and probabilistic views. *VLDB*, 2005.
8. A. Deutsch and Y. Papakonstantinou. Privacy in database publishing. In *ICDT*, 2005.
9. O. Duschka, M. Genesereth, and A. Levy. Recursive query plans for data integration. *Journal of Logic Programming*, 43(1):49–73, 2000.
10. A. Evfimievski, J. Gehrke, and R. Srikant. Limiting privacy breaches in privacy preserving data mining. In *PODS*, 2003.
11. R. Fagin, P. Kolaitis, R. Miller, and L. Popa. Data exchange: Semantics and query answering. In *ICDT*, 2003.
12. M. Friedman, A. Levy, and T. Millstein. Navigational plans for data integration. In 16th *National Conference on Artificial Intelligence (AAAI),*, 1999.
13. G. Grahne and A. O. Mendelzon. Tableau techniques for querying information sources through global schemas. In *ICDT*, 1999.
14. A. Halevy. Logic-based techniques in data integration. In *Logic Based Artificial Intelligence*, 2000.
15. C. Koch. Query rewriting with symmetric constraints. In *FoIKS*, 2002.
16. M. Lenzerini. Data integration: A theoretical perspective. In *PODS*, 2002.
17. G. Miklau, D. Suciu. Controlling access to published data using cryptography. *VLDB*, 2003.
18. G. Miklau and D. Suciu. A formal analysis of information disclosure in data exchange. In *SIGMOD Conference*, 2004.
19. A. Nash and A. Deutsch. Privacy in GLAV information integration. Technical Report CS2006-0869, University of California San Diego, 2006. http://db.ucsd.edu/people/alin.
20. S. Rizvi, A. O. Mendelzon, S. Sudarshan, and P. Roy. Extending query rewriting techniques for fine-grained access control. In *SIGMOD Conference*, 2004.
21. L. Segoufin and V. Vianu. Views and queries: Determinacy and rewriting. In *PODS*, 2005.
22. J. D. Ullman. Information integration using logical views. In *ICDT*, 1997.
23. C. Yu, L. Popa. Constraint-based XML query rewriting for data integration. *SIGMOD*, 2004.

Unlocking Keys for XML Trees

Sven Hartmann and Sebastian Link*

Information Science Research Centre, Massey University, New Zealand
{s.hartmann,s.link}@massey.ac.nz

Abstract. We review key constraints in the context of XML as introduced by Buneman et al. We show that one of the proposed inference
rules is not sound in general, and the axiomatisation proposed for XML
keys is incomplete even if key paths are simple. Therefore, the axiomatisation and also the implication problem for XML keys are still unsolved.

We propose a set of inference rules that is indeed sound and complete
for the implication of XML keys with simple key paths. Our completeness proof enables us to characterise the implication of XML keys in
terms of the reachability problem of nodes in a digraph. This results in a
quadratic time algorithm for deciding XML key implication, and shows
that reasoning for XML keys is practically efficient.

1   Introduction

The eXtensible markup language (XML,[6]) has recently evolved to the standard for data exchange on the Web, and also represents a uniform model for
data integration. It provides a high degree of syntactic flexibility but has little
to offer to specify the semantics of its data. Consequently, the study of integrity
constraints has been recognised as one of the most important yet challenging
areas of XML research [15,28,31,33]. The importance of XML constraints is due
to a wide range of applications ranging from schema design, query optimisation,
efficient storing and updating, data exchange and integration, to data cleaning [15]. Therefore, several classes of integrity constraints have been defined for
XML including keys [8], path constraints [10,11], inclusion constraints [16,17]
and functional dependencies [3,20,22,32]. However, for almost all classes of constraints the complex structure of XML data results in decision problems that are
intractable. It is therefore a major challenge to find natural and useful classes of
XML constraints that can be reasoned about efficiently [15,16,17,28,31]. Prime
candidates of such classes are absolute and relative keys [8,9] that are defined
independently from any specification such as a DTD [6] or XSD [30]. Keys are
based on the representation of XML data as trees. This is commonly used by
DOM [2], XSL [24], and XML Schema [30]. Figure 1 shows such a representation
in which nodes are annotated by their type: E for element, A for attribute, and
S for string (PCDATA).

---

* This research is supported by Marsden Funding, the Royal Society of New Zealand.

T. Schwentick and D. Suciu (Eds.): ICDT 2007, LNCS 4353, pp. 104–118, 2007.

Keys are defined in terms of path expressions, and determine nodes either relative to a set of context nodes or the root. Nodes are determined by (complex) values on some selected subnodes. In Figure 1, an example of a reasonable absolute key is that the *isbn* values identify the *book* node. That is, the *isbn* subnodes of different *book* nodes must have different values.

In contrast, an *author* cannot be identified in the entire tree by its *first* and *last* subnodes since the same author can have written more than one book. However, the *author* can indeed be identified by its *first* and *last* subnodes relatively to the *book* node. That is, for each individual *book* node, different *author* subnodes must differ on their *first* or *last* subnodes.

⟨**db**⟩
  ⟨**book isbn**=*0198532741*⟩
    ⟨**title**⟩ *Toposes and Local Set Theories* ⟨**/title**⟩
    ⟨**author**⟩⟨**first**⟩ *John* ⟨**/first**⟩⟨**last**⟩ *Bell* ⟨**/last**⟩⟨**/author**⟩
  ⟨**/book**⟩
  ⟨**book isbn**=*0720428440*⟩
    ⟨**title**⟩ *A course in mathematical logic* ⟨**/title**⟩
    ⟨**author**⟩⟨**first**⟩ *John* ⟨**/first**⟩⟨**last**⟩ *Bell* ⟨**/last**⟩⟨**/author**⟩
    ⟨**author**⟩⟨**first**⟩ *Moshe* ⟨**/first**⟩⟨**last**⟩ *Machover* ⟨**/last**⟩⟨**/author**⟩
  ⟨**/book**⟩
⟨**/db**⟩

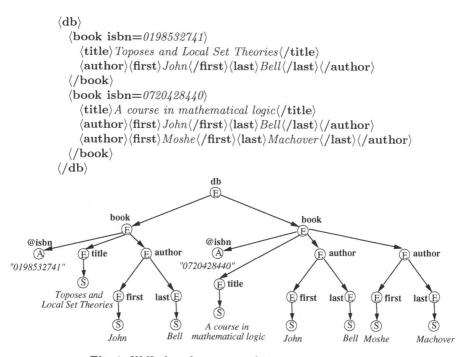

Fig. 1. XML data fragment and its tree representation

Contributions. We review XML key constraints. We show that one of the inference rules for key implication [9] is only sound for keys with simple key path expressions [8], but not sound in general as stated in [9]. The incorrectness is not just a minor detail but shows that the choice of a path language for defining XML keys can be crucial. We demonstrate that the axiomatisation proposed in [9] is not only incomplete in the general case but already incomplete in the case of simple key path expressions, i.e., for XML keys as defined in [8].

Since keys have had a significant impact on XML [8,9] we believe that it is important to provide an axiomatisation and show that automated reasoning about XML keys is practically efficient. We propose an axiomatisation of XML keys with simple key path expressions. Our completeness proof is based on a characterisation of key implication in terms of reachability of nodes in a digraph. Utilising the efficient evaluation of Core XPath queries [18] this results in a decision procedure for XML key implication that is quadratic in the size of the keys given. The simplicity of our algorithm is a result of the technique used for proving the completeness of our inference rules. Notice that the original (flawed) technique resulted in a heptic (n^7) algorithm, cf. [9].

Related Work. Constraints have been extensively studied in the context of the relational model of data, some excellent surveys include [14,29]. Dependencies have also been investigated in nested data models, cf. [19,21,27]. Recent work on XML constraints include [3,4,8,9,10,11,16,17,32], for a brief survey see [15].

2   Prerequisites

We review the definition of keys and their properties [8,9]. Throughout the paper we assume familiarity with basic concepts from graph theory [23].

2.1   The XML Tree Model

XML documents can be modelled as node-labelled trees. We assume that there is a countably infinite set $\mathbf{E}$ denoting element tags, a countably infinite set $\mathbf{A}$ denoting attribute names, and a singleton $\{S\}$ denoting text (PCDATA). We further assume that these sets are pairwise disjoint, and put $\mathcal{L} = \mathbf{E} \cup \mathbf{A} \cup \{S\}$. We refer to the elements of $\mathcal{L}$ as *labels*.

An *XML tree* is a 6-tuple $T = (V, lab, ele, att, val, r)$ where V denotes a set of nodes; *lab* is a mapping $V \to \mathcal{L}$ assigning a label to every node in V; a node v in V is called an *element (E) node* if $lab(v) \in \mathbf{E}$, an *attribute (A) node* if $lab(v) \in \mathbf{A}$, and a text (S) node if $lab(v) = S$; *ele* and *att* are partial mappings defining the edge relation of T: for any node v in V, if v is an element node, then $ele(v)$ is a list of element and text nodes in V and $att(v)$ is a set of attribute nodes in V; if v is an attribute or text node then $ele(v)$ and $att(v)$ are undefined; *val* is a partial mapping assigning a string to each attribute and text node: for any node v in V, if v is an A or S node then $val(v)$ is a string, and $val(v)$ is undefined otherwise; and r is the unique and distinguished root node.

An XML tree is said to be *finite* if V is finite. For a node $v \in V$, each node w in $ele(v)$ or $att(v)$ is called a *child* of v, and we say that there is an edge (v, w) from v to w in T. An XML tree has a tree structure: for each node $v \in V$, there is a unique (directed) path of edges from the root r to v.

We can now define value equality for pairs of nodes in XML trees. Informally, two nodes u and v of an XML tree T are value equal if they have the same label and, in addition, either they have the same string value if they are S or A nodes, or their children are pairwise value equal if they are E nodes. More formally, two nodes $u, v \in V$ are *value equal*, denoted by $u =_v v$, if and only if the following conditions are satisfied:

(a) $lab(u) = lab(v)$,

(b) if u, v are A or S nodes, then $val(u) = val(v)$,

(c) if u, v are E nodes, then *(i)* if $att(u) = \{a_1, \ldots, a_m\}$, then $att(v) = \{a'_1, \ldots, a'_m\}$ and there is a permutation π on $\{1, \ldots, m\}$ such that $a_i =_v a'_{\pi(i)}$ for $i = 1, \ldots, m$, and *(ii)* if $ele(u) = [u_1, \ldots, u_k]$, then $ele(v) = [v_1, \ldots, v_k]$ and $u_i =_v v_i$ for $i = 1, \ldots, k$.

That is, two nodes u and v are value equal whenever the subtrees rooted at u and v are isomorphic by an isomorphism that is the identity on string values. For example, the first and second *author* node (according to document order) in Figure 1 are value equal.

2.2 Path Languages

In order to define keys we need a path language that is expressive enough to be practical, yet sufficiently simple to be reasoned about efficiently. This is the case for the path languages PL_s and PL [8,9].

Table 1. The path languages PL_s and PL

Path Language	Syntax
PL_s	$P ::= \varepsilon \mid \ell.P$
PL	$Q ::= \varepsilon \mid \ell \mid Q.Q \mid \_^*$

A *path expression* is a (possibly empty) finite list of symbols. In this paper, a *simple path expression* is a path expression that consists of labels from $\mathcal{L}$. We use the languages PL_s and PL to describe path expressions. Both languages are fragments of regular expressions. PL_s *expressions* and PL *expressions* are defined by the grammars in Table 1. Herein, ε denotes the empty path expression, "." denotes the concatenation of two path expressions, and ℓ denotes any element of $\mathcal{L}$. The language PL is a generalisation of PL_s that allows the distinguished symbol "$\_^*$" to occur. We call $\_^*$ the *don't care* symbol. It serves as a combination of the wildcard "$\_$" and the Kleene star "*". Note that every PL_s expression is a PL expression, too.

We now introduce some more terminology [8,9] used throughout this paper. Note that for PL expressions, the equalities $Q.\varepsilon = \varepsilon.Q = Q$ for all $Q \in PL$, and $\_^*.\_^* = \_^*$ hold. A PL expression Q in *normal form* [8,9] does not contain consecutive $\_^*$, and it does not contain ε unless $Q = \varepsilon$. A PL expression can be transformed into normal form in linear time, just by removing superfluous $\_^*$ and ε symbols. To simplify discussion, we usually assume that PL expressions are already given in normal form. The *length* $|Q|$ of a PL expression Q is the number of labels in Q plus the number of $\_^*$ in the normal form of Q. The empty path expression ε has length 0.

When replacing all $\_^*$ in a PL expression Q by simple path expressions, we obtain a simple path expression P and write $P \in Q$. Thus, a PL expression Q gives rise to a regular language of simple path expressions $P \in Q$. In particular, a PL_s expression represents a single simple path expression. For convenience, we will sometimes refer to PL_s expressions as simple path expressions, too.

We will use path expressions to describe sets of paths in an XML tree T. Recall that each attribute or text node is a leaf in T. Therefore, a path expression is said to be *valid* if it does not contain a label $\ell \in \mathbf{A}$ or $\ell = S$ in a position other than the last one. In the sequel, we use a valid PL expression to represent only valid simple path expressions. For example, _*.*author* is a valid PL expression that represents (among others) the valid simple path expression *book.author*.

A path p is a sequence of pairwise distinct nodes $v_0, \ldots, v_m$ where (v_{i-1}, v_i) is an edge for $i = 1, \ldots, m$. We call p a path from v_0 to v_m, and say that v_m is *reachable* from v_0 following the path p. The path p gives rise to a valid simple path expression $lab(v_1). \cdots .lab(v_m)$, which we denote by $lab(p)$. Let P be a simple path expression, and Q a PL expression. A path p is called a P-*path* if $lab(p) = P$, and a Q-*path* if $lab(p) \in Q$. If p is a path from v to w, then w is said to be reachable from v *following* a P-path or Q-path, respectively. We also write $T \models P(v, w)$ and $T \models Q(v, w)$ when w is reachable from v following a P-path or Q-path, respectively, in an XML tree T. For example, in the XML tree in Figure 1, all *first* nodes are reachable from the root following a *book.author.first*-path. Consequently, they are also reachable from the root following a _*.*first*-path.

For a node v of an XML tree T, let $v[\![Q]\!]$ denote the set of nodes in T that are reachable from v by following the PL expression Q, i.e., $v[\![Q]\!] = \{w \mid T \models Q(v, w)\}$. We shall use $[\![Q]\!]$ as an abbreviation for $r[\![Q]\!]$ where r is the root of T. For example, let v be the second *book* node in Figure 1. Then $v[\![author]\!]$ is the set of all *author* nodes that are children of the second book. Furthermore, $[\![\_*.author]\!]$ is the set of all *author* nodes in the entire XML tree.

For nodes v and v' of T, the *value intersection* of $v[\![Q]\!]$ and $v'[\![Q]\!]$ is given by $v[\![Q]\!] \cap_v v'[\![Q]\!] = \{(w, w') \mid w \in v[\![Q]\!], w' \in v'[\![Q]\!], w =_v w'\}$ [9]. That is, $v[\![Q]\!] \cap_v v'[\![Q]\!]$ consists of all those node pairs in T that are value equal and are reachable from v and v', respectively, by following Q-paths.

A PL expression Q is said to be *contained* in a PL expression Q', denoted by $Q \subseteq Q'$, if for any XML tree T and any node v of T we have $v[\![Q]\!] \subseteq v[\![Q']\!]$. That is, every node that is reachable from v by following a Q-path is also reachable from v by following a Q'-path. Note that $Q \subseteq Q'$ holds if and only if every valid path expression $P \in Q$ satisfies $P \in Q'$ [9]. The *containment problem* of PL is to decide, given any PL expressions Q and Q', whether $Q \subseteq Q'$ holds. The containment problem of PL is decidable in $\mathcal{O}(|Q| \times |Q'|)$ time [9].

Note that although we have presented the language PL using the syntax of regular expressions, there is an easy conversion of PL expressions to *XPath* [12] expressions, just be replacing "_*" of a PL expression with "//", and "." with "/". Also, if a PL expression is meant to start from the root, the converted path is preceded with the symbol "/".

The choice of a path language is directly influenced by the complexity of its containment problem. Buneman et al. [8,9] argue that PL is simple yet expressive enough to be adopted by XML designers and maintained by systems for XML applications.

2.3   Keys for XML

In [9], Buneman et al. define a key φ as an expression $(Q, (Q', \{Q_1, \ldots, Q_k\}))$ where Q, Q', Q_i are PL expressions such that $Q.Q'.Q_i$ is a valid PL expression for all $i = 1, \ldots, k$. Herein, Q is called the *context path*, Q' is called the *target path*, and $Q_1, \ldots, Q_k$ are called the *key paths* of φ.

An XML tree T satisfies the key $(Q, (Q', \{Q_1, \ldots, Q_k\}))$ if and only if for any node $q \in [\![Q]\!]$ and any nodes $q'_1, q'_2 \in q[\![Q']\!]$ such that there are nodes $x_i \in q'_1[\![Q_i]\!], y_i \in q'_2[\![Q_i]\!]$ with $x_i =_v y_i$ for all $i = 1, \ldots, k$, then $q'_1 = q'_2$ [9]. More formally, $\forall q \in [\![Q]\!] \forall q'_1, q'_2 \in q[\![Q']\!]$

$$\left(\bigwedge_{1 \leq i \leq k} q'_1[\![Q_i]\!] \cap_v q'_2[\![Q_i]\!] \neq \emptyset \right) \Rightarrow q'_1 = q'_2.$$

Moreover, Buneman et al. [9] present a finite set of inference rules which they state is sound and complete for the implication of XML keys, as well as an implication decision algorithm based on this axiomatisation.

Table 2. An axiomatisation of XML keys whose key paths are PL_s expressions

$\dfrac{}{(Q, (\varepsilon, S))}$ (epsilon)	$\dfrac{(Q, (Q', S \cup \{\varepsilon, P\}))}{(Q, (Q', S \cup \{\varepsilon, P.P'\}))}$ (prefix-epsilon)	$\dfrac{(Q, (Q', S))}{(Q, (Q', S \cup \{P\}))}$ (superkey)
$\dfrac{(Q, (Q'.P, \{P'\}))}{(Q, (Q', \{P.P'\}))}$ (subnodes)	$\dfrac{(Q, (Q', S))}{(Q'', (Q', S))} Q'' \subseteq Q$ (context-path-containment)	$\dfrac{(Q, (Q', S))}{(Q, (Q'', S))} Q'' \subseteq Q'$ (target-path-containment)
$\dfrac{(Q, (Q'.Q'', S))}{(Q.Q', (Q'', S))}$ (context target)	$\dfrac{(Q, (Q'.P, \{\varepsilon, P'\}))}{(Q, (Q', \{\varepsilon, P.P'\}))}$ (subnodes-epsilon)	$\dfrac{(Q, (Q', \{P.P_1, \ldots, P.P_k\})), \ (Q.Q', (P, \{P_1, \ldots, P_k\}))}{(Q, (Q'.P, \{P_1, \ldots, P_k\}))}$ (interaction)

Let $\mathfrak{S}$ denote the set of inference rules from Table 2 without the *subnodes-epsilon rule*. This is the axiomatisation proposed in [9] when only PL_s expressions are allowed for the key paths. Unfortunately, $\mathfrak{S}$ turns out to be incomplete since the *subnodes-epsilon rule* is sound for the implication of XML keys and independent from $\mathfrak{S}$.

The soundness of the *subnodes-epsilon* rule is not difficult to see. Suppose an XML tree T violates $(Q, (Q', \{\varepsilon, P.P'\}))$. Then there is some node $q \in [\![Q]\!]$ and some nodes $q'_1, q'_2 \in q[\![Q']\!]$ such that $q'_1 \neq q'_2$, $q'_1 =_v q'_2$, and there exist $p'_1 \in q'_1[\![P.P']\!]$ and $p'_2 \in q'_2[\![P.P']\!]$ such that $p'_1 =_v p'_2$. By definition, there exists some $p_1 \in q'_1[\![P]\!]$ such that $p'_1 \in p_1[\![P']\!]$. Since $q'_1 =_v q'_2$ it is easy to see that there exists some node $p_2 \in q'_2[\![P]\!]$ such that $p_1 \neq p_2$, $p_1 =_v p_2$ and $p'_2 \in p_2[\![P']\!]$. But then $p_1 \in q[\![Q'.P]\!]$ and $p_2 \in q[\![Q'.P]\!]$. Hence, T also violates $(Q, (Q'.P, \{\varepsilon, P'\}))$.

Moreover, the *subnodes-epsilon* rule is independent from $\mathfrak{S}$, i.e., there is a finite set $\Sigma \cup \{\varphi\}$ of XML keys such that φ cannot be derived from Σ by $\mathfrak{S}$, but φ can be derived from Σ using $\mathfrak{S}$ and the *subnodes-epsilon* rule. A simple example is given by $\Sigma = \{(\varepsilon, (A.B, \{\varepsilon, C\}))\}$ and $\varphi = (\varepsilon, (A, \{\varepsilon, B.C\}))$. In fact, *subnodes* is the only inference rule in $\mathfrak{S}$ that allows us to make an infix of the target path in the premise of a rule a prefix of a key path in the conclusion of the rule. Since *subnodes* only permits a singleton as the set of key paths, and the other inference rules do not allow us to generate conclusions with a single key path from premises that have at least two key paths, it is impossible to derive φ from Σ using $\mathfrak{S}$. On the other hand, however, φ can be inferred from Σ by a single application of *subnodes-epsilon*. The soundness of the *subnodes-epsilon* rule shows that φ is implied by Σ, but φ cannot be inferred from Σ by $\mathfrak{S}$. Consequently, $\mathfrak{S}$ is incomplete, even for the implication of XML keys with PL_s expressions as key paths.

In the more general case where one allows key paths to be in PL the *subnodes* rule

$$\frac{(Q, (Q'.Q'', \{P\}))}{(Q, (Q', \{Q''.P\}))}$$

is not even sound for the implication of XML keys. A simple counter-example is the XML tree T illustrated in Figure 2. T satisfies the absolute key $\sigma = (\varepsilon, (a.\_^*.b.c.\_^*.d, \{e\}))$, but violates the absolute key $\varphi = (\varepsilon, (a.\_^*.b, \{c.\_^*.d.e\}))$ since $v_3, v_6 \in [\![a.\_^*.b]\!]$, $v_3 \neq v_6$ and $v_3[\![c.\_^*.d.e]\!] \cap_v v_6[\![c.\_^*.d.e]\!] = \{(v_{10}, v_{10})\}$, i.e., φ is not implied by σ. However, φ can be inferred from σ using the *subnodes* rule. Therefore, the inference rules proposed in [9] are not sound for the implication of keys as defined in [9]. Unfortunately, this is not just a minor detail since the completeness proof [9] makes use of the *subnodes* rule and is therefore not correct. Consequently, there is no completeness proof at all. The conference paper [7] contains a much more restrictive definition of value intersection which leaves the *subnodes* rule sound in the presence of arbitrary PL expressions for the key paths, but this does not affect the incorrectness of the results in the journal paper [9].

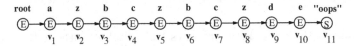

Fig. 2. The *subnodes* rule is not sound for key paths in PL

In this paper we study the implication of XML keys with simple key paths.

Definition 1. *A key constraint φ for XML (or short XML key) is an expression $(Q, (Q', S))$ where Q, Q' are PL expressions and S is a non-empty finite set of PL_s expressions such that $Q.Q'.P$ are valid PL expressions for all P in S. Herein, Q is called the* context path, *Q' is called the* target path, *and the elements of S are called the* key paths *of φ. If $Q = \varepsilon$, we call φ an* absolute key; *otherwise φ is called a* relative key. □

Let $\mathcal{K}$ denote the language of XML keys. For an XML key φ, we use Q_φ to denote its context path, Q'_φ to denote its target path, and $P^\varphi_1, \ldots, P^\varphi_{k_\varphi}$ to denote its key paths, where k_φ is the number of its key paths. The size $|\varphi|$ of a key φ is defined as the sum of the lengths of all path expressions in φ, i.e., $|\varphi| = |Q_\varphi| + |Q'_\varphi| + \sum_{i=1}^{k_\varphi} |P^\varphi_i|$.

Example 1. We formalise the examples from the introduction. In an XML tree that satisfies the absolute key $(\varepsilon, (\_^*.\text{book}, \{\text{isbn}\}))$ one will never be able to find two different *book* nodes that have value equal *isbn* subnodes. Furthermore, under a *book* node in an XML tree that satisfies the relative key $(\_^*.\text{book}, (\text{author}, \{\text{first}, \text{last}\}))$ one will never find two different *author* subnodes that are value equal on their *first* and *last* subnodes. □

It is stated in [8] "that allowing arbitrary path expressions for the P_i [key paths] merely complicates the definition of key but does not change much in the way of the theory". This is not true since the *subnodes* rule is sound according to the original XML key definition [8] but not if the P_is are arbitrary PL expressions as the example above shows.

We will prove that the inference rules from [9] together with the *subnodes-epsilon* rule are sound and complete for the implication of XML keys as defined in Definition 1.

Theorem 1. *The inference rules from Table 2 are sound and complete for the implication of XML keys in $\mathcal{K}$.* □

3   An Axiomatisation

Let Σ be a finite set of keys in $\mathcal{K}$. An XML tree T *satisfies* Σ if and only if T satisfies every $\sigma \in \Sigma$. Let $\Sigma \cup \{\varphi\}$ be a finite set of keys in $\mathcal{K}$. We say that Σ *(finitely) implies* φ, denoted by $\Sigma \models_{(f)} \varphi$, if and only if every (finite) XML tree T that satisfies Σ also satisfies φ. The *(finite) implication problem* is to decide, given any finite set of keys $\Sigma \cup \{\varphi\}$, whether $\Sigma \models_{(f)} \varphi$. For a set Σ of keys in $\mathcal{K}$, let $\Sigma^* = \{\varphi \in \mathcal{K} \mid \Sigma \models \varphi\}$ be its *semantic closure*, i.e., the set of all keys implied by Σ. Finite and unrestricted implication problem coincide for the class of keys in $\mathcal{K}$ [9]. We will therefore commonly speak of the *implication problem* for keys in $\mathcal{K}$.

The notion of derivability $(\vdash_\mathfrak{R})$ with respect to a set $\mathfrak{R}$ of inference rules can be defined analogously to the notion in the relational data model [1, pp. 164-168]. For a set Σ of keys in $\mathcal{K}$, let $\Sigma^+_\mathfrak{R} = \{\varphi \mid \Sigma \vdash_\mathfrak{R} \varphi\}$ be its *syntactic closure* under inference using $\mathfrak{R}$.

The aim in this section is to demonstrate that the set $\mathfrak{R}$ of inference rules in Table 2 is *sound* (i.e., $\Sigma^+_\mathfrak{R} \subseteq \Sigma^*$) and *complete* (i.e., $\Sigma^* \subseteq \Sigma^+_\mathfrak{R}$) for the implication of keys as defined in Definition 1.

Our completeness argument is fundamentally different from the technique proposed in [9]. Buneman et al. [9] apply the following strategy: for any $\varphi \notin \Sigma^+$ they construct a finite XML tree T that violates φ. Subsequently, they *chase* those keys in Σ which are violated by T and maintain at the same time the violation of φ. Eventually, this results into a chased version of T which finitely satisfies all keys in Σ and violates φ. This would show that φ is not implied by Σ. However, the completeness proof is flawed since it requires the soundness of the *subnodes* rule, but the *subnodes* rule is not sound as discussed above. Moreover, the *subnodes-epsilon* rule is sound and independent from the inference rules of [9]. Therefore, the rules are not complete even for the original definition of XML keys [8] whose key paths are PL_s expressions.

Our technique does not use a chase: we will first represent $\varphi \notin \Sigma^+$ in terms of a finite node-labelled tree $T_{\Sigma,\varphi}$, and then calculate the impact of each key in Σ on a finite XML tree T that satisfies Σ, but violates φ. We keep track of the impacts by inserting edges into a node-labelled digraph $G_{\Sigma,\varphi}$, called witness graph. Finally, we apply a reachability algorithm to $G_{\Sigma,\varphi}$ to generate the desired XML tree T. This approach turns out to provide even more than just proving completeness. In fact, Σ implies φ if and only if there is a path from a distinguished node q'_φ to a distinguished node q_φ in $G_{\Sigma,\varphi}$. We will see later on that this observation results in a surprisingly efficient decision procedure for the implication problem of XML keys.

3.1   Mini-trees and Witness Graphs

Let $\Sigma \cup \{\varphi\}$ be a finite set of keys in $\mathcal{K}$. Let $\mathcal{L}_{\Sigma,\varphi}$ denote the set of all labels $\ell \in \mathcal{L}$ that occur in path expressions of keys in $\Sigma \cup \{\varphi\}$, and fix a label $\ell_0 \in \mathbf{E} - \mathcal{L}_{\Sigma,\varphi}$. Further, let O_φ and O'_φ be the PL_s expressions obtained from the PL expressions Q_φ and Q'_φ, respectively, when replacing each $\_^*$ by ℓ_0.

Let p be an O_φ-path from a node r_φ to a node q_φ, let p' be an O'_φ-path from a node r'_φ to a node q'_φ and, for each $i = 1, \ldots, k_\varphi$, let p_i be a P_i^φ-path from a node r_i^φ to a node x_i^φ, such that the paths $p, p', p_1, \ldots, p_{k_\varphi}$ are mutually node-disjoint. From the paths $p, p', p_1, \ldots, p_{k_\varphi}$ we obtain the *mini-tree* $T_{\Sigma,\varphi}$ by identifying the node r'_φ with q_φ, and by identifying each of the nodes r_i^φ with q'_φ. Note that q_φ is the unique node in $T_{\Sigma,\varphi}$ that satisfies $q_\varphi \in [\![O_\varphi]\!]$, and q'_φ is the unique node in $T_{\Sigma,\varphi}$ that satisfies $q'_\varphi \in q_\varphi[\![O'_\varphi]\!]$.

In the sequel, we will discuss how to construct an XML tree from $T_{\Sigma,\varphi}$ that could serve as a counter-example for the implication of φ by Σ. A major step in this construction is the duplication of certain nodes of $T_{\Sigma,\varphi}$. To begin with, we determine those nodes of $T_{\Sigma,\varphi}$ for which we will generate two value equal copies in a possible counter-example tree. The *marking* of the mini-tree $T_{\Sigma,\varphi}$ is a subset $\mathcal{M}$ of the node set of $T_{\Sigma,\varphi}$: if for all $i = 1, \ldots, k_\varphi$ we have $P_i^\varphi \neq \varepsilon$, then $\mathcal{M}$ consists of the leaves of $T_{\Sigma,\varphi}$, and otherwise $\mathcal{M}$ consists of all descendant-or-selfs of q'_φ in $T_{\Sigma,\varphi}$. The nodes in $\mathcal{M}$ are said to be *marked*.

Example 2. The left of Figure 3 shows the mini-tree $T_{\Sigma,\varphi}$ for the key $\varphi = (\varepsilon, (\_^*.\text{book}, (\text{author}, \{\text{first,last}\})))$ and some Σ, where *library* is the fixed label chosen from $\mathbf{E} - \mathcal{L}_{\Sigma,\varphi}$. The marking of the mini-tree consists of its leaves (emphasised by $\times$). $\qquad\square$

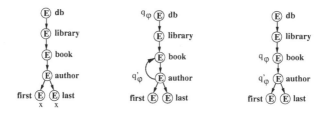

Fig. 3. A mini-tree and two witness graphs

We use mini-trees to calculate the impact of a key in Σ on a possible counter-example tree for the implication of φ by Σ. To distinguish keys that have an impact from those that do not, we introduce the notion of *applicability*.

Definition 2. *Let $T_{\Sigma,\varphi}$ be the mini-tree of the key φ with respect to Σ, and let $\mathcal{M}$ be its marking. A key σ is said to be* applicable *to φ if and only if there are nodes $w_\sigma \in [Q_\sigma]$ and $w'_\sigma \in w_\sigma[Q'_\sigma]$ in $T_{\Sigma,\varphi}$ such that $w'_\sigma[P_i^\sigma] \cap \mathcal{M} \neq \emptyset$ for all $i = 1,\ldots,k_\sigma$. We say that w_σ and w'_σ* witness the applicability *of σ to φ.* □

Example 3. Let Σ consist of the two keys $\sigma_1 = (\varepsilon, (\_^*.\text{book}, \{\text{isbn}\}))$ and $\sigma_2 = (\_^*.\text{book}, (\text{author}, \{\text{first,last}\}))$, and let $\varphi = (\varepsilon, (\_^*.\text{book.author}, \{\text{first,last}\}))$. We find that σ_1 is not applicable to φ, while σ_2 is indeed applicable to φ. □

We define the *witness graph* $G_{\Sigma,\varphi}$ as the node-labelled digraph obtained from $T_{\Sigma,\varphi}$ by inserting additional edges: for each key $\sigma \in \Sigma$ that is applicable to φ and for each pair of nodes $w_\sigma \in [Q_\sigma]$ and $w'_\sigma \in w_\sigma[Q'_\sigma]$ that witness the applicability of σ to φ, $G_{\Sigma,\varphi}$ should contain the edge (w'_σ, w_σ). Subsequently, we refer to these additional edges as *witness edges*, while the original edges from $T_{\Sigma,\varphi}$ are referred to as *downward edges* of $G_{\Sigma,\varphi}$. This is motivated by the fact that for every witness w_σ and w'_σ, the node w'_σ is a descendant-or-self of the node w_σ in $T_{\Sigma,\varphi}$, and thus the witness edge (w'_σ, w_σ) is an upward edge or loop in $G_{\Sigma,\varphi}$.

Example 4. Let $\Sigma = \{\sigma_1, \sigma_2\}$ as in Example 3, and let φ be the key $(\varepsilon, (\_^*.\text{book.author}, \{\text{first,last}\}))$. The witness graph $G_{\Sigma,\varphi}$ is illustrated in the middle of Figure 3. It contains a witness edge arising from σ_2. □

Example 5. Let Σ consist of the single key $\sigma = (\_^*.\text{book}, (\text{author}, \{\varepsilon\}))$, and let $\varphi = (\_^*.\text{book}, (\text{author}, \{\text{first,last}\}))$. The witness graph $G_{\Sigma,\varphi}$ is illustrated in the right of Figure 3. It does not contain any witness edges since σ is not applicable to φ due to $q'_\varphi[\varepsilon] \cap \mathcal{M} = \emptyset$. □

3.2 Reachability vs. Derivability

We show that if there is a dipath from q'_φ to q_φ in $G_{\Sigma,\varphi}$, then $\varphi \in \Sigma^+$. In other words, if $\varphi \notin \Sigma^+$, then there is no dipath from q'_φ to q_φ in $G_{\Sigma,\varphi}$.

The proof idea of the *Main Lemma* is illustrated in Figure 4. If there is a dipath D from q'_φ to q_φ in the witness graph $G_{\Sigma,\varphi}$, then D takes the form illustrated in the left of Figure 4 resulting from applicable keys $\sigma_1, \ldots, \sigma_n \in \Sigma$. For the existence of derivable keys applicable to φ we can assume without loss of generality that $\Sigma = \Sigma_{\mathfrak{R}}^+$. Notice that the *context-target* rule can be applied to extend context paths by shortening target paths appropriately. Hence, there are applicable keys in Σ that give rise to a dipath D' from q'_φ to q_φ that takes the form illustrated in the middle of Figure 4. The inference rules from Table 2 show that there is a single key $\sigma \in \Sigma$ that gives rise to a dipath D_0 from q'_φ to q_φ in $G_{\Sigma,\varphi}$ illustrated in the right of Figure 4.

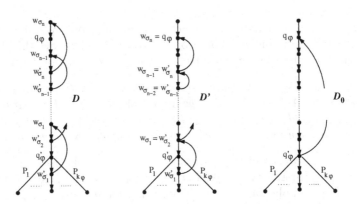

Fig. 4. Proof idea of main lemma

Lemma 1 (Main Lemma). *Let* $\Sigma \cup \{\varphi\}$ *be a finite set of XML keys in* $\mathcal{K}$. *If* q_φ *is reachable from* q'_φ *in the witness graph* $G_{\Sigma,\varphi}$, *then* $\varphi \in \Sigma^+$.   □

Example 6. In RSA the modulus n is the product of two large primes p and q which are part of the user's private key. *Common modulus attacks* are avoided by choosing a distinct modulus n for each user, i.e., we specify the key $(\varepsilon, (group.user, \{private.p, private.q\}))$ denoted by σ_1. Let σ_2 denote $(group, (user.private, \{p,q\}))$ stating that *private* keys can be identified by their prime numbers p and q relatively to the user's *group*; and let φ denote $(\varepsilon, (group.user.private, \{p,q\}))$ stating that there are no two private keys that contain the same primes p and q. Finally, let $\Sigma = \{\sigma_1, \sigma_2\}$. The mini-tree $T_{\Sigma,\varphi}$ and witness graph $G_{\Sigma,\varphi}$ are shown as first and second picture of Figure 5, respectively. We apply *context-target* to σ_2 to derive $(group.user, (private, \{p,q\}))$ denoted by σ'_2. Let $\Sigma' = \{\sigma_1, \sigma'_2\}$. The witness graph $G_{\Sigma',\varphi}$ is shown as third picture in Figure 5. An application of the *interaction* rule to σ_1 and σ'_2 results in φ which shows that $\varphi \in \Sigma^+$, illustrated on the right of Figure 5.   □

3.3   An Illustration of the Completeness Argument

Let $\Sigma \cup \{\varphi\}$ be a finite set of keys in $\mathcal{K}$ such that $\varphi \notin \Sigma^+$. In order to show completeness one needs to demonstrate that $\varphi \notin \Sigma^*$. Indeed, we can construct a finite XML tree T which satisfies Σ, but violates φ. Since $\varphi \notin \Sigma^+$ we know by Lemma 1 that q_φ is not reachable from q'_φ in $G_{\Sigma,\varphi}$. Let u denote the bottom-most

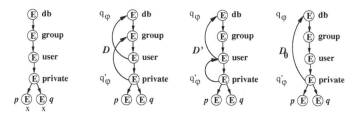

Fig. 5. Example of Main Lemma

descendant-or-self of q_φ in $T_{\Sigma,\varphi}$ such that q_φ is still reachable from u in $G_{\Sigma,\varphi}$. Further, u must be a proper ancestor of q'_φ because otherwise u and thus q_φ were reachable from q'_φ in $G_{\Sigma,\varphi}$. Let T_0 denote a copy of the path from r to u, and T_1, T_2 denote two node-disjoint copies of the subtree of $T_{\Sigma,\varphi}$ rooted at u. T_1 and T_2 are populated with text-leaves such that a node of T_1 and a node of T_2 become value-equal precisely when they are copies of the same marked node in $T_{\Sigma,\varphi}$. The counter-example tree T is obtained from T_0, T_1, T_2 by identifying the terminal node of T_0 with the roots of T_1 and T_2.

The left side of Figure 6 shows a counter-example tree T for the implication of φ by $\Sigma = \{\sigma_1, \sigma_2\}$ from Example 4. In this case, u is the single db-node in $T_{\Sigma,\varphi}$, and T_1, T_2 are two node-disjoint copies of the entire tree $T_{\Sigma,\varphi}$. Furthermore, T_1 and T_2 carry the same text under their *first*-nodes and their *last*-nodes, respectively, and carry different text anywhere else. T itself is obtained by identifying the three copies of the db-node from T_0, T_1 and T_2.

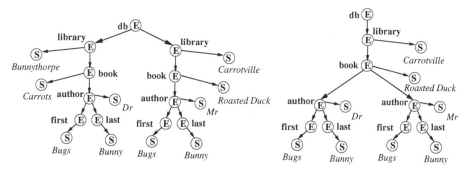

Fig. 6. Counter-example trees for the implication of φ by $\Sigma = \{\sigma_1, \sigma_2\}$ from Example 4, and for the implication of φ by σ in Example 5

4 Deciding Implication

We will show in this section how our technique of proving completeness can be applied to obtain an algorithm for deciding XML key implication in time quadratic in the size of the constraints. Notice that the heptic time algorithm from [9] is flawed since it is based on the soundness of the subnodes rule. Even if only PL_s expressions are considered for the key paths, the algorithm is still flawed since it is based on the incomplete set $\mathfrak{S}$ of inference rules.

4.1   The Algorithm

The first step is to show that XML key implication can be completely charac-
terised in terms of the reachability problem of nodes in the witness graph.

Theorem 2. *Let $\Sigma \cup \{\varphi\}$ be a finite set of keys in $\mathcal{K}$. We have $\Sigma \models \varphi$ if and
only if q_φ is reachable from q'_φ in $G_{\Sigma,\varphi}$.*   □

Theorem 2 suggests to utilise the following algorithm for deciding XML key
implication. Our technique for proving the completeness of our inference rules
results in a very compact and easily comprehensible algorithm.

Algorithm 1 (*XML Key*-Implication)
Input: finite set $\Sigma \cup \{\varphi\}$ of XML keys

Output: yes, if $\Sigma \models \varphi$; no, if $\Sigma \not\models \varphi$

Method:
(1)   Construct $G_{\Sigma,\varphi}$ from Σ and φ;
(2)   **IF** q_φ is reachable from q'_φ in $G_{\Sigma,\varphi}$ **THEN RETURN(yes)**
(3)   **ELSE RETURN(no)**.

The correctness of Algorithm 1 is an immediate consequence of Theorem 2.

4.2   The Time Complexity

We analyse the time complexity of Algorithm 1. The problem of deciding whether
q_φ is reachable from q'_φ in $G_{\Sigma,\varphi}$ can be solved by applying a depth-first search
algorithm to $G_{\Sigma,\varphi}$ with root q'_φ. This algorithm works in time linear in the
number of edges of $G_{\Sigma,\varphi}$ [23]. Since the number of nodes in $G_{\Sigma,\varphi}$ is just $|\varphi| + 1$,
step (2) of Algorithm 1 can be executed in $\mathcal{O}(|\varphi|^2)$ time. It therefore remains to
investigate the time complexity for generating the witness graph $G_{\Sigma,\varphi}$ from Σ
and φ. This can be done as follows:

1. Initialise $G_{\Sigma,\varphi}$ with $T_{\Sigma,\varphi}$;
2. For all $\sigma \in \Sigma$, add the edge (w'_σ, w_σ) to $G_{\Sigma,\varphi}$ whenever w_σ and w'_σ witness
   the applicability of σ to φ (and the edge does not already exist).

A semi-naive way to execute the last of these steps is to evaluate $w'_\sigma[\![P_i^\sigma]\!]$ for
$i = 1, \ldots, k_\sigma$, for all $w'_\sigma \in w_\sigma[\![Q'_\sigma]\!]$ and all $w_\sigma \in [\![Q_\sigma]\!]$. Recall that a query of the
form $v[\![Q]\!]$ is a *Core XPath* query and can be evaluated on a node-labelled tree
T in $\mathcal{O}(|T| \times |Q|)$ time [18]. Hence, we can evaluate $w'_\sigma[\![P_i^\sigma]\!]$ for all $i = 1, \ldots, k_\sigma$
in time $\mathcal{O}(|\varphi| \times |\sigma|)$. Since $[\![Q_\sigma]\!]$ and $w_\sigma[\![Q'_\sigma]\!]$ contain at most $|\varphi|$ nodes each, this
step can be executed in $\mathcal{O}(|\varphi|^3 \times |\sigma|)$ time for each σ. If $||\Sigma||$ denotes the sum
of all sizes $|\sigma|$ for $\sigma \in \Sigma$, then we need $\mathcal{O}(||\Sigma|| \times |\varphi|^3)$ time to generate $G_{\Sigma,\varphi}$.

Using a more involved analysis of witness edges, we can show that q_φ is
reachable from q'_φ in $G_{\Sigma,\varphi}$ if and only if q_φ is reachable from q'_φ in $H_{\Sigma,\varphi}$ -
where $H_{\Sigma,\varphi}$ is a subgraph of $G_{\Sigma,\varphi}$ in which certain witness edges are omitted.
Moreover, $H_{\Sigma,\varphi}$ can be computed in time $\mathcal{O}(||\Sigma|| \times |\varphi|)$. Hence, we obtain:

Theorem 3. *Let $\Sigma \cup \{\varphi\}$ be a finite set of XML keys in $\mathcal{K}$. The implication
problem $\Sigma \models \varphi$ can be decided in $\mathcal{O}(|\varphi| \times (||\Sigma|| + |\varphi|))$ time.*   □

5   Future Work

One area that warrants future research is the study of keys with respect to more expressive path languages [5,13,25,26,34]. In particular, the problems of axiomatising and developing efficient algorithms that decide the implication of XML keys as defined in [9] are still open.

A different way of increasing the expressiveness is to view keys from a different angle. Indeed, keys restrict the number of nodes, which have the same value on certain selected subnodes, to 1. It is therefore natural to introduce numerical keys that simply restrict the number of nodes, having the same value on certain selected subnodes, to an arbitrary finite number. We can axiomatise this class of XML constraints and provide practically efficient algorithms to reason about them. Due to lack of space we omit details. Efficient reasoning about such constraints allows to precompute upper bounds on the number of query answers.

6   Conclusion

We have reviewed the key constraint language for XML [8,9] and observed that their axiomatisation [9] is not sound for XML key implication in general [9] and not complete even for XML keys with simple key path expressions [8]. Based on this observation we have provided an axiomatisation of XML keys as defined in [8]. Our technique allows us to characterise XML key implication in terms of the reachability problem for nodes in a digraph. This results in a first correct decision procedure, that is also practically efficient, i.e., quadratic in the size of the input. Keys form a very natural class of XML constraints that can be utilised effectively by designers, and the complexity of their associated decision problems indicates that they can be maintained efficiently by database systems for XML applications.

References

1. S. Abiteboul, R. Hull, and V. Vianu. *Foundations of Databases*. Addison-Wesley, 1995.
2. V. Apparao et al. Document object model (DOM) level 1 specification, W3C recommendation, oct. 1998. http://www.w3.org/TR/REC-DOM-Level-1/.
3. M. Arenas and L. Libkin. A normal form for XML documents. *TODS*, 29(1):195–232, 2004.
4. M. Arenas and L. Libkin. An information-theoretic approach to normal forms for relational and XML data. *J. ACM*, 52(2):246–283, 2005.
5. M. Benedikt, W. Fan, and G. Kuper. Structural properties of XPath fragments. *TCS*, 336(1):3–31, 2005.
6. T. Bray, J. Paoli, C. M. Sperberg-McQueen, E. Maler, and F. Yergeau. Extensible markup language (XML) 1.0 (third edition) W3C recommendation, feb. 2004. http://www.w3.org/TR/2004/REC-xml-20040204/.
7. P. Buneman, S. Davidson, W. Fan, C. Hara, and W. Tan. Reasoning about keys for XML. In *DBPL*, pages 133–148, 2001.

8. P. Buneman, S. Davidson, W. Fan, C. Hara, and W. Tan. Keys for XML. *Computer Networks*, 39(5):473–487, 2002.

9. P. Buneman, S. Davidson, W. Fan, C. Hara, and W. Tan. Reasoning about keys for XML. *Inf. Syst.*, 28(8):1037–1063, 2003.

10. P. Buneman, W. Fan, J. Siméon, and S. Weinstein. Constraints for semi-structured data and XML. *SIGMOD Record*, 30(1):47–54, 2001.

11. P. Buneman, W. Fan, and S. Weinstein. Path constraints in semistructured databases. *JCSS*, 61(2):146–193, 2000.

12. J. Clark and S. DeRose. XML path language (XPath) version 1.0, W3C recommendation, nov. 1999. http://www.w3.org/TR/xpath.

13. A. Deutsch and V. Tannen. Containment and integrity constraints for XPath. In *KRDB*, 2001.

14. R. Fagin and M. Y. Vardi. The theory of data dependencies. In *ICALP*, pages 1–22, 1984.

15. W. Fan. XML constraints. In *DEXA Workshops*, pages 805–809, 2005.

16. W. Fan and L. Libkin. On XML integrity constraints in the presence of DTDs. *J. ACM*, 49(3):368–406, 2002.

17. W. Fan and J. Siméon. Integrity constraints for XML. *JCSS*, 66(1):254–291, 2003.

18. G. Gottlob, C. Koch, and R. Pichler. Efficient algorithms for processing XPath queries. *TODS*, 30(2):444–491, 2005.

19. C. Hara and S. Davidson. Reasoning about nested functional dependencies. In *PODS*, pages 91–100, 1999.

20. S. Hartmann and S. Link. More functional dependencies for XML. In *ADBIS*, number 2798 in LNCS, pages 355–369. Springer, 2003.

21. S. Hartmann and S. Link. Multivalued dependencies in the presence of lists. In *PODS*, pages 330–341, 2004.

22. S. Hartmann and T. Trinh. Axiomatising functional dependencies for XML with frequencies. In *FoIKS*, number 3861 in LNCS, pages 159–178. Springer, 2006.

23. D. Jungnickel. *Graphs, Networks and Algorithms*. Springer, 1999.

24. M. Kay. XSL transformations (XSLT) version 2.0 W3C candidate recommendation, nov. 2005. http://www.w3.org/TR/xslt20/.

25. G. Miklau and D. Suciu. Containment and equivalence for a fragment of XPath. *J. ACM*, 51(1):2–45, 2004.

26. F. Neven and T. Schwentick. XPath containment in the presence of disjunction, DTDs, and variables. In *ICDT*, pages 315–329, 2003.

27. J. Paredaens, P. De Bra, M. Gyssens, and D. Van Gucht. *The Structure of the Relational Database Model*. Springer, 1989.

28. D. Suciu. On database theory and XML. *SIGMOD Record*, 30(3):39–45, 2001.

29. B. Thalheim. *Dependencies in Relational Databases*. Teubner, 1991.

30. H. Thompson, D. Beech, M. Maloney, and N. Mendelsohn. XML Schema Part 1: Structures Second Edition, W3C Recommendation, 28 Oct. 2004. http://www.w3.org/TR/xmlschema-1/.

31. V. Vianu. A web odyssey: from Codd to XML. *SIGMOD Record*, 32(2):68–77, 2003.

32. M. Vincent, J. Liu, and C. Liu. Strong functional dependencies and their application to normal forms in XML. *TODS*, 29(3):445–462, 2004.

33. J. Widom. Data management for XML: Research directions. *Data Eng. Bull.*, 22(3):44–52, 1999.

34. P. Wood. Containment for XPath fragments under DTD constraints. In *ICDT*, pages 300–314, 2003.

Characterization of the Interaction
of XML Functional Dependencies with DTDs

Łucja Kot and Walker White

Department of Computer Science
Cornell University, Ithaca, NY 14853, USA
Phone: (607) 255-9537; Fax: (607) 255-4428
{lucja,wmwhite}@cs.cornell.edu

Abstract. With the rise of XML as a standard model of data exchange, XML functional dependencies (XFDs) have become important to areas such as key analysis, document normalization, and data integrity. XFDs are more complicated than relational functional dependencies because the set of XFDs satisfied by an XML document depends not only on the document values, but also the tree structure and corresponding DTD. In particular, constraints imposed by DTDs may alter the implications from a base set of XFDs, and may even be inconsistent with a set of XFDs. In this paper we examine the interaction between XFDs and DTDs. We present a sound and complete axiomatization for XFDs, both alone and in the presence of certain classes of DTDs; we show that these DTD classes induce an axiomatic hierarchy. We also give efficient implication algorithms for those classes of DTDs that do not use disjunction or nesting.

1   Introduction

Functional dependencies have proved to be a very useful class of integrity constraints for traditional database systems. They are integral to key analysis, normalization, and query optimization [1]. As XML is increasingly becoming the standard model of data exchange, there is much interest in formulating a definition of XML functional dependency. In addition to the benefits found in relational databases, a proper XFD definition would also aid in many new areas, such as verifying data consistency, preserving semantics during data exchange, and XML-SQL translation [10].

Several different XFD definitions have been suggested [3,20,14,19,16,13]. The major XFD definitions are similar to the relational definition except that, instead of attributes and table rows, they use path identifiers and subtrees. Informally, these definitions say that an XFD $A \rightarrow B$ is satisfied in a document if, for any two subtrees, whenever they agree on the paths in A, they also agree on the paths in B. The definitions differ primarily in how they choose subtrees, specify path identifiers, or test equality between XML nodes.

XFDs differ from their relational counterparts in that they must take into account the tree structure of XML documents. For example, a language for defining XFDs must allow us to specify when one path is a prefix of another. Another issue is the definition of equality: nodes can be compared by identity or value equality. In the relational model, no duplicate tuples are allowed, and so value equality is sufficient in FDs. However, in

T. Schwentick and D. Suciu (Eds.): ICDT 2007, LNCS 4353, pp. 119–133, 2007.

an XML document, we can have two different subtrees that are isomorphic and have exactly the same values. This is a clear instance of data duplication, but one allowed by the data model. Therefore, if XFDs are to be used for keys or normalization, they must be able to detect identity (in)equality between nodes. Finally, as XML represents semi-structured data that is often incomplete, XFDs must properly handle null values.

The implication problem is fundamental to all of the applications mentioned above [1]; hence this has been the focus of much of the work on XFDs. There are two important approaches to the implication problem. One approach is that of efficient decision algorithms, which allow us to determine whether an XFD is implied by a set of XFDs; some feasible decision algorithms have been discovered already [3]. The other approach is axiomatization, which often gives us slower decision algorithms, but which is important for understanding the underlying theory of XFDs [1]. For example, every child XML node has a unique parent node. Thus for any two path identifiers q and p, where p is an identifier for the parent of q, every XML document satisfies the XFD $q \to p$. A decision algorithm would allow us to check for *each specific* instance of parent-child p, q that $q \to p$ holds. However, an axiomatization would allow us to prove this entire general class of XFDs.

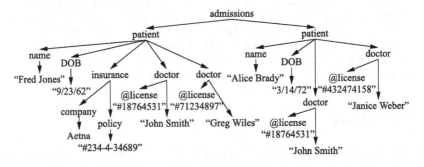

Fig. 1. XML Document for Medical Admissions

The implication problem becomes more complicated in the presence of a DTD. Consider the XML document illustrated in Figure 1. This document represents admissions at a special charity hospital and has the following entry in its DTD:

```
<!ELEMENT patient (name,DOB,insurance?,doctor,doctor)>
```

In particular, each patient must have a recommendation from exactly two doctors (who are unordered), and may or may not have insurance. Note that in this DTD, every patient has exactly one name node. So every document conforming to this DTD must satisfy the XFD $p \to q$, where p is a path identifier for a patient node, and q is a path identifier for the name node of that patient. This suggests that we should be able to use the structure of a DTD to make deductions about classes of XFDs satisfied by conforming documents. While there are several decision algorithms for XFDs conforming to certain classes of DTDs, to our knowledge there is no existing sound and complete axiomatization for XFDs with identity equality in the presence of a DTD.

1.1 Contributions

This paper is a study of the theory of XFDs and their interaction with various classes of DTDs, focusing on axiomatization and the implication problem. In this paper, we make the following contributions.

- We adapt the definition of XFDs presented in [3] to include documents without a DTD so that we can identify the base theory of XFDs.
- We adapt the chase algorithm to XFDs, and use it to improve existing bounds on the implication problem for XFDs, in some cases to linear time.
- We use the chase to formulate the first sound and complete axiomatization for XFD implication (using identity equality), in the absence of a DTD.
- We expand these techniques to explore the interactions between XFDs and several classes of DTDs. In particular, for all DTDs that can be rewritten without disjunction or nesting, we present an efficient chase algorithm for checking implication, as well as a sound and complete axiomatization of the same problem.

The remainder of the paper is organized as follows: Section 2 introduces the preliminary notation, while Section 3 presents our definition of XFDs. Sections 4 and 5 are devoted, respectively, to the implication problem in the absence and in the presence of a DTD. We discuss related work in Section 6 and conclude in Section 7.

2 Preliminaries

2.1 The Document Model

Throughout this paper, our notation is similar to that in the literature [3], though with some noticeable differences. These differences are necessary because this existing notation requires that an XML document have a corresponding DTD. In order to study the theory of XFDs, we need to decouple the definition of an XFD from a DTD.

Our model for an XML document is a tree representing the underlying DOM structure. We associate each part of the document, including text and attribute data, with a labeled node in the tree. For these labels, we have two disjoint sets EL and VAL. The set EL is the label alphabet for the XML nodes and the attribute names, while VAL is the alphabet of attribute values.

Formally, our model is the same in as Arenas and Libkin [3] with only two minor modifications. First, our alphabet EL contains two special elements ρ and α. The label ρ is used to identify the unique root element of each XML tree. This corresponds to the <?xml> tag in an XML document, and is necessary because documents without a DTD have no constraints on the root label.

The label α is used to decouple an attribute from its value. Within any XML document, an attribute is split into two tree nodes: one for its identifier and one for its value. The value node is labeled by α, and is the sole child of the identifier for that attribute. Furthermore, we have a function that maps each α node to is value in VAL. The introduction of α is a purely technical device; it simplifies the notation in settings where we need to refer to both the address and the value of attribute nodes.

To illustrate this model, consider the XML document from Figure 1. Our model would represented this document by the labeled tree in Figure 2.

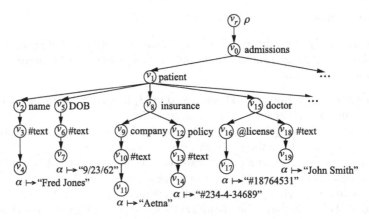

Fig. 2. Encoding of Medical XML Document

A path identifier is a finite list of labels in EL. For clarity, we separate the elements in a path identifier by periods, such as ρ.admissions.patient. We say that a path identifier *p occurs* in a tree T if there is a path $v_1, v_2, \cdots v_n$ in T such that the labels for the v_i form a string equal to p. For the rest of the paper, we refer to path identifiers as *paths*, with the understanding that a single identifier may represent more than one actual path in the tree. We say that a path is *rooted* if its first identifier is ρ. We denote the set of all rooted paths that occur in T as paths(T); note that this is a prefix-closed set.

Finally, we work with two kinds of equality on the nodes of T: identity equality and value equality. We compare internal tree nodes by identity; on the other hand, we compare α leaf nodes by their value in VAL.

2.2 DTDs

Our definition of a DTD is the standard one [3], namely a pair $D = (E, P)$, where E is a finite subset of EL and P is a set of productions that map elements of E to regular expressions over E. As in the definition in Arenas and Libkin [3], we ignore order in these regular expressions. This is acceptable because XFDs are not influenced by document order.

It is usual notation, when working with DTDs, to use arrows in the notation for productions (i.e. $a \rightarrow bc^*$). In this paper, we need to avoid a notational conflict with another sense of $\rightarrow$, which is used for XFDs. Therefore, we use $\rightsquigarrow$ instead for DTD productions. Informally, a document T satisfies D, written $T \vDash D$, if for each node v, the labels of the children of v can be produced from the label for v via P. A more formal definition is available in Arenas and Libkin [3].

We assume that all DTDs considered from now on are consistent (i.e. there is at least one finite tree satisfying the DTD). Furthermore, we denote by paths(D) all the possible rooted paths that may occur in any T such that $T \vDash D$.

We now define several classes of DTDs, according to the complexity of the regular expressions present in the productions. Bear in mind that we disregard order in defining these classes. Our DTD classes form a hierarchy and they are described below in increasing order of generality. We note that given a DTD, deciding which class it belongs to may be nontrivial in the worst case. However, we do not expect this to be an issue in practice, as humans do not typically write DTDs with complex nested regular expressions.

Simple DTDs: Our definition of a simple DTD is similar to that given in Arenas and Libkin [3]. Given an alphabet A, a regular expression over A is called *trivial* if it is of the form $s_1 \cdots s_n$, where for each s_i there is a letter $a_i \in A$ such that s_i is either $a_i, a_i?, a_i^+$ or a_i^*, and for $i \neq j$, $a_i \neq a_j$. A simple DTD is one where the right-hand side of any production is trivial. An example of a simple DTD is

$$\rho \rightsquigarrow ab^*, \ a \rightsquigarrow c^*, \ b \rightsquigarrow d^+e^*$$

#-DTDs: #-DTDs are a proper extension of simple DTDs. This extension allows productions having more than one occurrence of the same alphabet symbol (the # is intended to represent the concept of number). In other words, a #-DTD is an simple DTD which allows the right hand side to contain expressions of the form a_i^n. This class includes any DTD which does not use disjunction or nesting in its productions. (Nesting refers to parenthesised expressions in productions such as $\rho \rightsquigarrow (aab)^+$, which induces a correlation on the numbers of a and b children of the root). An example of a non-simple #-DTD is

$$\rho \rightsquigarrow aaab^*, \ a \rightsquigarrow c^*, \ b \rightsquigarrow ddeee^*$$

The DTD for the example in Figure 1 is a concrete example of a #-DTD. Every patient must have two recommending doctors. We give no preference to either doctor, and we may want to assert an XFD from the `license` number of a `doctor` to its text content, so we do not wish to give the doctors different tags.

Arbitrary DTDs: Arbitrary DTDs represent the most general class of DTDs. They allow all features, including arbitrary disjunction and nesting.

2.3 Mapping an XML Tree to a Nested Relation

Many existing definitions of XFDs implicitly rely on the nested relational structure of XML documents. In order to use the existing theory of relational functional dependencies, we make this connection explicit. To each tree T, we associate a nested relation $R(T)$, which we unnest to a flat relation $U(R(T))$. Note however, that this translation is conceptual only; we do not normally materialize $U(R(T))$.

In this section, we give a high-level illustration of $U(R(T))$; a more formal construction, together with a discussion of the close relationship between $U(R(T))$ and $tuples_D(T)$ from Arenas and Libkin [3], appears in the expanded version of this paper [15]. Our illustration makes use of the example in Figure 3. We have separated the tree elements v_i from their labels in EL to make clear the difference between nodes and their labels.

We start with a tree T for an XML document. First, we must normalize the tree to make it suitably homogeneous. For each path p that occurs in T, we take each prefix q of p. For each occurrence of q in T, we guarantee that q can be extended to a path matching p by adding special null nodes as necessary. In Figure 3, $\rho.a.b.f.\alpha$ matches a path in the tree, so we have to extend the second path matching $\rho.a.b$ with null nodes

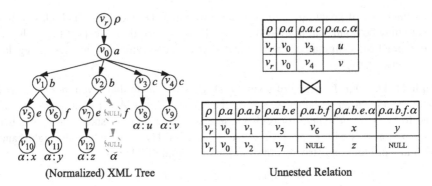

ρ	$\rho.a$	$\rho.a.c$	$\rho.a.c.\alpha$
v_r	v_0	v_3	u
v_r	v_0	v_4	v

$\bowtie$

ρ	$\rho.a$	$\rho.a.b$	$\rho.a.b.e$	$\rho.a.b.f$	$\rho.a.b.e.\alpha$	$\rho.a.b.f.\alpha$
v_r	v_0	v_1	v_5	v_6	x	y
v_r	v_0	v_2	v_7	NULL	z	NULL

(Normalized) XML Tree   Unnested Relation

Fig. 3. Mapping an XML Document to an Unnested Relation

to extend it to $\rho.a.b.f.\alpha$. If we add only one instance of every required null node, the normalization is unique.

After normalizing the tree, we take each maximal rooted path p occurring in the tree. We make a table with an attribute for each non-empty prefix of p. For each match to p in the normalized tree, we construct a row in this table. In this case, each attribute corresponds to a unique node v and we assign this attribute v if v is an internal node (i.e. the label is not α) or is null; otherwise we assign it the attribute value for α in VAL. The top table on the right hand side of Figure 3 represents the table for the path $\rho.a.c.\alpha$.

We then join all of these tables together. For each pair of tables, we use the common prefix of the pair as our join key. The bottom table on the right hand side of Figure 3 is the result of joining the tables for $\rho.a.b.e.\alpha$ and $\rho.a.b.f.\alpha$.

3   XML Functional Dependencies

Given the basic notation, we can now define XFDs, and describe the implication and consistency problems. As we mentioned before, our definition of XFDs must account explicitly for the possibility of null values. Several means of handling null values have been suggested for the relational model [4,17]. We adopt the definition in [4], which is also the one used in Arenas and Libkin [3]: given a relation R over a set of attributes U and $A, B \subseteq U$, $A \to B$ holds if for any two tuples $t_1, t_2 \in R$ that agree and are nonnull on all of A, the t_i are equal (though possibly both null) for each attribute in B.

3.1   Tree Patterns and Functional Dependencies

Relational functional dependencies are defined on tuples in the relation. The corresponding notion for an XML tree is a match for a *tree pattern*. Syntactically, a tree pattern φ is a document in which none of the attribute nodes (i.e. nodes labeled α) are yet mapped to a value in VAL. A *simple* pattern is a tree pattern where no node has two children with the same label $l \in$ EL. In a simple pattern, every rooted path occurs at most once; from now, we assume that all patterns are simple.

In order to use tree patterns to define XML functional dependencies, we must first define what it means to *match* a pattern in a document T. Intuitively, we want to match the pattern in the document "as far as possible", allowing incomplete matches only when the document does not allow a full match. Formally, given a tree T and a pattern φ, a match for φ in T is a function $\mu : nodes(\varphi) \to nodes(T) \cup \{null\}$ where

- μ maps the root of φ to the root of T.
- For all nodes v, $\mu(v)$ is either null, or it preserves the label of v.
- If v' is a child of v and $\mu(v')$ is not null, then $\mu(v)$ is also not null and $\mu(v')$ is a child of $\mu(v)$.
- If v' is a child of v and $\mu(v')$ is null while $\mu(v)$ is not, then $\mu(v)$ could not have had any child with the same label as v' (i.e. no "premature" null values are allowed).

For any path $p \in \varphi$, we use $\mu(p)$ to represent the image under μ for the node at the end of this path. We let $\mathcal{M}_{\varphi,T} = \{ \mu \mid \mu \text{ is a match for } \varphi \text{ in } T \}$.

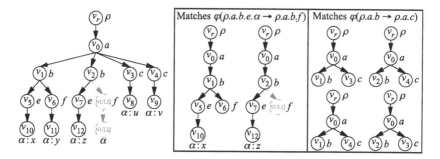

Fig. 4. Sample Tree Pattern Matches

Definition 1. *A functional dependency* $\sigma = A \to B$ *consists of two subsets* $A, B \subseteq$ PATHS. *We let* $\varphi(\sigma)$ *be the smallest tree pattern (with respect to number of nodes) in which all paths in A and B occur; note that this pattern is unique. Furthermore, we let* $=_{fd}$ *be an equality relation that compares nodes by identity equality if they are not attribute nodes (i.e. labeled by α), and by value equality otherwise. The dependency holds if, for any two matches* $\mu_1, \mu_2 \in \mathcal{M}_{\varphi(\sigma),T}$, *whenever we have* $\mu_1(p), \mu_2(p) \neq$ *null and* $\mu_1(p) =_{fd} \mu_2(p)$ *for all* $p \in A$, *then for all* $q \in B$, *either* $\mu_1(q) = \mu_2(q) =$ *null or* $\mu_1(q) =_{fd} \mu_2(q)$.

We illustrate this definition in Figure 4. Recall that our patterns are simple, and so each path in the pattern must occur exactly once. This means that there are only two matches for the pattern $\varphi(\rho.a.b.e.\alpha \to \rho.a.b.f)$ within this tree; no match for a simple pattern can contain both v_7 and v_6. If $x \neq z$ then the corresponding XFD is satisfied, otherwise it is not, as the f node is null in one match and non-null in another. Similarly, there are four matches for the pattern $\varphi(\rho.a.b \to \rho.a.c)$ in Figure 4; this XFD can never be satisfied in this tree.

Lemma 1.

1. *A tree pattern XFD $A \to B$ holds on T if and only if the relational FD $A \to B$ holds on $U(R(T))$.*
2. *Tree tuple XFDs [3] are expressible as tree pattern XFDs.*

3.2 The Implication Problem

Our primary area of focus is the implication problem. Given an XFD σ and document T, we write $T \vDash \sigma$ to mean σ holds in T. Given a set Σ, we write $T \vDash \Sigma$ if every $\tau \in \Sigma$ holds in T. Finally, we write $\Sigma \vDash \sigma$ to mean that, for all $T \vDash \Sigma$, $T \vDash \sigma$. Similarly, for a DTD D, $\Sigma \vDash_D \sigma$ means that, for any $T \vDash \Sigma$ and $T \vDash D$, we have $T \vDash \sigma$. Given (Σ, σ) [or in the case of a DTD, (Σ, σ, D)], the implication problem is to decide whether $\Sigma \vDash \sigma$ [respectively, $\Sigma \vDash_D \sigma$].

As in the relational literature, we allow implication to be unrestricted (i.e. the documents can be potentially infinite). However, finite and unrestricted implication coincide in the absence of a DTD, and in the presence of a nonrecursive DTD [15]. Dealing with unrestricted implication means that we have to be able to reason about trees of infinite height and/or branching. However, for any particular problem instance, we need only consider a finite subtree of any document. For details, see [15].

In our chase algorithm, we will assume that each instance (Σ, σ) is given so that σ has the form $A \to b$, with b a single path, and all $C \to d \in \Sigma$ have a single path on the right-hand side as well. As we will see from the soundness of our axiomatization in Section 4.2, this assumption is without loss of generality. By making it, we can give a clearer presentation and properly compare our complexity results with existing work, which makes the same assumption [3]. If our input is not in this form, conversion is polynomial, so tractability is not affected.

4 Implication Without a DTD

Before we understand how DTDs affect the XFDs satisfied by a document, we must first understand the theory of XFDs alone.

4.1 Chase Algorithm for XFD Implication

This section presents a fast algorithm for deciding XFD implication. This algorithm is essentially the standard chase algorithm adapted to XML documents. Suppose $\sigma = A \to b$. We set up a tableau $\mathcal{T}$ as follows: there are two rows, and one column for every path (and prefix of a path) in A and b. In the ρ column and in each column corresponding to a path in A itself, we insert two identical variables from some indexed set $\{v_i\}_{i \in I}$; however, no variables are repeated between columns. For all other entries in the tableau, we assign unique variables.

Consider, as an example, the dependency $\{\rho.a.b, \rho.a.c\} \to \rho.a.d.e$. This corresponds to the tableau in Figure 5. Next, we define the set $\widehat{\Sigma}$ of functional dependencies that are used to chase on $\mathcal{T}$. We let X be the set of attributes of $\mathcal{T}$ (equal to paths($\varphi(\sigma)$)); $\widehat{\Sigma}$ consists exactly of Σ plus the following additional dependencies:

- $p.d \rightarrow p$ for every $p.x \in X, x \in \mathrm{EL}$ (non-attribute parents are unique).
- $p \rightarrow p.\alpha$ for every $p.\alpha \in X$ (attributes have unique values).

ρ	$p.a$	$p.a.b$	$p.a.c$	$p.a.d$	$p.a.d.e$
v_1	v_2	v_3	v_4	v_5	v_7
v_1	v_9	v_3	v_4	v_6	v_8

Fig. 5. Tableau for $\{\rho.a.b, \rho.a.c\} \rightarrow \rho.a.d.e$

The algorithm now involves chasing with $\widehat{\Sigma}$. At each step of the chase we have a dependency $C \rightarrow d$ and attempt to unify the two variables in the d column. This is a legal move if either (or both) the following hold:

1. All C column values of both rows are equal.
2. Let q be the longest prefix of d on which the two rows agree. The rows agree on all paths in C of the form $q.x.t$, $x \in \mathrm{EL}$, where $q.x$ is a prefix of d.

The correctness of the first chase rule is clear, as it is the standard one. To understand the second rule, consider the tableau $\mathcal{T}$ represented by the first two rows in Figure 6, and suppose we are chasing with the dependency $\{\rho.a.b, \rho.a.c\} \rightarrow \rho.a.c.f$. This tableau corresponds to the tree on the right hand side of Figure 6. However, when we convert this tree T back to its relation $U(R(T))$, the tree structure gives us two additional rows to the tableau. And from these two new rows we see that we need to unify v_8 and v_9 to satisfy our dependency.

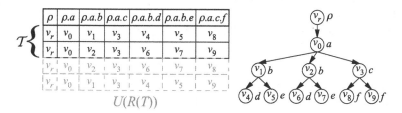

Fig. 6. Chasing with $\{\rho.a.b, \rho.a.c\} \rightarrow \rho.a.c.f$

One way to solve this problem is to construct our tableau so that it is closed under transformation to a tree and back to $U(R(T))$. However, the size of this tableau could be exponential in the size of our XFD σ. Fortunately, the regularity of the tree structure makes this unnecessary. We see that the two rows in the tableau for Figure 6 have the same value of $\rho.a.c$. As $\rho.a.b$ is a branch independent of $\rho.a.c$, the tree structure ensures that the equality between the values for $\rho.a.c$ is enough to unify $\rho.a.c.f$. The second chase rule generalizes this idea, allowing us to restrict our chase to just two rows.

When the chase terminates (as it clearly must), we can construct a tree T_{chase} from the tableau. By the following theorem, the values in the two columns for d are equal if and only if $\Sigma \vDash \sigma$.

Theorem 1. *After the chase terminates, $T_{chase} \models \sigma$ if and only if $\Sigma \models \sigma$.*

Computing the chase naively is $O(|\Sigma||\sigma|)$. We have at most $|\sigma|$ iterations of the outer loop, and finding a dependency that satsifies either rule 1 or rule 2 requires a scan of Σ. There is the issue that we are chasing with $\widehat{\Sigma}$ and not Σ. However, the functional dependencies in $\widehat{\Sigma} \setminus \Sigma$ depend on a single column and can be attached to that column for constant time evaluation.

It is easy to create a data structure that tracks, for each $C \to d \in \Sigma$, the greatest prefix of d unified in the chase so far. This allows us to adapt rule 2 to the linear time chase presented in Beeri and Bernstein [5]. We refer the reader to [15] for details.

Corollary 1. *Given (Σ, σ), implication can be decided in $O(|\Sigma| + |\sigma|)$ time.*

4.2 Axiomatization

Nonnull constraints and fictitious functional dependencies. Given the chase algorithm, we can now extract an axiomatization using traditional techniques[1]. Our axiomatization requires that our axiom language be able to express two additional types of constraints on XML documents. The first are the nonnull constraints; intuitively, certain nodes in a tree may not be null provided that certain other nodes are not null. For example, the root may never be null, and every nonnull node must have a nonnull parent. Formally, for $A, B \subseteq$ PATHS, we say that $nn(A, B)$ if in the smallest tree pattern for A and B, whenever the paths in A are not null, neither are the paths in B.

The second constraint is a variation on the FD concept. Following Atzeni and Morfuni [4], we refer to these constraints as fictitious functional dependencies (FFDs).

Definition 2. *A fictitious functional dependency $\sigma = A \xrightarrow{C} B$ consists of three subsets $A, B, C \subseteq$ PATHS. We let $\varphi(\sigma)$ be the smallest tree pattern in which all paths in A, B, and C occur, and let $=_{fd}$ be as in a normal XFD. The dependency holds if, for any two matches $\mu_1, \mu_2 \in M_{\varphi(\sigma),T}$, whenever we have $\mu_1(p) =_{fd} \mu_2(p)$ for all $p \in A$, and $\mu_1(s) \neq$ null for all $s \in C$, then for all $q \in B$, either $\mu_1(q) = \mu_2(q) =$ null or $\mu_1(q) =_{fd} \mu_2(q)$.*

It is absolutely essential to note that the condition $\mu_1(p)$ and $\mu_2(p) \neq$ null for all $p \in A$, present for ordinary XFDs, is missing from the above definition. Thus the matches are now no longer required to be nonnull on A, only equal. For example, suppose we add an additional node v_{13} to the tree in Figure 3; we add this node as a child of v_2 and label it e (the label of v_7). Then this tree satisfies the XFD $p.a.b.f \to p.a.e$ because there is a unique occurrence of each path below v_1, but it does not satisfy the FFD $p.a.b.f \xrightarrow{p.a.b} p.a.e$.

The Axiomatization. To axiomatize XFDs, we start with the axioms that Atzeni and Morfuni [4] introduced for relation FDs in the presence of null values. We let $X, Y, Z, W \subseteq$ PATHS. The following set of 12 axioms are sound and complete for relational FDs in the presence of nulls.

1. If $Y \subseteq X$, then $nn(X, Y)$.
2. If $nn(X, Y)$ then $nn(XZ, YZ)$.

3. If $nn(X, Y)$ and $nn(Y, Z)$ then $nn(X, Z)$
4. If $Y \subseteq X$, then $X \rightarrow Y$
5. If $X \rightarrow Y$, then $XZ \rightarrow YZ$
6. If $X \rightarrow Y$ and $X \rightarrow Z$, then $X \rightarrow YZ$
7. If $X \rightarrow YZ$, then $X \rightarrow Y$ and $X \rightarrow Z$
8. If $Y \subseteq X \subseteq Z$ then $X \xrightarrow{Z} Y$ (reflexivity for FFDs)
9. If $X \xrightarrow{Z} Y$ and $W \subseteq Z$, then $XW \xrightarrow{Z} YW$ (augmentation for FFDs)
10. If $X \xrightarrow{W} Y$ and $Y \xrightarrow{W} Z$ then $X \xrightarrow{W} Z$ (transitivity for FFDs)
11. If $X \rightarrow Y$ and $X \subseteq Z$ then $X \xrightarrow{Z} Y$ (FDs to FFDs)
12. If $X \xrightarrow{Z} p$ and $nn(Xp, Z)$ then $X \rightarrow p$ (FFDs to FDs)

We introduce an additional technical axiom for working with FFDs.

13. If $X \xrightarrow{Z} Y$ and $nn(W, Z)$ then $X \xrightarrow{W} Y$

Furthermore, we need several axioms to capture the tree structure of an XML document. We let $p, q \in$ PATHS, q is a prefix of $p, x, y \in$ EL, $x \neq \alpha$.

14. $nn(\rho)$ (root is never null)
15. $X \rightarrow \rho$ (root is unique)
16. $nn(p, q)$ (if a node is not null, neither are any of its ancestors).
17. $p.x \rightarrow p$ (every non-attribute child has a unique parent).
18. $p \rightarrow p.\alpha$ (unique attribute child)

Finally, we need one axiom to capture the ability to "splice" paths together as we saw with the second chase rule illustrated in Figure 6. For this axiom, if $s \in$ PATHS, let $s.Y$ denote a set of paths all having s as a prefix.

19. If $X, q.Y \xrightarrow{Z} q.y.s$, q not a prefix of any path in X, where $X, q.Y \subseteq Z$ and $q.y.W \subseteq q.Y$ includes all paths in $q.Y$ with $q.y$ as a prefix, then $q, q.y.W \xrightarrow{Z} q.y.s$.

Theorem 2. *Axioms 1-19 are sound and complete for XFD implication without a DTD.*

5   XFDs in the Presence of a DTD

Our chase algorithm and axiomatization for XFDs can be extended to documents that conform to certain classes of DTDs.

5.1   Simple DTDs

The chase algorithm. It is possible to modify our chase algorithm from Section 4.1 to include the presence of a simple DTD. For a problem instance (Σ, σ), we set up the tableau exactly as before, with a column for every path and prefix of a path in $\varphi(\sigma)$. However, in addition, we add a column for every path $p \in$ paths(Σ) such that D enforces $nn(\varphi(\sigma), p)$.

As before, we define the extension $\widehat{\Sigma}$ of Σ. However, we also add XFDs of the form $p.d_1 \rightarrow p.d_1.d_2$ for every column $p.d_1.d_2$ such that D contains a production of the form

$d_1 \leadsto d_2\gamma$ or $d_1 \leadsto d_2?\gamma$, $d_2 \notin \gamma$. These additional XFDs represent the unique child constraints specified by D.

With this new tableau and $\widehat{\Sigma}$ we run the chase as before; the values in the b column are equal if and only if $\Sigma \models_D \sigma$. To see this, we construct a tree T_{chase} from the tableau. Note that this tree may not satisfy the DTD D; however, we can extend T_{chase} to a document $\langle T_{chase} \rangle_D$ that does.

Theorem 3. *After the chase terminates, $\langle T_{chase} \rangle_D \models \sigma$ if and only if $\Sigma \models_D \sigma$.*

The only additional cost for running this chase comes from the additional number of columns and the additional XFDs for the DTD D. This allows us to improve on the previous quadratic bound obtained in [3] for this variant of the implication problem:

Corollary 2. *Given (Σ, σ, D) with D a simple DTD, implication can be decided in $O(|\Sigma| + |\sigma| + |D|)$ time.*

Axiomatization. To axiomatize XFD implication for simple DTDs, we need only account for the additional XFDs that we added to $\widehat{\Sigma}$ in the chase. However, instead of an additional axiom, we add an *axiom schema*. That is, the actual axioms depend on our DTD D, but we have a single schema for specifying these axioms from the DTD.

Theorem 4. *In the presence of a simple DTD D, a sound and complete set of axioms for (unrestricted) XFD implication includes exactly Axioms 1-19 from Section 4.2 with*

20. $nn(p.x, p.x.y)$, for each production $x \leadsto y\gamma$, $x \leadsto y^+\gamma \in D$
    (*i.e. the DTD does not allow certain children to be null*).
21. $p.x \to p.x.y$, for each production $x \leadsto y\gamma$, $x \leadsto y?\gamma \in D$, where $\gamma \in (\text{EL} - \{y\})^*$
    (*i.e. XFDs enforced by the DTD*).

5.2 #-DTDs

The implication problem in the presence of #-DTDs is more complicated because it is possible for these DTDs to be inconsistent with an XFD. Consider the DTD of the example in Figure 1, with the XFD $p \to q$, where p is a path identifier for a patient, and q is a path identifier for a recommending doctor. This XFD is inconsistent with our DTD; there is no document that can satisfy both the DTD and the functional dependency.

For many classes of DTDs, consistency is trivial, in the sense that there is no set of XFDs inconsistent with the DTD. #-DTDs are the lowest class in our hierarchy for which consistency becomes an issue. Consistency and implication are in fact related problems, as the former can be reduced to the latter [11].

However, in our extension of the chase algorithm and our axiomatization to #-DTDs, we solve the consistency problem directly. In particular, given an instance (Σ, σ, D) of an implication problem, if Σ and D are inconsistent then $\Sigma \models_D \sigma$ is trivially true. Therefore, out algorithm for deciding implication in the presence of #-DTDs starts by checking for inconsistency directly, in order to rule out this case.

To make this possible, we introduce a quadratic time algorithm for checking consistency of a set of XFDs Σ with a #-DTD. In this paper, we only present a naïve exponential algorithm. The details of the polynomial algorithm can be found in [15]. Our algorithm rests on the fact that issues of consistency can be decided on the smallest tree satisfying D.

Lemma 2. *Let T_D be the smallest tree such that $T_D \vDash D$. (Σ, D) is consistent if and only we can assign attribute values to any α-nodes in T_D so that $T_D \vDash \Sigma$.*

With this in mind, our algorithm is as follows:

1. Construct the minimal T_D from D. Initialize all the attribute nodes to different values from VAL, and convert T_D to the flat relation $U(R(T_D))$.
2. Partition Σ into Σ_a, which contains all the XFDs with an attribute node on the right-hand side, and $\Sigma_i = \Sigma \setminus \Sigma_a$.
3. Treat $U(R(T_D))$ as a very large chase tableau, and perform a standard relational chase (no use of the second rule) on it with Σ. Any unification from Σ_a is allowed to proceed normally, but any attempt at a unification from Σ_i causes the algorithm to return "no".
4. If the chase completes successfully, return "yes".

Lemma 3. *There is an assignment of attribute values to attribute nodes of T_D under which $T_D \vDash \Sigma$ if and only if the algorithm returns "yes".*

This algorithm is possibly exponential because of the duplicate paths that may appear in T_D, resulting in a large $U(R(T_D))$. However, using special encoding techniques to compress duplicate paths, we can implement this algorithm in polynomial time.

Proposition 1. *Given a pair (Σ, D) where D is a #-DTD, checking consistency requires $O(|D| + |\Sigma|^2)$ time.*

The chase algorithm. As we mentioned above, our first step in handling any implication problem instance (Σ, σ, D), is to determine whether (Σ, D) is consistent. A second special situation that can arise is that, while Σ is consistent with D, we cannot have a tree T such that $T \vDash D$, $T \vDash \Sigma$ and T contains even one nonnull match for all of $\varphi(\sigma)$. This can happen, for instance, in the case where D has productions $\rho \rightsquigarrow a^*b, a \rightsquigarrow cc$, $\Sigma = \{\rho.a \rightarrow \rho.a.c\}$ and $\sigma = \rho.b \rightarrow \rho.a$. Clearly there is only one tree satisfying D and Σ: the tree consisting of the root and one b child. On this one tree, σ also holds, precisely because there is no nonnull match for all of $\varphi(\sigma)$. In cases like this one also, $\Sigma \vDash_D \sigma$ vacuously. Fortunately, we can adapt our consistency checking algorithm to check for this case as well, without affecting the complexity.

Having ruled out the above two "pathological" cases, we can decide implication by using exactly the same chase that we used for simple DTDs. That gives us the result below. This proof of this theorem is quite technical; see [15].

Theorem 5. *Given (Σ, σ, D) where D is a #-DTD, implication can be decided in $O(|\Sigma|^2 + |\sigma| + |D|)$ time.*

Axiomatization. To axiomatize implication for #-DTDs, we need to account for the two pathological cases described above. Mathematically, the pathological cases arise because the DTD prevents certain XFDs from holding unless all matches of the left-hand side are null. Again, this requires the introduction of an axiom schema.

Theorem 6. *In the presence of a simple DTD D, a sound and complete set of axioms for (unrestricted) XFD implication includes exactly Axioms 1-21 from Section 5.1 with*

22. *If $p.x \xrightarrow{X} p.x.y$, then for $W \xrightarrow{X,p.x} Z$, for all W, Z and all $x \rightsquigarrow yy\gamma \in D$.*

5.3 Arbitrary DTDs

It is known that the presence of even very limited disjunction in a DTD makes the complexity of the implication problem rise to co-NP complete. For arbitrary DTDs, implication is co-NP hard and computable in co-NEXPTIME, while consistency is NP-hard and computable in NEXPTIME [2].

As for axiomatization, Arenas and Libkin [3] have shown that axiomatization is also difficult in the presence of disjunction; they prove that in their axiom language (which is less rich than ours) no finite axiomatization is possible for arbitrary DTDs. We note, however, that this result need not carry over to all possible axiom languages.

6 Related Work

In the relational model, functional dependencies [1] and chase algorithms [1,5] have been studied extensively. Our axiomatization draws on the theory developed for relational FDs in the presence of null values [4,17]. Functional dependencies have also been studied for nested relations [12].

In XML, functional dependencies have attracted much research attention [3,20,14,19,16,13]; see [21] for a survey. Our work uses a definition of XFD that is equivalent to the one in [3]; we have highlighted throughout the paper how our results extend these. The other FD definitions in the literature differ from ours in several ways. However, we believe that our definitions allow us to strike a good balance between generality of the framework and the ability to obtain strong tractability and axiomatization results.

Finally, there has been much work on other constraints in XML documents, notably keys [7], foreign keys [11], path constraints [8] and XICs [9]. For a recent, general survey on XML constraints, see [10]. DTDs are known to interact in a complex fashion with keys [11] and to affect the satisfiability and containment of XPath queries [18,6].

7 Future Directions

Several areas emerge as obvious directions for future work. While we know that axiomatization and the implication problem become intractable in the presence of disjunction, these problems are still open for DTDs with nested operations. In addition, the language used in the definition of XFDs can be made richer, for instance by adding wildcard descendant navigation to our tree patterns. Furthermore, our investigation of XFD interaction with DTDs can be broadened to include other popular XML constraint specifications, such as XML Schema.

Acknowledgments

We thank Al Demers, Johannes Gehrke, Dexter Kozen, David Martin, Millist Vincent and the anonymous reviewers for valuable suggestions that helped improve this paper.

References

1. S. Abiteboul, R. Hull, and V. Vianu. *Foundations of Databases*. Addison-Wesley, 1995.
2. M. Arenas. *Design Principles for XML Data*. PhD thesis, University of Toronto, 2005.
3. M. Arenas and L. Libkin. A normal form for XML documents. *ACM TODS*, 29(1):195–232, 2004.
4. P. Atzeni and N. Morfuni. Functional dependencies and constraints on null values in database relations. *Information and Control*, 70(1):1–31, 1986.
5. C. Beeri and P. Bernstein. Computational problems related to the design of normal form relational schemas. *ACM TODS*, 4(1):pp. 30 – 59, 1979.
6. Michael Benedikt, Wenfei Fan, and Floris Geerts. XPath satisfiability in the presence of DTDs. In *Proc. PODS*, pages 25–36, 2005.
7. P. Buneman, S. Davidson, W. Fan, C. Hara, and W. Tan. Reasoning about keys for XML. *Inf. Syst.*, 28(8):1037–1063, 2003.
8. P. Buneman, W. Fan, and S. Weinstein. Path constraints in semistructured and structured databases. In *Proc. PODS*, pages 129–138, 1998.
9. A. Deutsch and V. Tannen. Containment and integrity constraints for XPath. In *KRDB*, 2001.
10. W. Fan. XML constraints: Specification, analysis, and applications. In *Proc. DEXA*, pages 805–809, 2005.
11. W. Fan and L. Libkin. On XML integrity constraints in the presence of DTDs. In *Proc. PODS*, 2001.
12. C. Hara and S. Davidson. Reasoning about nested functional dependencies. In *Proc. PODS*, pages 91–100, 1999.
13. S. Hartmann and S. Link. More functional dependencies for XML. In *ADBIS*, pages 355–369, 2003.
14. S. Hartmann and S. Link. On functional dependencies in advanced data models. In *Electronic Notes in Theoretical Computer Science*, volume 84. Elsevier Science B. V., 2003.
15. Ł. Kot and W. White. Characterization of XML functional dependencies and their interaction with DTDs. Technical Report 2006-2039, Cornell University, July 2006.
16. M. Lee, T. Ling, and W. Low. Designing functional dependencies for XML. In *Proc. EDBT*, pages 124–141, 2002.
17. M. Levene and G. Loizou. Axiomatisation of functional dependencies in incomplete relations. *Theor. Comput. Sci.*, 206(1-2):283–300, 1998.
18. F. Neven and T. Schwentick. XPath containment in the presence of disjunction, DTDs, and variables. In *Proc. ICDT*, pages 315–329, 2003.
19. K. Schewe. Redundancy, dependencies and normal forms for XML databases. In *ADC*, pages 7–16, 2005.
20. M. Vincent, J. Liu, and C. Liu. Strong functional dependencies and their application to normal forms in XML. *ACM TODS*, 29(3):445–462, 2004.
21. J. Wang. A comparative study of functional dependencies for XML. In *APWeb*, pages 308–319, 2005.

Axiomatizing the Logical Core of XPath 2.0[*]

Balder ten Cate and Maarten Marx

ISLA – Informatics Institute, Universiteit van Amsterdam
balder.tencate@uva.nl, marx@science.uva.nl

Abstract. The first aim of this paper is to present the logical core of XPath 2.0: a logically clean, decidable fragment, which includes most navigational features of XPath 2.0 (complex counting conditions and data joins are not supported, as they lead to undecidability). The second aim is to provide a list of equations completely axiomatizing query equivalence in this language (i.e., all other query equivalences can be derived from these).

The introduction of *Core XPath*, the navigational core of XPath 1.0 [8], has been a very fruitful move. It has given rise to many new results enhancing our understanding of XPath. The full language of XPath 1.0 is too rich for a rigorous logical analysis, and Core XPath is a concise and well defined sublanguage, for which a detailed analysis *is* feasible (e.g., concerning its expressive power and complexity). Many of these results were established by relating Core XPath to other, more familiar logical languages on trees such as *first-order logic* or *MSO*, and applying known results and techniques for the latter.

XPath 2.0, the successor of XPath 1.0, has received less attention in the theoretical literature. In particular, no concrete proposal for its logical core has been made. One feature of XPath 2.0 is that it is expressively complete for first-order logic (in fact, it was designed to be). This does not mean that there are no interesting and challenging open problems for this language! In this paper we address one interesting problem, concerning query equivalence.

We identify the logical core of XPath 2.0, which we call *Core XPath 2.0*, and we present a complete axiomatization of query equivalence for this language, in the form of a finite list of remarkably simple algebraic equations. Our results might serve as a step towards improved *query optimization* methods for XPath 2.0 and XQuery (note that XQuery contains XPath 2.0 as a sublanguage).

Our axiomatization is based on a number of other results, including (*i*) a known complete axiomatization of Tarski's algebra of binary relations [16], which can be seen as a sublanguage of Core XPath 2.0, and (*ii*) an axiomatization of the first-order theory of finite trees based on [6].

To summarize, the main contributions are:

1. the definition of the logical core of XPath 2.0, together with an analysis of the redundancies in the language,
2. a finite list of equations axiomatizing query equivalence in this language.

---

[*] The full version of this paper is available at http://staff.science.uva.nl/~bcate

T. Schwentick and D. Suciu (Eds.): ICDT 2007, LNCS 4353, pp. 134–148, 2007.
© Springer-Verlag Berlin Heidelberg 2007

It is worth noting that, in *relational* database theory, complete axiomatizations of query equivalence are rather scarse. SQL and datalog both have undecidable query equivalence problems, and hence query equivalence is not recursively axiomatizable for these languages (on finite structures). Entailment relations between different types of constraints *have* been successfully axiomatized [1].

Organization of the paper. Section 1 defines Core XPath 2.0 and establishes some simple equivalences. Section 2 shows undecidability of query equivalence for a number of extensions of Core XPath 2.0. Section 3 contains axiomatizations both for Core XPath 2.0 and for its variable free fragment. We conclude in section 4.

1   A Decidable Logical Core of XPath 2.0

In this section, we define the syntax and semantics of the logical core of XPath 2.0, and we discuss some basic properties of this language, as well as how it relates to other languages (viz. *first-order logic* and *relation algebra*).

1.1   Design Choices

The following two criteria guided our choice of XPath 2.0 operators to be included in the navigational core: (*i*) expressions should manipulate *sets of nodes*, just as in Core XPath. This leads to a simple set theoretic semantics; (*ii*) the query equivalence problem should be decidable. Undecidability would imply non-axiomatizability, because the models we are concerned with are finite.

These criteria have the following repercussions:

1. In Core XPath 2.0, all expressions manipulate sets of nodes. More precisely, the meaning of each path expression is a function that, given a node (the *"context node"*) returns a set of nodes (the *"answer set"*). In contrast, in XPath 2.0, path expressions return *sequences* of elements, of various types. In particular, the `for` construct returns unsorted sequences, possibly containing duplicates. In our logic, we treat `for $i in` R `return` S as equivalent to (`for $i in` R `return` S)/., which always returns a document-order sorted list without duplicates.
2. In order to keep the logic decidable, we excluded the positional and aggregate functions `position()`, `last()` and `count()` and value comparison operators. Section 2 presents undecidability results in the presence of these functions.

The crucial differences with Core XPath are that besides union, also Boolean intersection and complementation can be applied to path expressions, and that the language contains variables, node comparison tests, and the `for`-loop.

1.2   Syntax and Semantics of Core XPath 2.0

We are ready to define the *Navigational Core of XPath 2.0*. The grammar of Core XPath 2.0 is given in Fig. 1. Just like in Core XPath, it has productions for path expressions PathExpr and filter expressions TestExpr. In addition, there is the node comparison expression CompTest.

Axis	:=	self | child | parent | descendant | ancestor
		| following_sibling | preceding_sibling
NameTest	:=	QName | *
Step	:=	Axis::NameTest
NodeRef	:=	. | $i
PathExpr	:=	Step | NodeRef | ()
		| PathExpr/PathExpr
		| PathExpr union PathExpr
		| PathExpr intersect PathExpr
		| PathExpr except PathExpr
		| PathExpr[TestExpr]
		| for $i in PathExpr return PathExpr
TestExpr	:=	PathExpr | CompTest | not TestExpr
		| TestExpr and TestExpr | TestExpr or TestExpr
CompTest	:=	NodeRef is NodeRef

Fig. 1. Syntax of Core XPath 2.0

The semantics is provided in Fig. 2. Expressions are evaluated on finite un-ranked node-labeled and sibling-ordered trees as usual. Because of the variables in the language we need an assignment function g mapping variables to nodes. For g an assignment, $\$i$ a variable and x a node, $g_x^{\$i}$ denotes the assignment which is just like g except that $g(\$i) = x$. The value of a NodeRef expression a relative to an assignment g and a node x, denoted by $[a]^{g,x}$, is x if $a = .$, or $g(a)$ if a is a variable.

Given a model and an assignment g, the meaning $[\![R]\!]^g$ of a PathExpr R is always a binary relation. Of course this is just another way of specifying a function from the set of nodes to the powerset of the set of nodes (the answer-set semantics).

The meaning of a TestExpr expression is given by the function $[\![\cdot]\!]^g_{\mathsf{Test}}$, which always yields a set of nodes: $x \in [\![\mathsf{TestExpr}]\!]^g_{\mathsf{Test}}$ if and only if TestExpr evaluates to true at node x. It is straightforward to check that the given semantics extends the semantics of Core XPath given in e.g. [8], and agrees with the official XPath 2.0 semantics as presented in e.g., [12], provided sequences are treated as nodesets.

Definition 1. *Two path expressions R, S are said to be equivalent if for every model, for every assignment g, $[\![R]\!]^g = [\![S]\!]^g$.*

Remark. We excluded the attribute axis because it only adds expressivity in the presence of data value comparisons. Because we focus on relative path equiv-alence, we also excluded the absolute path expression $/R$. This is term definable as $(\mathtt{ancestor} :: * \; \mathtt{union} \; \mathtt{self} :: *)[\mathtt{not} \; \mathtt{ancestor} :: *]/R$.

Syntactic sugar. XPath 2.0 contains a number of extra axes, operations and functions that, when restricted to the navigational fragment, are just syntac-tic sugar. They are listed in Fig. 3. As indicated, all these connectives can be

$$
\begin{aligned}
[\![\text{Axis::NameTest}]\!]^g &= \{(x,y) \mid x(\text{Axis})y \text{ and } y \text{ satisfies NameTest}\} \\
[\![.]\!]^g &= [\![\text{self} :: *]\!]^g \\
[\![\$i]\!]^g &= \{(x,y) \mid g(i) = y\} \\
[\![()]\!]^g &= \emptyset \\
[\![R/S]\!]^g &= [\![R]\!]^g \circ [\![S]\!]^g \\
[\![R \text{ union } S]\!]^g &= [\![R]\!]^g \cup [\![S]\!]^g \\
[\![R \text{ intersect } S]\!]^g &= [\![R]\!]^g \cap [\![S]\!]^g \\
[\![R \text{ except } S]\!]^g &= [\![R]\!]^g \setminus [\![S]\!]^g \\
[\![R[T]]\!]^g &= \{(x,y) \in [\![R]\!]^g \mid y \in [\![T]\!]^g_{\text{Test}}\} \\
[\![\text{for } \$i \text{ in } R \text{ return } S]\!]^g &= \{(x,y) \mid \exists z ((x,z) \in [\![R]\!]^g \text{ and } (x,y) \in [\![S]\!]^{g^{\$i}_z})\} \\
\\
[\![\text{PathExpr}]\!]^g_{\text{Test}} &= \{x \mid \exists y (x,y) \in [\![\text{PathExpr}]\!]^g\} \\
[\![\text{not } T]\!]^g_{\text{Test}} &= Nodes \setminus [\![T]\!]^g_{\text{Test}} \\
[\![T1 \text{ and } T2]\!]^g_{\text{Test}} &= [\![T1]\!]^g_{\text{Test}} \cap [\![T2]\!]^g_{\text{Test}} \\
[\![T1 \text{ or } T2]\!]^g_{\text{Test}} &= [\![T1]\!]^g_{\text{Test}} \cup [\![T2]\!]^g_{\text{Test}} \\
[\![a \text{ is } b]\!]^g_{\text{Test}} &= \{x \mid [\![a]\!]^{g,x} = [\![b]\!]^{g,x}\}.
\end{aligned}
$$

Fig. 2. Semantics of the Navigational Core of XPath 2.0

term-defined in terms of the connectives of Fig. 1. With the exception of the if-then-else construct, all definitions are linear.

1.3   Some Convenient Shorthand Notations

We will be making use of a slightly more compact notation in following sections. We will use $\downarrow, \downarrow^+, \uparrow, \uparrow^+, \rightarrow, \rightarrow^+, \leftarrow, \leftarrow^+$ and . as shorthands for the respective axes child::*, descendant::*, parent::*, ancestor::*, (following_sibling::* except following_sibling::*/following_-sibling::*), following_sibling::*, (preceding_sibling::* except preceding_sibling::*/preceding_sibling::*), preceding_sibling::*, and self::*. We will use $\top$ as shorthand for the universal relation $(\uparrow^+ \text{ union } .)/(\downarrow^+ \text{ union } .)$ and $\bot$ as shorthand for (). We will use $\ll$ to denote the document order (depth-first left-to-right) relation in a tree, as defined by $\downarrow^+ \text{ union } (\uparrow^+ \text{ union } .)/ \rightarrow^+ /(\downarrow^+ \text{ union } .)$. Finally, we will use the function $(\cdot)^{\smile}$, which, when applied to a path expression, yields its converse:

$$
\begin{aligned}
(\text{Axis} :: \text{NameTest})^{\smile} &\equiv \text{self} :: \text{NameTest}/\text{Axis}^{\smile} :: * \\
.^{\smile} &\equiv . \\
\$i^{\smile} &\equiv .[. \text{ is } \$i]/\top \\
()^{\smile} &\equiv () \\
(R/T^{\smile} &\equiv T^{\smile}/R^{\smile} \\
(R \text{ union } T)^{\smile} &\equiv R^{\smile} \text{ union } T^{\smile} \\
(R \text{ intersect } T)^{\smile} &\equiv R^{\smile} \text{ intersect } T^{\smile} \\
(R \text{ except } T)^{\smile} &\equiv R^{\smile} \text{ except } T^{\smile} \\
(R[X])^{\smile} &\equiv .[X]/R^{\smile}
\end{aligned}
$$

where Axis$^{\smile}$ is the converse of Axis (i.e., $\downarrow^{\smile}=\uparrow$, etc). The reader may verify that $R^{\smile}$ indeed defines the converse of R, i.e., $(x,y) \in [\![R^{\smile}]\!]^g$ iff $(y,x) \in [\![R]\!]^g$.

Definable path expressions:

```
descendant_or_self :: NameTest  ≡  descendant :: NameTest union self :: NameTest
ancestor_or_self :: NameTest    ≡  ancestor :: NameTest union self :: NameTest
following : NameTest             ≡  (ancestor :: * union self :: *)/following_sibling/
                                      (descendant :: NameTest union self :: NameTest)
preceding : NameTest            ≡  (ancestor :: * union self :: *)/preceding_sibling/
                                      (descendant :: NameTest union self :: NameTest)
if T then R else S              ≡  .[T]/R union .[not T]/S
```

Definable node expressions:

```
true()                         ≡  .
false()                        ≡  ()
exists(R)                      ≡  R
empty(R)                       ≡  not (R)
some $i in R satisfies T       ≡  for $i in R return .[T]
every $i in R satisfies T      ≡  not (for $i in R return .[not (T)])
```

Fig. 3. Definable XPath 2.0 operations

1.4 Relations with Other Languages

First order logic. XPath 2.0 was designed to be expressively complete for first-order queries [12]. More precisely, we mean here first-order logic in the signature with binary relations symbols $<$ and $\prec$ denoting the *descendant* and *following sibling* relations, and arbitrarily many unary predicates for the node tags. It is easy to see that there are linear translations between the two languages. In the absence of data value comparions the for-loop and the variables are not even needed for expressive completeness: even Core XPath extended with the **except** operator is already expressively complete for this first-order language [13]. Whether this holds in the presence of data value comparisons depends on a longstanding open problem in finite model theory, namely whether FO has a finite variable property on finite ordered structures [5].

A complete axiomatization of the first-order theory of finite node-labelled sibling ordered trees (in the signature described above) is given in Fig. 4.

Theorem 1. *The FO theory of finite node-labelled sibling ordered trees is completely axiomatized by the axioms and axiom scheme in Fig. 4.*

The proof is given in the full version of this paper.

Relation Algebra. The variable free fragment of Core XPath 2.0 (which already has the full expressive power of Core XPath 2.0) is closely related to Tarski's algebra of binary relations ("Relation Algebra") [16] Cf., also [11,9]. This elegant and purely algebraic language consists of

- atomic expressions denoting binary relations (over some set)
- constants $\top$, $\bot$ and ., denoting the total relation, the empty relation and the identity relation, respectively.

QT1.	$\forall xyz(x < y \wedge y < z \rightarrow x < z)$	$<$ is transitive
QT2.	$\neg \exists x(x < x)$	$<$ is irreflexive
QT3.	$\forall xy(x < y \rightarrow \exists z(x <_{imm} z \wedge z \leq y))$	immediate children
QT4.	$\exists x \forall y \neg(y < x)$	there is a root
QT5.	$\forall xyz(x < z \wedge y < z \rightarrow x \leq y \vee y \leq x)$	linearly ordered ancestors

QT6.	$\forall xyz(x \prec y \wedge y \prec z \rightarrow x \prec z)$	$\prec$ is transitive
QT7.	$\neg \exists x(x \prec x)$	$\prec$ is irreflexive
QT8.	$\forall xy(x \prec y \rightarrow \exists z(x \prec_{imm} z \wedge z \preceq y))$	immediately next sibling
QT9.	$\forall x \exists y(y \preceq x \wedge \neg \exists z(z \prec y))$	there is a least sibling
QT10.	$\forall xy((x \prec y \vee y \prec x) \leftrightarrow (\exists z(z <_{imm} x \wedge z <_{imm} y) \wedge x \neq y))$	
		$\prec$ linearly orders *siblings*

QT11. $\forall xy(x = y \vee x < y \vee y < x \vee \exists x'y'(x' < x \wedge y' < y \wedge (x' \prec y' \vee y' \prec x')))$

connectedness

Ind. $\forall x(\forall y(x \ll y \rightarrow \phi(y)) \rightarrow \phi(x)) \rightarrow \forall x.\phi(x)$

where

$x <_{imm} y$ is shorthand for $x < y \wedge \forall z(x < z \rightarrow y \leq z)$,

$x \prec_{imm} y$ is shorthand for $x \prec y \wedge \forall z(x \prec z \rightarrow y \preceq z)$, and

$x \ll y$ is shorthand for $x < y \vee \exists x'y'(x' \leq x \wedge y' \leq y \wedge x' \prec y')$

Fig. 4. Axioms of the FO theory of finite trees

- operators for taking *union* ($\cup$), *intersection* ($\cap$), *complement* ($-$), *composition* ($/$) and *converse* ($\cdot^{\smile}$).

As the reader can observe, the main syntactic differences between the variable free fragment of Core XPath and Relation Algebra are (*i*) Relation Algebra has a converse operator, while in Core XPath 2.0 each individual expression has a definable converse, (*ii*) Relation Algebra uses a unary complementation operator, whereas Core XPath 2.0 uses relative complementation, (*iii*) Relation Algebra includes a constant $\top$ denoting the universal relation, whereas in Core XPath 2.0 the universal relation is defined by (ancestor::* union self::*)/(descendant::* union self::*), (*iv*) Core XPath 2.0 features *predicates*, which are not present in Relation Algebras.

These differences in syntax are mostly cosmetic. The most important difference between Relation Algebra and Core XPath 2.0 lies in the *semantics*: Core XPath 2.0 is interpreted on finite trees whereas Relation Algebra is traditionally concerned with arbitrary relations. Still, in this paper, we will make important use of known results about Relation Algebra.

2   Undecidable Extensions

Because we want to axiomatize query equivalence on finite models it is neccessay that query equivalence is decidable. Here we show how value comparisons and functions as position(), last(), and count() can lead to undecidability.

Positional information. XPath supports reference to positional information in predicates, via the functions position(), last(), and count(). For example, `child::*[position()=1]` and `child::*[position()=last()]` (abbreviated as `child::*[1]` and `child::*[last()]`, respectively) return the first and last child of the context node, in document order. The simplest type of position predicates, of the form $R[k]$ or $R[\texttt{last()}-k]$, is quite harmless. They can be eliminated at the cost of an exponential blowup, using the following equivalences:

$$R[1] \quad\equiv R \texttt{ except } (R/\lll)$$
$$R[k+1] \equiv (R \texttt{ intersect } (R[k]/\lll))[1]$$

and symmetrically for $R[\texttt{last()}-k]$. These equivalences may be added to the axiomatisation we will give below in order to obtain completeness w.r.t. this enrichment of the language.

More advanced use of positional information quickly makes the logic undecidable:

Theorem 2. *Core XPath 2.0 extended with expressions of any of the following forms can define the* equilevel *predicate, and hence is undecidable:*

- $R[\texttt{count}(R') = \texttt{count}(R'')]$, *or*
- $R[\texttt{position()} = \texttt{count}(R')]$ *(equivalently written as $R[\texttt{count}(R')]$), or*
- $R[\texttt{position()} = \texttt{last()}/2]$ *(equivalently written as $R[\texttt{last()}/2]$)*

The *equilevel* predicate holds between two nodes if they are at the same distance from the root. First order logic on trees with the equilevel predicate is known to be undecidable [15]. More details, as well as a proof of Theorem 2, can be found in the full version of this paper.

Comparison operators. XPath 2.0 has three sets of operators to compare nodes. Here we just discuss the three types of *equality*: =, eq and is. Each takes two path expressions as input. = and eq compare the data values of input nodes (in XPath terminology, the *atomization* of the input), while is compares node identity. a eq b is true if the nodes a and b have the same data value, and a is b is true if a and b are the same node. = can be defined in terms of eq: $R=S$ iff some r in R satisfies some s in S satisfies r eq s (recall from Fig. 3 that some can be expressed in terms of for). Node equality is term definable in XPath 2.0 using intersection (see axiom Eq1 in Fig. 7). Data value equality quickly leads to undecidability: already in the context of Core XPath [7]; or in first order logic with three variables having only the child relation interpreted on unary trees [3]. Both proofs use Post's correspondence problem. In our setting, we can use the equilevel predicate again: one can force that two nodes have the same data value iff they are at the same distance from the root.

3   A Complete Equational Calculus

In this section, we will give a complete equational axiomatization of equivalence in Core XPath 2.0. First, we axiomatize the variable free fragment, and then we show how the axiomatization can be extended to the full language of Core XPath 2.0. We will make use of the shorthand notations introduced in Section 1.3. All missing proofs can be found in the full version of this paper.

3.1   The Variable Free Fragment

The *variable free fragment* of Core XPath 2.0 is the fragment without variables, for and node comparison tests. It is closely related to Tarski's algebra of binary relations ("Relation Algebra") [16]. Unlike the latter, however, it is interpreted on a specific class of structures, namely *finite node-labelled sibling-ordered trees* ("finite trees", for short). The calculus we will present essentially extends a known complete axiomatization of Relation Algebra with axioms that capture the special properties of these structures.

We do not enforce that, as in real XML document trees, each node is labelled by exactly one node label. Given a finite alphabet, this can always be enforced.

Our axioms are given in Fig. 5. Keep in mind that these axioms describe *relative path equivalence* (as opposed to *equivalence when evaluated at the root*). We leave it to the reader to check that axioms in Fig. 5 are indeed sound.

In this table, and in what follows, we use $R \subseteq S$ as shorthand for $S \equiv S \cup R$. We say that R is *provably equivalent* to S in our calculus (notation: $R \equiv^* S$), if the equivalence of R and S can be proved from substitution instances of the axioms using the *transitivity, symmetry and reflexivity of* $\equiv$ and *replacement of equals by equals* (if $R \equiv S$ and T' is obtained from T by replacing some occurences of R by S, then $T \equiv T'$). Likewise, we use $\subseteq^*$ for provable *containment*.

It is sometimes easier to prove mutual containment of two expressions than equivalence. Fortunately, the two are equivalent:

Fact 1. *For all expressions R and S, $R \equiv^* S$ iff both $R \subseteq^* S$ and $S \subseteq^* R$.*

In proofs of containment, the following fact can be very useful. Call a subexpression of an expression R positive (negative), if it occurs under the scope of an even (odd) number of polarity switching operators. Here, by polarity switching operators we mean **not** and **except**, and the latter is only counted as polarity switching with respect to the *second* argument.

Fact 2 (Monotonicity ([10])). *Suppose $R \subseteq^* S$, and let T' be obtained from T by replacing some positive occurences of R by S, and/or replacing some negative occurences of S by R. Then $T \subseteq^* T'$.*

In the completeness proof we will use the derivable equivalences listed in Fig. 6.

Lemma 1. *All equivalences and containments in Fig. 6 are derivable.*

Let us now proceed to prove completeness. First, we need to establish an important lemma. For any path expression R, let us use the following shorthands:

$$
\begin{array}{lll}
\mathsf{first\text{-}pair}(R) & := & R \text{ except } (\gg /R/\top \text{ union } R/ \ll) \\
\mathsf{other\text{-}pair}(R) & := & (\top \text{ except } .)/R/\top \text{ union } \top/R/(\top \text{ except } .)
\end{array}
$$

Observe that $\mathsf{first\text{-}pair}(R)$ denotes *the subrelation of R consisting only of the first pair, in lexicographic document order*, and $\mathsf{other\text{-}pair}(R)$ holds of all pairs (x, y) for which R *contains some different pair* (x', y') (i.e., such that $x' \neq x$ or $y' \neq y$). The following lemma combines these two, and shows that $\mathsf{first\text{-}pair}(R)$ always holds of at most one pair.

Axioms of Boolean Algebra and Relation Algebra

BA1.	R union $(S$ union $T)$	$\equiv$	$(R$ union $S)$ union T
BA2.	R intersect $(S$ intersect $T)$	$\equiv$	$(R$ intersect $S)$ intersect T
BA3.	R union S	$\equiv$	S union R
BA4.	R intersect S	$\equiv$	S intersect R
BA5.	R union $(S$ intersect $T)$	$\equiv$	$(R$ union $S)$ intersect $(R$ union $T)$
BA6.	R intersect $(S$ union $T)$	$\equiv$	$(R$ intersect $S)$ union $(R$ intersect $T)$
BA7.	R union $(R$ intersect $S)$	$\equiv$	R
BA8.	R intersect $(R$ union $S)$	$\equiv$	R
BA9.	R union $(\top$ except $R)$	$\equiv$	$\top$
BA10.	R intersect $(\top$ except $R)$	$\equiv$	$\bot$
BA11.	R intersect $(\top$ except $S)$	$\equiv$	R except S
RA1.	$(R/S)/T$	$\equiv$	$R/(S/T)$
RA2.	$R/.$	$\equiv$	R
RA3.	$(R$ union $S)/T$	$\equiv$	(R/T) union (S/T)
RA7.	$(S/(\top$ except $(S^{\smile}/R)))$	$\subseteq$	$\top$ except R

Axioms for eliminating predicates

Pred1.	$R[X$ and $Y]$	$\equiv$	$R[X][Y]$
Pred2.	$R[X$ or $Y]$	$\equiv$	$R[X]$ union $R[Y]$
Pred3.	$R[\text{not}(X)]$	$\equiv$	R except $R[X]$
Pred4.	$R[S]$	$\equiv$	$R/((S/\top)$ intersect $.)$

Axioms for finite trees:

Tr1.	$\downarrow^+ / \downarrow^+$	$\subseteq$	$\downarrow^+$
Tr2.	$\downarrow^+$ intersect $\uparrow^+$	$\equiv$	$\bot$
Tr3a.	$\downarrow^+$	$\equiv$	$\downarrow$ union $(\downarrow / \downarrow^+)$
Tr3b.	$\downarrow$	$\equiv$	$\downarrow^+$ except $(\downarrow^+ / \downarrow^+)$
Tr4.	$.[\uparrow]$	$\equiv$	$.[\uparrow^+ [\text{not}(\uparrow)]]$
Tr5.	$\downarrow^+ / \uparrow^+$	$\equiv$	$\downarrow^+$ union $.[\downarrow]$ union $.[\downarrow]/ \uparrow^+$
Tr6.	$\rightarrow^+ / \rightarrow^+$	$\subseteq$	$\rightarrow^+$
Tr7.	$\rightarrow^+$ intersect $\leftarrow^+$	$\equiv$	$\bot$
Tr8a.	$\rightarrow^+$	$\equiv$	$\rightarrow$ union $(\rightarrow / \rightarrow^+)$
Tr8b.	$\rightarrow$	$\equiv$	$\rightarrow^+$ except $(\rightarrow^+ / \rightarrow^+)$
Tr9.	$.[\leftarrow]$	$\equiv$	$.[\leftarrow^+ [\text{not}(\leftarrow)]]$
Tr10.	$\rightarrow^+$ union $\leftarrow^+$	$\equiv$	$(\uparrow / \downarrow)$ except $.$
Tr11.	$.$ union $\uparrow^+$ union $\downarrow^+$ union $(\uparrow^* / \rightarrow^+ / \downarrow^*)$ union $(\uparrow^* / \leftarrow^+ / \downarrow^*)$	$\equiv$	$\top$
Ind.	$\top[R]$	$\equiv$	$\top[R$ except $(R/ \lll)]]$

Axioms for tag-names:

Tag1.	$Axis::NameTest$	$\equiv$	$Axis::*/\text{self}::NameTest$
Tag2.	$\text{self}::NameTest$	$\subseteq$	$.$

Fig. 5. Axioms for Core XPath 2.0 query equivalence

RA4.	$(R \text{ union } S)^{\smile}$	$\equiv$	$R^{\smile} \text{ union } S^{\smile}$
RA5.	$(R/S)^{\smile}$	$\equiv$	$S^{\smile}/R^{\smile}$
RA6.	$(R^{\smile})^{\smile}$	$\equiv$	R
RA8.	$R/(S \text{ union } T)$	$\equiv$	$R/S \text{ union } R/T$
RA9.	$./R$	$\equiv$	R
RA10.	$R/\bot$	$\equiv$	$\bot$
RA11.	$\top/\top$	$\equiv$	$\top$
RA12.	$.^{\smile}$	$\equiv$	$.$
RA13.	$\bot^{\smile}$	$\equiv$	$\bot$
RA14.	$\top^{\smile}$	$\equiv$	$\top$
RA15.	$(R \text{ intersect } S)^{\smile}$	$\equiv$	$R^{\smile} \text{ intersect } S^{\smile}$
RA16.	$(R \text{ except } S)^{\smile}$	$\equiv$	$R^{\smile} \text{ except } S^{\smile}$
RA17.	$(\top \text{ except } R/S)/S^{\smile}$	$\subseteq$	$(\top \text{ except } R)$
RA18.	$(R \text{ intersect } .)/(R \text{ intersect } .)$	$\equiv$	$(R \text{ intersect } .)$
RA19.	$(R \text{ intersect } .)^{\smile}$	$\equiv$	$(R \text{ intersect } .)$
RA20.	$((R/\top) \text{ intersect } .)/\top$	$\equiv$	$R/\top$
Pred6.	R/S	$\equiv$	$R[S]/S$
Pred7.	$R[S[T]]$	$\equiv$	$R[S/T]$
Pred8.	$(R[S])^{\smile}$	$\equiv$	$.[S]/R^{\smile}$
Pred9.	$\top[S]/R$	$\equiv$	$\top[R^{\smile}/S]$
Pred10.	$R[S \text{ and } \text{not}(T)]$	$\subseteq$	$R[(S \text{ except } T)]$

Fig. 6. Derivable equivalences

Lemma 2. first-pair(R) intersect other-pair(first-pair(R)) $\equiv^* \bot$

The intuition behind the next lemma is best understood as follows: if $R \not\equiv^* \top$, for some path expression R, then first-pair($\top$ except R) acts as a witness of this fact: it denotes a pair that is a counterexample to the validity of R.

Lemma 3. *For all path expressions R, $R \equiv^* \top$ iff* first-pair($\top$ except R) $\subseteq^* R$.

Theorem 3 (Completeness). *For all equivalent variable-free expressions R and S, $R \equiv^* S$.*

Proof. The proof essentially proceeds in two steps: first, we will prove completeness with respect to arbitrary structures (i.e., possibly infinite, and in which the atomic expressions $\downarrow^+, \rightarrow^+$, etc. can denote arbitrary binary relations), then we prove completeness with respect to actual finite trees. Throughout the proof, we will restrict attention to expressions without predicates. This is safe because, by the axioms *Pred1–Pred4*, every expression is provably equivalent to one that does not contain predicates.

Call an expression *consistent* if it is not provably equivalent to $\bot$. To prove completeness of our axiomatization, it suffices to show that every consistent expression is satisfiable (in a finite tree). For, suppose $R \not\equiv^* S$. Then, by Fact 1, either $R \not\subseteq^* S$ or $S \not\subseteq^* R$, which implies that either R except S or S except R

is consistent. Any finite tree model in which either of these expressions is satisfied constitutes a counterexample for the equivalence of R and S.

Call a set of expressions consistent if no intersection of finitely many elements of the set is provably equivalent to $\perp$. A *maximal consistent set* ("MCS") is a consistent set of expressions Γ, such that, for any expression R, either $R \in \Gamma$ or ($\top$ except R) $\in \Gamma$.

Claim. Every consistent expression can be extended to an MCS.

Proof of claim. This follows from the fact that our axiomatization includes the axioms of Boolean Algebra.   ⊣

Claim. For every consistent set of expressions Γ there is a model M (not necessarily a finite tree) and a pair (d, e) of elements of the domain of M, such that $(d, e) \in [\![\Gamma]\!]^M$.

Proof of claim. This follows from a result of Venema [18], who showed that this claim holds for any axiomatization of Relation Algebra that includes *BA1–RA7*, and such that for each expression R there is an expression R' such that

1. R' intersect other-pair(R') $\equiv \perp$ is provable.
2. $R' \subseteq R$ is provable iff $R \equiv \top$ is provable.

Lemma 2 and 3 show that our axiomatization indeed satisfies this property (pick R' to be first-pair($\top$ except R)).   ⊣

Claim. Let Γ be any MCS, and let $(d, e) \in [\![\Gamma]\!]^M$ for some model M. Then M satisfies all FO axioms in Fig. 4.

Proof of claim. First, we will show that *Tr1*, ..., *Tr11* hold in M. Let $R \equiv S$ be any of these axioms (recall that we treat $R \subseteq S$ as being shorthand for $S \equiv S \cup R$). Then Γ must contain the expression $\top$ except ($\top/((R$ except $S)$ union $(S$ except $R))/\top$), for otherwise, by maximality, Γ would have to contain $\top/((R$ except $S)$ union $(S$ except $R))/\top$, which would immediately yield inconsistency.

It follows that the axioms *Tr1*, ..., *Tr11* all hold in M, and hence M satisfies the first-order properties defined by these axioms, which include the first-order formulas *QT1*, ..., *QT11* of Fig. 4.

Similarly, one can show that all instances of the *Ind* axiom hold in M. Here, we use the fact that Relation Algebra is expressively complete for the three-variable fragment of first-order logic [17], and that, on models satisfying *QT1–QT11*, every first-order formulas in at most two free variables is equivalent to one containing at most three variables in total [13].[1]   ⊣

It follows by Theorem 1 that every first-order formula, and therefore also every Core XPath 2.0 expression, satisfied in M is satisfied in some finite tree.   □

---

[1] In [13] this three-variable property was proved with respect to the class of finite trees, but the proof generalizes to models satisfying *QT1–QT11*.

Axioms enforcing that each variable denotes a constant function:

Var1. $\top/\$i$ $\equiv$ $\$i$

Var2. $\$i/(\top \text{ except } .)$ $\equiv$ $\top \text{ except } \$i$

Axiom for node-equality tests:

Eq1. $R[S \text{ is } T]$ $\equiv$ $R[S \text{ intersect } T]$

Rule for eliminating variables in a derivation:

Name.   From $\$i/R \equiv \$i/S$ derive $R \equiv S$, provided $\$i$ does not occur in R and S

Axioms for `for`**:**

For1. $\$x/\text{for } \$y \text{ in } R \text{ return } S$ $\equiv$ $\$x/R/(\text{for } \$y \text{ in } . \text{ return } \$x/S)$

For2. $\$x/\text{for } \$y \text{ in } . \text{ return } S$ $\equiv$ $\$x/S^{\$y}_{\$x}$

    where $S^{\$y}_{\$x}$ is the result of replacing all free occurences of $\$y$ by $\$x$,
    provided that this is a safe substitution.

Fig. 7. Additional axioms for variables and `for`

3.2   Adding Variables

We will now extend our axiomatization to the full language of Core XPath 2.0, including variables and `for`-expressions. The extra axioms and rule of inference that we need are given in Fig. 7.

The *For2* axiom deserves special attention, as it involves variable substitution. As is customary for quantified logics such as first-order logic, we prohibit unsafe substitution. For example, replacing the free occurence of $\$j$ by $\$i$ in `for` $\$i$ `in` $\downarrow$ `return` $\$i/ \downarrow[\text{not}(. \text{ is } \$j)]$ constitutes an *unsafe* substitution, because it has the side-effect that the variable becomes bound by the `for`-quantifier.

The inference rule *Name* allows us, when trying to prove equivalence of two expressions, to assign a variable to the current node. This sometimes makes it easier to prove the equivalence.

Lemma 4 (A variant of the Name rule). *For all path expressions R and S, and for all variables $\$i$ not occuring in R and S, if $(\$i/R/\top \text{ union } (\top \text{ except } (\top/R/\top)) \subseteq^* S \text{ then } S \equiv^* \top$.*

Theorem 4 (Completeness). *For all equivalent expressions R, S, $R \equiv^* S$.*

Proof. The completeness proof proceeds as before, with two important differences: (i) the language now contains variables and for-clauses. However, most of this proof, we will treat these simply as atomic expressions (thus we treat expressions of the form `for` $\$i$ `in` R `return` S as atomic, ignoring their internal structure). (ii) we use a more refined MCS construction:

Claim. Every consistent expression can be extended to an MCS Γ satisfying the following additional condition: *for each expression R there is a variable $\$i$ such that if $(\top/R/\top) \in \Gamma$ then $(\$i/R/\top) \in \Gamma$.*

Proof of claim. Let S be the given consistent expression, and let $R_1, R_2, \ldots$ be an enumeration of all (countably many) expressions of the language. For each R_k ($k \in \mathbb{N}$) pick a variable $\$i_k$ distinct from $\$i_1, \ldots, \$i_{k-1}$ and not occurring in $R_1, \ldots, R_k$. It is not hard to see that this can be done. Let

$$\Sigma_\ell = \{S\} \cup \{(\$i_k/R_k/\top) \text{ union } (\top \text{ except } \top/R_k/\top) \mid k \leq \ell\}$$

and let $\Sigma = \bigcup_{\ell \in \mathbb{N}} \Sigma_\ell$. We claim that each Σ_ℓ is consistent, and hence also Σ is consistent. The proof is by induction on Σ_ℓ. For $\ell = 0$, $\Sigma_\ell = \{S\}$, which is consistent by assumption. Next, suppose, for the sake of contradiction, that Σ_ℓ is consistent but $\Sigma_{\ell+1}$ is not. Then it follows by Boolean reasoning that $((\$i_{\ell+1}/R_{\ell+1}/\top) \text{ union } (\top \text{ except } \top/R_{\ell+1}/\top)) \equiv^* (\top \text{ except } \bigcap \Sigma_\ell)$. By Lemma 4, this implies that $\bigcap \Sigma_\ell \equiv^* \bot$, a contradiction.

Finally, any MCS extending Σ will satisfy the required property.   ⊣

Next, we proceed as before: given a consistent expression R, we extend it to a maximal consistent set Γ, and construct a model M with elements d, e such that $(d, e) \in [\![\Gamma]\!]^M$. Recall that we treat variables and for-clauses as atomic expressions, interpreted by the model. Now, the axioms *Var1* and *Var2* ensure that each variable denotes a constant function. As we will see next, the axioms *For1* and *For2* also force *for-clauses* to have the correct denotation.

A special feature of Venema's [18] model construction is that every element d of the domain of M is uniquely identified by some expression R, in the sense that $[\![R]\!]^M = \{(d, d)\}$. It follows by the construction of the MCS that d is also uniquely identified by a variable $\$i$, in the sense that $rng([\![\$i]\!]) = \{d\}$. It follows by the axioms *For1* and *For2* that for-clauses are correctly interpreted in M.   □

3.3 Further Remarks on the Axiomatization

Minimality. Our axiomatization was not intended to be a minimal list of axioms. Rather than being concise, our aim was to formulate the axioms as naturally as possible. It is quite likely that some of the axioms can be derived from others.

Stronger forms of completeness. Properly speaking, many of our axioms should be called *axiom schemes*. For instance, *BA1* says that R union (S union T) is equivalent to $(R$ union $S)$ union T *for all path expressions R, S and T*. This leads to an interesting question: let $\mathcal{R}$ and $\mathcal{S}$ be two path expressions containing "path-variables" $R, S, \ldots$, such that $\mathcal{R}$ is equivalent to $\mathcal{S}$ *under all assignments of path expressions to these path-variables*. Then can we derive $\mathcal{R} \equiv \mathcal{S}$ as a scheme in our axiomatization? The answer is negative. In fact, no recursive axiomatization of Core XPath 2.0 can be complete in this strong sense, for the following reason.

Theorem 5. *Equivalence of Core XPath 2.0 path expressions containing a single path-variable is undecidable.*

Proof (sketch). It follows from results in [4,16] that the equivalence problem for expressions of Tarski's relation algebra in a single binary relation, over finite models is undecidable. In terms of XPath, this means that equivalence of

Core XPath 2.0 path expressions containing a variable standing for an arbitrary binary relation is undecidable. Since, within any given XML document, all binary relations are definable in Core XPath 2.0, this problem coincides with the equivalence problem for Core XPath 2.0 path expressions containing a variable standing for a Core XPath 2.0 path expression.   □

Sequence semantics versus set semantics. The soundness of some of our axioms (in particular, *RA2* and *Pred2–Pred4*) depends on the set-theoretic semantics we provided for Core XPath 2.0. If, as in the official XPath 2.0 semantics, expressions are taken to manipulate *sequences* rather than sets of nodes, these axioms no longer hold. However, our results are still meaningful in this setting.

First, observe that, if $\equiv$ is interpreted as *equivalence up to sorting and duplicate removal*, henceforth $\equiv_{sdr}$, then all axioms remain sound. Secondly, all equivalences *derivable* from the axioms remain sound, because $\equiv_{srd}$ is an equivalence relation, and it admits *replacement of equals by equals* (e.g., if $R \equiv_{sdr} R'$ and $S \equiv_{sdr} S'$ then for \$i in R return $S \equiv_{sdr}$ for \$i in R' return S'). Thus, all derivable equivalences hold, if equivalence is interpreted as equivalence up to sorting and duplicate removal. In fact, it is not hard to see that both axiomatizations (the one from Section 3.1 and the one from Section 3.2) are complete under this interpretation. In particular, for any path expression R, $R \equiv^* \bot$ iff R is unsatisfiable according to the sequence semantics.

4   Conclusions

We have defined the navigational core of XPath 2.0, analogously to Core XPath, and we gave an intuitive and rather simple axiomatization of the equivalence of relative path expressions by combining three sets of algebraic axioms: Tarski's axiom system RA of relation algebras, a first order axiomatization of the theory of finite ordered trees, and an axiomatization of the variable binder.

We have provided axiomatizations for the complete Core XPath 2.0 language and its equally expressive fragment without the for-loop and variables. By the linear embedding of first order logic, Core XPath 2.0 inherits its non-elementary space lower bound for query equivalence [14]. Still, we hope that our axiomatizations will be useful for query optimization. The connection with Tarski's relation algebras might be fruitfully exploited by using results from the relation algebra theorem proving community [2].

Of particular practical importance seems to be the elimination of the for-loop and the use of variables. Empirical tests have shown us that rewritings into the for-free fragment can lead to speedups of up to 3 orders of magnitude with commercial XQuery processors. We obtained these results with the following two queries:

(1) descendant :: * [P] except (descendant :: * [not Q]/descendant :: *)
(2) for \$start in . return descendant :: * [P and (#)],
    with (#) the test expression
        every \$i in ancestor :: * [ancestor :: * [. is \$start]] satisfies \$i[Q].

where P and Q are filter expressions of the form @attribute='value'. Both express the relation (child :: * [Q])*/child :: * [P], with (·)* the transitive closure operation. By completeness, our axiom system can derive their equivalence. An important issue is whether such query rewritings can be performed efficiently.

References

1. S. Abiteboul, R. Hull, and V. Vianu. *Foundations of databases*. Addison-Wesley, 1995.
2. R. Berghammer, G. Schmidt, and M. Winter. RelView and Rath - two systems for dealing with relations. In *Theory and Applications of Relational Structures as Knowledge Instruments*, pages 1–16. LNCS, Nr.2929, 2003.
3. M. Bojanczyk, A. Muscholl, Th. Schwentick, L. Segoufin, , and C. David. Two-variable logic on words with data. In *Proceedings LICS'06*, pages 7–16, 2006.
4. E. Börger, E. Grädel, and Y. Gurevich. *The Classical Decision Problem*. Springer Verlag, 1997.
5. A. Dawar. How many first-order variables are needed on finite ordered structures? In S. Artemov et al., editor, *We will show them: Essays in Honour of Dov Gabbay*, pages 489–520. College Publications, 2005.
6. H.C. Doets. *Completeness and Definability: Applications of the Ehrenfeucht Game in Intensional and Second-Order Logic*. PhD thesis, Department of Mathematics and Computer Science, University of Amsterdam, 1987.
7. F. Geerts and W. Fan. Satisfiability of XPath queries with sibling axes. In *Proceedings DBPL '05*, pages 122–137, 2005.
8. G. Gottlob, C. Koch, and R. Pichler. Efficient algorithms for processing XPath queries. In *VLDB'02*, pages 95–106, 2002.
9. M. Gyssens, J. Paredaens, D. Van Gucht, and G. Fletcher. Structural characterizations of the semantics of XPath as navigation tool on a document. In *Proceedings PODS'06*, pages 318–327, 2006.
10. L. Henkin, J. D. Monk, and A. Tarski. *Cylindric Algebras, Part II*. North-Holland, 1985.
11. J. Hidders. Satisfiability of XPath expressions. In *Proceedings DBPL*, number 2921 in LNCS, pages 21–36, 2003.
12. M. Kay. *XPath 2.0 Programmer's Reference*. Wrox, 2004.
13. M. Marx. Conditional XPath. *ACM Transactions on Database Systems (TODS)*, 30(4):929–959, December 2005.
14. K. Reinhardt. The complexity of translating logic to finite automata. In E. Grädel et al., editor, *Automata, Logics, and Infinite Games*, volume 2500 of *LNCS*, pages 231–238. Springer, 2002.
15. J. Rogers. *A Descriptive Approach to Language Theoretic Complexity*. CSLI Press, 1998.
16. A. Tarski. On the calculus of relations. *Journal of Symbolic Logic*, 6:73–89, 1941.
17. A. Tarski and S. Givant. *A Formalization of Set Theory without Variables*, volume 41. AMS Colloquium publications, Providence, Rhode Island, 1987.
18. Y. Venema. *Many–Dimensional Modal Logic*. PhD thesis, Institute for Logic, Language and Computation, University of Amsterdam, 1992.

Query Evaluation on a Database Given by a Random Graph

Nilesh Dalvi

University of Washington, Seattle

Abstract. We consider random graphs, and their extensions to random structures, with edge probabilities of the form $\beta n^{-\alpha}$, where n is the number of vertices, α, β are fixed and $\alpha > 1$ ($\alpha > $ arity $- 1$ for structures of higher arity). We consider conjunctive properties over these random graphs, and investigate the problem of computing their asymptotic conditional probabilities. This provides us a novel approach to dealing with uncertainty in databases, with applications to data privacy and other database problems.

1 Introduction

Let $\mathcal{R} = \{R_1, R_2, \ldots, R_m\}$ be a vocabulary of relation symbols, and $A(R_i)$ denote the arity of relation R_i. We fix two functions $\alpha, \beta : \mathcal{R} \to \mathbb{R}^+$ that map relations to positive real numbers, where α satisfies $\alpha(R_i) > A(R_i)-1$ for all $R_i \in \mathcal{R}$. For any $n > 0$, denote μ_n the probability distribution over the structures with domain $[n]$ given by the following experiment: for each $R_i \in \mathcal{R}$ and $t \in [n]^{A(R_i)}$, choose t to be in R_i with probability $\beta(R_i)n^{-\alpha(R_i)}$. Let $CQ(c, \neq)$ denote the class of boolean conjunctive properties (queries) with constants (c) and inequalities $(\neq)$, i.e. formulas of the form: $\exists x_1 \exists x_2 ... (A_1 \wedge A_2 \wedge \cdots \wedge A_k)$ where each A_i is a predicate of the form $R_i(y_1, \cdots, y_j)$, or $y_1 \neq y_2$, where $y_1, \ldots, y_j$ denote variables or constants. $CQ(c)$, $CQ(\neq)$, and CQ denote the classes of conjunctive queries without $\neq$, without constants, and without either $\neq$ or constants respectively.

In this paper, we study the probabilities of conjunctive properties over the class μ_n of random structures. Lynch [17] has shown that if we consider the set of first order properties, of which conjunctive properties are a subset, then for each property q, $\mu_n(q)$ is either $cn^{-d} + o(n^{-d})$ for some $c > 0, d \geq 0$, or is $e^{-\Omega(n^k)}$ for some $k > 0$. Thus, the probability of every first order property is either asymptotically equal to a polynomial in $1/n$ or is exponentially small. Further, the problem of determining which of the two cases hold for a given query is undecidable.

Here we show that when q is a conjunctive query, then we always have $\mu_n(q) = cn^{-d} + o(n^{-d})$. A consequence is that for any two conjunctive queries q, v, the quantity $\mu(q \mid v) = \lim_{n \to \infty} \mu_n(q \mid v) = \lim_n \mu_n(q \wedge v)/\mu_n(v)$ exists and is a real number in $[0, 1]$. In this paper we investigate the complexity of computing this limit, in various settings, and the main result is below.

T. Schwentick and D. Suciu (Eds.): ICDT 2007, LNCS 4353, pp. 149–163, 2007.
© Springer-Verlag Berlin Heidelberg 2007

Problem	Combined Complexity (inputs: q, v, v')	Data Complexity (inputs: v, v'; fixed: q)
Compute $\mu(q \mid v)$	#coNP-complete	#coNP-complete
Decide if $\mu(q \mid v) = 0$	Θ_2^p-complete	Θ_2^p-complete
Decide if $\mu(q \mid v) \in (0,1)$	Σ_2^p-complete	Θ_2^p-complete
Decide if $\mu(q \mid v) = 1$	Π_2^p-complete	Θ_2^p-complete
Decide if $\mu(q \mid v) < p$ for $p \in (0,1)$	P.coNP-complete	P.coNP-complete
Decide $\mu(q \mid v) < \mu(q \mid v')$	P.coNP-complete	P.coNP-complete
Decide $\mu(q \mid v) < \mu(q \mid vv')$	P.coNP-complete.	P.coNP-complete

Fig. 1. Summary of Main Results

Theorem 1. *Fig. 1 shows the complexities of various decision problems and computation problems concerning their asymptotic conditional probabilities. Upper bounds hold for $q, v, v' \in CQ(c, \neq)$; lower bounds hold for both $q, v, v' \in CQ(c)$ and for $q, v, v' \in CQ(\neq)$. For $q, v, v' \in CQ$ all problems are in PTIME.*

1.1   Motivation

Our motivation comes from the following problem in databases: evaluate a property q of an unknown database instance I given some facts v about the instance. The problem appears in a wide range of applications, for instance in *data privacy* [8] where we want to analyze a sensitive query using published facts, in *data integration* [12,15] where we want to answer queries using views and in *cardinality estimation* [10,2] where we want to estimate the size of a query using known statistics about the data. In many applications, the standard approach is to use the notion of *certain answers* [12], where the property q is said to be *certain* if it is true on every possible instance I that is consistent with the facts v. However, this approach has two limitations that make it unsuitable for certain applications. First, it does not revel anything about tuples that are not certain answers to the query, whereas in applications like data privacy, we are interested in knowing which tuples are more (or less) likely to be the query answers given the facts in v. The second limitation of the approach is that it cannot incorporate any knowledge about the relative likelihood of possible instances. Applications often have auxiliary information, like statistical knowledge, that makes certain instances more likely than others. In data privacy setting, it is important to take the auxiliary information into account; in cardinality estimation this is often the only kind of information available.

Example 1. (K-Anonymity) Suppose a medical agency wants to publish its data patients data for research purposes, but wants to protect the identity of individual patients. The data is in the table `Patients(name, age, zipcode, disease)`. The agency publishes the following view:

Diseases(age, zipcode, disease) :− Patients(name, age, zipcode, disease)

In addition, suppose the following view is publically known:

Name(name, age, zipcode) :− Patients(name, age, zipcode, disease)

The contents of the views are given below. Note that some of the values in the view are partially hidden.

Names =

name	age	zipcode
JOHN	25	98190
MARY	25	98192
MARK	31	98100
FRANK	31	98111
LARRY	32	98100

Diseases =

age	zipcode	disease
25	9819*	FLU
25	9819*	FEVER
31	981**	FLU
**	*****	CANCER

We want to analyze the information given by $v = \{Diseases, Names\}$ about the following query $q(name, disease)$:− Patients(name, age, zipcode, disease). The Diseases table is *2-anonymous* [19], meaning that for every tuple in the Diseases table, there are at least two individuals that may have that record. For instance, the tuple *(25, 98192, FLU)* could either refer to *JOHN* or *MARY* or a third person that does not appear in the views. There are no certain answers to the query.

The technique of k-anonymization guarantees that each record in the published data refers to at least k individuals. However, Machanavajjhala et al. [19] have shown that k-anonymization does not guarantee data privacy when the attacker has auxiliary/background knowledge about the data, and they raise the problem of analyzing data privacy in the presence of such information. Examples of background information are: (i) every (age, zipcode) occurs four times in expectation and (ii) around 80% of all the patients have *FLU*. We need a framework where we can use such statistics on the data and evaluate the likelihood that a particular tuple is the answer to the query given the views.

Bayesian Approach. In order to provide such a framework, we consider an alternative approach to the problem using a technique from knowledge representation based on *degrees of beliefs* [3]. Here the uncertainty about the underlying database is expressed as a probability distribution $\mathbf{P}$, called the *prior probability distribution*, or simply the *prior*, which is an assessment of the likelihood of each data instance to occur before observing any facts about the database. Starting from this prior distribution, any subsequent knowledge v about the database is encapsulated by conditioning $\mathbf{P}$ on v. Thus, the probability that the database satisfies a property q is given by the conditional probability $\mathbf{P}(q \mid v)$. Query evaluation thus amounts to computing the conditional probabilities on the prior.

Example 2. Let us revisit Example 1 where we have the relation Patients(name, age, zipcode, disease), where each attribute takes value from a domain[1] of size n. Suppose that the only background knowledge we have is that the expected

---

[1] Assume for simplicity that all attributes take values from the same domain.

size of the table is 100. Consider the following probability distribution: there are n^4 tuples that are possible over the domain, pick each of them randomly and independently with probability $100/n^4$. The resulting distribution is a sparse random structure with each tuple having probability $p(n) = 100/n^4$. Further, it is easy to see that the expected size of Patients under this distribution is 100.

Now suppose we want to check if $q \equiv$ Patients($JOHN, 25, 98190, CANCER$) is true given the views $v = \{$Names, Patients$\}$. We compute the probability that q is true given v, i.e. the quantity $\mathbf{P}(q \mid v)$. It can be shown that $\mathbf{P}(q \mid v) = 1/101 + O(1/n)$. Intuitively, there are 100 records expected in the database, so there is around $1/100$ chance that the facts Names($JOHN, 25, 98190$) and Diseases($**, *****, CANCER$) talk about the same tuple.

Using a Sparse Random Graph as a Prior. Choosing a suitable prior distribution is an important step in this analysis, and the problem is well studied in the area of Knowledge Representation [3]. In our previous work [6], we look at this problem from a database perspective. We consider a framework for specifying prior knowledge about the database that allows statistics like the expected size of a relation, the expected number of distinct values of an attribute and integrity constraints like functional dependencies and inclusion dependencies. Under this framework, we describe how to represent such prior knowledge as a probability distribution using a technique from Knowledge Representation called *entropy maximization*. Applying this technique to Example 2, with the statistics that the expected size of Patients relation is 100, we get exactly the probability distribution where each tuple is chosen independently with probability $100/n^4$, which is a sparse random structure.

Other Prior Distributions. The probability distribution in Example 2 belongs to a special class of sparse random structures where $p_{R_i}(n) = c_i n^{-Arity(R_i)}$ for each R_i. We studies these distributions in one of our previous works [5]. One of the properties of these distributions is that with high probability, all the tuples in the structure are disjoint. For instance, in Example 2, all the zipcode values in the Patients tables are distinct with high probability. If we want to incorporate the knowledge that each zipcode is expected to have 10 records, we can add this statistics in our framework to obtain a new prior distribution. In this new distribution, the tuples are not independent since each zipcode value occurs 10 times in expectation, hence the new distribution will not be a random structure. In [6], we show that statistics like these can be captured using a generalization of random structures. For lack of space, we only describe results in this paper for random structures, but the results also extend to these generalized random structures described in [6].

Domain Size. Given a sparse random structure with probability distribution μ_n, and conjunctive properties q and v, we seek the conditional probability $\mu_n(q \mid v)$. In general, we do not know the domain size, n. But the domain is usually large. Hence, we study the behavior of conditional probability for large n by looking at the limit $\lim_{n \to \infty} \mu_n(q \mid v)$, which we denote $\mu(q \mid v)$. Below, we describe some specific problems related to the computation of $\mu(q \mid v)$ motivated by the data privacy application.

Data Privacy. Here, the owner of a database wishes to publish certain facts about a private database, while keeping certain sensitive information hidden. There are two basic problems. The first is *leakage*: does the view v leak information about a sensitive property s ? Various authors [8,20,14] have modeled non-leakage by requiring the *a priori* probability of s to be close to the *a posteriori* probability after seeing v, i.e. $\mathbf{P}(s) \approx \mathbf{P}(s \mid v)$. We make this precise by requiring $\mu(s \mid v) = \mu(s)$, which amounts to $\mu(s \mid v) = 0$ since, as we show, $\mu(s) = 0$ for all practical queries. The second problem is *usage*: a legitimate user wants to check a property q over the data, by examining v, and this amounts to checking $\mu(q \mid v) = 1$. In addition to these basic questions, we consider two more complex questions motivated by real application scenarios. In *collusion detection* we know that $\mu(s \mid v) = \mu(s \mid v') = 0$ and have to decide if $\mu(s \mid v, v') = 0$. In *relative security* the data owner has already published some view v, possibly leaking some information about the secret s: the damage cannot be undone, but the data owner wants to publish a second view v' and wants to know if there any additional leakage, i.e. $\mu(s \mid v, v') > \mu(s \mid v)$?

Query Evaluation. Vardi [23] has studied the query evaluation problem in databases: given I, q, decide if $I \models q$. In the *combined complexity* both I and q vary, while in the *data complexity*, q is fixed and I varies. The problem we investigate in this paper is related to query evaluation: evaluate q on the observations v, i.e. compute $\mu(q \mid v)$. The database is given by v, with the unknown part filled in by the random graph. Data complexity corresponds here to a fixed q and a variable v.

1.2   Related Work

The study of convergence laws for logical statements on random graphs has been a widely explored areas of model theory. Fagin [9] and Glebskiĭ et al. [11] considered random graphs with $p(n)$ a constant and proved a 0-1 law for statements of first order logic. However, asymptotic limits for *conditional* probabilities do not always exist [9] for this class of graphs, and even the problem of determining if they exist is undecidable [16]. The class of random graphs with edge probabilities of the form $\beta n^{-\alpha}$ with $\alpha > 1$ have also been studied before and there are results on the existence of asymptotic probabilities for statements of first order logic [21,17,18]. However, existence of asymptotic conditional probabilities, and the complexity of computing them, has not been studies previously. The applications of sparse random graphs and their generalizations [5,6] have been discussed before, but again these works did not study the complexity of query evaluation.

2   Computing Asymptotic Probabilities

For a conjunctive query q given by Eq.(1) let $goals(q)$ denote the set of its relational predicates (i.e. of the form $R_i(y_1, \cdots, y_j)$, and called "subgoals"),

$Var(q) = \{x_1, x_2, \ldots\}$ the set of variables, $Const(q)$ the set of constants mentioned in q. Here we show that the asymptotic conditional probabilities always exist for conjunctive queries and are computable. The basic result is:

Theorem 2. *For any conjunctive query* $q \in CQ(c, \neq)$*, there exists two constants* $\mathrm{coeff}(q)$ *and* $\exp(q)$*, such that*

$$\mu_n(q) = \mathrm{coeff}(q)(1/n)^{\exp(q)} + o((1/n)^{\exp(q)})$$

Corollary 1. *For* $q \in CQ(c, \neq)$*, the asymptotic probability* $\mu(q)$ *always exists. It equals* $\mathrm{coeff}(q)$ *if* $\exp(q) = 0$ *and 0 otherwise.*

Corollary 2. *For* $q_1, q_2 \in CQ(c, \neq)$*, the conditional asymptotic probability,* $\mu(q_1 \mid q_2)$*, always exists and is as follows:*

$$\mu(q_1 \mid q_2) = \begin{cases} 0 & \exp(q_1 q_2) > \exp(q_2) \\ \frac{\mathrm{coeff}(q_1 q_2)}{\mathrm{coeff}(q_2)} & \exp(q_1 q_2) = \exp(q_2) \end{cases}$$

In the remainder of the section, we show how to compute $coeff(q)$ and $exp(q)$. For a subgoal $g \in goals(q)$, let $\alpha(g)$ and $\beta(g)$ denote $\alpha(R)$ and $\beta(R)$ where R is the relation to which g refers. Define

$$V(q) = \text{the number of distinct variables in } q$$
$$\alpha(q) = \sum\{\alpha(g) \mid g \in goals(q)\}$$
$$\beta(q) = \prod\{\beta(g) \mid g \in goals(q)\}$$
$$D(q) = \alpha(q) - V(q)$$

A *substitution* η for a query q is a mapping $\eta : Var(q) \to Var(q) \cup Const(q)$ that does not violate the inequalities in q. We denote $\eta(q)$ the result of applying η to the subgoals of q. For example, if $q \leftarrow R(a, x), R(x, y), R(y, z), x \neq y$ then the substitution $\eta = \{x \to b, y \to y, z \to y\}$ is defined on q and by applying it we obtain the query $q_0 = \eta(q)$, $q_0 \leftarrow R(a, b), R(b, y), R(y, y), b \neq y$. If $\eta(q)$ results in duplicate subgoals, we remove duplicates[2]. We call a query of the form $\eta(q)$ a *unifying query* for q, since it unifies some of the subgoals in q, and denote with $UQ(q)$ the set of all unifying queries for q up to isomorphism. Let P be the partition on $goals(q)$ induced by η, where two subgoals g, g' are in the same equivalence class if $\eta(g) = \eta(g')$. Call η a *most general unifier* if, for any other unifier η' inducing P there exists a substitution θ s.t. $\eta' = \theta \circ \eta$. In this case we call $\eta(q)$ a *most general unifying query* of q, and we define $\mathrm{MGUQ}(q)$ the set of most general unifying queries of q (up to isomorphism). Define:

$$E(q) = \min\{D(q_0) \mid q_0 \in \mathrm{MGUQ}(q)\}$$
$$\mathrm{MGUQ}^0(q) = \{q_0 \mid q_0 \in \mathrm{MGUQ}(q), D(q_0) = E(q)\}$$
$$aut(q) = |\{\eta \mid \eta(q) \text{ is isomorphic to } q\}|$$

---

[2] While this sounds evident, we insist on it because the functions $D(-)$ and $\beta(-)$ return different (and wrong) results if we fail to eliminate duplicates.

We view a subset $q_1 \subseteq goals(q)$ as another conjunctive query, $q_1 = \exists x_1 \exists x_2 \ldots$ $(\bigwedge_{g \in q_1} g)$. Construct a graph whose nodes are $goals(q)$ and edges are pairs of sub-goals that share a variable, and consider all queries $q_1, q_2, \ldots$ given by its connected components. We write $q_i \simeq q_j$ to denote that the queries q_i and q_j are isomorphic, and let k be the number of distinct isomorphism types among queries q_i with $D(q_i) = 0$. Define the following partition on $goals(q)$ into $k + 2$ classes:

- $q_N = \bigcup \{q_i \mid D(q_i) < 0\}$.
- $q_P = \bigcup \{q_i \mid D(q_i) > 0\}$.
- $r_1^{t_1}, \cdots, r_k^{t_k}$, where $D(r_i) = 0$, $r_i^{t_i} = \bigcup \{q_j \mid q_j \simeq r_i\}$, $t_i = \mid \{q_j \mid q_j \simeq r_i\} \mid$.

We call q_P the *kernel* of q and we call $r_1^{t_1}, \cdots, r_k^{t_k}$ the *zero subgoals* or q.

Let $\Gamma(x, m) = \sum_{j=1}^{m} x^j e^{-m}/j$ be the Poisson distribution function. Given a query q_s of the form $r_1^{t_1}, \cdots, r_k^{t_k}$, define

$$f(q_S) = \prod_{i=1}^{k} (1 - \Gamma(\frac{\beta(r_i)}{aut(r_i)}, t_i))$$

If q_S is empty, then $f(q_S) = 1$. Given a set Q_s, where each element is a query of the form q_S, define

$$F(Q_s) = \sum_{S \subseteq Q_s} (-1)^{|S|} f(\wedge_{q_s \in S} f(q_s)$$

Now we are ready to describe the *coeff*(q). Group the queries in $\mathrm{MGUQ}^0(q)$ so that all queries that have the same kernel are in one group. Define a pair (q_P, Q_s) for each group where q_P is the kernel, and Q_s is the set consisting of sets of zero sub-goals of all queries in the group. Let $G(q)$ be the set of such pairs and let

$$C(q) = \sum_{(q_P, Q_s) \in G(q)} \frac{\beta(q_P)}{aut(q_P)} F(Q_s)$$

Theorem 3. *For any* $q \in CQ(c, \neq)$, $exp(q) = max(E(q), 0)$ *and* coeff$(q) = C(q)$.

Example 3. For a simple illustration, consider the following query q. Assume $\alpha(R) = 4$.

$$\exists x \exists y \exists z \exists u \exists v. R(a, x, y, c), R(z, z, u, c) R(v, a, b, c), y \neq b$$

Here a, b, c are constants. Define:

$$q_1 \equiv \exists y \exists v. R(a, a, y, c), R(v, a, b, c), y \neq b$$
$$q_2 \equiv \exists x \exists y. R(a, x, y, c), R(a, a, b, c), y \neq b$$

Then $\mathrm{MGUQ} = \{q, q_1, q_2\}$, $D(q) = 7$, $D(q_1) = D(q_2) = 6$, hence $exp(q) = 6$, $\mathrm{MGUQ}^0 = \{q_1, q_2\}$, $G(q) = \{(q_1, \emptyset), (q_2, \emptyset)\}$, $aut(q_1) = aut(q_2) = 1$ and $\beta(q) = 2\beta^2(R)$. Thus: $\mu_n(q) = 2\beta^2(R)/n^6 + o(1/n^6)$

3 Complexity Results

We state, explain, and expand here our complexity results that were briefly mentioned in Th. 1.

3.1 Computing *coeff* and *exp*

A direct application of the definitions for $exp(q)$ and $coeff(q)$ leads to an exponential time algorithm. The following gives a tight bound on their complexity:

Theorem 4. $\forall \mathcal{C} \in \{CQ(c), CQ(\neq), CQ(c, \neq)\}$

1. *The problem: given* $q \in \mathcal{C}$ *and a number* k, *decide if* $\exp(q) < k$, *is* NP-*complete.*
2. *The problem: given* $q \in \mathcal{C}$ *compute* $coeff(q)$, *is* #coNP-*complete.*

The complexity class #coNP [13] is the class of counting problems of the following form

$$f(A) = \#x \; \forall y \; R(x, y, A)$$

where R is some polynomial function. Thus, #coNP counts the number of x that satisfies a certain property where checking the property itself requires an coNP machine.

For pure conjunctive queries, we have:

Theorem 5. *Given a query* $q \in CQ$ *over some fixed schema, both* $\exp(q)$ *and* $coeff(q)$ *can be computed in* PTIME.

For $q \in CQ$ one can compute $exp(q)$ in PTIME because here it is always possible to unify completely all subgoals referring to the same relation name, and this unifier has the minimal D. (However, to compute $coeff(q)$ one needs to consider additional unifiers, but it can still be done in polynomial time for a fixed schema). It follows that for conjunctive queries q, v, $\mu(q \mid v)$ can be computed in PTIME and all the problems we described in Sec 1 have PTIME complexity.

Pure conjunctive queries are not very interesting because in practice there is not much we can express without constants. For example, in k-anonymity we need constants to refer to the constants being published and need $\neq$ to state that two published rows correspond to distinct rows in the data. We consider only $CQ(c)$, $CQ(\neq)$, and $CQ(c, \neq)$ in the rest of the paper.

3.2 Conditional Probabilities

We now consider the two decision problems for conditional probabilities that we formulated in Sec 1: deciding $\mu(q \mid v) = 0$ and deciding $\mu(q \mid v) = 1$.

In the following discussion, $\mathcal{C}$ denotes any of $CQ(c), CQ(\neq), CQ(c, \neq)$: all results hold for any of these three classes. Let $S \subseteq [0, 1]$. We define the Asymptotic Conditional Probability problem for S to be:

$$\text{ACP}^S = \{(q, v) \mid q, v \in \mathcal{C}, \mu(q \mid v) \in S\}$$

We only consider the cases when $S = \{0\}$, $(0, 1)$ or $\{1\}$.

Theorem 6. $\mathrm{ACP}^{\{0\}}$ *is* Θ_2^p-*complete.* $\mathrm{ACP}^{(0,1)}$ *is* Σ_2^p-*complete.* $\mathrm{ACP}^{\{1\}}$ *is* Π_2^p-*complete.*

The complexity class Θ_2^p [24], also referred to as $\mathsf{P}^{\mathsf{NP}[O(\log n)]}$, is the class of languages that can be decided by a polynomial time oracle Turing-machine that makes $O(\log n)$ calls to an NP oracle. Thus, $\Theta_2^p \subseteq P^{\mathsf{NP}} = \Delta_2^p \subseteq \Pi_2^p, \Sigma_2^p$.

The $\mathrm{ACP}^{\{1\}}$ property is related to query containment, a well studied problem in finite model theory. For boolean queries containment becomes logical implication, and $v \Rightarrow q$ iff $\forall n.\mu_n(q \mid v) = 1$, while $\mathrm{ACP}^{\{1\}}$ means $\lim_n \mu_n(q \mid v) = 1$. The complexity of query containment for CQ is NP-complete[4]. Similarly ACP^0 is related to non-containment, which, by complementation, is coNP-complete.

Data complexity. We study two notions of data complexity. In the first setting, we fix the query and study the complexity as a function of the size of the view. For a query q and set $S \subseteq [0, 1]$ we define the following problem:

$$\mathrm{ACP}_q^S = \{v \mid \mu(q \mid v) \in S\}$$

Theorem 7. *Let q be any query in $CQ(c, \neq)$ and S be any of $\{0\}$, $(0, 1)$ and $\{1\}$. Then, ACP_q^S is in Θ_2^p. Further, there exists a query $q \in CQ(c, \neq)$ such that ACP_q^S is Θ_2^p-complete.*

In the second setting, we fix the query as well as a non-boolean view definition and study complexity as a function of the size of the view instance. A non-boolean conjunctive query V is a formula Eq.(1) possibly with free variables. For example the following query V has free variables $\{x, y\}$:

$$\exists z R(x, a, z), S(z, y) \tag{1}$$

Let $\bar{V} = V_1, \ldots, V_m$ be a set of non-boolean views and let $\bar{J} = J_1, \ldots, J_m$ be sets of tuples, with J_i having the same arity as the arity of V_i. Denote $v_i \equiv V_i/J_i$ the boolean conjunctive query stating that all tuples in J_i must be in the result of V_i. For example, if V is given by Eq 1, and $J = \{(a, b), (c, b)\}$, then $V/J \equiv \exists z_1 \exists z_2 R(a, a, z_1), S(z_1, b), R(c, a, z_2), S(z_2, b)$.

For a query q, view definitions $\bar{V}$, and set $S \subseteq [0, 1]$ we define the following problem:

$$\mathrm{ACP}_{q,\bar{V}}^S = \{J \mid \mu(q \mid \bar{V}/\bar{J}) \in S\}$$

Theorem 8. *For any $q, \bar{V} \in CQ(c, \neq)$ and $S \in \{\{0\}, (0, 1), \{1\}\}$, the problem $\mathrm{ACP}_{q,\bar{V}}^S$ is in Θ_2^p. Further, there exists $q, \bar{V} \in CQ(c, \neq)$ such that $\mathrm{ACP}_{q,\bar{V}}^S$ is Θ_2^p-complete.*

Here, too, the problem $\mathrm{ACP}_{q,\bar{V}}^{\{1\}}$ is related to another well studied problem in the literature: the query answering using views problem, under the open world assumption [12]. Indeed, the latter is $\forall n.\mu_n(q \mid \bar{V}/\bar{J}) = 1$, since this means that q is true on all instances I consistent with the observations J, i.e. q is "certain". This problem is known to be in PTIME [1], even for $CQ(c, \neq)$. (One can also check it immediately, since it can be restated as the containment problem $\bar{V}/\bar{J} \subseteq q$, where q is a fixed query.)

$\mu(q \mid v_1)$	$\mu(q \mid v_2)$	$\mu(q \mid v_1v_2)$	v_1	v_2	q
0	0	0	$R(a_1, -)$	$R(a_2, -)$	$R(-, b)$
0	0	(0,1)	$R(a, -)$	$R(-, b)$	$R(a, b)$
0	0	1	$R(a, b, -)$	$R(-, b, c)$	$R(a, b, c)$
0	(0,1)	0	$R(a, b, d)$	$R(a, b, -), R(-, -, c)$	$R(a, -, c)$
0	(0,1)	(0,1)	$R(a, -)$	$R(a, -), R(-, b)$	$R(a, b)$
0	(0,1)	1	$R(a, b, -)$	$R(a, -, -), R(-, b, c)$	$R(a, b, c)$
0	1	0	$R(a, b, d)$	$R(a, b, -), R(-, b, c)$	$R(a, b, c)$
0	1	(0,1)	$R(-, b, d)$	$R(a, b, -), R(-, b, c)$	$R(a, b, c)$
0	1	1	$R(-, b, c)$	$R(a, b, -), R(-, b, c)$	$R(a, b, c)$
(0,1)	(0,1)	0	$R(a, b, -), R(-, -, c), R(a, e, d)$	$R(a, e, -), R(-, -, c), R(a, b, d)$	$R(a, -, c)$
(0,1)	(0,1)	(0,1)	$R(a, -), R(-, b)$	$R(a, -), R(-, b)$	$R(a, b)$
(0,1)	(0,1)	1	$R(a, b, -), R(-, -, c)$	$R(a, -, -), R(-, b, c)$	$R(a, b, c)$
(0,1)	1	0	$R(a, b, -), R(-, -, c), R(a, e, d)$	$R(a, e, -), R(-, e, c), R(a, b, d)$	$R(a, -, c)$
(0,1)	1	(0,1)	$R(a, e, -, -), R(-, -, c, f), R(a, b, g, -)$	$R(a, b, -, -), R(-, b, c, h)$	$R(a, -, c, -)$
(0,1)	1	1	$R(a, b, -), R(-, -, c)$	$R(a, -, c), R(-, b, c)$	$R(a, b, c)$
1	1	0	$R(a, b, -), R(-, b, c), R(a, e, d)$	$R(a, e, -), R(-, e, c), R(a, b, d)$	$R(a, -, c)$
1	1	(0,1)	$R(a, b, -), R(-, b, c), R(-, e, d)$	$R(a, e, -), R(-, e, c), R(-, b, d)$	$R(a, -, c)$
1	1	1	$R(a, b, -), R(-, b, c)$	$R(a, -, c), R(a, b, -)$	$R(a, b, c)$

Fig. 2. Each of the 27 classes $\mathrm{ACP}^S_{S_1, S_2}$ is nonempty, assuming $\alpha(R) = A(R)$

3.3   Complex Problems

Collusions. For $S, S_1, S_2 \in \{0, (0, 1), 1\}$, denote $\mathrm{ACP}^S_{S_1, S_2}$ the problem of deciding, for queries (q, v_1, v_2), whether $(q, v_1 v_2) \in \mathrm{ACP}^S$ given that $(q, v_1) \in \mathrm{ACP}^{S_1}$ and $(q, v_2) \in \mathrm{ACP}^{S_2}$.

Theorem 9. *The complexity of $\mathrm{ACP}^S_{S_1, S_2}$ is same as that of ACP^S.*

The theorem essentially contains 27 statements, for all combinations of S_1, S_2, S. A priori, it is not even clear why all the 27 classes $\mathrm{ACP}^S_{S_1, S_2}$ are nonempty. To see that, Fig. 2 shows for each class $\mathrm{ACP}^S_{S_1, S_2}$ an example of v_1, v_2 and q in that class. For queries, we use the shorthand notation where each "-" stands for a unique existentially quantified variable. There are less than 27 entries due to the symmetry between S_1 and S_2.

Fig. 2 reveals an interesting and counter-intuitive phenomenon, which we refer to as the *non-monotonicity of information disclosure*: publishing more information results in less information disclosure. For example, the entry corresponding to 1, 1, 0 shows that with v_1, v_2, q as given in the figure, we have $\mu(q \mid v_1) = \mu(q \mid v_2) = 1$ but $\mu(q \mid v_1 v_2) = 0$. Here the query q is very likely true given either v_1 or v_2 alone but is very likely false given both v_1 and v_2.

Relative Security. Finally, we explain the last three entries in Fig. 1 The complexity class P.coNP, also called probabilistic coNP, is the set of languages L for which there is a coNP Turing machine M that uses random bits such that for all strings x: (1) $x \in L \Rightarrow Pr(M \text{ accepts } x) > 1/2$, and (2) $x \notin L \Rightarrow Pr(M \text{ accepts } x) \leq 1/2$.

4   Proofs of Main Results

We include here some proofs and defer the rest to our technical report [7].

Recall the definition of *zero sub-goals* and expression for $exp(q)$ and $coeff(q)$ from Sec. 2. In all the proofs in this section, we consider only those queries that do not have any zero sub-goals and that they do not have any non-trivial automorphisms, i.e $aut(q) = 1$. We call such queries *simple conjunctive queries*. It is tedious but straightforward to incorporate zero-subgoals and automorphisms in these results, and we omit their discussion here.

For simple conjunctive queries, the expression for *exp* and *coeff* can be simplified to $exp(q) = \min_\eta D(\eta(q))$ and $coeff(q) = \sum_{\eta|D(\eta(q))=exp(q)} \beta(\eta(q))$.

Proposition 1. *Given a conjunctive query q, the complexity of evaluating* coeff(q) *is #coNP-complete.*

Proof. *coeff*(q) is simply the size of the set

$$\{(\eta, k) \mid \forall \eta_0 D(\eta(q)) \leq D(\eta_0(q)) \wedge k < \beta(\eta(q))\}$$

Thus, computing *coeff*(q) is in #coNP.

To prove the #coNP-hardness, we will give a reduction from #NSAT. In #NSAT, we are given a *3-CNF* formula ϕ where the set of variables can be partitioned into two sets X and Y, and we need to count the number of assignments of X that can be extended to an assignment of ϕ. #NSAT is known [22] to be #coNP-hard.

Given any *3-CNF* formula ϕ over variables X and Y, we construct two queries q_1 and q_2. Let ϕ have c clauses and let $|X| = k$. The vocabulary consists of a relation R of arity 4 and a relation S of arity 3 with $\beta(R) = \beta(S) = B$, where B is some integer greater than 2^k. We create a unique constant k_x for each variable x a unique constant k_C for each clause C in ϕ, and two extra constants t and f. The query q consists of $q_1 q_2$ where q_1 and q_2 are two queries as described below.

q_1 is constructed as follows. For each clause $C(x, y, z)$ in ϕ, q_1 contains 7 subgoals of the form $R(k_C, v_i, v_j, v_k)$, where v_i, v_j and v_k are such that $C(v_i, v_j, v_k)$ is true. In addition, for each variable $x \in X$ in ϕ, v contains three subgoals $S(k_x, x, x)$, $S(k_x, t, -)$ and $S(k_x, f, -)$.

q_2 is constructed as follows. For each clause $C(x, y, z)$ in ϕ, q_2 contains a subgoal $R(k_C, x', y', z')$, where x', y' and z' are variables. Also, for each variable $x \in X$ in ϕ, v contains a subgoal $S(k_x, -, x')$.

Claim: $\#\phi = (coeff(q_1 q_2) \bmod B^{7c+2k+1}) / B^{7c+2k}$.

To verify the claim, lets first look at the unifiers of just q_1. Each $S(k_x, x, x)$ can be unified with either $S(k_x, t, -)$ or $S(k_x, f, -)$. There are 2^k such unifiers, one corresponding to each assignment of t or f to variables in X. If η is any such unifier, $\beta(\eta(q_1)) = B^{7c+2k}$ since there are $7c + 2k$ subgoals.. Further, if η corresponds to an assignment that can be extended to an assignment of ϕ, then q_2 can be completely mapped to q_1, i.e. $\eta(q_1)q_2 \equiv \eta(q_1)$.

There are two cases, $\#\phi$ is either 0 or its greater than 0. In the latter case, there is at least one η with the property that $\eta(q_1)q_2 \equiv \eta(q_1)$. Every such η adds the term B^{7c+2k} to the *coeff* resulting in $coeff(q_1 q_2) = \#\phi * B^{7c+2k}$. The claim follows since B is chosen to be greater than 2^k and $\#\phi$ is at most 2^k. In the former case, when $\#\phi = 0$, every minimal unifier of $q_1 q_2$ must contain at least $7c + 2k + 1$ subgoals, so $coeff(q_1 q_2)$ is a multiple of $B^{7c+2k+1}$. The claim follows.

Theorem 10. $ACP^{\{1\}}$ *is Π_2^p-complete.*

Proof. We first show that $ACP^{\{1\}}$ belongs to Π_2^p. $(q, v) \in ACP^{\{1\}}$ can be restated as

$$\forall \eta_0 (\forall \eta_1 D(\eta_0(v)) \leq D(\eta_1(v)) \Rightarrow \exists \eta_2 \; \eta_2(qv) = \eta_0(v))$$

Thus, $ACP^{\{1\}} \in \Pi_2^p$.

For completeness, we give a reduction from the $\forall \exists SAT$ problem defined below, which is known to be Π_2^p-complete.

$\forall \exists SAT = \{(X, Y, \phi(X, Y)) \mid X, Y$ sets of variables, $\phi(X, Y)$ a *3CNF* formula, and $\forall X \exists Y \phi(X, Y)\}$

Given $(X, Y, \phi(X, Y))$, we construct two conjunctive queries q and v. The vocabulary consists of R, S of arities 4 and 2 respectively, and there are two constants t and f.

The query v is constructed as follows. Every clause $C(x, y, z)$ in $\phi(X, Y)$, which is a disjunction of x, y and z or their negations, contributes seven subgoals to v. These are of the form $R(k_C, v_i, v_j, v_k)$, where k_C is a unique constant for each clause and each of v_i, v_j, v_k is either t or f so that the resulting assignment makes the clause true. Every $x \in X$ contributes four subgoal to v given by $S(k_x, t, -), S(k_x, f, -), S(k_x, -, 0)$ and $S(k_x, -, 1)$, where k_x is a unique constant for each x.

The query q is constructed as follows. Corresponding to every clause $C(x, y, z)$ in ϕ, there is a subgoal $R(k_C, x, y, z)$, where k_C is the same constant for the clause as used in the definition of v and x, y, z are variables. For each $x \in X$, there is a subgoal $G(k_x, x, 0)$, where again k_x is the same constant used in v for variable x.

Claim: $(q, v) \in ACP^{\{1\}}$ *iff* $(X, Y, \phi(X, Y)) \in \forall \exists SAT$.

To see this, let us analyze the set $\text{MGUQ}^0(v)$. The subgoals corresponding to R relations cannot be unified with anything else, as all of them contain only constants. The S subgoals corresponding to two different x cannot be unified because of the k_x constants. For same $x \in X$, the four S subgoals can be maximally unified in two possibles ways leading to $S(k_x, t, 0), S(k_x, f, 1)$ or $S(k_x, f, 0), S(k_x, t, 1)$. The choice can be made independently for each x. Thus, the size of $\text{MGUQ}^0(v)$ is $2^{|X|}$. Now, $\mu(q \mid v) = 1$ iff for each of the query v_i in $\text{MGUQ}^0(v)$, q can be mapped to v_i. Each v_i, for each x, contains exactly one of $S(k_x, t, 0)$ and $S(k_x, f, 0)$. The subgoal $S(k_x, x, 0)$ in q has to map to this subgoal. Thus, x will be equated to t or f. After all the S subgoals in q are mapped, each of the X variables will have a truth assignment. As we iterate over v_i, we get all possibles truth assignments for X. Also, after X is given a truth assignment, all the R subgoals of q must map to one of the subgoals of v. This is possible iff the Y variables can be given a truth assignment so that all clauses in ϕ are satisfied. This proves that $(q, v) \in ACP^{\{1\}}$ iff $(X, Y, \phi(X, Y)) \in \forall \exists SAT$. Thus, $ACP^{\{1\}}$ is Π_2^p-complete.

Theorem 11. $ACP^{(0,1]}$ *is* Θ_2^p-*complete.*

Wagner [24] has provided a very useful tool for proving Θ_2^p-hardness of problems, which we state below.

Theorem 12 (Wagner [24]). *Let D be an* NP-*complete set and let A be any arbitrary set. Let χ_D be the characteristic function of D. If there exists a polynomial-time computable function f such that*

$$|\{i \mid x_i \in D\}| is\ odd \Leftrightarrow f(x_1, \ldots, x_{2k}) \in A$$

for all $k \geq 1$ and $x_1, \ldots, x_{2k}$ with $\chi_D(x_1) \geq \cdots \geq \chi_D(x_{2k})$, then A is Θ_2^p-complete[3].

Before we give the proof of Thm. 11, we need few results. Call a *3-CNF* formula with k clauses *almost satisfiable* if there exists an assignment that satisfies at least $k - 1$ clauses.

Lemma 1. *There exists a polynomial-time function F such that if ϕ is a 3-CNF formula, $F(\phi)$ is an almost satisfiable 3-CNF formula with the property $\phi \Leftrightarrow F(\phi)$.*

Lemma 2. *There exists PTIME functions g, h s.t. if ϕ_1 and ϕ_2 are almost satisfiable formulas, then $\phi_1 \Rightarrow \phi_2$ iff $\mu(g(\phi_1, \phi_2) \mid h(\phi_1, \phi_2)) > 0$.*

Proof. For each ϕ_i ($i = 1, 2$), we define two conjunctive queries $q_1(\phi_i)$ and $q_2(\phi_i)$. $q_1(\phi_i)$ is a query over a relation R_i of arity 4. Corresponding to each clause $C(x, y, z)$ in ϕ_i, there are seven subgoals in $q_1(\phi_i)$ of the form $R_i(k_C, v_j, v_k, v_l, 0)$, where k_C is a unique constant for each clause and $(v_j, v_k, v_l) \in \{t, f\}^3$ such that $C(v_j, v_k, v_l)$ is true. We call these the *type-0 subgoals* since all of them end with the constant 0. In addition, $q_1(\phi_i)$ contains eight more subgoals of the form $R_i(x_i, v_j, v_k, v_l, 1)$, where x_i is a variable and $(v_j, v_k, v_l) \in \{t, f\}^3$. We call these the *type-1 subgoals*. $q_2(\phi_i)$ is also a query over R_i. For each clause $C(x, y, z)$ in ϕ_i, $q_1(\phi_i)$ contains a subgoal $R_i(k_C, x, y, z, -)$ where x, y, z are variables. Let S be a new relation and a, b, c fresh constants:

$$g(\phi_1, \phi_2) = q_2(\phi_2)$$
$$h(\phi_1, \phi_2) = q_1(\phi_1)q_2(\phi_1)q_1(\phi_2)S(x_1, x_2, c), S(a, b, c)$$

We will show that g and h satisfy the required property, i.e. $\phi_1 \Rightarrow \phi_2$ iff $\mu(g(\phi_1, \phi_2) \mid h(\phi_1, \phi_2)) > 0$. Let us first analyze the set $\text{MGUQ}^0(h(\phi_1, \phi_2))$. Also, assume without loss of generality that ϕ_1 and ϕ_2 have distinct set of variables. Then, the sub-query $q_1(\phi_1)q_1(\phi_2)$ cannot be further unified. There are two cases: **(i)** ϕ_1 is satisfiable. Then, the sub-query $q_2(\phi_1)$ can be completely mapped to the type-0 subgoals of $q_1(\phi_1)$. Further, $S(x_1, x_2, c)$ can be unified with $S(a, b, c)$. The resulting query is the only one in $\text{MGUQ}^0(h(\phi_1, \phi_2))$. Note that it equates x_2 to b. **(ii)** ϕ_2 is not satisfiable. Then, $q_2(\phi_1)$ cannot be completely mapped to the

---

[3] The class Θ_2^p is referred to as P_{bf}^{NP} in [24].

type-0 subgoals of $q_1(\phi_1)$. But since ϕ_2 is almost satisfiable, all but one subgoal of $q_2(\phi_1)$ can be mapped to the type-0 subgoals. The remaining subgoal can be unified with a type-1 subgoal, by equating x_1 with the constant for the corresponding clause. $S(x_1, x_2, c)$ can no more be unified with $S(a, b, c)$, since x_1 has been equated with a different constant. One can easily check that the resulting query is the only one in $\mathrm{MGUQ}^0(h(\phi_1, \phi_2))$. Also note that x_2 is still a free variable in this query. In both cases, there is a unique query in $\mathrm{MGUQ}^0(h(\phi_1, \phi_2))$. Call it q_0. $\mu(g(\phi_1, \phi_2) \mid h(\phi_1, \phi_2)) > 0$ holds iff $g(\phi_1, \phi_2) = q_2(\phi_2)$ maps to q_0. If ϕ_1 is not satisfiable, q_0 contains $q_1(\phi_2)$ as a sub-query, otherwise it contains $q_1(\phi_2)$ with x_2 equated to b. If ϕ_2 is satisfiable, it can be mapped to the type-1 subgoal of $q_1(\phi_2)$, and hence can be mapped to q_0. If ϕ_2 is not satisfiable, it can still be mapped to $q_1(\phi_2)$ by using a type-1 subgoal, but then x_2 should be a free variable, i.e., ϕ_1 should also be not satisfiable. Hence, $\mu(g(\phi_1, \phi_2) \mid h(\phi_1, \phi_2)) > 0$ iff $\phi_1 \Rightarrow \phi_2$.

Proof. (**Thm. 11**) First we show that $\mathrm{ACP}^{(0,1]}$ belongs to Θ_2^p. By Cor. 2, $(q, v) \in \mathrm{ACP}^{(0,1]}$ iff $exp(v) = exp(qv)$. The language $\{(q, k) \mid exp(q) \leq k\}$ is in NP since given any (q, k), one only needs to check if there is a substitution η with $D(\eta(q)) \leq k$. Further, $exp(q)$ cannot exceed $D(q)$, which is polynomial in size of q. Thus, $exp(q)$ is determined by a binary search issuing $O(\log n)$ queries to an NP oracle. Since $exp(v) = exp(qv)$ can be checked by explicitly computing $exp(v)$ and $exp(qv)$, we have $\mathrm{ACP}^{(0,1]} \in \Theta_2^p$. For completeness, let $D = \textit{3-SAT}$ be the set of all satisfiable 3-CNF formulas. We know D is NP-complete. Let $x_1, \ldots, x_{2k}$ be s.t. $\chi_D(x_1) \geq \cdots \geq \chi_D(x_{2k})$. For $i = 1, \ldots, k$, let $Q_i = g(F(x_{2i-1}), F(x_{2i}))$ and $V_i = h(F(x_{2i-1}), F(x_{2i}))$, where F, g, h are functions as defined in Lemmas 1 and 2. Assume that Q_i and V_i use different set of relations for different i. Let $v = V_1 V_2 \ldots V_k$ and $q = Q_1 Q_2 \ldots Q_k$. Then, $\mu(v \mid q) = \prod_{i=1}^k \mu(V_i \mid Q_i)$. By Lemma 2, $\mu(V_i \mid Q_i) > 0 \Leftrightarrow \chi_D(x_{2i-1}) = \chi_D(x_{2i})$. Thus, $\mu(v \mid q) > 0 \Leftrightarrow |\{i \mid x_i \in D\}|$ is odd. By Thm. 12, ACP^1 is Θ_2^p-complete.

5   Conclusions

We investigate the complexity of a new approach to incompleteness in databases, based on Bayes's notion of a prior probability distribution. In this new framework we study the complexity of several fundamental problems, with applications to information disclosure and query answering using views, and provide tight complexity bounds.

Acknowledgments. This work was partially supported by the grants NSF SEIII 0513877, NSF 61-2252, and NSF IIS-0428168.

References

1. Serge Abiteboul and Oliver M. Duschka. Complexity of answering queries using materialized views. In *PODS*, pages 254–263, 1998.
2. Brian Babcock and Surajit Chaudhuri. Towards a robust query optimizer: a principled and practical approach. In *SIGMOD*, pages 119–130, 2005.

3. Fahiem Bacchus, Adam J. Grove, Joseph Y. Halpern, and Daphne Koller. From statistical knowledge bases to degrees of belief. *Artificial Intelligence*, 87(1-2):75–143, 1996.

4. Ashok K. Chandra and Philip M. Merlin. Optimal implementation of conjunctive queries in relational data bases. In *STOC*, pages 77–90, 1977.

5. Nilesh Dalvi, Gerome Milkau, and Dan Suciu. Asymptotic conditional probabilities for conjunctive queries. In *ICDT*, 2005.

6. Nilesh Dalvi and Dan Suciu. Query answering using probabilistic views. In *VLDB*, pages 805–816, 2005.

7. Nilesh Dalvi and Dan Suciu. Query evaluation on a database given by a random graph, April 2006.

8. Alexandre Evfimievski, Johannes Gehrke, and Ramakrishnan Srikant. Limiting privacy breaches in privacy preserving data mining. In *PODS*, pages 211–222, 2003.

9. R. Fagin. Probabilities on finite models. *Journal of Symbolic Logic*, 41(1):50–58, 1976.

10. Lise Getoor, Benjamin Taskar, and Daphne Koller. Selectivity estimation using probabilistic models. In *SIGMOD*, pages 461–472, 2001.

11. Y. V. Glebskiĭ, D. I. Kogan, M. I. Liogon'kiĭ, and V. A. Talanov. Range and degree of realizability of formulas in the restricted predicate calculus. *Kibernetika*, 2:17–28, 1969. [Engl. Transl. Cybernetics, vol. 5, 142–154 (1972)].

12. Alon Y. Halevy. Answering queries using views: A survey. *The VLDB Journal*, 10(4):270–294, 2001.

13. Lane A. Hemaspaandra and Heribert Vollmer. The satanic notations: Counting classes beyond #p and other definitional adventures. Technical report, Rochester, NY, USA, 1994.

14. Daniel Kifer and J. E. Gehrke. Injecting utility into anonymized datasets. In *SIGMOD*, 2006.

15. Maurizio Lenzerini. Data integration: a theoretical perspective. In *PODS*, pages 233–246, 2002.

16. M. I. Liogon'kiĭ. On the conditional satisfyability ratio of logical formulas. *Mathematical Notes of the Academy of the USSR*, 6:856–861, 1969.

17. James F. Lynch. Probabilities of sentences about very sparse random graphs. *random struct. algorithms*, 3(1):33–54, 1992.

18. James F. Lynch. Infinitary logics and very sparse random graphs. In *Logic in Computer Science*, pages 191–198, 1993.

19. Ashwin Machanavajjhala, Johannes Gehrke, Daniel Kifer, and Muthuramakrishnan Venkitasubramaniam. l-diversity: Privacy beyond k-anonymity. In *ICDE*, page 24, 2006.

20. Gerome Miklau and Dan Suciu. A formal analysis of information disclosure in data exchange. In *SIGMOD*, 2004.

21. J. Spencer and S. Shelah. Zero-one laws for sparse random graphs. *J. Amer. Math. Soc.*, pages 97–115, 1988.

22. L. Valiant. The complexity of computing the permanent. *Theoretical Computer Science*, 8:189–201, 1979.

23. Moshe Y. Vardi. The complexity of relational query languages. In *STOC*, pages 137–146, 1982.

24. K. W. Wagner. More complicated questions about maxima and minima, and some closures of NP. *Theor. Comput. Sci.*, 51(1-2):53–80, 1987.

The Limits of Querying Ontologies

Riccardo Rosati

Dipartimento di Informatica e Sistemistica
Università di Roma "La Sapienza"
Via Salaria 113, 00198 Roma, Italy
rosati@dis.uniroma1.it

Abstract. We study query answering in Description Logics (DLs). In particular, we consider conjunctive queries, unions of conjunctive queries, and their extensions with safe negation or inequality, which correspond to well-known classes of relational algebra queries. We provide a set of decidability, undecidability and complexity results for answering queries of the above languages over various classes of Description Logics knowledge bases. In general, such results show that extending standard reasoning tasks in DLs to answering relational queries is unfeasible in many DLs, even in inexpressive ones. In particular: (i) answering even simple conjunctive queries is undecidable in some very expressive DLs in which standard DL reasoning is decidable; (ii) in DLs where answering (unions of) conjunctive queries is decidable, adding the possibility of expressing safe negation or inequality leads in general to undecidability of query answering, even in DLs of very limited expressiveness. We also highlight the negative consequences of these results for the integration of ontologies and rules. We believe that these results have important implications for ontology-based information access, in particular for the design of query languages for ontologies.

1 Introduction

Description Logics (DLs) [5] are currently playing a central role in the research on ontologies and the Semantic Web. Description Logics are a family of knowledge representation formalisms based on first-order logic (in fact, almost all DLs coincide with decidable fragments of function-free first-order logic with equality) and exhibiting well-understood computational properties. DLs are currently the most used formalisms for building ontologies, and have been proposed as standard languages for the specification of ontologies in the Semantic Web [24].

Recently, a lot of research and implementation work has been devoted to the extension of DL knowledge bases towards expressive query languages: one of main motivations for this effort is to provide users of the Semantic Web with more powerful ontology accessing tools than the ones deriving from the standard reasoning services provided by DL knowledge bases [17]. To this aim, relational database query languages have been considered as very promising query languages for DLs, in particular *conjunctive queries* (CQs) and *unions of conjunctive queries* (UCQs). A lot of the current research in DLs is studying

T. Schwentick and D. Suciu (Eds.): ICDT 2007, LNCS 4353, pp. 164–178, 2007.

this problem, and many results have recently been obtained, both from the theoretical side (see Section 2) and the implementation side (see e.g., [21,26]).

These studies are in principle very close to relational databases, not only because of the common query language, but also because, from the semantic viewpoint, query answering in DLs corresponds to a well-known problem in database theory, namely query answering over databases with incomplete information [18,29], or query answering in databases under Open-World Assumption [31]. Then, of course, there is an important difference between the two settings, which lies in the different "schema language" adopted: DLs and relational schemas indeed correspond to two different subsets of function-free first-order logic. Nevertheless, there are well-known and important correspondences between DLs and (relational) data models (see e.g., [12,8]): more generally, the relationship between DLs and databases is now quite well-assessed.

In this paper we study query answering over Description Logics knowledge bases. In particular, we do not restrict our attention to (unions of) conjunctive queries, and analyze several subclasses of first-order queries.[1] In particular, we consider CQs, UCQs, and their extensions with safe negation ($CQ^{\neg s}$s, $UCQ^{\neg s}$s) and inequality ($CQ^{\neq}$s, $UCQ^{\neq}$s), which correspond to well-known classes of relational algebra queries.

We provide a set of decidability, undecidability and complexity results for answering queries of the above languages over various classes of Description Logics knowledge bases. In particular, we mainly consider the following, rather inexpressive, DLs: $RDFS(DL)$ [16], $\mathcal{EL}$ [4], $DL\text{-}Lite_R$ [9], and $\mathcal{AL}$ [5]. Many of the results obtained for such logics extend to more expressive DLs. A summary of the results obtained is reported in Figure 1 (Section 6).

In general, such results show that extending standard reasoning tasks in DLs to answering relational queries is unfeasible in many DLs, even in rather inexpressive ones. In particular:

- answering CQs and UCQs is already an unsolvable problem in decidable fragments of FOL, in particular in $\mathcal{L}^2$, the two-variable fragment of function-free FOL, which is very close to many DLs, and in which all standard DL reasoning tasks are decidable;
- in DLs where CQs and UCQs are decidable, adding safe negation generally leads to undecidability of query answering (even in DLs of very limited expressiveness);
- in the same way, adding inequality (and more generally, comparison operators) generally leads to undecidability of query answering.

We believe that these results have important implications for ontology-based information access, in particular for the design of query languages for ontologies, since they clearly highlight critical combinations of DL constructs and query constructs with respect to the decidability and complexity of query answering.

---

[1] We recall that, even for empty knowledge bases, the problem of answering arbitrary first-order queries is undecidable, both over finite and over unrestricted models [28].

Finally, we briefly point out that the above results have also important consequences in the design of rule layers for the Semantic Web, which is currently under standardization by the Rule Interchange Format (RIF) working group[2] of the World Wide Web Consortium (W3C). Indeed, almost all the rule formalisms proposed in this setting allow for posing relational queries (e.g., are able to express forms of Datalog queries). The results reported in this paper establish that not only recursion may lead to undecidability of reasoning in DL knowledge bases augmented with rules (which has been shown in [20,13]), but also the presence of very restricted forms of nonrecursive negation and/or inequality in the rules might easily lead to undecidability of reasoning.

2   Description Logics and Query Languages

In this section we briefly introduce Description Logics and the query languages analyzed in the paper.

2.1   Description Logics

We now briefly recall Description Logics (DLs). We assume that the reader is familiar with first-order logic (FOL). For a more detailed introduction to DLs, we refer the reader to [5].

We start from an alphabet of concept names, an alphabet of role names and an alphabet of constant names. Concepts correspond to unary predicates in FOL, roles correspond to binary predicates, and constants corresponds to FOL constants.

Starting from concept and role names, *concept expressions* and *role expressions* can be constructed, based on a formal syntax. Different DLs are based on different languages concept and role expressions. Details on the concept and role languages for the DLs considered in this paper are reported below.

A *concept inclusion* is an expression of the form $C_1 \sqsubseteq C_2$, where C_1 and C_2 are concept expressions. Similarly, a *role inclusion* is an expression of the form $R_1 \sqsubseteq R_2$, where R_1 and R_2 are role expressions.

An *instance assertion* is an expression of the form $A(a)$ or $P(a, b)$, where A is a concept expression, P is a role expression, and a, b are constant names. We do not consider complex concept and role expressions in instance assertions, since we are interested in data complexity of query answering, as explained below.

A *DL knowledge base* is a pair $\langle \mathcal{T}, \mathcal{A} \rangle$, where $\mathcal{T}$, called the *TBox*, is a set of concept and role inclusions, and $\mathcal{A}$, called the *ABox*, is a set of instance assertions.

The DLs mainly considered in this paper are the following (from now on, we use the symbol A to denote a concept name and the symbol P to denote a role name):

---

[2] http://www.w3.org/2005/rules/

- $DL\text{-}Lite_{RDFS}$ is the DL whose language for concept and role expressions is defined by the following abstract syntax:

$$C_L ::= A \mid \exists R$$
$$C_R ::= A$$
$$R ::= P \mid P^-$$

  and both concept inclusions of the form $C_L \sqsubseteq C_R$ and role inclusions $P_1 \sqsubseteq P_2$ are allowed in the TBox. Such DL corresponds to (a subset of) RDFS [1], the schema language for RDF.[3]

- $DL\text{-}Lite_R$ is the DL whose language for concept and role expressions is defined by the following abstract syntax:

$$C_L ::= A \mid \exists R$$
$$C_R ::= A \mid \neg C_R \mid \exists R$$
$$R ::= P \mid P^-$$

  and both concept inclusions of the form $C_L \sqsubseteq C_R$ and role inclusions $R_1 \sqsubseteq R_2$ are allowed in the TBox.

- $\mathcal{EL}$ is the DL whose language for concept expressions is defined by the following abstract syntax:

$$C ::= A \mid C_1 \sqcap C_2 \mid \exists P.C$$

  and only concept inclusions $C_1 \sqsubseteq C_2$ are allowed in the TBox.

- $\mathcal{AL}$ is the DL whose language for concept expressions is defined by the following abstract syntax:

$$C ::= A \mid \top \mid \bot \mid \neg A \mid C_1 \sqcap C_2 \mid \exists P \mid \forall P.C$$

  and only concept inclusions $C_1 \sqsubseteq C_2$ are allowed in the TBox.

- $\mathcal{ALC}$ is the DL whose language for concept expressions is defined by the following abstract syntax:

$$C ::= A \mid \neg C \mid C_1 \sqcap C_2 \mid \exists P.C$$

  and only concept inclusions $C_1 \sqsubseteq C_2$ are allowed in the TBox.

- $\mathcal{ALCHIQ}$ is the DL whose language for concept and role expressions is defined by the following abstract syntax:

$$C ::= A \mid \neg C \mid C_1 \sqcap C_2 \mid (\geq n\,R\,C)$$
$$R ::= P \mid P^-$$

  and both concept inclusions $C_1 \sqsubseteq C_2$ and role inclusions $R_1 \sqsubseteq R_2$ are allowed in the TBox.

---

[3] $DL\text{-}Lite_{RDFS}$ is very similar to the description logic $RDFS(DL)$ defined in [16].

Besides the inclusions defined by the concept and role expressions introduced above, in the following we will also consider role inclusions of the form $\neg P_1 \sqsubseteq P_2$, where P_1, P_2 are role names.

We give the semantics of DLs through the well-known translation of DL knowledge bases into FOL theories with counting quantifiers (see [5]).

$$\rho_{fol}(\langle \mathcal{T}, \mathcal{A} \rangle) = \rho_{fol}(\mathcal{T}) \cup \rho_{fol}(\mathcal{A})$$
$$\rho_{fol}(C_1 \sqsubseteq C_2) = \forall x. \rho_{fol}(C_1, x) \rightarrow \rho_{fol}(C_2, x)$$
$$\rho_{fol}(R_1 \sqsubseteq R_2) = \forall x. \rho_{fol}(R_1, x, y) \rightarrow \rho_{fol}(R_2, x, y)$$
$$\rho_{fol}(A, x) = A(x)$$
$$\rho_{fol}(\neg C, x) = \neg \rho_{fol}(C, x)$$
$$\rho_{fol}(C_1 \sqcap C_2, x) = \rho_{fol}(C_1, x) \wedge \rho_{fol}(C_2, x)$$
$$\rho_{fol}(\exists R, x) = \exists y. \rho_{fol}(R, x, y)$$
$$\rho_{fol}(\exists R.C, x) = \exists y. \rho_{fol}(R, x, y) \wedge \rho_{fol}(C, y)$$
$$\rho_{fol}((\geq n\, R\, C), x) = \exists^{\geq n} y. \rho_{fol}(R, x, y) \wedge \rho_{fol}(C, y)$$
$$\rho_{fol}(P, x, y) = P(x, y)$$
$$\rho_{fol}(P^-, x, y) = P(y, x)$$
$$\rho_{fol}(\neg P, x, y) = \neg P(x, y)$$

A *model* of a DL-KB $\mathcal{K} = \langle \mathcal{T}, \mathcal{A} \rangle$ is a FOL model of $\rho_{fol}(\mathcal{K})$. Therefore, DLs inherit the classical semantics of FOL, hence, in every interpretation, constants and predicates are interpreted over a non-empty interpretation domain which is either finite or countably infinite. In this paper the only reasoning service we are interested in is query answering, whose semantics is defined in the following subsection.

We will also mention the following logics: (i) the DL $\mathcal{DLR}$ [11], which extends $\mathcal{ALCHIQ}$ essentially through the use of n-ary relations, and for which decidability results on query answering are known; (ii) $\mathcal{L}^2$, i.e., the two-variable fragment of function-free first-order logic with equality [7]; (iii) $\mathcal{C}^2$, i.e., the extension of the two-variable fragment $\mathcal{L}^2$ through *counting quantifiers* [15]. The above two fragments of FOL are very much related to DLs, since almost all DLs are subsets of $\mathcal{L}^2$ or $\mathcal{C}^2$. Indeed, it can be easily seen that the above mentioned DLs and fragments of FOL satisfy the following partial order with respect to their relative expressive power (see [5] for details):

$$\text{DL-Lite}_{RDFS} \subset \text{DL-Lite}_R \subset \mathcal{ALCHIQ} \subset \mathcal{DLR}$$
$$\mathcal{EL} \subset \mathcal{ALC} \subset \mathcal{ALCHIQ} \subset \mathcal{C}^2$$
$$\mathcal{AL} \subset \mathcal{ALC} \subset \mathcal{L}^2 \subset \mathcal{C}^2$$
$$\text{DL-Lite}_R \subset \mathcal{L}^2$$

2.2   Queries

We now introduce the query languages that will be considered in the paper. A *union of conjunctive queries* (UCQ) is an expression of the form

$$\{ \boldsymbol{x} \mid conj_1(\boldsymbol{x}, \boldsymbol{c}) \vee \ldots \vee conj_m(\boldsymbol{x}, \boldsymbol{c}) \} \tag{1}$$

where each $conj_i(\boldsymbol{x}, \boldsymbol{c})$ is an expression of the form $conj_i(\boldsymbol{x}, \boldsymbol{c}) = \exists \boldsymbol{y}.a_1 \wedge \ldots \wedge a_n$ in which each a_i is an atom whose arguments are terms from the sets of variables

x, y, and from the set of constants c and such that each variable from x and y occurs in at least one atom a_i. The variables x are called the head variables (or distinguished variables) of the query.

A UCQ with safe negation ($\text{UCQ}^{\neg s}$) is an expression of the form (1) in which each a_i is either an atom or a negated atom (a negated atom is an expression of the form $\neg a$ where a is an atom) and such that in each $conj_i(x, c)$ each variable from x and y occurs in at least one positive atom.

A UCQ with inequalities ($\text{UCQ}^{\neq}$) is an expression of the form (1) in which each $conj_i(x, c)$ is a conjunction $\exists y.a_1 \wedge \ldots \wedge a_n$ where each a_i is either an atom or an expression of the form $z \neq z'$, where z and z' are variables.

A UCQ with universally quantified negation ($\text{UCQ}^{\neg \forall}$) is a UCQ with negated atoms in which the variables that only appear in negated atoms are universally quantified. Formally, a $\text{UCQ}^{\neg \forall}$ is an expression of the form (1) in which each $conj_i(x, c)$ is of the form

$$\exists y.\forall z.conj(x, y, z, c)$$

where $conj$ is a conjunction of literals (atoms and negated atoms) whose arguments are terms from the sets of variables x, y, z and from the set of constants c, in which each variable from x and y occurs in positive atoms, and *each variable in z only occurs in negated atoms*. An example of a $\text{UCQ}^{\neg \forall}$ is the following:

$$\{x \mid (\exists y, z.\forall w.r(x, y) \wedge \neg s(y, z) \wedge \neg t(w, z)) \vee (\exists y.\forall u.r(x, y) \wedge \neg s(x, u))\}$$

Notice that all the classes of queries above considered correspond to classes of relational algebra queries (hence they are classes of *domain-independent* first-order queries) [3].

We call a UCQ a *conjunctive query* (CQ) when $m = 1$. Analogously, we define the notions of CQ with negation ($\text{CQ}^{\neg}$), safe negation ($\text{CQ}^{\neg s}$), inequalities ($\text{CQ}^{\neq}$), and universally quantified negation ($\text{CQ}^{\neg \forall}$).

A *Boolean* CQ is a CQ without head variables, i.e., an expression of the form $conj_1(x, c) \vee \ldots \vee conj_m(x, c)$. Since it is a sentence, i.e., a closed first-order formula, such a query is either true or false in a database. In the same way, we define the Boolean version of the other kinds of queries introduced above. Finally, the *arity* of a query is the number of head variables, while the *size* of a CQ q is the number of atoms in the body of q.

The semantics of queries in DL knowledge bases is immediately obtained by adapting the well-known notion of *certain answers* in indefinite databases (see e.g. [29]). Let q be a query of arity n, let $x_1, \ldots, x_n$ be its head variables, and let $c = c_1, \ldots, c_n$ be a n-tuple of constants. We denote by $q(c)$ the Boolean query (i.e., the FOL sentence) obtained from q by replacing each head variable x_i with the constant c_i.

Let q be a query of arity n. A n-tuple c of constants occurring in $\mathcal{K}$ is a *certain answer* to q in $\mathcal{K}$ iff, for each model $\mathcal{I}$ of $\mathcal{K}$, $\mathcal{I}$ satisfies the sentence $q(c)$ (in this case we write $\mathcal{I} \models q(c)$). For a Boolean query q, we say that *true* is a certain answer to q in $\mathcal{K}$ iff, for each model $\mathcal{I}$ of $\mathcal{K}$, $\mathcal{I} \models q$.

Finally, in this paper we focus on *data complexity* of query answering, which is a notion borrowed from relational database theory [30]. First, we recall that there is a recognition problem associated with query answering, which is defined as follows. We have a fixed TBox $\mathcal{T}$ expressed in a DL $\mathcal{DL}$, and a fixed query q: the *recognition problem* associated to $\mathcal{T}$ and q is the decision problem of checking whether, given an ABox $\mathcal{A}$, and a tuple $\boldsymbol{c}$ of constants, we have that $\langle \mathcal{T}, \mathcal{A} \rangle \models q(\boldsymbol{c})$. Notice that neither the TBox nor the query is an input to the recognition problem.

Let $\mathcal{C}$ be a complexity class. When we say that query answering for a certain DL $\mathcal{DL}$ *is in $\mathcal{C}$ with respect to data complexity*, we mean that the corresponding recognition problem is in $\mathcal{C}$. Similarly, when we say that query answering for a certain DL $\mathcal{DL}$ is *$\mathcal{C}$-hard with respect to data complexity*, we mean that the corresponding recognition problem is $\mathcal{C}$-hard.

2.3   Previous Results on Query Answering in DLs

So far, only conjunctive queries and union of conjunctive queries have been studied in DLs. In particular, the first results in this field appear in [20], which proves that answering CQs and UCQs is decidable in $\mathcal{ALCNR}$, a DL whose expressiveness lies between $\mathcal{ALC}$ and $\mathcal{ALCHIQ}$. Then, in [11] it has been shown that answering CQs and UCQs is decidable in the very expressive Description Logic $\mathcal{DLR}$. The same paper also establishes undecidability of answering $CQ^{\neq}$s in $\mathcal{DLR}$, which so far is the only known result for DLs concerning the classes of queries (apart from CQs and UCQs) studied in this paper. Another decidability result appears in [21] and concerns answering conjunctive queries in $\mathcal{ALCIHQ}(\mathbf{D})$, which is the extension of $\mathcal{ALCHIQ}$ with concrete domains.

As for computational characterizations of query answering in DLs, the above mentioned work [20] has shown that the data complexity of answering CQs and UCQs in $\mathcal{ALCNR}$ is CONP-complete. Then, [27] presents the first algorithm for answering conjunctive queries over a description logic with transitive roles. Moreover, [10] provides a set of lower bounds for answering conjunctive queries in many DLs, while in [22] it has been shown that the complexity of answering conjunctive queries in $\mathcal{SHIQ}$ (which is the extension of $\mathcal{ALCHIQ}$ with transitive roles) is CONP-complete, for CQs in which transitive roles do not occur. This result (with the same restriction on roles occurring in queries) has been further extended in in [23] to unions of conjunctive queries, and in [14] to CQs for $\mathcal{SHOQ}$, a DL which extends $\mathcal{ALCHIQ}$ with transitive roles and *nominals*, but does not allow for expressing inverse roles anymore.

3   Results for Positive Queries

We start our analysis of query answering in DLs by considering, among the queries introduced in the previous section, the classes of positive queries. Thus, we first examine conjunctive queries, and then consider unions of conjunctive queries. In both cases, we identify sets of expressive features of a DL which are sufficient to make query answering undecidable.

Theorem 1. *Let $\mathcal{DL}$ be any DL such that: (i) its concept language allows for binary concept disjointness $(A_1 \sqsubseteq \neg A_2)$, concept disjunction $(C_1 \sqcup C_2)$, unqualified existential quantification $(\exists R)$, and universal quantification $(\forall R.C)$; (ii) it allows for concept inclusions and role inclusions of the form $\neg P_1 \sqsubseteq P_2$, where P_1, P_2 are role names. Then, answering UCQs in $\mathcal{DL}$ is undecidable.*

Proof (sketch). The proof is by a reduction from the unbounded tiling problem [6]. Let $(\mathcal{S}, \mathcal{H}, \mathcal{V})$ be an instance of the tiling problem, where $\mathcal{S} = \{t_1, \ldots, t_n\}$ is a finite set of tiles, and $\mathcal{H}$ and $\mathcal{V}$ are binary relations over $\mathcal{S} \times \mathcal{S}$. For each $i \in \{1, \ldots, n\}$, let $T_h^i = \{t_{h_1^i}, \ldots, t_{h_{k_i}^i}\}$ be the subset of $\mathcal{S}$ such that $T_h^i = \{x \in \mathcal{S} \mid (t_i, x) \in \mathcal{H}\}$, and let $T_v^i = \{t_{v_1^i}, \ldots, t_{v_{j_i}^i}\}$ be the subset of $\mathcal{S}$ such that $T_v^i = \{x \in \mathcal{S} \mid (t_i, x) \in \mathcal{V}\}$.

Now let $\mathcal{T}$ be the following TBox (in which we use a set of concept names $T_1, \ldots, T_n$ in one-to-one correspondence with the elements $t_1, \ldots, t_n$ of $\mathcal{S}$, and the roles H, V and $\overline{V}$):

$$\top \sqsubseteq \exists H$$
$$\top \sqsubseteq \exists V$$
$$\top \sqsubseteq T_1 \sqcup \ldots \sqcup T_n$$
$$T_i \sqsubseteq \neg T_j \quad \text{for each } i \neq j, \ i, j \in \{1, \ldots, n\}$$
$$T_i \sqsubseteq \forall H.T_{h_1^i} \sqcup \ldots \sqcup T_{h_{k_i}^i} \quad \text{for each } i \in \{1, \ldots, n\}$$
$$T_i \sqsubseteq \forall V.T_{v_1^i} \sqcup \ldots \sqcup T_{v_{j_i}^i} \quad \text{for each } i \in \{1, \ldots, n\}$$
$$\neg V \sqsubseteq \overline{V}$$

and let q be the CQ $\exists x_1, x_2, y_1, y_2.H(x_1, x_2) \wedge V(x_1, y_1) \wedge H(y_1, y_2) \wedge \overline{V}(x_2, y_2)$. We prove that there exists a model M for $\mathcal{T}$ such that q is false in M iff the tiling problem instance $(\mathcal{S}, \mathcal{H}, \mathcal{V})$ has a solution. □

Notice that the two-variable fragment $\mathcal{L}^2$ satisfies the conditions of Theorem 1 (in the sense that a DL satisfying the conditions of Theorem 1 can be translated into an equivalent $\mathcal{L}^2$ theory), which implies the following property.

Corollary 1. *Answering CQs in $\mathcal{L}^2$ is undecidable.*

Actually, the above property shows that answering CQs is undecidable already in a very small fragment of $\mathcal{L}^2$.

We point out that, although the syntax of the description logic $\mathcal{DLR}$ satisfies the conditions of the above theorem, such theorem actually does not apply to $\mathcal{DLR}$, due to a different interpretation of negated roles in $\mathcal{DLR}$ with respect to the standard semantics [11].

Then, we analyze unions of conjunctive queries. The next two theorems identify two sets of DL constructs which are sufficient to make query answering undecidable.

Theorem 2. *Let $\mathcal{DL}$ be any DL whose concept language allows for unqualified existential quantification $(\exists P)$ and concept disjunction $(C_1 \sqcup C_2)$, and which allows for concept inclusions and role inclusions of the form $\neg P_1 \sqsubseteq P_2$, where P_1, P_2 are role names. Then, answering UCQs in $\mathcal{DL}$ is undecidable.*

Proof (sketch). The proof is analogous to the proof of Theorem 1. The only difference is that the concept inclusions defined in the above proof and involving either concept disjointness or universal quantification are encoded by suitable Boolean CQs that are added to the query, thus producing a UCQ.   □

The proof of the next theorem is based on a reduction from the word problem for semigroups to answering UCQs in a description logic $\mathcal{DL}$.

Theorem 3. *Let $\mathcal{DL}$ be any DL whose concept language allows for unqualified existential quantification ($\exists R$) and inverse roles ($\exists P^-$), and which allows for concept inclusions and role inclusions of the form $\neg P_1 \sqsubseteq P_2$, where P_1, P_2 are role names. Then, answering UCQs in $\mathcal{DL}$ is undecidable.*

Then, we provide an upper bound for the data complexity of answering UCQs in the DL $\mathcal{EL}$ (we recall that hardness with respect to PTIME has been proved in [9]).

Theorem 4. *Answering UCQs in $\mathcal{EL}$ is in PTIME with respect to data complexity.*

Proof (sketch). We prove the thesis by defining a query reformulation algorithm for $\mathcal{EL}$. More precisely, we define an algorithm perfectRefEL that takes as input an $\mathcal{EL}$ TBox $\mathcal{T}$ and a UCQ q, and computes (in a finite amount of time) a positive Datalog query q' which constitutes a *perfect rewriting* [19] of the query q, in the sense that, for each ABox $\mathcal{A}$, the set of certain answers of q in $\langle \mathcal{T}, \mathcal{A} \rangle$ is equal to the answers returned by the standard evaluation of the Datalog query q' in the ABox $\mathcal{A}$ considered as a relational database. Since the evaluation of a positive Datalog query is in PTIME with respect to data complexity, and since the computation of the reformulation q' is independent of the data, it follows that the data complexity of answering UCQs in $\mathcal{EL}$ is in PTIME.   □

4   Results for Queries with Inequality

We now give decidability and complexity results for answering queries with inequality in DL knowledge bases. We first examine CQ$^{\neq}$s, then we turn our attention to UCQ$^{\neq}$s.

We first prove undecidability of answering CQ$^{\neq}$s in $\mathcal{AL}$.

Theorem 5. *Answering CQ$^{\neq}$s in $\mathcal{AL}$ is undecidable.*

Proof (sketch). Again, the proof is by reduction from the tiling problem. Let $(\mathcal{S}, \mathcal{H}, \mathcal{V})$ be an instance of the tiling problem, where $\mathcal{S} = \{t_1, \ldots, t_n\}$ is a finite set of tiles, $\mathcal{H}$ and $\mathcal{V}$ are binary relations over $\mathcal{S} \times \mathcal{S}$. For each $i \in \{1, \ldots, n\}$, let $\mathcal{T}_h^i = \{t_{h_1^i}, \ldots, t_{h_{k_i}^i}\}$ be the subset of $\mathcal{S}$ such that $\mathcal{T}_h^i = \{x \in \mathcal{S} \mid (t_i, x) \notin \mathcal{H}\}$, and let $\mathcal{T}_v^i = \{t_{v_1^i}, \ldots, t_{v_{j_i}^i}\}$ be the subset of $\mathcal{S}$ such that $\mathcal{T}_v^i = \{x \in \mathcal{S} \mid (t_i, x) \notin \mathcal{V}\}$.

Now let $\mathcal{T}$ be the following TBox:

$$\top \sqsubseteq \exists H$$
$$\top \sqsubseteq \exists V$$
$$\neg T_1 \sqcap \ldots \sqcap \neg T_n \sqsubseteq \bot$$
$$T_i \sqsubseteq \neg T_j \quad \text{for each } i \neq j,\ i,j \in \{1,\ldots,n\}$$
$$T_i \sqsubseteq \forall H.\neg T_{h_1^i} \sqcap \ldots \sqcap \neg T_{h_{k_i}^i} \quad \text{for each } i \in \{1,\ldots,n\}$$
$$T_i \sqsubseteq \forall V.\neg T_{v_1^i} \sqcap \ldots \sqcap \neg T_{v_{j_i}^i} \quad \text{for each } i \in \{1,\ldots,n\}$$

and let $q = \exists x_1, x_2, y_1, y_2.H(x_1,x_2) \wedge V(x_1,y_1) \wedge H(y_1,y_2) \wedge V(x_2,y_2') \wedge y_2 \neq y_2'$. We prove that there exists a model M for $\mathcal{T}$ such that q is false in M iff the tiling problem instance $(\mathcal{S}, \mathcal{H}, \mathcal{V})$ has a solution. $\qquad\square$

The above theorem improves the undecidability result of containment of CQ$^{\neq}$s presented in [11].

Then, we consider the DL $DL\text{-}Lite_R$: for this logic, we prove the following hardness result.

Theorem 6. *Answering CQ$^{\neq}$s in DL-Lite$_R$ is* CONP-*hard with respect to data complexity.*

Proof (sketch). The proof is by reduction from satisfiability of a 3-CNF propositional formula. The reduction is inspired by an analogous reduction reported in [2] which proves CONP-hardness of answering CQ$^{\neq}$s using views. $\qquad\square$

Finally, we show a (quite obvious) property which allows us to immediately define upper bounds for answering CQ$^{\neq}$s in the DLs $DL\text{-}Lite_{RDFS}$ and $\mathcal{EL}$. In the following, we call *singleton interpretation for* $\mathcal{K}$ an interpretation whose domain Δ is a singleton $\{d\}$, all constants occurring in $\mathcal{K}$ are interpeted as d, the interpretation of every concept name A is Δ, and the interpretation of every role name P is $\Delta \times \Delta$.

Theorem 7. *Let* $\mathcal{DL}$ *be a DL such that, for each DL-KB* $\mathcal{K}$, *any singleton interpretation for* $\mathcal{K}$ *is a model of* $\mathcal{K}$. *Then, answering CQ$^{\neq}$s in* $\mathcal{DL}$ *has the same complexity as answering CQs.*

It is immediate to see that both $DL\text{-}Lite_{RDFS}$ and $\mathcal{EL}$ satisfy the condition of the above theorem.[4] This allows us to extend the computational results of answering CQs to the case of CQ$^{\neq}$s for both the above DLs.

For UCQ$^{\neq}$s, we start by considering DLs allowing for inverse roles and unqualified existential quantification in concept expressions.

The proof of the next theorem is based on a reduction from the word problem for semigroups.

---

[4] Notice, however, that this property does not hold anymore if the Unique Name Assumption (UNA) [5] is adopted in such description logics (i.e., different constant names must be interpreted as different elements of the domain). Anyway, all the other results of this paper also hold in the case when the DL adopts the UNA.

Theorem 8. *Let $\mathcal{DL}$ be any DL whose concept language allows for unqualified existential quantification ($\exists R$) and inverse roles ($\exists P^-$), and which only allows for concept inclusions in the TBox. Then, answering $UCQ^{\neq}s$ in $\mathcal{DL}$ is undecidable.*

Notice that the above theorem holds for the description logic $DL\text{-}Lite_R$.

Then, we turn our attention to the description logic $\mathcal{EL}$, and prove a result analogous to the previous theorem (whose proof is obtained by slightly modifying the reduction of the previous proof).

Theorem 9. *Answering $UCQ^{\neq}s$ in $\mathcal{EL}$ is undecidable.*

Finally, in a similar way we prove the same undecidability result for the description logic $\mathcal{AL}$.

Theorem 10. *Answering $UCQ^{\neq}s$ in $\mathcal{AL}$ is undecidable.*

Actually, the above theorem implies undecidability of answering $UCQ^{\neq}s$ already in $\mathcal{FL}^-$, which is obtained from $\mathcal{AL}$ disallowing negation on atomic concepts [5].

Finally, we turn our attention to answering $UCQ^{\neq}s$ in $DL\text{-}Lite_{RDFS}$, and are able to easily prove the following upper bound.

Theorem 11. *Answering $UCQ^{\neq}s$ in $DL\text{-}Lite_{RDFS}$ is in* LOGSPACE *with respect to data complexity.*

5   Results for Queries with Negation

In this section, among the queries introduced in Section 2, we consider the classes containing forms of negation. So we first consider $CQ^{\neg s}$s, then $UCQ^{\neg s}$s, and finally $UCQ^{\neg\forall}$s.

We start by proving that answering $CQ^{\neg s}$s is undecidable in the description logic $\mathcal{AL}$ (the proof of next theorem is again by reduction from the tiling problem, in a way similar to the proof of Theorem 5).

Theorem 12. *Answering $CQ^{\neg s}$s in $\mathcal{AL}$ is undecidable.*

Then, we show a hardness result for answering $CQ^{\neg s}$s in $DL\text{-}Lite_R$.

Theorem 13. *Answering $CQ^{\neg s}$s in $DL\text{-}Lite_R$ is* CONP-*hard with respect to data complexity.*

Proof (sketch). We prove the thesis by a reduction from graph 3-colorability. Let $G = (V, E)$ be a directed graph. We define the $DL\text{-}Lite_R$-KB $\mathcal{K} = \langle \mathcal{T}, \mathcal{A} \rangle$, where $\mathcal{T}$ is the following TBox (independent of the graph instance):

$$
\begin{array}{lll}
Red \sqsubseteq \neg Green & \exists EdgeR \sqsubseteq Red & \exists EdgeR^- \sqsubseteq \neg Red \\
Red \sqsubseteq \neg Blue & \exists EdgeG \sqsubseteq Green & \exists EdgeG^- \sqsubseteq \neg Green \\
Green \sqsubseteq \neg Blue & \exists EdgeB \sqsubseteq Blue & \exists EdgeB^- \sqsubseteq \neg Blue
\end{array}
$$

and $\mathcal{A}$ is the following ABox: $\mathcal{A} = \{Edge(v_1, v_2) \mid (v_1, v_2) \in E\}$. Finally, let q be the $CQ^{\neg s}$ $\exists x, y.Edge(x, y) \wedge \neg EdgeR(x, y) \wedge \neg EdgeG(x, y) \wedge \neg EdgeB(x, y)$. We prove that G is 3-colorable iff $true$ is not a certain answer to q in $\mathcal{K}$.   □

Notice that the above theorem actually proves CONP-hardness of answering $CQ^{\neg s}$s already for DLs much less expressive than $DL\text{-}Lite_R$, i.e., for the DL obtained from $DL\text{-}Lite_R$ by eliminating both role inclusions and existential quantification on the right-hand side of concept inclusions.

Finally, we turn our attention to the description logics $DL\text{-}Lite_{RDFS}$ and $\mathcal{EL}$, and prove a property analogous to Theorem 7. We call *saturated interpretation for* $\mathcal{K}$ an interpretation whose domain Δ is in one-to-one correspondence with the constants occurring in $\mathcal{K}$, all constants are interpreted according to such correspondence, the interpretation of every concept name A is Δ, and the interpretation of every role name P is $\Delta \times \Delta$.

Theorem 14. *Let $\mathcal{DL}$ be a DL such that, for each DL-KB $\mathcal{K}$, any saturated interpretation for $\mathcal{K}$ is a model of $\mathcal{K}$. Then, answering $CQ^{\neg s}$s in $\mathcal{DL}$ has the same complexity as answering CQs.*

It is immediate to see that both $DL\text{-}Lite_{RDFS}$ and $\mathcal{EL}$ satisfy the condition of the above theorem. This allows us to extend the computational results of answering CQs to the case of $CQ^{\neg s}$s for both the above DLs.

Then, we analyze $UCQ^{\neg s}$s. First, we prove a very strong undecidability result.

Theorem 15. *Let $\mathcal{DL}$ be any DL allowing for unqualified existential quantification ($\exists P$) in concept expressions. Answering $UCQ^{\neg s}$s in $\mathcal{DL}$ is undecidable.*

Proof (sketch). Given a tiling problem instance $(\mathcal{S}, \mathcal{H}, \mathcal{V})$ as in the proof of Theorem 1, we define the following TBox $\mathcal{T}$: $\{\top \sqsubseteq Point, \top \sqsubseteq \exists H, \top \sqsubseteq \exists V\}$. Then, let q be the $UCQ^{\neg s}$ containing the following conjunctions:

$\exists x.Point(x) \wedge \neg T_1(x) \wedge \ldots \wedge \neg T_n(x)$
$\exists x.T_i(x) \wedge T_j(x)$ for each $i \neq j$, $i, j \in \{1, \ldots, n\}$
$\exists x_1, x_2, y_1, y_2.H(x_1, x_2) \wedge V(x_1, y_1) \wedge H(y_1, y_2) \wedge \neg V(x_2, y_2)$
$\exists x, y.T_i(x) \wedge H(x, y) \wedge \neg T_{h_1^i}(y) \wedge \ldots \wedge \neg T_{h_{k_i}^i}(y)$ for each $i \in \{1, \ldots, n\}$
$\exists x, y.T_i(x) \wedge V(x, y) \wedge \neg T_{v_1^i}(y) \wedge \ldots \wedge \neg T_{v_{j_i}^i}(y)$ for each $i \in \{1, \ldots, n\}$

We prove that there exists a model M for $\mathcal{T}$ such that q is false in M iff the tiling problem instance $(\mathcal{S}, \mathcal{H}, \mathcal{V})$ has a solution.   □

The above theorem implies that answering $UCQ^{\neg s}$s is undecidable in all the DLs analyzed in this paper, with the exception of $DL\text{-}Lite_{RDFS}$, in which the concept inclusions defined in the above proof cannot be expressed. So we turn our attention to answering $UCQ^{\neg s}$s in $DL\text{-}Lite_{RDFS}$, and prove the following computational characterization.

Theorem 16. *Answering $UCQ^{\neg s}$s in $DL\text{-}Lite_{RDFS}$ is CONP-complete with respect to data complexity.*

	CQ	UCQ	$CQ^{\neq}$	$UCQ^{\neq}$	$CQ^{\neg s}$	$UCQ^{\neg s}$	$UCQ^{\neg \forall}$
$DL\text{-}Lite_{RDFS}$	$\leq$LOGSPACE [10]	$\leq$LOGSPACE [10]	$\leq$LOGSPACE [10]+Thm. 7	$\leq$LOGSPACE Thm. 11	$\leq$LOGSPACE [10]+Thm. 14	$=$coNP Thm. 16	UNDEC. Thm. 17
$DL\text{-}Lite_{R}$	$\leq$LOGSPACE [10]	$\leq$LOGSPACE [10]	$\geq$coNP Thm. 6	UNDEC. Thm. 8	$\geq$coNP Thm. 13	UNDEC. Thm. 15	UNDEC. Thm. 17
$\mathcal{EL}$	$=$PTIME $\geq$: [10] $\leq$: Thm. 4	$=$PTIME $\geq$: [10] $\leq$: Thm. 4	$=$PTIME $\geq$: [10] $\leq$: Thm.7+4	UNDEC. Thm. 9	$=$PTIME $\geq$: [10] $\leq$: Thm.14+4	UNDEC. Thm. 15	UNDEC. Thm. 17
$\mathcal{AL}$, $\mathcal{ALC}$, $\mathcal{ALCHIQ}$	$=$coNP $\geq$: [10] $\leq$: [22]	$=$coNP $\geq$: [10] $\leq$: [23]	UNDEC. Thm. 5	UNDEC. Thm. 10	UNDEC. Thm. 12	UNDEC. Thm. 15	UNDEC. Thm. 17
$\mathcal{DLR}$	$\geq$ coNP[10] DECID. [11]	$\geq$ coNP[10] DECID. [11]	UNDEC. [11]	UNDEC. [11]	UNDEC. Thm. 12	UNDEC. Thm. 15	UNDEC. Thm. 17
$\mathcal{L}^2$	UNDEC. Thm. 1	UNDEC. Thm. 1	UNDEC. Thm. 1	UNDEC. Thm. 1	UNDEC. Thm. 1	UNDEC. Thm. 1	UNDEC. Thm. 1

Fig. 1. Summary of results

Finally, we turn our attention to unions of conjunctive queries with universally quantified negation, and show that answering queries of this class is undecidable in every DL.

The proof of the next theorem is based on a reduction from the word problem for semigroups.

Theorem 17. *Answering $UCQ^{\neg \forall}s$ is undecidable in every DL.*

This result identifies a very restricted fragment of FOL queries for which query answering is undecidable, independently of the form of the knowledge base/FOL theory to which they are posed.

6   Summary of Results and Conclusions

The table displayed in Figure 1 summarizes the results presented in this paper (as well as the already known results for the DLs considered in this paper). In the table, each column corresponds to a different query language, while each row corresponds to a different DL. Each cell reports the data complexity of query answering in the corresponding combination of DL and query language. If the problem is decidable, then hardness ($\geq$) and/or membership ($\leq$) and/or completeness ($=$) results are reported (with reference to the Theorem or the publication which proves the result).

Besides the considerations reported in the introduction about these results, a further interesting aspect is the existence of cases in which adding the possibility of expressing unions changes the complexity of query answering. E.g., in the case of $\mathcal{EL}$, adding the possibility of expressing unions (i.e., going from CQs to UCQs) in the presence of safe negation or inequality makes query answering undecidable, while it is decidable in the absence of unions in queries.

These results are of course only a small step towards a thorough analysis of expressive query languages in DLs. Among the DLs and the query languages studied in this paper, two interesting open problems concern the full computational characterization of answering $CQ^{\neg s}s$ and $CQ^{\neq}s$ in $DL\text{-}Lite_R$. Actually, even decidability of query answering in these cases is still unknown.

Finally, we remark that the present research is related to the work reported in [25], which presents a similar analysis for the same query classes in relational databases with incomplete information (instead of DL knowledge bases). However, we point out that none of the results reported in the present paper can be (either directly or indirectly) derived from the proofs of the results in [25], due to the deep differences between the database schema language considered there and the DLs examined in this paper.

Acknowledgments. The author wishes to warmly thank Giuseppe De Giacomo and Maurizio Lenzerini for their precious comments. This research has been partially supported by FET project TONES (Thinking ONtologiES), funded by the EU under contract number FP6-7603, by project HYPER, funded by IBM through a Shared University Research (SUR) Award grant, and by MIUR FIRB 2005 project "Tecnologie Orientate alla Conoscenza per Aggregazioni di Imprese in Internet" (TOCAI.IT).

References

1. http://www.w3.org/TR/rdf-schema/.
2. S. Abiteboul and O. Duschka. Complexity of answering queries using materialized views. unpublished manuscript, available at ftp://ftp.inria.fr/INRIA/Projects/gemo/gemo/GemoReport-383.pdf, 1999.
3. S. Abiteboul, R. Hull, and V. Vianu. *Foundations of Databases.* Addison Wesley Publ. Co., 1995.
4. F. Baader, S. Brandt, and C. Lutz. Pushing the $\mathcal{EL}$ envelope. In *Proc. of IJCAI 2005*, pages 364–369, 2005.
5. F. Baader, D. Calvanese, D. McGuinness, D. Nardi, and P. F. Patel-Schneider, editors. *The Description Logic Handbook: Theory, Implementation and Applications.* Cambridge University Press, 2003.
6. R. Berger. The undecidability of the dominoe problem. *Mem. Amer. Math. Soc.*, 66:1–72, 1966.
7. A. Borgida. On the relative expressiveness of description logics and predicate logics. *Artificial Intelligence*, 82(1–2):353–367, 1996.
8. A. Borgida, M. Lenzerini, and R. Rosati. Description logics for data bases. In Baader et al. [5], chapter 16, pages 462–484.
9. D. Calvanese, G. De Giacomo, D. Lembo, M. Lenzerini, and R. Rosati. DL-Lite: Tractable description logics for ontologies. In *Proc. of AAAI 2005*, pages 602–607, 2005.
10. D. Calvanese, G. De Giacomo, D. Lembo, M. Lenzerini, and R. Rosati. Data complexity of query answering in description logics. In *Proc. of KR 2006*, 2006.
11. D. Calvanese, G. De Giacomo, and M. Lenzerini. On the decidability of query containment under constraints. In *Proc. of PODS'98*, pages 149–158, 1998.
12. D. Calvanese, M. Lenzerini, and D. Nardi. Unifying class-based representation formalisms. *J. of Artificial Intelligence Research*, 11:199–240, 1999.
13. D. Calvanese and R. Rosati. Answering recursive queries under keys and foreign keys is undecidable. In *Proc. of KRDB 2003*. CEUR Electronic Workshop Proceedings, http://ceur-ws.org/Vol-79/, 2003.

14. B. Glimm, I. Horrocks, and U. Sattler. Conjunctive query answering for description logics with transitive roles. In *Proc. of DL 2006*. CEUR Electronic Workshop Proceedings, `http://ceur-ws.org/Vol-189`, 2006.

15. E. Grädel, P. G. Kolaitis, and M. Y. Vardi. On the decision problem for two-variable first-order logic. *Bulletin of Symbolic Logic*, 3(1):53–69, 1997.

16. B. C. Grau. A possible simplification of the semantic web architecture. In *Proc. of the 13th Int. World Wide Web Conf. (WWW 2004)*, pages 704–713, 2004.

17. I. Horrocks and S. Tessaris. Querying the Semantic Web: a formal approach. In *Proc. of ISWC 2002*, volume 2342 of *LNCS*, pages 177–191. Springer, 2002.

18. T. Imielinski and W. L. Jr. Incomplete information in relational databases. *J. of the ACM*, 31(4):761–791, 1984.

19. M. Lenzerini. Data integration: A theoretical perspective. In *Proc. of PODS 2002*, pages 233–246, 2002.

20. A. Y. Levy and M.-C. Rousset. Combining Horn rules and description logics in CARIN. *Artificial Intelligence*, 104(1–2):165–209, 1998.

21. B. Motik. *Reasoning in Description Logics using Resolution and Deductive Databases*. PhD thesis, University of Karlsruhe, 2005.

22. M. M. Ortiz, D. Calvanese, and T. Eiter. Characterizing data complexity for conjunctive query answering in expressive description logics. In *Proc. of AAAI 2006*, 2006.

23. M. M. Ortiz, D. Calvanese, and T. Eiter. Data complexity of answering unions of conjunctive queries in $\mathcal{SHIQ}$. In *Proc. of DL 2006*. CEUR Electronic Workshop Proceedings, `http://ceur-ws.org/Vol-189`, 2006.

24. P. F. Patel-Schneider, P. J. Hayes, I. Horrocks, and F. van Harmelen. OWL web ontology language; semantics and abstract syntax. W3C candidate recommendation, http://www.w3.org/tr/owl-semantics/, november 2002.

25. R. Rosati. On the decidability and finite controllability of query processing in databases with incomplete information. In *Proc. of PODS 2006*, pages 356–365, 2006.

26. E. Sirin and B. Parsia. Optimizations for answering conjunctive abox queries: First results. In *Proc. of DL 2006*. CEUR Electronic Workshop Proceedings, `http://ceur-ws.org/Vol-189`, 2006.

27. S. Tessaris. *Questions and Answers: Reasoning and Querying in Description Logic*. PhD thesis, University of Manchester, Department of Computer Science, Apr. 2001.

28. B. Trahtenbrot. Impossibility of an algorithm for the decision problem in finite classes. *Transactions of the American Mathematical Society*, 3:1–5, 1963.

29. R. van der Meyden. The complexity of querying indefinite data about linearly ordered domains. *J. of Computer and System Sciences*, 54(1):113–135, 1997.

30. M. Y. Vardi. The complexity of relational query languages. In *Proc. of STOC'82*, pages 137–146, 1982.

31. M. Y. Vardi. On the integrity of databases with incomplete information. In *Proc. of PODS'82*, pages 252–266, 1982.

Complexity of Consistent Query Answering in Databases Under Cardinality-Based and Incremental Repair Semantics

Andrei Lopatenko[1,*] and Leopoldo Bertossi[2]

[1] Free University of Bozen-Bolzano
Faculty of Computer Science Bozen-Bolzano, Italy
`lopatenko@inf.unibz.it`
[2] Carleton University, School of Computer Science
Ottawa, Canada
`bertossi@scs.carleton.ca`

Abstract. A database D may be inconsistent wrt a given set IC of integrity constraints. Consistent Query Answering (CQA) is the problem of computing from D the answers to a query that are consistent wrt IC. Consistent answers are invariant under all the *repairs* of D, i.e. the consistent instances that minimally depart from D. Three classes of repair have been considered in the literature: those that minimize set-theoretically the set of tuples in the symmetric difference; those that minimize the changes of attribute values, and those that minimize the cardinality of the set of tuples in the symmetric difference. The latter class has not been systematically investigated. In this paper we obtain algorithmic and complexity theoretic results for CQA under this cardinality-based repair semantics. We do this in the usual, static setting, but also in a dynamic framework where a consistent database is affected by a sequence of updates, which may make it inconsistent. We also establish comparative results with the other two kinds of repairs in the dynamic case.

1 Introduction

The purpose of *consistent query answering* (CQA) is to compute query answers that are consistent with certain integrity constraints (ICs) that the database as a whole may fail to satisfy. Consistent answers have been characterized as those that are invariant under minimal forms of restoration of the consistency of the database [1, 5]. A particular and first notion of minimal restoration of consistency was captured in [1] in terms of database *repairs*, i.e. consistent database instances that share the schema with the original database, but differ from the latter by a *minimal set of whole tuples under set inclusion*. In this paper we call this semantics "the S-repair semantics", for being set oriented. In [5, 15, 1, 7, 3, 9], complexity bounds for CQA under the S-repair semantics have been reported.

Two other repair semantics naturally arise and have been considered in the literature. The *A-repair semantics* is based on changing in a minimal way *attribute*

---

* Current affiliation: Google, Zürich.

values in database tuples in order to restore consistency. CQA under the A-repair semantics has also been investigated [29, 14, 4, 12]. The *C-repair semantics* is based on repairs of the original database that minimize the *cardinality* of the set of tuples by which the instances differ [2]. This semantics has received much less attention so far.

Example 1. Consider a database schema $P(X, Y, Z)$ with the functional dependency $X \rightarrow Y$. The inconsistent instance $D = \{P(a, b, c), P(a, c, d), P(a, c, e)\}$, seen as a set of ground atoms, has two S-repairs, $D_1 = \{P(a, b, c)\}$ and $D_2 = \{P(a, c, d), P(a, c, e)\}$, because the symmetric set differences with D, $\Delta(D, D_1)$ and $\Delta(D, D_2)$, are minimal under set inclusion. However, only for D_2 the cardinality $|\Delta(D, D_2)|$ of the symmetric set difference is minimum; and D_2 is the only C-repair.

The query $P(x, y, z)$ has consistent answers (a, c, d) and (a, c, e) under the C-repair semantics (they are classic answers in the only C-repair), but none under the S- repair semantics (the two S-repairs share no classic answers).   □

The consistent query answers under C-repairs form a superset of the consistent answers under S-repairs, because every C-repair is also an S-repair. Actually, in situations where the S-repair semantics does not give any consistent answers, the C-repair semantics may return answers. These answers could be further filtered out according to other criteria at a post-processing stage. For example, in the extreme case where there is only one database tuple in semantic conflict with a possibly large set of other tuples, the existence of an S-repair containing the only conflicting tuple would easily lead to an empty set of consistent answers. The C-repair semantics would not allow such a repair (c.f. Example 3 below).

Furthermore, the C-repair semantics has the interesting property that CQA, a form of *cautious* or *certain* reasoning (declaring true what is true in *all* repairs), and its *brave* or *possible* version (i.e. true in *some* repair), are mutually reducible in polynomial time and share the same data complexity. This is established in Section 3 by proving first some useful graph-theoretic lemmas about maximum independent sets that are interesting in themselves, and have a wider applicability in the context of CQA.

In [2], C-repairs were specified using disjunctive logic programs with stable model semantics [17] and weak cardinality constraints [6]. In this paper, applying the graph-theoretic techniques and results mentioned above, we obtain the first non-trivial complexity results for CQA under the C-repair semantics. Our emphasis is on CQA, as opposed to computing or checking specific repairs.

All the complexity bounds on CQA given so far in the literature, no matter which repair semantics is chosen, consider *the static case*: Given a snapshot of a database, a set of integrity constraints, and a query, the problems are the computation and verification of consistent answers to the query. In this paper we also take into account dynamic aspects of data, studying the complexity of CQA when the consistency of a database may be affected by update actions.

Example 2. (example 1 continued) The C-repair $D_2 = \{P(a,c,d), P(a,c,e)\}$ is obviously consistent, however after the execution of the update operation $insert(P(a,f,d))$ it becomes inconsistent. In this case, the only C-repair of $D_2 \cup \{P(a,f,d)\}$ is D_2 itself. So, CQA from $D_2 \cup \{P(a,f,d)\}$ amounts to classic query answering from D_2. However, if we start from the consistent instance $D' = \{P(a,c,d)\}$, executing the same update operation leads to two C-repairs, D' and also $\{P(a,f,d)\}$, and now CQA from $D' \cup \{P(a,f,d)\}$ is different from classic query answering from D', because two repairs have to be considered. □

Understanding and handling CQA in a dynamic setting is crucial for its applicability. Incremental methods should be developed, since it would be inefficient to compute a materialized repair of the database or a consistent answer to a query from scratch after every update.

While we think that the right repair semantics may be application dependent, being able to compare the possible semantics in terms of complexity may also shed some light on what may be the repair semantics of choice. This comparison should consider both static and incremental CQA, because a specific semantics might be better than others in terms of complexity when the database is affected by certain updates. In this paper we compare the C-repair semantics with the S- and A-repair semantics mentioned before, and both in the static and incremental settings.

In Section 3 we prove that static CQA under C-repairs is $P^{NP(log(n))}$-hard for denial constraints and ground atomic queries; which contrasts with the *PTIME* result for S-repairs in [9]. On the other side, in Section 4, we prove that incremental CQA, i.e. CQA in the dynamic setting, under the C-repair semantics is in *PTIME* for denial constraints and conjunctive queries; and that the same problem under S-repairs is *coNP*-hard (in data).

The naive algorithms for incremental CQA under the C-repair semantics are polynomial in data, but exponential in the size of the update sequence. In consequence, we also study the *parameterized complexity* [10, 13] of incremental CQA under the C-repair semantics, being the parameter the size of the update sequence. We establish that the problem is *fixed parameter tractable* (FPT).

For establishing comparisons with the C-repair semantics, we obtain new results on the static and incremental complexity both under the classic, i.e. S-repair semantics, and the A-repair semantics. We prove, for the former, that incremental CQA is coNP-hard; whereas for the latter, static and incremental CQA become both P^{NP}-hard in data.

We concentrate on relational databases and denial integrity constraints, which include most of the constraints found in applications where inconsistencies naturally arise, e.g. census-like databases [4], experimental samples databases, biological databases, etc. Complexity results refer to data complexity. For complexity theory we refer to [26]; and to [13] for parameterized complexity. Proofs of the results in this paper can be found in [22].

2   Semantics for Consistent Query Answering

A relational database instance D is a finite set of ground atoms $R(\bar{t})$ (also called *database tuples*[1]), where R is a relation in the schema $\mathcal{D}$, and $\bar{t}$ is a finite sequence of constants from the domain $\mathcal{U}$. A database atom is of the form $R(\bar{t})$, where R is a predicate in $\mathcal{D}$, and $\bar{t}$ may contain constants or variables. A database literal is a database atom or a negation of a database atom. With $\Delta(D', D)$ we denote the symmetric difference $(D' \smallsetminus D) \cup (D \smallsetminus D')$ between instances D, D', conceived both as sets of ground atoms.

The relational schema $\mathcal{D}$ determines a first-order language $L(\mathcal{D})$ based on the relation names, the elements of $\mathcal{U}$, and extra built-in predicates. In the language $L(\mathcal{D})$, integrity constraints are sentences, and queries are formulas, usually with free variables. We assume in this paper that sets IC of ICs are always consistent in the sense that they are simultaneously satisfiable as first-order sentences. A database is *consistent* wrt to a given set of integrity constraints IC if the sentences in IC are all true in D, denoted $D \models IC$. An answer to a query $Q(\bar{x})$, with free variables $\bar{x}$, is a tuple $\bar{t}$ that makes Q true in D when the variables in $\bar{x}$ are interpreted as the corresponding values in $\bar{t}$, denoted $D \models Q[\bar{t}]$.

Definition 1. For a database D, integrity constraints IC, and a partial order $\preceq_{D,\mathcal{S}}$ over databases that depends on the original database D and a repair semantics $\mathcal{S}$, a *repair of D wrt IC under $\mathcal{S}$* is an instance D' such that: (a) D' has the same schema and domain as D; (b) $D' \models IC$; and (c) there is no D'' satisfying (a) and (b), such that $D'' \prec_{D,\mathcal{S}} D'$, i.e. $D'' \preceq_{D,\mathcal{S}} D'$ and not $D' \preceq_{D,\mathcal{S}} D''$. The set of all repairs is denoted with $Rep(D, IC, \mathcal{S})$.   □

The class $Rep(D, IC, \mathcal{S})$ depends upon the semantics $\mathcal{S}$, that determines the partial order $\preceq$ and the way repairs can be obtained, e.g. by allowing both insertions and deletions of whole database tuples [1], or deletions of them only [9], or only changes of attribute values [29, 4, 12], etc. (c.f. Definition 2.) We summarize here the most common repair semantics.

Definition 2. (a) *S-repair semantics* [1]: $D' \preceq_{D,S} D''$ iff $\Delta(D', D) \subseteq \Delta(D'', D)$.
(b) *C-repair semantics*: $D' \preceq_{D,C} D''$ iff $|\Delta(D', D)| \leq |\Delta(D'', D)|$.
(c) *A-repair semantics*: $D' \preceq_{D,A} D''$ iff $f(D, D') \leq f(D, D'')$, where f is a fixed numerical aggregation function over differences of attribute values.   □

More details about the A-repair semantics can be found in Section 4.3. Particular cases of A-repairs can be found in [14, 12], where the aggregation function to be minimized is the number of all attribute changes; and in [4], where the function is the overall quadratic difference obtained from the changes in numerical attributes between the original database and the repair. S-repairs and C-repairs are "tuple-based", in the sense that consistency is restored by inserting and/or deleting whole database tuples; whereas A-repairs are obtained by changing attributes values in existing tuples only.

---

[1] We also use the term *tuple* to refer to a finite sequence $\bar{t} = (c_1, \ldots, c_n)$ of constants of the database domain $\mathcal{U}$, but a *database tuple* is a ground atomic sentence with predicate in $\mathcal{D}$ (excluding built-ins predicates, like comparisons).

In Example 1, attribute-based repairs could be $\{P(a, c, c), P(a, c, d), P(a, c, e)\}$, suggesting that we made a mistake in the second argument of the first tuple, but also $\{P(a, b, c), P(a, b, d), P(a, b, e)\}$. If the aggregate function in Definition 2(c) is the number of changes in attribute values, the former would be a repair, but not the latter. A-repairs may not be S- or C-repairs if the changes of attribute values have to be simulated via deletions followed by insertions.

Definition 3. Let D be a database, IC a set of ICs, and $Q(\bar{x})$ a query. (a) A ground tuple $\bar{t}$ is a *consistent answer* to Q wrt IC under semantics $\mathcal{S}$ if for every $D' \in Rep(D, IC, \mathcal{S})$, $D' \models Q[\bar{t}]$. (b) $Cqa(Q, D, IC, \mathcal{S})$ is the set of consistent answers to Q in D wrt IC under semantics $\mathcal{S}$. If Q is a sentence (a boolean query), $Cqa(Q, D, IC, \mathcal{S}) := \{yes\}$ when $D' \models Q$ for every $D' \in Rep(D, IC, \mathcal{S})$, and $Cqa(Q, D, IC, \mathcal{S}) := \{no\}$, otherwise. (c) $CQA(Q, IC, \mathcal{S}) := \{(D, \bar{t}) \mid \bar{t} \in Cqa(Q, D, IC, \mathcal{S})\}$ is the *decision problem of consistent query answering.*   □

Denial constraints are integrity constraints expressed by $L(\mathcal{D})$-sentences of the form $\forall \bar{x} \neg (A_1 \wedge \ldots \wedge A_m \wedge \gamma)$, where each A_i is a database atom and γ is a conjunction of comparison atoms. In particular, functional dependencies (FDs), e.g. $\forall x \forall y \forall z \neg (R(x, y) \wedge R(x, z) \wedge y \neq z)$, are denial constraints. For denial ICs, tuple-based repairs are obtained by tuple deletions only [9].

3   Complexity of CQA Under the C-Repair Semantics

As a consequence of the specification of C-repairs as the stable models of disjunctive logic programs with non-prioritized weak constraints [2] and the results in [6], we obtain that an upper bound on the data complexity of CQA under the C-repair semantics is the class $\Delta_3^P(log(n))$.

In [3], *conflict graphs* were first introduced to study the complexity of CQA for aggregate queries wrt FDs under the S-repair semantics. They have as vertices the database tuples; and edges connect two tuples that simultaneously violate a FD. There is a one-to-one correspondence between S-repairs of the database and the set-theoretically *maximal* independent sets in the conflict graph. Similarly, there is a one-to-one correspondence between C-repairs and *maximum* independent sets in the same graph (but now they are maximum in cardinality).

Conflict graphs for databases wrt general denial constraints become *conflict hypergraphs* [9] that have as vertices the database tuples, and as hyperedges the (set theoretically minimal) collections of tuples that simultaneously violate one of the denial constraints. The size of the hypergraph (including vertices and hyperedges) is polynomial in the size of the database, because we have a fixed set of denial constraints. The correspondence for conflict graphs between repairs and independent sets −maximum or maximal depending on the semantics− still holds for hypergraphs, where an independent set in an hypergraph is a set of vertices that does not contain any hyperedges [9].

Notice that, unless an IC forces a particular tuple not to belong to the database,[2] every tuple in the original database belongs to some S-repair, but

---

[2] We do not consider in this work such *non generic* ICs [5].

not necessarily to a C-repair (c.f. Example 1, where the tuple $P(a, b, c)$ does not belong to the only C-repair).

In consequence, testing membership of vertices to some maximum independent set becomes a relevant for C-repairs. The complexity of this problem will determine the complexity of CQA under the C-repair semantics. For this purpose we will use some graph-theoretic constructions and lemmas about maximum independent sets, whose proofs use a self-reducibility property of independent sets that can be expressed as follows: For any graph G and vertex v, every maximum independent set that contains v (meaning maximum among the independent sets that contain v) consists of vertex v together with a maximum independent set of the graph G' that is obtained from G by deleting all vertices adjacent to v.

To keep the presentation simpler, we concentrate mostly on conflicts graphs and FDs. However, the results obtained carry over to denial constraints and their hypergraphs. Notice, as a motivation for the next lemmas, that a ground atomic query is consistently true when it belongs, as a database tuple, i.e. as a vertex in the conflict graph, to all the maximum independent sets of the conflict graph.

Lemma 1. Consider a graph G and a vertex v in it. (a) For the graph G' obtained by adding a new vertex v' that is connected only to the neighbors of v, the following properties are equivalent: 1. There is a maximum independent set of G containing v. 2. v belongs to every maximum independent set of G'. 3. The sizes of maximum independent sets in G and G' differ by one.

(b) There is a graph G' extending G that can be constructed in logarithmic space, such that v belongs to all maximum independent sets of G iff v belongs to some maximum independent set of G'.   □

From this lemma and the membership to $FP^{NP(log(n))}$ of computing the size of a maximum clique in a graph [21], we obtain

Lemma 2. The problems of deciding for a vertex in a graph if it belongs to some maximum independent set and if it belongs to all maximum independent sets are both in $P^{NP(log(n))}$.   □

Theorem 1. For functional dependencies and ground atomic queries, CQA under the C-repair semantics belongs to $P^{NP(log(n))}$.   □

Considering the maximum independent sets, i.e. C-repairs, as a collection of possible worlds, the previous lemma shows a close connection between the *certain* C-repair semantics (true in *every* repair), that is the basis for CQA, and the *possible* C-repair semantics (true in *some* repair). CQA under these semantics and functional dependencies are polynomially reducible to each other; actually also for negations of ground atomic queries.

Lemma 3. The following problems are mutually *LOGSPACE*-reducible to each other: (1) *Certain positive:* Given a vertex v and a graph G, decide if v belongs to every maximum independent set of G. (2) *Certain negative:* Given a vertex v and a graph G, decide if all the maximum independent sets of G do not contain v. (3) *Possible negative:* Given a vertex v and a graph G, decide if there is a maximum independent set of G that does not contain v. (4) *Possible positive:* Given a vertex v and a graph G, decide if v belongs to at least one maximum independent set of G. □

Since the negation $\neg R(\bar{t})$ of a ground atomic query $R(\bar{t})$ is consistently true wrt the C-repair semantics iff the vertex corresponding to $R(\bar{t})$ in the conflict graph does not belong to any maximum independent set, using Lemma 3 we can extend Theorem 1 to conjunctions of literals.[3] Actually, since Lemmas 1, 2 and 3 still hold for hypergraphs, we obtain

Theorem 2. For denial constraints and queries that are conjunctions of literals, CQA under the C-repair semantics belongs to $P^{NP(log(n))}$. □

Now we will represent the maximum independent sets of a graph as C-repairs of an inconsistent database wrt a denial constraint. This is interesting, because conflict graphs for databases wrt denial constraints are, as indicate before, actually conflict hypergraphs.

Lemma 4. There is a fixed database schema $\mathcal{D}$ and a denial constraint φ in $L(\mathcal{D})$, such that for every graph G, there is an instance D over $\mathcal{D}$, whose C-repairs wrt φ are in one-to-one correspondence with the maximum independent sets of G. Furthermore, D can be built in polynomial time in the size of G. □

From Lemma 4 and the $P^{NP(log(n))}$-completeness of determining the size of a maximum clique [21], we obtain

Theorem 3. Determining the size of a C-repair for denial constraints is complete for $FP^{NP(log(n))}$. □

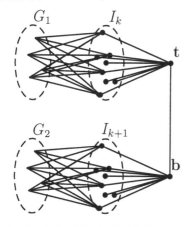

Fig. 1. The block $B_k(G, t)$

In order to obtain hardness for CQA under the C-repair semantics, we need to construct the block graph $B_k(G, \mathbf{t})$ (c.f. Figure 1), consisting of two copies G_1, G_2 of G, and two internally disconnected subgraphs I_k, I_{k+1}, with k and $k+1$ vertices, resp. Every vertex in G (G') is connected to every vertex in I_k (resp. I_{k+1}).

Lemma 5. Given a graph G and a number k, a graph $B_k(G, \mathbf{t})$ can be computed in polynomial time in the size of G, where $\mathbf{t}$ is a distinguished vertex in it that belongs to all its maximum independent sets iff the cardinality of a maximum independent set of G is equal to k. □

---

[3] This can also be obtained, less directly, from the closure of $P^{NP(log(n))}$ under complement.

Lemma 6. Deciding if a vertex belongs to all maximum independent sets of a graph is $P^{NP(log(n))}$-hard.   □

This result can be proved by reduction from the following $P^{NP(log(n))}$-complete decision problem [21]: Given a graph G and an integer k, is the size of a maximum clique in G equivalent to 0 *mod* k? G is reduced to a graph G' that is built by combining a number of versions of the block construction in Figure 1. Now, the graph G' used in Lemma 6 can be represented according to Lemma 4 as a database consistency problem, and in this way we obtain

Theorem 4. For denial constraints, CQA under the C-repair semantics for queries that are conjunctions of ground literals is $P^{NP(log(n))}$-complete.   □

This theorem still holds for ground atomic queries, which is interesting, because for this kind of queries and denial constraints CQA under the S-repair semantics is in *PTIME* [9].

4   Incremental Complexity of CQA

Assume that we have a consistent database instance D wrt to IC. D may become inconsistent after the execution of an update sequence U composed of operations of the forms $insert(R(\bar{t}))$, $delete(R(\bar{t}))$, meaning insert/delete tuple $R(\bar{t})$ into/from D, or $change(R(\bar{t}), A, a)$, for changing value of attribute A in $R(\bar{t})$ to a, with $a \in \mathcal{U}$. We are interested in whether we can find consistent query answers from the possibly inconsistently updated database $U(D)$ more efficiently by taking into account the previous consistent database state.

Definition 4. For a consistent database D wrt IC, and a sequence U of update operations $U_1, \ldots, U_m$, *incremental consistent query answering* for query Q is CQA for Q wrt IC from instance $U(D)$, that results from applying U to D.   □

Update sequences U will be atomic, in the sense that they are completely executed or not. This allows us to concentrate on "minimized" versions of update sequences, e.g. containing only insertions and/or attribute changes when dealing with denial constraints, because deletions do not cause any violations. We are still interested in data complexity, i.e. wrt the size $|D|$ of the original database. In particular, m is fixed, and usually small wrt $|D|$.

A notion of incremental complexity has been introduced in [23], and also in [20] under the name of *dynamic complexity*. There, the instance that is updated can be arbitrary, and the question is about the complexity for the updated version when information about the previous instance can be used. In our case, we are assuming that the initial database is consistent. As opposed to [23, 20], where new incremental or dynamic complexity classes are introduced, we appeal to those classic complexity classes found at a low level in the polynomial hierarchy.

4.1   Incremental Complexity: C-Repair Semantics

In contrast to static CQA for the C-repair semantics, it holds

Theorem 5. For the C-repair semantics, first-order boolean queries, denial constraints, and update sequences U of fixed length m applied to D, incremental CQA is in *PTIME* in $|D|$.   □

The proof of this theorem provides an upper bound of of $O(m \cdot n^m)$, that is polynomial in the size n of the initial database, but exponential in m, which makes the problem tractable in data, but with the size of the update sequence in the exponent. We are interested in determining if queries can be consistently answered in time $O(f(m) \times n^c)$, for a constant c and a function $f(m)$ depending only on m. In this way we isolate the complexity introduced by U.

The area of parameterized complexity studies this kind of problems [19, 25]. A decision problem with inputs of the form (I, p), where p is a distinguished parameter of the input, is *fixed parameter tractable*, and by definition belongs to the class *FPT* [10], if it can be solved in time $O(f(|p|) \cdot |I|^c)$, where c and the hidden constant do not depend on $|p|$ or $|I|$ and f does not depend on $|I|$.

Definition 5. Given a query Q, ICs IC, and a ground tuple $\bar{t}$, *parameterized incremental CQA* is the decision problem $CQA^P(Q, IC) := \{(D, U, \bar{t}) \mid D$ is an instance, U an update sequence , $\bar{t}$ is consistent answer to Q in $U(D)\}$, whose parameter is U, and consistency of answers refers to C-repairs of $U(D)$.   □

We keep Q and IC fixed in the problem definition because, except for the parameter U, we are interested in data complexity.

Theorem 6. For functional dependencies and queries that are conjunctions of literals, parameterized incremental CQA is in *FPT*.   □

The *vertex cover problem*, of deciding if graph G has a vertex cover (VC) of size no bigger than k, belongs to the class *FPT*, i.e. there is a polynomial time parameterized algorithm $VC(G, k)$ for it [10]; actually one that runs in time $O(1.2852^k + k \cdot n)$, being n the size of G [8].

The algorithm whose existence is claimed in Theorem 6 is as follows: Let G be the conflict graph associated to the database obtained after the insertion of m tuples. By binary search, calling each time $VC(G, \_)$, it is possible to determine the size of a minimum VC for G. This gives us the minimum number of tuples that have to be removed in order to restore consistency; and can be done in time $O(log(m) \cdot (1.2852^m + m \cdot n))$, where n is the size of the original database. In order to determine if a tuple $R(\bar{t})$ belongs to every maximum independent set, i.e. if it is consistently true, compute the size of a minimum VC for $G \smallsetminus \{R(\bar{t})\}$. The two numbers are the same iff the answer is *yes*. The total time is still $O(log(m) \cdot (1.2852^m + m \cdot n)))$, which is linear in the size of the original database. The same algorithm applies if, in addition to tuple insertions, we also have changes of attribute values in the update part; of course, still under the C-repair semantics.

Theorem 6 uses the membership to *FPT* of the VC problem, which we apply to conflict graphs for functional dependencies. However, the result can be extended to denials constraints and their conflict hypergraphs. In our case, the maximum size of an hyperedge is the maximum number of database atoms in a denial constraint, which is determined by the fixed database schema. If this number is d, then we are in the presence of the so-called *d-hitting set problem*, consisting in finding the size of a minimum hitting set for an hypergraph with hyperedges bounded in size by d. This problem is in *FPT* [24].

Theorem 7. For denial constrains and queries that are conjunctions of literals, parameterized incremental CQA is in *FPT*.   □

Using the reductions in Section 3, this result can be extended to incremental CQA under the *possible* C-repair semantics.

4.2   Incremental Complexity: S-Repair Semantics

Incremental CQA for non-quantified conjunctive queries under denial constraints belongs to *PTIME*, which can be established by applying the algorithm in [9] for the static case to $U(D)$.

However, for quantified conjunctive queries the situation may change. Actually, by reduction from static CQA for conjunctive queries and denial ICs under the S-repair semantics, which is *coNP*-hard [9], we obtain

Theorem 8. Under the S-repair semantics, incremental CQA for conjunctive queries and denial constraints is *coNP*-hard.   □

We can see that, for denial constraints, static CQA under the C-repair semantics seems to be harder than under the S-repair semantics ($P^{NP(log(n))}$- vs. *coNP*-hard). On the other side, incremental CQA under the S-repair semantics seems to harder than under the C-repair semantics (*coNP*-hard vs. *PTIME*). The reason is that for the C-repair semantics the cost of a repair cannot exceed the size of the update, whereas for the S-repair semantics the cost of a repair may be unbounded wrt the size of an update.

Example 3. Consider a schema $R(\cdot), S(\cdot)$ with the denial constraint $\forall x \forall y \neg (R(x) \wedge S(y))$; and the consistent database $D = \{R(1), \ldots, R(n)\}$, with an empty table for S. After the update $U = insert(S(0))$, the database becomes inconsistent, and the S-repairs are $\{R(1), \ldots, R(n)\}$ and $\{S(0)\}$. However, only the former is a C-repair, and is at a distance 1 from the original instance, i.e. as the size of the update. However, the second S-repair is at a distance n.   □

4.3   Incremental Complexity: A-Repair Semantics

Before addressing the problem of incremental complexity, we give a complexity lower bound for the *weighted* version of static CQA for the A-repair semantics. In this case, we have a numerical weight function w defined on triples of the form $(R(\bar{t}), A, newValue)$, where $R(\bar{t})$ is a database tuple stored in the database, A is an attribute of R, and $newValue$ is a new value for A in $R(\bar{t})$. The *weighted A-repair semantics* (wA-repair semantics) is just a particular case of Definition 2(c), where the distance is given by an aggregation function g applied to the set of numbers $\{w(R(\bar{t}), A, newValue) \mid R(\bar{t}) \in D\}$.

Typically, g is the sum, and the weights are $w(R(\bar{t}), A, newValue) = 1$ if $R(\bar{t})[A]$ is different from $newValue$, and 0 otherwise, where $R(\bar{t})[A]$ is the projection of database tuple $R(\bar{t})$ on attribute A, i.e. just the number of changes is counted [14]. In [4], g is still the sum, but w is given by $w(R(\bar{t}), A, newValue) = \alpha_A \cdot (R(\bar{t})[A] - newValue)^2$, where α_A is a coefficient introduced to capture the relative importance of attribute A or scale factors. In these cases, w does not depend on D. However, if the weight function w depended on the size of D, w should become part of the input for the decision problem of CQA.

Theorem 9. Static CQA for ground atomic queries and denial constraints under the wA-repair semantics is P^{NP}-hard. □

In order to obtain a hardness result in the incremental case and for denial constraints (for which we are assuming update sequences do not contain tuple deletions), we can use the kind of A-repairs introduced in [4].

Theorem 10. Incremental CQA for atomic queries and denial constraints under the wA-repair semantics is P^{NP}-hard. □

These results still hold for tuple insertions as update actions, the fixed weight function that assigns value 1 to every change, and the sum as aggregation function. In case we have numerical values as in [4] or a bounded domain, we can obtain as in [4, theorem 4(b)] that the problems in Theorems 9 and 10 belong both to Π_2^P.

Under the A-repair semantics, if the update sequence consist of *change* actions, then we can obtain polynomial time incremental CQA under the additional condition that the set of attribute values than can be used to restore consistency is bounded in size, independently from the database (or its active domain). Such an assumption can be justified in several applications, like in census-like databases that are corrected according to inequality-free denial constraints that force the new values to be taken at the border of a database independent region [4]; and also in applications where denial constraints, this time containing inequalities, force the attribute values to be taken in a finite, pre-specified set. The proof is similar to the one of Theorem 5, and the polynomial bound now also depends on the size of the set of candidate values.

Theorem 11. For a database independent and bounded domain of attribute values, incremental CQA under the A-repair semantics, for first-order boolean queries, denial constraints, and update sequences containing only *change* actions is in *PTIME* in the size of the original database. □

Now, we present a lower bound for CQA under the A-repair semantics for *first-order ICs* and tuple deletions, which now may affect their satisfaction.

Lemma 7. For any planar graph G with vertices of degree at most 4, there exists a regular graph G' of degree 4 that is 4-colorable, such that G' is 3-colorable iff G is 3-colorable. G' can be built in polynomial time in $|G|$. □

Notice that graph G, due to its planarity, is 4-colorable. The graph G', is an extension of graph G that may not be planar, but preserves 4-Colorability. We use the construction in Lemma 7 as follows: Given any planar graph G of degree 4, construct graph G' as in the lemma, which is regular of degree 4 and 4-colorable. Its 4-colorability is encoded as a database problem with a fixed set of first-order constraints. Since G' is 4-colorable, the database is consistent. Furthermore, G' uses all the 4 colors in the official table of colors, as specified by the ICs. In the update part, deleting one of the colors leaves us with the problem of coloring G' with only three colors (under an A-repair semantics only changes of colors are allowed to restore consistency), which is possible iff the original graph G is 3-colorable. Deciding about the latter problem is NP-complete [16]. We obtain

Theorem 12. For ground atomic queries, first-order ICs, and update sequences consisting of tuple deletions, incremental CQA under the A-repair semantics is $coNP$-hard.   □

To obtain this result it is good enough to use the sum as the aggregation function and the weight function that assigns 1 to each change. Clearly, this lower bound also applies to update sequences containing any combination of *insert, delete, change*.

5   Conclusions

The dynamic scenario for consistent query answering that considers possible updates on a database had not been considered before in the literature. Doing incremental CQA on the basis of the original database and the sequence of updates is an important and natural problem. Developing algorithms that take into account previously obtained consistent answers that are possible cached and the updates at hand is a crucial problem for making CQA scale up for real database applications. Much research is still needed in this direction.

In this paper we have concentrated mostly on complexity bounds for this problem under different semantics. When we started obtaining results for incremental CQA under repairs that differ from the original instance by a minimum number of tuples, i.e. C-repairs, we realized that this semantics had not been sufficiently explored in the literature in the static version of CQA, and that a full comparison was not possible. In the first part of this paper we studied the complexity of CQA for the C-repair semantics and denial constraints. In doing so, we developed graph-theoretic techniques for polynomially reducing each of the certain and possible (or cautious and brave) C-repair semantics for CQA to the other. A similar result does not hold for the S-repair semantics, conjunctive queries, and denial constraints: CQA (under the *certain* semantics) is $coNP$-complete [9], but is in $PTIME$ for the *possible* semantics.

The complexity of CQA in a P2P setting was studied in [18], including a form a cardinality-based repairs. However, a different semantics is used, which makes it difficult to compare results. Actually, in that setting it is possible that repairs do not exist, whereas in our case, since S-repairs always exist [1], also C-repairs exist. The complexity result for CQA in [18], that seems to be shared by C- and S-repairs, is obtained on the basis of the complexity of checking the existence of repairs (a problem that in our case is trivial).

The C-repair semantics can be generalized considering weights on tuples. Under denial constraints, this means that it may be more costly to remove certain tuples than others to restore consistency. More precisely, database tuples $R(\bar{t})$ have associated numerical costs $w(R(\bar{t}))$, that become part of the input for the CQA decision problem. Now, the partial order between instances is given by $D_1 \preceq_{D,wC} D_2$ iff $|D \triangle D_1|_w \leq |D \triangle D_2|_w$, where, for a set of database tuples S, $|S|_w$ is the sum of the weights of the elements of S. It can be proved that CQA for ground atomic queries wrt denial constraints under this semantics belongs to P^{NP} [22, proposition 5].

Furthermore, it possible to reduce CQA under the C-repair semantics to CQA under *least-squares* A-repairs semantics that minimizes the sum of the quadratic differences between numerical values [4], which is a particular case of the general semantics studied in Section 4.3.

Theorem 13. Given a database schema $\mathcal{D}$, a set IC of denial constraints in $L(\mathcal{D})$, and a ground atomic query $Q \in L(\mathcal{D})$, there are a schema $\mathcal{D}'$ with some fixable numerical attributes, a set IC' of ICs in $L(\mathcal{D}')$, and a query $Q' \in L(\mathcal{D}')$, such that: For every database D over $\mathcal{D}$, there is a database D' over $\mathcal{D}'$ that can be computed from D in $LOGSPACE$ (in data) for which it holds: Q is consistently true wrt IC in D under the C-repairs semantics iff Q' is consistently true wrt to IC' in D' under the least-squares A-repair semantics. □

This result also applies to other numerical A-repair semantics as discussed in [4], and is about data complexity. For fixed $\mathcal{D}, IC, Q, D$, also fixed $\mathcal{D}', IC', Q'$ can be obtained in $LOGSPACE$ from $\mathcal{D}, IC, Q$. Theorem 13, together with Theorem 4, allows us to obtain a simple proof of the $P^{NP(\log n)}$-hardness of the least-squares repair semantics. In [4], P^{NP}-hardness is obtained for the latter as a better lower bound, but the proof is more complex. This theorem can be extended to the weighted C-repair semantics if integer numerical weights are used.

Our results show that the incremental complexity is lower than the static one in several useful cases, but sometimes the complexity cannot be lowered. It is a subject of ongoing work the development of concrete and explicit algorithms for incremental CQA.

We obtained the first results about fixed parameter tractability for incremental CQA, where the input, for a fixed database schema, can be seen as formed by the original database and the update sequence, whose length is the relevant parameter. This problem requires additional investigation. In particular, the parameterized complexity of incremental CQA under the S- and A-repair semantics has to be investigated, and a more complete picture still has to emerge.

It would be interesting to examine the area of CQA in general from the point of view of parameterized complexity, including the static case. Natural candidates to be a parameter in the classic, static setting could be: (a) the number of inconsistencies in the database, (b) the degree of inconsistency, i.e. the maximum number of violations per database tuple, (c) complexity of inconsistency, i.e. the length of the longest path in the conflict graph or hypergraph. These parameters may be practically significant, since in many applications, like census application [4], inconsistencies are "local".

We considered a version of incremental CQA that assumes that the database is already consistent before updates are executed, a situation that could have been achieved because no previous updates violated the given semantic constraints or a repaired version was chosen before the new updates were executed.

We are currently investigating the dynamic case of CQA in the frameworks of *dynamic complexity* [20, 28] and *incremental complexity* as introduced in [23]. In this case we start with a database D that is not necessarily consistent on which a sequence of basic update operations $U_1, U_2, ..., U_m$ is executed. A clever algorithm for CQA may create or update intermediate data structures at each atomic update step, to help obtain answers at subsequent steps. We are interested in the complexity of CQA after a sequence of updates, when the data structures created by the query answering algorithm at previous states are themselves updatable and accessible.

Acknowledgments.   Research supported by NSERC, and EU projects: Knowledge Web, Interop and Tones. L. Bertossi is Faculty Fellow of IBM Center for Advanced Studies (Toronto Lab.). L. Bertossi appreciates the hospitality and support of Enrico Franconi and the KRDB group in Bolzano. We are grateful to Jan Chomicki, Jörg Flum, and anonymous referees for many useful comments.

References

[1] Arenas, M., Bertossi, L. and Chomicki, J. Consistent Query Answers in Inconsistent Databases. *Proc. ACM Symposium on Principles of Database Systems (PODS 99)*, ACM Press, 1999, pp. 68-79.

[2] Arenas, M., Bertossi, L. and Chomicki, J. Answer Sets for Consistent Query Answering in Inconsistent Databases. *Theory and Practice of Logic Programming*, 2003, 3(4-5):393-424.

[3] Arenas, M., Bertossi, L., Chomicki, J., He, X., Raghavan, V. and Spinrad, J. Scalar Aggregation in Inconsistent Databases. *Theoretical Computer Science*, 2003, 296:405–434.

[4] Bertossi, L., Bravo, L., Franconi, E. and Lopatenko, A. Fixing Numerical Attributes under Integrity Constraints. *Proc. Tenth International Symposium on Database Programming Languages (DBPL 05)*, Springer LNCS 3774, 2005, pp. 262-278.

[5] Bertossi, L. and Chomicki, J. Query Answering in Inconsistent Databases. In *Logics for Emerging Applications of Databases*. Springer, 2003, pp. 43-83.

[6] Buccafurri, F., Leone, N. and Rullo, P. Enhancing Disjunctive Datalog by Constraints. *IEEE Transactions on Knowledge and Data Engineering*, 2000, 12(5):845-860.

[7] Calì, A., Lembo, D. and Rosati, R. Complexity of Query Answering over Inconsistent and Incomplete Databases. *Proc. ACM Symposium on Principles of Database Systems (PODS 03)*, ACM Press, 2003, pp. 260-271.

[8] Chen, J., Kanj, I. and Jia, W. Vertex Cover: Further Observations and Further Improvements. In *Proc. 25th International Workshop on Graph-Theoretic Concepts in Computer Science (WG 99)*, Springer LNCS 1665, 1999, pp. 313-324.

[9] Chomicki, J. and Marcinkowski, J. Minimal-Change Integrity Maintenance using Tuple Deletions. *Information and Computation*, 2005, 197(1-2):90-121.

[10] Downey, R.G. and Fellows, M.R. *Parameterized Complexity*. Springer, Monographs in Computer Science, 1999.

[11] Eiter, T. and Gottlob, G. On the Complexity of Propositional Knowledge Base Revision, Updates, and Counterfactuals. *Artificial Intelligence*, 1992, 57(2-3):227-270.

[12] Flesca, S., Furfaro, F. Parisi, F. Consistent Query Answers on Numerical Databases under Aggregate Constraints. *Proc. Tenth International Symposium on Database Programming Languages (DBPL 05)*, Springer LNCS 3774, 2005, pp. 279-294.

[13] Flum, J. and Grohe, M. *Parameterized Complexity Theory*. Texts in Theoretical Computer Science, Springer Verlag, 2006.

[14] Franconi, E., Laureti Palma, A., Leone, N., Perri, S. and Scarcello, F. Census Data Repair: a Challenging Application of Disjunctive Logic Programming. In *Proc. Logic for Programming, Artificial Intelligence, and Reasoning (LPAR 01)*, Springer LNCS 2250, 2001, pp. 561-578.

[15] Fuxman, A. and Miller, R. First-Order Query Rewriting for Inconsistent Databases. *Proc. International Conference on Database Theory (ICDT 05)*, Springer LNCS 3363, 2004, pp. 337-351.

[16] Garey, M., Johnson, D. and Stockmeyer, L. Some Simplified NP-Complete Graph Problems. *Theoretical Computer Science*, 1976, 1(3):237–267.

[17] Gelfond, M. and Lifschitz, V. Classical Negation in Logic Programs and Disjunctive Databases. *New Generation Computing*, 1991, 9:365-385.

[18] Greco, G. and Scarcello, F. On the Complexity of Computing Peer Agreements for Consistent Query Answering in Peer-to-Peer Data Integration Systems. *Proc. International Conference on Information and Knowledge Management (CIKM 05)*, ACM Press, 2005, pp. 36-43.

[19] Grohe, M. Parameterized Complexity for the Data-base Theorist. *SIGMOD Record*, 2002, 31(4):86-96.

[20] Immerman, N. *Descriptive Complexity*. Graduate Texts in Computer Science. Springer, 1999.

[21] Krentel, M. The Complexity of Optimization Problems. *J. Computer and Systems Sciences*, 1988, 36:490-509.

[22] Lopatenko, A. and Bertossi, L. Complexity of Consistent Query Answering in Databases under Cardinality-Based and Incremental Repair Semantics. Corr Archiv paper cs.DB/0604002.

[23] Miltersen, P.B., Subramanian, S., Vitter, J.S. and Tamassia, R. Complexity Models for Incremental Computation. *Theoretical Computer Science*, 1994, 130(1):203-236.

[24] Niedermeier, R. and Rossmanith, P. An Efficient Fixed-Parameter Algorithm for 3-Hitting Set. *Journal of Discrete Algorithms*, 2003, 1(1):89-102.

[25] Papadimitriou, C.H. and Yannakakis, M. On the Complexity of Database Queries. *J. Comput. Syst. Sci.*, 1999, 58(3):407-427.

[26] Papadimitriou, C. *Computational Complexity*. Addison-Wesley, 1994.

[27] Robertson, N., Sanders, D.P., Seymour, P. and Thomas, R. Efficiently Four-Coloring Planar Graphs. In *Proc. 28th ACM Symposium on the Theory of Computing (STOC 96)*, ACM Press, 1996, pp. 571-575.

[28] Weber, V. and Schwentick, T. Dynamic Complexity Theory Revisited. *Proc. Annual Symposium on Theoretical Aspects of Computer Science (STACS 05)*, Springer LNCS 3404, 2005, pp. 256-268.

[29] Wijsen, J. Condensed Representation of Database Repairs for Consistent Query Answering. *Proc. International Conference on Database Theory (ICDT 03)*, Springer LNCS 2572, 2003, pp. 378-393.

World-Set Decompositions: Expressiveness and Efficient Algorithms

Lyublena Antova, Christoph Koch, and Dan Olteanu

Lehrstuhl für Informationssysteme
Universität des Saarlandes, Saarbrücken, Germany
{lublena, koch, olteanu}@infosys.uni-sb.de

Abstract. Uncertain information is commonplace in real-world data management scenarios. An important challenge in this context is the ability to represent large sets of possible instances (worlds) while supporting efficient storage and processing. The recent formalism of *world-set decompositions (WSDs)* provides a space-efficient representation for uncertain data that also supports scalable processing. WSDs are *complete* for finite world-sets in that they can represent any finite set of possible worlds. For possibly infinite world-sets, we show that a natural generalization of WSDs precisely captures the expressive power of c-tables. We then show that several important problems are efficiently solvable on WSDs while they are NP-hard on c-tables. Finally, we give a polynomial-time algorithm for factorizing WSDs, i.e. an efficient algorithm for minimizing such representations.

1 Introduction

Recently there has been renewed interest in incomplete information databases. This is due to the important applications of systems for representing incomplete information in data cleaning and integration and more generally in all forms of information systems that have to deal with uncertainty.

An important concept in this context are *strong representation systems* [18,3,17], that is, formalisms for representing sets of possible worlds that are closed under query operations in a given query language. The prototypical strong representation system are the so-called *c-tables* [18,15,16]. Two recent works presented strong, indeed *complete*, representation systems for finite sets of possible worlds. The approach of the *Trio x-relations* [8] relies on a form of intensional information ("lineage") only in combination with which the formalism is strong. In [6] large sets of possible worlds are managed using *world-set decompositions (WSDs)*. The approach is based on relational decomposition to permit space-efficient representation. [6] describes a prototype implementation and shows the efficiency and scalability of the formalism in terms of storage and query evaluation in a large census data scenario.

While there have been numerous other approaches to dealing with incomplete information, such as closing possible worlds semantics using certain answers [1,7,12], constraint or database repair [13,10,9], and probabilistic ranked retrieval [14,4], strong representation systems form a compositional framework

T. Schwentick and D. Suciu (Eds.): ICDT 2007, LNCS 4353, pp. 194–208, 2007.

Table 1. Decision Problems for Representation Systems

Input	Representation system $\mathcal{W}$, instance $I = (R^I)$, tuple t
Problems	Tuple Possibility: $\qquad\qquad\qquad\qquad\quad\exists \mathcal{A} \in rep(\mathcal{W}) : t \in R^{\mathcal{A}}$
	Tuple Certainty: $\qquad\qquad\qquad\qquad\qquad\forall \mathcal{A} \in rep(\mathcal{W}) : t \in R^{\mathcal{A}}$
	Instance Possibility: $\qquad\qquad\qquad\qquad\exists \mathcal{A} \in rep(\mathcal{W}) : R^I = R^{\mathcal{A}}$
	Instance Certainty: $\qquad\qquad\qquad\qquad\forall \mathcal{A} \in rep(\mathcal{W}) : R^I = R^{\mathcal{A}}$
	Tuple Q-Possibility (query Q fixed): $\quad\exists \mathcal{A} \in rep(\mathcal{W}) : t \in Q(\mathcal{A})$
	Tuple Q-Certainty (query Q fixed): $\quad\forall \mathcal{A} \in rep(\mathcal{W}) : t \in Q(\mathcal{A})$
	Instance Q-Possibility (query Q fixed): $\exists \mathcal{A} \in rep(\mathcal{W}) : R^I = Q(\mathcal{A})$
	Instance Q-Certainty (query Q fixed): $\forall \mathcal{A} \in rep(\mathcal{W}) : R^I = Q(\mathcal{A})$

that is minimally intrusive by not requiring to lose information, even about the lack of information, present in an information system. (In fact, computing certain answers entails a loss of possible but uncertain information.) Strong representation systems can be nicely combined with the other approaches; for example, data transformation queries and data cleaning steps effected within a strong representation systems framework can be followed by a query with ranked retrieval or certain answers semantics, closing the possible worlds semantics.

The main goal of this work is to develop expressive yet efficient representation systems for incomplete information. In [17], a strong argument is made supporting c-tables as a benchmark for the expressiveness of representation systems; we concur. Concerning efficient processing, we adopt v-tables as a lower bound regarding succinctness and complexity. The main development of this paper is a representation system that combines, in a sense, the best of all worlds: (1) It is just as expressive as c-tables, (2) it is exponentially more succinct than unions of v-tables, and (3) on the classical decision problems, the complexity bounds are not worse than those for v-tables.

In more detail, the technical contributions of this paper are as follows:

- We introduce gWSDs, an extension of the WSD model of [6] with variables and (in)equality conditions.
- We show that gWSDs are expressively equivalent to c-tables and are therefore a strong representation system for full relational algebra.
- We study the complexity of the main data management problems [3,18] regarding WSDs and gWSDs, summarized in Table 1. Table 2 compares the complexities of these problems in our context to those of existing strong representation systems like the well-behaved ULDBs of Trio[1] and c-tables.
- We present an efficient algorithm for optimizing gWSDs, i.e., for computing an equivalent gWSD whose size is smaller than that of a given gWSD. In the case of WSDs, this is a minimization algorithm that produces the unique maximal decomposition of a given WSD.

One can argue that gWSDs are a practically more applicable representation formalism than c-tables: While having the same expressive power, many

---

[1] The complexity results for Trio are from [8] and were not verified by the authors.

Table 2. Comparison of data complexities for standard decision problems. (* Result for positive relational algebra.)

	v-tables [3]	gWSD	Trio [8]	c-tables [3]
Tuple Possibility	PTIME	PTIME	PTIME	NP-complete
Tuple Certainty	PTIME	PTIME	PTIME	coNP-compl.
Instance Possibility	NP-complete	NP-complete	NP-hard	NP-complete
Instance Certainty	PTIME	PTIME	NP-hard	coNP-compl.
Tuple Q-Possibility	PTIME*	PTIME*	?	NP-complete
Tuple Q-Certainty	coNP-compl.	coNP-compl.	?	coNP-compl.
Instance Q-Possibility	NP-complete	NP-complete	NP-hard	NP-complete
Instance Q-Certainty	coNP-compl.	coNP-compl.	NP-hard	coNP-compl.

important problems are easier to solve. Indeed, as shown in Table 2, the complexity results for gWSDs on the most important decision problems are identical to those for the much weaker v-tables. At the same time WSDs are still concise enough to support the space-efficient representation of very large sets of possible worlds (cf. the experimental evaluation on WSDs in [6]). Also, while gWSDs are strictly stronger than Trio, the complexity characteristics are better.

The results on finding maximal product decompositions relate to earlier work done by the database theory community on relational decomposition given schema constraints (cf. e.g. [2]). Our algorithms do not assume such constraints and only take a snapshot of a database at a particular point in time into consideration. Consequently, updates may require to alter a decomposition. Nevertheless, our results may be of interest independently from WSDs as for instance in certain scenarios with very dense relations, decompositions may be a practically relevant technique for efficiently storing and querying large databases.

Note that we do not consider probabilistic approaches to representing uncertain data (e.g. the recent work [14]) in this paper. However, there is a natural and straightforward probabilistic extension which directly inherits many of the properties studied in this paper, see [6].

The structure of the paper basically follows the list of contributions. Due to space limitations, we have to refer to the technical report [5] for the proofs of a number of results presented in this paper.

2 Preliminaries

We use the named perspective of the relational model and relational algebra with the operations selection σ, projection π, product $\times$, union $\cup$, difference $-$, and renaming δ.

A *relation schema* is a construct of the form $R[U]$, where R is a relation name and U is a nonempty set of attribute names.[2] Let $\mathbf{D}$ be an infinite set of atomic values, the *domain*. A *relation* over schema $R[A_1, \ldots, A_k]$ is a finite set

---

[2] For technical reasons involving the WSDs presented later, we exclude nullary relations and will represent these (e.g., when obtained as results from a Boolean query) using unary relations over a special constant "true".

of tuples $(A_1 : a_1, \ldots, A_k : a_k)$ where $a_1, \ldots, a_k \in \mathbf{D}$. A *relational schema* is a tuple $\Sigma = (R_1[U_1], \ldots, R_k[U_k])$ of relation schemas. A *relational structure (or database)* $\mathcal{A}$ over schema Σ is a tuple $(R_1^{\mathcal{A}}, \ldots, R_k^{\mathcal{A}})$, where each $R_i^{\mathcal{A}}$ is a relation over schema $R_i[U_i]$. When no confusion may occur, we will also use R rather than $R^{\mathcal{A}}$ to denote one particular relation over schema $R[U]$. For a relation R, $\mathsf{sch}(R)$ denotes the set of its attributes, $ar(R)$ its arity and $|R|$ the number of tuples in R.

A set of *possible worlds* (or *world-set*) over schema Σ is a set of databases over schema Σ. Let $\mathbf{W}$ be a set of finite structures, and let rep be a function that maps each $\mathcal{W} \in \mathbf{W}$ to a world-set of the same schema. Then $(\mathbf{W}, rep)$ is called a *strong representation system* for a query language if, for each query Q of that language and each $\mathcal{W} \in \mathbf{W}$ such that the schema of Q is consistent with the schema of the worlds in $rep(\mathcal{W})$, there is a structure $\mathcal{W}' \in \mathbf{W}$ such that $rep(\mathcal{W}') = \{Q(\mathcal{A}) \mid \mathcal{A} \in rep(\mathcal{W})\}$.

2.1 Tables

We now review a number of representation systems for incomplete information that are known from earlier work (cf. e.g. [16,2]).

Let $\mathbf{X}$ be a set of variables. We call an equality of the form $x = c$ or $x = y$, where x and y are variables from $\mathbf{X}$ and c is from $\mathbf{D}$ an *atomic condition*, and will define *(general) conditions* as Boolean combinations (using conjunction, disjunction, and negation) of atomic conditions.

Definition 1 (c-table). A *c-multitable* [18,16] over schema $(R_1[U_1], \ldots, R_k[U_k])$ is a tuple

$$\mathcal{T} = (R_1^{\mathcal{T}}, \ldots, R_k^{\mathcal{T}}, \phi^{\mathcal{T}}, \lambda^{\mathcal{T}})$$

where each $R_i^{\mathcal{T}}$ is a set of $ar(R_i)$-tuples over $\mathbf{D} \cup \mathbf{X}$, $\phi^{\mathcal{T}}$ is a Boolean combination over equalities on $\mathbf{D} \cup \mathbf{X}$ called the *global condition*, and function $\lambda^{\mathcal{T}}$ assigns each tuple from one of the relations $R_1^{\mathcal{T}}, \ldots, R_k^{\mathcal{T}}$ to a condition (called the *local condition* of the tuple). A c-multitable with $k = 1$ is called a *c-table*.

The semantics of a c-multitable $\mathcal{T}$, called its *representation* $rep(\mathcal{T})$, is defined via the notion of a valuation of the variables occurring in $\mathcal{T}$ (i.e., those in the tuples as well as those in the conditions). Let $\nu : \mathbf{X} \to \mathbf{D}$ be a valuation that assigns each variable in $\mathcal{T}$ to a domain value. We overload ν in the natural way to map tuples and conditions over $\mathbf{D} \cup \mathbf{X}$ to tuples and formulas over $\mathbf{D}$.[3] A *satisfaction* of $\mathcal{T}$ is a valuation ν such that $\nu(\phi^{\mathcal{T}})$ is true. A satisfaction ν takes $\mathcal{T}$ to a relational structure $\nu(\mathcal{T}) = (R_1^{\nu(\mathcal{T})}, \ldots, R_k^{\nu(\mathcal{T})})$ where each relation $R_i^{\nu(\mathcal{T})}$ is obtained as $R_i^{\nu(\mathcal{T})} := \{\nu(t) \mid t \in R_i^{\mathcal{T}} \wedge \nu(\lambda^{\mathcal{T}}(t))$ is true$\}$. The representation of $\mathcal{T}$ is now given by its satisfactions, $rep(\mathcal{T}) := \{\nu(\mathcal{T}) \mid \nu$ is a satisfaction of $\mathcal{T}\}$. $\qquad \square$

Proposition 1 ([18]). *The c-multitables are a strong representation system for relational algebra.*

---

[3] Done by extending ν to be the identity on domain values and to commute with the tuple constructor, the Boolean operations, and equality.

We consider two important restrictions of c-multitables.

1. By a *g-multitable* [3], we refer to a c-multitable in which the global condition ϕ^T is a conjunction of possibly negated equalities and λ^T maps each tuple to "true".
2. A *v-multitable* is a g-multitable in which the global condition ϕ^T is a conjunction of equalities.

Without loss of generality, we may assume that the global condition of a g-multitable is a conjunction of *inequalities* and the global condition of a v-multitable is simply "true".[4] Subsequently, we will always assume these two normal forms and omit local conditions from g-multitables and both global and local conditions from v-multitables.

$$\phi^T = (x \neq y)$$

R^T	A	B
	x	1
	2	x

S^T	C
	y
	3

R	A	B
	1	1
	2	1

S	C
	2
	3

$$\nu : \begin{cases} x \mapsto 1 \\ y \mapsto 2 \end{cases}$$

(a)   (b)   (c)

Fig. 1. A g-multitable T (a), possible world $\mathcal{A}$ (b), and a valuation s.t. $\nu(T) = \mathcal{A}$ (c)

Example 1. Consider the g-multitable $T = (R^T, S^T, \phi^T)$ of Figure 1 (a). Then the valuation of Figure 1 (c) satisfies the global condition of T, as $\nu(x) \neq \nu(y)$. Thus $\mathcal{A} \in rep(T)$, where $\mathcal{A}$ is the structure from Figure 1 (b). ☐

Remark 1. It is known from [18] that v-tables are not a strong representation system for relational selection, but for the fragment of relational algebra built from projection, product, and union.

The definition of c-multitables used here is from [16]. The original definition from [18] has been more restrictive in requiring the global condition to be "true". While c-tables without a global condition are strictly weaker (they cannot represent the empty world-set), they nevertheless form a strong representation system for relational algebra.

In [2], the global conditions of c-multitables are required to be conjunctions of equalities and inequalities. It will be a corollary of a result of this paper (Theorem 2) that this definition is equivalent to c-multitables with arbitrary global conditions. ☐

3   Representation Systems

This section studies a number of new representation systems, leading from sets of tables to product decompositions.

---

[4] Each g-multitable resp. v-multitable can be reduced to one in this normal form by variable replacement and the removal of tautologies such as $x = x$ or $1 = 1$ from the global condition.

3.1   Tabsets and Tabset Tables

We consider finite sets of multitables as representation systems, and will refer to such constructs as *tabsets* (rather than as *multitable-sets*, to be short).

A c-(resp., g-, v-)tabset $\mathbf{T} = \{\mathcal{T}_1, \ldots, \mathcal{T}_n\}$ is a finite set of c-(g-, v-)multitables. The representation of a tabset is the union of the representations of the constituent multitables,

$$rep(\mathbf{T}) := rep(\mathcal{T}_1) \cup \cdots \cup rep(\mathcal{T}_n).$$

We next construct an *inlined* representation of a tabset as a single table by turning each multitable into a single tuple.

Let $\mathbf{A}$ be a g-tabset over schema Σ. For each $R[U]$ in Σ, let $|R|_{\max} = \max\{|R^{\mathcal{A}}| : \mathcal{A} \in \mathbf{A}\}$ denote the maximum cardinality of R in any multitable of $\mathbf{A}$. Given a g-multitable $\mathcal{A} \in \mathbf{A}$ with $R^{\mathcal{A}} = \{t_1, \ldots, t_{|R^{\mathcal{A}}|}\}$, let inline$(R^{\mathcal{A}})$ be the tuple obtained as the concatenation (denoted $\circ$) of the tuples of $R^{\mathcal{A}}$ padded with a special symbol $\perp$ up to arity $|R|_{\max} \cdot ar(R)$,

$$\text{inline}(R^{\mathcal{A}}) := t_1 \circ \cdots \circ t_{|R^{\mathcal{A}}|} \circ \underbrace{(\perp, \ldots \ldots \ldots, \perp)}_{(|R|_{\max} - |R^{\mathcal{A}}|) \cdot ar(R)}.$$

Then tuple

$$\text{inline}(\mathcal{A}) := \text{inline}(R_1^{\mathcal{A}}) \circ \cdots \circ \text{inline}(R_{|\Sigma|}^{\mathcal{A}})$$

encodes all the information in $\mathcal{A}$.

Definition 2 (gTST). The *g-tabset table (gTST)* of a g-tabset $\mathbf{A}$ is the pair (W, λ) consisting of the table[5] $W = \{\text{inline}(\mathcal{A}) \mid \mathcal{A} \in \mathbf{A}\}$ and the function λ which maps each tuple inline$(\mathcal{A})$ of W to the global condition of $\mathcal{A}$.   □

A vTST (TST) is obtained in strict analogy, omitting λ (λ and variables).

To compute inline$(R^{\mathcal{A}})$, we have fixed an arbitrary order of the tuples in $R^{\mathcal{A}}$. We represent this order by using indices d_i to denote the i-th tuple in $R^{\mathcal{A}}$ for each g-multitable $\mathcal{A}$, if that tuple exists. Then the TST has schema

$$\{R.d_i.A_j \mid R[U] \text{ in } \Sigma, 1 \leq i \leq |R|_{\max}, A_j \in U\}.$$

An example translation from a tabset to a TST is given in Figure 2.

The semantics of a gTST (W, λ) as a representation system is given in strict analogy with tabsets,

$$rep(W, \lambda) := \bigcup \{rep(\text{inline}^{-1}(t), \lambda(t)) \mid t \in W\}.$$

Remark 2. Computing the inverse of "inline" is an easy exercise. In particular, we map inline$(R^{\mathcal{A}})$ to $R^{\mathcal{A}}$ as

$$(a_1, \ldots, a_{ar(R) \cdot |R|_{\max}}) \mapsto \{(a_{ar(R) \cdot k+1}, \ldots, a_{ar(R) \cdot (k+1)}) \mid 0 \leq k < |R|_{\max},$$
$$a_{ar(R) \cdot k+1} \neq \perp, \ldots, a_{ar(R) \cdot (k+1)} \neq \perp\}.$$

---

[5] Note that this table may contain variables and occurrences of the $\perp$ symbol.

	ϕ^A			ϕ^B			ϕ^C	
R^A A B	S^A C		R^B A B	S^B C		R^C A B	S^C C	
a_1 a_2	a_5		b_1 b_2			c_1 c_2	c_3	
a_3 a_4	a_6		b_3 b_4				c_4	
			b_5 b_6				c_5	

(a) Three $(R[A,B], S[C])$-multitables $\mathcal{A}$, $\mathcal{B}$, and $\mathcal{C}$.

$R.d_1.A$	$R.d_1.B$	$R.d_2.A$	$R.d_2.B$	$R.d_3.A$	$R.d_3.B$	$S.d_1.C$	$S.d_2.C$	$S.d_3.C$	λ
a_1	a_2	a_3	a_4	$\perp$	$\perp$	a_5	a_6	$\perp$	ϕ^A
b_1	b_2	b_3	b_4	b_5	b_6	$\perp$	$\perp$	$\perp$	ϕ^B
c_1	c_2	$\perp$	$\perp$	$\perp$	$\perp$	c_3	c_4	c_5	ϕ^C

(b): TST of tabset $\{\mathcal{A}, \mathcal{B}, \mathcal{C}\}$.

Fig. 2. Translation from a tabset (a) to a TST (b)

By construction, the gTST capture the g-tabsets and thus the c-tables.

Proposition 2. *The g-(resp., v-)TST capture the g-(v-)tabsets.*

Finally, there is an noteworthy normal form for gTSTs.

Proposition 3. *The gTST in which λ maps each tuple to a unique common global condition ϕ, i.e. $\lambda : \cdot \mapsto \phi$, capture the gTST.*

Proof. Given a g-tabset $\mathbf{A}$, w.l.o.g., we may assume that no two g-multitables from $\mathbf{A}$ share a common variable, either in the tables or the conditions, and that all global conditions in $\mathbf{A}$ are satisfiable. (Otherwise we could safely remove some of the g-multitables in $\mathbf{A}$.) But, then, ϕ is simply the conjunction of the global conditions in $\mathbf{A}$. For any tuple t of the gTST of $\mathbf{A}$, the g-multitable $(\text{inline}^{-1}(t), \phi)$ is equivalent to $(\text{inline}^{-1}(t), \lambda(t))$. $\square$

Proviso. We will in the following write gTSTs as pairs (W, ϕ), where W is the table and ϕ is a single global condition shared by the tuples of W.

3.2 World-Set Decompositions

We are now ready to define world-set decompositions, our main vehicle for efficient yet expressive representation systems.

A *product m-decomposition* of a relation R is a set of non-nullary relations $\{C_1, \ldots, C_m\}$ such that $C_1 \times \cdots \times C_m = R$. The relations $C_1, \ldots, C_m$ are called *components*. A product m-decomposition of R is *maximal(ly decomposed)* if there is no product n-decomposition of R with $n > m$.

Definition 3 (attribute-level gWSD). Let (W, ϕ) be a gTST. Then an *attribute-level world-set m-decomposition (m-gWSD)* of (W, ϕ) is a pair of a product m-decomposition of W together with the global condition ϕ. $\square$

R	A	B
d_1	1	2
d_2	5	6

R	A	B
d_1	1	2

R	A	B
d_1	3	4
d_2	5	6

R	A	B
d_1	3	4

C_1	$R.d_1.A$	$R.d_1.B$
	1	2
	3	4

$\times$

C_2	$R.d_2.A$	$R.d_2.B$
	5	6
	$\perp$	$\perp$

Fig. 3. Four worlds and a corresponding 2-WSD

We also consider two important simplifications of (attribute-level) gWSDs, those without inequalities (called vWSDs), i.e., without a global condition, and vWSDs without variables (called WSDs). An example of a WSD is shown in Figure 3.

The semantics of a gWSD is given by its exact correspondence with a gTST,

$$rep \underbrace{(\{C_1, \ldots, C_m\}, \phi)}_{\text{gWSD}} := rep \underbrace{(C_1 \times \cdots \times C_m, \phi)}_{\text{gTST}}.$$

To decompose W, we treat its variables and the $\perp$-value as constants. Clearly, **A** and any gWSD of **A** represent the same set of possible worlds.

It immediately follows from the definition of WSDs that

Proposition 4. *Any finite set of possible worlds can be represented as a 1-WSD.*

Corollary 1. *WSDs are a strong representation system for any relational query language.*

The lack of power to express inequalities, despite the ability to express disjunction, keeps vWSDs (and thus equally v-tabsets) from being strong.

Proposition 5. *vWSDs are a strong representation system for projection, product and union but do not form a strong representation system for selection or difference.*

A proof of this is given in [5].

Remark 3. Note that verifying nondeterministically that a structure $\mathcal{A}$ is a possible world of gWSD $(\{C_1, \ldots, C_m\}, \phi)$ is easy: all we need is choose one tuple from each of the component tables $C_1, \ldots, C_m$, concatenate them into a tuple t, and check whether a valuation exists that satisfies ϕ and takes inline$^{-1}(t)$ to $\mathcal{A}$.

Already the vWSDs are exponentially more succinct than the v-tabsets. As is easy to verify,

Proposition 6. *Any v-tabset representation of the WSD*

$$\left\{ \begin{array}{c|c} C_1 & R.d_1.A \\ \hline & a_1 \\ & b_1 \end{array} \quad \cdots \quad \begin{array}{c|c} C_n & R.d_n.A \\ \hline & a_n \\ & b_n \end{array} \right\}$$

where the a_i, b_i are distinct domain values takes space exponential in n.

This greater succinctness is obtained at a price:

Theorem 1. *Given an attribute-level (g)WSD $\mathcal{W}$, checking whether the empty world is in $rep(\mathcal{W})$ is NP-complete.*

A proof of this is given in [5]. Note that this NP-hardness is a direct consequence of the succinctness increase in gWSDs as compared to gTSTs. On gTSTs, checking for the empty world is a trivial operation.

Corollary 2. *Tuple certainty is coNP-hard for attribute-level WSDs.*

This problem remains in coNP even for general gWSDs. Nevertheless, since computing certain answers is a central task related to incomplete information, we will consider also the following restriction of gWSDs. As we will see, this alternative definition yields a representation system in which the tuple and instance certainty problems are in polynomial time while the formalism is still exponentially more succinct than gTSTs.

Definition 4 (gWSD). An attribute-level gWSD is called a *tuple-level gWSD* if for any two attributes A_i, A_j from the schema of relation R, and any tuple id d, the attributes $R.d.A_i, R.d.A_j$ of the component tables are in the same component schema. □

In other words, in tuple-level gWSDs, values for one and the same tuple cannot be split across several components – that is, here the decomposition is less fine-grained than in attribute-level gWSDs. In the remainder of this paper, we will exclusively study tuple-level (g-, resp. v-)WSDs, and will refer to them as just simply (g-, v-)WSDs. Obviously, tuple-level (g)WSDs are just as expressive as attribute-level (g)WSDs, since they all are just decompositions of 1-(g)WSDs.

However, tuple-level (g)WSDs are less succinct than attribute-level (g)WSDs. For example, any tuple-level WSD equivalent to the attribute-level WSD

$$\left\{ \begin{array}{c|c} C_1 & R.d.A_1 \\ \hline & a_1 \\ & b_1 \end{array} \quad \cdots \quad \begin{array}{c|c} C_n & R.d.A_n \\ \hline & a_n \\ & b_n \end{array} \right\}$$

must be exponentially larger. Note that the WSDs of Proposition 6 are tuple-level.

4   Main Expressiveness Result

In this section we study the expressive power of gWSDs. We show that gWSDs and c-multitables are equivalent in expressive power, that is, for each gWSD one can find an equivalent c-multitable that represents the same set of possible worlds and vice versa. Thus, gWSDs form a strong representation system for relational algebra.

Theorem 2. *The gWSDs capture the c-multitables.*

Corollary 3. *gWSDs are a strong representation system for relational algebra.*

Corollary 4. *The g-tabsets capture the c-tabsets.*

That is, disjunction on the level of entire tables plus conjunctions of inequalities as global conditions, as present in g-tables, are enough to capture the full expressive power of c-tables. In particular, we are able to eliminate all local conditions.

We prove Theorem 2 by providing back and forth translations between c-multitables and gWSDs.

Lemma 1. *gWSDs can be translated in linear time into equivalent c-multitables.*

Proof (Sketch). Let $\mathcal{W} = (\{C_1, \ldots, C_m\}, \phi)$ be a (tuple-level) m-gWSD over relational schema $(R_1[U_1], \ldots, R_k[U_k])$, where $C_j = \{w_1, \ldots, w_{n_j}\}$. We define a translation f from $\mathcal{W}$ to an equivalent c-multitable $\mathcal{T} = (R_1^{\mathcal{T}}, \ldots, R_k^{\mathcal{T}}, \phi^{\mathcal{T}}, \lambda^{\mathcal{T}})$ in the following way.

1. The global condition ϕ of $\mathcal{W}$ becomes the global condition $\phi^{\mathcal{T}}$ of the c-multitable $\mathcal{T}$.
2. For each relation schema $R[U]$ we create a table $R^{\mathcal{T}}$ with the same schema.
3. We translate each component $C_j = \{w_1, \ldots, w_{n_j}\}$ of $\mathcal{W}$ in the following way. Let $w_i \in C$. Let d be a tuple identifier for a relation R defined in C_j and t be the tuple for d in w_i. If t is not a $\perp$-tuple, then we add the tuple t with local condition $\lambda^{\mathcal{T}}(t)$ to $R^{\mathcal{T}}$, where $R^{\mathcal{T}}$ is the corresponding table from the c-multitable. The local condition $\lambda^{\mathcal{T}}(t)$ is defined as

$$\lambda^{\mathcal{T}}(t) = \begin{cases} true & n_j = 1 \\ (x_j = i) & 1 \leq i < n_j \\ (x_j \neq 1 \wedge \ldots \wedge x_j \neq n_j - 1) & 1 < i = n_j. \end{cases}$$

Here x_j is a new variable for the component C_j not occurring in $\mathcal{W}$, which encodes to which row of component C_j a tuple belongs to.

The proof of the correctness of the translation is given in [5]. □

Example 2. Consider the 1-gWSD $(\{C_1\}, \phi)$ given in Figure 4(a). The first tuple of C_1 encodes a g-table R with a single tuple (with identifier d_1), and the second tuple of C_1 encodes two v-tuples with identifiers d_1 and d_2. The encoding of C_1 as a c-table T with global condition $\phi^{\mathcal{T}}$ is given in Figure 4(b). □

C_1	$R.d_1.A$	$R.d_1.B$	$R.d_2.A$	$R.d_2.B$
	x	y	$\perp$	$\perp$
	1	z	z	3

$\phi = (x \neq 1) \wedge (x \neq y) \wedge (z \neq 2)$

(a) 1-gWSD

T	A	B	$cond$
			$\phi^{\mathcal{T}} = (x \neq 1) \wedge (x \neq y) \wedge (z \neq 2)$
	x	y	$(x_1 = 1)$
	1	z	$(x_1 \neq 1)$
	z	3	$(x_1 \neq 1)$

(b) c-table equivalent to the 1-gWSD (a)

Fig. 4. Translating gWSDs into c-multitables

For the other, somewhat more involved direction,

Lemma 2. *Any c-multitable can be represented by an equivalent gWSD.*

Due to space limitations, we have to refer to [5] for a proof.

5   Complexity of Managing gWSDs

We consider the decision problems defined in Section 1. Note that in the literature the tuple (q-)possibility and (q-)certainty problems are sometimes called bounded or restricted (q-)possibility, and (q-)certainty respectively, and the instance (q-)possibility and (q-)certainty are sometimes called (q-)membership and (q-)uniqueness [3]. A comparison of the complexity results for these decision problems in the context of gWSDs to those of c-tables [3] and Trio [8] is given in Table 2. Remarkably, gWSDs and WSDs have the same complexities for all these decision problems. We next state the results and give some of their proofs.

Theorem 3. *Tuple possibility and certainty are in PTIME for gWSDs.*

Proof. Given a tuple-level gWSD $W = (\{C_1, \ldots, C_m\}, \phi)$ and a tuple t.

Tuple Possibility: Tuple t is in at least one world of $rep(W)$ if and only if there are i, j such that $(t_1, \ldots, t_k) \in C_i$ and $\theta(t_j) = t$ for a mapping θ from variables and domain values to domain values that is the identity on the domain values and for which $\theta(\phi)$ is true. Thus, all we have to do is iterate over each tuple t_j occurring in a component tuple (looking at the components individually; this requires a linear scan over W), and try to fix θ on the variables that appear in t_j such that $\theta(t_j) = t$. If this is possible for t_j, we map the remaining variables x to new domain values 'x'. This will render $\theta(\phi)$ true and consequently t part of a possible world iff ϕ is satisfiable, a condition that is easy to check since ϕ is simply a conjunction of inequalities.

Tuple certainty: Tuple t is certain exactly if ϕ is unsatisfiable or there is a component C_i such that each tuple of C_i contains t (without variables).

Suppose ϕ is satisfiable and for each component C_i there is at least one tuple $w_i \in C_i$ that does not contain t. Then there is a world-tuple $w \in C_1 \times \cdots \times C_m$ such that tuple t does not occur in w. If there is a mapping θ that maps some tuple in w to t and for which $\theta(\phi)$ is true, then there is also a mapping θ' such that $\theta'(w)$ does not contain t but $\theta'(\phi)$ is true. Thus t is not certain. □

Theorem 4. *Instance possibility is in NP for gWSDs and NP-hard for WSDs.*

Proof (Sketch). A proof of this result is presented in [5]; here we only give a brief sketch. Checking membership in NP is straightforward once we have guessed which tuples from the gWSD components constitute the input instance. NP-hardness can be shown by reduction from Exact Cover by 3-Sets. Given a set X with $|X| = 3q$ and a set C of 3-subsets of X, we turn X into a unary relation and C into a ternary relation. We construct a WSD by taking q copies of C as component relations. There is an exact cover of X by 3-sets from C iff X is a world in the WSD representation. □

Theorem 5. *Instance certainty is in PTIME for gWSDs.*

Proof. Given an instance I and a gWSD $\mathcal{W}$ representing a relation R, the problem is equivalent to checking for each world $\mathcal{A} \in rep(\mathcal{W})$ whether (1) $I \subseteq R^{\mathcal{A}}$ and (2) $R^{\mathcal{A}} \subseteq I$. Test (1) is reducible to checking whether each tuple from I is certain in R, and is thus in PTIME (cf. Theorem 3). For (2), we check in PTIME whether there is a non $\perp$-tuple in some world of $rep(\mathcal{W})$ that is not in the instance I. If $\mathcal{W}$ has variables then it cannot represent certain instances. $\square$

Theorem 6. *Tuple q-possibility is in PTIME for gWSDs and pos. rel. algebra.*

A proof is given in [5]. Note that by adding negation to the query language, tuple q-possibility becomes NP-hard even for v-tables where each variable occurs at most once (also called Codd tables) [3].

Theorem 7. *Tuple and instance q-certainty are coNP-complete for gWSDs.*

Proof. Hardness follows from the PTIME reduction of v-tables to gWSDs and the coNP-hardness of tuple and instance q-certainty problems even for Codd tables, i.e., v-tables where each variable occurs at most once [3]. Completeness follows from the PTIME reduction of gWSDs to c-tables (Lemma 1) and coNP-completeness of c-tables for both problems. $\square$

Theorem 8. *Instance q-possibility is NP-complete for gWSDs.*

6   Optimizing gWSDs

In this section we study the problem of optimizing a given gWSD by further decomposing its components using the product operation. We note that product decomposition corresponds to the notion of *relational factorization*. We then define this new notion and study some of its properties, like uniqueness and primality or minimality. It turns out that any relation admits a unique minimal factorization, and there is an algorithm that can compute it efficiently. Because gWSD components are special relations with variables and the $\perp$-symbol, they can admit several minimal factorizations and our efficient algorithm can not always find one of them (but it can still find good non-optimal factorizations by treating variables as constants). However, the (tuple-level) WSDs admit prime factorizations that are unique modulo the $\perp$-symbol[6] and can be efficiently computed by a trivial extension of our algorithm with the tuple-level constraint.

6.1   Prime Factorizations of Relations

Definition 5. Let there be schemata $R[U]$ and $Q[U']$ such that $\emptyset \subset U' \subseteq U$. A *factor* of a relation R over schema $R[U]$ is a relation Q over schema $Q[U']$ such that there exists a relation R' with $R = Q \times R'$.

---

[6] Two tuples $(A_1 : \perp, \ldots, A_n : \perp)$ and $(A_1 : a_1, \ldots, A_n : a_n)$ of a relation defined by a (g)WSD, where at least one a_i is $\perp$, are equivalent modulo the $\perp$-symbol.

A factor Q of R is called *proper*, if $Q \neq R$. A factor Q is *prime*, if it has no proper factors. Two relations over the same schema are *coprime*, if they have no common factors.

Definition 6. Let R be a relation. A *factorization* of R is a set $\{C_1, \ldots, C_n\}$ of factors of R such that $R = C_1 \times \ldots \times C_n$.

In case the factors $C_1, \ldots, C_n$ are prime, the factorization is said to be *prime*. From the definition of relational product and factorization, it follows that the schemata of the factors $C_1, \ldots, C_n$ are a disjoint partition of the schema of R.

Proposition 7. *For each relation a prime factorization exists and is unique.*

6.2   Computing Prime Factorizations

This section first gives two important properties of relational factors and factorizations. Based on them, it further devises an efficient yet simple algorithm for computing prime factorizations.

Proposition 8. *Let there be two relations S and F, an attribute A of S and not of F, and a value $v \in \pi_A(S)$. Then, for some relations R, E, and I holds*

$$S = F \times R \Leftrightarrow \sigma_{A=v}(S) = F \times E \text{ and } \sigma_{A \neq v}(S) = F \times I.$$

Corollary 5. *A relation S is prime iff $\sigma_{A=v}(S)$ and $\sigma_{A \neq v}(S)$ are coprime.*

The algorithm prime-factorization given in Figure 5 computes the prime factorization of an input relation S as follows. It first finds the trivial prime factors with one attribute and one value (line 1). These factors represent the prime factorization of S, in case the remaining relation is empty (line 2). Otherwise, the remaining relation is disjointly partitioned in relations Q and R (line 4) using *any* selection with constant $A = v$ such that Q is smaller than R (line 3). The prime factors of Q are then probed for factors of R and in the positive case

---

algorithm prime-factorization (S)
// Input: Relation S over schema $S[U]$.
// Result: Prime factorization of S as a set Fs of its prime factors.

1. $Fs := \{\{\pi_B(S)\} \mid B \in U, |\pi_B(S)| = 1\}; \ S := S \div \prod_{F \in Fs} (F);$
2.   **if** $S = \emptyset$ **then return** Fs;
3.   **choose any** $A \in \text{sch}(S), v \in \pi_A(S)$ **such that** $|\sigma_{A=v}(S)| \leq |\sigma_{A \neq v}(S)|$;
4. $Q := \sigma_{A=v}(S); \ R := \sigma_{A \neq v}(S);$
5.   **foreach** $F \in$ prime-factorization(Q) **do**
6.   **if** $(R \div F) \times F = R$ **then** $Fs := Fs \cup \{F\};$
7.   **if** $\prod_{F \in Fs} (F) \neq S$ **then** $Fs := Fs \cup \{S \div \prod_{F \in Fs} (F)\};$
8.   **return** Fs;

Fig. 5. Computing the prime factorization of a relation

become prime factors of S (lines 5 and 6). This property is ensured by Proposition 8. The remainder of Q and R, which does not contain factors common to both Q and R, becomes a factor of S (line 7). According to Corollary 5, this factor is also prime.

Theorem 9. *The algorithm of Figure 5 computes the prime factorization of any relation.*

Our relational factorization is a special case of algebraic factorization of Boolean functions, as used in multilevel logic synthesis [11]. In this light, our algorithm can be used to algebraically factorize disjunctions of conjunctions of literals. A factorization is then a conjunction of factors, which are disjunctions of conjunctions of literals. This factorization is only algebraic, because Boolean identities (e.g., $x \cdot x = x$) do not make sense in our context and thus are not considered (Note that Boolean factorization is NP-hard, see e.g., [11]).

The algorithm of Figure 5 computes prime factorizations in polynomial time and linear space, as stated by the following theorem.

Theorem 10. *The prime factorization of a relation S with arity m and size n is computable in time $O(m \cdot n \cdot \log n)$ and space $O(n)$.*

We can further trade the space used to explicitly store the temporary relations Q, R, and the factors for the time needed to recompute them. For this, the temporary relations computed at any recursion depth i are defined *intentionally* as queries constructed using the chosen selection parameters. This leads to a sublinear space complexity at the expense of an additional logarithmic factor for the time complexity.

Proposition 9. *The prime factorization of a relation S with arity m and size n is computable in time $O(m \cdot n \cdot \log^2 n)$ and space $O(m \cdot \log n)$.*

Remark 4. An important property of our algorithm is that it is polynomial in both the arity and the size of the input relation S. If the arity is considered constant, then a trivial prime factorization algorithm (yet exponential in the arity of S) can be devised as follows: First compute the powerset $PS(U)$ over the set U of attributes of S. Then, test for each set $U' \in PS(U)$ whether $\pi_{U'}(S) \times \pi_{U-U'}(S) = S$ holds. In the positive case, a factorization is found with factors $\pi_{U'}(S)$ and $\pi_{U-U'}(S)$, and the same procedure is now applied to these factors until all prime factors are found.   □

6.3   Optimization Flavors

The gWSD optimization discussed here is a facet of the more general problem of finding minimal representations for a given g-tabset or world-set. To find a minimal representation for a given g-tabset **A**, one has to take into account all possible inlinings for the g-tables of **A** in g-tabset tables. Recall from Section 3 that we consider a fixed arbitrary inlining order of the tuples of the g-tables in **A**. Such an order is supported by common *identifiers* of tuples from different worlds, as maintained in virtually all representation systems [18,3,16,8] and *exploited* in practitioner's representation systems such as [8,4]. We note that when no correspondence between tuples from different worlds has to be preserved, smaller representations of the same world-set may be possible.

Acknowledgments. The authors were supported in part by DFG project grant KO 3491/1-1. The first author was supported by the International Max Planck Research School for Computer Science, Saarbrücken, Germany.

References

1. S. Abiteboul and O. M. Duschka. "Complexity of Answering Queries Using Materialized Views". In *Proc. PODS*, pages 254–263, 1998.
2. S. Abiteboul, R. Hull, and V. Vianu. *Foundations of Databases*. Addison-Wesley, 1995.
3. S. Abiteboul, P. Kanellakis, and G. Grahne. On the representation and querying of sets of possible worlds. *Theor. Comput. Sci.*, 78(1):158–187, 1991.
4. P. Andritsos, A. Fuxman, and R. J. Miller. Clean answers over dirty databases: A probabilistic approach. In *Proc. ICDE*, 2006.
5. L. Antova, C. Koch, and D. Olteanu. World-set decompositions: Expressiveness and efficient algorithms. Technical Report INFOSYS-TR-2006-12, Saarland University.
6. L. Antova, C. Koch, and D. Olteanu. 10^{10^6} worlds and beyond: Efficient representation and processing of incomplete information. In *Proc. ICDE*, 2007.
7. M. Arenas, L. E. Bertossi, and J. Chomicki. "Answer sets for consistent query answering in inconsistent databases". *TPLP*, 3(4–5):393–424, 2003.
8. O. Benjelloun, A. D. Sarma, A. Halevy, and J. Widom. ULDBs: Databases with uncertainty and lineage. In *Proc. VLDB*, 2006.
9. L. E. Bertossi, L. Bravo, E. Franconi, and A. Lopatenko. "Complexity and Approximation of Fixing Numerical Attributes in Databases Under Integrity Constraints". In *Proc. DBPL*, pages 262–278, 2005.
10. P. Bohannon, W. Fan, M. Flaster, and R. Rastogi. "A Cost-Based Model and Effective Heuristic for Repairing Constraints by Value Modification". In *Proc. SIGMOD*, June 2005.
11. R. K. Bryant. Factoring logic functions. *IBM J. Res. Develop.*, 31(2), 1987.
12. D. Calvanese, G. D. Giacomo, M. Lenzerini, and R. Rosati. "Logical Foundations of Peer-To-Peer Data Integration". In *PODS 2004*, pages 241–251, 2004.
13. J. Chomicki, J. Marcinkowski, and S. Staworko. "Computing consistent query answers using conflict hypergraphs". In *Proc. CIKM*, pages 417–426, 2004.
14. N. Dalvi and D. Suciu. Efficient query evaluation on probabilistic databases. In *Proc. VLDB*, pages 864–875, 2004.
15. G. Grahne. Dependency satisfaction in databases with incomplete information. In *Proc. VLDB*, pages 37–45, 1984.
16. G. Grahne. *The Problem of Incomplete Information in Relational Databases*. Number 554 in LNCS. Springer-Verlag, 1991.
17. T. J. Green and V. Tannen. "Models for Incomplete and Probabilistic Information". In *International Workshop on Incompleteness and Inconsistency in Databases (IIDB)*, 2006.
18. T. Imielinski and W. Lipski. Incomplete information in relational databases. *Journal of ACM*, 31:761–791, 1984.

On the Expressiveness of Implicit Provenance in Query and Update Languages

Peter Buneman[1,*], James Cheney[1,*], and Stijn Vansummeren[2,**]

[1] University of Edinburgh, Scotland
[2] Hasselt University and Transnational University of Limburg, Belgium

Abstract. Information concerning the origin of data (that is, its *provenance*) is important in many areas, especially scientific recordkeeping. Currently, provenance information must be maintained explicitly, by added effort of the database maintainer. Since such maintenance is tedious and error-prone, it is desirable to provide support for provenance in the database system itself. In order to provide such support, however, it is important to provide a clear explanation of the behavior and meaning of existing database operations, both queries and updates, with respect to provenance. In this paper we take the view that a query or update *implicitly* defines a provenance mapping linking components of the output to the originating components in the input. Our key result is that the proposed semantics are expressively complete relative to natural classes of queries that *explicitly* manipulate provenance.

1   Introduction

The *provenance* of data – its origins and how it came to be included in a database – has recently sparked interest in database research [4,12,14]. The topic is particularly important in those scientific databases, sometimes referred to as *curated* databases, that are constructed by a labor-intensive process of copying, correcting and annotating data from other sources. The value of curated databases lies in their organization and in the trustworthiness of their data. Provenance is particularly important in assessing the latter. In practice, provenance – if it is recorded at all – is recorded manually, which is both time-consuming and error-prone. Automated provenance recording support is desirable, and for this it is essential to have a proper semantic foundation to guide us on what should be recorded and to understand what effect database operations have on provenance.

We focus on a specific kind of provenance associated with the copying and modification of data by query and update languages. We use a formalization based on the "tagging" or "propagation" approach of Wang and Madnick [15] and Bhagwat et al. [3]. In this approach, it is assumed that each input data item has an identifying color. Existing database operations are then given a new semantics as functions mapping such colored databases to colored databases in

---

* Supported by the UK EPSRC (Digital Curation) and the Royal Society.
** Postdoctoral Fellow of the Research Foundation - Flanders (FWO).

T. Schwentick and D. Suciu (Eds.): ICDT 2007, LNCS 4353, pp. 209–223, 2007.

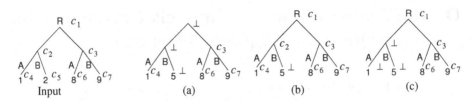

Fig. 1. Color propagation for query (a) and updates (b) and (c)

which colors are propagated along with their data item during computation of the output. The provenance of a data item in the output is then simply that input data item with the same color. To illustrate this approach, consider a table $R(A, B)$ with tuples $\{(1, 2), (8, 9)\}$, and consider the following SQL query.

$$\text{(select * from } R \text{ where } A \text{ <> } 1)$$
$$\text{union (select } A, \text{ 5 as } B \text{ from } R \text{ where } A = 1) \qquad (a)$$

The input tree at the left of Fig. 1 is a representation of R in which the atomic data values, the tuples and the table R itself are all annotated with colors $c_1, c_2, \ldots$. We could then define the colored semantics of query (a) to map the input to the colored table represented by the tree (a) in Fig. 1. This defines the provenance of the atom 1 in the output to be the corresponding atom in R, the provenance of the tuple $(8, 9)$ to be the second tuple in R, and so on. The color $\perp$ indicates that a data item is introduced by the query itself. Hence, this particular colored semantics takes the view that queries construct new tables and that the second **select** subquery constructs a new tuple rather than copying an existing one.

Color-propagating functions from colored databases to colored databases can hence be used to formally define the provenance behavior of existing database operations. By "color-propagating" we mean that the function should only use colors to indicate the origin of output items: if the function is applied to a recolored version of the input, then it should produce an output with the same recoloring applied. In particular, the input colors cannot influence the uncolored part of the output and the function's behavior is insensitive to the actual choice of colors used in the input. We shall refer to such propagating functions as *provenance-aware operations*.

The particular provenance ascribed to query (a) in Fig. 1 has the property that if an output item j has the same color as an input item i, then i and j are identical. We shall call provenance-aware operations with this property *copying*. A copying operation has the property that if some item is colored $\perp$ ("blank"), all items that contain it will also be colored $\perp$.

The provenance of query (a) described in Fig. 1 is exactly the "intuitive" or "default" provenance of SQL queries proposed by Bhagwat et al. [3], although they only consider provenance of atomic values. In particular, the default provenance is always copying, as it views constant and tuple constructors in queries as creating new items. Of course, this default semantics may not be the provenance semantics that a curator wants to give to a particular query. For this reason, [3] proposes an extension to query languages that allows provenance to be defined explicitly. Our first result is to propose a default provenance semantics for query languages, similar to that given in [15] and [3], and show that it is *complete* in the sense that it expresses exactly the explicitly definable provenance-aware operations that are copying. This shows that the default provenance semantics is a reasonable semantics for queries.

Turning to updates, we note that simple update languages, such as the expressions of SQL that modify data, do not express more database transformations than SQL queries do. As a result, update languages have largely been ignored in database theory. The following examples, however, show that the story is very different when we take account of provenance.

$$\text{update } R \text{ set } B = 5 \text{ where } A = 1 \qquad\qquad (b)$$

$$\text{delete from } R \text{ where } A = 1; \text{ insert into } R \text{ values } (1,5) \qquad (c)$$

Since updates do not construct new databases, but modify existing ones in-place, it is reasonable to define their provenance semantics in a way that agrees with how tuple identifiers are preserved in practical database management systems. For example, the provenance of updates (b) and (c) would behave on R as illustrated in Fig. 1(b) and Fig. 1(c), respectively. Note that this provenance semantics is no longer copying. For example, the provenance of the tuple $(1, 5)$ in Fig. 1(b) is the tuple $(1, 2)$ from the input, although they are clearly not identical. For this reason we introduce a weaker semantic restriction on provenance-aware operations, and consider the *kind-preserving* ones. By "kind-preserving" we mean that if output item j has the same color as input item i, then they are of the same *kind*: they are both sets, both tuples, or identical atoms. Kind-preserving operations allow the output type of an item to differ from its input type, and this is practically important in considering operations such as SQL's add column update, which extends a tuple but does not change its provenance.

We propose a default provenance semantics for updates as kind-preserving operations, and show this semantics to be complete in the sense that every explicitly definable kind-preserving provenance-aware operation can be expressed by the default provenance semantics of an update.

Most previous work on provenance focuses on the relational model. We shall work in the more general "nested relational" or complex object data model [1,7] for two reasons. First, as our examples indicate, we are interested in provenance at all levels: atoms, tuples, and tables (sets of tuples); a complex object model allows us to provide a uniform treatment of these levels. Second, complex object models are widely used in scientific data, where provenance is of paramount importance. Liefke and Davidson [11] proposed a simple and elegant language that extends SQL-style updates to complex objects. To be more precise about our completeness result for updates: it is the default provenance of this language that we show complete with regard to the explicitly definable, kind-preserving provenance-aware operations. It is therefore a natural choice for updating complex-object databases when one wants to record provenance.

Related work. There is a substantial body of research on provenance (sometimes termed *lineage* or *pedigree*) in both database and scientific computing settings, which is nicely surveyed in [4,12,14]. In early approaches to provenance [15,8] the provenance of an output tuple consists of sets of input tuples that directly or indirectly influenced the output. These techniques only track the provenance of tuples in relational data. In [6] a distinction is made between "why" and "where" provenance for queries in a tree-structured model. More recently, [5] investigated tracking where-provenance for manual updates to curated databases. The Trio project [2] has investigated the combination of tuple-level lineage with uncertainty and accuracy information.

There has also been significant work on the properties of "tagging" or "annotation" in databases. Tan [13] studied theoretical issues of query containment and equivalence in the presence of annotations. The DBNotes system [3] uses variations on why- and where-provenance to propagate annotations on source data through queries. Geerts et al. have developed Mondrian [10], a database system that supports *block annotations*, in which a color can be associated with a subset of the fields in a table, not just a single value.

Finally, provenance has also been studied in the geospatial and Grid computing communities [4,9,12]. Here, the motivation is to record the workflow that constructs large data sets in order to avoid repeated computation.

2 Preliminaries

Let us first sketch the languages used throughout this paper. As query languages, we employ the nested relational algebra $\mathcal{NRA}$ and the nested relational calculus $\mathcal{NRC}$ [7]. We also use the nested update language $\mathcal{NUL}$, based on the complex object update language $\mathcal{CUCA}$ [11], which generalizes familiar SQL updates to complex objects. All of these languages deal with complex objects in the form of nested relations, whose types are given by the following grammar:

$$s, t ::= b \mid s \times t \mid \{s\}.$$

Here, b ranges over some unspecified finite collection of base types like the booleans, the integers, and so on. We assume this collection to include at least the special base type *unit*. Types denote sets of *objects*. The type *unit* consists only of the empty tuple (); objects of $s \times t$ are pairs (v, w) with v and w objects of type s and t, respectively; and objects of $\{s\}$ are finite sets of objects, each of type s. We write $v : s$ to indicate that v is an object of type s. Furthermore, we feel free to omit parentheses and write $s_1 \times \cdots \times s_n$ for $(\ldots((s_1 \times s_2) \times s_3) \cdots \times s_n)$. Our results hold if we use labeled records instead of pairs; but the syntax of pairs is more manageable.

The expressions of $\mathcal{NRA}$, $\mathcal{NRC}$, and $\mathcal{NUL}$ are explicitly typed and are formed using the typing rules of Fig. 2. Here, we range over $\mathcal{NRA}$ expressions by $f, g,$ and h; over $\mathcal{NRC}$ expressions by e; and over $\mathcal{NUL}$ expressions by u. We will often omit the explicit type annotations in superscript when they are clear from the context.

EXPRESSIONS OF $\mathcal{NRA}$.

$$\frac{}{Ka:\ unit \to b} \qquad \frac{}{id^s:\ s \to s} \qquad \frac{h:\ r \to s \quad g:\ s \to t}{g \circ h:\ r \to t}$$

$$\frac{}{!^s:\ s \to unit} \qquad \frac{}{\pi_1^{s,t}:\ s \times t \to s} \qquad \frac{}{\pi_2^{s,t}:\ s \times t \to t} \qquad \frac{h:\ r \to s \quad g:\ r \to t}{\langle g, h \rangle:\ r \to s \times t}$$

$$\frac{}{\eta^s:\ s \to \{s\}} \qquad \frac{}{\mu^s:\ \{\{s\}\} \to \{s\}} \qquad \frac{}{K\{\}^s:\ unit \to \{s\}} \qquad \frac{}{\cup^s:\ \{s\} \times \{s\} \to \{s\}}$$

$$\frac{}{\rho_2^{s,t}:\ s \times \{t\} \to \{s \times t\}} \qquad \frac{f:\ s \to t}{map(f):\ \{s\} \to \{t\}} \qquad \frac{}{cond^t:\ s \times s \times t \times t \to t}$$

EXPRESSIONS OF $\mathcal{NRC}$.

$$\frac{}{a:\ b} \qquad \frac{}{x^s:\ s} \qquad \frac{e:\ t}{\lambda x^s.e:\ s \to t} \qquad \frac{e_1:\ s \to t \quad e_2:\ s}{e_1\ e_2:\ t}$$

$$\frac{}{():\ unit} \qquad \frac{e:\ s \times t}{\pi_1\ e:\ s} \quad \frac{}{\pi_2\ e:\ t} \qquad \frac{e_1:\ s \quad e_2:\ t}{(e_1, e_2):\ s \times t} \qquad \frac{}{\{\}^s:\ \{s\}} \qquad \frac{e:\ s}{\{e\}:\ \{s\}}$$

$$\frac{e_1:\ \{s\} \quad e_2:\ \{s\}}{e_1 \cup e_2:\ \{s\}} \qquad \frac{e_1:\ \{s\} \quad e_2:\ \{t\}}{\bigcup\{e_2 \mid x^s \in e_1\}:\ \{t\}} \qquad \frac{e_1:\ s \quad e_2:\ s \quad e_3:\ t \quad e_4:\ t}{\text{if } e_1 = e_2 \text{ then } e_3 \text{ else } e_4:\ t}$$

EXPRESSIONS OF $\mathcal{NUL}$.

$$\frac{}{skip^s:\ s \to s} \qquad \frac{u_1:\ r \to s \quad u_2:\ s \to t}{u_1; u_2:\ r \to t} \qquad \frac{e:\ t}{repl^s\ e:\ s \to t} \qquad \frac{u:\ s \to t}{[x^s]\,u:\ s \to t}$$

$$\frac{e:\ \{s\}}{insert\ e:\ \{s\} \to \{s\}} \qquad \frac{e:\ \{s\}}{remove\ e:\ \{s\} \to \{s\}} \qquad \frac{u:\ s \to t}{iter\ u:\ \{s\} \to \{t\}}$$

$$\frac{u:\ r \to t}{updl^s\ u:\ r \times s \to t \times s} \qquad \frac{u:\ s \to t}{updr^r\ u:\ r \times s \to r \times t}$$

Fig. 2. Expressions of $\mathcal{NRL}$

Semantics of $\mathcal{NRA}$. The $\mathcal{NRA}$ is an algebra of functions over complex objects. Every $\mathcal{NRA}$ expression $f:\ s \to t$ defines a function from s to t. The expression Ka is the constant function that always produces the atom a; id is the identity function; and $g \circ h$ is function composition, i.e., $(g \circ h)(v) = g(h(v))$. Then follow the pair operations: $!$ produces $()$ on all inputs; π_1 and π_2 are respectively the left and right projections; and $\langle g, h \rangle$ is pair formation: $\langle g, h \rangle(v) = (g\,v, h\,v)$. Next come the set operations: η forms singletons: $\eta(v) = \{v\}$; $K\{\}$ is the constant function that produces the empty set; $\cup$ is set union; μ flattens sets of sets: $\mu(\{V, \ldots, V'\}) = V \cup \cdots \cup V'$; ρ_2 is the right tensor product: $\rho_2(v, \{w, \ldots, w'\}) = \{(v, w), \ldots, (v, w')\}$; and $map(f)$ applies f to every object in its input set: $map(f)(\{v, \ldots, v'\}) = \{f(v), \ldots, f(v')\}$. Finally, *cond* is the conditional that, when applied to a tuple (v, v', w, w') returns w if $v = v'$, and returns w' otherwise.

Example 1. Here are some simple examples of the functions that are definable in $\mathcal{NRA}$. The relational projections $\Pi_1\colon \{s \times t\} \to \{s\}$ and $\Pi_2\colon \{s \times t\} \to \{t\}$ on sets of pairs are given by $\Pi_1 := map(\pi_1)$ and $\Pi_2 := map(\pi_2)$, respectively. The tensor product ρ_1 similar to ρ_2 but pairing to the left is defined as $\rho_1 := map(\langle \pi_2, \pi_1 \rangle) \circ \rho_2 \circ \langle \pi_2, \pi_1 \rangle$. Cartesian product of two sets is then readily defined as $cartprod := \mu \circ map(\rho_1) \circ \rho_2$.

Semantics of $\mathcal{NRC}$. The semantics of $\mathcal{NRC}$ is that of the first-order, simply typed lambda calculus with products and sets. As such, expression a denotes the constant a; x^s is the explicitly typed variable that can be bound to objects of type s; $\lambda x.e$ is standard lambda abstraction; and $e_1\,e_2$ is function application. Furthermore, expression $()$ denotes the empty tuple; (e_1, e_2) is pair construction; and $\pi_1\,e$ and $\pi_2\,e$ are respectively the left and right projection on pairs. Expression $\{\}$ denotes the empty set; $\{e\}$ is singleton construction; $e_1 \cup e_2$ is set union; and $\bigcup\{e_2 \mid x \in e_1\}$ is set comprehension. That is, $\bigcup\{e_2 \mid x \in e_1\} = f(v) \cup \cdots \cup f(v')$ where $f = \lambda x.e_2$ and e_1 denotes $\{v, \ldots, v'\}$. Finally, if $e_1 = e_2$ then e_3 else e_4 is the conditional expression that returns e_3 if the denotations of e_1 and e_2 are equal and returns e_4 otherwise.

Example 2. The left relational projection $\Pi_1\colon \{s \times t\} \to \{s\}$ on a sets of pairs is defined in $\mathcal{NRC}$ as $\lambda U.\bigcup\{\{\pi_1\,x\} \mid x \in U\}$. Right relational projection is defined similarly. SQL query (a) from the Introduction is defined in $\mathcal{NRC}$ as $e_{(a)} := \bigcup\{\text{if } \pi_1\,x = 1 \text{ then } \{(\pi_1\,x, 5)\} \text{ else } \{y\} \mid y \in R\}$. Here, the table $R(A, B)$ is represented as a set of pairs $R\colon \{b \times b\}$. Finally the expression,

$$\bigcup\{\bigcup\{\text{if } \pi_1\,x = \pi_1\,y \text{ then } \{((\pi_1\,x, \pi_2\,x), \pi_2\,y)\} \text{ else } \{\} \mid y \in S\} \mid x \in R\}$$

defines the relational join of two sets of pairs $R\colon \{r \times s\}$ and $S\colon \{r \times t\}$.

We note that the power of $\mathcal{NRC}$ is not restricted to simple select-project-join queries. It is well-known that the conditional expression allows definition of all other non-monotone operations such as difference, intersection, set membership testing, subset testing, and nesting [7]. Furthermore,

Proposition 1 ([7]). $\mathcal{NRA} \equiv \mathcal{NRC}$ *in the sense that every function definable by an expression* $f\colon s \to t$ *in* $\mathcal{NRA}$ *is definable by a closed expression* $e\colon s \to t$ *in* $\mathcal{NRC}$, *and vice versa.*

Semantics of $\mathcal{NUL}$. Note that most $\mathcal{NUL}$ updates syntactically contain $\mathcal{NRC}$ expressions. Each $\mathcal{NUL}$ update $u\colon s \to t$ defines a function that intuitively modifies objects of type s "in-place" to objects of type t. First, we have some "control" updates: skip is the trivial update with $\mathsf{skip}(v) = v$; while $u_1; u_2$ is update composition: $(u_1; u_2)(v) = u_2(u_1(v))$. The expression repl e replaces the input object by the object denoted by e. Next, $[x]\,u$ binds all free occurrences of x in $\mathcal{NRC}$ expressions occurring in u to the input object and then performs u. For example, $([x]\,\mathsf{repl}\,(x, x))(v) = (v, v)$. Note that the value of x is immutable; it is not affected by the changes u makes to the input object. In particular,

$[x]\,(\mathsf{repl}();\mathsf{repl}(x,x))$ is equivalent to $[x]\,\mathsf{repl}(x,x)$. Next come the set updates: $(\mathsf{insert}\ e)(V) = V \cup W$ where W is the denotation of e; $(\mathsf{remove}\ e)(V) = V - W$ where W is the denotation of e; and $\mathsf{iter}\ u$ applies u to every object in its input: $(\mathsf{iter}\ u)(\{v,\ldots,v'\}) = \{u(v),\ldots,u(v')\}$. Finally we have the updates on pairs: $(\mathsf{updl}\ u)(v,w) = (u(v),w)$ and $(\mathsf{updr}\ u)(v,w) = (v,u(w))$.

Example 3. We express the SQL updates (b) and (c) from the Introduction in $\mathcal{NUL}$. Here, the table $R(A,B)$ is represented as an object $R\colon \{b \times b\}$, which serves as the context object for the $\mathcal{NUL}$ updates. Example (b) is expressed as $u_{(b)} := \mathsf{iter}\,\big([x]\,\mathsf{updr}\ \mathsf{repl}(\text{if } \pi_1\,x = 1 \text{ then } 5 \text{ else } \pi_2\,x)\big)$. Example (c) is expressed as $u_{(c)} := [x]\,\mathsf{remove}\bigcup\{\text{if } \pi_1\,y = 1 \text{ then } \{y\} \text{ else } \{\} \mid y \in x\};\ \mathsf{insert}\,\{(1,5)\}$. We can also express schema modifying updates such as `alter table` R `drop column` B that transforms $R\colon \{b \times b\}$ into $R\colon \{b\}$ in $\mathcal{NUL}$ by $\mathsf{iter}\,([x]\,\mathsf{repl}\,\pi_1\,x)$.

Theorem 1. *$\mathcal{NRA}$, $\mathcal{NRC}$, and $\mathcal{NUL}$ are all equally expressive.*

Hence, we may view expressions in each of the three languages as "syntactic sugar" for expressions in the other languages. This allows us to freely combine $\mathcal{NRA}$, $\mathcal{NRC}$, and $\mathcal{NUL}$ into the single nested relational language $\mathcal{NRL}$.

3 A Model of Provenance

In this section we begin our study of provenance. Let *color* be an additional base type (not included in the unspecified collection of base types of $\mathcal{NRL}$) whose infinite set of elements we will refer to as *colors*. Let the *color-extended types* be the types in which *color* may also occur:

$$\mathbf{s},\mathbf{t} := color \mid b \mid \mathbf{s} \times \mathbf{t} \mid \{\mathbf{s}\}.$$

To avoid possible confusion, $\mathbf{r},\mathbf{s}$, and $\mathbf{t}$ will range over color-extended types and r, s and t will range over ordinary $\mathcal{NRL}$ types. Let $\mathbf{s} * \mathbf{t}$ be the type of objects of type $\mathbf{s}$ that are recursively paired with objects of type $\mathbf{t}$:

$$color*\mathbf{t} := color \times \mathbf{t} \quad b*\mathbf{t} := b\times\mathbf{t} \quad (\mathbf{r}\times\mathbf{s})*\mathbf{t} := (\mathbf{r}*\mathbf{t}\times\mathbf{s}*\mathbf{t})\times\mathbf{t} \quad \{\mathbf{s}\}*\mathbf{t} := \{\mathbf{s}*\mathbf{t}\}\times\mathbf{t}$$

We then define the type $\underline{s}$ of *colored objects of type* s as $s * color$. A colored object is hence an object in which each subobject is paired with a color. Let $\perp$ be a special color that describes the provenance of newly created objects. A *distinctly colored* object is a colored object in which $\perp$ does not occur and in which each other color occurs at most once.

As we have already illustrated in the Introduction, we can describe the provenance behavior of database operations by color-propagating functions from distinctly colored objects to colored objects. For our further formalisation it is more convenient, however, to consider color-propagating functions $f\colon \underline{s} \to \underline{t}$ that operate on *all* colored objects. Here, *color-propagating* means that f cannot let input colors influence the uncolored part of the output and that f's behavior is insensitive to the actual colors used in the input. In particular, a function

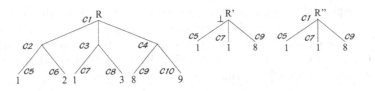

Fig. 3. The provenance semantics of left relational projection

$g: \underline{b} \times \underline{b} \to \underline{b}$ that outputs $(1, \text{red})$ when its two input atoms are colored equally, but outputs $(2, \text{blue})$ otherwise is not color-propagating. Formally, we require that $f \circ \alpha_{\underline{s}}^* = \alpha_{\underline{t}}^* \circ f$ for any "recoloring" $\alpha: color \to color$ that maps $\bot$ to $\bot$. Here, $\alpha_{\underline{r}}^*: \underline{r} \to \underline{r}$ is the canonical extension of α to type $\underline{r}$:

$$\alpha_{\underline{b}}^* := id \times \alpha \qquad \alpha_{\underline{r} \times \underline{r}'}^* := (\alpha_{\underline{r}}^* \times \alpha_{\underline{r}'}^*) \times \alpha \qquad \alpha_{\{\underline{r}\}}^* := map(\alpha_{\underline{r}}^*) \times \alpha,$$

where $h \times h'$ is an abbreviation of $\langle h \circ \pi_1, h' \circ \pi_2 \rangle$. Note that "color-propagating" is a different concept than "generic w.r.t. colors" since α above is not required to be bijective. Also note that this definition ensures that all colors in $f(v)$, except $\bot$, also occur in v. Finally, note that the behavior of f is fully determined by its behavior on distinctly colored objects, as the following lemma shows.

Lemma 1. *If $f: \underline{s} \to \underline{t}$ and $g: \underline{s} \to \underline{t}$ are two color-propagating functions such that $f(v) = g(v)$ for each distinctly colored $v: \underline{s}$, then $f \equiv g$.*

Proof. Let $w: \underline{s}$ be arbitrary and fix some distinctly colored $v: \underline{s}$ that equals w modulo colors. Then there obviously exists some recoloring α such that $\alpha_{\underline{s}}^*(v) = w$. Hence, $f(w) = f(\alpha_{\underline{s}}^*(v)) = \alpha_{\underline{t}}^*(f(v)) = \alpha_{\underline{t}}^*(g(v)) = g(\alpha_{\underline{s}}^*(v)) = g(w)$. □

Database operations are typically "domain-preserving" and are hence limited in their ability to create new atomic data values. In particular, if $o: s \to t$ is a query or update that creates atom a (in the sense that a appears in $o(v)$ but not in v for some v), then a appears as a constant in o. We want our concept of "provenance-aware operation" to reflect this behavior. We therefore define $f: \underline{s} \to \underline{t}$ to be *bounded-inventing* if there exists a finite set A of atoms such that for every distinctly colored $v: \underline{s}$ and every $(a, c): \underline{b}$ occurring in $f(v)$, if f says that it created a (i.e., if $c = \bot$), then $a \in A$.

Definition 1. *A* provenance-aware database operation *(pado for short) is a color-propagating, bounded-inventing function $f: \underline{s} \to \underline{t}$.*

It is important to note that a pado may define an object in the output to come from multiple parts in the input. For example, we will define the provenance semantics of the left relational projection Π_1 such that it maps the colored object $R: \{b \times b\}$ from Fig. 3 to R' in that figure. Note that atom 1 originated from both the first and the second pair in the input, as it appears both with colors c_5 and c_7 in R'.

In what follows, we will consider two natural classes of pados: copying and kind-preserving. Intuitively, a pado is *copying* if every object in the output that was not created by f was copied verbatim from the input.

Definition 2 (Copying). *A pado* $f: \underline{s} \rightarrow \underline{t}$ *is copying if for every* $v: \underline{s}$ *and every colored subobject* $(w, c): \underline{r}$ *of* $f(v)$, *if* $c \neq \perp$ *then* (w, c) *occurs in* v.

Similarly, a pado is kind-preserving if every subobject in the output that was not created by f originates from an object in the input of the same kind. In particular, every copying pado is also kind-preserving.

Definition 3 (Kind-preserving). *A pado* $f: \underline{s} \rightarrow \underline{t}$ *is* kind-preserving *if for every* $v: \underline{s}$ *and every colored subobject* $(w, c): \underline{r}$ *of* $f(v)$, *if* $c \neq \perp$ *then there exists* (u, c) *in* v *such that* u *and* v *are of the same kind: they are both sets, both pairs, or the same atom.*

Define $\mathcal{NRL}(color)$ to be the extension of $\mathcal{NRL}$ with the base type *color* in which $\perp$ is the only color that may appear as a constant. Since $\mathcal{NRL}(color)$ can explicitly manipulate colors, it is a natural language for the "explicit" definition of pados and a suitable benchmark to compare proposals for "standard" provenance semantics of query and update languages against. Define $\mathcal{CP}$ and $\mathcal{KP}$ as the sets of closed expressions in $\mathcal{NRL}(color)$ defining respectively copying and kind-preserving pados:

$$\mathcal{CP} := \{ f \mid f: \underline{s} \rightarrow \underline{t} \text{ in } \mathcal{NRL}(color) \text{ defines a copying pado} \},$$
$$\mathcal{KP} := \{ f \mid f: \underline{s} \rightarrow \underline{t} \text{ in } \mathcal{NRL}(color) \text{ defines a kind-preserving pado} \}.$$

Note that $\mathcal{CP}$ and $\mathcal{KP}$ are semantically defined. In fact both $\mathcal{CP}$ and $\mathcal{KP}$ are undecidable: a standard reduction from the satisfiability problem of the relational algebra shows that checking if an $\mathcal{NRL}(color)$ expression is color-propagating, bounded-inventing, copying, or kind-preserving are all undecidable.

4   Provenance for Query Languages

In this section we give an intuitive provenance-aware semantics for $\mathcal{NRA}$ and $\mathcal{NRC}$ expressions. Concretely, we take the view that queries construct new objects. As such, all objects constructed by a constant, pair, or set constructor (including union and map/comprehension) during a query are colored $\perp$. Objects copied from the input retain their color. The provenance semantics $\mathcal{P}[f]: \underline{s} \rightarrow \underline{t}$ of an $\mathcal{NRA}$ expression $f: s \rightarrow t$ is formally defined in Fig. 4 by translation into $\mathcal{NRL}(color)$. There, we write $(g \times h)$ as a shorthand for $\langle g \circ \pi_1, h \circ \pi_2 \rangle$; $\perp$ as a shorthand for $K\perp \circ !$; Π_1 as a shorthand for the left relational projection $map(\pi_1)$; and $val_{\underline{s}}: \underline{s} \rightarrow s$ for the function that forgets colors:

$$val_{\underline{b}} := \pi_1 \qquad val_{\underline{s \times t}} := (val_{\underline{s}} \times val_{\underline{t}}) \circ \pi_1 \qquad val_{\{\underline{s}\}} := map(val_{\underline{s}}) \circ \pi_1.$$

Note that $\mathcal{P}[cond]$ ignores colors during comparison: applied to a colored tuple $((v, v', w, w'), c)$ it returns w if $val(v) = val(v')$, and w' otherwise.

The provenance semantics $\mathcal{P}[e]: \underline{s}$ and $\mathcal{P}[e']: \underline{s} \rightarrow \underline{t}$ of $\mathcal{NRC}$ expressions $e: s$ and $e': s \rightarrow t$ is also defined in Fig. 4 by translation into $\mathcal{NRL}(color)$.

PROVENANCE SEMANTICS OF $\mathcal{N}\mathcal{R}\mathcal{A}$.

$$\mathcal{P}[Ka] := Ka \times \bot$$
$$\mathcal{P}[!] := ! \times \bot$$
$$\mathcal{P}[\langle g, h \rangle] := (\mathcal{P}[g] \times \mathcal{P}[h]) \times \bot$$
$$\mathcal{P}[K\{\}] := K\{\} \times \bot$$
$$\mathcal{P}[map(f)] := map(\mathcal{P}[f]) \times \bot$$

$$\mathcal{P}[id^s] := id^{\underline{s}}$$
$$\mathcal{P}[\pi_1] := \pi_1 \circ \pi_1$$
$$\mathcal{P}[\eta] := \eta \times \bot$$
$$\mathcal{P}[\cup] := \cup \times \bot$$
$$\mathcal{P}[cond] := cond \circ (val \times val \times id \times id) \circ \pi_1$$

$$\mathcal{P}[g \circ h] := \mathcal{P}[g] \circ \mathcal{P}[h]$$
$$\mathcal{P}[\pi_2] := \pi_2 \circ \pi_1$$
$$\mathcal{P}[\mu] := \mu \circ \Pi_1 \times \bot$$
$$\mathcal{P}[\rho_2] := \rho_2 \times \bot$$

PROVENANCE SEMANTICS OF $\mathcal{N}\mathcal{R}\mathcal{C}$.

$$\mathcal{P}[a] := (a, \bot)$$
$$\mathcal{P}[x^s] := x^{\underline{s}}$$
$$\mathcal{P}[()] := ((), \bot)$$
$$\mathcal{P}[\pi_2 \, e] := \pi_2 \, \pi_1 \, \mathcal{P}[e]$$
$$\mathcal{P}[\{\}] := (\{\}, \bot)$$
$$\mathcal{P}[\{e\}] := (\{\mathcal{P}[e]\}, \bot)$$

$$\mathcal{P}[\lambda x^s . e] := \lambda x^{\underline{s}} . \mathcal{P}[e]$$
$$\mathcal{P}[e_1 \, e_2] := \mathcal{P}[e_1] \, \mathcal{P}[e_2]$$
$$\mathcal{P}[\pi_1 \, e] := \pi_1 \, \pi_1 \, \mathcal{P}[e]$$
$$\mathcal{P}[(e_1, e_2)] := ((\mathcal{P}[e_1], \mathcal{P}[e_2]), \bot)$$
$$\mathcal{P}[e_1 \cup e_2] := ((\pi_1 \, \mathcal{P}[e_1] \cup \pi_1 \, \mathcal{P}[e_2]), \bot)$$
$$\mathcal{P}[\bigcup \{e_2 \mid x^s \in e_1\}] := (\bigcup \{\pi_1 \, \mathcal{P}[e_2] \mid x^{\underline{s}} \in \pi_1 \mathcal{P}[e_1]\}, \bot)$$

$$\mathcal{P}[\text{if } e_1 = e_2 \text{ then } e_3 \text{ else } e_4] := \text{if } val(\mathcal{P}[e_1]) = val(\mathcal{P}[e_2]) \text{ then } \mathcal{P}[e_3] \text{ else } \mathcal{P}[e_4]$$

PROVENANCE SEMANTICS OF $\mathcal{N}\mathcal{U}\mathcal{L}$.

$$\mathcal{P}[\text{skip}^s] := \text{skip}^{\underline{s}}$$
$$\mathcal{P}[\text{repl}^s \, e] := \text{repl}^{\underline{s}} \, \mathcal{P}[e]$$
$$\mathcal{P}[\text{insert } e] := \text{updl insert } (\pi_1 \, \mathcal{P}[e])$$
$$\mathcal{P}[\text{updl } u] := \text{updl updl } \mathcal{P}[u]$$
$$\mathcal{P}[\text{remove } e] := \text{updl } ([x] \text{ remove } \{y \mid y \in x, val(y) \in val(\mathcal{P}[e])\})$$

$$\mathcal{P}[u; u'] := \mathcal{P}[u]; \mathcal{P}[u']$$
$$\mathcal{P}[[x^s] \, u] := [x^{\underline{s}}] \, \mathcal{P}[u]$$
$$\mathcal{P}[\text{iter } u] := \text{updl iter } \mathcal{P}[u]$$
$$\mathcal{P}[\text{updr } u] := \text{updl updr } \mathcal{P}[u]$$

Fig. 4. Provenance semantics of $\mathcal{N}\mathcal{R}\mathcal{A}$, $\mathcal{N}\mathcal{R}\mathcal{C}$, and $\mathcal{N}\mathcal{U}\mathcal{L}$

Example 4. The provenance semantics $\mathcal{P}[\Pi_1]$ of the $\mathcal{N}\mathcal{R}\mathcal{A}$ expression Π_1 defining the left relational projection from Example 1 maps the colored set $R : \{b \times b\}$ from Fig. 3 to the colored set R' in that figure. The provenance semantics of the $\mathcal{N}\mathcal{R}\mathcal{C}$ expression Π_1 defining the left relational projection from Example 2 has the same behavior. The provenance semantics of the $\mathcal{N}\mathcal{R}\mathcal{A}$ expression *cartprod* from Example 1 maps the colored pair $v : \{b\} \times \{b\}$ from Fig. 5 to the colored set $w : \{b \times b\}$ in that figure. The provenance semantics $\mathcal{P}[e_{(a)}]$ of the $\mathcal{N}\mathcal{R}\mathcal{C}$ expression $e_{(a)}$ from Example 2 that defines query (a) from the Introduction has already been illustrated: it maps the colored set R from Fig. 1 to the colored set in Fig. 1(a).

Note that expressions that are equivalent under the normal semantics need not be equivalent under the provenance semantics. For example, $map(id)$ is equivalent to id, but $\mathcal{P}[map(id)]$ is not equivalent to $\mathcal{P}[id]$ as the set returned by $\mathcal{P}[map(id)]$ is colored with $\bot$, while $\mathcal{P}[id]$ retains the original color from the input. Likewise, if x is a variable of type $s \times t$ then $(\pi_1 \, x, \pi_2 \, x)$ is equivalent to x, but $\mathcal{P}[(\pi_1 \, x, \pi_2 \, x)]$ is not equivalent to $\mathcal{P}[x]$.

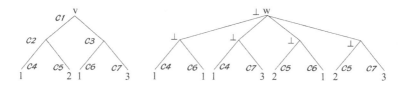

Fig. 5. The provenance semantics of cartesian product

Define $\mathcal{PNRA}$ and $\mathcal{PNRC}$ as the languages we obtain by interpreting $\mathcal{NRA}$ and $\mathcal{NRC}$ under the new provenance semantics:

$$\mathcal{PNRA} := \{\ \mathcal{P}[f] \mid f \text{ expression in } \mathcal{NRA}\ \},$$
$$\mathcal{PNRC} := \{\ \mathcal{P}[e] \mid e \text{ expression in } \mathcal{NRC}\ \}.$$

Proposition 2. *$\mathcal{PNRA} \equiv \mathcal{PNRC}$ in the sense that every function definable by an expression $\mathcal{P}[f]\colon \underline{s} \to \underline{t}$ in $\mathcal{PNRA}$ is definable by a closed expression $\mathcal{P}[e]\colon \underline{s} \to \underline{t}$ in $\mathcal{PNRC}$, and vice versa.*

Hence, the equivalence of $\mathcal{NRA}$ and $\mathcal{NRC}$ (as stated by Proposition 1) continues to hold under the provenance semantics. In particular, we may continue to view expressions in $\mathcal{NRA}$ and $\mathcal{NRC}$ as "syntactic sugar" for expressions in the other language whenever convenient – even when we consider provenance. On the other hand, in order to study the expressive power of provenance in these languages it suffices to study the expressiveness of $\mathcal{PNRA}$ or $\mathcal{PNRC}$ alone. For example, the following is straightforward to prove by induction on f:

Proposition 3. *Every $\mathcal{PNRA}$ expression $\mathcal{P}[f]\colon \underline{s} \to \underline{t}$ defines a copying pado.*

It readily follows from Proposition 2 that every $\mathcal{PNRC}$ expression also defines a copying pado. The key result of this section is that the converse also holds:

Theorem 2. *Every function in CP is also definable by a closed expression $\mathcal{P}[f']\colon \underline{s} \to \underline{t}$ in $\mathcal{PNRC}$.*

This theorem essentially follows from the following observations. First, Theorem 1 continues to hold in the presence of the base type *color*. Hence, every pado in CP can be expressed by some closed expression $f\colon \underline{s} \to \underline{t}$ in $\mathcal{NRC}(color)$. Second, the color-propagation of f implies that f is "polymorphic on colors" in the sense that we can substitute the colors in f by objects of some other type as follows. Let r be an arbitrary type, let $g\colon r$ be a closed $\mathcal{NRC}$ expression, and let $\mathcal{T}[f, g]\colon s * r \to t * r$ be the $\mathcal{NRC}$ expression we obtain by replacing every occurrence of *color* in a type annotation in f by r and subsequently replacing every occurrence of the constant $\bot$ in f by g.

Example 5. Let $f\colon \underline{b} \times \{b\} \to \underline{b} \times \{b\}$ be as below. Then $\mathcal{T}[f, g]$ is as shown.

$$f = \lambda x^{\underline{b} \times \{b\}}.\Big(\big((5, \bot), (\pi_1\,\pi_2\,\pi_1\,x \cup \{\pi_1\,\pi_1\,x\}, \bot)\big), \bot\Big),$$
$$\mathcal{T}[f, g] = \lambda x^{(b \times \{b\}) * r}.\Big(\big((5, g), (\pi_1\,\pi_2\,\pi_1\,x \cup \{\pi_1\,\pi_1\,x\}, g)\big), g\Big).$$

Note that $T[f,g]$ propagates the objects of type r from input to output in the same way as f propagates colors, where g takes the role of $\bot$. What is more, $P[T[f,g]]$: $\underline{s} * \underline{r} \to \underline{t} * \underline{r}$ propagates the *colored* objects of type $\underline{r}$ from input to output in the same way as f propagates colors. The formal statement of this claim is as follows.

Let r and s be types and let ϕ: $color \to \underline{r}$ be a function. We define w: $\underline{s} * \underline{r}$ to be *a substitution of the colors in* v: $\underline{s}$ *relative to* ϕ, denoted by $v \approx_s^\phi w$, by induction on s:

- $(a, c) \approx_b^\phi (((a, c'), \phi(c)), c'')$ with c' and c'' arbitrary;
- $((v, v'), c) \approx_{s \times s'}^\phi (((w, w'), \phi(c)), c')$ if $v \approx_s^\phi w$ and $v' \approx_{s'}^\phi w'$; and
- $(\{v, \dots, v'\}, c) \approx_{\{s\}}^\phi ((\{w, \dots, w'\}, \phi(c)), c')$ if $v \approx_s^\phi w, \dots, v' \approx_s^\phi w'$.

Proposition 4 (Color polymorphism). *Let* f: $\underline{s} \to \underline{t}$ *be a closed expression in* $\mathcal{NRC}(color)$ *defining a color-propagating function; let* g: r *be a closed expression in* $\mathcal{NRC}$; *and let* ϕ: $color \to \underline{r}$ *be a function such that* $\phi(\bot) = P[g]$. *Then* $f(v) \approx_t^\phi P[T[f,g]](w)$ *for every* v: $\underline{s}$ *and every* w: $\underline{s} * \underline{r}$ *with* $v \approx_s^\phi w$.

Let us now sketch how color polymorphism allows us to prove Theorem 2. In general, given a particular copying pado f: $\underline{s} \to \underline{t}$ in $\mathcal{NRC}(color)$ the proof constructs a type r and closed expressions g: r, enc: $s \to s * r$, and dec: $t * r \to t$ such that $P[enc]$: $\underline{s} \to \underline{s} * \underline{r}$ encodes the colors in $\underline{s}$ as colored objects of type $\underline{r}$ in $\underline{s} * \underline{r}$ and $P[dec]$: $\underline{t} * \underline{r} \to \underline{t}$ decodes the colored objects of $\underline{r}$ in $\underline{t} * \underline{r}$ back into their original colors. The copying property of f is crucial for the decoding step. Theorem 2 then follows as f is expressed in $\mathcal{PNRC}$ by $P[dec \circ T[f,g] \circ enc]$.

The construction. To illustrate the construction, assume that f: $b \times \{b\} \to b \times \{b\}$ is a copying pado in $\mathcal{NRC}(color)$. We will only motivate why $\overline{f}$ is equivalent to $P[dec \circ T[f,g] \circ enc]$ on *distinctly* colored objects. Equivalence on arbitrary colored object then follows by Lemma 1, as both f and $P[dec \circ T[f,g] \circ enc]$ are color-propagating. Furthermore, we will use tuples of arbitrary arity, as these can readily be simulated in the $\mathcal{NRC}$. For example, (x, y, z) is an abbreviation of $((x, y), z)$ and the projection π_i^n that retrieves the i-th component of an n-tuple is an abbreviation of $\pi_2 \pi_1 x$.

Let s abbreviate $b \times \{b\}$. Roughly speaking, we want $P[enc]$: $\underline{s} \to \underline{s} * \underline{r}$ to substitute every color in a distinctly colored object v: $\underline{s}$ by the unique colored subobject of v that is colored by c. In particular, $\underline{r}$ must hence be big enough to store all colored subobjects of v. Hereto, we take $r = b \times \{b\} \times (b \times \{b\}) \times \{unit\}$, where the first three components will be used to store colored subobjects from v, and the last type $\{unit\}$ will be used as an extra boolean flag that indicates the encoding of $\bot$. The following expressions can then be used to "inject" subobjects of v into r and to encode $\bot$:

$$put^b : b \to r := \lambda x^b.(x, e_{\{b\}}, e_s, \{\}) \quad put^{\{b\}} : \{b\} \to r := \lambda x^{\{b\}}.(e_b, x, e_s, \{\})$$
$$put^s : s \to r := \lambda x^s.(e_b, e_{\{b\}}, x, \{\}) \quad g : r \qquad := (e_b, e_{\{b\}}, e_s, \{()\}).$$

Here, e_b: b, $e_{\{b\}}$: $\{b\}$, and e_s: s are arbitrary but fixed closed $\mathcal{NRC}$ expressions. For example, e_s could be $(a, \{\})$ with a: b an arbitrary constant.

We now construct enc such that if $v\colon \underline{s}$ is distinctly colored and $\phi\colon color \to \underline{r}$ is the function that maps $\bot$ to $\mathcal{P}[g]$ and that maps every color c occurring in v to $\mathcal{P}[put^{s'}](v_c)$ where $v_c\colon \underline{s'}$ is the unique subobject of v colored by c, then $v \approx_{\underline{s}}^{\phi} \mathcal{P}[enc](v)$. Hereto, it suffices to let enc be

$$\lambda x^s.\Big(\big((\pi_1\,x,\,put^b(\pi_1\,x)),\,(\textstyle\bigcup\{\{(y,\,put^b(y))\} \mid y \in \pi_2\,x\},\,put^{\{b\}}(\pi_2\,x))\big),\,put^s(x)\Big).$$

Let $w\colon \underline{s*r}$ abbreviate $\mathcal{P}[\mathcal{I}[f,g] \circ enc](v)$. Then $f(v) \approx_{\underline{s}}^{\phi} w$ by color polymorphism since $v \approx_{\underline{s}}^{\phi} \mathcal{P}[enc](v)$. That is, subobjects of type $\underline{r}$ in w are substitutions of the colors in $f(v)$ relative to ϕ. By inspecting these objects we can decode w back into $f(v)$ as follows. Let c be the color of $f(v)$, i.e., let $c = \pi_2(f(v))$. First, we note that we can check in $\mathcal{PNRC}$ whether $c = \bot$ in the sense that $\mathcal{P}[\lambda x.\text{if } \pi_2\,x = g \text{ then } e_1 \text{ else } e_2](w)$ executes $\mathcal{P}[e_1]$ if $c = \bot$, and executes $\mathcal{P}[e_2]$ otherwise. To prove this claim, it suffices to show that $c = \bot$ iff $val(\mathcal{P}[\pi_2](w)) = val(\mathcal{P}[g])$. Suppose that $c = \bot$. Because $f(v) \approx_{\underline{s}}^{\phi} w$, it is easily seen that $\mathcal{P}[\pi_2](w) = \phi(c) = \phi(\bot) = \mathcal{P}[g]$, and hence also $val(\mathcal{P}[\pi_2](w)) = val(\mathcal{P}[g])$. For the only-if direction, suppose for the purpose of contradiction that $val(\mathcal{P}[\pi_2](w)) = val(\mathcal{P}[g])$ but $c \neq \bot$. Since f is color-propagating, every color different from $\bot$ occurring in $f(v)$ must also occur in v. Hence, c occurs in v, and thus $\phi(c) = \mathcal{P}[put^{s'}](v_c)$. Because $f(v) \approx_{\underline{s}}^{\phi} w$, it is easily seen that $\mathcal{P}[\pi_2](w) = \phi(c) = \mathcal{P}[put^{s'}](v_c)$. By construction, however, $val(\mathcal{P}[put^{s'}](v')) \neq val(\mathcal{P}[g])$ for any s' and any $v'\colon \underline{s'}$. Hence, $val(\mathcal{P}[\pi_2](w)) = val(\mathcal{P}[put^{s'}](v_c)) \neq val(\mathcal{P}[g])$, which gives us the desired contradiction.

We now claim that $\mathcal{P}[dec]$ with $dec\colon s*r \to s$ defined as follows successfully decodes w back into $f(v)$.

$$
\begin{aligned}
dec &:= \lambda x.\ \text{if } \pi_2\,x = g \text{ then } \big(dec^b(\pi_1\,\pi_1\,x),\,dec^{\{b\}}(\pi_2\,\pi_1\,x)\big) \text{ else } \pi_3^4(\pi_2\,x) \\
dec^b &:= \lambda x.\ \text{if } \pi_2\,x = g \text{ then } inv(\pi_1\,x) \text{ else } \pi_1^4(\pi_2\,x) \\
dec^{\{b\}} &:= \lambda x.\ \text{if } \pi_2\,x = g \text{ then } \textstyle\bigcup\{\{dec^b(y)\} \mid y \in \pi_1\,x\} \text{ else } \pi_2^4(\pi_2\,x).
\end{aligned}
$$

Here, $inv := \lambda x.\text{if } x = a_1 \text{ then } a_1 \text{ else } \ldots \text{ else if } x = a_k \text{ then } a_k \text{ else } x$, where $\{a_1, \ldots, a_k\}$ is the finite set of constants testifying that f is bounded inventing.

To see why $\mathcal{P}[dec](w) = f(v)$, first consider the case where $c \neq \bot$. Because f is copying, we know that $f(v) = v_c$ with $v_c\colon \underline{s}$ the unique subobject of v colored by c. Hence, $\mathcal{P}[dec](w) = \mathcal{P}[\pi_3^4](\mathcal{P}[\pi_2](w)) = \mathcal{P}[\pi_3^4](\phi(c)) = \mathcal{P}[\pi_3^4](\mathcal{P}[put^s](v_c))$. It is not hard to see that the latter is precisely $v_c = f(v)$, as desired.

Next, consider the case where $c = \bot$. Then $f(v)$ is a "newly constructed" colored pair. Hence, to decode w into $f(v)$, $\mathcal{P}[dec]$ first decodes $w_1 := \mathcal{P}[\pi_1\,\pi_1](w)$ and $w_2 := \mathcal{P}[\pi_2\,\pi_1](w)$ into $\pi_1(f(v))$ and $\pi_2(f(v))$ respectively, and constructs a new pair to put them in. Here, $\mathcal{P}[dec^b]$ and $\mathcal{P}[dec^{\{b\}}]$ decode w_1 and w_2 using essentially the same reasoning as $\mathcal{P}[dec]$: first they inspect the colors of w_1 and w_2, extracting the correct value from the $\underline{r}$-component if the color is not $\bot$, and by "reconstructing" the object otherwise.

This concludes the proof illustration of Theorem 2. As a corollary to Proposition 2, Proposition 3, and Theorem 2 we immediately obtain:

Corollary 1. *$\mathcal{PNRA}$, $\mathcal{PNRC}$, and $\mathcal{CP}$ are all equally expressive.*

5   Provenance for Updates

In this section we give an intuitive provenance-aware semantics for updates. Concretely, we take the view that updates do not construct new objects, but modify existing ones. As such, objects retain their colors during an update.

The provenance semantics $\mathcal{P}[u]\colon \underline{s} \to \underline{t}$ of a $\mathcal{NUL}$ update $u\colon s \to t$ is formally defined in Fig. 4 by translation into $\mathcal{NRL}(color)$. Here, $\mathcal{P}[e]$ is the provenance semantics of $\mathcal{NRC}$ expression e as defined in Section 4 and $\{y \mid y \in x, val(y) \in val(\mathcal{P}[e])\}$ abbreviates the expression

$$\bigcup\{\text{if } val(y) \in val(\mathcal{P}[e]) \text{ then } \{y\} \text{ else } \{\} \mid y \in x\},$$

where the conditional if $e_1 \in e_2$ then e_3 else e_4 is known to be expressible in $\mathcal{NRL}$ [7]. Note in particular that the provenance semantics of remove e ignores colors when selecting the objects to remove.

Example 6. The provenance semantics of the $\mathcal{NUL}$ update iter $([x]$ repl $\pi_1 x)$ from Example 3 maps the colored set $R\colon \{\underline{b \times b}\}$ from Fig. 3 to the colored set R'' in that figure. Note in particular that the set itself retains its color. This is in contrast to the provenance semantics of the relational projection Π_1, as we have explained in Example 4. The provenance semantics of the updates $u_{(b)}$ and $u_{(c)}$ from Example 3 that express respectively the SQL updates (b) and (c) from the Introduction has already been illustrated in the Introduction. In particular, $\mathcal{P}[u_{(b)}]$ maps the colored set R from Fig. 1 to the colored set in Fig. 1(b), while $\mathcal{P}[u_{(c)}]$ maps R to the colored set in Fig. 1(c).

Define $\mathcal{PNUL}$ as the language we obtain by interpreting $\mathcal{NUL}$ under the new provenance semantics:

$$\mathcal{PNUL} := \{\mathcal{P}[u] \mid u \text{ expression in } \mathcal{NUL}\}.$$

It is easy to show that $\mathcal{PNUL} \subseteq \mathcal{KP}$; that is, every $\mathcal{P}[u]$ defines a kind-preserving pado. The key result of this section is that the converse also holds. The proof uses the same "color polymorphism" technique we have used for queries.

Theorem 3. $\mathcal{KP} \equiv \mathcal{PNUL}$ *in the sense that every function definable by an expression* $f\colon \underline{s} \to \underline{t}$ *in* $\mathcal{KP}$ *is also definable by a closed update* $\mathcal{P}[u]\colon \underline{s} \to \underline{t}$ *in* $\mathcal{PNUL}$, *and vice versa.*

6   Discussion

Our goal in this paper has been to achieve an understanding of how query and update languages manipulate provenance. Although the completeness results from Sects. 4 and 5 show why our proposed provenance semantics is sensible, there are several issues that must be tackled before we can build a practical system that records provenance.

Space and processing overhead are concerns even for simple, manual updates [5]. From a space-efficiency point of view, it may be desirable to "merge" objects in the same set that are equal modulo colors. For example, we could collapse the two occurrences of atom 1 in R' of Fig. 3 into a single atom colored by the set $\{c_5, c_7\}$ [15,3]. Query rewriting is also problematic. In Sect. 4 we noted that expressions that are equivalent under traditional semantics are no longer equivalent when provenance is considered. This may affect query optimisation.

There is also the issue of aggregation queries such as **select** A, **sum**(B) **from** R **group by** A. This particular aggregation could be expressed in $\mathcal{NRL}$ by adding a function $sum\colon \{int\} \to int$. Since the output of sum is a new data value, we could define $\mathcal{P}[sum] := \langle sum, K\bot \circ \,! \rangle$, but it is surely more satisfactory to record some form of *workflow* provenance, as known from the geospatial and Grid computing communities [4,9,12], that tells us how the sum was formed. Another problem is that $\mathcal{P}[sum]$ is no longer bounded-inventing, a problem that also arises when we want to consider external user-defined functions. We hope to generalize our approach to address these issues.

References

1. S. Abiteboul, R. Hull, and V. Vianu. *Foundations Of Databases.* Addison-Wesley, 1995.
2. O. Benjelloun, A. D. Sarma, A. Halevy, and J. Widom. ULDBs: databases with uncertainty and lineage. In *VLDB 2006*, pages 953–964, 2006.
3. D. Bhagwat, L. Chiticariu, W. Tan, and G. Vijayvargiya. An annotation management system for relational databases. In *VLDB 2004*, pages 900–911, 2004.
4. R. Bose and J. Frew. Lineage retrieval for scientific data processing: a survey. *ACM Comput. Surv.*, 37(1):1–28, 2005.
5. P. Buneman, A. Chapman, and J. Cheney. Provenance management in curated databases. In *SIGMOD 2006*, pages 539–550, 2006.
6. P. Buneman, S. Khanna, and W. Tan. Why and where: A characterization of data provenance. In *ICDT 2001*, volume 1973 of *LNCS*, pages 316–330. Springer, 2001.
7. P. Buneman, S. A. Naqvi, V. Tannen, and L. Wong. Principles of programming with complex objects and collection types. *Theor. Comp. Sci.*, 149(1):3–48, 1995.
8. Y. Cui, J. Widom, and J. L. Wiener. Tracing the lineage of view data in a warehousing environment. *ACM Trans. Database Syst.*, 25(2):179–227, 2000.
9. I. Foster and L. Moreau, editors. *Proceedings of the 2006 International Provenance and Annotation Workshop*, volume 4145 of *LNCS*. Springer-Verlag, 2006.
10. F. Geerts, A. Kementsietsidis, and D. Milano. Mondrian: Annotating and querying databases through colors and blocks. In *ICDE 2006*, page 82, 2006.
11. H. Liefke and S. B. Davidson. Specifying updates in biomedical databases. In *SSDBM*, pages 44–53, 1999.
12. Y. Simmhan, B. Plale, and D. Gannon. A survey of data provenance in e-science. *SIGMOD Record*, 34(3):31–36, 2005.
13. W. Tan. Containment of relational queries with annotation propagation. In *DBPL 2003*, volume 2921 of *LNCS*, pages 37–53. Springer, 2003.
14. W. Tan. Research problems in data provenance. *IEEE Data Engineering Bulletin*, 27(4):45–52, 2004.
15. Y. R. Wang and S. E. Madnick. A polygen model for heterogeneous database systems: The source tagging perspective. In *VLDB 1990*, pages 519–538, 1990.

Trajectory Databases: Data Models, Uncertainty and Complete Query Languages

Bart Kuijpers and Walied Othman

Theoretical Computer Science Group
Hasselt University & Transnational University of Limburg, Belgium

Abstract. Moving objects produce trajectories. We describe a data model for trajectories and trajectory samples and an efficient way of modeling uncertainty via beads for trajectory samples. We study transformations for which important physical properties of trajectories, such as speed, are invariant. We also determine which transformations preserve beads. We give conceptually easy first-order complete query languages and computationally complete query languages for trajectory databases, which allow to talk directly about speed and beads. The queries expressible in these languages are invariant under speed- and bead-preserving transformations.

1 Introduction and Summary

The research on spatial databases, which started in the 1980s from work in geographic information systems, was extended in the second half of the 1990s to deal with spatio-temporal data. One particular line of research in this field, started by Wolfson, concentrated on *moving object databases* (MODs) [4,12], a field in which several data models and query languages have been proposed to deal with moving objects whose position is recorded at, not always regular, moments in time. Some of these models are geared towards handling uncertainty that may come from various sources (measurements of locations, interpolation, ...) and often ad-hoc query formalisms have been proposed [11]. For an overview of models and techniques for MODs, we refer to the book by Güting and Schneider [4].

In this paper, we focus on the trajectories that are produced by moving objects and on managing and querying them in a database. We therefore think it is more appropriate to talk about *trajectory databases*, rather than to refer to the moving objects that produce these trajectories. We give a data model for trajectory data, an efficient way of modeling uncertainty, we study transformations for which important physical properties of trajectories are invariant and we give first-order complete and computationally complete query languages for queries invariant under these transformations.

We propose two types of trajectory data, namely *trajectories*, which are curves in the plane (rationally parameterized by time) and *trajectory samples*, which are well-known in MODs, namely finite sequences of time-space points. A trajectory database contains a finite number of labeled trajectories or trajectory samples. There are various ways to reconstruct trajectories from trajectory samples, of

T. Schwentick and D. Suciu (Eds.): ICDT 2007, LNCS 4353, pp. 224–238, 2007.

which linear interpolation is the most popular in the literature [4]. However, linear interpolation relies on the (rather unrealistic) assumption that between sample points, a moving object moves at constant minimal speed. It is more realistic to assume that moving objects have some physically determined speed bounds. Given such upper bounds, an uncertainty model has been proposed which constructs *beads* between two consecutive time-space points in a trajectory sample. Basic properties of this model were discussed a few years ago by Egenhofer et al. [1,7] and Pfoser et al. [9], but beads were already known in the time-geography of Hägerstrand in the 1970s [6]. A bead is the intersection of two cones in the time-space space and all possible trajectories of the moving object between the two consecutive time-space points, given the speed bound, are located within the bead. Beads manage uncertainty more efficiently than other approaches based on cylinders [12] (by a factor of 3).

Speed is not only important in obtaining good uncertainty models, but also many relevant queries on trajectory data involve physical properties of trajectories of which speed is the most important. Geerts proposed a model which works explicitly with the equations of motion of the moving objects, rather than with samples of trajectories, and in which the velocity of a moving object is directly available and used [3]. If we are interested in querying about speed, it is important to know which transformations of the time-space space preserve the speed of a moving object. We characterize this group $\mathcal{V}$ of transformations as the combinations of affinities of time with orthogonal transformations of space composed with a spatial scaling (that uses the same scale factor as the temporal affinity) and translations. In [2], transformations that leave the velocity vector invariant were discussed, but starting from spatial transformation that are a function of time alone. Our result holds in general. We also show that the group $\mathcal{V}$ contains precisely the transformations that preserve beads. So, the queries that involve speed are invariant under transformations of $\mathcal{V}$, as are queries that speak about uncertainty in term of beads. Therefore, if we are interested in querying about speed and dealing with uncertainty via beads, it is advisable to use a query language that expresses queries invariant under transformations of $\mathcal{V}$. Beads have never before been considered in the context of query languages.

As a starting point to query trajectory (sample) databases, we take a two-sorted logic based on first-order logic extended with polynomial constraints in which we have trajectory label variables and real variables. This logic has been studied well in the context of constraint databases [8] and also allows the expression of speed and beads. We remark that the $\mathcal{V}$-invariant queries form an undecidable class, and we show that this fragment is captured by a three-sorted logic, with trajectory label variables, time-space point variables and speed variables, that uses two very simple predicates: $\mathsf{Before}(p, q)$ and $\mathsf{minSpeed}(p, q, v)$. For time-space points p and q, the former expresses that the time-component of p is smaller than that of q. The latter predicate expresses that the minimal constant speed to travel from p to q is v. This logic also allows polynomial constraints on speed variables. We show that using these two, conceptually intuitive, predicates, all the $\mathcal{V}$-invariant first-order queries can be expressed. This language allows one to express all queries concerning speed on trajectory data and all queries concerning uncertainty in terms of beads on trajectory samples. In particular, a predicate inBead(r, p, q, v) can be defined in this logic, expressing that r is in the bead of p and q with maximal speed v.

We also show that a programming language, based on this three-sorted logic, in which relations can be created and which has a while-loop with first-order stop conditions, is sound and complete for the computable $\mathcal{V}$-invariant queries on trajectory (sample) databases. The proofs of these sound and completeness results are inspired by earlier work on complete languages for spatial [5] and spatio-temporal databases [2]. Compared to [2], the language we propose is far more user oriented since it is not based on geometric but speed-oriented predicates. We remark that the completeness and soundness results presented in this paper hold for arbitrary spatio-temporal data, but we present them for trajectory (sample) data. In any case, in all the presented languages it is expressible that an output relation is a trajectory (sample) relation.

This paper is organized as follows. In Section 2, we give definitions and results concerning trajectories and Section 3 deals with uncertainty via beads. Trajectory databases and queries are discussed in Section 4 and results on complete query languages are in Section 5.

2   Trajectories and Trajectory Samples

2.1   Definitions and Basic Properties

Let $\mathbf{R}$ denote the set of real numbers. We will restrict ourselves to the real plane $\mathbf{R}^2$ (although all definitions and results can be generalized to higher dimensions).

Definition 1. A *trajectory* T is the graph of a mapping $I \subseteq \mathbf{R} \to \mathbf{R}^2 : t \mapsto \alpha(t) = (\alpha_x(t), \alpha_y(t))$, i.e., $T = \{(t, \alpha_x(t), \alpha_y(t)) \in \mathbf{R} \times \mathbf{R}^2 \mid t \in I\}$. The *image of the trajectory* T is the image of the mapping α that describes T. The set I is called the *time domain* of T. □

Often, in the literature, conditions are imposed on the nature of the mappings α_x and α_y. For instance, they may be assumed to be continuous, piecewise linear [4], differentiable, or C^∞ [11]. For reasons of finite representability, we assume that I is a (possibly unbounded) interval and that α_x and α_y are continuous semi-algebraic functions (i.e., they are given by a combination of polynomial inequalities in x and t and y and t respectively). For example, the set $\{(t, \frac{1-t^2}{1+t^2}, \frac{2t}{1+t^2}) \mid 0 \le t \le 1\}$ describes a trajectory on a quarter of a circle. In this example, α_x is given by the formula $x(1 + t^2) = 1 - t^2 \wedge 0 \le t \le 1$.

Definition 2. A *trajectory sample* is a list $\langle (t_0, x_0, y_0), (t_1, x_1, y_1), ..., (t_N, x_N, y_N) \rangle$, with $x_i, y_i, t_i \in \mathbf{R}$ for $i = 0, ..., N$ and $t_0 < t_1 < \cdots < t_N$. □

For the sake of finite representability, we may assume that the time-space points (t_i, x_i, y_i), have rational coordinates. This will be the case in practice, since these points are typically the result of observations.

A classical model to reconstruct a trajectory from a sample is the *linear-interpolation model* [4], where the unique trajectory, that contains the sample and that is obtained by assuming that the trajectory is run through at constant lowest speed between any two consecutive sample points, is constructed. For a sample $S = \langle(t_0, x_0, y_0), (t_1, x_1, y_1), ..., (t_N, x_N, y_N)\rangle$, the trajectory $LIT(S) := \bigcup_{i=0}^{N-1}\{(t, \frac{(t_{i+1}-t)x_i+(t-t_i)x_{i+1}}{t_{i+1}-t_i}, \frac{(t_{i+1}-t)y_i+(t-t_i)y_{i+1}}{t_{i+1}-t_i}) \mid t_i \leq t \leq t_{i+1})\}$ is called the *linear-interpolation trajectory* of S.

We now define the speed of a trajectory.

Definition 3. Let $T = \{(t, \alpha_x(t), \alpha_y(t)) \in \mathbf{R} \times \mathbf{R}^2 \mid t \in I\}$ be a trajectory. If α_x and α_y are differentiable in $t_0 \in I$, then the *velocity vector of T in t_0* is defined as $(1, \frac{d\alpha_x(t_0)}{dt}, \frac{d\alpha_y(t_0)}{dt})$ and the length of the projection of this vector on the (x, y)-plane is called the *speed of T in t_0*. □

Let $S = \langle(t_0, x_0, y_0), (t_1, x_1, y_1), ..., (t_N, x_N, y_N)\rangle$ be a sample. Then for any t, with $t_i < t < t_{i+1}$, the velocity vector of $LIT(S)$ in t is $(1, \frac{x_{i+1}-x_i}{t_{i+1}-t_i}, \frac{y_{i+1}-y_i}{t_{i+1}-t_i})$ and the corresponding speed is the minimal speed at which this distance between (x_i, y_i) and (x_{i+1}, y_{i+1}) can be covered. At the moments $t_0, t_1, ..., t_N$ the velocity vector and speed of $LIT(S)$ may not be defined.

2.2 Transformations of Trajectories

Now, we study transformations of trajectories under mappings $f : \mathbf{R} \times \mathbf{R}^2 \to \mathbf{R} \times \mathbf{R}^2 : (t, x, y) \mapsto (f_t(t, x, y), f_x(t, x, y), f_y(t, x, y))$. We assume that f preserves the temporal order of events (for a technical definition we refer to [2]). It has been shown that this is equivalent to the assumption that f_t is a monotone increasing function of time alone, i.e., that $(t, x, y) \mapsto f_t(t)$ [2]. We further assume transformations to be bijective and differentiable. We remark that if f is as above and f_t is a monotone increasing function of t, then f maps trajectories to trajectories.

If $f : \mathbf{R} \times \mathbf{R}^2 \to \mathbf{R} \times \mathbf{R}^2$ transforms a trajectory, then we can roughly say that $df = \begin{pmatrix} \frac{\partial f_t}{\partial t} & 0 & 0 \\ \frac{\partial f_x}{\partial t} & \frac{\partial f_x}{\partial x} & \frac{\partial f_x}{\partial y} \\ \frac{\partial f_y}{\partial t} & \frac{\partial f_y}{\partial x} & \frac{\partial f_y}{\partial y} \end{pmatrix}$, the *derived transformation of f*, transforms in each point of the trajectory the velocity vector.

Theorem 1. *A mapping $f : \mathbf{R} \times \mathbf{R}^2 \to \mathbf{R} \times \mathbf{R}^2 : (t, x, y) \mapsto (f_t(t, x, y), f_x(t, x, y), f_y(t, x, y))$ preserves at all moments the speed of trajectories and preserves the order of events if and only if*

$$f(t, x, y) = a \cdot \begin{pmatrix} 1 & 0 & 0 \\ 0 & a_{11} & a_{12} \\ 0 & a_{21} & a_{22} \end{pmatrix} \begin{pmatrix} t \\ x \\ y \end{pmatrix} + \begin{pmatrix} b \\ b_1 \\ b_2 \end{pmatrix},$$

with $a, b, b_1, b_2 \in \mathbf{R}$, $a > 0$, and the matrix $\begin{pmatrix} a_{11} & a_{12} \\ a_{21} & a_{22} \end{pmatrix} \in \mathbf{R}^{2 \times 2}$ defining an orthogonal transformation (i.e., its inverse is its transposed). We denote the group of these transformations by $\mathcal{V}$.

Proof. Let $f : (t, x, y) \mapsto (f_t(t, x, y), f_x(t, x, y), f_y(t, x, y))$ be a transformation. If f preserves the order of events, then everywhere $\frac{\partial f_t}{\partial x} = 0$, $\frac{\partial f_t}{\partial y} = 0$ and $\frac{\partial f_t}{\partial t} > 0$ [2], which means that f_t is a reparameterization of time, i.e., $(t, x, y) \mapsto f_t(t)$.

Consider a trajectory $T = \{(t, \alpha_x(t), \alpha_y(t)) \in \mathbf{R} \times \mathbf{R}^2 \mid t \in I\}$. The trajectory T will be transformed to a trajectory $f(T)$ given by $\beta : \mathbf{R} \to \mathbf{R} \times \mathbf{R}^2 : \tau \mapsto (\tau, \beta_x(\tau), \beta_y(\tau))$. Since f_t is a reparameterization of time, we can write $\tau = f_t(t)$ and $t = f_t^{-1}(\tau)$. The mapping f transforms $(t, \alpha_x(t), \alpha_y(t))$ into $f(T)$ which is $(f_t(t), f_x(t, \alpha_x(t), \alpha_y(t)), f_y(t, \alpha_x(t), \alpha_y(t)))$ and which can be written as $(\tau, f_x(f_t^{-1}(\tau), \alpha_x(f_t^{-1}(\tau)), \alpha_y(f_t^{-1}(\tau))), f_y(f_t^{-1}(\tau), \alpha_x(f_t^{-1}(\tau)), \alpha_y(f_t^{-1}(\tau))))$. This trajectory is given as β (depending on the parameter τ).

We assume that f preserves, at all moments in time, the speed of trajectories, which means that the length of $(1, \partial\alpha_x(t)/\partial t, \partial\alpha_y(t)/\partial t)$ equals that of $(1, \partial\beta_x(\tau)/\partial\tau, \partial\beta_y(\tau)/\partial\tau)$. Since $(f \circ \alpha)'(t)$ and $\frac{\partial\beta(\tau)}{\partial t}$ have to be equal, and since $(f \circ \alpha)'(t) = df_{\alpha(t)} \circ \alpha'(t)$ and $\frac{\partial\beta(\tau)}{\partial t} = \beta'(\tau) \cdot \frac{\partial\tau(t)}{\partial t} = \beta'(\tau) \cdot f_t'(t)$, we have $df_{\alpha(t)} \circ \alpha'(t) = \beta'(\tau) \cdot f_t'(t)$ which means $\left(\frac{1}{f_t'(t)} \cdot df_{\alpha(t)}\right) \circ \alpha'(t) = \beta'(\tau)$ and that $\frac{1}{f_t'(t)} \cdot df_{(t,x,y)}$ must be an isometry of $\mathbf{R} \times \mathbf{R}^2$ for each (t, x, y).

Let A be the matrix associated to the linear mapping $\frac{1}{f_t'(t)} \cdot df_{(t,x,y)}$. Since this linear transformation must be orthogonal, we have that $A \cdot A^T = A^T \cdot A = I$ and $\det(A) = \pm 1$. These conditions lead to the following equations. Firstly, $(\frac{\partial f_t}{\partial t} \frac{\partial f_x}{\partial t})/(f_t'(t))^2 = 0$, which means $\frac{\partial f_x}{\partial t} = 0$, because $\frac{\partial f_t}{\partial t} > 0$. Similarly, we have that $\frac{\partial f_y}{\partial t} = 0$. Secondly, $(\partial f_x/\partial x)^2 + (\partial f_x/\partial y)^2 = (f_t'(t))^2$. We remark that the right-hand side is time-dependent and the left-hand side isn't, and vice versa the left-hand side is dependent on only spatial coordinates and the right-hand side isn't, which means both sides must be constant. This implies that $f_t(t) = at + b$ where $a > 0$ since f_t is assumed to be an increasing function. The condition $(\frac{\partial f_x}{\partial x})^2 + (\frac{\partial f_x}{\partial y})^2 = a^2$ is known as a *differential equation of light rays* [10], and has the solution $f_x(x, y) = a_{11}x + a_{12}y + b_1$, where $a_{11}^2 + a_{12}^2 = a^2$ and where b_1 is arbitrary. Completely analogue, we obtain $f_y(x, y) = a_{21}x + a_{22}y + b_2$ where $a_{21}^2 + a_{22}^2 = a^2$ and where b_2 is arbitrary.

Thirdly, $\left(\frac{\partial f_x}{\partial x} \frac{\partial f_y}{\partial x} + \frac{\partial f_y}{\partial y} \frac{\partial f_x}{\partial y}\right)/(f_t'(t))^2 = 0$. And finally, $\det(A) = \pm 1$ gives $a_{11}a_{22} - a_{12}a_{21} = \pm 1$. If we write $a_{ij}' = \frac{a_{ij}}{a}$, then we all these equations lead to the following form of f: $f(t, x, y) =$

$$a \cdot \begin{pmatrix} 1 & 0 & 0 \\ 0 & a_{11}' & a_{12}' \\ 0 & a_{11}' & a_{22}' \end{pmatrix} \begin{pmatrix} t \\ x \\ y \end{pmatrix} + \begin{pmatrix} b \\ b_1 \\ b_2 \end{pmatrix}$$

where $a > 0$, and the matrix of the a_{ij}' determines an orthogonal transformation of the plane. It is also clear that transformations of the above form preserve at any moment the speed of trajectories. This completes the proof. $\square$

Examples of speed-preserving transformations include the spatial translations and rotations, temporal translations and scalings of the time-space space.

3 Uncertainty Via Beads

In 1999, Pfoser et al. [9], and later Egenhofer et al. [1,7], introduced the notion of *beads* in the moving object database literature to model uncertainty. Before Wolfson used *cylinders* to model uncertainty [4,12]. However, cylinders give less precision (by a factor of 3, compared to beads). Let S be a sample $\langle (t_0, x_0, y_0), (t_1, x_1, y_1), ..., (t_N, x_N, y_N)\rangle$. Basically, the cylinder approach to managing uncertainty, depends on an uncertainty threshold value $\varepsilon > 0$ and gives a buffer of radius ε around $LIT(S)$. In the bead approach, for each pair $(t_i, x_i, y_i), (t_{i+1}, x_{i+1}, y_{i+1})$ in the sample S, their bead related does not depend on a uncertainty threshold value $\varepsilon > 0$, but rather on a maximal velocity value v_{max} of the moving object.

Definition 4. Given $(t_i, x_i, y_i), (t_{i+1}, x_{i+1}, y_{i+1})$, with $t_i < t_{i+1}$ and $v_{max} > 0$, the *bead of* $(t_i, x_i, y_i, t_{i+1}, x_{i+1}, y_{i+1}, v_{max})$, denoted $B(t_i, x_i, y_i, t_{i+1}, x_{i+1}, y_{i+1}, v_{max})$, is the set $\{(t, x, y) \in \mathbf{R} \times \mathbf{R}^3 \mid (x - x_i)^2 + (y - y_i)^2 \leq (t - t_i)^2 v_{max}^2 \wedge (x - x_{i+1})^2 + (y - y_{i+1})^2 \leq (t_{i+1} - t)^2 v_{max}^2 \wedge t_i \leq t \leq t_{i+1}\}$. ☐

The bead in Figure 1 shows at each moment a *disk* or a *lens*.

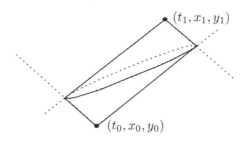

Fig. 1. An example of a bead $B(t_0, x_0, y_0, t_1, x_1, y_1, 1)$

We remark that for a sample $S = \langle (t_0, x_0, y_0), (t_1, x_1, y_1), ..., (t_N, x_N, y_N)\rangle$ the set $\bigcup_{i=0}^{N-1} B(t_i, x_i, y_i, t_{i+1}, x_{i+1}, y_{i+1}, v_{max})$ is called the *bead chain* of S [1].

Suppose we transform a bead $B(t_i, x_i, y_i, t_{i+1}, x_{i+1}, y_{i+1}, v_{max})$ by a function $f : \mathbf{R} \times \mathbf{R}^2 \to \mathbf{R} \times \mathbf{R}^2 : (t, x, y) \mapsto (f_t(t), f_x(t, x, y), f_y(t, x, y))$, with f_t strictly monotone, as we have done earlier with trajectories. We ask which class of transformations map a bead to a bead. Also here we assume transformations to be bijective and differentiable.

Theorem 2. *Let* $f : \mathbf{R} \times \mathbf{R}^2 \to \mathbf{R} \times \mathbf{R}^2 : (t, x, y) \mapsto (f_t(t), f_x(t, x, y), f_y(t, x, y))$ *be a transformation that preserves the order of events. Then for arbitrary time-space points* (t_i, x_i, y_i) *and* $(t_{i+1}, x_{i+1}, y_{i+1})$ *with* $t_i < t_{i+1}$ *and arbitrary* $v_{max} > 0$, $f(B(t_i, x_i, y_i, t_{i+1}, x_{i+1}, y_{i+1}, v_{max}))$ *is also a bead if and only if*

$$f(t, x, y) = \begin{pmatrix} a & 0 & 0 \\ 0 & ca_{11} & ca_{12} \\ 0 & ca_{21} & ca_{22} \end{pmatrix} \begin{pmatrix} t \\ x \\ y \end{pmatrix} + \begin{pmatrix} b \\ b_1 \\ b_2 \end{pmatrix},$$

with $a, b, c, b_1, b_2 \in \mathbf{R}$, $a, c > 0$, and the matrix of the a_{ij} defining an orthogonal transformation. Furthermore, if these conditions are satisfied, then $f(B(t_i, x_i, y_i, t_{i+1}, x_{i+1}, y_{i+1}, v_{\max})) = B(f(t_i, x_i, y_i), f(t_{i+1}, x_{i+1}, y_{i+1}), \frac{cv_{\max}}{a})$.

Proof. Let f be a transformation of $\mathbf{R} \times \mathbf{R}^2$ that preserves the order of events. Suppose that for any bead $B = B(t_i, x_i, y_i, t_{i+1}, x_{i+1}, y_{i+1}, v_{\max})$, $f(B)$ is a bead.

Let us first consider the special case, $v_{max} = \frac{d((x_i, y_i), (x_{i+1}, y_{i+1}))}{(t_{i+1} - t_i)}$ (this means that the maximal speed is also the minimal speed). Then the bead B is the straight line segment between (t_i, x_i, y_i) and $(t_{i+1}, x_{i+1}, y_{i+1})$ in the (t, x, y)-space. This segment is not parallel to the (x, y)-plane (like all beads that are lines). Since B is one-dimensional and since $f(B)$ is assumed to be a bead and since $f(B)$ at any moment consists of one point also $f(B)$ must be a straight line segment not parallel to the (x, y)-plane in the (t, x, y)-space. We can conclude that f maps line segments not parallel to the (x, y)-plane to line segments not parallel to the (x, y)-plane.

Secondly, let us consider a bead B with $(x_i, y_i) = (x_{i+1}, y_{i+1})$ and $v_{\max} > 0$. This bead consists of a cone between t_i and $(t_i + t_{i+1})/2$ with top (t_i, x_i, y_i) and base the disk $D = \{((t_i + t_{i+1})/2, x, y) \mid (x - x_i)^2 + (y - y_i)^2 \leq v_{\max}^2 ((t_{i+1} - t_i)/2)^2\}$ and a cone between $(t_i + t_{i+1})/2$ and t_{i+1} with top (t_{i+1}, x_i, y_i) and the same disk D as base. Consider the straight line segments emanating from the top (t_i, x_i, y_i) and ending in the central disk D. They are mapped to straight line segments in $f(B)$ (as we have argued before) that emanate from the top $f(t_i, x_i, y_i)$ of $f(B)$ and that end up in some figure $f(D)$ in the hyperplane $t = f_t((t_i + t_{i+1})/2)$. Since $f(B)$ is assumed to be a bead, the image of the bottom cone of B is again a cone, and the aforementioned figure $f(D)$ in the hyperplane $t = f_t((t_i + t_{i+1})/2)$ is also a closed disk. The same holds for the top cone of B. This half of B is mapped to a cone with top $f(t_{i+1}, x_{i+1}, y_{i+1})$ and base $f(D)$.

Therefore, $f(B)$ is the union of two cones, one with top $f(t_i, x_i, y_i)$, the other with top $f(t_{i+1}, x_i, y_i)$ and both with base $f(D)$. Since $f(B)$ is a bead that at no moment in time is a lens, it must itself be a bead with equally located tops. This means that $f_x(t_i, x_i, y_i) = f_x(t_{i+1}, x_i, y_i)$ and $f_y(t_i, x_i, y_i = f_y(t_{i+1}, x_i, y_i)$. In other words, the functions f_x and f_y are independent of t. This argument also shows that $f_t((t_i + t_{i+1})/2)$ is the middle of $f_t(t_i)$ and $f_t(t_{i+1})$. This means that for any t_i and t_{i+1}, $f_t((t_i + t_{i+1})/2) = \frac{1}{2}(f_t(t_i) + f_t(t_{i+1}))$. It is then easy to show that, $f_t(t) = at + b$ with $a > 0$.

So, we have shown that a bead-preserving transformation f is of the form $f(t, x, y) = (at + b, f_x(x, y), f_y(x, y))$. Now we determine f_x and f_y. If we restrict ourselves to a (x, y)-plane at some moment t between t_i and t_{i+1}, the bead $B = B(t_i, x_i, y_i, t_{i+1}, x_i, y_i, v_{\max})$ shows a disk. Since $f(B)$ is a bead again, it will also show a disk at $f_t(t)$. Since f_x and f_y are independent of t, they map disks on disks, hence distances between points are all scaled by a positive factor c by this transformation. To determine what f_x and f_y look like we can restrict ourselves to a mapping from $\mathbf{R}^2$ to $\mathbf{R}^2$, since f_x and f_y depend only on x and y. Consider the transformation $\tilde{f}(x, y) = (f_x(x, y), f_y(x, y))$, we know now that for all points $\mathbf{x}$ and $\mathbf{y}$ in $\mathbf{R}^2$, $\|\mathbf{x} - \mathbf{y}\| = \frac{1}{c}\|\tilde{f}(\mathbf{x}) - \tilde{f}(\mathbf{y})\|$. Now consider $\hat{f} = \frac{1}{c}\tilde{f}$, this means $\|\mathbf{x} - \mathbf{y}\| = \|\hat{f}(\mathbf{x}) - \hat{f}(\mathbf{y})\|$ and thus $\hat{f}$ is an isometry. Just like before (cfr. speed preserving-transformations), we can conclude that $\tilde{f}(x,y) = (f_x(x,y), f_y(x,y))$ is a plane-similarity, i.e., composed of a linear plane isometry, a scaling and a translation.

We know that $(x' - x'_i)^2 + (y' - y'_i)^2 = c^2((x - x_i)^2 + (y - y_i)^2)$ and that $(t' - t'_i)^2 = a^2(t - t_i)^2$. That means that if B is a bead between the points (t_1, x_1, y_1) and (t_2, x_2, y_2) and speed v_{max}, then B' is a bead between the points (t'_1, x'_1, y'_1) and (t'_2, x'_2, y'_2) and speed $v'_{max} = \frac{c.v_{max}}{a}$. This has to hold for all beads, hence all v_{max} since degenerate beads must be transformed to degenerate beads. This concludes the proof since it is clear that all transformations of this form also map beads to beads. $\qquad \square$

From this result it follows that if f maps a bead B with maximal speed $v_{\max}$ to a bead $f(B)$, the latter has maximal speed $\frac{cv_{\max}}{a}$. So, we get the following.

Corollary 1. *If $f : \mathbf{R} \times \mathbf{R}^2 \to \mathbf{R} \times \mathbf{R}^2$ is a transformation that preserves the order of events, then f maps beads to beads with the same speed, if and only if, f preserves the speed of trajectories (i.e., f belongs to $\mathcal{V}$ defined in Theorem 1).* $\qquad \square$

4   A Model for Trajectory Databases and Queries

4.1   Trajectory and Trajectory Sample Databases and Queries

We assume the existence of an infinite set $\mathsf{Labels} = \{a, b, ..., a_1, b_1, ..., a_2, b_2, ...\}$ of *trajectory labels*. We now define the notion of trajectory (sample) database.

Definition 5. *A trajectory relation R is a finite set of tuples (a_i, T_i), $i = 1, ..., r$, where $a_i \in \mathsf{Labels}$ can appear only once and where T_i is a trajectory. Similarly, a trajectory sample relation R is a finite set of tuples $(a_i, t_{i,j}, x_{i,j}, y_{i,j})$, with $i = 1, ..., r$ and $j = 0, ..., N_i$, such that $a_i \in \mathsf{Labels}$ cannot appear twice in combination with the same t-value and such that $\langle (t_{i,0}, x_{i,0}, y_{i,0}), (t_{i,1}, x_{i,1}, y_{i,1}), ..., (t_{i,N_i}, x_{i,N_i}, y_{i,N_i}) \rangle$ is a trajectory sample.*

A trajectory (sample) database is a finite collection of trajectory (sample) relations. $\qquad \square$

Without loss of generality, we will assume in the sequel that a database consists of one relation. In Section 2, we have discussed how we finitely represent trajectories and trajectory samples.

Now, we define the notion of a trajectory database query. We distinguish between trajectory database transformations and boolean trajectory queries.

Definition 6. *A (sample-)trajectory database transformation is a partial computable function from (sample-)trajectory relations to (sample-)trajectory relations. A boolean (sample-)trajectory database query is a partial computable function from (sample-)trajectory relations to $\{0, 1\}$.* $\qquad \square$

When we say that a function is computable, this is with respect to some fixed encoding of the trajectory (sample) relations (e.g., rational polynomial functions represented in dense or sparse encoding of polynomials; or rational numbers represented as pairs of natural numbers in bit representation).

4.2 $\mathcal{V}$-Equivalent Trajectory Databases and $\mathcal{V}$-Invariant Queries

Definition 7. Let R and S be trajectory (sample) databases. We say that R and S are $\mathcal{V}$-*equivalent*, if there is bijection $\mu :$ Labels $\rightarrow$ Labels and a speed-preserving transformation $f \in \mathcal{V}$ such that $(\mu \times f)(R) = S$.   □

In this paper, we are especially interested in transformations and queries that are invariant under elements of $\mathcal{V}$.

Definition 8. A trajectory (sample) database transformation Q is $\mathcal{V}$-*invariant* if for any trajectory (sample) databases S_1 and S_2 which are $\mathcal{V}$-equivalent by $\mu \times f$, also $(\mu \times f)(Q(S_1)) = Q(S_2)$ holds.

A boolean trajectory (sample) database query Q is $\mathcal{V}$-*invariant* if for any $\mathcal{V}$-equivalent trajectory (sample) databases R and S, $Q(R) = Q(S)$.   □

5   Complete Query Languages for Trajectory Databases

5.1   First-Order Queries on Trajectory (Sample) Databases

A first query language for trajectory (sample) databases we consider is the following extension of first-order logic over the real numbers, which we refer to as $\mathsf{FO}(+, \times, <, 0, 1, S)$.

Definition 9. The language $\mathsf{FO}(+, \times, <, 0, 1, S)$ is a two-sorted logic with *label variables* $a, b, c, \ldots$ (possibly with subscripts) that refer to trajectory labels and *real variables* $x, y, z, \ldots$ (possibly with subscripts) that refer to real numbers. The atomic formulas of $\mathsf{FO}(+, \times, <, 0, 1, S)$ are

- $P(x_1, \ldots, x_n) > 0$, where P is a polynomial with integer coefficients in the real variables $x_1, \ldots, x_n$;
- $a = b$; and
- $S(a, t, x, y)$ (S ia a 4-ary predicate).

The formulas of $\mathsf{FO}(+, \times, <, 0, 1, S)$ are built from the atomic formulas using the logical connectives $\wedge, \vee, \neg, \ldots$ and quantification over the two types of variables: $\exists x, \forall x$ and $\exists a, \forall a$.   □

The label variables are assumed to range over the labels occurring in the input database and the real variables are assumed to range over $\mathbf{R}$. The formula $S(a, t, x, y)$ expresses that a tuple (a, t, x, y) belongs to the input database. The interpretation of the other formulas is standard. It is well-known that $\mathsf{FO}(+, \times, <, 0, 1, S)$-expressible queries can be evaluated effectively [8].

The $\mathsf{FO}(+, \times, <, 0, 1, S)$-sentence

$$\exists a \exists b (\neg (a = b) \wedge \forall t \forall x \forall y S(a, t, x, y) \leftrightarrow S(b, t, x, y)), \tag{†}$$

for example, expresses the boolean trajectory query that says that there are two identical trajectories in the input database with different labels.

The FO$(+, \times, <, 0, 1, S)$-formula

$$S(a, t, x, y) \wedge t \geq 0 \qquad\qquad (*)$$

returns the subtrajectories of the input trajectories at positive time moments.

Boolean queries can be expressed by sentences in FO$(+, \times, <, 0, 1, S)$ (for example, the sentence (†)). Trajectory transformations can be expressed by formulas $\varphi(a, t, x, y)$ in FO$(+, \times, <, 0, 1, S)$ with four free variables (for example, the formula $(*)$). We remark that not every FO$(+, \times, <, 0, 1, S)$-formula $\varphi(a, t, x, y)$ defines a trajectory relation on input a trajectory. However, it can be syntactically guaranteed that the output of such a query is a trajectory (sample), since this can be expressed in FO$(+, \times, <, 0, 1, S)$. Indeed, it is expressible that a semi-algebraic set is a function and also that it is continuous. By combining a formula $\varphi(a, t, x, y)$ with a guard that expresses that the output of $\varphi(a, t, x, y)$ is a trajectory, we can determine a closed or safe fragment of FO$(+, \times, <, 0, 1, S)$ for transforming trajectories.

Property 1. There is a FO$(+, \times, <, 0, 1, S)$-formula that expresses that S is a trajectory (sample). □

5.2 A Point-Based First-Order Language for Trajectory (Sample) Databases

In this section, we consider a first-order query language, FO(Before, minSpeed, $\tilde{S}$), for trajectory (sample) databases.

Definition 10. FO(Before, minSpeed, $\tilde{S}$) is a three-sorted logic with *label variables* $a, b, c, \ldots$ (possibly with subscripts) that refer to labels of trajectories; *point variables* $p, q, r, \ldots$ (possibly with subscripts), that refer to time-space points (i.e., elements of $\mathbf{R} \times \mathbf{R}^2$); and *speed variables* $u, v, w, \ldots$ (possibly with subscripts), that refer to speed values (i.e., elements of $\mathbf{R}^+$).

The atomic formulas of FO(Before, minSpeed, $\tilde{S}$) are

- $P(v_1, \ldots, v_n) > 0$, where P is a polynomial with integer coefficients in the velocity variables $v_1, \ldots, v_n$;
- equality for all types of variables; and
- $\tilde{S}(a, p)$ (here $\tilde{S}$ is a binary predicate);
- Before(p, q), minSpeed(p, q, v).

The formulas of FO(Before, minSpeed, $\tilde{S}$) are built from the atomic formulas using the logical connectives $\wedge, \vee, \neg, \ldots$ and quantification over the three types of variables: $\exists a, \forall a, \exists p, \forall p$ and $\exists v, \forall v$. □

The label variables are assumed to range over the labels occurring in the input database, the point variables are assumed to range over the set of time-space points $\mathbf{R} \times \mathbf{R}^2$ and the velocity variables are assumed to range over the positive real numbers $\mathbf{R}^+$.

If p is a time-space point, then we denote its time-component by p_t and its spatial coordinates by p_x and p_y. The formula $S(a,p)$ expresses that a tuple (a, p_t, p_x, p_y) belongs to the input database. The atomic formula $\mathsf{Before}(p, q)$ expresses that $p_t \le q_t$. The atomic formula $\mathsf{minSpeed}(p, q, v)$ expresses that $(p_x - q_x)^2 + (p_y - q_y)^2 = v^2(p_t - q_t)^2 \wedge (\neg q_t \le p_t)$, in other words, that v is the minimal speed to go from the spatial projection of p to that of q in the time-interval that separates them.

For example, the $\mathsf{FO}(\mathsf{Before}, \mathsf{minSpeed}, \tilde{S})$-sentence

$$\exists a \exists b (\neg(a = b) \wedge \forall p \tilde{S}(a, p) \leftrightarrow \tilde{S}(b, p)) \tag{$\dagger'$}$$

equivalently expresses ($\dagger$). To define equivalence of (queries expressible by) formulas in $\mathsf{FO}(\mathsf{Before}, \mathsf{minSpeed}, \tilde{S})$ and $\mathsf{FO}(+, \times, <, 0, 1, S)$, we define the canonical mapping $can : (a, p) \mapsto (a, p_t, p_x, p_y)$. If $\tilde{A}$ is an instance of $\tilde{S}$, then $id \times can(\tilde{A})$ is an instance of S. We say that a formula $\tilde{\varphi}(a, p)$ in $\mathsf{FO}(\mathsf{Before}, \mathsf{minSpeed}, \tilde{S})$ and a formula $\varphi(a, t, x, y)$ in $\mathsf{FO}(+, \times, <, 0, 1, S)$ express *equivalent* transformations if for any $\tilde{A}$, $id \times can(\{(a, p) \mid \tilde{A} \models \tilde{\varphi}(a, p)\}) = \{(a, t, x, y) \mid id \times can(A) \models \varphi(a, t, x, y)\}$. For boolean queries the definition is analogue.

For the formula $(*)$, there is no equivalent in $\mathsf{FO}(\mathsf{Before}, \mathsf{minSpeed}, \tilde{S})$. The reason for this is given by the following theorem in combination with the observation that the formula $(*)$ does not express a $\mathcal{V}$-invariant transformation.

Theorem 3. *A $\mathcal{V}$-invariant trajectory (sample) transformation or a boolean trajectory (sample) query is expressible in $\mathsf{FO}(+, \times, <, 0, 1, S)$ if and only if it is expressible in $\mathsf{FO}(\mathsf{Before}, \mathsf{minSpeed}, \tilde{S})$.*

Before giving the proof of Theorem 3, we introduce some more predicates on time-space points and speed values, which will come in handy later on:

- $\mathsf{inBead}(r, p, q, v)$ expresses that $r = (r_t, r_x, r_y)$ belongs to the bead $B(p_t, p_x, p_y, q_t, q_x, q_y, v)$ (assuming that $p_t \le q_t$);
- $\mathsf{Between}^2(p, q, r)$ expresses that the three co-temporal points p, q and r are collinear and that q is between p and r;
- $\mathsf{Between}^{1+2}(p, q, r)$ expresses that the three points p, q and r are collinear and that q is between p and r;
- $\mathsf{EqDist}(p_1, q_1, p_2, q_2)$ expresses that the distance between the co-temporal points p_1 and q_1 is equal to the distance between the co-temporal points p_2 and q_2;
- $\mathsf{Perp}(p_1, q_1, p_2, q_2)$ expresses that the vectors $\overrightarrow{p_1 q_1}$ and $\overrightarrow{p_2 q_2}$ of the co-temporal points p_1, q_1, p_2 and q_2 are perpendicular.

Lemma 1. *The expressions* $\mathsf{inBead}(r, p, q, v)$, $\mathsf{Between}^2(p, q, r)$, $\mathsf{Between}^{1+2}(p, q, r)$, $\mathsf{EqDist}(p_1, q_1, p_2, q_2)$, *and* $\mathsf{Perp}(p_1, q_1, p_2, q_2)$ *can all be expressed in the logic* $\mathsf{FO}(\mathsf{Before}, \mathsf{minSpeed})$. $\qquad\square$

Proof. In the proof of Theorem 3, a key predicate to simulate addition and multiplication in $\mathsf{FO}(\mathsf{Before}, \mathsf{minSpeed})$ is $\mathsf{Between}^2$. Here, we only sketch how this predicate can be expressed. We omit the other expressions.

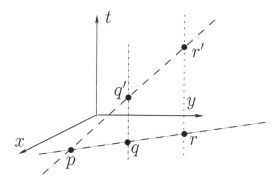

Fig. 2. The geometric construction of Between^2

First, we introduce predicates to denote co-spatiality and co-temporality. Equality of the spatial coordinates, $=_S (p, q)$, is expressed as $\exists v(\mathsf{minSpeed}(p, q, v) \wedge v = 0) \vee p = q$. Co-temporality of time-space points, $=_T (p, q)$, is expressed as $\mathsf{Before}(p, q) \wedge \mathsf{Before}(q, p)$. With the help of these predicates we can express $\mathsf{Between}^2(p, r, q)$ as

$$=_T(p, r) \wedge =_T(r, q) \wedge \neg(p = r \vee r = q \vee p = q) \wedge$$
$$\exists r' \exists q' \exists v (=_S(r, r') \wedge =_S(q, q') \wedge \neg\mathsf{Before}(r', p) \wedge \neg\mathsf{Before}(q', r') \wedge$$
$$\mathsf{minSpeed}(p, q', v) \wedge \mathsf{minSpeed}(p, r', v) \wedge \mathsf{minSpeed}(r', q', v)).$$

The first line states that p, q and r should be co-temporal and distinct. Next we say that there exist points r' and q' with the same spatial coordinates as r and q respectively. The last line states that p, r' and q' are collinear and that r' is between p and q'. Therefore the projected points p, r and q are also collinear and r is between p and q. The above expression describes the geometric construction illustrated in Figure 2. □

For the purpose of the proof of Theorem 3, we need to give a more general definition of $\mathcal{V}$-invariance of $\mathsf{FO}(\mathsf{Before}, \mathsf{minSpeed}, \tilde{S})$-formulas.

Definition 11. A $\mathsf{FO}(\mathsf{Before}, \mathsf{minSpeed}, \tilde{S})$-formula $\varphi(a_1, ..., a_n, p_1, ..., p_m, v_1, ..., v_k)$ expresses a $\mathcal{V}$-invariant query Q if for any trajectory (sample) databases S_1 and S_2 for which there is a bijection $\mu : \mathsf{Labels} \to \mathsf{Labels}$ and a transformation $f \in \mathcal{V}$ such that $(\mu \times f)(S_1) = S_2$, also $(\mu^n \times f^m \times \mathsf{id}^k)(Q(S_1)) = Q(S_2)$. □

This definition corresponds to the definition for transformations and boolean queries (Definition 8), if we take $n = m = 1$, $k = 0$ and $n = m = k = 0$.

Proof (of Theorem 3). We have to prove soundness and completeness.
Soundness: Firstly, we show that every $\mathsf{FO}(\mathsf{Before}, \mathsf{minSpeed}, \tilde{S})$-formula is equivalently expressible in $\mathsf{FO}(+, \times, <, 0, 1, S)$ and that every query expressible in $\mathsf{FO}(\mathsf{Before}, \mathsf{minSpeed}, \tilde{S})$ is $\mathcal{V}$-invariant.

We assume prenex normal form for formulas, and translate the atomic formulas first. Logical connectives, and finally quantifiers, can then be added in a straightforward manner. A label variable is left unchanged. A point variable p is simulated by three real variables p_x, p_y and p_t and a speed variable v is simulated by a real variable v and when it appears it is accompanied with the restriction $v \geq 0$. An appearance of the trajectory predicate $\tilde{S}(a, p)$ is translated into $S(a, p_t, p_x, p_y)$. By switching to coordinate representations, the predicates minSpeed(p, q, v) and Before(p, q) are translated to $(p_x - q_x)^2 + (p_y - q_y)^2 = v^2 (p_t - q_t)^2 \wedge (\neg q_t \leq p_t)$ and $p_t \leq q_t$ respectively. Polynomial constraints on speed variables are literally translated (adding $v \geq 0$). Logical connectives, and finally quantifiers, can then be added in a straightforward manner ($\exists p$ is translated to $\exists p_t \exists p_x \exists p_y$).

Speed-preserving transformations preserve the order of events. That means the predicate Before is $\mathcal{V}$-invariant. The predicate minSpeed is also $\mathcal{V}$-invariant. If f belongs to $\mathcal{V}$, then we know from Theorem 1 that f is the composition of a scaling by a positive factor a and an orthogonal transformation and a translation. Suppose that $f(p_t, p_x, p_y) = (p'_t, p'_x, p'_y) = p'$ and $f(q_t, q_x, q_y) = (q'_t, q'_x, q'_y) = q'$. Then $(p'_x - q'_x)^2 + (p'_y - q'_y)^2 = v^2(p'_t - q'_t)^2 = a^2((p_x - q_x)^2 + (p_y - q_y)^2) = v^2 a^2(p_t - q_t)^2$. So, minSpeed$(p, q, v)$ holds if and only if minSpeed(p', q', v) holds.

The polynomial constraints on speed variables are by definition $\mathcal{V}$-invariant (see Definition 11). Now, it is easy to show, by induction on the syntactic structure of FO(Before, minSpeed, $\tilde{S}$)-formulas that they are all $\mathcal{V}$-invariant.

Completeness: Now, we show that every $\mathcal{V}$-invariant trajectory query, expressible in FO($+, \times, <, 0, 1, S$), can equivalently be expressed in FO(Before, minSpeed, $\tilde{S}$). We will sketch the proof, as a rigorous proof easily becomes long and tedious. The general strategy that we outline is based on proof strategies introduced in [5] for spatial data and later developed for spatio-temporal data in [2]. Label variables are literally translated. The real variables are translated into point variables and we simulate addition and multiplication operations and order in a "computation plane". To do this we need a coordinate system for $\mathbf{R} \times \mathbf{R}^2$ that is the image of the standard coordinate system of $\mathbf{R} \times \mathbf{R}^2$ under some element of $\mathcal{V}$. Let (u_0, u_1, u_2, u_3) be such a coordinate system, meaning u_0, u_2 and u_3 are co-temporal, $\overrightarrow{u_0 u_1}$, $\overrightarrow{u_0 u_2}$ and $\overrightarrow{u_0 u_3}$ are perpendicular and have equal length and u_0 is a point Before u_1. All of this is expressible in FO(Before, minSpeed, $\tilde{S}$) with the predicates introduced in Lemma 1. The predicate CoSys(u_0, u_1, u_2, u_3) expresses that (u_0, u_1, u_2, u_3) is the image of the standard coordinate system under some speed-preserving transformation. Next all real variables are directly translated into point variables on the line $u_0 u_2$, the idea is to translate a real variable x to a point variable p^x with a cross ratio (u_0, u_2, p^x) equal to x. Using only Between[2] we can express all addition and multiplication operations in the plane spanned by the co-temporal points u_0, u_2 and u_3.

At this point, we have in our translated formula too many free variables, since we translated variables, which represent coordinates, to point variables and added a coordinate system. We need to introduce new point variables and express that the translated coordinate point variables are coordinates for these new point variables. Thus linking every triple of coordinate point variables on the line $u_0 u_2$ with a single point variable. This can be done with a predicate $\mathsf{Coordinates}(u_0, u_1, u_2, u_3, t, x, y, u)$ which expresses that the cross ratios (u_0, u_2, t), (u_0, u_2, x) and (u_0, u_2, y) are the coordinates for the point variable u with respect to the coordinate system (u_0, u_1, u_2, u_3). This can be done using only the predicate $\mathsf{Between}^{1+2}$ as was shown in [5]. The relation S is translated in a similar straight-forward manner. Finally we add existential quantifiers for all the coordinate point variables and for the points u_0, u_1, u_2 and u_3. □

As a corollary of Theorem 3 and Property 2, is the following.

Property 2. There is a $\mathsf{FO(Before, minSpeed}, \tilde{S})$-formula that expresses that $\tilde{S}$ is a trajectory (-sample). □

5.3   Computationally Complete Query Language for Trajectory (Sample) Databases

In this section, we consider computationally complete query languages for trajectory (sample) databases. We start by extending the logic $\mathsf{FO(Before, minSpeed}, \tilde{S})$ with a sufficient supply of relation variables (of all arities), assignment statements and while-loops. Afterward, we will prove that this extended language is computationally sound and complete for $\mathcal{V}$-invariant computable queries on trajectory (sample) databases.

Definition 12. A program in $\mathsf{FO(Before, minSpeed}, \tilde{S})$+while is a finite sequence of *assignment statements* and *while-loops*:

- An *assignment statement* is of the form

$$\tilde{R} := \{(a_1, \ldots, a_k, p_1, \ldots, p_l, v_1, \ldots, v_m) \mid \varphi(a_1, \ldots, a_k, p_1, \ldots, p_l, v_1, \ldots, v_m)\};$$

  where $\tilde{R}$ is a relation variable of arity k in the label variables, arity l in the time-space point variables and arity m in the speed variables, and φ is a formula in the language $\mathsf{FO(Before, minSpeed}, \tilde{S})$ extended with the relation labels that were previously introduced in the program.
- A *while-loop*

$$\textbf{while } \varphi \textbf{ do } P;$$

  contains a sentence φ in $\mathsf{FO(Before, minSpeed}, \tilde{S})$ extended with previously introduced relation labels and a $\mathsf{FO(Before, minSpeed}, \tilde{S})$+while-program P (again extended with previously introduced relation labels).
- One relation variable is designated as an output relation $\tilde{R}_{out}$. The program ends once that particular relation variable has been assigned a value.   □

The semantics of $\mathsf{FO(Before, minSpeed}, \tilde{S})$+while should be clear and is like that of $\mathsf{FO}(+, \times, <, 0, 1, S)$+while. A program defines a query on a trajectory (sample) database. Indeed, given an input relation, as soon as a value is assigned to the relation $\tilde{R}_{out}$, the program halts and returns an output; or the program might loop forever on that input. Thus, a program defines a partial function from input to output relations. We remark that the output relation is computable from the input.

Once we have fixed a data model for trajectories or trajectory samples (see Section 2) and concrete data structures to implement the data model, we say that a partial function on trajectory (sample) databases is *computable*, if there exists a Turing machine that computes the function, given the particular data encoding and data structures (see [8] for details).

We omit the proof of the following result.

Theorem 4. FO(Before, minSpeed, $\tilde{S}$)+while *is sound and complete for the computable $\mathcal{V}$-invariant queries on trajectory (sample) databases.*   □

Acknowledgments. This research has been partially funded by the European Union under the FP6-IST-FET programme, Project n. FP6-14915, GeoPKDD: Geographic Privacy-Aware Knowledege Discovery and Delivery, and by the Research Foundation Flanders (FWO-Vlaanderen), Research Project G.0344.05.

References

1. M. Egenhofer. Approximation of geospatial lifelines. In *SpadaGIS, Workshop on Spatial Data and Geographic Information Systsems*, 2003. Electr. proceedings, 4p.
2. F. Geerts, S. Haesevoets, and B. Kuijpers. A theory of spatio-temporal database queries. In *Database Programming Languages (DBPL'01)*, volume 2397 of *Lecture Notes in Computer Science*, pages 198–212. Springer, 2002 (a full version will appear in ACM Transactions on Computational Logic).
3. Floris Geerts. Moving objects and their equations of motion. In *Constraint Databases (CDB'04)*, volume 3074 of *Lecture Notes in Computer Science*, pages 41–52. Springer, 2004.
4. R. Güting and M. Schneider. *Moving Object Databases*. Morgan Kaufmann, 2005.
5. M. Gyssens, J. Van den Bussche, and D. Van Gucht. Complete geometric query languages. *J. Comput. System Sci.*, 58(3):483–511, 1999.
6. T. Hägerstrand What about People in Regional Science? *Papers of the Regional Science Association* vol.24, 1970, pp.7-21.
7. K. Hornsby and M. Egenhofer. Modeling moving objects over multiple granularities. *Annals of Mathematics and Artificial Intelligence*, 36(1–2):177–194, 2002.
8. J. Paredaens, G. Kuper, and L. Libkin, editors. *Constraint databases*. Springer-Verlag, 2000.
9. D. Pfoser and C. S. Jensen. Capturing the uncertainty of moving-object representations. In *Advances in Spatial Databases (SSD'99)*, volume 1651 of *Lecture Notes in Computer Science*, pages 111–132, 1999.
10. A. D. Polyanin, V. F. Zaitsev, and A. Moussiaux. *Handbook of First Order Partial Differential Equations*. Taylor & Francis, 2002.
11. J. Su, H. Xu, and O. Ibarra. Moving objects: Logical relationships and queries. In *Advances in Spatial and Temporal Databases (SSTD'01)*, volume 2121 of *Lecture Notes in Computer Science*, pages 3–19. Springer, 2001.
12. O. Wolfson. Moving objects information management: The database challenge. In *Proceedings of the 5th Intl. Workshop NGITS*, pages 75–89. Springer, 2002.

Complexity of Typechecking XML Views of Relational Databases

Piotr Wieczorek[*]

Institute of Computer Science, University of Wrocław,
Joliot-Curie 15, PL-50-383 Wrocław, Poland
`piotr.wieczorek@ii.uni.wroc.pl`

Abstract. The typechecking problem for transformations of relational data into tree data is the following: given a TreeQL program P (called *transformation*), and a DTD d (called *output type*), decide whether for every database instance D the result of the transformation P of D is of a type consistent with d (see [2]). TreeQL programs with projection-free conjunctive queries and DTDs with arbitrary regular expressions are considered here.

A non-elementary upper bound for the typechecking problem is given in [2] (although in a more general setting, where equality and negation in projection-free conjunctive queries and additional universal integrity constraints are allowed).

In this paper we show that the typechecking problem is in coNEXP-TIME.

As an intermediate step we consider the following problem, which can be formulated in a language independent of XML notions. Given a set of triples of the form (φ, k, j), where φ is a projection-free conjunctive query and k, j are natural numbers, decide whether there exists a database D such that for each triple (φ, k, j) in the set, there exists a natural number α, such that there are exactly $k + j * \alpha$ tuples satisfying the query φ in D. Our main technical contribution consists of a NEXPTIME algorithm for the last problem.

1   Introduction

During the last years XML has become the standard in data exchange in the web. Often the actual data resides in relational databases. In order to be published such data should be transformed to XML. XML documents have their *types* — a type is a tree language. There are many formalisms to define a type e.g. RE-LAX NG, which can define the full class of regular tree languages or DTD/XML Schema, which can define some fragments of this class. Typically, a community agrees on a certain type and then all members of the community publish documents consistent with the type. Here comes the problem of typechecking for transformations of relational data into tree data: for a given transformation, an

---

[*] Partially supported by Polish Ministry of Science and Higher Education research project N206022 31/3660, 2006/2009.

T. Schwentick and D. Suciu (Eds.): ICDT 2007, LNCS 4353, pp. 239–253, 2007.

output type and a set of integrity constraints, decide whether every database satisfying the integrity constraints is transformed to a tree consistent with the output type. Thus the problem can be parameterized by:

– the class of transformations,
– the class of output tree languages,
– the class of integrity constraints.

Alon et al. [2] present a study of decidability and complexity of many versions of the problem. As a formalism to define transformations the authors introduce TreeQL programs. TreeQL is an abstraction of practical languages such as RXL (SilkRoute [4]). A TreeQL program is a tree with each node labeled with a symbol from a finite alphabet and with a logical formula, which in our paper is always a projection-free conjunctive query. The result of a transformation of a relational structure is a tree reflecting the structure of the program tree, such that each node t of the program tree is substituted by as many nodes as there are tuples in the database satisfying the formula being the label of t. The nodes of the output tree inherit, as their labels, the symbols that label nodes of the program tree. The output type is specified by a DTD — a formalism which puts local restrictions on trees, that is, it restricts how the sequence of child labels of a node looks like.

Decidability results in [2] include a coNEXPTIME upper bound on typecheck-ing TreeQL programs with conjunctive queries (with negation and equality), DTDs with star-free regular languages as the output types and the integrity con-straints in $FO(\exists^*\forall^*)$. When arbitrary regular expressions are allowed in DTDs the authors show decidability of typechecking TreeQL programs with projection-free conjunctive queries[1] (with negation and equality) and integrity constraints in $FO(\forall^*)$. In the latter case, however, the complexity is prohibitively high – the proof uses a combinatorial argument based on Ramsey's Theorem and yields a non-elementary upper bound. It was left as an open problem in [2] whether the bound can be improved. We show that such an improvement is possible, at least for a restricted case. We show a coNEXPTIME upper bound on the typechecking problem for DTDs with arbitrary regular expressions as the output types and projection-free conjunctive queries in TreeQL programs, but without integrity constraints.

Our approach is as follows. Inspired by the notion of *the modulo property* [2], we perform the reduction of the complement of the typechecking problem to the following problem. Given a set of triples of the form (φ, k, j), where φ is a projection-free conjunctive query and k, j are natural numbers, decide whether there exists a database D such that for each triple (φ, k, j) in the set, there exists a natural number α, such that there are exactly $k + j * \alpha$ tuples satisfying the query φ in D. Notice, that a triple (φ, k, j) is a kind of a constraint on a relational database. We call such constraints *modulo constraints*. Our main technical contribution consists of a NEXPTIME algorithm for the problem of

---

[1] If conjunctive queries with projections are allowed, the problem (even in our simple setting) is not known to be decidable.

satisfiability of a set of modulo constraints. We use an elementary technique, namely a direct construction of a counterexample database of exponential size (by a counterexample database we mean such a database that is transformed to a tree not in the output tree language).

Related work. Recently the problem of typechecking gained a lot of attention in literature, especially in the context of typechecking XML-to-XML transformations, which, since relational structures can easily be encoded as XML trees, is closely related to ours. In the context we are given input and output tree languages and a transformation and we are asked whether every tree in the input tree language is transformed to a tree in the output language. The problem was studied in [7], where the input and output types were regular tree languages and transformations were expressed by k-pebble transducers. As long as the data values in trees are not considered, the problem is decidable, however the complexity is non-elementary. If the nodes in trees can be equipped with data values from an infinite domain, in addition to the tags from a finite alphabet, then, as it was shown in [3], the problem quickly gets undecidable and in the decidable cases the complexity is rather high. In [5] and [6] Martens and Neven considered transformations in a form of a single top-down traversal of the input tree, during which every node can be replaced by a new tree or deleted. Such transformations can be used for restructuring and filtering rather than for advanced querying, but on the other hand, the obtained complexity results range from EXPTIME to PTIME.

Outline of the paper. The rest of the paper is organized as follows. In Sect. 2 we give the necessary preliminaries. In a short Sect. 3 we state Theorem 1, which is our main theorem, and formulate an intermediate result – the main lemma needed for the proof of Theorem 1. In Sect. 4, which is the main technical part, we prove the intermediate result. Finally, in Sect. 5 we use some of the ideas from [2] and show how the intermediate result implies the main result.

2 Preliminaries

XML and XML Types. We abstract XML documents as ordered, unranked, finite trees whose nodes are labeled with symbols from some finite alphabet Σ (see Fig. 1). We denote the label of the node v by $lab(v)$ and the root node of the tree t by $root(t)$. A *Document Type Definition (DTD)* is a way of defining a tree language. A DTD d defines for each symbol $\sigma \in \Sigma$ a regular language $d(\sigma)$. We say that a tree t is consistent with d if for every node v of t with children $v_1, \ldots, v_n$ the word $lab(v_1) \ldots lab(v_n)$ is in the regular language $d(lab(v))$. If v is a leaf, then the empty word ϵ has to be in $d(lab(v))$. The language of trees consistent with a DTD d is denoted by $L(d)$.

Databases and queries. Let S be a vocabulary consisting of relational symbols. A *database over S* is a finite structure over S ([1]). We denote the domain of a structure $\mathcal{A}$ by $dom(\mathcal{A})$. In the paper we consider also structures over vocabularies containing constant symbols. A *projection-free conjunctive query* *(projection-free CQ)* $\varphi(x_1, \ldots, x_n)$ is a conjunction of atomic formulas over vocabulary S. By $\mathrm{Vars}(\varphi)$ we denote the set of variables of φ (note that all variables in projection-free CQs are free). Let $\varphi(\bar{x})$ be a projection-free CQ, $\mathcal{A}$ a database and $\bar{a}$ a tuple of elements in $\mathcal{A}$. We define $\mathcal{A} \models \varphi(\bar{a})$ in the usual way.

TreeQL and typechecking. The following definitions come from [2], but are tailored for our setting.

Definition 1. *1. A TreeQL program is an ordered, unranked tree P with labels.*

  - *the root is labeled with an element from alphabet Σ.*
  - *every non-root element node is labeled with a pair (σ, φ), where $\sigma \in \Sigma$ and φ is a projection-free CQ. The formula in a node v is denoted by $\mathrm{formula}(v)$.*
  - $\mathrm{Vars}(\mathrm{formula}(v)) \subseteq \mathrm{Vars}(\mathrm{formula}(v'))$, *for all non-root nodes v and v', where v' is a descendant of v.*

 2. Let $\mathcal{A}$ be a database and P a TreeQL program. A tree $P(\mathcal{A})$ generated from $\mathcal{A}$ is defined as follows:

  - *The root is $(\mathrm{root}(P), \emptyset)$.*
  - *The non-root nodes consist of pairs (v, θ), where v is a non-root node of P and θ is a substitution for variables $\mathrm{Vars}(\mathrm{formula}(v))$, such that $\mathcal{A} \models \varphi[\theta]$, for every formula φ labeling v or labeling an ancestor of v in P.*
  - *The edges in $P(\mathcal{A})$ are $((v, \theta), (v', \theta'))$ such that v' is a child of v in P and θ' is an extension of θ (i.e. θ' agrees with θ on variables in the formula in v).*
  - *Sibling nodes in $P(\mathcal{A})$ are ordered as follows: if v and v' are siblings in P and v occurs before v', then all nodes (v, θ) occur before all nodes (v', θ') in $P(\mathcal{A})$. For a given v in P, the ordering of nodes (v, θ) and (v, θ') is irrelevant in our setting, so it is not considered here (see remark below).*
  - *Finally, the label of a node (v, θ) is the Σ-label of v in P.*

Remark. We use the following observation from [2]. If d is a DTD then d does not distinguish among trees $P(\mathcal{A})$ for distinct orderings of the nodes (v, θ) and (v, θ'), for each v in P. As we consider DTDs as XML types, we abstract from the ordering of such nodes.

Definition 2. *A TreeQL program P typechecks with respect to an output type d iff $P(\mathcal{A}) \subseteq L(d)$, for every database $\mathcal{A}$.*

Example 1. Consider a database $\mathcal{A}$ containing information about car owners, with two relations `PERSON(Id, FirstName, LastName)` and `CARS(Id, Car)`:

PERSON	Id	FirstName	LastName
	1	John	Smith
	2	John	Doe

CARS	Id	Car
	1	Ferrari
	2	Porsche
	2	Ferrari
	2	Mini

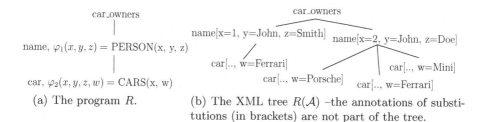

(a) The program R.

(b) The XML tree $R(\mathcal{A})$ –the annotations of substitutions (in brackets) are not part of the tree.

Fig. 1. A TreeQL query and its result (Example 1)

In Fig. 1 we present a program R and a tree $R(\mathcal{A})$ resulting from the transformation of the database $\mathcal{A}$ by the program R. The tree $R(\mathcal{A})$ is consistent with the following DTD d: $d(\texttt{car\_owners}) = \texttt{name}^*$, $d(\texttt{name}) = \texttt{car}^*$, $d(\texttt{car}) = \epsilon$.

3   Our Main Result

Now we are able to formulate our main theorem.

Theorem 1 (Main Theorem). *The problem of typechecking a TreeQL program with projection-free conjunctive queries w.r.t. DTD with arbitrary regular expressions is in coNEXPTIME.*

The rest of the paper is devoted to the proof of Theorem 1.

Definition 3. *A set of modulo constraints Γ is a finite set of triples of the form (φ, k, j), where φ is a projection-free conjunctive query and k, $j \in \mathbb{N}$. We say that a database $\mathcal{A}$ satisfies a set of modulo constraints Γ (we write $\mathcal{A} \models \Gamma$) iff for each $(\varphi_i, k_i, j_i) \in \Gamma$ there exists $\alpha_i \in \mathbb{N}$ such that:*

$$|\{\bar{t} \,|\, \mathcal{A} \models \varphi_i(\bar{t})\}| = k_i + (\alpha_i * j_i)$$

Of course, we assume that $0 \in \mathbb{N}$, so in particular Γ can contain some triples of the form $(\varphi, k, 0)$.

Now, we formulate the intermediate result, which is the main technical contribution of this paper.

Theorem 2 (Intermediate Result). *Let Γ be a set of constraints with projection-free conjunctive queries. The problem whether there exists a database $\mathcal{A}$ such that $\mathcal{A} \models \Gamma$ is in NEXPTIME.*

In Sect. 4 we prove the intermediate result, and in Sect. 5 we show how it implies the main result.

4   Proof of the Intermediate Result

We use the following notation. Let Γ be a set of modulo constraints, then: Γ_{CONST} is the set of *constant* constraints: $\Gamma_{\text{CONST}} = \{(\varphi, k, j) \in \Gamma \,|\, j = 0\}$, and Γ_{PROP} is the set of *proper* constraints: $\Gamma_{\text{PROP}} = \{(\varphi, k, j) \in \Gamma \,|\, j > 0\}$. Of course, we have: $\Gamma = \Gamma_{\text{CONST}} \cup \Gamma_{\text{PROP}}$. In the sequel, when talking about the modulo constraints we sometimes omit the word *modulo*.

A *canonical structure* $\mathcal{C}_\varphi$ for a projection-free CQ φ is defined as usually: elements of $\mathcal{C}_\varphi$ are variables and constants of φ and relations of $\mathcal{C}_\varphi$ consist of tuples of variables and constants from conjuncts of φ.

Outline of the proof. We present an algorithm, which for a satisfiable set of (modulo) constraints $\Gamma = \Gamma_{\text{CONST}} \cup \Gamma_{\text{PROP}}$ constructs a witness database $\mathcal{B}$ of exponential size w.r.t. the size of Γ. The general idea of the algorithm is to guess a database $\mathcal{A}_{\text{CONST}}$ satisfying Γ_{CONST} and then to satisfy the proper constraints Γ_{PROP} one by one, by extending the database $\mathcal{A}_{\text{CONST}}$ with some number of copies of canonical structures of the formulas of Γ_{PROP}. But won't satisfying a constraint in such a way cause some of the constraints, which have been already satisfied, to fail? In Sect. 4.2 we show that the problem can be overcome if constraints are in some normal form, and if the order in which we try to satisfy them is correct. Earlier, in Sect. 4.1 we show that, for each set of modulo constraints, one can construct, in NEXPTIME an equisatisfiable set of constraints which is in the desired normal form.

Operation REPLACE. Suppose that formulas $\varphi_1, \ldots, \varphi_n$ in some constraints $(\varphi_i, k_i, j_i) \in \Gamma_{\text{PROP}}$ (for $i \in \{1, \ldots, n\}$) are equivalent (i.e. canonical structures C_{φ_i} are isomorphic). We define a single constraint (φ_1, k, j), where j is the least common multiple of the numbers $j_1, \ldots, j_n$ (recall that $j_i > 0$ in constraints in Γ_{PROP}) and k is the smallest number such that, for each $i = 1, \ldots, n$, there exists $\alpha_i \in \mathbb{N}$ such that it holds $k = k_i + \alpha_i * j_i$. Using Chinese Remainder Theorem it is possible to show that if the constraints are satisfiable such a number k exists, otherwise we know that the constraints are inconsistent and the algorithm stops.

This allows us to define an operation REPLACE. The operation transforms a set of proper constraints Γ by replacing each set of constraints having equivalent formulas with a single constraint, while preserving satisfiability. After applying the operation, there are no two distinct constraints in REPLACE(Γ) with equivalent formulas. Notice that equivalence of CQs is in NP, so we do not run out of time.

Lemma 1. *For every set of proper constraints Γ and every database $\mathcal{A}$ we have $\mathcal{A} \models \Gamma$ iff $\mathcal{A} \models \text{REPLACE}(\Gamma)$.*

Dealing with constant constraints. In the following lemma we show that given a satisfiable set of constraints $\Gamma = \Gamma_{\text{CONST}} \cup \Gamma_{\text{PROP}}$, it is possible to guess a database $\mathcal{A}_{\text{CONST}}$ of at most exponential size, such that $\mathcal{A}_{\text{CONST}} \models \Gamma_{\text{CONST}}$.

Lemma 2. *Let $\Gamma = \Gamma_{\text{CONST}} \cup \Gamma_{\text{PROP}}$ be a set of constraints. If there exists a database $\mathcal{A}$ such that $\mathcal{A} \models \Gamma$ then there exists a database $\mathcal{A}_{\text{CONST}}$ such that $\mathcal{A}_{\text{CONST}} \models \Gamma_{\text{CONST}}$. The size of $\mathcal{A}_{\text{CONST}}$ is at most exponential w.r.t. $|\Gamma|$.*

Proof (sketch). Consider the database $\mathcal{A}$ and the set $\Gamma = \Gamma_{\text{CONST}} \cup \Gamma_{\text{PROP}}$. Since $\mathcal{A} \models \Gamma$ obviously we have $\mathcal{A} \models \Gamma_{\text{CONST}}$. Let $\mathcal{A}_{\text{CONST}}$ be a substructure of $\mathcal{A}$ which consists exactly of the elements from $\mathcal{A}$ that are in some tuple satisfying a formula in a constraint from Γ_{CONST} or are a constant in Γ.

The number of such elements is bounded by the sum of the number of constants in Γ and the number of constraints in Γ_{CONST} multiplied by the maximal number of variables in formulas in Γ_{CONST} and the value of the maximal number k from Γ_{CONST}. Hence, the size of $\mathcal{A}_{\text{CONST}}$ is at most exponential w.r.t. $|\Gamma|$. Clearly, $\mathcal{A}_{\text{CONST}}$ satisfies Γ_{CONST}. □

From now on we assume that the set of constraints $\Gamma = \Gamma_{\text{CONST}} \cup \Gamma_{\text{PROP}}$ and the database $\mathcal{A}_{\text{CONST}}$ are fixed. All databases which we are going to consider will be superstructures of $\mathcal{A}_{\text{CONST}}$. We extend the vocabulary provided by Γ with a new set of constants $\text{dom}(\mathcal{A}_{\text{CONST}})$, interpreted as elements of $\mathcal{A}_{\text{CONST}}$.

4.1   Construction of a Modified Set of Constraints

The algorithm starts the modifications with a set Γ_{PROP} and goes through three steps. Each of these steps will produce an equisatisfiable set of constraints that will be the input of the next step. All steps are of a similar structure:

1. For each constraint t from the input set, a set Γ_t of new constraints is generated.
2. The set $\text{REPLACE}(\bigcup \Gamma_t)$ is returned as the output of the step.

Step 1. Each constraint $t = (\varphi, k, j)$ asserts the existence of exactly $k + \alpha * j$, for some $\alpha \in \mathbb{N}$, tuples $\bar{a}$ of elements of a database such that $\varphi(\bar{a})$ is true. In this step we want to fix which variables are substituted with elements of $\mathcal{A}_{\text{CONST}}$. Thus we have to produce separate constraints for each (possibly partial) substitution of variables of φ with elements of $\mathcal{A}_{\text{CONST}}$. Additionally, we ensure that such a substitution is final i.e. we forbid the substitution of remaining variables to the constants in the resulting constraints.

Recall the basic intuition behind the algorithm – for each proper constraint, we want to extend $\mathcal{A}_{\text{CONST}}$ with copies of the canonical structure of the formula in the constraint. After Step 1 it is clear how to do it – the elements of the canonical structure corresponding to the constants should be identified with elements of $\mathcal{A}_{\text{CONST}}$ and the other elements should be fresh.

Consider a constraint $t = (\varphi, k, j) \in \Gamma_{\text{PROP}}$. We define Γ_t to be the set of triples of the form $(\psi_\theta, k_\theta, j)$, for each $V \subseteq \text{Vars}(\varphi)$ and $\theta \colon V \to \text{dom}(\mathcal{A}_{\text{CONST}})$, where:

$$\psi_\theta = \varphi[\theta] \wedge \text{NotConstants}(\text{Vars}(\varphi[\theta])).$$

By $\varphi[\theta]$ we mean the result of the substitution θ on φ. $\text{NotConstants}(X)$ is the conjunction of inequalities of the form $x \neq c$, for each $x \in X$ and $c \in \text{dom}(\mathcal{A}_{\text{CONST}})$. The inequalities are introduced to ensure that for any database $\mathcal{A}$ such that $\mathcal{A} \models \Gamma_t$, in any tuple satisfying $\varphi[\theta]$ no variable from $\text{Vars}(\varphi[\theta])$ is substituted with an element from $\mathcal{A}_{\text{CONST}}$.

The numbers k_θ are guessed in such a way that $\sum_\theta k_\theta = k + \alpha * j$, for some $\alpha \in \mathbb{N}$. It is enough to consider the numbers bounded by $k + j$. Intuitively numbers k_θ determine how the total number of tuples satisfying the constraint $t = (\varphi, k, j)$ is distributed among its versions $\varphi[\theta]$, for all θ. We define $\Gamma_1 = \text{REPLACE}(\bigcup_{t \in \Gamma_0} \Gamma_t)$.

Lemma 3

1. *Let $\mathcal{A}$ be a database, such that $\mathcal{A}_{\text{CONST}} \subseteq \mathcal{A}$ and $\mathcal{A} \models \Gamma$. There exists a choice of the numbers k_θ in Γ_1 such that $\mathcal{A} \models \Gamma_1$.*
2. *If there exists $\mathcal{A}' \supseteq \mathcal{A}_{\text{CONST}}$ such that $\mathcal{A}' \models \Gamma_{\text{CONST}}$ and $\mathcal{A}' \models \Gamma_1$ then $\mathcal{A}' \models \Gamma$.*
3. *The size of Γ_1 is exponential w.r.t. the size of Γ.*

Step 2

Definition 4. *Let $\mathcal{B}$ be a relational structure over the vocabulary containing relational symbols from Γ and constant symbols $\text{dom}(\mathcal{A}_{\text{CONST}})$. Define $GRAPH(\mathcal{B})$ to be a graph, whose vertices are the elements of $\mathcal{B}$ which are not a constant in $\text{dom}(\mathcal{A}_{\text{CONST}})$. There is an edge between vertices e_1, e_2 of $GRAPH(\mathcal{B})$ if there is a tuple $\bar{e}$ of elements of $\mathcal{B}$ containing both e_1 and e_2, such that an atom $R(\bar{e})$ is true in $\mathcal{B}$, for some relation R in $\mathcal{B}$.*

Consider a formula $\varphi(\bar{x})$ from one of the constraints from Γ_1. The formula $\varphi(\bar{x})$ is of the form $\bigwedge_k R_k(\bar{x}_k) \wedge \text{NotConstants}(\bar{x})$.

Notice that the set of vertices of $GRAPH(\mathcal{C}_\varphi)$ (i.e. the graph for the canonical structure for φ) is exactly the set of variables of φ.

Definition 5. *A connected subformula of φ is a formula $\varphi_D(\bar{x}_D)$ defined as $\bigwedge_{R \in D} R(\bar{x}_R) \wedge \text{NotConstants}(\bar{x}_D)$, where D is a maximal set of non-ground atoms (i.e. atoms with variables), such that $GRAPH(\mathcal{C}_{\varphi_D})$ is a connected component of $GRAPH(\mathcal{C}_\varphi)$.*

Notice, that the formula φ is a conjunction of its connected subformulas and its ground atoms. (i.e. atoms without variables).

Example 2. Consider following formula $\varphi(x_1, \ldots, x_5)$:

$$R_1(x_1, x_2) \wedge R_2(x_2, x_3, c_1, x_5, c_2) \wedge R_1(c_1, c_3) \wedge R_1(c_3, c_3)$$

$$\wedge R_1(x_4, c_1) \wedge R_1(c_2, x_4) \wedge \text{NotConstants}(\{x_1, \ldots, x_5\}),$$

where c_1, c_2, c_3 are constants from $\mathcal{A}_{\text{CONST}}$. Vertices of $GRAPH(\mathcal{C}_\varphi)$ are $\{x_1, \ldots, x_5\}$, and edges of $GRAPH(\mathcal{C}_\varphi)$ are $\{x_1, x_2\}$, $\{x_2, x_3\}$, $\{x_2, x_5\}$ and $\{x_3, x_5\}$. Clearly, $GRAPH(\mathcal{C}_\varphi)$ has two connected components, namely $\{x_1, x_2, x_3, x_5\}$ and $\{x_4\}$.

There are two connected subformulas of φ:

$$\varphi_1(x_1, x_2, x_3, x_5) = R_1(x_1, x_2) \wedge R_2(x_2, x_3, c_1, x_5, c_2) \wedge \text{NotConstants}(\{x_1, x_2, x_3, x_5\})$$

and

$$\varphi_2(x_4) = R_1(x_4, c_1) \wedge R_1(c_2, x_4) \wedge \text{NotConstants}(\{x_4\}).$$

Ground atoms of φ are $R_1(c_1, c_3)$ and $R_1(c_3, c_3)$.

The motivation for Step 2 can be best explained using the following example. Again, recall that our goal is to order the proper constraints in such a way that extending $\mathcal{A}_{\mathrm{CONST}}$ with the canonical structure of the formula in the constraint does not increase the number of tuples satisfying the earlier (in the order) constraints.

Example 3. Let $\varphi_1 = R_1(c_1, x_1) \wedge R_2(c_1, x_2) \wedge \mathrm{NotConstants}(\{\bar{x}\})$ and $\varphi_2 = R_1(c_1, x_1) \wedge R_2(c_1, x_2) \wedge R_3(c_1, x_3) \wedge \mathrm{NotConstants}(\{\bar{x}\})$. Thus φ_1 consists of two and φ_2 consists of three connected subformulas. Let t_1 be a constraint containing the formula φ_1 and t_2 a constraint containing the formula φ_2. Clearly, it is impossible to order t_1 and t_2 in a right way –adding a copy of the canonical structure $\mathcal{C}_{\varphi_2}$ changes the number of tuples satisfying φ_1, and, in presence of at least one copy of $\mathcal{C}_{\varphi_2}$, adding a copy of $\mathcal{C}_{\varphi_1}$ changes the number of tuples satisfying φ_2.

Step 2 is performed in order to avoid the problem from Example 3. The step consists of replacing each constraint t in Γ_1 with separate constraints for each connected subformula of the formula in t. We also forget about ground atoms in formulas in the constraints. The reason is that after Step 1 the ground atoms are already determined to be either true or false.

Let $t = (\varphi, k, j)$ be a constraint in Γ_1, let $\varphi_1, \ldots, \varphi_n$ be connected subformulas of φ and let $\psi_1, \ldots, \psi_l$ be ground atoms of φ. Let $m_i \in \{0, 1\}$ be 1 if ψ_i holds in $\mathcal{A}_{\mathrm{CONST}}$ and 0 otherwise (for $i = 1, \ldots, l$). Notice that the number of tuples satisfying t is the product of the numbers of tuples satisfying φ_i, (for $i = 1 \ldots, n$), times the product of m_i, for $i = 1, \ldots, l$.

Now, if $k > 0$ and some $m_i = 0$, we know that the constraints are inconsistent, so the algorithm can stop. If $k = 0$ and some $m_i = 0$ the constraint is satisfied in every superstructure of $\mathcal{A}_{\mathrm{CONST}}$ so we put $\Gamma_t = \emptyset$. If $k \geq 0$ and for all $i = 1, \ldots, l$ the number $m_i = 1$, then Γ_t consists of triples (φ_i, k_i, j), where the numbers $k_i \leq k + j$ are guessed such that $\prod_i k_i = k + \alpha * j$, for some $\alpha \in \mathbb{N}$.

We define $\Gamma_2 = \mathrm{REPLACE}(\bigcup_{t \in \Gamma_1} \Gamma_t)$.

Lemma 4.   *1. Let $\mathcal{A}$ be a database, such that $\mathcal{A} \supseteq \mathcal{A}_{\mathrm{CONST}}$ and $\mathcal{A} \models \Gamma_{\mathrm{CONST}} \cup \Gamma_1$. There exists a choice of the numbers k_i in Γ_2, such that $\mathcal{A} \models \Gamma_2$.*
2. For every database $\mathcal{A}'$ such that $\mathcal{A}' \supseteq \mathcal{A}_{\mathrm{CONST}}$ if $\mathcal{A}' \models \Gamma_{\mathrm{CONST}}$ and $\mathcal{A}' \models \Gamma_2$ then $\mathcal{A}' \models \Gamma$.
3. The size of Γ_2 is exponential w.r.t. the size of Γ.

Step 3. Consider a database $\mathcal{A}$, a formula $\varphi(\bar{x})$ from Γ_2 and a tuple $\bar{a}$ such that $\mathcal{A} \models \varphi(\bar{a})$. The substitution of elements $\bar{a}$ for variables $\bar{x}$ may map several variables from $\bar{x}$ to a single element a in $\bar{a}$. During Step 3 we replace each constraint t with separate constraints for all possible ways in which variables of the formula of t can be identified. We also disallow any further identification of variables in the resulting constraints Γ_3. In other words: if $\mathcal{A} \models \varphi(\bar{a})$ then there is a corresponding homomorphism from elements of the canonical structure $\mathcal{C}_\varphi$ to elements of $\mathcal{A}$. The goal of this step is to obtain a new set Γ_3 which can replace Γ_2, such that all homomorphisms, which correspond to the tuples satisfying formulas in Γ_3, are injective.

The following example explains why we need this step.

Example 4. Let $\varphi_1 = R(x_1, x_2) \wedge R(x_1, x_3)$ and $\varphi_2 = R(x_1, x_2)$. The formula φ_2 is, in fact, equal to the formula φ_1 with variables x_2 and x_3 identified. Let t_1 be a constraint containing the formula φ_1 and t_2 a constraint containing the formula φ_2. Similarly as in Example 3, these two constraints cannot be ordered properly. If we extend a database with the canonical structure $\mathcal{C}_{\varphi_1}$ we change the number of tuples satisfying φ_2 and vice versa.

Let $t = (\varphi, k, j)$ be a constraint in Γ_2. We define Γ_t to be the set of constraints of the form: $(\psi_\theta, k_\theta, j)$ for each $V \subseteq \text{Vars}(\varphi)$ and each $\theta \colon \text{Vars}(\varphi) \setminus V \to V$, where ψ_θ is:

$$\varphi[\theta] \wedge \text{INEQ}(\text{Vars}(\varphi[\theta])).$$

The numbers $k_\theta \leq k + j$ are guessed such that $\sum_\theta k_\theta = k + \alpha * j$, for some $\alpha \in \mathbb{N}$. $\text{INEQ}(\text{Vars}(\varphi[\theta]))$ is a conjunction of inequalities of the form $x \neq y$, for each pair of distinct variables $x, y \in \text{Vars}(\varphi[\theta])$. We introduce the inequalities to ensure that all variables which are not identified during this step have to be substituted with distinct elements of a database.

Finally, we define Γ_3 as $\text{REPLACE}(\bigcup_{t \in \Gamma_2} \Gamma_t)$.

The following lemma states the properties of Γ_3.

Lemma 5

1. Let $\mathcal{A}$ be a database, such that $\mathcal{A} \supseteq \mathcal{A}_{\text{CONST}}$ and $\mathcal{A} \models \Gamma_{\text{CONST}} \cup \Gamma_2$ There exists a choice of the numbers k_θ in Γ_3, such that $\mathcal{A} \models \Gamma_3$.
2. For every database $\mathcal{A}'$ such that $\mathcal{A}' \supseteq \mathcal{A}_{\text{CONST}}$ if $\mathcal{A}' \models \Gamma_{\text{CONST}}$ and $\mathcal{A}' \models \Gamma_3$ then $\mathcal{A}' \models \Gamma$.
3. The size of Γ_3 is exponential w.r.t. Γ.

4.2 Construction of an Exponential Database Satisfying Γ_3

In Sect. 4.1 we constructed, for a set Γ of modulo constraints a set Γ_3 of constraints which are satisfiable if and only if Γ are, and such that formulas in the constraints from Γ_3 have the following normal form:

(A) Each formula contains the NotConstants subformula, so that the variables cannot be substituted with elements $\text{dom}(\mathcal{A}_{\text{CONST}})$;
(B) each formula is connected and does not contain ground atoms;
(C) each formula contains the INEQ subformula, so that distinct variables cannot be substituted with the same element of a database.

Define a partial order $\leq_{part}$ on constraints from Γ_3 as follows: $(\varphi_1, k_1, j_1) \leq_{part}$ (φ_2, k_2, j_2) if there exists a tuple $\bar{a}$ of elements of $\mathcal{C}_{\varphi_2}$ such that $\mathcal{C}_{\varphi_2} \models \varphi_1(\bar{a})$. In other words: $(\varphi_1, k_1, j_1) \leq_{part} (\varphi_2, k_2, j_2)$ if $\mathcal{C}_{\varphi_1}$ is isomorphic to a substructure of $\mathcal{C}_{\varphi_2}$. We use the word *substructure* in a *positive* sense where $R(a, b)$ is a substructure of $R(a, b), R(b, a), R(a, c)$.

Let $\leq$ be some linear order on constraints from Γ_3 consistent with the partial order $\leq_{part}$. We write $(\varphi_1, k_1, j_1) < (\varphi_2, k_2, j_2)$ if $(\varphi_1, k_1, j_1) \leq (\varphi_2, k_2, j_2)$ and $\varphi_1 \neq \varphi_2$ (recall that formulas in Γ_3 are unique).

Lemma 6. *Let (φ, k, j) be a constraint in Γ_3 such that C_φ has exactly n automorphisms. There are exactly n tuples $\bar{a}$ such that $C_\varphi \models \varphi(\bar{a})$. Moreover, for every database $\mathcal{B}$ we have $|\{\bar{a} \mid \mathcal{B} \models \varphi(\bar{a})\}| = \alpha * n$, for some $\alpha \in \mathbb{N}$.*

Notice however, that the above lemma would not be true if conjunctive queries with projections were allowed.

Lemma 7. *Let (φ, k, j) be a constraint in Γ_3 and let $\mathcal{B}$ be a database such that $\mathcal{A}_{\text{CONST}} \subseteq \mathcal{B}$ and $\mathcal{B} \models \{t \in \Gamma_3 \mid t > (\varphi, k, j)\}$. If the constraints Γ_3 are satisfiable then there exists a database $\mathcal{B}' \supseteq \mathcal{B}$ such that $\mathcal{B}' \models \{t \in \Gamma_3 \mid t \geq (\varphi, k, j)\}$. The size of the database $\mathcal{B}'$ is at most $|\mathcal{B}| + |C_\varphi| * \delta$, where $\delta \in \mathbb{N}$ is bounded by the sum of k and j.*

Example 5. Consider constraints $t_1 = (\varphi_1, 2, 2)$ and $t_2 = (\varphi_2, 1, 6)$. Let $\varphi_1 = R(v, z_1) \wedge R(v, z_2) \wedge R'(a, b, z_1) \wedge \text{NotConstants}(v, z_1, z_2) \wedge \text{INEQ}(v, z_1, z_2)$ and $\varphi_2 = R(x, y) \wedge \text{NotConstants}(x, y) \wedge \text{INEQ}(x, y)$. Clearly: $t_1 > t_2$. There are two tuples $\bar{x}$ such that $C_{\varphi_1} \models \varphi_2(\bar{x})$. Let $\mathcal{B}$ be a database presented schematically at Fig. 2 such that $\mathcal{B} \models \{t_1\}$. Our algorithm constructs the database $\mathcal{B}' \models \{t_1, t_2\}$. In order to satisfy t_2 three copies of C_{φ_2} are added.

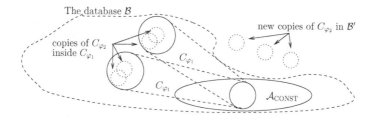

Fig. 2. The database $\mathcal{B}$ satisfying the constraint t_1 from Example 5

Proof (of Lemma 7). Let n be the number of automorphisms of C_φ. According to Lemma 6, the number $m = |\{\bar{b} \in \mathcal{B} \mid \mathcal{B} \models \varphi(\bar{b})\}|$ is a multiple of n.

Let m' be the smallest number such that m' is a multiple of n (including 0) and $m' + m = k + \alpha * j$, for some $\alpha \in \mathbb{N}$. If constraints Γ_3 are satisfiable such number m' exists and its value is bounded by $j * n + k$.

Let $x_1, \ldots, x_{|\text{Vars}(\varphi)|}$ be variables in φ. The database $\mathcal{B}'$ is defined as the union of the database $\mathcal{B}$ and $\frac{m'}{n}$ copies of the canonical structure C_φ, with constants $\text{dom}(\mathcal{A}_{\text{CONST}})$ from each copy of C_φ identified with elements of $\mathcal{A}_{\text{CONST}} \subseteq \mathcal{B}$. Formally, elements of $\mathcal{B}'$ are elements of $\mathcal{B}$ and new elements $e_{h,i}$, for $h = 1, \ldots, |\text{Vars}(\varphi)|$ and $i = 1, \ldots, \frac{m'}{n}$. Database $\mathcal{B}'$ is a superstructure of $\mathcal{B}$, and additionally for each conjunct $R(w_1, \ldots, w_l)$ in φ, for each $i = 1, \ldots, \frac{m'}{n}$, the atom $R(v_{1,i}, \ldots, v_{l,i})$ is true in $\mathcal{B}'$, where

$$v_{h,i} = \begin{cases} e_{g,i} & \text{if } w_h = x_g, \text{ where } g \in \{1, \ldots, |\text{Vars}(\varphi)|\} \\ a & \text{if } w_h = a, \text{ where } a \text{ is a constant,} \end{cases}$$

for $h = 1, \ldots, l$. Clearly, the size of $\mathcal{B}'$ is at most $|\mathcal{B}| + |C_\varphi| * \frac{m'}{n}$.

Now, we show that $\mathcal{B}' \models \{t \in \Gamma_3 \mid t \geq (\varphi, k, j)\}$. We will use the following observation:

Observation. Consider a constraint $(\varphi', k', j') \in \Gamma_3$, such that $(\varphi', k', j') \geq (\varphi, k, j)$. Each tuple $\bar{b}$ such that $\mathcal{B}' \models \varphi'(\bar{b})$ is contained in a single connected component of $\mathrm{GRAPH}(\mathcal{B}')$.

Proof (of the observation). This is since, by (A), the variables in φ' cannot be substituted with elements from $\mathcal{A}_{\mathrm{CONST}}$. and since, by (B), the graph of the canonical structure for φ' consists of a single connected component.   □

We show that $\mathcal{B}' \models (\varphi, k, j)$. Let us count the number of tuples $\bar{b}$ such that $\mathcal{B}' \models \varphi(\bar{b})$: there are m tuples consisting of elements of $\mathcal{B}$ and m' new tuples (by Lemma 6), such that the elements of each of them are all contained in some new copy of $\mathcal{C}_\varphi$. Since newly added copies of $\mathcal{C}_\varphi$ are the only new connected components of $\mathrm{GRAPH}(\mathcal{B}')$, it follows from the above observation that there are no new tuples satisfying φ in $\mathcal{B}'$. So there are exactly $m + m'$ tuples satisfying φ and $\mathcal{B}' \models (\varphi, k, j)$.

Now we need to prove that by extending the structure we did not spoil one of the old constraints. We claim that, for each constraint $(\varphi', k', j') \in \Gamma_3$, such that $(\varphi', k', j') > (\varphi, k, j)$, the number of tuples satisfying (φ', k', j') in $\mathcal{B}'$ is exactly the same as in $\mathcal{B}$: from the above observation it follows that each new tuple $\bar{b}$, such that $\mathcal{B}' \models \varphi'(\bar{b})$, must be contained in some copy of $\mathcal{C}_\varphi$. But this would mean that $\mathcal{C}_\varphi \models \varphi'(\bar{b})$, which would contradict $(\varphi', k', j') > (\varphi, k, j)$.   □

Let us now construct a sequence of databases $\mathcal{A}_i$, for $i = 0, \ldots, |\Gamma_3|$, such that the database $\mathcal{A}_i$ satisfies the set of first i (in the order $\leq$) constraints from Γ_3. We start from the database $\mathcal{A}_0 = \mathcal{A}_{\mathrm{CONST}}$. Then, for all $i = 1, \ldots, |\Gamma_3|$, we consider the i-th (in the order $\leq$) constraint from Γ_3 and obtain the database $\mathcal{A}_i$ from the database $\mathcal{A}_{i-1}$ using Lemma 7, which guarantees that finally: $\mathcal{A}' = \mathcal{A}_{|\Gamma_3|}$ satisfies Γ_3, and the size of $\mathcal{A}'$ is at most exponential in $|\Gamma|$.

So far, our nondeterministic algorithm has built a database $\mathcal{A}'$. As its last step it just verifies if $\mathcal{A}' \models \Gamma_3 \cup \Gamma_{\mathrm{CONST}}$. This would almost finish the proof of Theorem 2. The only thing which would still be in doubt is if in the process of satisfying the constraints from Γ_3 we did not spoil anything concerning the constant constraints Γ_{CONST}:

Lemma 8. *Let $\mathcal{A}'$ be the database resulting from the construction in the previous paragraphs. If there exists a database $\mathcal{A}$ such that $\mathcal{A} \supseteq \mathcal{A}_{\mathrm{CONST}}$ and $\mathcal{A} \models \Gamma_{\mathrm{CONST}} \cup \Gamma_3$ then $\mathcal{A}' \models \Gamma_{\mathrm{CONST}}$.*

Notice that Lemma 8 needs an additional assumption: that there exists $\mathcal{A} \supseteq \mathcal{A}_{\mathrm{CONST}}$ satisfying all the constraints $\Gamma_3 \cup \Gamma_{\mathrm{CONST}}$. Otherwise it might happen that new tuples satisfying the queries from Γ_{CONST} would appear in $\mathcal{A}'$, and thus the constraints from Γ_{CONST} would be violated in $\mathcal{A}'$. But if the constraints are satisfiable then our nondeterministic algorithm guessed $\mathcal{A}_{\mathrm{CONST}}$ correctly, and so we can be sure that such $\mathcal{A} \supseteq \mathcal{A}_{\mathrm{CONST}}$ indeed exists.

Observation. Let $(\varphi, k, j) \in \Gamma_3$. If $\mathcal{A}_{\text{CONST}} \cup \mathcal{C}_\varphi$ is a substructure of $\mathcal{A}'$ then $\mathcal{A}_{\text{CONST}} \cup \mathcal{C}_\varphi$ is also a substructure of $\mathcal{A}$. By $\mathcal{A}_{\text{CONST}} \cup \mathcal{C}_\varphi$ we mean here a union of the two structures, with constants from $\mathcal{C}_\varphi$ identified with the respective elements in $\mathcal{A}_{\text{CONST}}$. Again, the word *substructure* is used in a *positive* sense.

Proof (of the observation). Suppose $\mathcal{A}_{\text{CONST}} \cup \mathcal{C}_\varphi$ is a substructure of $\mathcal{A}'$. Then there exists a minimal number i such that $0 < i \leq |\Gamma_3|$ and $\mathcal{A}_{\text{CONST}} \cup \mathcal{C}_\varphi$ is a substructure of $\mathcal{A}_i$. Thus, at the i-th step of the construction of $\mathcal{A}'$, while processing some constraint $(\varphi', k', j') \in \Gamma_3$ we extended the database $\mathcal{A}_{i-1}$ with at least one copy of the canonical structure $\mathcal{C}_\varphi$. This means that $\mathcal{C}_\varphi$ must be a substructure of $\mathcal{C}_{\varphi'}$. Now there are 2 cases:

Case 1: $k' > 0$. Then $\mathcal{A}_{\text{CONST}} \cup \mathcal{C}_{\varphi'}$ is a substructure of $\mathcal{A}$, and so also $\mathcal{A}_{\text{CONST}} \cup \mathcal{C}_\varphi$ is a substructure of $\mathcal{A}$.

Case 2: $k' = 0$. Recall that we extended $\mathcal{A}_{i-1}$ because the number of tuples $\bar{b}$ such that $\mathcal{A}_{i-1} \models \varphi'(\bar{b})$ was not equal to $\alpha * j'$ for any $\alpha \in \mathbb{N}$, including $\alpha = 0$. Hence, $\mathcal{A}_{\text{CONST}} \cup \mathcal{C}_{\varphi'}$ is a substructure of A_{i-1}, but therefore $\mathcal{A}_{\text{CONST}} \cup \mathcal{C}_\varphi$ is a substructure of A_{i-1}. But this contradicts the minimality of i. □

Proof (of Lemma 9). For each $\mathcal{B}'$ being a substructure of $\mathcal{A}'$, of a form $\mathcal{A}_{\text{CONST}} \cup \mathcal{C}_\varphi$ (where φ is a formula in constraints from Γ_3) and such that $\text{GRAPH}(\mathcal{B}')$ is a connected component of $\text{GRAPH}(\mathcal{A}')$, fix one substructure $\mathcal{B}$ of $\mathcal{A}$ of the form $\mathcal{A}_{\text{CONST}} \cup \mathcal{C}_\varphi$ (existence of $\mathcal{B}$ is guaranteed by Observation) and define $h_\mathcal{B} \colon \mathcal{B}' \to \mathcal{B}$ as identity (or, to be more precise, as isomorphism).

We define a mapping $h \colon \mathcal{A}' \to \mathcal{A}$. For $c \in \mathcal{A}_{\text{CONST}}$ put $h(c) = c$. For $a \notin \mathcal{A}_{\text{CONST}}$ put $h(a) = h_\mathcal{B}(a)$, where $\mathcal{B}$ is such that $a \in \text{dom}(h_\mathcal{B})$. Notice that we used the fact that all connected components of $\text{GRAPH}(\mathcal{A}')$ are of the form $\text{GRAPH}(\mathcal{C}_\varphi)$ for some $(\varphi, k, j) \in \Gamma_3$.

Now, suppose that $\mathcal{A}' \not\models \Gamma_{\text{CONST}}$. So, there exists a tuple $\bar{a}$ of elements of $\mathcal{A}'$, containing some element(s) not in $\mathcal{A}_{\text{CONST}}$ such that for a constraint $(\psi, k, j) \in \Gamma_{\text{CONST}}$ it holds $\mathcal{A}' \models \psi(\bar{a})$. But then the tuple $h(\bar{a})$ contains some element(s) not in $\mathcal{A}_{\text{CONST}}$ and $\mathcal{A} \models \psi(h(\bar{a}))$. (this is since negation and inequality are not allowed in constraints from Γ_{CONST}). The last implies that $\mathcal{A} \not\models \Gamma_{\text{CONST}}$. □

5   From the Intermediate Result to the Main Result

In this section we use some of the ideas from [2] to show how Theorem 2 implies Theorem 1. We start with the following definition and lemma from [2].

Definition 6. *Let R be a TreeQL-program and let d be a DTD such that R does not typecheck with respect to d. Then:*

- *there is a path $\bar{v} = v_1, \ldots, v_k$ in the program R where*
    1. *v_1 is a child of the root;*
    2. *$lab(v_i) = (\sigma_i, \varphi_i(\bar{x}_1, \ldots, \bar{x}_i))$, for $i \in \{1, \ldots, k\}$;*
    3. *let $\bar{x} = \bar{x}_1, \ldots, \bar{x}_k$.*
       The node v_k has precisely n children with labels $(\delta_1, \psi_1(\bar{x}, \bar{y}_1))$, ..., $(\delta_n, \psi_n(\bar{x}, \bar{y}_n))$;
  and

– there is a database $\mathcal{A}$ with elements $\bar{a} = \bar{a}_1, \ldots, \bar{a}_k$ such that:
1. *$\mathcal{A}$ satisfies $\varphi_i(\bar{a}_1, \ldots, \bar{a}_i)$, for each $i = 1, \ldots, k$;*
2. *$\delta_1^{j_1} \ldots \delta_n^{j_n} \notin d(\sigma_k)$ where $j_i = |\{\bar{b} \mid \mathcal{A}$ satisfies $\psi_i(\bar{a}, \bar{b})\}|$, for all $i = 1, \ldots, n$.*

We say that $(\bar{v}, \mathcal{A}, \bar{a})$ is a breakpoint *for R and d.*

Lemma 9 ([2]). *Let $\delta_1, \ldots, \delta_n$ be symbols and let $\nu = (k_1, j_1), \ldots, (k_1, j_1)$ be a vector of n pairs of natural numbers. We denote by L_ν the language of all words of the form: $\delta_1^{k_1 + \alpha_1 * j_1} \ldots \delta_n^{k_n + \alpha_n * j_n}$ where each $\alpha_i \in \mathbb{N}$, $1 \leq i \leq n$. For each regular language r over alphabet $\{\delta_1, \ldots, \delta_n\}$, there exists a finite set $Vec(r)$ of vectors of pairs of natural numbers as above such that $\neg r \cap \delta_1^* \ldots \delta_n^* = \bigcup_{\nu \in \mathrm{Vec}(r)} L_\nu$.*

Moreover, the values of the numbers in $Vec(r)$ are bounded by the number of states of the deterministic automaton recognizing $\neg r$.

We briefly sketch the beginning of the proof of the non-elementary upper bound from [2], using the notation introduced in Definition 6. Assume that the program R does not typecheck w.r.t. d, then there exists a breakpoint $(\bar{v}, \mathcal{A}, \bar{a})$. Let r be the regular language $d(\sigma_k)$ specified by the DTD d. Consider the language $\neg r \cap \delta_1^* \ldots \delta_n^*$, it is the intersection of the language of children of the node v_k (i.e. $\delta_1^* \cdot \ldots \cdot \delta_n^*$) and the complement of r. From lemma 9 it follows that there exists a set of vectors $\mathrm{Vec}_{R,d,\bar{v}}$ such that $\neg r \cap \delta_1^* \ldots \delta_n^* = \bigcup_{\nu \in \mathrm{Vec}_{R,d,\bar{v}}} L_\nu$

Since $(\bar{v}, \mathcal{A}, \bar{a})$ is a breakpoint then there exists a vector $\nu = (k_1, j_1), \ldots, (k_n, j_n)$ in $\mathrm{Vec}_{R,d,\bar{v}}$, such that for each $l \in \{1, \ldots, n\}$ there exists $\alpha_l \in \mathbb{N}$ such that: $|\{\bar{b} \mid \mathcal{A} \models \psi_l(\bar{a}, \bar{b})\}| = k_l + \alpha_l * j_l$.

Then it is shown that it is always possible to find a substructure $\mathcal{A}'$ of $\mathcal{A}$ of a size bounded independently of $\mathcal{A}$ such that elements $\bar{a}$ are in $\mathcal{A}'$ and for each $l \in \{1, \ldots, n\}$ there exists $\alpha_l' \in \mathbb{N}$ such that: $|\{\bar{b} \mid \mathcal{A}' \models \psi_l(\bar{a}, \bar{b})\}| = k_l + \alpha_l' * j_l$.

In our proof we do not require the database $\mathcal{A}'$ to be a substructure of $\mathcal{A}$. This allows us to modify the structure, which makes it possible to achieve an exponential upper bound, however at the cost that we can no longer have universal formulas as integrity constraints.

Again, we use the same notation as in Definition 6. We begin by guessing a path $\bar{v} = v_1, \ldots, v_k$ in the program R, and a vector $\nu = (k_1, j_1), \ldots, (k_n, j_n)$ of as many pairs of natural numbers as the node v_k has children. The numbers in ν are bounded by the number of states of the DFA for $\neg r$. Hence, the sizes of binary representations of the numbers in ν are linear in DTD d. Then we have to check[2] whether the language $\{\delta_1^{k_1 + \alpha_1 * j_1} \ldots \delta_n^{k_n + \alpha_n * j_n} \mid \alpha_1, \ldots, \alpha_n \in \mathbb{N}\}$ is contained in $\neg r$. This step can be done in PSPACE. It is enough to check words with values of $\alpha_1, \ldots, \alpha_n$ bounded by the number of states of the DFA for $\neg r$. Each of these words (represented with all numbers written in binary) can be verified to be in $\neg r$ in PSPACE by checking whether a final state of the NFA for r can be reached by reading the word.

---

[2] This is to guarantee that if for some database $\mathcal{A}$ there exists a node (v_k, θ) in the output tree $R(\mathcal{A})$ such that the concatenation of symbols labeling children of (v_k, θ) is in the language defined by ν then $R(\mathcal{A})$ is not consistent with the DTD d.

Now, we construct a set of modulo constraints Γ over the vocabulary consisting of relational symbols in the program R and constants $\bar{a} = \bar{a}_1, \ldots, \bar{a}_k$:

1. For formulas $\varphi_1, \ldots, \varphi_k$ in nodes $v_1, \ldots, v_k$ we define the constraint t_0: $(\bigwedge_{i=1,\ldots,k} \varphi_i(\bar{a}_1, \ldots, \bar{a}_i), 1, 0)$. Notice that $\mathcal{A} \models t_0$ iff $\mathcal{A}$ satisfies $\varphi_i(\bar{a}_1, \ldots, \bar{a}_i)$, for each $i = 1, \ldots, k$.
2. For the l-th child $(l = 1, \ldots, n)$ of the node v_k we define the constraint $t_l = (\psi_l(\bar{a}, \bar{y}_l), k_l, j_l)$. Notice that $\mathcal{A} \models \bigcup_{l=1,\ldots,n} \{t_l\}$ iff $\delta_1^{j_1} \ldots \delta_n^{j_n}$ is in the language defined by ν, where j_l is $|\{\bar{b} \mid \mathcal{A} \models \psi_l(\bar{a}, \bar{b})\}|$, for all $l = 1, \ldots, n$.

Finally, Γ is defined as $\{t_0, \ldots, t_n\}$. We conclude with the following lemma, which completes the proof of Theorem 1.

Lemma 10

1. *If the program R does not typecheck w.r.t. d then there exists a choice of a path $\bar{v}$ in R and a choice of a vector ν, such that there exists a database $\mathcal{A}$ satisfying Γ.*
2. *For every choice of a path $\bar{v}$ in R and every choice of a vector ν, if there exists a database $\mathcal{A}$ satisfying Γ then R does not typecheck w.r.t. d.*
3. *The construction of Γ can be done in polynomial space.*

Acknowledgments. This paper would not have been possible without help of Jurek Marcinkowski, who spent a lot of time on discussions with me and suggested many ideas. Then I would like to thank Tomek Truderung for his suggestions and comments. I really appreciate all the help from both of them. Also, I thank the anonymous referees for their helpful comments.

References

1. S.Abiteboul, R. Hull, V. Vianu Foundations of Databases. Addison-Wesley 1995.
2. N. Alon, T. Milo, F. Neven, D. Suciu, V. Vianu Typechecking XML Views of Relational Databases, *ACM Transactions on Computational Logic*, Vol. 4, No. 3, July 2003, pages 315-354. (preliminary version in *Proceedings of the 16th LICS*, 421-430, 2001).
3. N. Alon, T. Milo, F. Neven, D. Suciu, and V. Vianu. XML with data values: Typechecking revisited. *Journal of Computer and System Sciences*, 66(4) pages 688-727, 2003.
4. M. Fernandez, D. Suciu, W. Tan. SilkRoute: Trading between relations and XML. In *Proceedings of the WWW9 Conference*. 2000, pages 723-746.
5. W. Martens and F. Neven. On the complexity of typechecking top-down XML transformations. *Theoretical Computer Science, 336(1)* pages 153-180, 2005.
6. W. Martens and F. Neven. Frontiers of tractability for typechecking simple XML transformations. *Journal of Computer and System Sciences, 2006.* to appear.
7. T. Milo, D. Suciu, and V. Vianu. Typechecking for XML transformers. *Journal of Computer and System Sciences*, 66(1) pages 66-97, 2003.

Exact XML Type Checking in Polynomial Time

Sebastian Maneth[1], Thomas Perst[2], and Helmut Seidl[2]

[1] Sydney Research Lab, National ICT Australia*
and School of Computer Science and Engineering, UNSW, Sydney, Australia
[2] Technische Universität München, Garching, Germany

Abstract. Stay macro tree transducers (smtts) are an expressive formalism for reasoning about XSLT-like document transformations. Here, we consider the exact type checking problem for smtts. While the problem is decidable, the involved technique of inverse type inference is known to have exponential worst-case complexity (already for top-down transformations without parameters). We present a new *adaptive* type checking algorithm based on forward type inference through exact characterizations of output languages. The new algorithm correctly type-checks all call-by-value smtts. Given that the output type is specified by a deterministic automaton, the algorithm is *polynomial-time* whenever the transducer uses only few parameters and visits every input node only constantly often. Our new approach can also be generalized from smtts to stay macro forest transducers which additionally support concatenation as built-in output operation.

1 Introduction

The extensible markup language XML is the current standard format for exchanging structured data. Its widespread use has initiated lots of work to support processing of XML on many different levels: customized query languages for XML, such as XQuery, transformation languages like XSLT, and programming language support either in the form of special purpose languages like XDuce, or of binding facilities for mainstream programming languages like JAXB. A central problem in XML processing is the *(static) type checking problem*: given an input and output type and a transformation f, can we statically check whether all outputs generated by f on valid inputs conform to the output type? Since XML types are intrinsically more complex than the types found in conventional programming languages, the type checking problem for XML poses new challenges on the design of type checking algorithms. The excellent survey [20] gives an overview of the different approaches to XML type checking.

In its most general setting, the type checking problem for XML transformations is undecidable. Hence, general solutions are bound to be approximative, but seem to work well for practical XSLT transformations [19]. Another approach is to restrict the types and transformations in such a way that type checking becomes decidable; we then refer to the problem as *exact XML type checking*. For the exact setting, types can be considered as regular or *recognizable* tree languages — thus capturing the expressive strength of virtually all known type formalisms for XML [21].

---

* National ICT Australia is funded through the Australian Governments *Backing Australias Ability* initiative, in part through the Australian Research Council.

T. Schwentick and D. Suciu (Eds.): ICDT 2007, LNCS 4353, pp. 254–268, 2007.

Even though the class of translations for which exact type checking is possible is surprisingly large [6,18,15], the price to be paid for exactness is also extremely high. The design space for exact type checking comes as a huge "exponential wasteland": even for simple top-down transformations, exact type checking is exponential-time complete [17]. For practical considerations, however, one is interested in useful subclasses of transformations for which exact type checking is tractable.

The fundamental work connecting pebble tree transducers with stay macro tree transducers [6] together with the type checking results of [15] have established (compositions of) stay macro tree transducers as an adequate formal model for XML transformations. In general, we are interested in type checking of transformations formulated through stay macro tree transducers (smtts). Given suitable descriptions (types) of admissible inputs and outputs for an smtt M, type checking M means to test whether all outputs produced by M on admissible inputs are again admissible. Our main result is: if admissible outputs are described by *deterministic* tree automata, then exact type checking can be done in polynomial time for a large class of practically interesting transformations obtained by putting only mild restrictions on the transducers.

Stay macro tree transducers are a combination of top-down tree transducers and macro grammars [9]. An smtt is a recursive first-order functional program that generates output trees by top-down pattern matching its first (tree) argument while possibly accumulating intermediate results in additional (tree) parameters. Alternatively, an smtt can be seen as a zero-pebble tree transducer without up-moves, but with states additionally equipped by accumulating parameters. We show that exact type checking can be solved in polynomial time for any transformation realized by one smtt which translates each node of the input tree at most once in each processing step (*linear* smtts) or, more generally, which translates every node only constantly often (*b-bounded copying* smtts). Note that no restriction is put on the copying that the smtt applies to its accumulating parameters: parameters may freely be copied! Note further that the above results hold for *nondeterministic* transducers with call-by-value semantics. Technically, our contributions are the following. First, we generalize the well-known triple construction for context-free grammars to provide a general construction for smtts to produce only output trees from the language accepted by some deterministic finite automaton. Secondly, we use stay moves to cut down the numbers of function calls in right-hand sides which crucially affect the complexity of the construction. Also, we present a formulation through Datalog to obtain a practically efficient implementation. Then we exhibit subclasses for which our approach to type checking is provably efficient and present an adaptive algorithm which is correct for arbitrary smtts but automatically meets the improved time bounds on the provably efficient sub-classes. Finally, the new approach is generalized from smtts to stay macro forest transducers which additionally provide built-in support for concatenation of forests.

Related Work. Approximative type checking for XML transformations is typically based on (subclasses of) recognizable tree languages. Using XPath as pattern language, XQuery [1] is a functional language for querying XML documents. It is strongly-typed and type checking is performed via type inference rules computing approximative types for each expression. Approximative type inference is also used in XDuce [13] and its follow-up version CDuce [10]; navigation and deconstruction are based on an extension of the pattern matching mechanism of functional languages with regular expression constructs. Recently, Hosoya et al. proposed a type checking system based on the approximative type inference of [12] for parametric polymorphism for XML [11]. Type variables are interpreted as markings indicating the parameterized subparts. In [19] a sound type checking algorithm is proposed (originally developed for the Java-based language XACT [14]) based on an XSLT flow analysis that determines the possible outcomes of pattern matching operations; for the benefit of better performance the algorithm deals with regular approximations of possible outputs.

Milo et al. [18] propose the k-pebble tree transducer (k-ptt) as a formal model for XML transformations, and show that exact type checking can be done for k-ptts using *inverse* type inference. The latter means to start with an output type O of a transformation f and then to construct the type of the inputs by backwards translating O through f. Each k-pebble transducer can be simulated by compositions of $k+1$ smtts [6], thus, type checking can be solved in time (iterated) exponential in the number of used pebbles. Recently [15] it was shown that inverse type inference can be done for a transformation language providing all standard features of most XML transformation languages using a simulation by at most three smtts. Inverse type inference is used in [16,17] to identify subclasses of top-down XML transformation which have tractable exact type checking. We note that the classes considered there are incomparable to the ones considered in this paper.

2   Stay Macro Tree Transducers

An XML document can be seen as a sequential representation of sequences of unranked trees also called hedges or *forests*. Here is a small example document:

```
<mbox>
  <mail>
    <sender> Homer Simpson </sender>
    <address> homer@simpson.com </address>
    <subject> CONFIDENTIAL </subject>
    <body> ... </body> </mail>
  <spam><mail> ...
    <subject> V.I.A.G.R.A. </subject>
    ... </mail></spam></mbox>
<trash> ... </trash>
```

This example represents a mail file, where the elements mbox and trash collect the incoming and deleted mails, respectively. Besides mail elements, the mbox also contains mails inside a spam element indicating that these mails have been identified as spam, e.g., by some automated filter.

Rather than on forests, stay macro tree transducers work on *ranked* trees. For a finite (ranked) alphabet Σ the set T_Σ of ranked trees over Σ is defined by: $t ::= a(t_1, \ldots, t_n) \mid b$, where $a, b \in \Sigma$ are symbols of rank n and zero, respectively; thus, we assume that we are given a fixed rank for every element of Σ. Often, we consider constructor applications together with leaf nodes by allowing n to equal 0. For a set

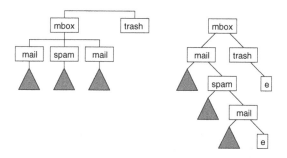

Fig. 1. An unranked forest and its binary encoding

$Y = \{y_1, y_2, \dots\}$ of variables of rank 0, $\mathcal{T}_\Sigma(Y)$ denotes the set of trees over Σ and Y. In the following we use the term 'tree' as a synonym for *ranked tree*.

In order to define stay macro tree transducers on XML documents, we rely on ranked tree representations of forests, e.g., through binary trees. The empty forest then is represented by a leaf e; the content of an element node a is coded as the left child of a while the forest of right siblings of a is represented as the right child (cf. first-child next-sibling encoding). Accordingly, the ranks of symbols are either zero or two.

Figure 1 illustrates this relationship between unranked trees and their representation as binary trees. Consider for example a transformation which cleans up the mail element by moving all sub-documents marked by spam into trash, while leaving all mail elements untouched. For our example document, the transformation produces:

```
<mbox>
  <mail>
    <sender> Homer Simpson </sender>
    <address> homer@simpson.com </address>
    <subject> CONFIDENTIAL </subject>
    <body> ... </body></mail></mbox>
<trash>
  <spam><mail> ...
    <subject> V.I.A.G.R.A. </subject>
    ... </mail></spam> ... </trash>
```

Using our representation of forests by binary trees (Fig. 1), this transformation is realized by a tree transducer with the following rules:

$$\begin{array}{ll}
1 & q(\mathtt{mbox}(x_1, x_2)) \qquad \to \mathtt{mbox}(q_1(x_1), p(x_2, q_2(x_1))) \\
2 & p(\mathtt{trash}(x_1, x_2), y_1) \to \mathtt{trash}(app(x_1, y_1), \mathtt{e}),
\end{array}$$

together with a function q_1 for collecting all ordinary mails in mbox

$$\begin{array}{ll}
3 & q_1(\mathtt{mail}(x_1, x_2)) \qquad \to \mathtt{mail}(cp(x_1), q_1(x_2)) \\
4 & q_1(\mathtt{spam}(x_1, x_2)) \qquad \to q_1(x_2) \\
5 & q_1(\mathtt{e}) \qquad\qquad\qquad \to \mathtt{e},
\end{array}$$

as well as a function q_2 for collecting the spam mails in mbox

$$
\begin{array}{lll}
_6 & q_2(\mathtt{mail}(x_1, x_2)) & \rightarrow q_2(x_2) \\
_7 & q_2(\mathtt{spam}(x_1, x_2)) & \rightarrow \mathtt{spam}(cp(x_1), q_2(x_2)) \\
_8 & q_2(\mathtt{e}) & \rightarrow \mathtt{e}
\end{array}
$$

where function *app* in line 2 is meant to copy the content of trash in front of the accumulating parameter, here containing the spam elements collected by the call q_2. Likewise, function *cp* is meant to produce an exact copy of its input.

Formally, a *stay macro tree transducer* M (smtt for short) is a tuple (Q, Σ, R, Q_0) where Q is the (ranked) set of function names (or states), Σ is the (ranked) alphabet of input and output symbols, $Q_0 \subseteq Q$ is the set of initial functions, and R is a finite set of rules of the form

$$
q(x_0, y_1, \ldots, y_k) \rightarrow t \qquad \text{or} \qquad q(\mathtt{a}(x_1, \ldots, x_n), y_1, \ldots, y_k) \rightarrow t
$$

where $q \in Q$ is of rank k, $\mathtt{a} \in \Sigma$ is of rank n, $x_0, x_1, \ldots, x_n$ are input variables, $y_1, \ldots, y_k, k \geq 0$ are the accumulating parameters of q, and t is an expression describing the output actions of the corresponding rule. Possible action expressions are:

$$
t \quad ::= \quad \mathtt{b}(t_1, \ldots, t_m) \mid y_j \mid q'(x_i, t_1, \ldots, t_m),
$$

where $\mathtt{b}$ is a label of an output node, y_j is one of the accumulating parameters $(1 \leq j \leq k)$, $q' \in Q$ of rank m, and x_i is one of the input variables of the left-hand side. Also, we assume that initial function symbols $q_0 \in Q_0$ have no accumulating parameters. The rules which do not process input symbols are called *stay*-rules. Transducers without stay-rules are also called (ordinary) mtts[1].

Intuitively, the meaning of the action expressions is as follows: The output can either be an element $\mathtt{b}$ whose content is recursively determined, the content of one of the accumulating parameters y_j, or a recursive call to some function q' on the i-th subtree of the current input node or on the current input node itself. Thus, the transformation of an smtt M starts at the root node of the input with one of the initial functions. A function q with actual accumulating parameters $t_1, \ldots, t_k$ is applied to an input subtree $s = \mathtt{a}(s_1, \ldots, s_n)$ as follows. If a stay rule $q(x_0, y_1, \ldots, y_k) \rightarrow t$ is chosen for q, s and the t_j are substituted in t for x_0 and the variables y_j, respectively. If an ordinary rule $q(\mathtt{a}(x_1, \ldots, x_n), y_1, \ldots, y_k) \rightarrow t'$ for q is chosen, the subterms s_i and t_j are substituted in t' for the variables x_i and y_j, respectively. Since function calls may be nested, the order in which they are evaluated matters. In *outside-in* (OI) or *call-by-name* evaluation order, outermost calls are evaluated first. The parameters of a function call may themselves contain function calls which then are transferred to the body in an unevaluated form [8]. In this paper, however, we consider the *inside-out* (IO) evaluation order. This

---

[1] Note that in [15], smtts are defined in a slightly different way. The rules there are of the form $q(x_0 \text{ as } \mathtt{a}(x_1, \ldots, x_n), \ldots) \rightarrow t$ where variable x_0 is bound to the current node and x_0 as well as $x_1, \ldots, x_n$ can occur in the right-hand side t. In our nondeterministic setting both formats can be converted into each other by means of a polynomial algorithm.

order corresponds to *call-by-value* parameter passing as provided by mainstream programming languages like C or OCaml. The inside-out strategy evaluates innermost calls first, meaning that fully evaluated output trees are passed in accumulating parameters.

As in [23], we will not use an operational semantics of smtts based on rewriting, but prefer a denotational formulation which greatly simplifies proof arguments. Thus, the meaning $[\![q]\!]$ of state q of M with k accumulating parameters is defined as a function from input trees to sets of trees with parameters in $Y = \{y_1, \ldots, y_k\}$, i.e., $[\![q]\!] : \mathcal{T}_\Sigma \to 2^{\mathcal{T}_\Sigma(Y)}$. When, during a computation, we evaluate an innermost call $q(s, t_1, \ldots, t_k)$, it suffices to substitute actual parameters t_j for the formal parameters y_j of all terms from $[\![q]\!](s)$ to obtain the set of produced outputs. The values $[\![q]\!]$ for all q are jointly defined as the least functions satisfying:

$$\begin{array}{llll}
[\![q]\!](s) & \supseteq [\![t[s/x_0]]\!] & \text{for rule} & q(x_0, \boldsymbol{y}) \to t \\
[\![q]\!](\mathsf{a}(s_1, \ldots, s_d)) & \supseteq [\![t'[s_1/x_1, \ldots, s_d/x_d]]\!] & \text{for rule} & q(\mathsf{a}(x_1, \ldots, x_d), \boldsymbol{y}) \to t'
\end{array}$$

where $\boldsymbol{y}$ denotes the sequence $y_1, \ldots, y_k$ and

$$\begin{array}{rl}
[\![y_j]\!] = & \{y_j\} \\
[\![\mathsf{b}(t_1, \ldots, t_m)]\!] = & \{\mathsf{b}(t_1', \ldots, t_m') \mid t_i' \in [\![t_i]\!]\} \\
[\![q'(s', t_1, \ldots, t_l)]\!] = & \{t'[t_1'/y_1, \ldots, t_l'/y_l] \mid t' \in [\![q']\!](s'), t_i' \in [\![t_i]\!]\},
\end{array}$$

Here, $t[t''/z]$ denotes the substitution of the tree t'' for all occurrences of the variable z in tree t. Note that the call-by-value semantics is reflected in the last equation: the same trees t_i' are used for all occurrences of a variable y_i in the tree t' corresponding to a potential evaluation of the function symbol q'. The transformation τ_M realized by the smtt M on an input tree s and sets S of input trees, respectively, is thus defined by:

$$\tau_M(s) = \bigcup \{[\![q_0]\!](s) \mid q_0 \in Q_0\} \quad \text{and} \quad \tau_M(S) = \bigcup \{\tau_M(s) \mid s \in S\}.$$

3   General Properties of SMTTs

Since we are concerned with techniques for type checking, we need to define the type of the input and output language of a transformation. Usually, types for XML documents are given by a document type definition (DTD) [28] or by a schema (using, e.g., RELAX NG [3]).

A convenient abstraction of the existing XML type formalisms are recognizable (or: regular) tree languages [21,22]. In the context of this work we use bottom-up tree automata to define recognizable tree languages. As usual, a *bottom-up finite state tree automaton* (fta) is a tuple $A = (P, \Sigma, \delta, F)$ where P is a finite set of states, $F \subseteq P$ is a set of accepting states, and $\delta \subseteq P \times \Sigma \times P^k$ is a set of transitions of the form $(p, \mathsf{a}, p_1 \ldots p_k)$ where a is a symbol of rank k from the alphabet Σ and $p, p_1, \ldots, p_k$ are states in P. A transition $(p, \mathsf{a}, p_1 \ldots p_k)$ denotes that if A arrives in state p_i after processing the tree t_i, then it can assign state p to the tree $\mathsf{a}(t_1, \ldots, t_k)$. A run of A on a tree $t \in \mathcal{T}_\Sigma$ is a mapping which assigns to each node v of t a state $r(v) \in P$ w.r.t. δ. The tree language $\mathcal{L}(A)$ accepted by A consists of the trees $t \in \mathcal{T}_\Sigma$ by which A can reach an accepting state.

Coming back to our example, an fta describing (the binary representation of) valid mailbox documents before applying the transformation can have as set of states $P = \{p_{\text{mbox}}, p_{\text{e}}, p_{\text{mail}}, p_{\text{trash}}, p_{\text{spam}}, p_{\text{content}}, \ldots\}$ and as set of transitions:

$$\delta = \{ \ (p_{\text{mbox}}, \text{mbox}, \ p_{\text{spam}}p_{\text{trash}}), \quad (p_{\text{e}}, \quad \text{e}),$$
$$(p_{\text{spam}}, \text{mail}, \ p_{\text{content}}p_{\text{spam}}), \ (p_{\text{spam}}, \text{mail}, p_{\text{content}}p_{\text{e}}),$$
$$(p_{\text{spam}}, \text{spam}, \ p_{\text{mail}}p_{\text{spam}}), \quad (p_{\text{spam}}, \text{spam}, p_{\text{mail}}p_{\text{e}}),$$
$$(p_{\text{mail}}, \text{mail}, \ p_{\text{content}}p_{\text{mail}}), \ (p_{\text{mail}}, \text{mail}, p_{\text{content}}p_{\text{e}}),$$
$$(p_{\text{trash}}, \text{trash}, \ p_{\text{spam}}p_{\text{e}}), \quad (p_{\text{mbox}}, \text{mbox}, p_{\text{e}}p_{\text{trash}}), \ldots \ \},$$

where p_{content} is the state characterizing valid content of mails where we have omitted further states and transitions for checking validity of, e.g., sender, address, subject, body etc. According to this automaton, mbox contains a possibly empty sequence of mail and spam elements where every spam element contains one mail element.

In the following, we will not mention explicitly given input types in our theorems. Instead, we implicitly assume that this type has been encoded into the smtt. This can be done as follows. Assume that the input type S is given by a (possibly nondeterministic) finite tree automaton A. From an smtt M, we then build a new smtt M_A whose function symbols are pairs consisting of a function of M and an automaton state of A. E.g., from a rule $q(a(x_1, x_2), y_1) \rightarrow b(q_1(x_1, y_1), q_2(x_2, y_1))$ we obtain the following new rule

$$\langle q, p \rangle(a(x_1, x_2), y_1) \rightarrow b(\langle q_1, p_1 \rangle(x_1, y_1), \langle q_2, p_2 \rangle(x_2, y_1))$$

if (p, a, p_1p_2) is a transition of A. Thus, the predecessor state p_i corresponds to the input variable x_i and therefore occurs in the right-hand side as the second component in recursive calls on x_i. In order to deal with variables x_i not occurring in the right-hand side, we introduce extra functions $\text{check}_{p'}$ for every state p' of A such that $\text{check}_{p'}(s, y_1)$ produces y_1 iff there is a run of A on s resulting in state p'. The new set of initial states then is the set of all pairs $\langle q_0, f \rangle$ consisting of an initial state of M and an accepting state of A. In particular, the new smtt M_A is of size $\mathcal{O}(|M| \cdot |A|)$. Since the construction of M_A does not add new function calls in rules of M, M_A is linear in $x_0, x_1, \ldots$ if M is, and M_A is syntactically b-bounded if M is, cf. Sections 4 and 5.

As usual, the *size* $|M|$ of an smtt M is the sum of the sizes of all its rules where the size of a rule is defined as the sum of the sizes of the terms representing the left- and right-hand sides of the rule. The size $|A|$ of a finite automaton A is defined analogously. The most basic problem for a given smtt M is to decide whether or not the translation of M is non-empty. For this problem we recall:

Theorem 1. *Deciding whether $\tau_M \neq \emptyset$ for an smtt M is DEXPTIME-complete.*

Proof. The lower bound follows since translation non-emptiness is DEXPTIME-hard already in absence of accumulating parameters, i.e., for top-down tree transducers [26].

Since we will heavily rely on this algorithm, we briefly sketch the construction for the upper bound. Assume that $M = (Q, \Sigma, R, Q_0)$ and, w.l.o.g., that for every function $q \in Q$ with k accumulating parameters there is a rule $q(x_0, y_1, \ldots, y_k) \rightarrow q(x_0, y_1, \ldots, y_k)$. These rules will be used when checking the nonemptiness of several states simultaneously where for some states stay moves are selected.

For every subset $B \subseteq Q$, we introduce a propositional variable $[B]$ where $[B] = $ true denotes the fact that $\exists t \in T_\Sigma \; \forall q \in B : \; [\![q]\!](t) \neq \emptyset$. In particular, for the empty set we have the fact $[\emptyset] \Leftarrow$ true. We then consider the set of all propositional implications

$$[B] \;\Leftarrow\; [B_1]$$

for all selections of rules $q(x_0, y_1, \ldots, y_k) \to t_q \;\in\; R, q \in B$, with $B_1 = \{p \in Q \mid \exists q \in B : \; p(x_0, \ldots) \text{ occurs in } t_q\}$, as well as all implications

$$[B] \;\Leftarrow\; [B_1] \wedge \ldots \wedge [B_n],$$

for which there exists an a and a selection of rules $q(a(x_1, \ldots, x_n), y_1, \ldots, y_k) \to t'_q \;\in\; R, q \in B$, where $B_i = \{p \in Q \mid \exists q \in B : \; p(x_i, \ldots) \text{ occurs in } t'_q\}$.

Let $\mathcal{C}_M$ denote this system of implications. By construction, the size of $\mathcal{C}_M$ is exponential in the size of M. Moreover, the translation of M is nonempty iff, for some $q \in Q_0$, $[\{q\}] = $ true follows from $\mathcal{C}_M$. Since systems of propositional Horn clauses can be solved in linear time, the assertion follows.   □

Next, we show how to effectively restrict a given smtt so that it only produces output trees in a given recognizable output tree language. In fact, the corresponding construction is a straightforward generalization of the triple construction known for context-free grammars. In case of smtts, the construction is simpler if we additionally assume that the recognizable tree language, is given by a *deterministic* finite tree automaton. As usual, we call an fta $A = (P, \Sigma, \delta, F)$ *deterministic* (dfta) if for each symbol $a \in \Sigma$ of rank $k \geq 0$ and every tuple $p_1 \ldots p_k$ of states, there is exactly one state p with $(p, a, p_1 \ldots p_k) \in \delta$, i.e., δ is a function $\delta : \Sigma \times P^k \to P$. For a given symbol a we also define $\delta_a : P^k \to P$.

In our example, the output type could, e.g., indicate that after transformation, the element mbox should contain only a list of mail elements. For this purpose we can use a deterministic fta with set of states $\{p_e, p_{trash}, p_{mail}, p_{spam}, p_{mbox}, p_{content}, p_{fail}, \ldots\}$, where state $p_{content}$ codes that a mail has a correct content. The leaf e is accepted by the state p_e. For all other symbols, we only list the transitions not resulting in the error state p_{fail}.

e	
	p_e

mbox	p_{trash}
p_{mail}	p_{mbox}
p_e	p_{mbox}

trash	p_e
p_{spam}	p_{trash}
p_{mail}	p_{trash}
p_e	p_{trash}

Each table represents δ for the label given in its upper left corner. States in the first row are possible states for the right child, and accordingly states in the first column are possible states for the left child. The transitions for mail and spam are defined as:

mail	p_e	p_{mail}	p_{spam}
$p_{content}$	p_{mail}	p_{mail}	p_{spam}

spam	p_e	p_{mail}	p_{spam}
$p_{content}$	p_{spam}	p_{spam}	p_{spam}

Theorem 2. *Assume M is an smtt and A is a dfta. Then there is an smtt M_A with*

$$\tau_{M_A}(t) \;=\; \tau_M(t) \cap \mathcal{L}(A)$$

for all $t \in \mathcal{T}_\Sigma$. The smtt M_A can be constructed in time $\mathcal{O}(N \cdot n^{k+1+d})$ where N is the size of M, k is the maximal number of accumulating parameters of a function symbol of M, d is the maximal number of function occurrences in any right-hand side, and n is the size of the finite tree automaton A.

Proof. Let $M = (Q, \Sigma, R, Q_0)$ and $A = (P, \Sigma, \delta, P_F)$. The set of function symbols of the new smtt M_A consists of all tuples $\langle q, p_0 p_1 \dots p_k \rangle$ where $q \in Q$ is a function symbol of the original smtt of rank k and $p_0, \dots, p_k \in P$ are states of the dfta A. The new function symbol $\langle q, p_0 \dots p_k \rangle$ is meant to generate all trees t with variables from $y_1, \dots, y_k$ for which there is a run of A starting at the leaves y_i with states p_i and reaching the root of t in state p_0. Therefore, the intersection smtt M_A has the rules:

$$\langle q, p_0 \dots p_k \rangle (r, y_1, \dots, y_k) \;\to\; t'$$

for every rule $q(r, y_1, \dots, y_k) \to t$ of M with either $r = x_0$ or $r = a(x_1, \dots, x_d)$, and $t' \in \mathcal{T}^{p_0 \dots p_k}[t]$. The sets $\mathcal{T}^{p_0 \dots p_k}[t]$ represent all right-hand sides, where the occurrences of variables y_i are annotated with state p_i and the root node is annotated with p_0. They are inductively defined by:

$$
\begin{aligned}
\mathcal{T}^{p_i p_1 \dots p_k}[y_i] &= \{y_i\} \\
\mathcal{T}^{p_0 p_1 \dots p_k}[a(t_1, \dots, t_m)] &= \{a(t'_1, \dots, t'_m) \mid \delta_a(p'_1, \dots, p'_m) = p_0 \wedge \\
&\qquad\qquad \forall i: t'_i \in \mathcal{T}^{p'_i p_1 \dots p_k}[t_i]\} \\
\mathcal{T}^{p_0 p_1 \dots p_k}[q'(x_j, t_1, \dots, t_m)] &= \{\langle q', p_0 p'_1 \dots p'_m \rangle (x_j, t'_1, \dots, t'_m) \mid \\
&\qquad\qquad \forall i: t'_i \in \mathcal{T}^{p'_i p_1 \dots p_k}[t_i]\}
\end{aligned}
$$

By fixpoint induction, we verify for every state q of rank $k \ge 0$, every input tree $s \in \mathcal{T}_\Sigma$ and states $p_0, \dots, p_k$ that:

$$[\![\langle q, p_0 \dots p_k \rangle]\!](s) = [\![q]\!](s) \cap \{t \in \mathcal{T}_\Sigma(Y) \mid \delta^*(t, p_1 \dots p_k) = p_0\} \quad (*)$$

where $Y = \{y_1, \dots, y_k\}$ and δ^* is the extension of the transition function of A to trees containing variables from Y, namely, for $\underline{p} = p_1 \dots p_k$:

$$
\begin{aligned}
\delta^*(y_i, \underline{p}) &= p_i \\
\delta^*(a(t_1, \dots, t_m), \underline{p}) &= \delta_a(\delta^*(t_1, \underline{p}), \dots, \delta^*(t_m, \underline{p}))
\end{aligned}
$$

The set of new initial function symbols then consists of all $\langle q_0, p_f \rangle$ where $q_0 \in Q_0$ and p_f is an accepting state of A. Then the correctness of the construction follows from $(*)$.

For an smtt of size N with at most k parameters and at most d occurrences of states in right-hand sides, and a tree automaton with n states, the intersection smtt is of size $\mathcal{O}(N \cdot n^{k+1+d})$: there can be in the worst case n^{k+1} copies of a rule of the smtt M, and for each function occurrence in the right-hand side we may choose an arbitrary output states. This completes the proof.   □

Note that in general, the number d of occurrences of states in a right-hand side can be arbitrarily large. SMtts, however, allow a construction which cuts down the depth of right-hand sides to at most 2. We have:

Proposition 3. *For every smtt M, an smtt M' can be constructed with:*

1. *The translations of M and M' agree;*
2. *Whenever a right-hand side t of M' is not contained in $T_{\Sigma}(Y)$, then the depth of t is bounded by 2;*
3. *The maximal number of states in a right-hand side of M' is at most $k + 1$;*
4. *The size of M' is bounded by $\mathcal{O}(|M| \cdot k^2)$*

where k is the maximum of the maximal rank of output symbols and the maximal number of accumulating parameters of a state of M.

The idea of Proposition 3 is to split the right-hand sides into their subterms and to organize the execution by stay-rules. In this way, for every internal (i.e., non-root and non-leaf) node (of rank r) in the right-hand side of a rule of M, the transducer M' has a new state of rank r. Clearly, r is bounded by the maximum rank of states and output symbols of M. Moreover, if the corresponding left-hand side of M is a state with m parameters, then each new state also has rank m. This means that m parameters are passed in each of the new rules, which explains the size increase of at most k^2. Note that, given some input tree s, if there is a computation of M using n sequential rule applications (in the conventional term rewriting sense), then there is a corresponding computation of M' with at most $c \cdot n$ rule applications, where c is the size of the largest right-hand side of the rules of M.

4 Linear SMTTs

In this section we prove that type checking is in PTIME for smtts with a bounded number of parameters which process every node of the input tree at most once. Syntactically, the latter can be guaranteed by requiring that in every right-hand side, each input variable x_i occurs at most once. Mtts satisfying this restriction are called *linear* [8].

Note that linearity for an smtt implies that the number of function calls in right-hand sides is bounded by the maximal rank of input symbols (in our case: 2). Here, we observe for linear smtts that their output languages can be described by means of rules where the input arguments of all occurring function symbols is simply deleted. Accordingly, the resulting rules no longer specify a transformation but generate output trees. A set of rules which we obtain in this way, constitutes a *context-free tree grammar* (cftg). As an example of a linear smtt consider the smtt q_1 (lines 3-5 in our mail transformation). The grammar characterizing q_1's output language looks as follows:

$$q_1 \rightarrow \mathtt{mail}(cp, q_1) \mid q_1 \mid \mathsf{e}$$

where q_1, cp are nonterminals. Note that selection of rules depending on input symbols now is replaced with nondeterministic choice.

Context-free tree grammars were invented in the 70s [24]. See [7] for a comprehensive study of their basic properties. Formally, a cftg G can be represented by a tuple (E, Σ, P, E_0) where E is a finite ranked set of function symbols or nonterminals, $E_0 \subseteq E$ is a set of initial symbols of rank 0, Σ is the ranked alphabet of terminal nodes and P is a set of rules of the form $q(y_1, \ldots, y_k) \rightarrow t$ where $q \in E$ is a nonterminal of rank $k \geq 0$. The right-hand side t is a tree built up from variables $y_1, \ldots, y_k$ by means of application of nonterminal and terminal symbols. In the example, we have represented the cftg only by its set of rules. As for smtts, inside-out (IO) and outside-in evaluation order for nonterminal symbols must be distinguished [7]. Here, we use the IO or call-by-value evaluation order. The least fixpoint semantics for the cftg G is obtained straightforwardly along the lines for smtts — simply by removing the corresponding input components (and the substitution σ when evaluating right-hand sides). In particular, this semantics assigns to every nonterminal q of rank $k \geq 0$, a set $[\![q]\!] \subseteq \mathcal{T}_\Sigma(Y)$ for $Y = \{y_1, \ldots, y_k\}$. The language generated by G is $\mathcal{L}(G) = \bigcup \{[\![q_0]\!] \mid q_0 \in E_0\}$.

By Corollary 5.7 of [8], the output language of a linear smtt M can be characterized by a cftg G_M which can be constructed from M in linear time. During this construction every rule $q(\pi, y_1, \ldots, y_k) \rightarrow t$ (π is either $\mathsf{a}(x_1, \ldots, x_n)$ or x_0) is rewritten as a production $q(y_1, \ldots, y_k) \rightarrow t'$, where t' is obtained from t by deleting all occurrences of input variables x_i. A formal proof that G_M indeed characterizes the output language of M can be found, e.g., in [8].

The characterization of smtt output languages by cftgs is useful because emptiness for (IO-)cftgs is decidable using a similar algorithm as the one for ordinary context-free (word) grammars (see, e.g., [4]). Thus we have:

Theorem 4. *It can be decided in linear time for a cftg G whether or not $\mathcal{L}(G) = \emptyset$.*

Here, we are interested in type checking transformations implemented through smtts, i.e., we want to check whether any output of an smtt M is accepted by an automaton A for the complement of the given output type. If M is linear, then the intersection smtt M_A is again linear — meaning that its range can be described by a cftg (thus generating all "illegal outputs" of M w.r.t. A). Therefore, Theorem 4 gives us:

Theorem 5. *Type checking for a linear smtt M can be done in time $\mathcal{O}(N \cdot n^{k+1+d})$ where N is the size of the smtt, k is the maximal number of accumulating parameters, d is the maximal rank of an input symbol and n is the size of a dfta for the output type.*

The complexity bound provided for the construction of Theorem 5 is a worst-case estimation. Instead, we want to point out that in case of linear smtts, the triple construction for M_A can be organized in such a way that only "useful" functions are constructed. In order to see this, we introduce for every q of M of rank k, a predicate $q/(k+1)$. Every rule $q(\_, y_1, \ldots, y_k) \rightarrow t$ of M then gives rise to the Datalog implication:

$$q(Y_0, \ldots, Y_k) \; \Leftarrow \; \mathcal{D}[t]_{Y_0}$$

where $\mathcal{D}[t]_X$ (X a variable) is defined by

$$
\begin{aligned}
\mathcal{D}[y_i]_X &= X \doteq Y_i \\
\mathcal{D}[\mathsf{a}(t_1, \ldots, t_m)]_X &= \delta(X, \mathsf{a}, X_1, \ldots, X_m) \wedge \mathcal{D}[t_1]_{X_1} \wedge \ldots \wedge \mathcal{D}[t_m]_{X_m} \\
\mathcal{D}[q'(t_1, \ldots, t_m)]_X &= q'(X, X_1, \ldots, X_m) \wedge \mathcal{D}[t_1]_{X_1} \wedge \ldots \wedge \mathcal{D}[t_m]_{X_m}
\end{aligned}
$$

and the variables $X_1, \ldots, X_m$ in the last two rows are fresh. For subsets $X, X_1, \ldots, X_k$ of the set of states of A, $\delta(X, \mathsf{a}, X_1, \ldots, X_k)$ denotes the fact that $(x, \mathsf{a}, x_1, \ldots, x_k)$ for all $x \in X$ and $x_i \in X_i$, $i = 1, \ldots, k$. A bottom-up evaluation of the resulting program computes for every $q/(k + 1)$, the set of all tuples $(p_0, \ldots, p_k)$ such that the translation of $\langle q, p_0 \ldots p_k \rangle$ is non-empty. If we additionally want to restrict these predicates only to tuples which may contribute to a terminal derivation of the initial nonterminal $\langle q_0, p_f \rangle$, we may top-down query the program with $\Leftarrow q_0(p_f)$. Practically, top-down solving organizes the construction such that only useful nonterminals of the intersection grammar are considered. Using this approach, the number of newly constructed nonterminals often will be much smaller than the bounds stated in the theorem.

The algorithm in the proof of Theorem 5 can also be applied to *non-linear* smtts. Then, the constructed Datalog program does no longer precisely characterize the nonempty functions of the intersection smtt because dependencies on input subtrees (viz. several function calls on the same input variable x_i) have been lost. Accordingly, a *superset* is returned. By means of cftgs, we can express this observation as follows:

Theorem 6. *Let G_M be the cftg constructed for an smtt M. Then $\tau_M(T_\Sigma) \subseteq \mathcal{L}(G_M)$.*

Since the cftg still provides a safe *superset* of produced outputs, type checking based on cftgs is sound in the sense that it accepts only correct programs. Consider a top-down transducer M with rule $q_0(x_0) \to c(p(x_0), p(x_0))$, where p realizes the identity using the rules $p(a(x_1)) \to a(p(x_1))$, $p(b(x_1)) \to a(p(x_1))$, $p(e) \to e$. In this case, the corresponding approximating cftg G_M is rather coarse: it generates $c(u, v)$ with $u, v \in \{a, b\}^* e$ (seen as monadic trees). Note, however, that exact tree copying can be realized through the use of parameters: the transducer with rules $q_0(x_0) \to q(x_0, p(x_0))$ and $q(x_0, y_1) \to c(y_1, y_1)$ realizes the same translation as M. However, now the cftg is not approximating but precisely captures the correct output language of M.

Note that when approximating the output languages of general smtts with cftgs, then we no longer may assume that the maximal number d of occurrences of nonterminals in a right-hand side of this grammar is bounded by a small constant. If d turns out to be unacceptably large, we still can apply Proposition 3 to limit the maximal number of occurrences of nonterminals in each right-hand side to a number k which is the maximum of the maximal rank of input symbols and the maximal number of parameters.

5 SMTTs with Bounded Copying

In this section we investigate in how far the exact techniques from the last section can be extended to more general classes of smtts. The goal again is to find precise and tractable characterizations of the output language. If the smtt is no longer linear, we must take into account that distinct function calls could refer to the same input node and therefore must be "glued together", i.e., be jointly evaluated.

In general, an arbitrary number of function calls may be applied to the same subdocument of the input. Quite a few useful transformations on the other hand consult every part of the input only a small number of times [25]. In our running example with `mail` and `spam`, every subtree of the input is processed at most twice. Therefore, we consider the subclass of smtts processing every subtree of the input at most b times. Thus in principle, b-bounded copying is a semantic property (cf. [5]).

Instead of dealing with a semantic definition, we find it more convenient to consider syntactic b-bounded copying only. For all states q of M, we define the maximal copy numbers $b[q]$ as the least fixpoint of a constraint system over $\mathcal{N} = \{-\infty < 1 < 2 < \ldots < \infty\}$, the complete lattice of natural numbers extended with $\pm\infty$. The constraint system consists of all constraints:

$$b[q] \geq 1$$

whenever q has a rule without calls in the right-hand side, together with all constraints:

$$b[q] \geq b[q_1] + \ldots + b[q_m]$$

where $q(\mathbf{a}(x_1, \ldots, x_l), y_1, \ldots, y_k) \to t$ is a rule of M and, for some i, $q_1, \ldots, q_m$ is the sequence of occurrences of calls $q_j(x_i, \ldots)$ for the same variable x_i in the right-hand side t. The constraints for stay-rules are constructed analogously. According to [27], the least solution of this constraint system can be constructed in linear time. Let $[q]$, q state of M, denote this least solution. Then the smtt M is *syntactically b-bounded* (*copying*) (or, a *b-smtt* for short) iff $[q] \leq b$ for all states of M. For the case where every input node is visited only a *small* number of times, we have:

Theorem 7. *For every syntactically b-bounded smtt M the following holds:*

1. *For every dfta A, the intersection smtt M_A is again syntactically b-bounded.*
2. *Translation emptiness can be decided in time $\mathcal{O}(|M|^b)$.*

Proof. For the first assertion, we claim that for every state q of M with k parameters, $b[q] \geq b[\langle q, p_0 \ldots p_k \rangle]$ for every sequence $p_0, \ldots, p_k$ of dfta states. This claim is easily verified by fixpoint induction w.r.t. the corresponding constraint systems characterizing $b[q]$ and $b[\langle q, p_0 \ldots p_k \rangle]$, respectively.

For a proof of the second assertion, we observe that, for syntactically b-bounded smtts, the propositional variables $[\{q\}]$, $q \in Q_0$, only depend on propositional variables $[B]$ for sets of states B of cardinality at most b.

Theorem 2 provides us with the technical background to prove our main theorem:

Theorem 8. *Type checking for a b-smtt M can be done in time $\mathcal{O}(N^b \cdot n^{b \cdot (k+1+d)})$ where N is the size of the smtt, k is the maximal number of accumulating parameters, d is the maximal rank of an input symbol and n is the size of a dfta for the output type.*

Instead of first testing b-boundedness and then running a specialized algorithm, we definitely prefer to have a general purpose algorithm which is correct for all smtts but additionally will meet the better complexity bounds on the exhibited subclasses. Indeed, our methods can be combined to construct such an adaptive algorithm. Given an smtt M and a dfta A, we proceed as follows:

1. For M, we compute an equivalent smtt M' where the numbers of occurrences of states in right-hand sides are bounded.
2. For M', we compute a safe superset of the states of the intersection smtt M'_A by means of top-down solving the corresponding Datalog program.
3. If no accepting states of A are found for the predicates $q_0/1$, q_0 initial state of M', the intersection is definitely empty, and we return.
   Otherwise, we precisely check the intersection smtt M'_A for emptiness through locally solving the corresponding system of propositional Horn clauses.

In the worst case, this algorithm will be exponential in the number of states of M and doubly exponential in the number of parameters and, due to the lower bounds for translation emptiness, nothing better can be hoped for. If on the other hand, the smtt is linear or syntactically b-bounded, the algorithm's complexity achieves the upper bounds of Theorems 5 and 8, respectively.

6   Macro Forest Transducers

Macro tree transducers have the disadvantage that they do not operate on forests directly. In [23], this limitation is lifted. Thus, *stay macro forest transducers* (smfts) generalize smtts by providing concatenation as additional operation on output forests. Although, smfts are more expressive than smtts, we obtain closure under intersection with recognizable forest languages also for output languages of smfts. This result is again based on a generalized triple construction. This time, however, we additionally must take care that our deterministic finite-state representation of the output type is compatible with concatenations. Therefore, we replace the concept of a dfta by a *finite forest monoid* (ffm) which is a finite monoid S extended with an operation up : $S \times \Sigma \to S$ that is used to handle upward movement in the forest (cf. [2]).

Since the notion of linearity for smfts is completely analogous to linearity for smtts, the type checking algorithm for a linear smft T is almost the same as for linear smtts. As in the ranked tree case, we can also extend the methods to syntactically b-bounded copying smfts (b-mfts) and obtain as our main result for smfts:

Theorem 9. *Type checking for a b-smft M can be done in time $\mathcal{O}(N^b \cdot n^{b \cdot (k+3)})$ where N is the size of the smft, k is the maximal number of accumulating parameters, and n is the size of a ffm for the output type.*

7   Conclusion

We have exhibited exact type checking algorithms for useful classes of XML transformations based on a precise characterization of output languages. For our approach, the input type could always be described by a nondeterministic finite automaton. In order to obtain tractable algorithms, we assumed for macro tree transducers, that output types are given as *deterministic* finite automata, whereas for macro forest transducers, we even assumed legal outputs to be represented by finite forest monoids. The latter was necessary to elegantly cope with the extra ability of concatenating separately produced output forests. Besides exact methods, we also provided approximate type checking based on context-free tree grammars. Finally, we combined our techniques to a simple adaptive algorithm which is provably efficient on the exhibited subclasses but may be promising also in other practical contexts. In case sets of possibly illegal outputs are described by cf tree grammars, we can also check in PTIME whether only *finitely many* illegal outputs may occur. This is called "almost always type checking" in [6]. It remains open in how far these techniques can be applied to smtts with outside-in (call-by-name) evaluation order.

References

1. S. Boag and D. Chamberlin et.al., editors. XQuery 1.0: An XML Query Language. World Wide Web Consortium Working Draft. Available at http://www.w3.org/TR/xquery/, 2003.
2. M. Bojańczyk and I. Walukiewicz. Unranked Tree Algebra. Technical report, University of Warsaw, 2005.
3. J. Clark and M. Murata et al. *RelaxNG Specification.* OASIS. Available online http://www.oasis-open.org/committees/relax-ng.
4. J. Engelfriet. Context-Free Graph Grammars. In G. Rozenberg and A. Salomaa, editors, *Handbook of Formal Languages*, pages 125–213. Springer-Verlag, Berlin, 1997.
5. J. Engelfriet and S. Maneth. Macro Tree Transducers, Attribute Grammars, and MSO Definable Tree Translations. *Inform. and Comput.*, 154(1):34–91, 1999.
6. J. Engelfriet and S. Maneth. A Comparison of Pebble Tree Transducers with Macro Tree Transducers. *Acta Informatica*, 39:613–698, 2003.
7. J. Engelfriet and E.M. Schmidt. IO and OI. (I&II). *J. Comp. Syst. Sci.*, 15:328–353, 1977. and 16:67–99, 1978.
8. J. Engelfriet and H. Vogler. Macro Tree Transducers. *J. Comp. Syst. Sci.*, 31:71–146, 1985.
9. M. J. Fischer. *Grammars with Macro-like Productions.* PhD thesis, Harvard University, Massachusetts, 1968.
10. A. Frisch. Regular Tree Language Recognition with Static Information. In *PLAN-X*, 2004.
11. H. Hosoya, A. Frisch, and G. Castagna. Parametric Polymorphism for XML. In *POPL*, pages 50–62. ACM Press, 2005.
12. H. Hosoya and B.C. Pierce. Regular expression pattern matching for XML. *Journal of Functional Programming*, 13(6):961–1004, 2002.
13. H. Hosoya and B.C. Pierce. XDuce: A Statically Typed XML Processing Language. *ACM Trans. Inter. Tech.*, 3(2):117–148, 2003.
14. C. Kirkegaard, A. Møller, and M.I. Schwartzbach. Static Analysis of XML Transformations in Java. *IEEE Trans. Soft. Eng.*, 30:181–192, 2004.
15. S. Maneth, A. Berlea, T. Perst, and H. Seidl. XML Type Checking with Macro Tree Transducers. In *PODS*, pages 283–294. ACM Press, 2005.
16. W. Martens and F. Neven. Frontiers of Tractability for Typechecking Simple XML Transformations. In *PODS*, pages 23–34. ACM Press, 2004.
17. W. Martens and F. Neven. On the complexity of typechecking top-down xml transformations. *Theor. Comput. Sci.*, 336:153–180, 2005.
18. T. Milo, D. Suciu, and V. Vianu. Typechecking for XML Transformers. *J. Comp. Syst. Sci.*, 66:66–97, 2003.
19. A. Møller, M. Olesen, and M. Schwartzbach. Static Validation of XSL Transformations. Technical Report RS-05-32, BRICS, October 2005.
20. A. Møller and M. I. Schwartzbach. The Design Space of Type Checkers for XML Transformation Languages. In *ICDT*, pages 17–36. Springer-Verlag, 2005.
21. M. Murata, D. Lee, and M. Mani. Taxonomy of XML Schema Languages using Formal Language Theory. In *Extreme Markup Languages*, 2000.
22. F. Neven. Automata Theory for XML Researchers. *SIGMOD Record*, 31(3):39–46, 2002.
23. T. Perst and H. Seidl. Macro Forest Transducers. *Inf. Proc. Letters*, 89:141–149, 2004.
24. W.C. Rounds. Mappings and Grammars on Trees. *Math. Systems Theory*, 4:257–287, 1970.
25. A. Schmidt, F. Waas, M. L. Kersten, M. J. Carey, I. Manolescu, and Ralph Busse. Xmark: A benchmark for XML data management. In *VLDB*, pages 974–985. Morgan Kaufmann, 2002.
26. H. Seidl. Haskell Overloading is DEXPTIME Complete. *Inf. Proc. Letters*, 52:57–60, 1994.
27. H. Seidl. Least Solutions of Equations over $\mathcal{N}$. In *ICALP*, pages 400–411. Springer, 1994.
28. W3C. *Extensible Markup Language (XML) 1.0*, second edition, 6 October 2000. Available online http://www.w3.org/TR/2000/REC-xml-20001006.

Optimizing Schema Languages for XML: Numerical Constraints and Interleaving

Wouter Gelade*, Wim Martens, and Frank Neven

Hasselt University and Transnational University of Limburg
School for Information Technology
{firstname.lastname}@uhasselt.be

Abstract. The presence of a schema offers many advantages in processing, translating, querying, and storage of XML data. Basic decision problems like equivalence, inclusion, and non-emptiness of intersection of schemas form the basic building blocks for schema optimization and integration, and algorithms for static analysis of transformations. It is thereby paramount to establish the exact complexity of these problems. Most common schema languages for XML can be adequately modeled by some kind of grammar with regular expressions at right-hand sides. In this paper, we observe that apart from the usual regular operators of union, concatenation and Kleene-star, schema languages also allow numerical occurrence constraints and interleaving operators. Although the expressiveness of these operators remain within the regular languages, their presence or absence has significant impact on the complexity of the basic decision problems. We present a complete overview of the complexity of the basic decision problems for DTDs, XSDs and Relax NG with regular expressions incorporating numerical occurrence constraints and interleaving. We also discuss chain regular expressions and the complexity of the schema simplification problem incorporating the new operators.

1 Introduction

XML is the lingua franca for data exchange on the Internet [1]. Within applications or communities, XML data is usually not arbitrary but adheres to some structure imposed by a schema. The presence of such a schema not only provides users with a global view on the anatomy of the data, but far more importantly, it enables automation and optimization of standard tasks like (*i*) searching, integration, and processing of XML data (cf., e.g., [11,20,23,40]); and, (*ii*) static analysis of transformations (cf., e.g., [2,15,24,30]). Decision problems like equivalence, inclusion and non-emptiness of intersection of schemas, hereafter referred to as *the basic decision problems*, constitute essential building blocks in solutions for the just mentioned optimization and static analysis problems. Additionally, the basic decision problems are fundamental for schema minimization (cf., e.g.,

---

* Research Assistant of the Fund for Scientific Research - Flanders (Belgium).

T. Schwentick and D. Suciu (Eds.): ICDT 2007, LNCS 4353, pp. 269–283, 2007.
© Springer-Verlag Berlin Heidelberg 2007

$$
\begin{array}{ll}
\text{shop} & \rightarrow \text{regular}^* \ \& \ \text{discount-box}^* \\
\text{regular} & \rightarrow \text{cd} \\
\text{discount-box} & \rightarrow \text{cd}^{[10,12]} \ \text{price} \\
\text{cd} & \rightarrow \text{artist} \ \& \ \text{title} \ \& \ \text{price}
\end{array}
$$

Fig. 1. A sample schema using the numerical occurrence and interleave operators. The schema defines a shop that sells CDs and offers a special price for boxes of 10–12 CDs.

[9,27]). Because of their widespread applicability, it is therefore important to establish the exact complexity of the basic decision problems for the various XML schema languages.

The most common schema languages for XML are DTD, XML Schema [36], and Relax NG [8] and can be modeled by grammar formalisms [29]. In particular, DTDs correspond to context-free grammars with regular expressions (REs) at right-hand sides, while Relax NG is abstracted by extended DTDs (EDTDs) [31] or equivalently, unranked tree automata [6], defining the regular unranked tree languages. While XML Schema is usually abstracted by unranked tree automata as well, recent results indicate that XSDs correspond to a strict subclass of the regular tree languages and are much closer to DTDs than to tree automata [26]. In fact, they can be abstracted by single-type EDTDs. As detailed in [25], the relationship between schema formalisms and grammars provides direct upper and lower bounds for the complexity of the basic decision problems.

A closer inspection of the various schema specifications reveals that the above abstractions in terms of grammars with regular expressions is too coarse. Indeed, in addition to the conventional regular expression operators like concatenation, union, and Kleene-star, the XML Schema and the Relax NG specification allow two other operators as well:

(1) Both the XML Schema and the Relax NG specification allow a certain form of unordered concatenation: the `ALL` and the `interleave` operator, respectively. This operator is actually the resurrection of the &-operator from SGML DTDs that was excluded from the definition of XML DTDs. Although there are restrictions on the use of `ALL` and `interleave`, we consider the operator in its unrestricted form. We refer by RE(&) to such regular expressions with the unordered concatenation operator.

(2) The XML Schema specification allows to express numerical occurrence constraints which define the minimal and maximal number of times a regular construct can be repeated. We refer by RE(#) to such regular expressions with numerical occurrence constraints.

We illustrate these additional operators in Figure 1. The formal definition is given in Section 2. Although the new operators can be expressed by the conventional regular operators, they cannot do so succinctly, which has severe implications on the complexity of the basic decision problems.

The goal of this paper is to study the complexity of the basic decision problems for DTDs, XSDs, and Relax NG with regular expressions extended with interleaving and numerical occurrence constraints. The latter class of regular expressions is denoted by $\mathrm{RE}(\#, \&)$. As observed in Section 5, the complexity of inclusion and equivalence of $\mathrm{RE}(\#, \&)$-expressions (and subclasses thereof) carries over to DTDs and single-type EDTDs. We therefore first establish the complexity of the basic decision problems for $\mathrm{RE}(\#, \&)$-expressions and frequently occurring subclasses. These results are summarized in Table 1 and Table 2. Of independent interest, we introduce $\mathrm{NFA}(\#, \&)$s, an extension of NFAs with counter and split/merge states for dealing with numerical occurrence constraints and interleaving operators. Finally, we revisit the simplification problem introduced in [26] for schemas with $\mathrm{RE}(\#, \&)$-expressions. That is, given an extended DTD, can it be rewritten into an equivalent DTD or a single-type EDTD?

In this paper, we do not consider deterministic or one-unambiguous regular expressions which form a strict subclass of the regular expressions [7]. The reason is two-fold. First of all, one-unambiguity is a highly debatable constraint (cf., e.g., pg 98 of [38] and [22,35]) which is only required for DTDs and XML Schema, not for Relax NG. Actually, the only direct advantage of one-unambiguity is that it gives rise to PTIME algorithms for some of the basic decision problems for standard regular expressions. The latter does not hold anymore for $\mathrm{RE}(\#, \&)$-expressions rendering the notion even less attractive. Indeed, already intersection for one-unambiguous regular expressions is PSPACE-hard [25] and inclusion for one-unambiguous $\mathrm{RE}(\#)$-expressions is coNP-hard [17]. A second reason is that, in contrast to conventional regular expressions, one-unambiguity is not yet fully understood for regular expressions with numerical occurrence constraints and interleaving operators. Some initial results are provided by Bruggemann-Klein, and Kilpeläinen and Tuhkanen who give algorithms for deciding one-unambiguity of $\mathrm{RE}(\&)$- and $\mathrm{RE}(\#)$-expressions, respectively [5,18]. No study investigating their properties has been undertaken. Such a study, although definitely relevant, is outside the scope of this paper.

Outline. In Section 2, we provide the necessary definitions. In Section 3, we define $\mathrm{NFA}(\#, \&)$. In Section 4 and Section 5, we establish the complexity of the basic decision problems for regular expressions and schema languages, respectively. We discuss simplification in Section 6. We conclude in Section 7. A version of this paper containing all proofs is available from the authors' webpages.

2 Definitions

2.1 Regular Expressions with Counting and Interleaving

For the rest of the paper, Σ always denotes a finite alphabet. A Σ-*symbol* (or simply symbol) is an element of Σ, and a Σ-*string* (or simply string) is a finite sequence $w = a_1 \cdots a_n$ of Σ-symbols. We define the length of w, denoted by $|w|$, to be n. We denote the empty string by ε. The set of *positions of w* is $\{1, \ldots, n\}$ and the *symbol of w at position i* is a_i. By $w_1 \cdot w_2$ we denote the *concatenation* of two strings w_1 and w_2. For readability, we usually denote the concatenation of w_1 and w_2 by $w_1 w_2$. The set of all strings is denoted by Σ^*. A

Table 1. Overview of new and known complexity results. All results are completeness results. The new results are printed in bold.

	INCLUSION	EQUIVALENCE	INTERSECTION
RE	PSPACE ([37])	PSPACE ([37])	PSPACE ([21])
RE(&)	EXPSPACE ([28])	EXPSPACE ([28])	**PSPACE**
RE(#) and RE(#, &)	**EXPSPACE**	**EXPSPACE**	**PSPACE**
NFA(#), NFA(&), and NFA(#, &)	**EXPSPACE**	**EXPSPACE**	**PSPACE**
DTDs with RE	PSPACE ([37])	PSPACE ([37])	PSPACE ([21])
DTDs with RE(#), RE(&), or RE(#, &)	**EXPSPACE**	**EXPSPACE**	**PSPACE**
single-type EDTDs with RE	PSPACE ([25])	PSPACE ([25])	EXPTIME ([25])
single-type EDTDs with RE(#), RE(&), or RE(#, &)	**EXPSPACE**	**EXPSPACE**	**EXPTIME**
EDTD with RE	EXPTIME ([34])	EXPTIME ([34])	EXPTIME ([33])
EDTDs with RE(#), RE(&), or RE(#, &)	**EXPSPACE**	**EXPSPACE**	**EXPTIME**

string language is a subset of Σ^*. For two string languages $L, L' \subseteq \Sigma^*$, we define their concatenation $L \cdot L'$ to be the set $\{w \cdot w' \mid w \in L, w' \in L'\}$. We abbreviate $L \cdot L \cdots L$ (i times) by L^i. By $w_1 \& w_2$ we denote the set of strings that is obtained by *interleaving* or *shuffling* w_1 and w_2 in every possible way. That is, for $w \in \Sigma^*$, $w \& \varepsilon = \varepsilon \& w = \{w\}$, and $a \cdot w_1 \& b \cdot w_2 = (\{a\} \cdot (w_1 \& b \cdot w_2)) \cup (\{b\} \cdot (a \cdot w_1 \& w_2))$. The operator $\&$ is then extended to languages in the canonical way.

The set of *regular expressions* over Σ, denoted by RE, is defined in the usual way: ε, and every Σ-symbol is a regular expression; and when r and s are regular expressions, then rs, $r + s$, and r^* are also regular expressions. By RE(#, &) we denote RE extended with two new operators: *interleaving* and *numerical occurrence constraints*. That is, when r and s are RE(#, &)-expressions then so are $r \& s$ and $r^{[k,\ell]}$ for $k, \ell \in \mathbb{N}$ with $k \leq \ell$ and $\ell > 0$. By RE(#) and RE(&), we denote RE extended only with counting and interleaving, respectively.

The language defined by a regular expression r, denoted by $L(r)$, is inductively defined as follows: $L(\varepsilon) = \{\varepsilon\}$; $L(a) = \{a\}$; $L(rs) = L(r) \cdot L(s)$; $L(r + s) = L(r) \cup L(s)$; $L(r^*) = \{\varepsilon\} \cup \bigcup_{i=1}^{\infty} L(r)^i$, $L(r^{[k,\ell]}) = \bigcup_{i=k}^{\ell} L(r)^i$; and, $L(r \& s) = L(r) \& L(s)$. The *size* of a regular expression r over Σ, denoted by $|r|$, is the number of Σ-symbols and operators occurring in r plus the sizes of the binary representations of the integers. By $r?$ and r^+, we abbreviate the expression $r + \varepsilon$ and rr^*, respectively. We assume familiarity with finite automata such as nondeterministic finite automata (NFAs) and deterministic finite automata (DFAs) [14].

2.2   Schema Languages for XML

The set of *unranked Σ-trees*, denoted by $\mathcal{T}_\Sigma$, is the smallest set of strings over Σ and the parenthesis symbols "(" and ")" such that, for $a \in \Sigma$ and $w \in (\mathcal{T}_\Sigma)^*$, $a(w)$ is in $\mathcal{T}_\Sigma$. So, a tree is either ε (empty) or is of the form $a(t_1 \cdots t_n)$ where each t_i is a tree. In the tree $a(t_1 \cdots t_n)$, the subtrees $t_1, \ldots, t_n$ are attached to the root labeled a. We write a rather than $a()$. Notice that there is no a priori bound on the number of children of a node in a Σ-tree; such trees are therefore *unranked*. For every $t \in \mathcal{T}_\Sigma$, the *set of nodes* of t, denoted by $\mathrm{Dom}(t)$, is the set defined as follows: (*i*) if $t = \varepsilon$, then $\mathrm{Dom}(t) = \emptyset$; and (*ii*) if $t = a(t_1 \cdots t_n)$, where each $t_i \in \mathcal{T}_\Sigma$, then $\mathrm{Dom}(t) = \{\varepsilon\} \cup \bigcup_{i=1}^n \{iu \mid u \in \mathrm{Dom}(t_i)\}$. In the sequel, whenever we say tree, we always mean Σ-tree. A *tree language* is a set of trees.

We make use of the following definitions to abstract from the commonly used schema languages:

Definition 1. Let $\mathcal{M}$ be a class of representations of regular string languages over Σ.

1. A *DTD($\mathcal{M}$)* over Σ is a tuple (Σ, d, s_d) where d is a function that maps Σ-symbols to elements of $\mathcal{M}$ and $s_d \in \Sigma$ is the start symbol. For convenience of notation, we denote (Σ, d, s_d) by d and leave the start symbol s_d implicit whenever this cannot give rise to confusion.

    A tree t *satisfies* d if (*i*) $\mathrm{lab}^t(\varepsilon) = s_d$ and, (*ii*) for every $u \in \mathrm{Dom}(t)$ with n children, $\mathrm{lab}^t(u1) \cdots \mathrm{lab}^t(un) \in L(d(\mathrm{lab}^t(u)))$. By $L(d)$ we denote the set of trees satisfying d.

2. An *extended DTD* (EDTD($\mathcal{M}$)) over Σ is a 5-tuple $D = (\Sigma, \Sigma', d, s, \mu)$, where Σ' is an alphabet of *types*, (Σ', d, s) is a DTD($\mathcal{M}$) over Σ', and μ is a mapping from Σ' to Σ.

    A tree t then *satisfies* an extended DTD if $t = \mu(t')$ for some $t' \in L(d)$. Here we abuse notation and let μ also denote its extension to define a homomorphism on trees. Again, we denote by $L(D)$ the set of trees satisfying D. For ease of exposition, we always take $\Sigma' = \{a^i \mid 1 \leq i \leq k_a, a \in \Sigma, i \in \mathbb{N}\}$ for some natural numbers k_a, and we set $\mu(a^i) = a$.

3. A *single-type EDTD* (EDTDst($\mathcal{M}$)) over Σ is an EDTD($\mathcal{M}$) $D = (\Sigma, \Sigma', d, s, \mu)$ with the property that for every $a \in \Sigma'$, in the regular expression $d(a)$ no two types b^i and b^j with $i \neq j$ occur.

We denote by EDTD, EDTD(#), EDTD(&), and EDTD(#,&), the classes EDTD(RE), EDTD(RE(#)), EDTD(RE(&)), and EDTD(RE(#, &)), respectively. The same notation is used for EDTDst and DTDs.

For clarity, we write $a \to r$ rather than $d(a) = r$ in examples and proofs. Following this notation, a simple example of an EDTD is the following:

$$
\begin{array}{ll}
\mathrm{shop}^1 \to (\mathrm{dvd}^1 + \mathrm{dvd}^2)^* \mathrm{dvd}^2 (\mathrm{dvd}^1 + \mathrm{dvd}^2)^* & \quad \mathrm{title}^1 \quad \to \varepsilon \\
\mathrm{dvd}^1 \to \mathrm{title}^1 \; \mathrm{price}^1 & \quad \mathrm{price}^1 \quad \to \varepsilon \\
\mathrm{dvd}^2 \to \mathrm{title}^1 \; \mathrm{price}^1 \; \mathrm{discount}^1 & \quad \mathrm{discount}^1 \to \varepsilon
\end{array}
$$

Here, dvd^1 defines ordinary DVDs, while dvd^2 defines DVDs on sale. The rule for shop^1 specifies that there should be at least one DVD on sale. Note that the above is not a single-type EDTD as dvd^1 and dvd^2 occur in the same rule.

As explained in [29,26], EDTDs and single-type EDTDs correspond to Relax NG and XML Schema, respectively.

2.3 Decision Problems

The following problems are fundamental to this paper.

Definition 2. Let $\mathcal{M}$ be a class of regular expressions, string automata, or extended DTDs. We define the following problems:

- INCLUSION for $\mathcal{M}$: Given two elements $e, e' \in \mathcal{M}$, is $L(e) \subseteq L(e')$?
- EQUIVALENCE for $\mathcal{M}$: Given two elements $e, e' \in \mathcal{M}$, is $L(e) = L(e')$?.
- INTERSECTION for $\mathcal{M}$: Given an arbitrary number of elements $e_1, \ldots, e_n \in \mathcal{M}$, is $\bigcap_{i=1}^{n} L(e_i) \neq \emptyset$?
- MEMBERSHIP for $\mathcal{M}$: Given an element $e \in \mathcal{M}$ and a string or a tree f, is $f \in L(e)$?

We recall the known results concerning the complexity of REs and EDTDs.

Theorem 3. *(1)* INCLUSION, EQUIVALENCE, *and* INTERSECTION *for REs are* PSPACE-*complete [21,37].*
(2) INCLUSION *and* EQUIVALENCE *for RE(&) are* EXPSPACE-*complete [28].*
(3) INCLUSION *and* EQUIVALENCE *for* $EDTD^{st}$ *are* PSPACE-*complete [25];* INTERSECTION *for* $EDTD^{st}$ *is* EXPTIME-*complete [25].*
(4) INCLUSION, EQUIVALENCE, *and* INTERSECTION *for EDTDs are* EXPTIME-*complete [33,34].*
(5) MEMBERSHIP *for RE(&) is* NP-*complete [28].*

3   Automata for Occurrence Constraints and Interleaving

We introduce the automaton model NFA($\#, \&$). In brief, an NFA($\#, \&$) is an NFA with two additional features: *(i)* split and merge transitions to handle interleaving; and, *(ii)* counting states and transitions to deal with numerical occurrence constraints. The idea of split and merge transitions stems from Jędrzejowicz and Szepietowski [16]. Their automata are more general as they can express shuffle-closure which is not regular. Counting states are also used in the counter automata of Kilpeläinen and Tuhkanen [19], and Reuter [32] although these counter automata operate quite differently from NFA($\#$)s. Zilio and Lugiez [10] also proposed an automaton model that incorporates counting and interleaving by means of Presburger formulas. None of the cited papers consider the complexity of the basic decision problems of their model. We will use NFA($\#, \&$)s for obtaining complexity upper bounds in Sections 4 and 5.

For readability, we denote $\Sigma \cup \{\varepsilon\}$ by Σ_ε. We then define an NFA($\#, \&$) as follows.

Definition 4. An NFA($\#, \&$) is a 5-tuple $A = (Q, \Sigma, s, f, \delta)$ where

- Q is a finite set of states. To every $q \in Q$, we associate a lower bound $\min(q) \in \mathbb{N}$ and an upper bound $\max(q) \in \mathbb{N}$.
- $s, f \in Q$ is the start and final state, respectively.
- δ is the transition relation and is a subset of the union of the following sets:

(1)	$Q \times \Sigma_\varepsilon \times Q$	ordinary transition (resets the counter)
(2)	$Q \times \{\text{store}\} \times Q$	transition that does not reset the counter
(3)	$Q \times \{\text{split}\} \times Q \times Q$	split transition
(4)	$Q \times Q \times \{\text{merge}\} \times Q$	merge transition

Let $\max(A) = \max\{\max(q) \mid q \in Q\}$ be the largest upper bound occurring in A. A *configuration* γ is a pair (P, α) where, $P \subseteq Q$ is a set of states and $\alpha : Q \to \{0, \ldots, \max(A)\}$ is the value function mapping states to the value of their counter. For a state $q \in Q$, we denote by α_q the value function mapping q to 1 and every other state to 0. The initial configuration γ_s is $(\{s\}, \alpha_s)$. The final configuration γ_f is $(\{f\}, \alpha_f)$. When α is a value function then $\alpha[q = 0]$ and $\alpha[q^{++}]$ denote the functions obtained from α by setting the value of q to 0 and incrementing the value of q by 1, respectively, while leaving all other values unchanged.

We now define the transition relation between configurations. Intuitively, the value of the state at which the automaton arrives is always incremented by one. When exiting a state, the state's counter is always reset to zero, except when we exit through a *counting transition*, in which case the counter remains the same. In addition, exiting a state through a non-counting transition is only allowed when the value of the counter lies between the allowed minimum and maximum. The latter, hence, ensures that the occurrence constraints are satisfied. *Split* and *merge transitions* start and close a parallel composition.

A configuration $\gamma' = (P', \alpha')$ *immediately follows* a configuration $\gamma = (P, \alpha)$ by reading $\sigma \in \Sigma_\varepsilon$, denoted $\gamma \to_{A,\sigma} \gamma'$, when one of the following conditions hold:

1. **(ordinary transition)** there is a $q \in P$ and $(q, \sigma, q') \in \delta$ such that $\min(q) \leq \alpha(q) \leq \max(q)$, $P' = (P - \{q\}) \cup \{q'\}$, and $\alpha' = \alpha[q = 0][q'^{++}]$. That is, A is in state q and moves to state q' by reading σ (note that σ can be ε). The latter is only allowed when the counter value of q is between the lower and upper bound. The state q is replaced in P by q'. The counter of q is reset to zero and the counter of q' is incremented by one.

2. **(counting transition)** there is a $q \in P$ and $(q, \text{store}, q') \in \delta$ such that $\alpha(q) < \max(q)$, $P' = (P - \{q\}) \cup \{q'\}$, and $\alpha' = \alpha[q'^{++}]$. That is, A is in state q and moves to state q' by reading ε when the counter of q has not reached its maximal value yet. The state q is replaced in P by q'. The counter of q is not reset but remains the same. The counter of q' is incremented by one.

3. **(split transition)** there is a $q \in P$ and $(q, \text{split}, q_1', q_2') \in \delta$ such that $\min(q) \leq \alpha(q) \leq \max(q)$, $P' = (P - \{q\}) \cup \{q_1', q_2'\}$, and $\alpha' = \alpha[q = 0][q_1'^{++}][q_2'^{++}]$. That is, A is in state q and splits into states q_1' and q_2' by reading ε when the counter value of q is between the lower and upper bound. The state q in P is replaced by (split into) q_1' and q_2'. The counter of q is reset to zero, and the counters of q_1' and q_2' are incremented by one.

4. **(merge transition)** there are $q_1, q_2 \in P$ and $(q_1, q_2, \text{merge}, q') \in \delta$ such that, for each $j = 1, 2$, $\min(q_j) \leq \alpha(q_j) \leq \max(q_j)$, $P' = (P - \{q_1, q_2\}) \cup \{q'\}$, and $\alpha' = \alpha[q_1 = 0][q_2 = 0][q'^{++}]$. That is, A is in states q_1 and q_2 and moves to state q' by reading ε when the respective counter values of q_1 and q_2 are between the lower and upper bounds. The states q_1 and q_2 in P are replaced by (merged into) q', the counters of q_1 and q_2 are reset to zero, and the counter of q' is incremented by one.

For a string w and two configurations γ, γ', we denote by $\gamma \Rightarrow_{A,w} \gamma'$ when there is a sequence of configurations $\gamma \rightarrow_{A,\sigma_1} \cdots \rightarrow_{A,\sigma_n} \gamma'$ such that $w = \sigma_1 \cdots \sigma_n$. The latter sequence is called a *run* when γ is the initial configuration γ_s. A string w is *accepted* by A iff $\gamma_s \Rightarrow_{A,w} \gamma_f$ with γ_f the final configuration. We usually denote $\Rightarrow_{A,w}$ simply by $\Rightarrow_w$ when A is clear from the context. We denote by $L(A)$ the set of strings accepted by A. The size of A, denoted by $|A|$, is $|Q| + |\delta| + \Sigma_{q \in Q} \log(\max(q))$. So, each $\max(q)$ is represented in binary.

An NFA(#) is an NFA(#, &) without split and merge transitions. An NFA(&) is an NFA(#, &) without counting transitions. An NFA is an NFA(#) without counting transitions. NFA(#, &) therefore accept all regular languages.

The next theorem shows the complexity of translating between RE(#, &) and NFA(#, &), and NFA(#, &) and NFA. In brief, the proof of part (1) is by induction on the structure of RE(#, &)-expressions. Figure 2 illustrates the inductive steps for expressions $r_1^{[k,\ell]}$ and $r_1 \& r_2$, employing counter, and split and merge states, respectively. For part (2), we define an NFA from an NFA(#, &) that keeps in its state the current configuration of the latter: i.e., a set of states and a value function.

Theorem 5. *(1) Given an RE(#, &)-expression r, an equivalent NFA(#, &) can be constructed in time polynomial in the size of r.*

(2) Given an NFA(#, &) A, an equivalent NFA can be constructed in time exponential in the size of A.

We next turn to the complexity of the basic decision problems for NFA(#, &).

Theorem 6. *(1)* EQUIVALENCE *and* INCLUSION *for NFA(#, &) is* EXPSPACE-*complete;*

(2) INTERSECTION *for NFA(#, &) is* PSPACE-*complete; and,*

(3) MEMBERSHIP *for NFA(#) is* NP-*hard,* MEMBERSHIP *for NFA(&) and NFA(#,&) is* PSPACE-*complete.*

We only provide some intuition. For part (1), membership in EXPSPACE follows directly from Theorem 5(2) and the fact that INCLUSION for NFAs is PSPACE-complete [37]. EXPSPACE-hardness follows from Theorem 5(1) and Theorem 7(3). For part (2), PSPACE-hardness follows from PSPACE-hardness of INTERSECTION for REs [21]. Membership in PSPACE is witnessed by an in parallel simulation of the given NFA(#, &)s on a guessed string. Finally, NP-hardness of MEMBERSHIP for NFA(#)s is by a reduction from INTEGER KNAPSACK, PSPACE-hardness of MEMBERSHIP for NFA(&)s is by a reduction from CORRIDOR TILING.

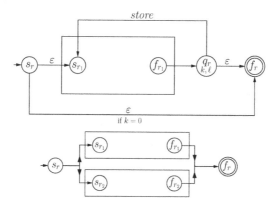

Fig. 2. From RE$(\#, \&)$ to NFA$(\#, \&)$

4   Complexity of Regular Expressions

Before we turn to schemas, we first deal with the complexity of regular expressions and frequently used subclasses.

Mayer and Stockmeyer already established the EXPSPACE-completeness of INCLUSION and EQUIVALENCE for RE$(\&)$ [28]. From Theorem 5(1) and Theorem 6(1) it then directly follows that adding numerical occurrence constraints does not increase the complexity. It further follows from Theorem 5(1) and Theorem 6(2), that INTERSECTION for RE$(\#, \&)$ is in PSPACE. We stress that the latter results could also have been obtained without making use of NFA$(\#, \&)$ but by translating RE$(\#, \&)$s directly to NFAs. However, in the case of INTERSECTION such a construction should be done in an on-the-fly fashion in order not to go beyond PSPACE. Although such an approach is possible, we prefer the shorter and more elegant construction using NFA$(\#, \&)$s. Finally, we show that INCLUSION and EQUIVALENCE of RE$(\#)$ is also EXPSPACE-hard. While Mayer and Stockmeyer reduce from REs with intersection [12], we employ a reduction from EXP-CORRIDOR TILING.

Theorem 7.   *1.* EQUIVALENCE *and* INCLUSION *for RE$(\#, \&)$ is in* EXPSPACE;
  2. INTERSECTION *for RE$(\#, \&)$ is* PSPACE-*complete; and,*
  3. EQUIVALENCE *and* INCLUSION *for RE$(\#)$ is* EXPSPACE-*hard.*

Proof. We prove (3). It suffices to show that it is EXPSPACE-hard to decide whether a given RE$(\#)$ defines Σ^*. The proof is a reduction from EXP-CORRIDOR TILING. A *tiling instance* is a tuple $T = (X, H, V, x_\perp, x_\top, n)$ where X is a finite set of tiles, $H, V \subseteq X \times X$ are the horizontal and vertical constraints, $x_\perp, x_\top \in X$, and n is a natural number in unary notation. A *correct exponential corridor tiling for T* is a mapping $\lambda : \{1, \dots, m\} \times \{1, \dots, 2^n\} \to X$ for some $m \in \mathbb{N}$ such that the following constraints are satisfied:

  - the first tile of the first row is $x_\perp$: $\lambda(1, 1) = x_\perp$;
  - the first tile of the m-th row is $x_\top$: $\lambda(m, 1) = x_\top$;

- all vertical constraints are satisfied: $\forall i < m, \forall j \leq 2^n, (\lambda(i,j), \lambda(i+1,j)) \in V$; and,
- all horizontal constraints are satisfied: $\forall i \leq m, \forall j < 2^n, (\lambda(i,j), \lambda(i,j+1)) \in H$.

The EXP-CORRIDOR TILING problem asks, given a tiling instance, whether there exists a correct exponential corridor tiling. The latter problem is easily shown to be EXPSPACE-complete [39].

We proceed with the reduction from EXP-CORRIDOR TILING. Thereto, let $T = (X, H, V, x_\perp, x_\top, n)$ be a tiling instance. We construct an RE(#)-expression r which defines the set of all strings iff there is no correct tiling for T. As EXPSPACE is closed under complement, the EXPSPACE-hardness of EQUIVALENCE and INCLUSION for RE(#) follows.

Let $\Sigma = X \cup \{\triangle\}$. For a set $S = \{s_1, \ldots, s_k\} \subseteq \Sigma$, we abuse notation and abbreviate $(s_1 + \cdots + s_k)$ simply by S. We represent a candidate tiling consisting of m rows $\rho_1, \ldots, \rho_m$ by the string $\triangle\rho_1\triangle \cdots \triangle\rho_m\triangle$. Here, every two successive rows are delimited by the symbol $\triangle$. We now define r as a disjunction of RE(#)-expressions where every disjunct catches an error in the candidate tiling. Therefore, when r is equivalent to Σ^* there can be no correct tiling for T. It remains to define the disjuncts constituting r:

1. The string does not start or end with $\triangle$: $X\Sigma^* + \Sigma^* X$.
2. There are no 2^n tiles between two successive delimiters:
   $\Sigma^*\triangle(X^{[0,2^n-1]} + X^{[2^n+1,2^n+1]}X^*)\triangle\Sigma^*$.
3. The first tile is not $x_\perp$: $\triangle x\Sigma^*$ for every $x \neq x_\perp$.
4. The first tile of the last row is not $x_\top$: $\Sigma^*\triangle xX^*\triangle$ for every $x \neq x_\top$.
5. Horizontal constraint violation: $\Sigma^* x_1 x_2 \Sigma^*$ for every $(x_1, x_2) \notin H$.
6. Vertical constraint violation: $\Sigma^* x_1 \Sigma^{[2^n,2^n]} x_2 \Sigma^*$ for every $(x_1, x_2) \notin V$.

Clearly, a Σ-string that does not satisfy any of the disjuncts in r is a correct tiling for T. Hence, $L(r) \neq \Sigma^*$ iff there is a correct tiling for T.   □

Bex et al. [4] established that the far majority of regular expressions occurring in practical DTDs and XSDs are of a very restricted form as defined next. The class of *chain regular expressions (CHAREs)* are those REs consisting of a sequence of factors $f_1 \cdots f_n$ where every factor is an expression of the form $(a_1 + \cdots + a_n)$, $(a_1 + \cdots + a_n)?$, $(a_1 + \cdots + a_n)^+$, or, $(a_1 + \cdots + a_n)^*$, where $n \geq 1$ and every a_i is an alphabet symbol. For instance, the expression $a(b + c)^* d^+ (e + f)?$ is a CHARE, while $(ab + c)^*$ and $(a^* + b?)^*$ are not.[1]

We introduce some additional notation to define subclasses and extensions of CHAREs. By CHARE(#) we denote the class of CHAREs where also factors of the form $(a_1 + \cdots + a_n)^{[k,\ell]}$ are allowed. For the following fragments, we list the admissible types of factors. Here, a, $a?$, a^* denote the factors $(a_1 + \cdots + a_n)$, $(a_1 + \cdots + a_n)?$, and $(a_1 + \cdots + a_n)^+$, respectively, with $n = 1$, while $a\#$ denotes $a^{[k,\ell]}$, and $a\#^{>0}$ denotes $a^{[k,\ell]}$ with $k > 0$.

---

[1] We disregard here the additional restriction used in [3] that every symbol can occur only once.

Table 2. Overview of new and known complexity results concerning Chain Regular Expressions. All results are completeness results, unless otherwise mentioned. The new results are printed in bold.

	INCLUSION	EQUIVALENCE	INTERSECTION
CHARE	PSPACE [25]	in PSPACE [37]	PSPACE [25]
CHARE(#)	**EXPSPACE**	**in EXPSPACE**	**PSPACE**
CHARE(a, a?)	coNP [25]	in PTIME [25]	NP [25]
CHARE(a, a^*)	coNP [25]	in PTIME [25]	NP [25]
CHARE(a, a?, a#)	**PSPACE-hard / in EXPSPACE**	**in PTIME**	**NP**
CHARE(a, a#$^{>0}$)	**in PTIME**	**in PTIME**	**in PTIME**

Table 2 lists the new and the relevant known results. We first show that adding numerical occurrence constraints to CHAREs increases the complexity of INCLUSION by one exponential. Again we reduce from EXP-CORRIDOR TILING.

Theorem 8. INCLUSION *for CHARE(#) is* EXPSPACE-*complete.*

Adding numerical occurrence constraints to the fragment CHARE(a, a?) and CHARE(a, a^*), makes INCLUSION PSPACE-hard but keeps EQUIVALENCE in PTIME and INTERSECTION in NP.

Theorem 9. *(1)* EQUIVALENCE *for CHARE(a, a?, a#) is in* PTIME.
(2) INCLUSION *for CHARE(a, a?, a#) is* PSPACE-*hard and in* EXPSPACE.
(3) INTERSECTION *for CHARE(a, a?, a#) is* NP-*complete.*

Finally, we exhibit a tractable subclass with numerical occurrence constraints:

Theorem 10. INCLUSION, EQUIVALENCE, *and* INTERSECTION *for CHARE(a, a#$^{>0}$) are in* PTIME.

5   Complexity of Schemas

5.1   DTDs and Single-Type EDTDs

In [25] it was shown for any subclass of the REs that the complexity of INCLUSION and EQUIVALENCE is the same as the complexity of the corresponding problem for DTDs and single-type EDTDs. We next generalize this result to RE($\#, \&$). As a corollary, all results of the previous section carry over to DTDs and single-type DTDs. The same holds for INTERSECTION and DTDs.

We call a complexity class $\mathcal{C}$ *closed under positive reductions* if the following holds for every $O \in \mathcal{C}$. Let L' be accepted by a deterministic polynomial-time Turing machine M with oracle O (denoted $L' = L(M^O)$). Let M further have the property that $L(M^A) \subseteq L(M^B)$ whenever $A \subseteq B$. Then L' is also in $\mathcal{C}$. For a more precise definition of this notion we refer the reader to [13]. For our purposes, it is sufficient that important complexity classes like PTIME, NP, coNP, PSPACE, and EXPSPACE have this property, and that every such class contains PTIME.

Proposition 11. *Let $\mathcal{R}$ be a subclass of $RE(\#, \&)$ and let $\mathcal{C}$ be a complexity class closed under positive reductions. Then the following are equivalent:*

(a) INCLUSION *for $\mathcal{R}$ expressions is in $\mathcal{C}$.*
(b) INCLUSION *for $DTD(\mathcal{R})$ is in $\mathcal{C}$.*
(c) INCLUSION *for $EDTD^{st}(\mathcal{R})$ is in $\mathcal{C}$.*

The corresponding statement holds for EQUIVALENCE.

The previous proposition can be generalized to INTERSECTION of DTDs as well. The proof carries over literally from [25].

Proposition 12. *Let $\mathcal{R}$ be a subclass of $RE(\#, \&)$ and let $\mathcal{C}$ be a complexity class which is closed under positive reductions. Then the following are equivalent:*

(a) INTERSECTION *for $\mathcal{R}$ expressions is in $\mathcal{C}$.*
(b) INTERSECTION *for $DTD(\mathcal{R})$ is in $\mathcal{C}$.*

The above proposition does not hold for single-type EDTDs. Indeed, there is a class of regular expressions $\mathcal{R}'$ for which INTERSECTION is NP-complete while INTERSECTION for $EDTD^{st}(\mathcal{R}')$ is EXPTIME-complete [25].

5.2   Extended EDTDs

We next consider the complexity of the basic decision problems for EDTDs with numerical occurrence constraints and interleaving. As the basic decision problems are EXPTIME-complete for EDTD(RE), the straightforward approach of translating every $RE(\#, \&)$-expression into an NFA and then applying the standard algorithms gives rise to a double exponential time complexity. By using $NFA(\#, \&)$, we can do better: EXPSPACE for INCLUSION and EQUIVALENCE, and, more surprisingly, EXPTIME for INTERSECTION.

Theorem 13. *(1)* EQUIVALENCE *and* INCLUSION *for $EDTD(\#, \&)$ is in* EX-
    PSPACE;
(2) EQUIVALENCE *and* INCLUSION *for $EDTD(\#)$ and $EDTD(\&)$ is* EXPSPACE-
    hard; and,
(3) INTERSECTION *for $EDTD(\#, \&)$ is* EXPTIME-*complete.*

Proof (Sketch).
    (1) Given two EDTDs $D_1 = (\Sigma, \Sigma_1', d_1, s_1, \mu_1)$ and $D_2 = (\Sigma, \Sigma_2', d_2, s_2, \mu_2)$, we compute a set E of pairs $(C_1, C_2) \in 2^{\Sigma_1'} \times 2^{\Sigma_2'}$ where $(C_1, C_2) \in E$ iff there exists a tree t such that $C_j = \{\tau \in \Sigma_j' \mid t \in L((D_j, \tau))\}$ for each $j = 1, 2$. Here, (D_j, τ) denotes the EDTD D_j with start symbol τ. So, every C_j is the set of types that can be assigned by D_j to the root of t. Or when viewing D_j as a tree automaton, C_j is the set of states that can be assigned to the root in a run on t. The tree t is called a *witness tree*. Then, $t \in L(D_1)$ (resp., $t \in L(D_2)$) if $s_1 \in C_1$ (resp. $s_2 \in C_2$). Hence, $L(D_1) \not\subseteq L(D_2)$ iff there exists a pair $(C_1, C_2) \in E$ with $s_1 \in C_1$ and $s_2 \notin C_2$.

Although each witness tree can have exponential depth and therefore double exponential size, we do not need to compute it directly. Instead, we compute the set E in a bottom-up fashion where we make use of an NFA($\#, \&$)-representation of the RE($\#, \&$)-expressions.

(2) Is immediate from Theorem 3(2) and Theorem 7(2).

(3) In brief, given a set of EDTDs, we construct an alternating polynomial space TM which incrementally guesses a tree defined by all schemas. To be precise, the algorithm guesses the first-child-next-sibling encoding of the unranked tree. Again, RE($\#, \&$)-expressions are translated into equivalent NFA($\#, \&$)s.□

6 Simplification

The simplification problem is defined as follows: Given an EDTD, check whether it has an equivalent EDTD of a restricted type, i.e., an equivalent DTD or single-type EDTD. In [26], this problem was shown to be EXPTIME-complete for EDTDs with standard regular expressions. We revisit this problem in the context of RE($\#, \&$).

Theorem 14. Given an EDTD($\#,\&$), deciding whether it is equivalent to an EDTDst($\#,\&$) or DTD($\#,\&$) is EXPSPACE-complete.

Proof (Sketch). We only show that the problem is hard for EXPSPACE. We use a reduction from universality of RE($\#, \&$), i.e., deciding whether an RE($\#, \&$)-expression is equivalent to Σ^*. The proof of Theorem 7(2) shows that the latter is EXPSPACE-hard. To this end, let r be an RE($\#, \&$)-expression over Σ and let b and s be two symbols not occurring in Σ. By definition, $L(r) \neq \emptyset$. Define $D = (\Sigma \cup \{b, s\}, \Sigma \cup \{s, b^1, b^2\}, d, s, \mu)$ as the EDTD with the following rules: $s \to (b^1)^* b^2 (b^1)^*$, $b^1 \to \Sigma^*$, and $b^2 \to r$, where for every $\tau \in \Sigma \cup \{s\}$, $\mu(\tau) = \tau$, and $\mu(b^1) = \mu(b^2) = b$. We claim that D is equivalent to a single-type DTD or a DTD iff $L(r) = \Sigma^*$. Clearly, if r is equivalent to Σ^*, then D is equivalent to the DTD (and therefore also to a single-type EDTD) with rules: $s \to b^*$ and $b \to \Sigma^*$. Conversely, suppose that there exists an EDTDst which defines the language $L(D)$. Towards a contradiction, assume that r is not equivalent to Σ^*. Let w_r be a string in $L(r)$ and let $w_{\neg r}$ be a Σ-string not in $L(r)$. Consider the trees $t_1 = s(b(w_r)b(w_{\neg r}))$ and $t_2 = s(b(w_{\neg r})b(w_r))$. Clearly, t_1 and t_2 are in $L(D)$. However, the tree $t = s(b(w_{\neg r})b(w_{\neg r}))$ obtained from t_1 by replacing its left subtree by the left subtree of t_2 is not in $L(D)$. According to Theorem 7.1 in [26], every tree language defined by a single-type EDTD is closed under such an exchange of subtrees. So, this means that $L(D)$ cannot be defined by an EDTDst, which leads to the desired contradiction.   □

7 Conclusion

The present work gives an overview of the complexity of the basic decision problems for abstractions of several schema languages including numerical occurrence constraints and interleaving. W.r.t. INTERSECTION the complexity remains the same, while for INCLUSION and EQUIVALENCE the complexity increases by one exponential for DTDs and single-type EDTDs, and goes from EXPTIME to EXPSPACE for EDTDs. The results w.r.t. CHAREs also follow this pattern. We further showed that the complexity of simplification increases to EXPSPACE.

We emphasize that this is a theoretical study delineating the worst case complexity boundaries for the basic decision problems. Although these complexities must be studied, we note that the regular expressions used in the hardness proofs do not correspond at all to those employed in practice. Further, w.r.t.XSDs, our abstraction is not fully adequate as we do not consider the one-unambiguity (or unique particle attribution) constraint. However, it is doubtful that this constraint is the right one to get tractable complexities for the basic decision problems. Indeed, already intersection for unambiguous regular expressions is PSPACE-hard [25] and inclusion for one-unambiguous RE($\#$)-expressions is coNP-hard [17]. It would therefore be desirable to find robust subclasses for which the basic decision problems are in PTIME.

References

1. S. Abiteboul, P. Buneman, and D. Suciu. *Data on the Web : From Relations to Semistructured Data and XML*. Morgan Kaufmann, 1999.
2. M. Benedikt, W. Fan, and F. Geerts. XPath satisfiability in the presence of DTDs. In *PODS 2005*, pages 25–36, 2005.
3. G.J. Bex, F. Neven, T. Schwentick, and K. Tuyls. Inference of concise DTDs from XML data. In *VLDB 2006*, pages 115–126, 2006.
4. G.J. Bex, F. Neven, and J. Van den Bussche. DTDs versus XML schema: A practical study. In *WebDB 2004*, pages 79–84, 2004.
5. A. Brüggemann-Klein. Unambiguity of extended regular expressions in SGML document grammars. In *ESA 1993*, pages 73–84, 1993.
6. A. Brüggemann-Klein, M. Murata, and D. Wood. Regular tree and regular hedge languages over unranked alphabets: Version 1, april 3, 2001. Technical Report HKUST-TCSC-2001-0, The Hongkong University of Science and Technology, 2001.
7. A. Brüggemann-Klein and D. Wood. One-unambiguous regular languages. *Information and Computation*, 142(2):182–206, 1998.
8. J. Clark and M. Murata. *RELAX NG Specification*. OASIS, December 2001.
9. J. Cristau, C. Löding, and W. Thomas. Deterministic automata on unranked trees. In *FCT 2005*, pages 68–79. Springer, 2005.
10. S. Dal-Zilio and D. Lugiez. XML schema, tree logic and sheaves automata. In *RTA*, pages 246–263, 2003.
11. Alin Deutsch, Mary F. Fernandez, and Dan Suciu. Storing Semistructured Data with STORED. In *SIGMOD 1999*, pages 431–442, 1999.
12. M. Fürer. The complexity of the inequivalence problem for regular expressions with intersection. In *ICALP 1980*, pages 234–245. Springer, 1980.
13. L. Hemaspaandra and M. Ogihara. *Complexity Theory Companion*. Springer, 2002.
14. J.E. Hopcroft, R. Motwani, and J.D. Ullman and. *Introduction to Automata Theory, Languages, and Computation*. Addison-Wesley, second edition, 2001.
15. H. Hosoya and B. C. Pierce. XDuce: A statically typed XML processing language. *ACM Trans. Inter. Tech.*, 3(2):117–148, 2003.

16. J. Jędrzejowicz and A. Szepietowski. Shuffle languages are in P. *Theoretical Computer Science*, 250(1-2):31–53, 2001.
17. P. Kilpeläinen. Inclusion of unambiguous #REs is NP-hard. Unpublished note, University of Kuopio, Finland, May 2004.
18. P. Kilpeläinen and R. Tuhkanen. One-unambiguity of regular expressions with numeric occurrence indicators. Tech. Rep. A/2006/2, Univ. Kuopio, Finland, 2006.
19. P. Kilpeläinen and R. Tuhkanen. Towards efficient implementation of XML schema content models. In *DOCENG 2004*, pages 239–241. ACM, 2004.
20. C. Koch, S. Scherzinger, N. Schweikardt, and B. Stegmaier. Schema-based scheduling of event processors and buffer minimization for queries on structured data streams. In *VLDB 2004*, pages 228–239, 2004.
21. D. Kozen. Lower bounds for natural proof systems. In *FOCS 1977*, pages 254–266. IEEE, 1977.
22. M. Mani. Keeping chess alive — Do we need 1-unambiguous content models? In *Extreme Markup Languages*, Montreal, Canada, 2001.
23. I. Manolescu, D. Florescu, and D. Kossmann. Answering XML Queries on Heterogeneous Data Sources. In *VLDB 2001*, pages 241–250, 2001.
24. W. Martens and F. Neven. Frontiers of tractability for typechecking simple XML transformations. *Journal of Computer and System Sciences*, 2006. To Appear.
25. W. Martens, F. Neven, and T. Schwentick. Complexity of decision problems for simple regular expressions. In *MFCS 2004*, pages 889–900, Berlin, 2004. Springer.
26. W. Martens, F. Neven, T. Schwentick, and G. J. Bex. Expressiveness and complexity of XML schema. *ACM Trans. Database Systems*, 31(3), 2006. To appear.
27. W. Martens and J. Niehren. Minimizing tree automata for unranked trees. In *DBPL 2005*, pages 232–246, 2005.
28. A. J. Mayer and L. J. Stockmeyer. Word problems — this time with interleaving. *Information and Computation*, 115(2):293–311, 1994.
29. M. Murata, D. Lee, M. Mani, and K. Kawaguchi. Taxonomy of XML schema languages using formal language theory. *ACM Trans. Inter. Tech.*, 5(4):1–45, 2005.
30. F. Neven and T. Schwentick. XPath containment in the presence of disjunction, DTDs, and variables. *Logical Methods in Computer Science*, page To appear, 2006.
31. Y. Papakonstantinou and V. Vianu. DTD inference for views of XML data. In *PODS 2000*, pages 35–46, New York, 2000. ACM Press.
32. F. Reuter. An enhanced W3C XML Schema-based language binding for object oriented programming languages. Manuscript, 2006.
33. H. Seidl. Deciding equivalence of finite tree automata. *SIAM Journal on Computing*, 19(3):424–437, 1990.
34. H. Seidl. Haskell overloading is DEXPTIME-complete. *Information Processing Letters*, 52(2):57–60, 1994.
35. C.M. Sperberg-McQueen. XML Schema 1.0: A language for document grammars. In *XML 2003*, 2003.
36. C.M. Sperberg-McQueen and H. Thompson. XML Schema. http://www.w3.org/XML/Schema, 2005.
37. L.J. Stockmeyer and A.R. Meyer. Word problems requiring exponential time: Preliminary report. In *STOC 1973*, pages 1–9. ACM Press, 1973.
38. E. van der Vlist. *XML Schema*. O'Reilly, 2002.
39. P. van Emde Boas. The convenience of tilings. In *Complexity, Logic and Recursion Theory*, volume 187 of *Lec. Notes in Pure and App. Math.*, pages 331–363. 1997.
40. G. Wang, M. Liu, J. X. Yu, B. Sun, G. Yu, J. Lv, and H. Lu. Effective schema-based XML query optimization techniques. In *IDEAS 2003*, pages 230–235, 2003.

Database Query Processing Using
Finite Cursor Machines

Martin Grohe[1], Yuri Gurevich[2], Dirk Leinders[3], Nicole Schweikardt[1],
Jerzy Tyszkiewicz[4], and Jan Van den Bussche[3]

[1] Humboldt-University Berlin
[2] Microsoft Research
[3] Hasselt University and Transnational University of Limburg
[4] University of Warsaw

Abstract. We introduce a new abstract model of database query processing, *finite cursor machines*, that incorporates certain data streaming aspects. The model describes quite faithfully what happens in so-called "one-pass" and "two-pass query processing". Technically, the model is described in the framework of abstract state machines. Our main results are upper and lower bounds for processing relational algebra queries in this model, specifically, queries of the semijoin fragment of the relational algebra.

1 Introduction

We introduce and analyze *finite cursor machines*, an abstract model of database query processing. Data elements are viewed as "indivisible" abstract objects with a vocabulary of arbitrary, but fixed, functions. Relational databases consist of finitely many finite relations over the data elements. Relations are considered as tables whose rows are the tuples in the relation. Finite cursor machines can operate in a finite number of *modes* using an *internal memory* in which they can store bit strings. They access each relation through finitely many cursors, each of which can read one row of a table at any time. The answer to a query, which is also a relation, can be given through a suitable output mechanism. The model incorporates certain "streaming" or "sequential processing" aspects by imposing two restrictions: First, the cursors can only move on the tables sequentially in one direction. Thus once the last cursor has left a row of a table, this row can never be accessed again during the computation. Second, the internal memory is limited. For our lower bounds, it will be sufficient to put an $o(n)$ restriction on the internal memory size, where n is the size (that is, the number of entries) of the input database. For the upper bounds, no internal memory will be needed. The model is clearly inspired by the *abstract state machine (ASM)* methodology [16], and indeed we will formally define our model using this methodology. The model was first presented in a talk at the ASM 2004 workshop [29].

Algorithms and lower bounds in various data stream models have received considerable attention in recent years both in the theory community (e.g., [1,2,5,6,

T. Schwentick and D. Suciu (Eds.): ICDT 2007, LNCS 4353, pp. 284–298, 2007.

13, 14, 18, 25]) and the database systems community (e.g., [3, 4, 7, 12, 15, 20, 26]).
Note that our model is fairly powerful; for example, the multiple cursors can
easily be used to perform multiple sequential scans of the input data. But more
than that; by moving several cursors asynchronously over the same table, entries
in different, possibly far apart, regions of the table can be read and processed
simultaneously. This way, different regions of the same or of different tables can
"communicate" with each other without requiring any internal memory, which
makes it difficult to use communication complexity to establish lower bounds.
The model is also powerful in that it allows arbitrary functions to access and
process data elements. This feature is very convenient to model "built in" standard operations on data types like integers, floating point numbers, or strings,
which may all be part of the universe of data elements.

Despite these powerful features, the model is weak in many respects. We
show that a finite cursor machine with internal memory size $o(n)$ cannot even
test whether two sets A and B, given as lists, are disjoint, even if besides the
lists A and B, also their reversals are given as input. However, if two sets A
and B are given as *sorted* lists, a machine can easily compute the intersection.
Aggarwal et al. [1] have already made a convincing case for combining streaming
computations with sorting, and we will consider an extension of the model with
a sorting primitive.

Our main results are concerned with evaluating *relational algebra queries* in
the finite cursor machine model. Relational algebra forms the core of the standard query language SQL and is thus of fundamental importance for databases.
We prove that, when all sorted versions of the database relations are provided
as input, every operator of the relational algebra can be computed, except for
the *join*. The latter exception, however, is only because the output size of a
join can be quadratic, while finite cursor machines by their very definition can
output only a linear number of different tuples. A *semijoin* is a projection of
a join between two relations to the columns of one of the two relations (note
that the projection prevents the result of a semijoin from getting larger than
the relations to which the semijoin operation is applied). The *semijoin algebra* is
then a natural fragment of the relational algebra that may be viewed as a generalization of acyclic conjunctive queries [9, 22, 21, 30]. When sorted versions of the
database relations are provided as input, semijoins can be computed by finite
cursor machines. Consequently, every query in the semijoin fragment of the relational algebra can be computed by a composition of finite cursor machines and
sorting operations. This is interesting because it models quite faithfully what is
called "one-pass" and "two-pass processing" in database systems [11]. The question then arises: are intermediate sorting operations really needed? Equivalently,
can every semijoin-algebra query already be computed by a single machine on
sorted inputs? We answer this question negatively in a very strong way, and this
is our main technical result: Just a composition of two semijoins $R \ltimes (S \ltimes T)$
with R and T unary relations and S a binary relation is not computable by a
finite cursor machine with internal memory size $o(n)$ working on sorted inputs.
This result is quite sharp, as we will indicate.

The paper is structured as follows: After fixing some notation in Section 2, the notion of finite cursor machines is introduced in Section 3. The power of $O(1)$-FCMs and of $o(n)$-FCMs is investigated in Sections 4 and 5. Some concluding remarks and open questions can be found in Section 6.

Due to space limitations, some technical details of our proofs had to be deferred to the full version of this paper, available on the authors' websites.

2   Preliminaries

Throughout the paper we fix an arbitrary, typically infinite, universe $\mathbb{E}$ of "data elements", and we fix a database schema $\mathcal{S}$. I.e., $\mathcal{S}$ is a finite set of relation names, where each relation name has an associated arity, which is a natural number. A database $\mathbf{D}$ with schema $\mathcal{S}$ assigns to each $R \in \mathcal{S}$ a finite, nonempty set $\mathbf{D}(R)$ of k-tuples of data elements, where k is the arity of R. In database terminology the tuples are often called *rows*. The *size* of database $\mathbf{D}$ is defined as the total number of rows in $\mathbf{D}$.

A *query* is a mapping Q from databases to relations, such that the relation $Q(\mathbf{D})$ is the answer of the query Q to database $\mathbf{D}$. The *relational algebra* is a basic language used in database theory to express exactly those queries that can be composed from the actual database relations by applying a sequence of the following operations: union, intersection, difference, projection, selection, and joins. The meaning of the first three operations should be clear, the *projection* operator $\pi_{i_1,\dots,i_k}(R)$ returns the projection of a relation R to its components $i_1,\dots,i_k$, the *selection* operator $\sigma_{p(i_1,\dots,i_k)}(R)$ returns those tuples from R whose i_1th, ..., i_kth components satisfy the predicate p, and the *join* operator $R \bowtie_\theta S$ (where θ is a conjunction of equalities of the form $\bigwedge_{s=1}^k x_{i_s} = y_{j_s}$) is defined as $\{(\bar{a},\bar{b}) : \bar{a} \in R,\ \bar{b} \in S,\ a_{i_s} = b_{j_s} \text{ for all } s \in \{1,\dots,k\}\}$. A natural sublanguage of the relational algebra is the so-called *semijoin algebra* where, instead of ordinary joins, only *semijoin* operations of the form $R \ltimes_\theta S$ are allowed, defined as $\{\bar{a} \in R : \exists \bar{b} \in S : a_{i_s} = b_{j_s} \text{ for all } s \in \{1,\dots,k\}\}$.

To formally introduce our computation model, we need some basic notions from mathematical logic such as (many-sorted) vocabularies, structures, terms, and atomic formulas.

3   Finite Cursor Machines

In this section we formally define *finite cursor machines* using the methodology of Abstract State Machines (ASMs). Intuitively, an ASM can be thought of as a transition system whose states are described by many-sorted first-order structures (or algebras)[1]. Transitions change the interpretation of some of the symbols—those in the *dynamic* part of the vocabulary—and leave the remaining

---

[1] Beware that "state" refers here to what for Turing machines is typically called "configuration"; the term "mode" is used for what for Turing machines is typically called "state".

symbols—those in the *static* part of the vocabulary—unchanged. Transitions are described by a finite collection of simple update rules, which are "fired" simultaneously (if they are inconsistent, no update is carried out). A crucial property of the sequential ASM model, which we consider here, is that in each transition only a limited part of the state is changed. The detailed definition of sequential ASMs is given in the Lipari guide [16], but our presentation will be largely self-contained.

We now describe the formal model of finite cursor machines.

The Vocabulary: The *static vocabulary* of a finite cursor machine (FCM) consists of two parts, Υ_0 (providing the background structure) and $\Upsilon_{\mathcal{S}}$ (providing the particular input).

Υ_0 consists of three sorts: Element, Bitstring, and Mode. Furthermore, Υ_0 may contain an arbitrary number of functions and predicates, as long as the output sort of each function is Bitstring. Finally, Υ_0 contains an arbitrary but finite number of constant symbols of sort Mode, called *modes*. The modes *init*, *accept*, and *reject* are always in Υ_0.

$\Upsilon_{\mathcal{S}}$ provides the input. For each relation name $R \in \mathcal{S}$, there is a sort Row_R in $\Upsilon_{\mathcal{S}}$. Moreover, if the arity of R is k, we have function symbols $attribute_R^i \colon \mathsf{Row}_R \to$ Element for $i = 1, \ldots, k$. Furthermore, we have a constant symbol $\perp_R$ of sort Row_R. Finally, we have a function symbol $next_R \colon \mathsf{Row}_R \to \mathsf{Row}_R$ in $\Upsilon_{\mathcal{S}}$.

The *dynamic vocabulary* Υ_M of an FCM M contains only constant symbols. This vocabulary always contains the symbol *mode* of sort Mode. Furthermore, there can be a finite number of symbols of sort Bitstring, called *registers*. Moreover, for each relation name R in the database schema, there are a finite number of symbols of sort Row_R, called *cursors on R*.

The Initial State: Our intention is that FCMs will work on databases. Database relations, however, are sets, while FCMs expect lists of tuples as inputs. Therefore, formally, the input to a machine is an *enumeration* of a database, which consists of enumerations of the database relations, where an enumeration of a relation is simply a listing of all tuples in some order. An FCM M that is set to run on an enumeration of a database $\mathbf{D}$ then starts with the following structure $\mathcal{M}$ over the vocabulary $\Upsilon_0 \cup \Upsilon_{\mathcal{S}} \cup \Upsilon_M$: The interpretation of Element is $\mathbb{E}$; the interpretation of Bitstring is the set of all finite bitstrings; and the interpretation of Mode is simply given by the set of modes themselves. For technical reasons, we must assume that $\mathbb{E}$ contains an element $\perp$. For each $R \in \mathcal{S}$, the sort Row_R is interpreted by the set $\mathbf{D}(R) \cup \{\perp_R\}$; the function $attribute_R^i$ is defined by $(x_1, \ldots, x_k) \mapsto x_i$, and $\perp_R \mapsto \perp$; finally, the function $next_R$ maps each row to its successor in the list, and maps the last row to $\perp_R$. The dynamic symbol *mode* initially is interpreted by the constant *init*; every register contains the empty bitstring; and every cursor on a relation R contains the first row of R.

The Program of an FCM: A *program* for the machine M is now a program as defined as a basic sequential program in the sense of ASM theory, with the important restriction that all basic updates concerning a cursor c on R must be of the form $c := next_R(c)$.

Thus, basic update rules of the following three forms are rules: $mode := t$, $r := t$, and $c := next_R(c)$, where t is a term over $\Upsilon_0 \cup \Upsilon_S \cup \Upsilon_M$, and r is a register and c is a cursor on R. The semantics of these rules is the obvious one: Update the dynamic constant by the value of the term. Update rules $r_1, \ldots, r_m$ can be combined to a new rule par $r_1 \ldots r_m$ endpar, the semantics of which is: Fire rules $r_1, \ldots, r_m$ in parallel; if they are inconsistent do nothing. Furthermore, if r_1 and r_2 are rules and φ is an atomic formula over $\Upsilon_0 \cup \Upsilon_S \cup \Upsilon_M$, then also if φ then r_1 else r_2 endif is a rule. The semantics is obvious.

Now, an FCM program is just a single rule. (Since finitely many rules can be combined to one using the par...end construction, one rule is enough.)

The Computation of an FCM: Starting with the initial state, successively apply the (single rule of the FCM's) program until $mode$ is equal to $accept$ or to $reject$. Accordingly, we say that M terminates and $accepts$, respectively, $rejects$ its input.

Given that inputs are $enumerations$ of databases, we must be careful to define the result of a computation on a database. We agree that an FCM $accepts$ a database $\mathbf{D}$ if it accepts $every$ enumeration of $\mathbf{D}$. This already allows us to use FCMs to compute decision queries. In the next paragraph we will see how FCMs can output lists of tuples. We then say that an FCM M computes a query Q if on each database $\mathbf{D}$, the output of M on any enumeration of $\mathbf{D}$ is an enumeration of the relation $Q(\mathbf{D})$. Note that later we will also consider FCMs working only on sorted versions of database relations: in that case there is no ambiguity.

Producing Output: We can extend the basic model so that the machine can output a list of tuples. To this end, we expand the dynamic vocabulary Υ_M with a finite number of constant symbols of sort Element, called $output\ registers$, and with a constant of sort Mode, called the $output\ mode$. The output registers can be updated following the normal rules of ASMs. In each state of the finite cursor machine, when the output mode is equal to the special value out, the tuple consisting of the values in the output registers (in some predefined order) is output; when the output mode is different from out, no tuple is output. The initial settings of the output registers and the output mode are as follows: each output register contains the value $\bot$; the output mode is equal to $init$. We denote the output of a machine M working on a database $\mathbf{D}$ by $M(\mathbf{D})$.

Space Restrictions: For considering FCMs whose bitstring registers are restricted in size, we use the following notation: Let M be a finite cursor machine and $\mathcal{F}$ a class of functions from $\mathbb{N}$ to $\mathbb{N}$. Then we say that M is an $\mathcal{F}$-$machine$ (or, an $\mathcal{F}$-FCM) if there is a function $f \in \mathcal{F}$ such that, on each database enumeration $\mathbf{D}$ of size n, the machine only stores bitstrings of length $f(n)$ in its registers. We are mostly interested in $O(1)$-FCMs and $o(n)$-FCMs. Note that the latter are quite powerful. For example, such machines can easily store the positions of the cursors. On the other hand, $O(1)$-machines are equivalent to FCMs that do not use registers at all (because bitstrings of constant length could also be simulated by finitely many $modes$).

Example 1. The following FCM program works on a ternary relation $R(A, B, C)$ and produces the sum of attributes A and B for each row with C at least 100.

if $outputmode = out$ then
par $outputmode := init$, $c := next_R(c)$ endpar
else if $outputmode <> out$ and $attribute_R^3(c) > 100$ then
par $outputmode := out$, $out_1 := attribute_R^1(c) + attribute_R^2(c)$ endpar
else $c := next_R(c)$ endif endif

3.1   Discussion of the Model

Storing Bitstrings instead of Data Elements: An important question about our model is the strict separation between data elements and bitstrings. Indeed, data elements are abstract entities, and our background structure may contain arbitrary functions and predicates, mixing data elements and bitstrings, with the important restriction that the output of a function is always a bitstring. At first sight, a simpler way to arrive at our model would be without bitstrings, simply considering an arbitrary structure on the universe of data elements. Let us call this variation of our model the "universal model".

Note that the universal model can easily become computationally complete. It suffices that finite strings of data elements can somehow be represented by other data elements, and that the background structure supplies the necessary manipulation functions for that purpose. Simple examples are the natural numbers with standard arithmetic, or the strings over some finite alphabet with concatenation. Thus, if we would want to prove complexity lower bounds in the universal model, while retaining the abstract nature of data elements and operations on them, it would be necessary to formulate certain logical restrictions on the available functions and predicates on the data elements. Finding interesting such restrictions is not clear to us. In the model with bitstrings, however, one can simply impose restrictions on the length of the bitstrings stored in registers, and that is precisely what we will do. Of course, the unlimited model with bitstrings can also be computationally complete. It suffices that the background structure provides a coding of data elements by bitstrings.

Element Registers: The above discussion notwithstanding, it might still be interesting to allow for registers that can remember certain data elements that have been seen by the cursors, but without arbitrary operations on them. Formally, we would expand the dynamic vocabulary Υ_M with a finite number of constant symbols of sort Element, called *element registers*. It is easy to see, however, that such element registers can already be simulated by using additional cursors, and thus do not add anything to the basic model.

Running Time and Output Size: A crucial property of FCMs is that all cursors are one-way. In particular, an FCM can perform only a linear number of steps where a cursor is advanced. As a consequence, an FCM with output can output only a linear number of different tuples. On the other hand, if the background structure is not restricted in any way, arbitrary computations on the register contents can occur in between cursor advancements. As a matter of fact, in this paper we will present a number of positive results and a number of negative results. For the positive results, registers will never be needed, and in particular, FCMs run in linear time. For the negative results, arbitrary computations on the registers will be allowed.

Look-ahead: Note that the terms in the program of an FCM can contain nested applications of the function $next_R$, such as $next_R(next_R(c))$. In some sense, such nestings of depth up to d correspond to a *look-ahead* where the machine can access the current cursor position as well as the next d positions. It is, however, straightforward to see that every k-cursor FCM with look-ahead $\leq d$ can be simulated by a $(k \times d)$-cursor FCM with look-ahead 0. Thus, throughout the remainder of this paper we will w.l.o.g. restrict attention to FCMs that have look-ahead 0, i.e., to FCMs where the function $next_R$ never occurs in if-conditions or in update rules of the form $mode := t$ or $r := t$.

The Number of Cursors: In principle we could allow more than constantly many cursors, which would enable us to store that many data elements. We stick with the constant version for the sake of technical simplicity, and also because our *upper* bounds only need a constant number of cursors. Note, however, that our main *lower* bound result can be extended to a fairly big number of cursors (cf. Remark 11).

4   The Power of $O(1)$-Machines

We start with a few simple observations on the database query processing capabilities of FCMs, with or without sorting, and show that sorting is really needed.

Let us first consider *compositions* of FCMs in the sense that one machine works on the outputs of several machines working on a common database.

Proposition 2. *Let $M_1, \ldots, M_r$ be FCMs working on a schema S, let S' be the output schema consisting of the names and arities of the output lists of $M_1, \ldots, M_r$, and let M_0 be an FCM working on schema S'. Then there exists an FCM M working on schema S, such that $M(\mathbf{D}) = M_0(\mathbf{D}')$, for each database $\mathbf{D}$ with schema S and the database $\mathbf{D}'$ that consists of the output relations $M_1(\mathbf{D}), \ldots, M_r(\mathbf{D})$.*

The proof is obvious: Each row in a relation R_i of database $\mathbf{D}'$ is an output row of a machine M_i working on $\mathbf{D}$. Therefore, each time M_0 moves a cursor on R_i, the desired finite cursor machine M will simulate that part of the computation of M_i on $\mathbf{D}$ until M_i outputs a next row.

Let us now consider the operators from relational algebra: Clearly, *selection* can be implemented by an $O(1)$-FCM. Also, *projection* and *union* can easily be accomplished if either duplicate elimination is abandoned or the input is given in a suitable order. *Joins*, however, are *not* computable by an FCM, simply because the output size of a join can be quadratic, while finite cursor machines can output only a linear number of different tuples.

In stream data management research [4], one often restricts attention to *sliding window joins* for a fixed window size w. This means that the join operator is successively applied to portions of the data, each portion consisting of a number w of consecutive rows of the input relations. It is then straightforward to obtain the following:

Proposition 3. *For every fixed window size $w \in \mathbb{N}$ there is an $O(1)$-FCM that implements the sliding window join operator of width w. However, no FCM (with registers of arbitrary size) can compute the full join of two relations of arity ≥ 2.*

Using more elaborate methods, we can moreover show that even checking whether the join is nonempty (so that output size is not an issue) is hard for FCMs. Specifically, we will consider the problem whether two sets intersect, which is the simplest kind of join. We will give two proofs: an elegant one for $O(1)$-machines, using a proof technique that is simple to apply, and an intricate one for more general $o(n)$-machines (Theorem 12). Note that the following result is valid for *arbitrary* (but fixed) background structures.

Theorem 4. *There is no $O(1)$-FCM that checks for two sets R and S whether $R \cap S \neq \emptyset$. (This holds even if also the reversals of R and S are supplied as input.)*

Proof. We give here the proof without the reversals; the proof with reversals can be obtained using the proof technique of our main result (Theorem 10). Let M be an $O(1)$-FCM that is supposed to check whether $R \cap S \neq \emptyset$. Without loss of generality, we assume that $\mathbb{E}$ is totally ordered by a predicate $<$ in Υ_0. Using Ramsey's theorem, we can find an infinite set $V \subseteq \mathbb{E}$ over which the truth of the atomic formulas in M's program on tuples of data elements only depends on the way these data elements compare w.r.t. $<$ (details on this can be found, e.g., in Libkin's textbook [24, Section 13.3]). Now choose $2n$ elements in V, for n large enough, satisfying $a_1 < a_1' < \cdots < a_n < a_n'$, and consider the run of M on $R = \{a_1, \ldots, a_n\}$ (listed in that order) and $S = \{a_n', \ldots, a_1'\}$. We say that a pair of cursors "checks" i if in some state during the run, one of the cursors is on a_i and the other one is on a_i'. By the way the lists are ordered, every pair of cursors can check only one i. Hence, some j is not checked. Now replace a_j' in S by a_j. The machine will not notice this, because a_j and a_j' have the same relative order with respect to the other elements in the lists. The intersection of R and S, however, is now nonempty, so M is wrong.   □

Of course, when the sets R and S are given as *sorted* lists, an FCM can easily compute $R \cap S$ by performing one simultaneous scan over the two lists. Moreover, while the full join is still not computable simply because its output is too large, the semijoin $R \ltimes S$ is also easily computed by an FCM on sorted inputs. Furthermore, the same holds for the difference $R - S$. These easy observations motivate us to extend FCMs with sorting, in the spirit of "two-pass query processing" based on sorting [11].

Formally, assume that $\mathbb{E}$ is totally ordered by a predicate $<$ in Υ_0. Then a relation of arity p can be sorted "lexicographically" in $p!$ different ways: for any permutation ρ of $\{1, \ldots, p\}$, let sort_ρ denote the operation that sorts a p-ary relation $\rho(1)$-th column first, $\rho(2)$-th column second, and $\rho(p)$-th column last. By an FCM *working on sorted inputs* of a database $\mathbf{D}$, we mean an FCM that gets all possible sorted orders of all relations of $\mathbf{D}$ as input lists. We then summarize the above discussion as follows:

Proposition 5. *Each operator of the semijoin algebra (i.e, union, intersection, difference, projection, selection, and semijoin) can be computed by an $O(1)$-FCM on sorted inputs.*

Corollary 6. *Every semijoin algebra query can be computed by a composition of $O(1)$-FCMs and sorting operations.*

Proof. Starting from the given semijoin algebra expression we replace each operator by a composition of one FCM with the required sorting operations.   □

The simple proof of the above corollary introduces a lot of intermediate sorting operations. In some cases, intermediate sorting can be avoided by choosing in the beginning a particularly suitable ordering that can be used by *all* the operations in the expression [28].

Example 7. Consider the query $(R - S) \ltimes_{x_2 = y_2} T$, where R, S and T are binary relations. Since the semijoin compares the second columns, it needs its inputs sorted on second columns first. Hence, if $R - S$ is computed on $\mathsf{sort}_{(2,1)}(R)$ and $\mathsf{sort}_{(2,1)}(S)$ by some machine M, then the output of M can be piped directly to a machine M' that computes the semijoin on that output and on $\mathsf{sort}_{(2,1)}(T)$. By compositionality (Proposition 2), we can then even compose M and M' into a single FCM. A stupid way to compute the same query would be to compute $R - S$ on $\mathsf{sort}_{(1,2)}(R)$ and $\mathsf{sort}_{(1,2)}(S)$, thus requiring a re-sorting of the output.

The question then arises: can intermediate sorting operations always be avoided? Equivalently, can every semijoin algebra query already be computed by a single machine on sorted inputs? We can answer this negatively. Our proof applies a known result from the classical topic of multihead automata, which is indeed to be expected given the similarity between multihead automata and FCMs.

Specifically, the *monochromatic 2-cycle* query about a binary relation E and a unary relation C asks whether the directed graph formed by the edges in E consists of a disjoint union of 2-cycles where the two nodes on each cycle either both belong to C or both do not belong to C. Note that this query is indeed expressible in the semijoin algebra as "Is $e_1 \cup e_2 \cup e_3$ *empty?*", where $e_1 := E - (E \underset{\substack{x_2=y_1 \\ x_1=y_2}}{\ltimes} E)$, where $e_2 := E \underset{\substack{x_2=y_1 \\ x_1 \neq y_2}}{\ltimes} E$, and where $e_3 := (E \underset{x_1=y_1}{\ltimes} C) \underset{x_2=y_1}{\ltimes}$
$((\pi_1(E) \cup \pi_2(E)) - C)$

(We use a nonequality in the semijoin condition, but that is easily incorporated in our formalism as well as computed by an FCM on sorted inputs.)

Theorem 8. *The monochromatic 2-cycle query is not computable by an $O(1)$-FCM on sorted inputs.*

Proof sketch. The proof is via a reduction from the Palindrome problem. As was proved by Hromkovič [19], the set of Palindromes cannot be decided by a one-way multi-head deterministic sensing finite state automaton (1DSeFA(k)). It can be shown that Hromkovič's proof can be generalized to the presence of an arbitrary but finite number of oblivious right-to-left heads that can only move from right to left on the input tape sensing other heads, but not read the symbols on the tape. Now let M be an $O(1)$-FCM that is supposed to solve the monochromatic 2-cycle query. Again using Ramsey's theorem, we can find an infinite set $V \subseteq \mathbb{E}$ over which the truth of the atomic formulas in M's program on tuples of data elements only depends on the way these data elements compare w.r.t. $<$. Hence, there is an $O(1)$-FCM M' with only $<$ in its rules, and equivalent to M over V. We now come to the reduction. For $a_1 < \cdots < a_n \in V$, with n large enough, fix relation E as $\{(a_i, a_{n-i+1}) \mid 1 \le i \le n\}$. Given a string $w = w_1 \cdots w_n$ over $\{0,1\}$, we define relation $C = \{a_i \mid w_i = 1\}$. It is then clear that w is a palindrome if and only if E and C form a positive instance to the monochromatic 2-cycle query. From FCM M' we can then construct a 1DSeFA(k) that would decide Palindrome, and thus arrive at a contradiction. □

An important remark is that the above proof only works if the set C is only given in ascending order. In practice, however, one might as well consider sorting operations in descending order, or, for relations of higher arity, arbitrary mixes of ascending and descending orders on different columns. Indeed, that is the general format of sorting operations in the database language SQL. We thus extend our scope to sorting in descending order, and to much more powerful $o(n)$-machines, in the next section.

5   Descending Orders and the Power of $o(n)$-Machines

We already know that the computation of semijoin algebra queries by FCMs and sortings in ascending order only requires intermediate sortings. So, the next question is whether the use of descending orders can avoid intermediate sorting. We will answer this question negatively, and will do this even for $o(n)$-machines (whereas Theorem 8 is proven only for $O(1)$-machines).

Formally, on a p-ary relation, we now have sorting operations $\mathsf{sort}_{\rho, f}$, where ρ is as before, and $f \colon \{1, \ldots, p\} \to \{\nearrow, \searrow\}$ indicates ascending or descending. To distinguish from the terminology of the previous section, we talk about an FCM working on *AD-sorted inputs* to make clear that both ascending and descending orders are available.

Before we show our main technical result, we remark that the availability of sorted inputs using descending order allows $O(1)$-machines to compute more relational algebra queries. Indeed, we can extract such a query from the proof of Theorem 8. Specifically, the "Palindrome" query about a binary relation R and a unary relation C asks whether R is of the form $\{(a_i, a_{n-i+1}) \mid i = 1, \ldots, n\}$ with $a_1 < \cdots < a_n$, and $C \subseteq \{a_1, \ldots, a_n\}$ such that $a_i \in C \Leftrightarrow a_{n-i+1} \in C$. We can express this query in the relational algebra (using the order predicate in selections). In the following proposition, the lower bound was already shown in Theorem 8, and the upper bound is easy.

Proposition 9. *The "Palindrome" query cannot be solved by an $O(1)$-FCM on sorted inputs, but can be solved by an $O(1)$-FCM on AD-sorted inputs.*

We now establish:

Theorem 10. *The query* $RST := $ *"Is* $R \ltimes_{x_1=y_1} (S \ltimes_{x_2=y_1} T)$ *nonempty?", where* R *and* T *are unary and* S *is binary, is not computable by any* $o(n)$-*FCM working on AD-sorted inputs.*

Proof. For the sake of contradiction, suppose M is a $o(n)$-FCM computing RST on sorted inputs. Without loss of generality, we can assume that M accepts or rejects the input only when all cursors are positioned at the end of their lists.

Let k be the total number of cursors of M, let r be the number of registers and let m be the number of modes occurring in M's program. Let $v := \binom{k}{2} + 1$.

Choose n to be a multiple of v^2, and choose $4n$ values in $\mathbb{E}$ satisfying $a_1 < a_1' < a_2 < a_2' < \cdots < a_n < a_n' < b_1 < b_1' < \cdots < b_n < b_n'$.

Divide the ordered set $\{1, \ldots, n\}$ evenly in v consecutive blocks, denoted by $B_1, \ldots, B_v$. So, B_i equals the set $\{(i-1)\frac{n}{v} + 1, \ldots, i\frac{n}{v}\}$. Consider the following permutation of $\{1, \ldots, n\}$:

$$\pi : \quad (i-1) \cdot \tfrac{n}{v} + s \; \mapsto \; (v-i) \cdot \tfrac{n}{v} + s$$

for $1 \leq i \leq v$ and $1 \leq s \leq \frac{n}{v}$. So, π maps subset B_i to subset B_{v-i+1}, and vice versa.

We fix the binary relation S of size $2n$ for the rest of this proof as follows:

$$S := \big\{(a_\ell, b_{\pi\ell}) : \ell \in \{1, .., n\}\big\} \cup \big\{(a_\ell', b_{\pi\ell}') : \ell \in \{1, .., n\}\big\}.$$

Furthermore, for all sets $I, J \subseteq \{1, \ldots, n\}$, we define unary relations $R(I)$ and $T(J)$ of size n as follows:

$$R(I) := \{a_\ell : \ell \in I\} \cup \{a_\ell' : \ell \in I^c\}$$
$$T(J) := \{b_\ell : \ell \in J\} \cup \{b_\ell' : \ell \in J^c\},$$

where I^c denotes $\{1, \ldots, n\} - I$. By $\mathbf{D}(I, J)$, we denote the database consisting of the lists $\mathsf{sort}_\nearrow(R(I))$, $\mathsf{sort}_\searrow(R(I))$, $\mathsf{sort}_\nearrow(T(J))$, $\mathsf{sort}_\searrow(T(J))$, and all sorted versions of S. It is easy to see that the nested semijoin of $R(I)$, S, and $T(J)$ is empty if, and only if, $(\pi(I) \cap J) \cup (\pi(I)^c \cap J^c) = \emptyset$. Therefore, for each I, the query RST returns *false* on instance $\mathbf{D}(I, \pi(I)^c)$, which we will denote by $\mathbf{D}(I)$ for short. Furthermore, we observe for later use:

the query RST on $\mathbf{D}(I, \pi(J)^c)$ returns *true* if, and only if, $I \neq J$.   (∗)

To simplify notation a bit, we will in the following use $R_\nearrow$ and $T_\nearrow$ to denote lists $\mathsf{sort}_\nearrow(R(I))$ and $\mathsf{sort}_\nearrow(T(I))$ sorted in ascending order, and we use $R_\searrow$ and $T_\searrow$ to denote the lists $\mathsf{sort}_\searrow(R(I))$ and $\mathsf{sort}_\searrow(T(I))$ sorted in descending order.

Consider a cursor c on list $R_\nearrow$ of the machine M. In a certain state (i.e., configuration), we say that c is on position ℓ on $R_\nearrow$ if M has executed $\ell-1$ update rules $c := next_{R_\nearrow}(c)$. I.e., if cursor c is on position ℓ on $R_\nearrow$, then c sees value a_ℓ or a_ℓ'. We use analogous notation for the sorted lists $R_\searrow$, $T_\nearrow$, and $T_\searrow$. I.e., if a cursor c is on position ℓ on $R_\searrow$ (resp. $T_\nearrow$, resp. $T_\searrow$), then c sees value $a_{n-\ell+1}$ or $a_{n-\ell+1}'$ (resp. b_ℓ or b_ℓ', resp. $b_{n-\ell+1}$ or $b_{n-\ell+1}'$).

Consider the run of M on $\mathbf{D}(I)$. We say that a pair of cursors of M *checks block* B_i if at some state during the run

- one cursor in the pair is on a position in B_i on $R_\nearrow$ (i.e., the cursor reads an element a_ℓ or a'_ℓ, for some $\ell \in B_i$) and the other cursor in the pair is on a position in B_{v-i+1} on $T_\nearrow$ (i.e., the cursor reads an element $b_{\pi\ell}$ or $b'_{\pi\ell}$, for some $\ell \in B_i$), or
- one cursor in the pair is on a position in B_{v-i+1} on $R_\searrow$ (i.e., the cursor reads an element a_ℓ or a'_ℓ, for some $\ell \in B_i$) and the other cursor in the pair is on a position in B_i on $T_\searrow$ (i.e., the cursor reads an element $b_{\pi\ell}$ or $b'_{\pi\ell}$, for some $\ell \in B_i$).

Note that each pair of cursors working on the ascendingly sorted lists $R_\nearrow$ and $T_\nearrow$ or on the descendingly sorted lists $R_\searrow$ and $T_\searrow$, can check at most one block. There are v blocks and at most $\binom{k}{2} < v$ cursor pairs. Hence, there is one block B_{i_0} that is not checked by any pair of cursors working on $R_\nearrow$ and $T_\nearrow$ or on $R_\searrow$ and $T_\searrow$. In order to also deal with pairs of cursors on $R_\nearrow$ and $T_\searrow$ or on $R_\searrow$ and $T_\nearrow$, we further divide each block B_i evenly into v consecutive subblocks, denoted by $B_i^1, \ldots, B_i^v$. So, B_i^j equals the set $\{(i-1)\frac{n}{v} + (j-1)\frac{n}{v^2} + 1, \ldots, (i-1)\frac{n}{v} + j\frac{n}{v^2}\}$. We say that a pair of cursors of M *checks subblock* B_i^j if at some state during the run

- one cursor in the pair is on a position in B_i^j on $R_\nearrow$ (thus reading an element a_ℓ or a'_ℓ, for some $\ell \in B_i^j$) and the other cursor in the pair is on a position in B_i^{v-j+1} on $T_\searrow$ (thus reading an element $b_{\pi\ell}$ or $b'_{\pi\ell}$, for some $\ell \in B_i^j$), or
- one cursor in the pair is on a position in B_{v-i+1}^{v-j+1} on $R_\searrow$ (thus reading an element a_ℓ or a'_ℓ, for some $\ell \in B_i^j$) and the other cursor in the pair is on a position in B_{v-i+1}^j on $T_\nearrow$ (thus reading an element $b_{\pi\ell}$ or $b'_{\pi\ell}$, for some $\ell \in B_i^j$).

Note that each pair of cursors working either on $R_\nearrow$ and $T_\searrow$ or on $R_\searrow$ and $T_\nearrow$, can check at most one subblock in B_{i_0}. There are v subblocks in B_{i_0} and at most $\binom{k}{2} < v$ cursor pairs. Hence, there is at least one subblock $B_{i_0}^{j_0}$ that is not checked by any pair of cursors working either on $R_\nearrow$ and $T_\searrow$ or on $R_\searrow$ and $T_\nearrow$. Note that, since the entire block B_{i_0} is not checked by any pair or cursors working either on $R_\nearrow$ and $T_\nearrow$ or on $R_\searrow$ and $T_\searrow$, the subblock $B_{i_0}^{j_0}$ is thus not checked by *any* pair of cursors (on $R_\nearrow$, $R_\searrow$, $T_\nearrow$, $T_\searrow$).

We say that M checks subblock B_i^j if at least one pair of cursors of M checks subblock B_i^j.

At this point it is useful to introduce the following terminology. By "block $B_{i_0}^{j_0}$ on R", we refer to the positions in $B_{i_0}^{j_0}$ of list $R_\nearrow$ and to the positions in $B_{v-i_0+1}^{v-j_0+1}$ of list $R_\searrow$, i.e., "block $B_{i_0}^{j_0}$ on R" contains values a_ℓ or a'_ℓ where $\ell \in B_{i_0}^{j_0}$. By "block $B_{i_0}^{j_0}$ on T", however, we refer to the positions in $B_{v-i_0+1}^{j_0}$ of list $T_\nearrow$ and to the positions in $B_{i_0}^{v-j_0+1}$ of list $T_\searrow$, i.e., "block $B_{i_0}^{j_0}$ on T" contains values $b_{\pi\ell}$ where $\ell \in B_{i_0}^{j_0}$. Note that this terminology is consistent with the way we have defined the notion of "checking a block".

It can be shown that there exist at least two different instances $\mathbf{D}(I)$ and $\mathbf{D}(J)$ with the following crucial properties:

1. The query RST returns *false* on $\mathbf{D}(I)$ and on $\mathbf{D}(J)$ (cf. $(*)$);
2. M does not check block $B_{i_0}^{j_0}$ on $\mathbf{D}(I)$, nor on $\mathbf{D}(J)$;
3. $\mathbf{D}(I)$ and $\mathbf{D}(J)$ differ on R and T only in block $B_{i_0}^{j_0}$; and
4. For each cursor c, when c has just left block $B_{i_0}^{j_0}$ (on R or T) in the run on $\mathbf{D}(I)$, the machine M is in the same state as when c has just left block $B_{i_0}^{j_0}$ in the run on $\mathbf{D}(J)$.

Let $\mathcal{V}_0, \mathcal{V}_1, \dots$ be the sequence of states in the run of M on $\mathbf{D}(I)$ and let $\mathcal{W}_0, \mathcal{W}_1, \dots$ be the sequence of states in the run of M on $\mathbf{D}(J)$. Let t_c^I and t_c^J be the points in time when the cursor c of M has just left block $B_{i_0}^{j_0}$ in the run on $\mathbf{D}(I)$ and $\mathbf{D}(J)$, respectively. Because of Property 4 above, $\mathcal{V}_{t_c^I}$ equals $\mathcal{W}_{t_c^J}$ for each cursor c. Note that the start states $\mathcal{V}_0$ and $\mathcal{W}_0$ are equal.

Now consider instance $\mathbf{D}_{\text{err}} := \mathbf{D}(I, \pi(J)^c)$. So, $\mathbf{D}_{\text{err}}$ has the same lists $R_\nearrow, R_\searrow$ as $\mathbf{D}(I)$ and the same lists $T_\nearrow, T_\searrow$ as $\mathbf{D}(J)$. It can now be shown that the (rejecting) runs of M on $\mathbf{D}(I)$ and $\mathbf{D}(J)$ can be combined to obtain a run of M on $\mathbf{D}_{\text{err}}$ which rejects $\mathbf{D}_{\text{err}}$. This is wrong, however, because due to $(*)$ the query RST returns *true* on $\mathbf{D}_{\text{err}}$. Finally, this completes the proof of Theorem 10. $\square$

Remark 11. **(a)** An analysis of the proof of Theorem 10 shows that we can make the following, more precise statement: *Let $k, m, r, s : \mathbb{N} \to \mathbb{N}$ such that*

$$k(n)^6 \cdot (\log m(n)) \cdot r(n) \cdot \max(s(n), \log n) = o(n).$$

Then for sufficiently large n, there is no FCM with at most $k(n)$ cursors, $m(n)$ modes, and $r(n)$ registers each holding bitstrings of length at most $s(n)$ that, for all unary relations R, T and binary relations S of size n decides if $R \ltimes_{x_1=y_1} (S \ltimes_{x_2=y_1} T)$ is nonempty. (In the statement of Theorem 10, k, m, r are constant.) This is interesting in particular because we can use a substantial number of cursors, polynomially related to the input size, to store data elements and still obtain the lower bound result.

(b) Note that Theorem 10 is sharp in terms of arity: if S would have been unary (and R and T of arbitrary arities), then the according RST query would have been computable on sorted inputs.

(c) Furthermore, Theorem 10 is also sharp in terms of register bitlength: Assume data elements are natural numbers, and focus on databases with elements from 1 to $O(n)$. If the background provides functions for setting and checking the i-th bit of a bitstring, the query RST is easily computed by an $O(n)$-FCM.

By a variation of the proof of Theorem 10 we can also show the following strengthening of Theorem 4:

Theorem 12. *There is no $o(n)$-FCM working on enumerations of unary relations R and S and their reversals, that checks whether $R \cap S \neq \emptyset$.*

Note that Theorems 10 and 12 are valid for arbitrary background structures.

6   Concluding Remarks

A natural question arising from Corollary 6 is whether finite cursor machines with sorting are capable of computing relational algebra queries *beyond* the semijoin algebra. The answer is affirmative:

Proposition 13. *The boolean query over a binary relation R that asks if $R = \pi_1(R) \times \pi_2(R)$ can be computed by an $O(1)$-FCM working on* $\mathsf{sort}_{(1,2),(\nearrow,\nearrow)}(R)$ *and* $\mathsf{sort}_{(2,1),(\nearrow,\nearrow)}(R)$.

The proof is straightforward. Note that, using an Ehrenfeucht-game argument, one can indeed prove that the query from Proposition 13 is not expressible in the semijoin algebra [23].

We have not been able to solve the following:

Problem 14. Is there a boolean relational algebra query that cannot be computed by any composition of $O(1)$-FCMs (or even $o(n)$-FCMs) and sorting operations?

Under a plausible assumption from parameterized complexity theory [10, 8] we can answer the $O(1)$-version of this problem affirmatively for FCMs with a decidable background structure.

There are, however, many queries that are not definable in relational algebra, but computable by FCMs with sorting. By their sequential nature, FCMs can easily compare cardinalities of relations, check whether a directed graph is regular, or do modular counting—and all these tasks are not definable in relational algebra. One might be tempted to conjecture, however, that FCMs with sorting cannot go beyond relational algebra with counting and aggregation, but this is false:

Proposition 15. *On a ternary relation G and two unary relations S and T, the boolean query "Check that $G = \pi_{1,2}(G) \times (\pi_1(G) \cup \pi_2(G))$, that $\pi_{1,2}(G)$ is deterministic, and that T is reachable from S by a path in $\pi_{1,2}(G)$ viewed as a directed graph" is not expressible in relational algebra with counting and aggregation, but computable by an $O(1)$-FCM working on sorted inputs.*

References

1. G. Aggarwal, M. Datar, S. Rajagopalan, and M. Ruhl. On the streaming model augmented with a sorting primitive. *FOCS 2004*, p 540–549.
2. N. Alon, Y. Matias, and M. Szegedy. The space complexity of approximating the frequency moments. *JCSS*, 58:137–147, 1999.
3. M. Altinel and M. Franklin. Efficient filtering of XML documents for selective dissemination of information. *VLDB 2000*, p 53–64.
4. B. Babcock, S. Babu, M. Datar, R. Motwani, and J. Widom. Models and issues in data stream systems. *PODS 2002*, p 1–16.
5. Z. Bar-Yossef, M. Fontoura, and V. Josifovski. On the memory requirements of XPath evaluation over XML streams. *PODS 2004*, p 177–188.
6. Z. Bar-Yossef, M. Fontoura, and V. Josifovski. Buffering in query evaluation over XML streams. *PODS 2005*, p 216–227.

7. C.Y. Chan, P. Felber, M.N. Garofalakis, and R. Rastogi. Efficient filtering of XML documents with XPath expressions. *The VLDB Journal*, 11:354–379, 2002.
8. R.G. Downey and M.R. Fellows. *Parameterized Complexity*. Springer, 1999.
9. R. Fagin. Degrees of acyclicity for hypergraphs and relational database schemes. *JACM*, 30:514–550, 1983.
10. J. Flum and M. Grohe. *Parameterized Complexity Theory*. Springer, 2006.
11. H. Garcia-Molina, J.D. Ullman, and J. Widom. *Database System Implementation*. Prentice Hall, 1999.
12. T.J. Green, G. Miklau, M. Onizuka, and D. Suciu. Processing XML streams with deterministic automata. *ICDT 2003*, p 173–189.
13. M. Grohe, C. Koch, and N. Schweikardt. Tight lower bounds for query processing on streaming and external memory data. *ICALP 2005*, p 1076–1088.
14. M. Grohe and N. Schweikardt. Lower bounds for sorting with few random accesses to external memory. *PODS 2005*, p 238–249.
15. A.K. Gupta and D. Suciu. Stream processing of XPath queries with predicates. *SIGMOD 2003*, p 419–430.
16. Y. Gurevich. Evolving algebras 1993: Lipari guide. In E. Börger, editor, *Specification and Validation Methods*, p 9–36. Oxford University Press, 1995.
17. L. Hella, L. Libkin, J. Nurmonen, and L. Wong. Logics with aggregate operators. *JACM*, 48(4):880–907, July 2001.
18. M. Henzinger, P. Raghavan, and S. Rajagopalan. Computing on data streams. *External Memory Algorithms. DIMACS Series In Discrete Mathematics And Theoretical Computer Science*, 50:107–118, 1999.
19. J. Hromkovič. One-way multihead deterministic finite automata. *Acta Informatica*, 19:377–384, 1983.
20. Y-N. Law, H. Wang, and C. Zaniolo. Query languages and data models for database sequences and data streams. *VLDB 2004*, p 492–503.
21. D. Leinders and J. Van den Bussche. On the complexity of division and set joins in the relational algebra. *PODS 2005*, p 76–83.
22. D. Leinders, M. Marx, J. Tyszkiewicz, and J. Van den Bussche. The semijoin algebra and the guarded fragment. *JoLLI*, 14(3):331–343, 2005.
23. D. Leinders, J. Tyszkiewicz, and J. Van den Bussche. On the expressive power of semijoin queries. *IPL*, 91(2):93–98, 2004.
24. L. Libkin. *Elements of Finite Model Theory*. Springer, 2004.
25. S. Muthukrishnan. *Data Streams: Algorithms and Applications*. Now Publishers Inc, 2005.
26. F. Peng and S.S. Chawathe. XPath queries on streaming data. *SIGMOD 2003*, p 431–442.
27. A.L. Rosenberg. On multi-head finite automata. In *Proceedings of the 6th IEEE Symposium on Switching Circuit Theory and Logical Design*, p 221–228, 1965.
28. D. Simmen, E. Shekita, and T. Malkemus. Fundamental techniques for order optimization. *SIGMOD 1996*, p 57–67.
29. J. Van den Bussche. Finite cursor machines in database query processing. In *Proceedings of the 11th International Workshop on ASMs*, p 61–61, 2004.
30. M. Yannakakis. Algorithms for acyclic database schemes. *VLDB 1981*, p 82–94.

Constant-Memory Validation of Streaming XML Documents Against DTDs

Luc Segoufin and Cristina Sirangelo

INRIA and Université Paris 11

Abstract. In this paper we investigate the problem of validating, with constant memory, streaming XML documents with respect to a DTD. Such constant memory validations can only be performed for some but not all DTDs. This paper gives a non trivial interesting step towards characterizing those DTDs for which a constant-memory on-line algorithm exists.

1   Introduction

The Extended Markup Language (XML) is emerging as the standard for data exchange on the Web. Many applications require on-line processing of large amounts of data in XML format using limited memory. Such processing includes querying XML documents, computing running aggregates of streams of numerical data, and validating XML documents against given Document Type Definitions (DTDs). For each query, for each aggregate and for each DTD, one issue is then to see what would be the minimal amount of memory which is really needed in order to process it on-line.

In this paper we are concerned with those validation problems that can be processed on-line and using a constant amount of memory. The problem of validating XML documents against a given DTD is to find out whether the document conforms the specification given by the DTD. We consider only simple DTDs that do not have any integrity constraint, and we want to perform this validation on-line. As we consider only simple DTDs, data values are not relevant for validation, and we can view our XML document as a stream of symbols representing the sequence of opening/closing tags of the document. Given such a stream, in a single pass and using a fixed amount of memory, depending on the DTD, but not on the size of the XML document, we want to be able to tell whether the document conforms the DTD or not. In other words, we are looking for a finite-state automaton (FSA) performing a pass on the XML document, as it streams through the network, and testing conformance with the DTD. An easy observation shows that this is not always possible for all DTDs ([4]).

As pointed out in [4], a FSA can certainly not check that the document is well-formed. By this we mean that the sequence of opening/closing tags is well balanced. But even if we take this for granted, and this is what we are going to do in this paper, many DTDs cannot be validated on-line using a FSA.

In this paper we tackle the question of finding those DTDs that can be validated on-line using a FSA. We call such DTDs *streamable* . The main questions we address are: Which are the streamable DTDs? Is it decidable whether a DTD is streamable? If a DTD is streamable can we compute a FSA which performs the validation?

T. Schwentick and D. Suciu (Eds.): ICDT 2007, LNCS 4353, pp. 299–313, 2007.

We don't provide a full answer to these questions, but we make a significant step towards answering them.

A simple observation made in [4] shows that if a DTD is not recursive then it is streamable. When the DTD is recursive, a FSA gets immediately lost in the depth of the tree and a first intuition that one could have is that it can only check locally whether two successive tags are consistent with those appearing in the DTD. This was the approach taken in [4]. Given a DTD τ, a *local-automaton* [1] for τ can be constructed which checks that each two successive letters are consistent with those appearing in τ. The hope was to prove that a DTD is streamable iff the set of trees accepted by the local-automaton for τ equals the set of trees valid for τ. In [4] it was shown that this is indeed the case for so called "fully-recursive" DTDs, but the paper ended with an example of a DTD showing that doing modulo-2 counting on the number of occurrences of two successive letters could be necessary to validate it on-line.

We thus generalize the notion of local-automaton by extending it using an arbitrary finite group operation on the occurrences of two successive letters. In that respect, a modulo-counting operation corresponds to the case finite groups generated by a single element. Given any finite group H and any DTD τ we define a notion of H-local-automaton for τ which extends local-automaton by combining it with computation in H. We conjecture that H-local-automata capture the notion of streamability: a DTD τ is streamable iff there exists a finite group H such that the H-*local-automaton* for τ defines the same set of trees than τ. We give a necessary and sufficient condition on a DTD τ to admit a H-local-automaton. This condition is expressed in terms of a word problem for finite groups. Unfortunately we don't know yet whether this condition is decidable or not. Recall that the word problem for finite groups is undecidable in general [3,5].

We also provide a decidable necessary and sufficient criterion on the DTDs τ for which there exists a finite commutative group H such that the H-local-automaton for τ defines the same set of trees as τ.

Maybe one of our most interesting contribution lies in the concepts we develop here in order to obtain our results. We believe that those will eventually be sufficient for finding the right characterization. We also think that they could be used in other contexts.

Related work. This paper can be seen as a continuation of [4]. In [4] several necessary conditions were given for a DTD to be streamable. We reuse one of them in an essential way in this paper, while the others will follow from our results. Those conditions were obtained using the notion of local-automaton that is also the starting brick of our construction here. In [4] a decidable characterization of DTDs streamable by a local-automaton was also given. Here we extend this result by providing a decidable characterization of DTDs streamable using a H-local-automaton for some finite commutative group H. The techniques we use in this paper are completely different than the one used in [4]. We have good hope that these new techniques could be pushed to eventually obtain the complete characterization of streamable DTDs.

---

[1] This automaton was called "standard automaton" in [4], but we believe that this terminology is misleading.

The work of [4] was also continued in [2]. In this paper some limited amount of memory was allowed by using restricted pushdown automata instead of FSA.

Testing whether a DTD is streamable can be seen as the problem of deciding which subclass of regular tree languages a FSA could accept when trees are coded à la XML, using a well-formed sequence of opening and closing tags. With this coding the string $ab\bar{b}c\bar{c}\bar{a}$ codes the tree rooted in a node labelled with a and having two children, the left one labelled with b and the right one labelled with c. The same question naturally arises with any other coding for trees. For instance one could use the functional coding which codes the tree above with the string $a(b()c())$. Using this coding one could now ask which are the regular tree languages a FSA could recognize. It is easy to see that this class is strictly contained in the class of tree languages recognized by a FSA using the XML coding. The reason is that when reading a closing bracket in the functional coding the FSA does not know the label of the node this bracket closes, while this is known in the case of the XML coding. In [1] a decidable characterization of streamable languages using the functional coding was given. It seems quite difficult to extend their ideas to the XML coding.

The paper is organized as follows. After introducing the necessary background notations in Section 2, we define in Section 3 the central notions of this paper: Graph of a DTD and separating group for a DTD. In Section 4 we define, for any finite group H, the notion of H-local-automaton for a DTD and show that the existence of a separating group for a DTD is equivalent to the existence of a H-local-automaton accepting exactly all the valid trees for this DTD. Finally in Section 5 we give a decidable characterization of those DTDs having a H-local-automaton, for some finite commutative group H, which accepts exactly all the valid trees.

2   Notations

We fix a finite set of labels Σ.

Trees. A *tree* with labels in Σ is a finite unranked ordered tree whose nodes have labels from Σ. To capture the on-line behavior, we will manipulate trees via string representations corresponding to a depth-first traversal or, equivalently, to the sequence of opening/closing tags of the document represented by t. To this end we view Σ as the set of opening tag symbols while $\bar{\Sigma} = \{\bar{a} \mid a \in \Sigma\}$ is the set of closing tag symbols. Now the string representation of a tree t is the string, also denoted by t, defined by induction as: if t has a single node of label a, then $t = a\bar{a}$. It t consists of a root labeled a and subtrees $t_1 \ldots t_k$ then t is the string $a\, t_1 \ldots t_k\, \bar{a}$.

For instance the string representation of the tree

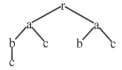

is the string $rabc\bar{c}b\bar{c}\bar{a}ab\bar{b}c\bar{c}\bar{a}\bar{r}$. We denote by $\mathcal{L}_{\text{tree}}$ the set of (string representation of) trees.

DTDs. A DTD consists of an extended context-free grammar where each rule associates to a label $a \in \Sigma$ a regular expression r_a over Σ, together with a distinguished initial symbol. A tree t is conform to a DTD τ (or t is valid w.r.t τ) if the label of its root is the label of the initial symbol of τ and, for each node $x \in t$ of label a, the sequence of labels of the children of x form a word of r_a. For instance the tree above is valid for the DTD[2]: $\begin{array}{l} r \to a^* \\ a \to bc \\ b \to c^? \\ c \to \epsilon \end{array}$. Since regular expressions are closed under union, we can assume w.l.o.g. that each DTD has a unique rule $a \to r_a$ for each symbol $a \in \Sigma$.

Each DTD τ, defines a language of trees, denoted $\mathcal{L}(\tau)$ consisting of all (string representation of) trees valid for τ.

Streaming. We are interested in DTDs τ whose membership problem can be solved using a finite memory device assuming that (the string representation of) the input tree is well formed (is in $\mathcal{L}_{\text{tree}}$). More formally we say that a DTD τ is *streamable* if there exists a regular language R over Σ such that $\mathcal{L}(\tau) = \mathcal{L}_{\text{tree}} \cap R$. If R is such that $\mathcal{L}(\tau) = \mathcal{L}_{\text{tree}} \cap R$ we say that R *recognizes* τ. For instance the DTD τ: $r \to a, a \to a \mid \epsilon$ is streamable as $\mathcal{L}(\tau) = \{r a^n \bar{a}^n \bar{r} \mid n \in \mathbb{N}\}$ which is $\mathcal{L}_{\text{tree}} \cap r a^* \bar{a}^* \bar{r}$. On the other hand it is not too difficult to show that the DTD $r \to aa, a \to a \mid \epsilon$ is not streamable. We are looking for a decidable characterization of streamable DTDs. In order to do so we associate in Section 3 a graph to any DTD and show in Section 4 how to construct from this graph a family of automata that could recognize the corresponding DTD.

3   DTDs, Graphs and Groups

In this Section we introduce the machinery necessary for stating our results.

Decomposition of a DTD. Given a DTD τ, we define a pre-order $\leq_\tau$ on Σ as follows. A label b is a successor of a label a relative to τ if there is a word w of r_a containing the label b. We then simply set $\leq_\tau$ as the reflexive transitive closure of this successor relation. This pre-order induces an equivalence relation $\sim_\tau$ on Σ: $a \sim_\tau b$ if $a \leq_\tau b \wedge b \leq_\tau a$. The set C_τ of equivalence classes of $\sim_\tau$ is now partially ordered by $\leq_\tau$.

Example 1. If τ is the following DTD: $\begin{array}{ll} r \to abc & a \to c \\ c \to edc \mid \epsilon & b \to a \\ d \to ad \mid ed \mid eb \mid \epsilon & e \to b \end{array}$
C_τ contains two equivalence classes, $\{r\}$ and $\{a, b, c, d, e\}$ and $r \leq_\tau a$.

Graph of a DTD. We now define the central notion used in this paper. For each class $\mathbf{c}$ of C_τ, we construct the labelled directed graph $G_\tau(\mathbf{c})$, denoted as the *graph of* $\mathbf{c}$ relative to τ. The intuition is that the graph of $\mathbf{c}$ relative to τ codes all the transitions between two successive letters of $\mathbf{c}$ occurring in τ.

More formally, the set of vertices of $G_\tau(\mathbf{c})$ is defined as $\{\hat{a} \mid a \in \mathbf{c}\} \cup \{a_\infty \mid a \in \mathbf{c}\}$. The nodes in $\{\hat{a} \mid a \in \mathbf{c}\}$ are called *inner nodes*. If v is a node of $G_\tau(\mathbf{c})$, $l(v)$ denotes

---

[2] $c^?$ is an abbreviation for $(c|\epsilon)$.

the label $a \in \mathbf{c}$ such that $v = \hat{a}$ or $v = a_\infty$. Given three labels a, b, d of $\mathbf{c}$, there is
an edge of label d from $\hat{a}$ to $\hat{b}$ in $G_\tau(\mathbf{c})$ whenever there is a word $w = w_1 a w_2 b w_3$ in
r_d such that all the labels occurring in w_2 are not in $\mathbf{c}$ (by definition they must belong
to classes $\mathbf{c}'$ of C_τ with $\mathbf{c} <_\tau \mathbf{c}'$). Given two labels a, d of $\mathbf{c}$, there is an edge of label
d from d_∞ to $\hat{a}$ whenever there is a word $w = w_1 a w_2$ in r_d such that all the labels
occurring in w_1 are not in $\mathbf{c}$. Given two labels a, d of $\mathbf{c}$, there is an edge of label d from
$\hat{a}$ to d_∞ whenever there is a word $w = w_1 a w_2$ in r_d such that all the labels occurring
in w_2 are not in $\mathbf{c}$. Given a label d of $\mathbf{c}$, there is an edge of label d from d_∞ to d_∞
whenever there is a word w in r_d such that all the labels occurring in w are not in $\mathbf{c}$.
No other edges occurs in $G_\tau(\mathbf{c})$. We view $G_\tau(\mathbf{c})$ as a simple directed graph. That is,
whenever there are several edges, with different labels, going from vertex $\hat{a}$ to vertex $\hat{b}$,
we replace them with a single edge whose label is the union of all the previous labels.
The graph G_τ is the disjoint union of all $G_\tau(\mathbf{c})$, $\mathbf{c} \in C_\tau$.

We illustrate this central concept with three examples that will be our running examples for the paper.

Continuation of Example 1. The graph of this DTD is (ignoring the trivial class containing only r):

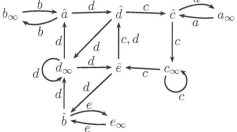

Example 2. Consider now the DTD τ: $r \to abc$ $\qquad\qquad\qquad\qquad$ $b \to a$
$$a \to ad \mid af \mid sd \mid sq \mid bf \mid bq \mid \epsilon \qquad f \to q$$
$$q \to sdch \mid sqg \mid fh \mid fg \mid \epsilon \qquad g \to q$$
$$c \to afg \qquad\qquad\qquad\qquad\qquad h \to q$$
$$d \to bfh \qquad\qquad\qquad\qquad\qquad s \to q$$

C_τ contains again two equivalence classes, one for $\{r\}$ and one for the remaining letters
(note that the last 5 rules are only here to make all the symbols but r equivalent according to $\sim_\tau$, they don't affect much the graph and are irrelevant for the rest of the paper).
The graph for this DTD looks like this. For the sake of simplicity we have ignored the
nodes $a_\infty, b_\infty, f_\infty, g_\infty, h_\infty, s_\infty, q_\infty$ and their corresponding edges which will not be
relevant in the sequel.

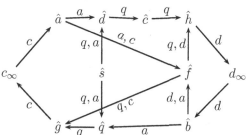

Example 3. Our third running example is with the DTD:

$r \to abc$

$u \to de \mid fe \mid fm \mid bh \mid jh \mid jm \mid qb \mid qxn \mid dn$ $j \to m$ $y \to j$

$z \to xn \mid dn \mid dw \mid fw \mid fm \mid jm \mid jy \mid xy$ $w \to y$ $a \to u$

$t \to bh \mid jh \mid jg \mid fg \mid fec$ $b \to t$ $m \to s$

$v \to adw \mid axy \mid jy \mid jg \mid fg \mid fw$ $h \to u$ $c \to z$

$s \to ax \mid qx \mid qb$ $f \to g$ $n \to w$

$e \to t$ $g \to v$ $d \to f$

$q \to u$ $x \to n$

Again C_τ contains two equivalence classes, one with only r and one with all the other labels. All the last rules are again irrelevant for the rest of the paper, they are only needed to have a unique class containing all the symbols but r. The graph is depicted below:

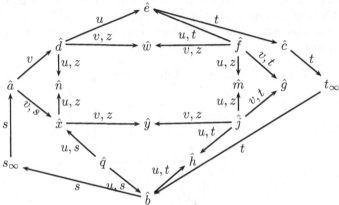

Paths. Given the graph G of a DTD, a path p is an arbitrary sequence of vertices such that for any two consecutive vertices of this sequence, there is an edge between them (not necessarily from the first one to the second one). A path p is *directed* if it traverses the edges in the direction induced by it. A path is *simple* if it traverses a vertex at most once. A path is a *cycle* if it starts and ends at the same vertex of G. A path of G_τ is *internal* if all its nodes, besides the first and last one, are inner nodes.

Continuation of Example 1. The path $b_\infty \hat{a} \hat{d} \hat{c}$ is simple, internal and directed. The path $\hat{d} \hat{e} d_\infty \hat{a} \hat{d}$ is a simple non-directed non-internal cycle.

Languages of internal paths. For each edge of G_τ from vertex $\hat{a}$ to vertex $\hat{b}$ we define $\mathcal{L}_\tau(\hat{a}, \hat{b})$ as the set of words $w \in \Sigma^*$, such that all letters of w are in a class strictly higher that the class of a, and there exists a label d of the edge such that $w_1 a w b w_2 \in r_d$ for some arbitrary strings w_1 and w_2. Similarly we define $\mathcal{L}_\tau(a_\infty, \hat{b})$, $\mathcal{L}_\tau(\hat{a}, b_\infty)$ and $\mathcal{L}_\tau(a_\infty, a_\infty)$. We extend this notion to any directed internal path p. Assume p is $v_1 \cdots v_n$. We set $\mathcal{L}_\tau(p) = \mathcal{L}_\tau(v_1, v_2)\, l(v_2)\, \mathcal{L}_\tau(v_2, v_3)\, l(v_3) \cdots l(v_{n-1})\, \mathcal{L}_\tau(v_{n-1}, v_n)$. Finally for each symbol d, let $\mathcal{L}_\tau(d)$ to be the union over all directed internal paths p, starting and ending in d_∞, of $\mathcal{L}_\tau(p)$. Note that we take this union over all directed internal paths, not just the simple ones (the path can go several time through the same node).

Continuation of Example 1. In this example we have $\mathcal{L}_\tau(d) = \{ad, eb, ed, \epsilon\}$ and $\mathcal{L}_\tau(c) = \{edc, \epsilon\}$.

NECESSARY CONDITION: A DTD τ satisfies condition $(*)$ if for all d, $\mathcal{L}_\tau(d) = r_d$.

All the three DTDs given in Example 1,2 and 3 satisfy the condition $(*)$. On the other hand, if we replace in the DTD of Example 1 the line $d \rightarrow ad \mid ed \mid eb \mid \epsilon$ with $d \rightarrow ad \mid eb \mid \epsilon$ the edges of the underlying graph remain the same (the new graph differs from the previous one only by the label of edge $(\hat{e}, \hat{d})$ which no longer contains d) but the DTD no longer satisfies the condition $(*)$. It follows from Theorem 1 below that this DTD is not streamable.

The following result is a rephrasing of the first necessary condition for streamability proved in [4].

Theorem 1. *If a DTD τ is streamable then it satisfies $(*)$.*

Based on this result, in the sequel we will represent our DTDs using their graph representation. We aim at characterizing those graphs that represent streamable DTDs. In order to do this we use the notions of *monochromatic cycles* and *dangerous cycles* that we introduce now.

Monochromatic cycles and dangerous cycles. The set MCycles(τ) of *monochromatic cycles of τ* is the set of all simple directed cycles p of G_τ such that there is a label $a \in \mathbf{c}$ which occurs as a label of all edges traversed by p.

A directed path of $G_\tau(\mathbf{c})$ from $\hat{a}$ to $\hat{b}$, is a *source path* if it consists of a simple internal directed path from $\hat{a}$ to d_∞, followed by a simple internal directed path from d_∞ to $\hat{b}$, for some label d of $\mathbf{c}$. A directed cycle p of G_τ is *dangerous* if the following holds:

- p traverses successively vertices $\hat{a}_n, \cdots, \hat{a}_1$ of G_τ by forming a source path from $\hat{a}_j$ to $\hat{a}_{j-1}, \forall j\ 1 < j < n+1$, and by forming a simple internal directed path p' from $\hat{a}_1$ to $\hat{a}_n$, where $a_1, \cdots, a_n$ is a sequence of labels of some class $\mathbf{c}$ such that all labels in the sequence are distinct, except possibly a_1 and a_n.
- There exists a label d of class $\mathbf{c}' <_\tau \mathbf{c}$ and a word w of r_d with
  $w = w_1 a_1 w_2 \cdots w_n a_n w_{n+1}$, where $w_1, \cdots, w_{n+1}$ are arbitrary strings over Σ.
- Either $w_1 a_1 \mathcal{L}_\tau(p') a_n w_{n+1} \not\subseteq r_d$ or
  for all internal directed paths p_{1n} in G_τ from $\hat{a}_1$ to $\hat{a}_n$,
  $a_1 w_2 a_2 \cdots w_n a_n \notin a_1 \mathcal{L}_\tau(p_{1n}) a_n$

We denote by DCycles(τ) the set of dangerous cycles of τ.

Continuation of Example 1. In this example the set MCycles(τ) contains the monochromatic cycles for d and c: $d_\infty \hat{a} \hat{d} d_\infty$, $d_\infty \hat{e} \hat{d} d_\infty$, $d_\infty \hat{e} \hat{b} d_\infty$, $d_\infty d_\infty$, $c_\infty \hat{e} \hat{d} \hat{c} c_\infty$, and $c_\infty c_\infty$. The graph also contains the dangerous cycle $d_\infty \hat{a} \hat{d} \hat{c} c_\infty \hat{e} \hat{b} d_\infty$. This cycle is dangerous because: 1) $r \rightarrow abc$, $\hat{b} d_\infty \hat{a}$ and $\hat{c} c_\infty \hat{e} \hat{b}$ are dangerous, and 2) $adc \notin r_r$.

Continuation of Example 2. In this example some of the monochromatic cycles in the set MCycles(τ) are: $c_\infty \hat{a} \hat{f} \hat{g} c_\infty$, $d_\infty \hat{b} \hat{f} \hat{h} d_\infty$ and $q_\infty \hat{s} \hat{d} \hat{c} \hat{h} q_\infty$. The graph also contains the dangerous cycle $c_\infty \hat{a} \hat{d} \hat{c} \hat{h} d_\infty \hat{b} \hat{q} \hat{g} c_\infty$. This cycle is dangerous because: 1) $r \to abc$, $\hat{b} \hat{q} \hat{g} c_\infty \hat{a}$ and $\hat{c} \hat{h} d_\infty \hat{b}$ are dangerous, and 2) $adc \notin r_r$.

Continuation of Example 3. In this example some of the monochromatic cycles in the set MCycles(τ) are: $s_\infty \hat{a} \hat{x} s_\infty \ v_\infty \hat{a} \hat{d} \hat{w} v_\infty \ u_\infty \hat{f} \hat{m} u_\infty$.

The graph has only one dangerous cycle $s_\infty \hat{a} \hat{d} \hat{e} \hat{c} t_\infty \hat{b} s_\infty$. This cycle is dangerous because 1) $r \to abc$, $\hat{b} s_\infty \hat{a}$ is dangerous, $\hat{c} t_\infty \hat{b}$ is also dangerous, and 2) $adec \notin r_r$.

Groups versus graphs. Let H be a finite group, G be a directed graph and μ be a mapping from the set of edges of G to H. This induces a mapping, which we also denote by μ, between sequences of edges of G into H such that $\mu(e_1 e_2) = \mu(e_1) \cdot \mu(e_2)$ where $\cdot$ is the group operation of H. In particular the mapping μ induces a homomorphism between the directed paths of G to H: If $p = v_1 \cdots v_n$ is a directed path of G then $\mu(p) = \mu((v_1, v_2))\mu((v_2, v_3)) \cdots \mu((v_{n-1}, v_n))$.

Given a DTD τ, a separating group for τ is a finite group H together with a mapping μ from G_τ to H such that $\forall p \in$ MCycles(τ), $\mu(p) = 1$ and $\forall p \in$ DCycles(τ), $\mu(p) \neq 1$ where 1 is the neutral element of H.

Continuation of Example 1. In this example there is no separating group for τ. Indeed assume there is a finite group H and a mapping μ from G_τ to H such that $\forall p \in$ MCycles(τ), $\mu(p) = 1$. Let x bet the edge $(\hat{e}, \hat{d})$. One label of x is d and by hypothesis all monochromatic cycles of d are mapped to 1 by μ. Simple algebraic computation shows that then $\mu(x) = \mu(p_d)$ where p_d is the path $(\hat{e}, \hat{b}, d_\infty, \hat{a}, \hat{d})$. Now c is also a label of x and similar algebraic computation shows that $\mu(x)\mu(p_c) = 1$ where p_c is the path $(\hat{d}, \hat{c}, c_\infty, \hat{e})$. This implies that $\mu(p) = 1$ where p is the path $p_d \cdot p_c$. But p is exactly the dangerous cycle of τ! Therefore any mapping μ sending all monochromatic cycles to the identity of H will also send a dangerous cycle to 1.

Continuation of Example 2. In this example there is a separating group for τ. Let H be the group of order 3 generated by one element: $H = \{1, x, x^2\}$ with $x^3 = 1$. Let μ be the mapping sending all edges to 1 except for the q-labelled edges $e_1 = (\hat{d}, \hat{c})$, $e_2 = (\hat{q}, \hat{g})$, $e_3 = (q_\infty, \hat{s})$. For those three edges we set $\mu(e_1) = \mu(e_2) = x$ and $\mu(e_3) = x^2 = x^{-1}$. Now one can verify that we do have $\mu(p) = 1$ for all $p \in$ MCycles(τ) (this is trivial for all monochromatic cycles of label different than q and can be done by hand for the others) but that $\mu(p) = x^2 \neq 1$ for the dangerous cycle p. Moreover, one can verify that the group H together with the mapping μ also separates all the other dangerous cycles of the graph from the monochromatic cycles. In particular it can be checked that for all dangerous cycles θ of the graph other than p, $\mu(\theta) = x \neq 1$.

Continuation of Example 3. In this example also there is a separating group for τ. Let H be any finite non-commutative group with α and β two elements of H which do no commute ($\alpha\beta \neq \beta\alpha$ or equivalently $\alpha^{-1}\beta^{-1}\alpha\beta \neq 1$). Let μ be the mapping that sends all edges to 1 except for $\mu((\hat{j}, \hat{m})) = \mu((\hat{d}, \hat{e})) = \mu((\hat{y}, z_\infty)) = \mu((u_\infty, \hat{f})) = \mu((v_\infty, \hat{a})) = \alpha, \mu((\hat{f}, \hat{g})) = \mu((\hat{c}, t_\infty)) = \mu((\hat{w}, v_\infty)) = \beta, \mu((\hat{x}, \hat{y})) = \mu((z_\infty, \hat{j})) = \mu((\hat{e}, u_\infty)) = \mu((\hat{m}, u_\infty)) = \alpha^{-1}, \mu((v_\infty, \hat{f})) = \mu((t_\infty, \hat{f})) = \beta^{-1}$, and $\mu((\hat{a}, \hat{d})) = \alpha^{-1}\beta^{-1}$. One can verify that we do have $\forall p \in$ MCycles(τ), $\mu(p) = 1$ but that for the dangerous cycle p we have $\mu(p) = \alpha^{-1}\beta^{-1}\alpha\beta \neq 1$.

The notions of monochromatic and dangerous cycles are motivated by the following result showing a sufficient condition for a DTD to be streamable. It is possible that this condition is also necessary, see Section 6.

Theorem 2. *If a DTD τ satisfies* ($*$) *and has a separating group, then τ is streamable.*

Theorem 2 follows from Theorem 4 below that shows how to construct, from a separating group for τ, a FSA that recognizes τ. Note that, although Theorem 4 is constructive, we do not know yet how to decide the existence of such a separating group nor whether we can construct it if it exists. In Section 5 we will construct such a separating group for a special case of DTDs and in Section 6 we will indicate the difficulty of testing the existence of a separating group.

4   Groups and Automata

Let τ be a DTD verifying ($*$). Let H be a finite group and μ be a mapping from edges of G_τ to H. From τ, H and μ we construct an automaton $A(\tau, H, \mu)$, called the *H-local-automaton* for τ which combines local tests on two consecutive symbols with operations in H. If H is a separating group for τ we show that $A(\tau, H, \mu)$ recognizes τ.

Let 1 be the neutral element of H and $\cdot$ be its group operation. Consider again the partition C_τ of Σ and its preorder $\leq_\tau$. For $d \in \Sigma$, recall the definition of $\mathcal{L}_\tau(d)$ given in Section 3.

For each class $\mathbf{c} \in C_\tau$ and $d \in \mathbf{c}$, we define an automaton $A_\mu(\mathbf{c}, d)$ by induction on $\leq_\tau$ as follows. The intuition is that $A_\mu(\mathbf{c}, d)$ is only concerned with symbols in classes higher or equal to $\mathbf{c}$ relative to $\leq_\tau$ and that it checks locally consistency with τ while simulating the product in H for successive pairs of symbols in $\mathbf{c}$: For each sequence of two successive symbols in $\mathbf{c}$ it checks whether this sequence is plausible in τ (by inspecting $G_\tau(\mathbf{c})$) and, if this is the case, simulates the product in H using this pair and μ. When a symbol in a higher class is read, local consistency with τ and the previous symbol read is checked and a subcomputation for the new class is started. Each subcomputation should start simulating the product in H at its neutral element 1 and ends only when the current value of this product is 1. In summary only local tests are performed against the DTD except for the product in H which is the only information which is carried over the tree.

Checking that any sequence of two successive symbols in $\mathbf{c}$ is plausible in τ can be read from $G_\tau(\mathbf{c})$: It amounts to check that, for any $a, b \in \mathbf{c}$, if $\bar{a}b$ occurs then $(\hat{a}, \hat{b}) \in G_\tau(\mathbf{c})$, if ab occurs then $(a_\infty, \hat{b}) \in G_\tau(\mathbf{c})$, if $a\bar{b}$ occurs then $a = b$ and $(a_\infty, a_\infty) \in G_\tau(\mathbf{c})$, and, if $\bar{a}\bar{b}$ occurs then $(\hat{a}, b_\infty) \in G_\tau(\mathbf{c})$.

The simulation of the product in H is done as follows. For each class $\mathbf{c} \in C_\tau$ and $d \in \mathbf{c}$, let $A_H(\mathbf{c}, d)$ be the automaton simulating the product in H for edges in $G_\tau(\mathbf{c})$ while ignoring the symbols not related to $\mathbf{c}$. It is defined formally as follows. Its states are elements of $(\Sigma \cup \bar{\Sigma}) \times H$. Its initial state is $(d, 1)$. When reading a symbol $\delta \in (\Sigma \cup \bar{\Sigma})$, it has a transition from (α, h) to (β, h') exactly when one of the condition below is satisfied.

- $\delta \in \mathbf{c}$, $\beta = \delta$, $\alpha = \bar{y}$ for $y \in \mathbf{c}$, $(\hat{y}, \hat{\delta})$ is an edge e of G_τ, and $h \cdot \mu(e) = h'$.
- $\delta \in \mathbf{c}$, $\beta = \delta$, $\alpha \in \mathbf{c}$, $(\alpha_\infty, \hat{\delta})$ is an edge e of G_τ, and $h \cdot \mu(e) = h'$.
- $\delta \in \bar{\mathbf{c}}$, $\beta = \delta$, $\alpha \in \mathbf{c}$, $\delta = \bar{a}$, $(\alpha_\infty, \alpha_\infty)$ is an edge e of G_τ, and $h \cdot \mu(e) = h'$.
- $\delta \in \bar{\mathbf{c}}$, $\beta = \delta$, $\alpha \in \bar{\mathbf{c}}$, $(\hat{y}', x'_\infty)$ is an edge e of G_τ where x' and y' are such that $\delta = \bar{x}'$ and $\alpha = \bar{y}'$, and $h \cdot \mu(e) = h'$.
- If $\delta \notin (\mathbf{c} \cup \bar{\mathbf{c}})$, $\alpha = \beta$ and $h = h'$ (those letters are ignored).

The set of final states of $A_H(\mathbf{c}, d)$ are all the states $(\bar{a}, h)$, $a \in \mathbf{c}$, such that $(\hat{a}, d_\infty)$ is an edge of $G_\tau(\mathbf{c})$ such that $h \cdot \mu((\hat{a}, d_\infty)) = 1$, together with all the states (d, h), such that (d_∞, d_∞) is an edge of $G_\tau(\mathbf{c})$ such that $h \cdot \mu((d_\infty, d_\infty)) = 1$.

It now remains to perform the local tests on how the class can interleave. This is also read from G_τ.

Let $\mathbf{c}$ be a maximal class of C_τ and let $d \in \mathbf{c}$. This is the simple case. Because the class is maximal, there is no interleaving authorized and $A_\mu(\mathbf{c}, d)$ needs only to simulate the product in H. In this case we let $A_\mu(\mathbf{c}, d) = A_H(\mathbf{c}, d)$.

Let now $\mathbf{c}$ be an arbitrary class and $d \in \mathbf{c}$. Assuming the definition of $A_\mu(\mathbf{c}', d')$ for each class $\mathbf{c}'$ and element $d' \in \mathbf{c}'$ such that $\mathbf{c} <_\tau \mathbf{c}'$, we define $A_\mu(\mathbf{c}, d)$. In this case we have to worry about symbols in higher classes and check for local consistency with τ. This is done as follows. We define next an automata $A_\tau(\mathbf{c}, d)$ that does this local consistency tests then we set $A_\mu(\mathbf{c}, d)$ as the product of $A_\tau(\mathbf{c}, d)$ with $A_H(\mathbf{c}, d)$. For each edge e of $G_\tau(\mathbf{c})$, recall the definition of $\mathcal{L}(e)$ as given in Section 3. For each edge e of $G_\tau(\mathbf{c})$, let A_e be the deterministic minimal automaton for $\mathcal{L}(e)$ and assume that these automata have pairwise disjoint sets of states. We build on these automata to construct $A_\tau(\mathbf{c}, d)$. $A_\tau(\mathbf{c}, d)$ contains all the states of the A_e together with one state q_x per symbol $x \in \Sigma \cup \bar{\Sigma}$. Let $e = (\alpha, \beta)$ be an edge of $G_\tau(\mathbf{c})$, let q_0^e be the initial state of A_e and F^e be its set of accepting states. For any transition (q, d', q') of A_e, where $d' \in \mathbf{c}'$, we add in $A_\tau(\mathbf{c}, d)$ a fresh new copy of $A_\mu(\mathbf{c}', d')$ with initial state q_0 and accepting set of states F, and we add in $A_\tau(\mathbf{c}, d)$ the transitions (q, d', q_0) and $(q_f, \bar{d}', q')$ for any $q_f \in F$. Depending on α and β we also add in $A_\tau(\mathbf{c}, d)$ the following transitions (with $a = l(\alpha)$ and $b = l(\beta)$).

- If α and β are inner nodes, we add transitions $q_{\bar{a}} \xrightarrow{\epsilon} q_0^e$ and $q_f^e \xrightarrow{b} q_b$ for any $q_f^e \in F^e$.

- If α is an inner node but β is not, we add transitions $q_{\bar{a}} \xrightarrow{\epsilon} q_0^e$ and $q_f^e \xrightarrow{\bar{b}} q_{\bar{b}}$ for any $q_f^e \in F^e$.

- If β is an inner node but α is not, we add transitions $q_a \xrightarrow{\epsilon} q_0^e$ and $q_f^e \xrightarrow{b} q_b$ for any $q_f^e \in F^e$.

- If both α and β are not inner nodes (then $\alpha = \beta$), we add transitions $q_a \xrightarrow{\epsilon} q_0^e$ and $q_f^e \xrightarrow{\bar{b}} q_{\bar{b}}$ for any $q_f^e \in F^e$.

The initial state of $A_\tau(\mathbf{c}, d)$ is the state q_d. The set of accepting states of $A_\tau(\mathbf{c}, d)$ are all the accepting states of the automata A_e where e is an edge ending in d_∞. This finishes the construction of $A_\tau(\mathbf{c}, d)$ and therefore of $A_\mu(\mathbf{c}, d)$.

Now set $A(\tau, H, \mu)$ as $A_\mu(\mathbf{c}, r)$ where r is the initial symbol of the DTD and $\mathbf{c}$ is the class of r. When H is the trivial group with one element, the $A(\tau, H, \mu)$ is exactly what was call "standard automaton" in [4]. We are now ready to state the main result of this paper.

Theorem 3. *Assume that τ satisfies $(*)$. There exists a separating group for τ iff there exists a finite group H and a mapping μ such that $A(\tau, H, \mu)$ recognizes τ.*

The proof of Theorem 3 is given in two steps. Theorem 4 below shows that if H is a separating group for τ then $A(\tau, H, \mu)$ recognizes τ. Next, Theorem 5 shows how to compute a separating group from a H-local-automaton recognizing τ.

Theorem 4. *If τ verifies $(*)$ and there exists a separating group H for τ via the mapping μ, then $A(\tau, H, \mu)$ recognizes τ.*

Proof. The proof of this theorem is very technical and will appear in the full version of this paper. We only outline it here. One first shows that if H and μ are such that for each $p \in \mathrm{MCycles}(\tau)$ $\mu(p) = 1$, then all trees valid with respect to τ are accepted by $A(\tau, H, \mu)$. This is done by induction on $\leq_\tau$ by noticing that in a valid tree, any sequence of labels of the children of a node induces a monochromatic cycle in G_τ.

The other direction, showing that $A(\tau, H, \mu)$ accepts only valid trees is more complicated and requires that H is a separating group and that τ verifies $(*)$. The proof is again done by induction on $\leq_\tau$. We only illustrate here the requirement on dangerous cycles on an example. Assume the DTD has initial symbol r with the rule $r \rightarrow abc$ and that a, b, c are symbols in the same class $\mathbf{c}$ and that no other classes are in τ. By construction $A(\tau, H, \mu)$ performs three successive "calls", to $A_\mu(\mathbf{c}, a)$, $A_\mu(\mathbf{c}, b)$, then $A_\mu(\mathbf{c}, c)$. Assume we have shown by induction that all trees accepted by $A_\mu(\mathbf{c}, a_i)$ are valid for τ, we show that this is the case for $A_\mu([r], r)$. Let t be a tree accepted by $A(\tau, H, \mu)$. We decompose the string t into $s_1 s_2 s_3$ where s_i is the substring read by $A_\mu(\mathbf{c}, a_i)$, where $a_1 = a, a_2 = b, a_3 = c$. Assume moreover that those substrings are as depicted in Figure 1.

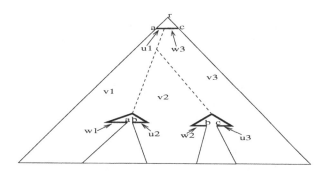

Fig. 1. Illustration of the run of $A(\tau, H, \mu)$. We have $s_i = u_i v_i w_i$, where u_i is the substring containing all the trees in s_i whose root is either the first symbol of s_i or one of its siblings, w_i is the substring containing all the trees in s_i whose root is either the last symbol of s_i or one of its siblings and v_i is the remaining part of s_i.

We further decompose s_i into $u_i v_i w_i$ as depicted in Figure 1. Let ν_i be the sequence of tree nodes consisting of the roots of the trees in u_i followed by the first node processed in v_i. Similarly let ω_i be the sequence of tree nodes consisting of the last node processed in v_i followed by the roots of the trees in w_i. As each of s_i is read by $A_\mu(\mathbf{c}, a_i)$, for all i, ν_i and ω_i correspond to paths in $G_\tau(\mathbf{c})$, which we denote as α_i and β_i, respectively. This implies that the path p formed by the path concatenation $\beta_3 \cdot \alpha_3 \cdot \beta_2 \cdot \alpha_2 \cdot \beta_1 \cdot \alpha_1$ is a cycle in τ.

By abuse of notations we denote by $\mu(s)$ the image by μ of the path induced by the sequence of symbols of s. We know that $\mu(s_1) = \mu(s_2) = \mu(s_3) = 1$. This implies – by denoting as v_i' and v_i'' the first and the last symbol of v_i, respectively – that $\mu(v_i) = \mu(u_i v_i')^{-1} \mu(v_i'' w_i)^{-1}$. By induction we know that any tree t' entirely contained in a s_i is valid for τ and therefore is such that $\mu(t') = 1$. This implies that $\mu(u_i v_i') = \mu(\alpha_i)$ and $\mu(v_i'' w_i) = \mu(\beta_i)$. Therefore $\mu(v_1)\mu(v_2)\mu(v_3) = \mu(p)^{-1}$. Now notice that there exist valid forests f_1, f_2 such that $v_1 f_1 v_2 f_2 v_3$ is a valid tree rooted in a label of class $\mathbf{c}$, thus $\mu(v_1 f_1 v_2 f_2 v_3) = 1$. This implies $\mu(v_1)\mu(v_2)\mu(v_3) = 1$. As H was a separating group for τ, this shows that p cannot be a dangerous cycle. Therefore (a, b) and (b, c) must be edges of $G_\tau(\mathbf{c})$ and the sequence of labels in the path $\alpha_1 \beta_3$ must be valid below the root. This implies that t is valid for τ. The general case requires more case analysis but the overall idea is the same.   □

Theorem 5. *Assume H and μ are such that $A(\tau, H, \mu)$ recognizes τ. Then there exists a finite group H', constructible from τ, H and μ, such that H' is a separating group for τ. Moreover if H is commutative then H' is also commutative.*

Proof. The proof will appear in the full version of this paper.   □

5   Commutative Separating Groups

In this section we provide a necessary and sufficient decidable condition for the existence of a commutative separating group for a DTD. Note that by Theorem 5 this implies a necessary and sufficient decidable condition for the existence of a H-local-automaton, H commutative, that recognizes a given DTD.

Throughout this section we consider a DTD τ satisfying the condition $(*)$. Let X_τ be the set of edges of G_τ and m the cardinality of X_τ. Let n be the number of cycles in MCycles(τ). Let $X_\tau = \{x_1, \ldots, x_m\}$ and MCycles$(\tau) = \{\pi_1, \ldots, \pi_n\}$.

We first fix some more notations on linear algebra. For any $r \in \mathbb{N}$, let $\mathbb{Z}^r$ denote the set of vectors of integers of size r, and $\mathbb{N}^r$ denote the set of vectors of non-negative integers of size r. For any $\bar{y} \in \mathbb{Z}^r$, the i-th component of $\bar{y}$ will be denoted as $\bar{y}[i]$. The maximum absolute value occurring in $\bar{y}$ is denoted by max $\bar{y}$.

For each $k \in \mathbb{N}$, and each $y, z \in \mathbb{N}$, $y \equiv_k z$ denotes that y and z agree modulo k and $[y]_k$ is the number between 0 and $k - 1$ equivalent to y modulo k, and $[\bar{y}]_k$ denotes its extension to $\mathbb{N}^r$. Moreover, for each $k \in \mathbb{N}$, the vector $\bar{k}^r$ is the vector of $\mathbb{N}^r$ which has all its components set to k. For each $i \leq r$, the vector ϵ_i^r denotes the vector of $\mathbb{N}^r$ having 1 on the i-th component, and 0 everywhere else.

For each path π of G_τ and for each edge $x_i \in X_\tau$ we denote as $|\pi|_{x_i}$ the number of times that π traverses x_i according to the edge orientation, and by $|\pi|_{x_i^-}$ the number of times that π traverses x_i in reverse direction. To each path π of G_τ, we associate a vector $\bar{\pi}$ of $\mathbb{Z}^m$ such that, for each $i = 1, \ldots, m$, $\bar{\pi}[i] = |\pi|_{x_i} - |\pi|_{x_i^-}$. Notice that if π is a directed path, $\bar{\pi}$ is a vector of $\mathbb{N}^m$, and if π is a simple path, then $\bar{\pi} \in \{-1, 0, 1\}$.

We denote as $\overline{\text{MCycles}(\tau)}$ the subgroup of $\mathbb{Z}^m$ generated by $\{\bar{\pi}_1, \ldots, \bar{\pi}_n\}$, that is $\overline{\text{MCycles}(\tau)} = \{\bar{y} \in \mathbb{Z}^m \mid \bar{y} = \sum_{i=1}^n \alpha_i \cdot \bar{\pi}_i, \ \alpha_i \in \mathbb{Z}, \ i = 1, .., n\}$.

All this notation is motivated by the following result:

Theorem 6. *Given a DTD τ satisfying $(*)$, there exists a commutative separating group for τ if and only if $\forall p \in \text{DCycles}(\tau)$, $\bar{p} \notin \overline{\text{MCycles}(\tau)}$.*

Proof. We first prove the "only if" part. Let $p \in \text{DCycles}(\tau)$ be such that $\bar{p} = \sum_{i=1}^n \alpha_i \cdot \bar{\pi}_i$, $\alpha_i \in \mathbb{Z}$ for $i = 1, .., n$.

Let D be the set of indices $i \in 1..n$ such that $\alpha_i \geq 0$, and R be the set of indices $i \in 1..n$ such that $\alpha_i < 0$, and let γ_i be the absolute value of α_i, for each $i = 1, .., n$. Then the following equality holds: $\bar{p} + \sum_{i \in R} \gamma_i \cdot \bar{\pi}_i = \sum_{i \in D} \gamma_i \cdot \bar{\pi}_i$

Suppose, by contradiction, that there exists a commutative separating group H with associated mapping μ from G_τ to H.

By commutativity of H, $\mu(p) = \prod_{j=1}^m \mu(x_j)^{\bar{p}[j]}$ and $\mu(\pi_i) = \prod_{j=1}^m \mu(x_j)^{\bar{\pi}_i[j]}$ for each $i = 1, .., n$. Let h_R be the element of H obtained as $h_R = \prod_{i \in R} \mu(\pi_i)^{\gamma_i}$; by commutativity of H, $h_R = \prod_{j=1}^m \mu(x_j)^{k_j}$, where $k_j = \sum_{i \in R} \gamma_i \cdot \bar{\pi}_i[j]$, for $j = 1, .., m$.

Similarly, Let h_D be the element of H obtained as $h_D = \prod_{i \in D} \mu(\pi_i)^{\gamma_i}$; by commutativity of H, $h_D = \prod_{j=1}^m \mu(x_j)^{k'_j}$, where $k'_j = \sum_{i \in D} \gamma_i \cdot \bar{\pi}_i[j]$, for $j = 1, .., m$.

Together with $\bar{p} + \sum_{i \in R} \gamma_i \cdot \bar{\pi}_i = \sum_{i \in D} \gamma_i \cdot \bar{\pi}_i$ this immediately implies that $\mu(p) = h_D \cdot h_R^{-1}$. As H is a separating group for τ, we have $h_R = h_D = 1$ therefore $\mu(p) = 1$ which is a contradiction.

We will now prove the "if" part. For each $p \in \text{DCycles}(\tau)$ we show that there exists a finite commutative group H_p and a homomorphism μ_p from G_τ to H_p, such that $\mu_p(p) \neq 1$ and $\mu_p(\pi_i) = 1$ for $i = 1, \ldots, n$. The desired commutative separating group for τ is the product of all H_p, for $p \in \text{DCycles}(\tau)$.

Given $p \in \text{DCycles}(\tau)$ such that $p \notin \overline{\text{MCycles}(\tau)}$ we effectively construct a separating commutative group for p.

For each edge x_j of X_τ, let D_j be the set of cycles of $\text{MCycles}(\tau)$ which traverse the edge x_j: $D_j = \{i \in 1..n \mid \bar{\pi}_i[j] = 1\}$.

For a vector $\bar{y} = (y_1, \ldots, y_m)$ over $\mathbb{N}^m$, we define the following formula of Presburger arithmetic:

$$\psi(\bar{y}) = \exists \alpha_1, \ldots, \alpha_n \bigwedge_{j=1}^m \left(y_j = \sum_{i \in D_j} \alpha_i \right)$$

By construction, ψ is satisfied by the vector associated to each cycle of $\text{MCycles}(\tau)$ and is not satisfied by $\bar{p}$; We will refer to this property saying that ψ is a separating formula for $\bar{p}$.

By Presburger quantifier elimination procedure, ψ can be transformed into an equivalent quantifier free formula $\varphi(\bar{y}) := \varphi_e(\bar{y}) \wedge \varphi_c(\bar{y})$, where, using matrix notation, φ_e and φ_c are formulas of the form:

$$\varphi_e(\bar{y}) := (A\bar{y} = B\bar{y}) \qquad \varphi_c(\bar{y}) := (C\bar{y} \equiv_\delta D\bar{y})$$

where $A, B \in \mathbb{N}^{m_e \times m}$ and $C, D \in \mathbb{N}^{m_c \times m}$, for some $m_e, m_c \in \mathbb{N}$.

From φ we define a new separating formula for $\bar{p}$, $\varphi_k(\bar{y})$, whose terms use only the modulo-congruence operator $\equiv_k$, for some $k \in \mathbb{N}$. We consider two cases:

1. $\varphi_c(\bar{p})$ is false. Then $\varphi_k(\bar{y}) := \varphi_c(\bar{y})$ and $k = \delta$.
2. $\varphi_e(\bar{p})$ is false. We choose $k = \max(A\bar{p} - B\bar{p}) + 1$ and take $\varphi_k(\bar{y}) := (A\bar{y} \equiv_k B\bar{y})$.

In both cases we have $\varphi_k(\bar{y}) := (E\bar{y} \equiv_k F\bar{y})$, where $E, F \in \mathbb{N}^{r \times m}$ for some $r \in \mathbb{N}$, and the vector of p does not satisfy the formula while it is satisfied by any cycles in $\mathrm{MCycles}(\tau)$. We now construct, from $\varphi_k(\bar{y})$, a commutative finite group H_p and a homomorphism μ_p from the paths of G_τ to H_p, such that $\mu_p(p) \neq 1$ and $\mu_p(\pi_i) = 1$ for all $i = 1 \ldots n$.

Let K be the commutative finite group whose elements are the pairs $(\bar{z}_1, \bar{z}_2) \in \mathbb{N}^r \times \mathbb{N}^r$ such that $\bar{z}_1 < \bar{k}^r \wedge \bar{z}_2 < \bar{k}^r$, with group composition defined by $(\bar{z}_1, \bar{z}_2) + (\bar{z}_3, \bar{z}_4) = ([\bar{z}_1 + \bar{z}_3]_k, [\bar{z}_2 + \bar{z}_4]_k)$. We define a mapping μ_K from the set of edges of G_τ to K as follows: for each edge $x_i \in X_\tau$, $\mu_K(x_i) = ([E\epsilon_i^m]_k, [F\epsilon_i^m]_k)$.

Let $K_=$ be the (normal) subgroup of K, consisting of all elements of the form $(\bar{z}, \bar{z})$. Let $H_p = K/K_=$, and set μ_p as the composition of μ_K with the quotient morphism. As $[E\bar{p}]_k \neq [F\bar{p}]_k$, $\mu_K(p) = ([E\bar{p}]_k, [F\bar{p}]_k)$ is not in $K_=$ thus, $\mu_p(p) \neq 1$.

Conversely if π is a cycle of $\mathrm{MCycles}(\tau)$, $[E\bar{\pi}]_k = [F\bar{\pi}]_k$, thus $\mu_p(\pi) = 1$. This concludes the proof of the Theorem.   □

An immediate corollary of Theorem 6 and of the constructiveness of its proof together with Theorem 4, is the following:

Corollary 1. *Given a DTD τ, it is decidable whether there exists a commutative separating group for τ, and if it exists, the group, and therefore a H-local-automaton recognizing τ, can be effectively computed.*

Continuation of Example 2. In this example a commutative separating group exists. We have already given an example of such a group. This group could also be obtained from Theorem 6. Indeed one can verify that the dangerous cycle $p = b_\infty \hat{q} \hat{g} c_\infty \hat{a} \hat{d} \hat{c} \hat{h} d_\infty \hat{b}$ is not a linear combination of monochromatic cycles as defined in the statement of Theorem 6.

Continuation of Example 3. This example shows that there exist DTDs for which no commutative separating group exists, but a separating group does exist. Indeed, the dangerous cycle $p = s_\infty \hat{a} \hat{d} \hat{e} \hat{c} t_\infty \hat{b} s_\infty$ for that DTD τ can be shown to be such that $\bar{p} \in \overline{\mathrm{MCycles}(\tau)}$ as follows. Let $\theta_1, \theta_2, \theta_3, \theta_4, \theta_5$ be the following non-directed cycles: $\theta_1 = \hat{d} \hat{n} \hat{x} \hat{y} \hat{j} \hat{m} \hat{f} \hat{w} \hat{d}$, $\theta_2 = \hat{d} \hat{e} \hat{f} \hat{m} \hat{j} \hat{h} \hat{b} \hat{q} \hat{x} \hat{n} \hat{d}$, $\theta_3 = \hat{d} \hat{w} \hat{f} \hat{g} \hat{j} \hat{y} \hat{x} \hat{a} \hat{d}$, $\theta_4 = \hat{f} \hat{e} \hat{c} t_\infty \hat{b} \hat{h} \hat{j} \hat{g} \hat{f}$, $\theta_5 = \hat{x} \hat{q} \hat{b} s_\infty \hat{a} \hat{x}$; it's easy to check that $\bar{\theta}_1$ is a linear sum (with weights 1 and -1) of monochromatic cycles whose labels are all in z, the same holds for $\bar{\theta}_2, \bar{\theta}_3, \bar{\theta}_4, \bar{\theta}_5$, using monochromatic cycles of label u, v, t and s, respectively.

As we alos have $\bar{p} = \sum_{i=1..5} \bar{\theta}_i$, $\bar{p} \in \overline{\mathrm{MCycles}(\tau)}$, thus no commutative separating group exists for that DTD.

Unfortunately, we are not yet able to extend Theorem 6 to non-commutative groups. See Section 6 for more details on this issue.

6 Discussion and Conclusion

The next step is obviously to prove whether it is decidable that a DTD has a separating group or not. We have seen that this is related to the word problem for finite groups.

The word problem for finite groups is whether, given a finite set F of words and a word w over a finite alphabet of the form $A \cup A^-$, there exists a finite group H and a morphism $\mu : (A \cup A^-)^* \to H$ interpreting words in F as the identity of H but such that $\mu(w) \neq 1_H$. We are interested in the case where $F = \text{MCycles}(\tau)$ and $w \in \text{DCycles}(\tau)$. This problem is undecidable in general [5]. But we are dealing with a very special case of the word problem as $\text{MCycles}(\tau)$ and $\text{DCycles}(\tau)$ have a lot of similarities being both defined via the same graph. It is thus quite possible that this special case is decidable. Note that we are not only interested in knowing whether such a separating group exists but also in constructing it.

It would also be interesting to know whether the notion of streamability coincides with the existence of a separating group for τ. We think that this might be the case and would like to argue here in favor of this conjecture. An obvious extension of the H-local-automaton would be to allow computation in an arbitrary monoid (instead of a group). We don't think that this will extend the expressive power. Indeed assume that a DTD τ is recognized by a H-local-automaton A where H is now just a monoid. Because we are dealing with DTDs, monoid computation of A on any valid subtrees should correspond to the identity. This is because neither the context nor the content of the subtree matters for the rest of the validation, therefore the automaton does not need to remember anything (besides the fact that the subtree is valid or not). Now, because of the local tests against the DTD, each time A has partially read a subtree and has not yet rejected it, there is always a way to complete it so that it is valid for the DTD. In other words, for any monoid element m (the current monoid state of A in the subtree), there is always a m' such that $m \cdot m' = 1$: The monoid needs to be right-invertible. The reason why we took groups instead of right-invertible monoids is more technical and might not be necessary. It is because we deal with cycles (monochromatic and dangerous) and therefore work modulo cyclic permutations. This implies that if $m \cdot m' = 1$ then the cyclic permutation $m' \cdot m$ of $m \cdot m'$ should also be 1. Thus the monoid is a group.

Finally it would be interesting to go beyond the class of DTDs as defined in this paper, and start with an arbitrary regular language. This would answer an open question raised in [4,1] and certainly requires more ideas than those presented here.

Acknowledgment. We thank Victor Vianu for all the interesting discussions we had with him on this subject.

References

1. V. Bárány and C. Löding and O. Serre. Regularity Problems for Visibly Pushdown Languages. In *STACS*, 2006.
2. C. Chitic and D. Rosu. On Validation of XML Streams Using Finite State Machines. In *WebDB*, 2004.
3. P.S. Novikov. On the algorithmic unsolvability of the word problem in group theory. In *Trudy Mat. Inst. Steklov*, 44, 1955. (in Russian)
4. L. Segoufin and V. Vianu. Streaming XML documents. In *PODS*, 2002.
5. A.M. Slobodskoi. Unsolvability of the universal theory of finite groups. In *Algebra and Logic*, 20, pp 139-156, 1981.

Preferentially Annotated Regular Path Queries

Gösta Grahne[1], Alex Thomo[2], and William Wadge[2]

[1] Concordia University, Montreal, Canada
grahne@cs.concordia.ca
[2] University of Victoria, Victoria, Canada
{thomo,wwadge}@cs.uvic.ca

Abstract. In this paper, we introduce preferential regular path queries. These are regular path queries whose symbols are annotated with preference weights for "scaling" up or down the intrinsic importance of matching a symbol against a (semistructured) database edge label. Annotated regular path queries are expressed syntactically as annotated regular expressions. We interpret these expressions in a uniform semiring framework, which allows different semantics specializations for the same syntactic annotations. For our preference queries, we study three important aspects: (1) (progressive) query answering (2) (certain) query answering in LAV data-integration systems, and (3) query containment and equivalence. In all of these, we obtain important positive results, which encourage the use of our preference framework for enhanced querying of semistructured databases.

1 Introduction

Regular path queries are one of the basic building blocks of virtually all the mechanisms for querying *semistructured data*, commonly found in information integration applications, Web and communication networks, biological data management, etc. Semistructured data is conceptualized as edge-labeled graphs, and regular path queries are in essence regular expressions over the edge symbols. The answer to a regular path query on a given graph (database) is the set of pairs of objects, which are connected by paths spelling words in the language of the regular path query.

Seen from a different angle, regular path queries provide the user with a simple way of expressing *preferences* for navigating database paths. Let us take an example from road network databases. Suppose that the user wants to retrieve all the pairs of objects preferentially connected by highways, and tolerating up to k provincial roads or city streets. Clearly, such preferences can easily be captured by the regular path query

$$Q = highway^* \parallel (road + street + \epsilon)^k,$$

where $\parallel$ is the shuffle operator.

It is exactly this ability of regular expressions to capture pattern preferences that has made them very popular, starting from the early days of computers.

T. Schwentick and D. Suciu (Eds.): ICDT 2007, LNCS 4353, pp. 314–328, 2007.

However, let us take a more careful look at the above example. It surely captures the user preferences, but in a "Boolean" way. A pair of objects will be produced as an answer if there exists a path between them satisfying the user query. In other words, there is just a "yes" or "no" qualification for the query answers. But, the answers are not equally good! A pair of objects connected by a *highway* path with only 1 intervening *road* is obviously a "better" answer than a pair of objects connected by a *highway* path with 5 intervening *roads*.

Clearly, preferences beyond the "Boolean" ones cannot be captured by simple regular path queries.

In this paper, we introduce *preferentially annotated regular path queries*, which are regular path queries (regular expressions) with a very simple syntactic addition: the user can annotate the symbols in the regular expressions with "markers" (typically natural numbers), which "strengthen" or "weaken" her (pattern) preferences. For example, she can write

$$Q = (highway : 0)^* \parallel (road : 1 + street : 2 + \epsilon)^k,$$

to express that she ideally prefers highways, then roads, which she prefers less, and finally she can tolerate streets, but with an even lesser preference. Given such a query, the system should produce first the pairs of objects connected by highways, then the pairs of objects connected by highways intervened by 1 road, and so on.

The above "so on" raises some important semantical questions. Is a pair of objects connected by a highway path intervened by two roads equally good as another pair of objects connected by a highway path intervened by one street only? Indeed, in this example, it might make sense to consider them equally good, and "concatenate" weights by summing them up.

However, let us consider another example regarding travel itineraries. Assume that the preferentially annotated user query is

$$Q = (viarail : 0)^* \parallel (greyhound : 1 + aircanada : 2 + \epsilon)^k.$$

Is now a pair of objects connected by a path with two *greyhound* segments equally equally preferable as a pair of objects connected with one *aircanada* segment? Here the answer is not clear anymore. If the user is afraid of flying, she might want to "concatenate" edge-weights by choosing the maximum of the weights. Then an itinerary with no matter how many *greyhound* segments is preferable to an itinerary containing only one flight segment.

We say that in the first case the preference semantics are "quantitative," while in the second case they are "qualitative." We study both semantics for regular path queries, and leave the choice as an option specified by the user during query time.

We also consider another choice of semantics, which is a hybrid between the quantitative and qualitative semantics. Continuing the travel itinerary example, by following a purely qualitative approach, *greyhound* itineraries are always preferrable to itineraries containing *aircanada* segments, while these itineraries are equally preferable, no matter how many lags the flight has. Although, there might be applications where such qualification is all what is needed, in the particular example we need to distinguish among itineraries on the same "level of discomfort." Namely, we should be able to (quantitatively) say for example that a direct *aircanada* route is preferable to an *aircanada* route with a stop-over, which again is preferrable to an *aircanada* route with three lags. Notably, such user preferences can concisely be captured by our hybrid semantics.

In total, from all the above, we have four kind of preference semantics: Boolean, quantitative, qualitative, and hybrid. Other semantics can also be proposed, tailored to specific applications. In all these semantics, we aggregate ("concatenate") preference markers or weights along edges of the paths, and then we aggregate path preferences when there are multiple paths connecting a pair of objects. Hence, we regard the preference annotations as elements of a semiring, with two operations: the "plus" and "times." The "times" aggregates the preferences along edges of a path, while the "plus" aggregates preferences among paths.

An interesting feature of our preference framework is that for all new semantics (quantitative, qualitative, and hybrid), the syntactic user interface (*i.e.* annotated regular expressions) is exactly the same. After the user writes the query, she also specifies which semantics the system should assume for answering the query. It is straightforward for the user to preferentially annotate regular path queries, and moreover, such annotation can be easily facilitated by system default values.

In this paper, we study three important aspects of our preferentially annotated queries. First, we focus on query answering and design a progressive algorithm, which produces the answer tuples in order of their "goodness" with respect to the user preferences. Notably, answering annotated regular path queries is computationally no more difficult than the answering of classical regular path queries. In both cases, a database object is accessed at most once.

Second, we turn our attention to query answering in data integration systems, in which we have only incomplete information about databases. Such systems have been the focus of many studies (cf. [2,3][1]) and reasoning about query answering in this setting is a very important technology. We introduce a technique, which we call "query sphering" and show how to progressively compute answer tuples in this variant of incomplete information.

Third, we study query containment and equivalence of prefential regular path queries. We show that containment is undecidable for the quantitative and the hybrid semantics and decidable for qualitative semantics. Then, we present an important class of queries for which the containment is decidable for both quantitative and hybrid semantics.

Due to space constraints we omit this third part. The interested reader can find it in the full version of the paper available online (see [7]). Also, the full proofs of most of our results can be found at this online reference.

The rest of the paper is organized as follows. In Section 2, we overview related work. In Section 3, we introduce the semiring framework for preferentially

---

[1] For the semistructured data case.

annotated regular path queries. In Section 4, we give a progressive algorithm for computing the answer to an annotated query. In Section 5, we define and reason about the certain answer to annotated queries in LAV data integration systems. In Section 6, we introduce the concept of query spheres and give a characterization of the certain answer in terms of query spheres. Finally, in Section 7, we present algorithms for computing query spheres under the different preference semantics.

2   Related Work

In relational databases, the most important work on preferences is by Chomicki in a series of papers. One of his recent papers, which gives a detailed overview of the field, is [4]. However, in Chomicki's work, the preference framework is about reasoning on fixed-arity tuples of attribute values. In contrast, here we define "structural" preferences, in the sense that they apply to the paths used for obtaining query answers. Because of this difference, the meaning of our "quantitative" and "qualitative" adjectives is different from the ones mentioned in [4].

Preferences for XML are studied by [9]. These preferences are aimed at comparing attribute values of XML elements rather than structure of (parts of) documents. As characterized by [4], the preferences of [9] seem to largely conform to the relational paradigm.

Regarding our qualitative preferences, they are similar in spirit with constraints in the framework of Infinitesimal Logic studied in [11]. However, [11] focuses on the relational case only.

In [5], weighted path queries are introduced. Syntactically, such queries are the same as our preferentially annotated queries. However, [5] do not give any semantics on their queries. Technically, one can use their query answering algorithm to answer our queries on a given database. However, we carefully study some important details of query answering, which are not taken into consideration in [5]. Moreover, query answering on a given database is not our most important contribution in this paper.

Regarding query answering (on a given database), one can also use, assuming quantitative semantics only, the algorithm of [6] for queries under distortions. In that paper, there are also some technical results, which can be adapted to help in some of our derivations. However, we do not do this, due to the high computational complexity of constructs in [6]. Rather, we devise new and better constructs, which are original and can contribute in research regarding formal languages as well. Such research will be mentioned in relevant places during the exposition of the paper.

Finally, [12] and [13] deal with distributed evaluation of weighted regular path queries. However, the algorithms of [12] and [13] apply to quantitative semantics only. We believe that they can also be adapted for other semantics as well, and thus, [12,13] should be considered to nicely complement this work regarding query answering on distributed databases.

3   Databases and Preferential Regular Path Queries

Databases and classical regular path queries. We consider a database to be an edge-labeled graph. Intuitively, the nodes of the database graph represent objects and the edges represent relationships between the objects.

Formally, let Δ be an alphabet. Elements of Δ will be denoted $r, s, \ldots$. As usual, Δ^* denotes the set of all finite words over Δ. Words will be denoted by $u, w, \ldots$. We also assume that we have a universe of objects, and objects will be denoted $a, b, c, \ldots,$. A *database DB* is then a graph (V, E), where V is a finite set of objects and $E \subseteq V \times \Delta \times V$ is a set of directed edges labeled with symbols from Δ.

Before introducing preferentially annotated regular path queries, it will help to first review the classical regular path queries.

A *regular path query* (RPQ) is a regular language over Δ. For the ease of notation, we will blur the distinction between regular languages and regular expressions that represent them. Let Q be an RPQ and $DB = (V, E)$ a database. Then, the *answer* to Q on DB is defined as

$$\mathrm{Ans}(Q, DB) = \{(a, b) \in V : \text{ for some } w \in Q,\ a \xrightarrow{w} b \text{ in } DB\},$$

where $\xrightarrow{w}$ denotes a path spelling the word w in the database.

Semirings and annotated regular path queries. By a *semiring* we mean a tuple $\mathscr{R} = (R, \oplus, \otimes, \mathbf{0}, \mathbf{1})$ such that

1. $(R, \oplus, \mathbf{0})$ is a commutative monoid with 0 as the identity element for $\oplus$.
2. $(R, \otimes, \mathbf{1})$ is a monoid with 1 as the identity element for $\otimes$.
3. $\otimes$ distributes over $\oplus$: for all $x, y, z \in R$,

$$(x \oplus y) \otimes z = (x \otimes z) \oplus (y \otimes z)$$
$$z \otimes (x \oplus y) = (z \otimes x) \oplus (z \otimes y).$$

4. $\mathbf{0}$ is an anihilator for $\otimes$: $\forall x \in R,\ x \otimes \mathbf{0} = \mathbf{0} \otimes x = \mathbf{0}$.

The *natural order* $\preceq$ on R is defined as: $x \preceq y$ if and only if $x \oplus y = x$. It is easily verified that $\preceq$ is a partial order.

In this paper, we will in addition require for semirings of preferences to have a *total* natural order. All the preference semirings mentioned in Introduction posses such an order.[2] Observe that $\mathbf{0}$ is the "biggest" element of the semiring, and it corresponds to the "infinitely worst" preference weight.

Now, let $\mathscr{R} = (R, \oplus, \otimes, \mathbf{0}, \mathbf{1})$ be a semiring as above. An $\mathscr{R}$-annotated language Q over Δ is a function

$$Q : \Delta^* \to R.$$

---

[2] We want to note here that for database paths, it is difficult to find intuitively plausible preference semantics, which would ask for a partial order only.

We will call such Q's *annotated queries* for short. Frequently, we will write $(w, x) \in Q$ instead of $Q(w) = x$. When such annotated queries are given by "annotated regular expressions," we have *annotated regular path queries* (ARPQ's). Computationally, ARPQ's are represented by "annotated automata."

An *annotated automaton* $\mathcal{A}$ is a quintuple $(P, \Delta, \mathcal{R}, \tau, p_0, F)$, where τ is a subset of $P \times \Delta \times R \times P$. Each annotated automaton $\mathcal{A}$ defines the annotated language (query) $[\mathcal{A}]$ defined by

$$[\mathcal{A}] = \{(w, x) \in \Delta^* \times R :$$
$$w = r_1 r_2 \ldots r_n, x = \oplus \{\otimes_{i=1}^n x_i : (p_{i-1}, r_i, x_i, p_i) \in \tau, p_n \in F\}\}.$$

Given a a database DB, and a query Q, annotated over a semiring $\mathcal{R} = (R, \oplus, \otimes, \mathbf{0}, \mathbf{1})$ we define the preferentially *weighted answer* of Q on DB as

$$\text{Ans}(Q, DB, \mathcal{R}) = \{(a, b, x) \in V \times V \times R :$$
$$x = \oplus\{\{y : (w, y) \in Q \text{ and } a \xrightarrow{w} b \text{ in } DB\} \cup \{\mathbf{0}\}\}.$$

Intuitively, we have $(a, b, \mathbf{0})$ as an answer to Q, if there is no path in DB spelling some word in Q.

Let us now discuss each of the preference semirings that we mentioned in Introduction. The *Boolean* semiring is

$$\mathcal{B} = (\{T, F\}, \vee, \wedge, F, T),$$

where T and F stand for "true" and "false" respectively, and $\vee$, $\wedge$ are the usual "and," and "or" Boolean operators. ARPQ's in the Boolean semiring correspond exactly to classical RPQ's. The user does not annotate explicitly the regular expression symbols by T or F. By default, all the symbols present in the query are assumed to be annotated with T. Also, the system produces only the "T-ranked" answers. In general, for any semiring it only makes sense to produce the answers, which are not ranked by the $\mathbf{0}$ of the semiring. In practice, a $\mathbf{0}$-ranked answer means in fact "no answer." For the $\mathcal{B}$ semiring, we formally have that

$$\text{Ans}(Q, DB, \mathcal{B}) = \{(a, b, T) : (a, b) \in \text{Ans}(Q, DB)\} \cup$$
$$\{(a, b, F) : (a, b) \notin \text{Ans}(Q, DB)\}.$$

It is easy to see that a Boolean annotated automaton $\mathcal{A} = (P, \Delta, \mathcal{B}, \tau, p_0, F)$ is indeed an "ordinary" finite state automaton $(P, \Delta, \tau, p_0, F)$.

In the case of *quantitative preferences* we have

$$\mathcal{N} = (\mathbb{N} \cup \{\infty\}, min, +, \infty, 0),$$

where min and $+$ are the usual operators for integers. This semiring is also known as the *tropical semiring* in the literature. The user annotates query symbols by natural numbers.

In the case of *qualitative preferences*, we have

$$\mathcal{F} = (\mathbb{N} \cup \{\infty\}, min, max, \infty, 0).$$

This semiring is also known as the *fuzzy semiring* in the literature. Similarly to the quantitative case, the user annotates query symbols by natural numbers. This is however, only syntactically "the same" as the quantitative case. The semantics of the two cases are different. The numbers here represent the "level of discomfort" for traversing database edges. As we mentioned in Introduction, it is the choice of the user to specify the semantics that she desires.

Finally, for hybrid preferences, the user again uses the same query syntax as for the quantitative and qualitative case. That is, the user annotates the query symbols with natural numbers. However, here the set $\mathbb{N}$ is just the "user interface." In fact the support set of the semiring $\mathscr{H}$, for hybrid preference semantics is

$$R = \{0, 1, 1^{(2)}, \ldots, 2, 2^{(2)}, \ldots\} \cup \{\infty\},$$

where the symbolic ingredients, n and i, of a semiring element $n^{(i)}$ are natural numbers. [Elements $1, 2, \ldots$ are shorthand for $1^{(1)}, 2^{(1)}, \ldots$.] Intuitively, n represents the level of discomfort, while i represents how many times a user is "forced to endure" that level of discomfort. While the subset $\{0, 1, 2, \ldots\}$ is the user interface for annotating queries, set R is richer in elements in order to allow for a finer ranking of query answers.

Regarding the semiring operations, we introduce

$$n^{(i)} \oplus m^{(j)} = \begin{cases} n^{(i)} & \text{if } n < m \\ m^{(j)} & \text{if } n > m \\ n^{(min\{i,j\})} & \text{if } n = m, \end{cases} \qquad n^{(i)} \otimes m^{(j)} = \begin{cases} n^{(i)} & \text{if } n > m \\ m^{(j)} & \text{if } n < m \\ n^{(i+j)} & \text{if } n = m \end{cases}$$

and for these we have $\mathbf{0} = \infty$, $\mathbf{1} = 0$. It is easy to verify that the semiring axioms are satisfied.

Reiterating, the user, the same as before, annotates query symbols with natural numbers representing her preferences. However, semantically the queries will be different from both the quantitative and qualitative case, while bearing similarities with both of them. Similarly with the qualitative semantics, only database edges matched by transitions annotated with the "worst" level of discomfort will really count in computing a preferential weight for a traversed path. On the other hand, differently from the qualitative semantics, and similarly with the quantitative semantics, paths with the the same "worst-level of discomfort" are comparable. Namely, the best path will be the one with the fewest "worst-level of discomfort" edges.

4   Answering Preferentially Annotated RPQ's

Our goal here is to not only compute preferentially weighted answers to a query, but to compute the answers in a progressive way, *i.e.* to compute the best answers first. First, we will review the well-known method for the evaluation of classical RPQ's (cf. [1]). In essence, the evaluation proceeds by creating state-object pairs from the query automaton and the database. For this, let $\mathcal{A}$ be an NFA that accepts an RPQ Q. Starting from an object a of a database DB, we first create the pair (p_0, a), where p_0 is the initial state in $\mathcal{A}$. Then, we create all the pairs (p, b) such that there exist a transition from p_0 to p in $\mathcal{A}$, and an edge from a to b in DB, and furthermore the labels of the transition and the edge match. In the same way, we continue to create new pairs from existing ones, until we are not anymore able to do so. In essence, what is happening is a lazy construction of a Cartesian product graph of the query automaton with the database graph. Of course, only a small (hopefully) part of the Cartesian product is really contructed depending on the selectivity of the query. The implicit assumption in [1] is that this part of the Cartesian product fits in main memory and each object is not accessed more than once in secondary storage.

After obtaining the above Cartesian product graph, producing query answers becomes a question of computing reachability of nodes (p, b), where p is a final state, from (p_0, a), where p_0 is the intial state. Namely, if (p, b) is reachable from (p_0, a), then (a, b) is a tuple in the query answer.

Now, when having instead an annotated query automaton, we can modify the classical matching algorithm to build an annotated (or weighted) Cartesian product graph. This can be achieved by assigning to the edges of this graph the corresponding (automaton) transition annotations (weights).

It is not difficult to see that, in order to compute preferentially weighted answers, we have to find, in the Cartesian product graph, the (semiring) shortest paths from (p_0, a) to all the nodes (p, b), where p is a final state in the query automaton $\mathcal{A}$.

In our algorithm, we, in a similar spirit with [1], lazily build the above mentioned Cartesian product. However, we also compute "on the fly" shortest paths needed for preferentially weighting the answer tuples.

Our algorithm is progressive, $i.e.$ it computes answer tuples (w.r.t. each potential starting object a) in the order of their preference rank. For this, Dijkstra's algorithm is the best choice (compared to Flloyd-Warshall algorithm). It fits perfectly with the lazy strategy of constructing the Cartesian product graph, and it reaches the b objects in a "best first" fashion. Our general algorithm, which works with all the proposed preference semirings is as follows.

Algorithm 1
Input: An ϵ-free automaton $\mathcal{A}$ for an $\mathcal{R}$-annotated query Q, and a database DB.
Output: $Ans(Q, DB, \mathcal{R})$.
Method: For each *potential* start object a^3 compute the set $Reach_a$ as follows.

1. Initialize $Reach_a$ to $\{(p_0, a, \mathbf{1}, \textit{false})\}$.
2. Repeat 3–5 until $Reach_a$ no longer changes.
3. Choose a quadruple $(p, b, x, \textit{false}) \in Reach_a$, such that

$$x = \oplus\{y : (p, b, y, \textit{false}) \in Reach\}.$$

Update $(p, b, x, \textit{false})$ to $(p, b, x, \textit{true})$.

---

[3] Finding potential start objects can be facilitated by classical indexes on the database edge labels.

4. If p is a final state, then insert (a, b, x) in $Ans(Q, DB, \mathscr{R})$.
5. If there is a transition (p, r, y, q) in $\mathcal{A}$ and there is an edge $b \xrightarrow{r} c$ in DB then add $(q, c, x \otimes y, false)$ to $Reach_a$.

5   Preferentially Ranked Answers on Possible Databases

In a semistructured LAV data integration system (cf. [2,10,3]), we do not have a database in the classical sense. Instead what we have is incomplete information, which is in the form of a set of "data-sources," characterized by an algebraic definition over a "global schema."

Each data-source also has a name, and the set of these names constitutes the "local schema." The LAV system also has a set of tuples over the local schema. The queries are formulated on the "integrated" global schema. Since the data exists in the local schema only, a translation from the global to the local schema has to be performed in order to be able to compute query answers.

When the user gives an ARPQ, the question is: What does it mean to preferentially answer such a query in a LAV system?

Formally, let Δ be the *global schema*. Let $\mathbf{S} = \{S_1, \ldots, S_n\}$ be a set of *data-source definitions*, with each S_i being a regular language over the global schema Δ. Associated with each data-source is a name s_i, for $i = 1, \ldots, n$. The *local schema* is the set $\Omega = \{s_1, \ldots, s_n\}$ of all the data-source names. There is a natural mapping between the local and global schema: for each $s_i \in \Omega$, we set $def(s_i) = S_i$. The mapping or substitution[4] *def* associates with each data-source name s_i the definition language S_i. The substitution *def* is applied to words, languages, and regular expressions in the usual way.

Let $\Omega = \{s_1, \ldots s_n\}$ be the local schema as before. Then, a *source collection* $\mathcal{S}$ over $(\mathbf{S}, \Omega)$ is a database over (D, Ω). As mentioned earlier, in a LAV system, the user formulates queries on the global schema, *i.e.* Δ, and the system has to compute the answer on the data available in the local schema, *i.e.* Ω. For this, we have to reason about hypothetical databases over (D, Δ) that a database over (D, Ω) could possibly represent.

A source collection $\mathcal{S}$ defines a set $poss(\mathcal{S})$ of databases over (D, Δ) as follows:

$$poss(\mathcal{S}) = \{DB \ : \ \text{there exists a path } a \xrightarrow{w \in S_i} b \text{ in } DB \text{ for each } (a, s_i, b) \in \mathcal{S}\}.$$

This definition reflects the intuition about the connection of an edge (a, s_i, b) in $\mathcal{S}$ with paths between a and b in hypothetical DB's.

For classical regular path queries, what we usually compute is the *certain answer* using $\mathcal{S}$, which is the set of all tuples, which are in the query answer on each possible database.

Consider a classical regular path query as a preferentially annotated query over the Boolean semiring $\mathscr{B}$. In a semiring terminology, what we do is an "∧" aggregation of query answers on the possible databases. Also, let us overload ∧ operator to work for answer tuples and sets as follows:

---

[4] In a language theoretic terminology.

$(a, b, x) \wedge (a, b, y) = (a, b, x \wedge y)$, and

$$\mathrm{Ans}(Q, DB_1, \mathscr{B}) \wedge \mathrm{Ans}(Q, DB_2, \mathscr{B}) =$$
$$\{(a, b, x \wedge y) : (a, b, x) \in \mathrm{Ans}(Q, DB_1, \mathscr{B}) \text{ and } (a, b, y) \in \mathrm{Ans}(Q, DB_2, \mathscr{B})\}.$$

Then, the certain answer w.r.t. $\mathcal{S}$ and "weighted" over $\mathscr{B}$ is

$$CAns(Q, \mathcal{S}, \mathscr{B}) = \bigwedge_{DB \in poss(\mathcal{S})} \mathrm{Ans}(Q, DB, \mathscr{B}),$$

It is easy to verify that this definition is equivalent with the definition of the certain answer given in other works as for example [2].

In fact, $\wedge$ for aggregating the answers on possible databases is the "dual operator" of $\vee$ used for aggregating paths when computing answers on databases.[5] Generalizing, in order to define the certain answer for other semirings, we introduce the $\odot$ operator, which is the dual of the path aggregation operator $\oplus$. Namely,

$$x \odot y = \begin{cases} x & \text{if } x \oplus y = y \\ y & \text{if } x \oplus y = x. \end{cases}$$

This is possible since $\oplus$ induces a total order, and so, $x \oplus y$ is equal to either x or y. Clearly, $\wedge$ is the dual of $\vee$ according to this definition. Observe also that the operator $\odot$ induces the reverse order (with respect to $\oplus$) among the elements of the semiring.

Similarly with the above overloading of $\wedge$, we overload $\odot$ to work with answer tuples and sets. Now, for a query Q, annotated over a preference semiring $\mathscr{R}$, we define the certain answer as

$$CAns(Q, \mathcal{S}, \mathscr{R}) = \bigodot_{DB \in poss(\mathcal{S})} \mathrm{Ans}(Q, DB, \mathscr{R}).$$

In the above definition, a tuple (a, b, x), with $x \neq \mathbf{0}$, will belong to $CAns(Q, \mathcal{S}, \mathscr{R})$ iff for each $DB \in poss(\mathcal{S})$ there exists $y \preceq x$ such that $(a, b, y) \in \mathrm{Ans}(Q, DB, \mathscr{R})$. This definition reflects the *certainty* that objects a and b are always connected with paths, which are preferentially weighted not more than x. As an example, consider the query

$$Q = (highway : 0)^* \| (road : 1 + \epsilon)^*,$$

and a source collection (consisting of single source with a single tuple) $\mathcal{S} = \{(a, s, b)\}$, with definition

$$S = highway^* \| (road + \epsilon)^5.$$

The possible databases for $\mathcal{S}$ are all those databases, which have at least a path (between a and b) labeled by highways intervened by at most 5 roads. Now

---

[5] The fact that this operator $\wedge$ is the same as the "multiplication" operator of the Boolean semiring for aggregating edge-weights along paths, is just a coincidence.

let us discuss the certain answer considering the semirings for the quantitative, qualitative, and hybrid preference semantics.

In the quantative case, $\odot$ is *max*, and we have $(a, b, 5)$ as a certain answer. The weight of 5 states exactly our certainty that in any possible database, there is a path from a to b, whose preferential weight w.r.t. the given query is not more than 5. Also, there exists a possible database in which the best path between a and b is exactly 5.

In the qualitative case, $\odot$ is again *max*. However, we have now $(a, b, 1)$ as a certain answer. The weight of 1 states our certainty that in any possible database, there is a path from a to b, and the level of discomfort (w.r.t. the query) for traversing that path is not more than 1.

Finally, in the hybrid case, $\odot$ is as follows

$$n^{(i)} \odot m^{(j)} = \begin{cases} m^{(j)} & \text{if } n < m \\ n^{(i)} & \text{if } n > m \\ n^{(max\{i,j\})} & \text{if } n = m. \end{cases}$$

We have that $(a, b, 1^{(5)})$ as a certain answer. This is because although the level of discomfort of the best path connecting a with b in any possible database is 1, in the worst case (of such best paths), we need to endure up to 5 times such discomfort (w.r.t. the query). Of course $1^{(5)}$ is infinitely better than 2.

6   Certain Answers Via Query Spheres

In [2], there is given an algorithm, which computes the certain answer of a classical RPQ Q given a source collection S. This translates into having available an algorithm for computing $CAns(Q, S, \mathscr{B})$.

Now, let Q be an ARPQ with annotations over a preference semiring $\mathscr{R}$. In this section, we cast computing tuples in $CAns(Q, S, \mathscr{R})$ into computing tuples in $CAns(Q, S, \mathscr{B})$, which is the Boolean certain answer of Q, after "collapsing" all the annotations in Q into element T of the Boolean semiring.

For this, we introduce the notion of "query spheres." We formally define the *y-sphere* of Q, where $y \in R$, as

$$Q^y = \{(w, x) \in \Delta^* \times R : (w, x) \in Q \text{ and } x \preceq y, \text{ or otherwise } y = \mathbf{0}\}.$$

Let $\mathcal{A}$ be an annotated automaton recognizing Q. Then, Q^y will be the query recognized by the automaton $\mathcal{A}^y$ obtained from $\mathcal{A}$ by retaining only (transition) paths weighted by some x, which is no more than y. We show in the next section how to obtain such automata for the different preference semirings that we consider.

Clearly, $Q^x \subseteq Q^y$ for $x \preceq y$.[6]

For semirings in which the notion of the "next" element is well defined, we give a necessary and sufficient condition for a tuple (a, b, y) to belong to

---

[6] It is this property that motivates the use of "query spheres."

$CAns(Q, \mathcal{S}, \mathcal{R})$. We give the following definition about the "next element" property of a semiring.

A semiring $\mathcal{R} = (R, \oplus, \otimes, \mathbf{0}, \mathbf{1})$ is said to be *discrete* iff for each $x \neq \mathbf{0}$ in R there exists y in R, such that (a) $x \prec y$, and (b) there does not exist z in R, such that $x \prec z \prec y$. The element y is called the *next element after* x.

Notably, all our preference semirings are discrete. Let $\mathcal{R}$ be a discrete semiring. Also, let y (as above) be the next element after (some) x. We can show that

Theorem 1

$(a, b, y) \in CAns(Q, \mathcal{S}, \mathcal{R})$ iff
$$(a, b, T) \in CAns(Q^y, \mathcal{S}, \mathcal{B}) \text{ and } (a, b, F) \in CAns(Q^x, \mathcal{S}, \mathcal{B}),$$
$(a, b, \mathbf{1}) \in CAns(Q, \mathcal{S}, \mathcal{R})$ iff $(a, b, T) \in CAns(Q^\mathbf{1}, \mathcal{S}, \mathcal{B})$.

From the above theorem, we conclude that if we are able to compute Q^y for each y (relevant to the query), then we could generate all the y-ranked tuples (a, b, y) of $CAns(Q, \mathcal{S}, \mathcal{R})$ by computing with the algorithm of [2] $CAns(Q^y, \mathcal{S}, \mathcal{B})$ and $CAns(Q^x, \mathcal{S}, \mathcal{B})$, and then taking the set difference of their T-tuples.

We present in the next section algorithms, which for a given y compute Q^y, for the different preference semirings that we study.

Now the question is, for what y's to apply the method suggested by Theorem 1 for generating (a, b, y) tuples of the certain answer? For this, let $z = \odot\{x : (w, x) \in Q\}$. We state the following theorem, which can be easily verified.

Theorem 2. $Q^z = Q$.

For the quantitative and qualitative semirings, the existence of a $z \prec \mathbf{0}$ (strict $\prec$) guarantees a terminating procedure for ranking all the tuples in the certain answer. Simply, one has to repeat the method of Theorem 1 starting with y equal to $\mathbf{1}$ and continuing for up to y equal to z. On the other hand, for the hybrid semiring a "global" (upper bound) z is not enough. Rather, we need to reason about "level-wise" z's, as we explain later in this section.

Quantitative case. Interestingly, determining whether there exists such a $z \prec \mathbf{0}$ coincides with deciding the "limitedness" problem for "distance automata." The later problem is widely known and positively solved in the literature (cf. for example [8]).

If the query automaton is limited in distance, and this limit is z, then we need to compute query spheres up to Q^z, which will be equivalent to Q. On the other hand, if the query automaton is not limited in distance, we can still apply the same procedure utilizing query spheres for ranking the tuples in the certain answer. However, the ranking in this case is only *eventually computable*.

In practice, the user might provide beside the query, also an upper bound z' on the preferential weight of the answers that she is interested to retrieve. In such a case, we need to compute not more than z' query spheres in order to return all the tuples weighted less or equal to z' in $CAns(Q, \mathcal{S}, \mathcal{R})$.

Qualitative case. Here, the existence of $z \prec \infty$ (semiring $\mathbf{0}$) is guaranteed. This is because z will be less or equal to the biggest transition weight in the query automaton.

Hybrid case. In this case, the existence of a global $z \prec \infty$ does not guarantee the ability to rank all the tuples in the certain answer. Rather we need for this the existence of the level-wise z's. Namely, we define the *upper bound for level n* as $z_n = \odot\{x : (w,x) \in Q \text{ and } x \prec n+1\}$ (strict $\prec$, and recall $n+1$ is a shorthand for $(n+1)^{(1)}$). If there exists $i \in \mathbb{N}$, such that $z_n = n^{(i)}$, we say that z_n is *finite*.

Now, if z_n is finite, then for determining the exact weight of the "n-range" tuples $(a, b, n^{(-)})$ in the certain answer, we need to compute query spheres from $Q^{(n^{(1)})}$ up to $Q^{(n^{(i)})}$.

If $z_n = z_m$ for $m \prec n$ (strictly), then there cannot be any n-range tuple in the certain answer.

On the other hand, if $z_n > n^{(i)}$ for each $i \in \mathbb{N}$, then the exact weight of the "n-range" tuples is only eventually computable.

Hence the question is how can we determine the existence of a finite z_n? For this, we first introduce the generalized query spheres $Q^{n^{(\infty)}} = \bigcup_{i=0}^{\infty} Q^{n^{(i)}}$. If z_n is finite, then there exists $j \in \mathbb{N}$, such that $Q^{n^{(\infty)}} = \bigcup_{i=0}^{j} Q^{n^{(i)}}$. But, the existence of such j can be found by deciding the limitedness of an automaton for $Q^{n^{(\infty)}}$. Thus, we state that

Theorem 3. z_n *is finite iff* $Q^{n^{(\infty)}}$ *is limited in distance.*

The question is, how can we compute $Q^{n^{(\infty)}}$? In essence we want to extract the paths in a query automaton $\mathcal{A} = (P, \Delta, \mathbb{N}, p_0, \tau_A, F)$, which are weighted strictly less than $n + 1$. Such paths cannot recognize words weighted more or equal to $n + 1$. In order to perform this extraction, we build a one-state mask automaton $\mathcal{M}_n$ on the alphabet $\{0, 1, \ldots, n\}$. Let τ_A be the transition relation of the query automaton $\mathcal{A}$. Then, $\mathcal{M}_n = (\{q\}, \{0, 1, \ldots, n\}, q, \tau_n, \{q\})$, where $\tau_n = \{(q, m, q) : (p, r, m, p') \in \tau_A \text{ and } m \leq n\}$.

Finally, we construct a Cartesian product automaton

$$\mathcal{C}_n = \mathcal{A} \times \mathcal{M}_n = (P_A \times \{q\}, \Delta, \tau, (p_0, q), F_A \times \{q\}),$$

where $\tau = \{((p, q), r, n, (p', q)) : (p, r, m, p') \in \tau_A \text{ and } (q, m, q') \in \tau_n\}$. It can be shown that

Theorem 4. *The weighted automaton* $\mathcal{C}_n$ *accepts exactly* $Q^{n^{(\infty)}}$.

Here again, the user can practically specify an upper bound k on the preferential weight of the tuples in each range that she is interested to exactly rank. Such a bound will serve as an accuracy index. By computing query spheres up to $Q^{(n^{(k)})}$, we accurately rank the n-range tuples having a weight, which is not more than $n^{(k)}$. Finally, we can "inaccurately" derive the rest of n-range tuples, by computing the whole $CAns(Q^{n^{(\infty)}}, \mathcal{S}, \mathcal{B})$. By "inaccurately" we mean that for the n-range tuples weighted more than $n^{(k)}$, we only know that their weight is from $n^{(k)}$ to $n + 1$ exclusive.

7 Computing Query Spheres

Quantitative Case. In this section we present an algorithm, which for any given number $k \in \mathbb{N}$ constructs the k-th sphere Q^k of an ARPQ Q.

For this, we build a mask automaton $\mathcal{M}_k$ on the alphabet $K = \{0, 1, \ldots, k\}$, which formally is as follows: $\mathcal{M}_k = (P_k, K, \tau_k, p_0, F_k)$, where $P_k = F_k = \{p_0, p_1, \ldots, p_k\}$, and

$$\tau_k = \{(p_i, n, p_{i+n}) : 0 \leq i \leq k, \text{ and } 0 \leq n \leq k - i\}.$$

The automaton $\mathcal{M}_k$ has a nice property. It captures all the possible paths (unlabeled with respect to Δ) with weight equal to k. Formally, we can show that

Theorem 5. $\mathcal{M}_k$ contains all the possible paths π with weight(π) $\leq k$, and it does not contain any path with weight greater than k.

Now by using $\mathcal{M}_k$, we can extract from a weighted automaton $\mathcal{A}$ for Q all the transition paths with a weight less or equal to k, giving so an effective procedure for computing the k-th sphere $Q^{(k)}$.

For this, let $\mathcal{A} = (P_{\mathcal{A}}, \Delta, \tau_{\mathcal{A}}, q_0, F_{\mathcal{A}})$ be a weighted automaton for Q. We construct a Cartesian product automaton

$$\mathcal{C}_k = \mathcal{A} \times \mathcal{M}_k = (P_{\mathcal{A}} \times P_k, \Delta, \tau, (q_0, p_0), F_{\mathcal{A}} \times F_k),$$

where $\tau = \{((q, p), r, n, (q', p')) : (q, r, n, q') \in \tau_{\mathcal{A}} \text{ and } (p, n, p') \in \tau_k\}$. We can show that

Theorem 6. The weighted automaton $\mathcal{C}_k$ accepts exactly the k-th sphere $Q^{(k)}$ of query Q.

It can be easily seen that the size of automaton $\mathcal{M}_k$ is $\mathcal{O}(k^2)$. Thus, the above algorithm for computing $Q^{(k)}$ through $\mathcal{C}_k$ is in fact exponential in k, since k is represented in a binary format. However, as we show by the next theorem, this is the best one could do unless $P = NP$. In fact, our suggested incremental computation of the certain answer is a parametrically optimal procedure. We can show that

Theorem 7. Our algorithm for computing $Q^{(k)}$ is essentially optimal.

Qualitative Case. Here the mask automaton is polynomial in k, and it coincides with the mask automaton for computing $Q^{k^{\infty}}$ in the hybrid case (see previous section). The procedure for computing query spheres is repeated as many times as the number of different annotations in the query automaton, *i.e.* the number of repetitions does not depend on k. Hence, we conclude that to compute the certain answer is polynomial in k for the qualitative case.

Hybrid Case. For computing a query sphere Q^y, where $y = n^{(k)}$, for $n, k \in \mathbb{N}$, we need to extract from a query automaton all the paths (not necessary simple) with (a) any number of transitions weighted strictly less than n, and (b) not more than k transitions weighted exactly n.

For this, we build a mask automaton $\mathcal{M}_{n,k}$ as follows:

$$\mathcal{M}_{n,k} = (P_{n,k}, \{0, 1, \ldots, n\}, \tau_{n,k}, p_0, F_{n,k}),$$

where $P_{n,k} = F_{n,k} = \{p_0, p_1, \ldots, p_k\}$, and

$$\tau_{n,k} = \{(p_i, m, p_i) : 0 \leq m < n \text{ and } 0 \leq i \leq k\} \cup$$
$$\{(p_i, n, p_{i+1}) : 0 \leq i < k\}.$$

Formally, we can show that

Theorem 8. $\mathcal{M}_k$ *contains all the possible paths* π *with* $weight(\pi) \leq n^{(k)}$, *and it does not contain any path with weight greater than* $n^{(k)}$.

Now by using $\mathcal{M}_{n,k}$, similarly with the previous cases, we can extract from an automaton $\mathcal{A}$ for Q all the transition paths weighted less or equal to $n^{(k)}$, giving so an effective procedure for computing the $Q^{(n^{(k)})}$ query sphere.

Observe that the above algorithm for computing $Q^{(n^{(k)})}$ is polynomial in n, but unfortunately exponential in k (due to a binary representation of n). It is open whether or not $Q^{(n^{(k)})}$ can be computed in better time with respect to k.

References

1. Abiteboul S., P. Buneman, and D. Suciu. *Data on the Web: From Relations to Semistructured Data and XML.* Morgan Kaufmann, San Francisco, CA, 1999.
2. Calvanese D., G. Giacomo, M. Lenzerini, and M. Y. Vardi. Answering Regular Path Queries Using Views. *Proc. of ICDE '00.*
3. Calvanese D., G. Giacomo, M. Lenzerini, and M. Y. Vardi. View-based Query Processing: On the Relationship between Rewriting, Answering and Losslessness. *Proc. of ICDT '05.*
4. Chomicki J. Preference formulas in relational queries. *ACM Trans. Database Syst.* 28 (4) : 427–466, 2003.
5. Flesca S., F. Furfaro, and S. Greco. Weighted Path Queries on Web Data. *Proc. of WebDB '01.*
6. Grahne, G., and A. Thomo. Query Answering and Containment for Regular Path Queries under Distortions. *Proc. of FoIKS '04.*
7. Grahne, G., A. Thomo, W. Wadge. Preferentially Annotated Regular Path Queries. http://www.cs.uvic.ca/~thomo/papers/icdt2007full.pdf
8. Hashiguchi K. Limitedness Theorem on Finite Automata with Distance Functions. *Journal of Computer and System Sciences* 24 (2) : 233–244, 1982.
9. Kiesling W., B. Hafenrichter, S. Fischer, and S. Holland. Preference XPATH – A query language for E-commerce. *Proc. of the 5th Int'l Conf. Wirtschaftsinformatik,* Augsburg, Germany, 2001.
10. Lenzerini M. Data Integration: A Theoretical Perspective. *Proc. of PODS '02.*
11. Ruchi A. A Framework for Expressing Prioritized Constraints Using Infinitesimal Logic *Master Thesis* University of Victoria, BC, Canada, 2005.
12. Stefanescu D. C., A. Thomo, and L. Thomo Distributed evaluation of generalized path queries. *Proc. of SAC '05.*
13. Stefanescu D. C., A. Thomo. Enhanced Regular Path Queries on Semistructured Databases. *Proc. of QLQP '05.*

Combining Incompleteness and Ranking in Tree Queries*

Benny Kimelfeld and Yehoshua Sagiv

The Selim and Rachel Benin School of Engineering and Computer Science
The Hebrew University of Jerusalem
Edmond J. Safra Campus, Jerusalem 91904, Israel
{bennyk,sagiv}@cs.huji.ac.il

Abstract. In many cases, users may want to consider incomplete answers to their queries. Often, however, there is an overwhelming number of such answers, even if subsumed answers are ignored and only maximal ones are considered. Therefore, it is important to rank answers according to their degree of incompleteness and, moreover, this ranking should be combined with other, conventional ranking techniques that are already in use (e.g., the relevance of answers to keywords). Query evaluation should take the ranking into account by computing answers incrementally, i.e., in ranked order. In particular, the evaluation process should generate the top-k answers efficiently.

We show how a semantics for incomplete answers to tree queries can be combined with common ranking techniques. In our approach, answers are *rewarded* for relevancy and *penalized* for incompleteness, where the user specifies the appropriate quantum. An incremental algorithm for evaluating tree queries is given. This algorithm enumerates in ranked order with polynomial delay, under query-and-data complexity. Our results are couched in terms of a formal framework that captures a variety of data models (e.g., relational, semistructured and XML).

1 Introduction

The conventional paradigm of querying large databases using structured queries has two major drawbacks. First, databases commonly store incomplete and irregular information; for example, when data is integrated from several heterogeneous sources. Consequently, there may be partial answers that are highly relevant. For dealing with this problem, the notion of *incomplete answers* has been studied [7, 9, 8]. The second drawback is that of overwhelming the user with many answers that largely differ in their semantic strength. This is a problem especially when queries involve fuzzy conditions [16] or when applying twig patterns to graph-structured XML [17, 12]. As a solution, *ranking* and evaluation in ranked order have been studied [11, 12, 14, 5, 15]. The second drawback is further intensified when allowing incomplete answers, since it increases both

---

* This research was supported by The Israel Science Foundation (Grant 893/05).

T. Schwentick and D. Suciu (Eds.): ICDT 2007, LNCS 4353, pp. 329–343, 2007.

the number of answers and the variation in the semantic strength due to missing information. Therefore, it is important to *combine* incompleteness and ranking.

Towards this end, we introduce an approach that features both ranking and incompleteness in tree queries. Our results are couched in an abstract data model that easily captures XML (including ID references) as well as relational data. Users can control the amount of missing information by specifying completeness constraints that generalize the existence constraints of [7, 9]. Answers are partial matches that correspond to a subtree of the query, satisfy the completeness constraints and are maximal (i.e., not subsumed by other answers). Ranking functions consist of two parts. One can express conventional ranking techniques that measure, for example, the relevance of objects to the query terms [2] or the proximity among matched objects [4, 10, 12]. The second part penalizes a partial answer for the missing information.

The main contribution of this paper is an algorithm for efficiently evaluating queries of the above type. Our algorithm enumerates the answers in ranked order with polynomial delay, under query-and-data complexity. In comparison to earlier work, the following should be noted. Efficient evaluation of incomplete answers to queries (which are not necessarily trees) was investigated in [7, 9, 8], but they did not consider ranking and their evaluation techniques cannot be easily adapted to enumerating with polynomial delay (even if ranking is not required). The algorithms of [11, 12] enumerate in ranked order with polynomial delay, but they strongly rely on the fact that answers are complete.

Our algorithm uses two reductions. The first is an adaptation of Lawler's procedure [13] that enumerates in ranked order by repeatedly using a subroutine that finds a top-ranked answer under constraints. This subroutine should be developed for the specific problem at hand. In our case, it is more difficult to do so, compared to [11, 12], for several reasons—one is that the constraints generated by Lawler's procedure are inherently different from the completeness constraints mentioned above. Consequently, the second reduction is that of applying a transformation that generates constraints of a new type. This is done by performing several reasoning steps starting with the original constraints. Finally, we compute bottom-up the top-ranked answer under the new constraints.

A related problem is that of computing full disjunctions [3, 1]. The techniques used in [1] for enumerating with polynomial delay can handle only a limited type of ranking functions (namely, "c-determined") and, therefore, cannot be applied here. We can handle more general ranking functions as well as completeness constraints, since queries are trees.

2   Data Model

2.1   Databases

Our results can be couched in a rather abstract data model that captures a variety of concrete models, including the semistructured and relational models. Formally, a *database* D consists of a set of *objects* that is denoted by $\mathcal{O}(D)$.

For example, in a relational database, an object is a tuple. Alternatively, a database can be an XML document, where the objects are the document nodes. For any given object, certain properties and tests can be computed by either using just the object itself or the whole database. For example, in the relational model, we can determine the name of the relation that contains a given object (i.e., tuple) or test whether there exists another object that is join consistent with the given one. Similarly, in an XML document, we can find the label of an object. Computations can be performed also w.r.t. (with respect to) pairs of objects, e.g., testing whether one given object of an XML document is the parent of the second given object. We only consider properties and tests that can be computed in polynomial time in the size of the database (typically they can even be evaluated much more efficiently, i.e., in logarithmic or constant time).

Example 1. As an example, the upper-right box in Figure 1 depicts a database D that is a labeled, directed graph where $\mathcal{O}(D)$ is the set of nodes. Each object is shown as a circle, with its identifier inside the circle and its label next to it.   □

2.2   Q-Trees and Complete Matches

We consider tree-structured queries over databases. A *query tree* T (abbr. *q-tree*) is directed tree with a designated node, called the *root* and denoted by $root(T)$, such that each node of T is reachable from $root(T)$ through a directed path. We use $\mathcal{N}(T)$ and $\mathcal{E}(T)$ to denote the set of nodes and the set of edges, respectively, of T. Each node n of a q-tree is associated with a predicate that gets a truth value when given a database D and an object $o \in D$. By a slight abuse of notation, however, the predicate for node n, denoted by $cond_n(X)$, is written as a unary predicate over database objects. Similarly, every edge e has a binary predicate $cond_e(X_1, X_2)$ over pairs of database objects (although, formally, the truth value depends also on the given database D and not just on the pair of objects o_1 and o_2 that are substituted for X_1 and X_2, respectively).

A q-tree can represent an XPath query or a twig pattern (and the underlying database can be a graph, as in [17, 12], and not just a tree document). Alternatively, a q-tree can be an acyclic join of some given relations.

A *complete match* (abbr. c-match) of a q-tree T in a database D is a mapping M from $\mathcal{N}(T)$ to $\mathcal{O}(D)$ that satisfies the node and edge predicates, i.e., for every node $n \in \mathcal{N}(T)$ and every edge $e = (n_1, n_2) \in \mathcal{E}(T)$, both $cond_n(M(n))$ and $cond_e(M(n_1), M(n_2))$ are true. Given a database D, the set of answers to T is usually defined as the set of all c-matches. However, we are interested in incomplete answers which are defined later in this section.

Example 2. Consider again Figure 1. A q-tree T is shown inside the dashed box, next to the database D that is described in Example 1. In this particular example, we use the following shorthand notation. Each node of T is denoted by n_l, where l is a label, and we assume that $cond_{n_l}(X)$ is the predicate "the label of object X is l." For each edge $e = (n_1, n_2)$, the predicate $cond_e(X_1, X_2)$

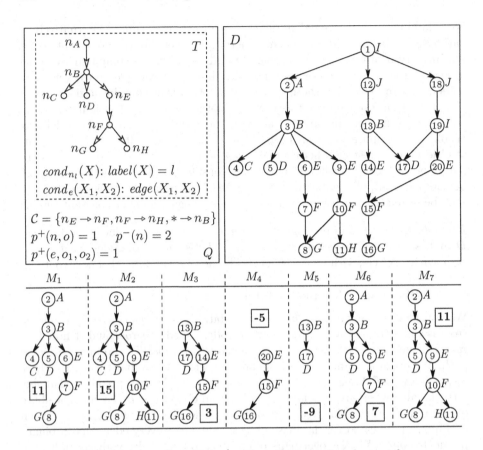

Fig. 1. A query $Q = \langle T, \mathcal{C}, p^+, p^- \rangle$, a database D and p-matches

simply means that the database D has an edge from object X_1 to object X_2. Thus, a c-match of T in the database D must preserve labels and edges. That is, a node n_l of T must be mapped to an object that has the label l while an edge of T must be mapped to an edge of D.

The c-match M_2 of T in D is shown at the bottom of Figure 1. Note that instead of defining the c-match M_2 explicitly, we show the image of M_2, i.e., the subtree of D that corresponds to T under M_2. The c-match M_2 is unambiguously derived from its image, since each node of T must be mapped to an object with a distinct label. For example, M_2 maps n_A to object 2 and n_F to object 10.   □

2.3   Partial and Maximal Matches

The c-match M_2 (from the above example) maps every node of the q-tree T to an object of D. Sometimes users want to consider *partial* matches that map only some of the nodes to objects while the remaining nodes are mapped to the *null* value, denoted by $\bot$. For a partial match to be meaningful, it must map a connected part of T to database objects.

Formally, consider a q-tree T and a database D. We say that M is a *partial match* (abbr. p-match) of T in D if there is a nonempty subtree T' of T, such that M is a c-match of T' in D and it maps the nodes of $\mathcal{N}(T) \setminus \mathcal{N}(T')$ to the null value. The set of nodes of T' is called the *domain* of M and is denoted by $\text{DOM}(M)$. Note that T' itself is a q-tree, but it does not necessarily have the same root as T. Also observe that a c-match is a special case of a p-match. We use $\mathcal{M}(T, D)$ to denote the set of all the p-matches of T in D.

We sometimes use $n \mapsto o$ to denote the fact that node n is mapped to object o. Consequently, a p-match M can be viewed as a set $\{n_1 \mapsto o_1, \ldots, n_j \mapsto o_j\}$ (and if some node does not appear at all in this set, then it is mapped to null). Note that by definition, the empty set is not a p-match. Thus, we use $\emptyset$ when we need to denote that there is no p-match that satisfies certain conditions.

Consider two p-matches M_1 and M_2 of a q-tree T. We say that M_2 *subsumes* M_1, denoted by $M_1 \sqsubseteq M_2$, if M_2 is equal to M_1 when the latter is nonnull, i.e., $\text{DOM}(M_1) \subseteq \text{DOM}(M_2)$ and for all nodes $n \in \text{DOM}(M_1)$, it holds that $M_1(n) = M_2(n)$. We say that M_2 *properly* subsumes M_1 if M_2 subsumes M_1 but the two are not identical, i.e., $M_1 \sqsubseteq M_2$ and $\text{DOM}(M_1) \subsetneq \text{DOM}(M_2)$).

Now, consider a subset $\mathcal{S}$ of $\mathcal{M}(T, D)$. A p-match $M \in \mathcal{M}(T, D)$ is said to be *maximal* w.r.t. $\mathcal{S}$ if $M \in \mathcal{S}$ and M is not properly subsumed by any p-match of $\mathcal{S}$. If M is maximal w.r.t. $\mathcal{M}(T, D)$, then we say that it is *globally* maximal.

As an example, consider again the q-tree T and the database D of Figure 1. Some of the p-matches of T in D are shown at the bottom of the figure. The p-matches M_1, M_2, M_3 and M_4 are globally maximal (and these are the only globally maximal p-matches) while the others are not. For example, the p-match M_5 is properly subsumed by the p-match M_3.

2.4 Edge-Completeness Constraints

Sometimes, when a user poses a q-tree T, she may also want to specify that some nodes of T must be assigned nonnull values. We actually allow more general constraints that can express predicates of the form "if node n_1 is assigned a nonnull value then so is n_2," where n_1 and n_2 are connected by an edge. Formally, given a q-tree T, an *edge-completeness constraint* (abbr. *ec-constraint*) has the form $n_1 \twoheadrightarrow n_2$, where either (n_1, n_2) or (n_2, n_1) is an edge of T. A p-match M of T in a database D *satisfies* $n_1 \twoheadrightarrow n_2$ if either $M(n_1) = \bot$ or $M(n_2) \neq \bot$. Note that since a p-match is only required to be nonnull on a subtree of T that does not necessarily have the same root as T, the constraint $n_1 \twoheadrightarrow n_2$ is nontrivial even if the direction of the edge is from n_2 to n_1. Given a set $\mathcal{C}$ of ec-constraints, we say that the p-match M satisfies $\mathcal{C}$ if M satisfies all the ec-constraints of $\mathcal{C}$.

As a special case, ec-constraints can express the predicate "node n must be assigned a nonnull value." As a shorthand notation, we use $* \twoheadrightarrow n$ to denote the set of ec-constraints that is satisfied by exactly all the p-matches that assign a nonnull value to n. The next example shows how this set is constructed.

Consider again Figure 1 and consider the specified set $\mathcal{C}$ of ec-constraints. In this specific example, $* \rightarrow n_B$ is a shorthand notation for $n_A \rightarrow n_B, n_C \rightarrow n_B,$ $n_D \rightarrow n_B, n_E \rightarrow n_B, n_F \rightarrow n_E, n_G \rightarrow n_F, n_H \rightarrow n_F$. In addition to $* \rightarrow n_B$, the set $\mathcal{C}$ also contains the constraints $n_E \rightarrow n_F$ and $n_F \rightarrow n_H$. Among the p-matches of this figure ($M_1, \ldots, M_7$), only M_2, M_5 and M_7 satisfy $\mathcal{C}$. M_4 does not satisfy $\mathcal{C}$ since it does not include n_B in its domain. M_1, M_3 and M_6 do not satisfy $\mathcal{C}$ since each one has n_F, but not n_H in its domain (thus, $n_F \rightarrow n_H$ is violated).

Consider a q-tree T with a set $\mathcal{C}$ of ec-constraints and a database D. A p-match M is maximal w.r.t. $\mathcal{C}$ if M satisfies $\mathcal{C}$ and there is no p-match M' that properly subsumes M and also satisfies $\mathcal{C}$. We use $\mathcal{M}_{|\mathcal{C}}^{max}(T, D)$ to denote the set of all p-matches of T in D that are maximal w.r.t. $\mathcal{C}$. In Figure 1, for example, $\mathcal{M}_{|\mathcal{C}}^{max}(T, D)$ consists of the p-matches M_2 and M_5. Note that M_2 is also globally maximal while M_5 is not.

2.5   Ranking P-Matches

In many cases, users may be overwhelmed by a huge number of p-matches. Therefore, ranking is important. But (to the best of our knowledge) ranking has not been discussed in the context of partial answers to queries. We propose to rank p-matches using two functions. The first, p^+, *rewards* a p-match for assigning nonnull values to nodes. The second, p^-, *penalizes* a p-match for missing information. These functions are formally described next.

Consider a q-tree T. The functions p^+ and p^- are associated with T. Given a p-match M of T in a database D, the function p^+ determines a nonnegative number, denoted by $p^+(n, M(n))$, for each node n of T that is mapped under M to an object of D, i.e., $n \in \text{DOM}(M)$. The function p^+ also determines a nonnegative number, denoted by $p^+(e, M(n_1), M(n_2))$, for each edge $e = (n_1, n_1)$, such that both n_1 and n_2 are in $\text{DOM}(M)$. Note that both $p^+(n, M(n))$ and $p^+(e, M(n_1), M(n_2))$ depend also on D, but by a slight abuse of notation, we do not show D explicitly as an argument of p^+ (and we do the same with p^-). The function p^- determines a nonnegative number, denoted by $p^-(n)$, for each node of T that is mapped to null. The *rank* of a p-match M, denoted by $rank(M)$, is obtained by adding all the rewards and subtracting all the penalties, that is,

$$rank(M) = \sum_{n \in \text{DOM}(M)} p^+(n, M(n)) + \sum_{\substack{e = (n_1, n_2) \in \mathcal{E}(T), \\ n_1, n_2 \in \text{DOM}(M)}} p^+(e, M(n_1), M(n_2)) - \sum_{\substack{n \in \mathcal{N}(T), \\ n \notin \text{DOM}(M)}} p^-(n).$$

As an example, consider the functions p^+ and p^- in Figure 1. Both are constant functions, i.e., the reward is always 1 and the penalty is always 2. The rank of each of the p-matches $M_1, \ldots, M_7$ is shown in a box next to the p-match.

Generally, prizes and penalties are not necessarily constant. For example, $p^+(n, o)$ can express ranking functions used in information retrieval [2], such as the relevance of object o to the keywords attached to node n of the query (e.g., a $tf \cdot idf$ formula), while $p^+(e, o_1, o_2)$ may represent the *semantic proximity* (e.g., *distance* [4, 10, 12]) between o_1 and o_2.

2.6   Queries and Answers

In our model, a query is a combination of a q-tree, ec-constraints and ranking. Formally, a *query* is a tuple $Q = \langle T, \mathcal{C}, p^+, p^- \rangle$, where T is a q-tree, $\mathcal{C}$ is a set of ec-constraints, p^+ is a reward function and p^- is a penalty function. Given a database D, the *answers* obtained by applying Q to D are the p-matches of $\mathcal{M}^{\max}_{|\mathcal{C}}(T, D)$. Therefore, the computational goal is defined as follows.

> *Given a query* $Q = \langle T, \mathcal{C}, p^+, p^- \rangle$ *and a database* D,
> *enumerate* $\mathcal{M}^{\max}_{|\mathcal{C}}(T, D)$ *in ranked order.*

Note that by "ranked order," we mean that if two p-matches M_1 and M_2 satisfy $rank(M_1) > rank(M_2)$, then M_1 should appear before M_2.

As an example, Figure 1 shows the query $Q = \langle T, \mathcal{C}, p^+, p^- \rangle$ in the upper-left box (each of the elements of Q has already been described earlier) and the database D in the upper-right box. The answers are the p-matches M_2 and M_5 depicted in that figure, where the rank of M_2, 15, is higher than that of M_5, which is -9.

3   Efficient Ranked Evaluation

3.1   Enumeration with Polynomial Delay

In order to discern between efficient and inefficient evaluations of queries in ranked order, we need to use the measure of *query-and-data* (i.e., combined) complexity. Furthermore, measuring the running time as a function of only the input size is inappropriate, since the output size could be exponential in the size of the input. In such cases, there are several notions of efficiency [6]. The conventional notion is *polynomial total time*, i.e., the time for evaluating the query is polynomial in the combined size of the input and the output. This notion, however, does not provide a sufficiently strong requirement for efficiency, since it does not capture the need to enumerate the answers *incrementally* in ranked order (or to obtain the top-k answers quickly). Therefore, we use the strongest notion in [6], namely, enumeration with *polynomial delay* that is defined as follows. After the algorithm prints the $(i - 1)$st answer, it generates the next (ith) answer in time that is polynomial in the size of the input (i.e., the query and the database). Polynomial delay implies, in particular, an efficient evaluation of the top-k answers, since we can stop the execution after printing the first k answers and the running time is only linear in k (and polynomial in the input).

3.2   Efficiency of Query Evaluation

Our main complexity result is that queries can be evaluated in ranked order with polynomial delay. We assume that the predicates attached to the nodes and edges of q-trees as well as the prize and penalty functions can all be evaluated in polynomial time in the size of T and D. In the next two sections, we prove the following for a query $Q = \langle T, \mathcal{C}, p^+, p^- \rangle$ and a database D.

Algorithm RANKEDEVALUATION(Q, D)

1: $Queue \leftarrow$ an empty priority queue, with priority based on $rank$
2: $M \leftarrow$ TOPRANKED($Q, D, \emptyset, \emptyset$)
3: **if** $M \neq \emptyset$ **then**
4:      $Queue$.INSERT($\langle \emptyset, \emptyset, M \rangle$)
5: **while** $Queue$ is not empty **do**
6:      $\langle Pos, Neg, M \rangle \leftarrow Queue$.REMOVETOP()
7:      $\{n_1, \ldots, n_k\} \leftarrow$ DOM(M) $\setminus$ DOM(Pos)
8:      **for** $i \leftarrow 1$ **to** k **do**
9:          $Pos_i \leftarrow Pos \cup \{n_1 \rightsquigarrow M(n_1), \ldots, n_{i-1} \rightsquigarrow M(n_{i-1})\}$
10:         $Neg_i \leftarrow Neg \cup \{n_i \not\rightsquigarrow M(n_i)\}$
11:         $M_i \leftarrow$ TOPRANKED(Q, D, Pos_i, Neg_i)
12:         **if** $M_i \neq \emptyset$ **then**
13:             $Queue$.INSERT($\langle Pos_i, Neg_i, M_i \rangle$)
14:     PRINT(M)

Fig. 2. Incrementally computing answers in sorted order

Theorem 1. *The answers of $\mathcal{M}_{|\mathcal{C}}^{\max}(T, D)$ can be enumerated in ranked order with polynomial delay, under query-and-data complexity.*

4   The Basic Enumeration Technique

By generalizing an algorithm of Yen [18], Lawler [13] developed a procedure for enumerating the top-k solutions to discrete optimization problems. The algorithm RANKEDEVALUATION(Q, D) of Figure 2 is an adaptation of this procedure. The input is a query $Q = \langle T, \mathcal{C}, p^+, p^- \rangle$ and a database D. The algorithm uses two types of constraints (in addition to the ec-constraints of $\mathcal{C}$). A *positive* constraint has the form $n \rightsquigarrow o$ and a *negative* constraint has the form $n' \not\rightsquigarrow o'$, where n and n' are nodes of the q-tree T while o and o' are objects of D. A p-match $M \in \mathcal{M}_{|\mathcal{C}}^{\max}(T, D)$ satisfies $n \rightsquigarrow o$ if $M(n) = o$. M satisfies $n' \not\rightsquigarrow o'$ if $M(n) \neq o$ (in particular, note that $M(n) \neq o$ holds if $n \notin$ DOM(M), i.e., $M(n) = \perp$). We use Pos and Pos_i to denote sets of positive constraints whereas Neg and Neg_i denote sets of negative constraints. DOM(Pos) denotes the set of all the nodes that appear on the left side of some constraint of Pos.

RANKEDEVALUATION uses a priority queue, denoted by $Queue$. Each element of $Queue$ represents a subset of $\mathcal{M}_{|\mathcal{C}}^{\max}(T, D)$ that is characterized by sets of positive and negative constraints. At any given time, the elements of $Queue$ correspond to disjoint subsets that cover all the answers that have not yet been printed. In particular, an element of $Queue$ is a triplet $\langle Pos, Neg, M \rangle$, where Pos and Neg are sets of positive and negative constraints, respectively, and M is the top-ranked p-match among all the p-matches of $\mathcal{M}_{|\mathcal{C}}^{\max}(T, D)$ that satisfy Pos and Neg. Priority in $Queue$ is based on the ranking function $rank$; that is, the top element of $Queue$ is a triplet $\langle Pos, Neg, M \rangle$, such that $rank(M) \geq rank(M')$ for all triplets $\langle Pos', Neg', M' \rangle$ of $Queue$. The operations on $Queue$ take logarithmic time in the size of $Queue$ (hence, polynomial time in Q and D).

The first element inserted into $Queue$ (Lines 2–4) represents the whole set $\mathcal{M}_{|\mathcal{C}}^{\max}(T, D)$. In the loop of Lines 5–14, each iteration starts by removing the top element $\langle Pos, Neg, M \rangle$ from $Queue$. The p-match M is printed in Line 14. Let $n_1, \ldots, n_k$ be the set of all the nodes of $\text{DOM}(M)$ that do not appear in Pos, i.e., $\{n_1, \ldots, n_k\} = \text{DOM}(M) \setminus \text{DOM}(Pos)$. In Lines 8–13, we partition all the p-matches represented by $\langle Pos, Neg, M \rangle$, except for M, into k disjoint subsets by creating the elements $\langle Pos_i, Neg_i, M_i \rangle$ $(1 \le i \le k)$ and inserting them into $Queue$ (whenever M_i exists, i.e., $M_i \ne \emptyset$). The set Pos_i is obtained from Pos by adding the constraints $n_j \rightsquigarrow M(n_j)$ for $j = 1, \ldots, i-1$. The set Neg_i is obtained from Neg by adding the constraint $n_i \not\rightsquigarrow M(n_i)$. The top-ranked p-match $M_i \in \mathcal{M}_{|\mathcal{C}}^{\max}(T, D)$ that satisfies Pos_i and Neg_i is generated in Line 11 by executing the algorithm $\text{TOPRANKED}(Q, D, Pos_i, Neg_i)$, which is described in the next section. Designing this algorithm is the main difficulty in applying Lawler's procedure to a specific enumeration problem. The correctness and running time of $\text{RANKEDEVALUATION}(Q, D)$ are stated by the next lemma. To prove it, we need to show that the original method of [13] remains correct even when using non-binary variables and allowing incomplete (yet maximal) assignments.

Lemma 1. *Consider a query $Q = \langle T, \mathcal{C}, p^+, p^- \rangle$ and a database D. The algorithm $\text{RANKEDEVALUATION}(Q, D)$ enumerates $\mathcal{M}_{|\mathcal{C}}^{\max}(T, D)$ in ranked order with polynomial delay if TOPRANKED is correct and runs in polynomial time.*

5   Finding Top-Ranked P-Matches Under Constraints

Throughout this section, $Q = \langle T, \mathcal{C}, p^+, p^- \rangle$ denotes a query, D is a database, and Pos and Neg are sets of positive and negative constraints, respectively. Our goal is to describe the algorithm TOPRANKED for finding a top-ranked answer of $\mathcal{M}_{|\mathcal{C}}^{\max}(T, D)$ that satisfies Pos and Neg (in addition to $\mathcal{C}$). The main idea is to transform all the constraints of the sets $\mathcal{C}$, Pos and Neg into *negative rules* (which are similar to negative constraints but applied differently) and then use an algorithm for finding the top answer under such rules.

5.1   Negative Rules

In the algorithm of Figure 2, negative constraints are used for selecting answers. That is, a negative constraint $n' \not\rightsquigarrow o'$ is applied to $\mathcal{M}_{|\mathcal{C}}^{\max}(T, D)$ and the result comprises all p-matches that satisfy that constraint. In this section, we use negative constraints in a different way, similarly to the role of ec-constraints in defining the set $\mathcal{M}_{|\mathcal{C}}^{\max}(T, D)$. To emphasize this difference, we use the term *negative rules* instead of negative constraints. However, the definition of when a p-match satisfies a negative rule remains the same.

Given a set NR of negative rules, we use $\mathcal{M}_{|NR}^{\max}(T, D)$ to denote the set of all p-matches of the q-tree T in the database D that are maximal w.r.t. NR. In other words, $M \in \mathcal{M}_{|NR}^{\max}(T, D)$ if M satisfies all the negative rules of NR and there is no p-match M' that properly subsumes M and also satisfies NR.

We also use the following notation. Given a set $\mathcal{P}$ of p-matches and a set C of constraints, $[\mathcal{P}]_{|C}$ denotes the set of all p-matches of $\mathcal{P}$ that satisfy C. Note that TOPRANKED should find a top-ranked p-match of $[\mathcal{M}_{|C}^{\max}(T, D)]_{|\,Pos \cup Neg}$.

Consider the query $Q = \langle T, C, p^+, p^- \rangle$, the database D and a set NR of negative rules. Recall that $n \mapsto o$ means that node n of T is mapped to object o. We say that $n \mapsto o$ is *legal* if $cond_n(o)$ holds and, in addition, NR does not contain the rule $n \not\leadsto o$. Now, suppose that $n \mapsto o$ is legal and let n' be connected to n by an edge e (i.e., either $e = (n, n') \in \mathcal{E}(T)$ or $e = (n', n) \in \mathcal{E}(T)$). We say that $n' \mapsto o'$ *complies* with $n \mapsto o$ if $n' \mapsto o'$ is legal and, in addition, if $(n, n') \in \mathcal{E}(T)$, then $cond_e(o, o')$ holds, and otherwise $cond_e(o', o)$ holds.

5.2 Transforming Constraints into Negative Rules

Positive Constraints. First, we transform positive constraints into negative and ec-constraints by applying POS-TRANS of Figure 3. This operation replaces each positive constraint $n \leadsto o$ of Pos with constraints that are added to Neg and C as follows. The ec-constraint $* \to n$ is added to C. For each object $o' \in \mathcal{O}(D)$, such that $n \mapsto o'$ is legal (w.r.t. the empty set of negative rules) and $o' \neq o$, the negative constraint $n \not\leadsto o'$ is added to Neg. Let Neg' and C' be the sets of constraints when POS-TRANS terminates, after starting with Pos, Neg and C.

Lemma 2. $[\mathcal{M}_{|C}^{\max}(T, D)]_{|\,Pos \cup Neg} = [\mathcal{M}_{|C'}^{\max}(T, D)]_{|\,Neg'}$.

Edge-Completeness Constraints. After eliminating the positive constraints, we apply the operation EC-TRANS of Figure 3 that transforms ec-constraints into negative rules. Consider an ec-constraint $n_1 \to n_2$ of C'. Suppose that o_1 is an object, such that $n_1 \mapsto o_1$ is legal (w.r.t. NR) but there is no object o_2, such that $n_2 \mapsto o_2$ complies with $n_1 \mapsto o_1$. Clearly, in this case, n_1 cannot be mapped to o_1. Hence, EC-TRANS adds the negative rule $n_1 \not\leadsto o_1$ to NR. Note that adding rules to NR may create new opportunities to add more rules and, hence, the loop of Line 2 is repeated while NR changes. It can be shown that the final result does not depend on the order of iterating through ec-constraints and objects in Lines 3 and 4. Let NR denote the set of negative rules that is obtained from the empty one by applying EC-TRANS when starting with C'.

Lemma 3. $\mathcal{M}_{|C'}^{\max}(T, D) = \mathcal{M}_{|NR}^{\max}(T, D)$.

Negative Constraints. Negative constraints are transformed into negative rules by applying the operation NEG-TRANS of Figure 3 that repeatedly adds negative constraints to Neg'' (which is initially equal to Neg') and finally computes the union of Neg'' and NR. Constraints are added to Neg'' as follows. Consider two neighbors n and $\hat{n}$ of T and an object o of D, such that $n \mapsto o$ is

---

Operation POS-TRANS

1: **for all** positive constraints $n \rightsquigarrow o \in Pos$ **do**
2:    $\mathcal{C} \leftarrow \mathcal{C} \cup \{* \rightarrow n\}$
3:    **for all** $o' \in \mathcal{O}(D)$, such that $n \mapsto o'$ is legal and $o' \neq o$ **do**
4:        $Neg \leftarrow Neg \cup \{n \not\rightsquigarrow o'\}$

Operation EC-TRANS

1: $NR \leftarrow \emptyset$
2: **while** NR changes **do**
3:    **for all** ec-constraints $n_1 \rightarrow n_2 \in \mathcal{C}'$ **do**
4:        **for all** objects $o_1 \in \mathcal{O}(D)$, such that $n_1 \mapsto o_1$ is legal **do**
5:            $O = \{o_2 \in \mathcal{O}(D) \mid n_2 \mapsto o_2 \text{ complies with } n_1 \mapsto o_1\}$
6:            **if** $O = \emptyset$ **then**
7:                $NR \leftarrow NR \cup \{n_1 \not\rightsquigarrow o_1\}$

Operation NEG-TRANS

1: $Neg'' \leftarrow Neg'$
2: **while** Neg'' changes **do**
3:    **for all** $n \in \mathcal{N}(T)$ and $o \in \mathcal{O}(D)$, such that $n \mapsto o$ is legal **do**
4:        **for all** neighbors $\hat{n}$ of n **do**
5:            $O' \leftarrow \{o' \in \mathcal{O}(D) \mid \hat{n} \mapsto o' \text{ complies with } n \mapsto o\}$
6:            $\hat{O} \leftarrow \{\hat{o} \in O' \mid \hat{n} \not\rightsquigarrow \hat{o} \in Neg''\}$
7:            **if** $O' \neq \emptyset$ and $\hat{O} = O'$ **then**
8:                $Neg'' \leftarrow Neg'' \cup \{n \not\rightsquigarrow o\}$
9: $NR' \leftarrow NR \cup Neg''$

Operation TRANSFORM

1: apply POS-TRANS
2: apply EC-TRANS
3: apply NEG-TRANS
4: **return** NR'

Fig. 3. Transformations of constraints

legal (w.r.t. the set NR that was generated by the previous transformation). If there is at least one object $\hat{o}$, such that $\hat{n} \mapsto \hat{o}$ complies with $n \mapsto o$ and, moreover, for all such objects $\hat{o}$, the constraint $\hat{n} \not\rightsquigarrow \hat{o}$ is in Neg'', then add $n \not\rightsquigarrow o$ to Neg''. Again, it can be shown that the final result does not depend on the order of iterating over nodes and objects. The result of NEG-TRANS is NR', namely, the union of NR and Neg''.

Algorithm TopMaxMatch(Q, D, NR)

1: let $Q = \langle T, \mathcal{C}, p^+, p^- \rangle$
2: **for all** $n \in \mathcal{N}(T)$ and $o \in \mathcal{O}(D)$ **do**
3:    $r[n, o] \leftarrow -\infty$, $f[n, o] \leftarrow -\infty$, $m[n, o] \leftarrow \emptyset$
4: **for all** $n \in \mathcal{N}(T)$ in bottom-up order **do**
5:    **for all** $o \in \mathcal{O}(D)$, such that $n \mapsto o$ is legal **do**
6:       $m[n, o] \leftarrow \{n \mapsto o\}$
7:       $r[n, o] \leftarrow p^+(n, o)$
8:       **for all** edges $e = (n, \hat{n}) \in \mathcal{E}(T)$ **do**
9:          $\hat{O} = \{o' \in \mathcal{O}(D) \mid \hat{n} \mapsto o' \text{ complies with } n \mapsto o\}$
10:          **if** $\hat{O} = \emptyset$ **then**
11:             $N \leftarrow \mathcal{N}(T_{\hat{n}})$
12:             $r[n, o] \leftarrow r[n, o] - \sum_{n' \in N} p^-(n')$
13:          **else**
14:             $\hat{o} = argmax_{o'}\{r[\hat{n}, o'] + p^+(e, o, o') \mid o' \in O\}$
15:             $m[n, o] \leftarrow m[n, o] \cup m[\hat{n}, \hat{o}]$
16:             $r[n, o] \leftarrow r[n, o] + r[\hat{n}, \hat{o}] + p^+(e, o, \hat{o})$
17: **for all** $n \in \mathcal{N}(T)$ **do**
18:    $N \leftarrow \mathcal{N}(T) \setminus \mathcal{N}(T_n)$
19:    **for all** $o \in \mathcal{O}(D)$ **do**
20:       $f[n, o] \leftarrow r[n, o] - \sum_{n' \in N} p^-(n')$
21: let *Top* be the set of all p-matches $m[n, o]$ with the maximal $f[n, o]$
22: **return** a p-match $m[n, o] \in Top$, such that n has a minimal depth in T

Fig. 4. Finding the top-ranked p-match of $\mathcal{M}^{\mathsf{max}}_{|NR}(T, D)$

Lemma 4. $[\mathcal{M}^{\mathsf{max}}_{|NR}(T, D)]_{| Neg'} = \mathcal{M}^{\mathsf{max}}_{|NR'}(T, D)$.

The Complete Transformation. To conclude, the operation Transform of Figure 3 describes the complete transformation. Recall that the input consists of a query $Q = \langle T, \mathcal{C}, p^+, p^- \rangle$, a database D, and sets *Pos* and *Neg* of positive and negative constraints, respectively. Pos-Trans is applied first, followed by EC-Trans and, finally, Neg-Trans. Correctness of Transform, i.e., $[\mathcal{M}^{\mathsf{max}}_{|\mathcal{C}}(T, D)]_{| Pos \cup Neg} = \mathcal{M}^{\mathsf{max}}_{|NR'}(T, D)$, follows from Lemmas 2, 3 and 4.

5.3 Finding Top-Ranked P-Matches Under Negative Rules

We now describe the algorithm TopMaxMatch of Figure 4 for finding the top-ranked p-match of $\mathcal{M}^{\mathsf{max}}_{|NR}(T, D)$. The input is a query $Q = \langle T, \mathcal{C}, p^+, p^- \rangle$, a database D and a set NR of negative rules. The algorithm finds the top-ranked p-match M of $\mathcal{M}^{\mathsf{max}}_{|NR}(T, D)$ according to the ranking defined by p^+ and p^-.

In the algorithm, T_n denotes the subtree of T that is rooted at node n, i.e., the subtree that consists of n and all of its descendants. The algorithm uses three arrays r, f and m that are indexed by a node $n \in \mathcal{N}(T)$ and an object $o \in \mathcal{O}(D)$. When the execution terminates, $m[n, o]$ contains a top-ranked p-match of $\mathcal{M}^{\max}_{|NR}(T_n, D)$ that maps n to o; however, if $n \mapsto o$ is illegal, then $m[n, o] = \emptyset$. The rank of the p-match $m[n, o]$ is w.r.t. T_n (i.e., the penalties for the nodes of $\mathcal{N}(T) \setminus \mathcal{N}(T_n)$ are not taken into account) and it is stored in $r[n, o]$. The real rank of $m[n, o]$ (i.e., w.r.t. T) is eventually stored in $f[n, o]$. Next, we describe the algorithm in detail.

In Lines 1–3, we initialize the arrays r and f to $-\infty$, and m to $\emptyset$. In Lines 4–16, we construct the arrays r and m. Lines 6–16 are executed for each node n and object o, such that $n \mapsto o$ is legal. The nodes n of T are traversed in a bottom-up order. When the iteration terminates, $m[n, o]$ and $r[n, o]$ hold their final values. Line 6 sets $m[n, o]$ to the p-match that maps n to o and the prize for this match is assigned to $r[n, o]$ in Line 7. If n is a leaf in T, then $m[n, o]$ and $r[n, o]$ already hold their final values. Otherwise, Lines 9–16 are executed for each child $\hat{n}$ of n in T. Consider such a child $\hat{n}$ and let e be the edge $(n, \hat{n})$. In Line 9, we define the set $\hat{O}$ of all objects o' of D, such that $\hat{n} \mapsto o'$ complies with $n \mapsto o$. If $\hat{O}$ is empty, then we cannot add $\hat{n}$ to the domain of $m[n, o]$ and, in Lines 11–12, we subtract from $r[n, o]$ the penalties for all the descendants of $\hat{n}$, including $\hat{n}$ itself. If $\hat{O}$ is not empty, then we choose from $\hat{O}$ an object $\hat{o}$, such that the value $r[\hat{n}, \hat{o}] + p^+(e, o, \hat{o})$ is maximal. Then, in Lines 15–16, we add all the mappings defined for $m[\hat{n}, \hat{o}]$ to $m[n, o]$ and add to $r[n, o]$ the value $r[\hat{n}, \hat{o}] + p^+(e, o, \hat{o})$.

In Lines 17–20, we construct the array f. For each n and o, the value of $f[n, o]$ is obtained from $r[n, o]$ by simply subtracting the penalties for the nodes of T that are neither n nor descendants of n. Finally, in Lines 21–22, a top-ranked p-match of $\mathcal{M}^{\max}_{|NR}(T, D)$ is returned. Line 21 constructs the set Top of all the p-matches $m[n, o]$, such that the value of $f[n, o]$ is the largest in f. Not all p-matches of Top are necessarily maximal. Hence, Line 22 returns a p-match $m[n, o]$ in Top, such that n is closest to the root of T, since this is a maximal p-match of $\mathcal{M}^{\max}_{|NR}(T, D)$.

Lemma 5. *Upon termination of* TopMaxMatch(Q, D, NR), *the following hold for each* $n \in \mathcal{N}(T)$ *and* $o \in \mathcal{O}(D)$, *such that* $n \mapsto o$ *is legal.*

1. $m[n, o]$ *is a top-ranked p-match of* $\mathcal{M}^{\max}_{|NR}(T_n, D)$ *that maps* n *to* o;
2. $r[n, o]$ *stores the rank of* $m[n, o]$ *w.r.t.* T_n; *and*
3. $f[n, o]$ *stores the rank of* $m[n, o]$ *w.r.t.* T.

Corollary 1. TopMaxMatch(Q, D, NR) *returns, in polynomial time, a top-ranked p-match of* $\mathcal{M}^{\max}_{|NR}(T, D)$, *or* $\emptyset$ *if no such p-match exists.*

We conclude Section 5 with the following theorem that shows the correctness and efficiency of the algorithms we presented.

Theorem 2. *Consider a query* $Q = \langle T, \mathcal{C}, p^+, p^- \rangle$ *and a database* D. *Suppose that Pos and Neg are sets of positive and negative constraints, respectively. Let* NR' *be obtained by applying* Transform. TopMaxMatch(Q, D, NR') *returns a top-ranked p-match of* $[\mathcal{M}^{\max}_{|\mathcal{C}}(T, D)]_{|\,Pos \cup Neg}$, *or* $\emptyset$ *if no such p-match exists. Furthermore, both* Transform *and* TopMaxMatch *have a polynomial running time.*

6   Conclusion

We have investigated how to combine incompleteness and ranking in tree queries. Our results apply to the semistructured data model (including XML with ID references) and can be translated into the relational models. Our semantics for answers to queries deploys the notion of partial, yet maximal matches. This approach extends earlier work [7, 9] by allowing the root to be matched with any data object (rather than just a specified root object). Furthermore, answers may assign the null value to the root of the query. Our edge-completeness constraints over query answers extend the existence constraints of [7]. The user can rank answers according to the degree of incompleteness (by penalizing nodes that are assigned the null value) and combine it with known ranking paradigms commonly in use, e.g., relevance of objects to query terms [2] and proximity among objects [4, 10, 12] (by rewarding nodes and edges associated with nonnull values).

To characterize the efficiency of an evaluation algorithm, one has to measure the delay between successive answers when presenting them in ranked order. We developed an evaluation algorithm that enumerates answers in ranked order with polynomial delay under query-and-data complexity. Our algorithm employs an adaptation of Lawler's technique [13] that reduces ranked evaluation to the problem of finding the top-ranked answer under positive and negative constraints (in addition to the edge-completeness constraints that define the set of all answers). For solving the latter problem, all the constraints are transformed into negative rules by means of a reasoning process. Finally, a bottom-up algorithm computes the top-ranked p-match that satisfies the negative rules. It is important to observe that the transformation of the constraints to negative rules does not use the ranking function. Therefore, we can use any ranking function for which the top-ranked p-match under negative rules can be found efficiently.

This work can be extended in several directions. The first is allowing projection in queries. The naive approach of applying the projection as a postprocessing step can lead to an exponential delay, since it may generate redundant answers. After applying a projection, there are two kinds of redundant answers: *repeated answers* and *subsumed answers*. Our algorithms can be extended to handle the first kind of redundancy. An open problem is whether our result holds if subsumption among the projected answers is not allowed.

The second extension is generalizing the ranking function. For example, we can adapt our algorithm to ranking functions that have some properties of monotonicity. More specifically, we can allow the "branch-monotonic" functions of [12]. As another example, we can allow negative prizes and penalties. More formally, we can show that one can enumerate all the maximal answers in ranked order, even under negative prizes and penalties. However, in this case there is an apparent contradiction between the notions of ranking and maximal answers, since one p-match can properly subsume another p-match that has a higher rank. In future work, we intend to explore suitable semantics that allow negative prizes and penalties without overwhelming the user with all the partial matches.

Finally, we can show that our result holds even if edge-completeness constraints are used differently from the definition in the paper when determining the set of all answers. Specifically, instead of defining answers as the p-matches that are maximal w.r.t. the ec-constraints, they can be defined as the globally maximal p-matches that satisfy the ec-constraints. Our algorithm can be modified to handle the new definition.

Acknowledgment

The authors thank anonymous referees for helpful comments and suggestions.

References

[1] S. Cohen, I. Fadida, Y. Kanza, B. Kimelfeld, and Y. Sagiv. Full disjunctions: Polynomial-delay iterators in action. In *VLDB*, 2006.
[2] N. Fuhr and K. Großjohann. XIRQL: A query language for information retrieval in XML documents. In *SIGIR*, 2001.
[3] C. Galindo-Legaria. Outerjoins as disjunctions. In *SIGMOD*, 1994.
[4] R. Goldman, N. Shivakumar, S. Venkatasubramanian, and H. Garcia-Molina. Proximity search in databases. In *VLDB*, 1998.
[5] I. F. Ilyas, W. G. Aref, and A. K. Elmagarmid. Supporting top-k join queries in relational databases. In *VLDB*, 2003.
[6] D. Johnson, M. Yannakakis, and C. Papadimitriou. On generating all maximal independent sets. *Information Processing Letters*, 27, 1988.
[7] Y. Kanza, W. Nutt, and Y. Sagiv. Queries with incomplete answers over semistructured data. In *PODS*, 1999.
[8] Y. Kanza, W. Nutt, and Y. Sagiv. Querying incomplete information in semistructured data. *J. Comput. Syst. Sci.*, 64(3), 2002.
[9] Y. Kanza and Y. Sagiv. Flexible queries over semistructured data. In *PODS*, 2001.
[10] B. Kimelfeld and Y. Sagiv. Finding and approximating top-k answers in keyword proximity search. In *PODS*, 2006.
[11] B. Kimelfeld and Y. Sagiv. Incrementally computing ordered answers of acyclic conjunctive queries. In *NGITS*, 2006.
[12] B. Kimelfeld and Y. Sagiv. Twig patterns: From XML trees to graphs. In *WebDB*, 2006.
[13] E. L. Lawler. A procedure for computing the k best solutions to discrete optimization problems and its application to the shortest path problem. *Management Science*, 18, 1972.
[14] A. Natsev, Y. C. Chang, J. R. Smith, C. S. Li, and J. S. Vitter. Supporting incremental join queries on ranked inputs. In *VLDB*, 2001.
[15] M. Theobald, R. Schenkel, and G. Weikum. An efficient and versatile query engine for TopX search. In *VLDB*, 2005.
[16] A. Trotman and B. Sigurbjörnsson. Narrowed Extended XPath I (NEXI). In *INEX*, 2004.
[17] Z. Vagena, M. M. Moro, and V. J. Tsotras. Twig query processing over graph-structured XML data. In *WebDB*, 2004.
[18] J. Y. Yen. Another algorithm for finding the k shortest loopless network paths. In *Proc. 41st Mtg. Operations Research Society of America*, volume 20, 1972.

Structural Recursion on Ordered Trees and List-Based Complex Objects
Expressiveness and PTIME Restrictions

Edward L. Robertson[1], Lawrence V. Saxton[2],
Dirk Van Gucht[1], and Stijn Vansummeren[3],[*]

[1] Indiana University, USA
[2] University of Regina, Canada
[3] Hasselt University and Transnational University of Limburg, Belgium

Abstract. XML query languages need to provide some mechanism to inspect and manipulate nodes at all levels of an input tree. In this paper we investigate the expressive power provided in this regard by structural recursion. We show that the combination of vertical recursion down a tree combined with horizontal recursion across a list of trees gives rise to a robust class of transformations: it captures the class of all primitive recursive queries. Since queries are expected to be computable in at most polynomial time for all practical purposes, we next identify a restriction of structural recursion that captures the polynomial time queries. Although this restriction is semantic in nature, and therefore undecidable, we provide an effective syntax. We also give corresponding results for list-based complex objects.

1 Introduction

Over the past few years, the ordered, node-labeled tree data model of XML has emerged as the standard format for representing and exchanging data on the web. Often, there is no a priori bound on the width and depth of such trees. As such, an XML query language needs to provide some mechanism to inspect and manipulate nodes at all levels. XQuery, the standard XML query language currently under development by the World Wide Web Consortium [4,14], uses *recursion* for this purpose. For example, to compute the table of contents of books in which sections can be arbitrarily nested, one would write:

```
function toc(t) {
    for s in t/section return <section>{ s/title, toc(s) }</section>
};

<toc> toc(book)</toc>
```

Here, *toc* is a recursive function returning for each **section** child s of its input tree t a new **section** node containing the title and table of contents of s.

---

[*] Postdoctoral Fellow of the Research Foundation - Flanders (FWO).

T. Schwentick and D. Suciu (Eds.): ICDT 2007, LNCS 4353, pp. 344–358, 2007.

XQuery allows arbitrary recursive function definitions, resulting in a Turing complete language. Turing completeness is an undesirable property for a query language however, as it makes optimization difficult and allows non-terminating queries. Therefore, it is desirable to look for suitable restrictions of arbitrary recursion in XQuery. Non-termination can be prevented by closely tying recursion to the structure of the data being operated upon, i.e., by restricting to *structural recursion*. For example, a structural recursive function computing on a tree t can only recursively call itself on the children of t. The function *toc* defined above is an example of such a structural recursion. Similarly, a structural recursive function computing on a list l can only recursively call itself on the tail of l. A typical example of such a structural recursion is the list reversal function *rev*:

function $rev(l)$ { if $empty(l)$ then l else $rev(tl(l)), hd(l)$ };

Here hd returns the head of a nonempty list, tl returns the tail of a nonempty list, and the comma operator is concatenation of lists.

In this paper, we study the properties of structural recursion as a candidate replacement of arbitrary recursion in XQuery. In particular, we study the combination of vertical structural recursion down trees and horizontal structural recursion across lists of trees (as trees and lists of trees both naturally occur in the XQuery data model [4,14].

Structural recursion is an important primitive in database theory. It has been used to query (nested) collections based on sets, or-sets, pomsets, bags, and lists [8,17,21,24]; unordered trees and graphs [7]; and sequences and text documents [5]. Unrestricted structural recursion leads to highly expressive query languages. For example, Buneman et al. have shown [8] that structural recursion on nested relations is equivalent to the powerset algebra of Abiteboul and Beeri [1], which by a result of Hull and Su, captures exactly the class of elementary nested relational queries [20] (i.e., the queries with hyper-exponential time data complexity). Furthermore, Immerman et al. [21] and Suciu and Wong [27] have shown that, in the presence of object invention, the class of functions $f \colon \mathbb{N} \times \cdots \times \mathbb{N} \to \mathbb{N}$ representable with structural recursion on sets coincides with the class of primitive recursive functions [6]. The resulting language is hence strictly more powerful than the elementary queries. This result was later extended to structural recursion on (nested) bags by Libkin and Wong [24].

Since tree construction is a form of object invention, it should come as no surprise that a similar result also hold for structural recursion in XQuery. We actually obtain a slightly stronger result than that of Immerman et al.: not only does the class of functions $f \colon \mathbb{N} \times \cdots \times \mathbb{N} \to \mathbb{N}$ representable in our language coincide with the class of primitive recursive functions, but the class of expressible *queries* coincides with the class of queries that have primitive recursive time data complexity.

From a complexity point of view, structural recursion is hence too powerful a primitive, as queries are expected to be computable in at most polynomial time for all practical purposes. A restriction of structural recursion to polynomial time is therefore desirable. Nevertheless, this restriction should still enable all polynomial time queries.

The first such restriction was given by Immerman et al. for structural recursion on sets, by disallowing all forms of nesting [21]. The resulting language captures exactly the polynomial time flat relational queries. Their restriction does not transfer to nested data models or data models with duplicates such as bags or lists, however. As such, it is not directly applicable to structural recursion in XQuery. A different restriction technique, known as *bounded recursion* dates back to Cobham [11], and was applied to structural recursion on flat lists by Grumbach and Milo [17]. Bounded recursion is best explained by means of an example. Consider the unbounded function that computes a list of size exponential in the size of l:

function $explist(l)$ {if $empty(l)$ then l else $explist(tl(l)), explist(tl(l))$};

Since *explist* generates exponential output, it certainly cannot be evaluated in polynomial time. Bounded recursion prevents the expression of *explist* by requiring each recursive function definition to halt computation whenever the result becomes larger than some explicitly given size bound b. That is, with bounded recursion, *explist* is required to have the following form:

function $explist'(l, b)$ {
  if $empty(l)$ then l else
    let $r = explist'(tl(l), b), explist'(tl(l), b)$ in
    if $sizeof(r) \leq sizeof(b)$ then r else $explist'(tl(l), b)$
};

In particular, the size of $explist'(l, b)$ is always bounded by the size of b. Since the value for b will ultimately be computed by an expression that does not involve recursion, the size of recursively computed outputs is always polynomial, and this guarantees that all expressible queries can be evaluated in polynomial time (see [11,17] for details). This way of bounding recursion has also been applied to query languages over nested relations and bags based on inflationary fixpoint operators [12,25,26].

Although bounded recursion is useful for capturing polynomial time, it is unsatisfactory from a practical point of view, as the programmer is required to give explicit complexity bounds upon each recursive function invocation. More intrinsic restrictions of structural recursion on the bitstrings by means of *predicative recursion* were proposed by Bellantoni and Cook [3] and Leivant [23]. Their restrictions were later generalized to arbitrary recursive functions operating on ranked trees generated by a free term algebra by Caseiro [9]. Her techniques were later explained by means of a type system based on linear and modal logic in the context of a higher-order functional programming language by Hofmann [18,19].

In this paper, we apply Caseiro's observations and ideas to structural recursion operating on lists and *unranked* trees to obtain an intrinsic restriction that captures exactly the class of polynomial time queries. In particular, we prevent the definition of *explist* above by disallowing all forms of *doubling* like $explist(tl(l)), explist(tl(l))$. Although this restriction is semantical in nature, and therefore undecidable, we provide an effective syntax for it.

For the formal development of our results, we find it convenient to not study structural recursion directly in XQuery itself, but in the *Nested Tree Calculus* $\mathcal{NTC}$. The $\mathcal{NTC}$ can be viewed as the combination of non-recursive for-let-where-return XQuery $\mathcal{XQ}$ and a complex object calculus for nested lists $\mathcal{COC}$. These languages blend naturally together, as it has repeatedly been observed in the literature that there is a close correspondence between $\mathcal{XQ}$ and calculi for complex objects [15,22,29]. In fact, we show $\mathcal{NTC}$ to be a *conservative* extension of both $\mathcal{XQ}$ and $\mathcal{COC}$, even in the presence of (restricted) structural recursion. As a consequence, results about (restricted) structural recursion in $\mathcal{NTC}$ transfer immediately to the respective sublanguages. As an important corollary we obtain that our polynomial time restriction of structural recursion also allows to capture the polynomial time queries on nested lists. Hence, suitably restricted structural recursion provides an elegant alternative to the rather awkward *list-trav* iteration construct of Colby et al. [13], which also captures polynomial time on nested lists.

Organization. This paper is further organized as follows. We start by introducing our data model and the notion of a query in Section 2. Next, we define the Nested Tree Calculus $\mathcal{NTC}$ and structural recursion in Section 3. The expressive power of structural recursion in $\mathcal{NTC}$ is in studied in Section 4, where we also show how to restrict it to polynomial time. Finally, we show $\mathcal{NTC}$ to be a conservative extension of both $\mathcal{XQ}$ and $\mathcal{COC}$ in Section 5.

2   Preliminaries

Our data model is a combination of the tree-based data model of XQuery and the list-based complex object data model [8]. That is, we consider the types given by the following grammar:

$$\sigma, \tau ::= \mathsf{atom} \mid \mathsf{tree} \mid \sigma \times \tau \mid [\tau].$$

Semantically, a type denotes a set of *values*. The values of the base type atom are *atoms* like the integers, the strings, and so on. The elements of the base type tree are finite trees. Here, a tree is a pair $\langle a \rangle\, v$ with a an atom and v a finite list of trees. Values of the product type $\sigma \times \tau$ are pairs (v, w) with v and w values of type σ and τ, respectively. Finally, values of the list type $[\tau]$ are finite lists of values of type τ. Note that our types are not meant to describe the structure of trees (as e.g., XML Schema types [28] do). They are used solely to define our data model and to structure $\mathcal{NTC}$ expressions.

According to the XQuery data model, an XQuery value is either an atomic data value; an ordered tree; a list of atoms; or a list of trees [4,14]. Arbitrary nested combinations of atoms, pairs, lists, and trees are not allowed. Conversely, the list-based complex object data model typically does not include trees. We therefore formally define an *XQuery type* (xq-type for short) to be either atom; tree; $[\mathsf{atom}]$; or $[\mathsf{tree}]$, while a *complex object type* (co-type for short) is a type in which tree does not occur.

Notational convention. In what follows, we will range over atoms by letters from the beginning of the alphabet. Also, we will denote the empty list by $[\,]$, non-empty lists by for example $[a, b, c]$, and the concatenation of two lists l_1 and l_2 by $l_1 + l_2$. Following [8], we write $v \uparrow l$ for $[v] + l$. We feel free to omit parentheses in types and write $\tau_1 \times \cdots \times \tau_n$ for $(\ldots ((\tau_1 \times \tau_2) \times \tau_3) \cdots \times \tau_n)$. Finally, we write $v : \tau$ to indicate that v is a value of type τ.

Queries. Queries on values are defined by extending the classical definition of Chandra and Harel [10] for relations. That is, a *query* is a function $q\colon \sigma \to \tau$ that maps values in σ to values in τ, for some types σ and τ. If $\sigma = \sigma' \times \cdots \times \sigma''$ where $\sigma', \ldots, \sigma'', \tau$ are xq-types, then q is an *xquery*. Similarly, if σ and τ are co-types, then q is a *complex object query*. Queries must be computable and generic (i.e., they must treat all but a finite set of atoms in uninterpreted way [2]). We will use the *domain Turing machine* of Hull and Su [20] as our model of computation. Domain Turing machines (DTMs for short) are augmented Turing machines that are specifically designed to express generic computations; in particular, they can work directly with an *infinite* alphabet on their tape. In contrast to normal Turing machines, there is hence no need to (rather clumsily) encode atoms as strings over finite alphabets. Nevertheless, DTMs can be simulated by ordinary Turing machines while respecting the complexity classes considered in this paper [20].

  A query $q\colon \sigma \to \tau$ is said to *run in polynomial (resp. primitive recursive [6]) time* if there exists a DTM M that, starting from the standard encoding of a value $v\colon \sigma$, produces the standard encoding of $q(v)$ in at most polynomially many (resp. primitive recursive many) steps in terms of the size of the input. Note that the query itself is fixed (i.e., we consider data complexity, not combined complexity). Here, the standard encoding $str(v)$ of a value v on a DTM tape is as follows. The type constructor symbols $(,), [,$ and $]$ are part of the tape alphabet, as are all of the atoms. Then a is encoded by itself; $\langle a \rangle \, v$ is encoded by the string $(str(a)\, str(v))$; (v, w) is encoded by $(str(v) \ldots str(w))$; and $[v, \ldots, w]$ is encoded by $[str(v) \ldots str(w)]$. We write $\mathbf{s}\,(v)$ for the length of $str(v)$.

3   Query Languages

In this section, we define the *Nested Tree Calculus* $\mathcal{NTC}$, a first-order calculus that extends both non-recursive for-let-where-return XQuery and a complex object calculus for nested lists. We will show in Section 5 that $\mathcal{NTC}$ is a *conservative* extension of these languages, even in the presence of structural recursion. As a consequence, in order to prove our expressiveness results claimed in the Introduction, it suffices to prove them for $\mathcal{NTC}$; they immediately transfer to the respective sublanguages.

3.1   Nested Tree Calculus

To avoid confusion, we note that $\mathcal{NTC}$ is a first-order language; structural recursion operators will be added in Section 3.2. The expressions of $\mathcal{NTC}$ are explicitly typed, and are formed according to the typing rules of Fig. 1. There

$$\frac{}{x^\tau:\tau} \qquad \frac{}{a:\text{atom}} \qquad \frac{e_1:\sigma \quad e_2:\sigma \quad e_3:\tau \quad e_4:\tau}{\text{if } e_1 = e_2 \text{ then } e_3 \text{ else } e_4:\tau} \qquad \frac{e:\sigma \quad e':\tau}{(e,e'):\sigma\times\tau}$$

$$\frac{e:\sigma\times\tau \quad e':\tau'}{\text{case } e \text{ of } \{(x^\sigma,y^\tau)\to e'\}:\tau'} \qquad \frac{}{[\,]:[\tau]} \quad \frac{e:\tau}{[e]:[\tau]} \quad \frac{e_1:[\tau] \quad e_2:[\tau]}{e_1 +\!\!+ e_2:[\tau]}$$

$$\frac{e:[\sigma] \quad e_1':\tau \quad e_2':\tau}{\text{case } e \text{ of } \{[\,]\to e_1';\ x^\sigma\!\uparrow\! y^{[\sigma]}\to e_2'\}:\tau} \qquad \frac{e:[\sigma] \quad e':[\tau]}{\text{for } x^\sigma \text{ in } e \text{ return } e':[\tau]}$$

$$\frac{e_1:\text{atom} \quad e_2:[\text{tree}]}{\langle e_1\rangle\, e_2:\text{tree}} \qquad \frac{e:\text{tree} \quad e':\sigma}{\text{case } e \text{ of } \{\langle x^{\text{atom}}\rangle\, y^{[\text{tree}]}\to e'\}:\sigma}$$

$$\frac{e:\tau}{\lambda x^\sigma.e:\sigma\to\tau} \qquad \frac{f:\sigma\to\tau \quad e:\sigma}{fe:\tau}$$

Fig. 1. Expressions of $\mathcal{NTC}$

are two sorts of expressions: *value expressions* and *function expressions*. Value expressions like $a:\text{atom}$ intuitively evaluate to values and are typed by a normal type, while function expressions like $\lambda x^\sigma e$ intuitively evaluate to queries and are typed by a function type $\sigma\to\tau$. Note that variables are also explicitly typed; we write x^τ to denote that x is a variable of type τ. To ease notation, we will often omit the explicit type annotations in superscript when they are clear from the context. We use an ML-like notation for value inspection. For example, $\text{case } e \text{ of } \{(x,y)\to e'\}$ should be understood to be the expression that first evaluates e to a pair (v,w) and then evaluates e' with x bound to v and y bound to w. This non-standard syntax for inspection of pairs, lists, and trees will allow us to easily define our polynomial time restriction in Section 4. The set $FV(e)$ of *free variables* of an expression e is defined as usual, with lambda abstraction and the case expressions acting as binders. For example, $FV(\lambda x.e) = FV(e) - \{x\}$ and $FV(\text{case } e \text{ of } \{[\,]\to e_1;\ x\!\uparrow\! y\to e_2\}) = FV(e)\cup FV(e_1)\cup(FV(e_2)-\{x,y\})$. We will refer to expressions without free variables such as $\lambda x.(x,x)$ as *closed expressions*.

Semantics. Intuitively, a value expression $e:\tau$ evaluates to a value in τ when given values for its free variables, while a function expression $f:\sigma\to\tau$ evaluates to a query mapping values in σ to values in τ. Formally, a value expression $e:\tau$ denotes a value $[\![e]\!]_\kappa$ under context κ, while a function expression $f:\sigma\to\tau$ denotes a query $[\![f]\!]_\kappa$ under context κ. Here, a *context* κ is a function from variables to values respecting types (i.e., $\kappa(x):\tau$ for all x^τ). We denote by $x:v,\kappa$ the context that equals κ on all variables except x, which it maps to v. The denotation of all expressions is inductively defined in Table 1. It is easy to see that the denotation of an expression depends only on its free variables: if κ and κ' agree on $FV(e)$ then $[\![e]\!]_\kappa = [\![e]\!]_{\kappa'}$. As such, the input context to an expression can always be finitely represented. Moreover, the denotation of closed expressions e without free variables is independent of the context. We simply write $[\![e]\!]$ in that case.

Syntactic sugar. We will abbreviate $\lambda x.\text{case } x \text{ of } \{(x_1,x_2)\to e\}$ by $\lambda(x_1,x_2).e$. Furthermore, we abbreviate $\text{case } e \text{ of } \{(x,y)\to x\}$ and $\text{case } e \text{ of } \{(x,y)\to y\}$ by $\pi_1(e)$ and $\pi_2(e)$, respectively. Similarly, we abbreviate $\text{case } e \text{ of } \{\langle x\rangle\, y\to x\}$

Table 1. Semantics of $\mathcal{NTC}$

$$
\begin{aligned}
[\![x]\!]_\kappa &= \kappa(x) \\
[\![a]\!]_\kappa &= a \\
[\![\text{if } e_1 = e_2 \text{ then } e_3 \text{ else } e_4]\!]_\kappa &= \begin{cases} [\![e_3]\!]_\kappa & \text{if } [\![e_1]\!]_\kappa = [\![e_2]\!]_\kappa \\ [\![e_4]\!]_\kappa & \text{otherwise} \end{cases} \\
[\![(e, e')]\!]_\kappa &= ([\![e]\!]_\kappa, [\![e']\!]_\kappa) \\
[\![\text{case } e \text{ of } \{(x, y) \to e'\}]\!]_\kappa &= [\![e']\!]_{x:\, v, y:\, w, \kappa} \quad \text{where } [\![e]\!]_\kappa = (v, w) \\
[\![\,[\,]\,]\!]_\kappa &= [\,] \\
[\![[e]]\!]_\kappa &= [[\![e]\!]_\kappa] \\
[\![e \,\text{+\!\!+}\, e']\!]_\kappa &= [\![e]\!]_\kappa \,\text{+\!\!+}\, [\![e']\!]_\kappa \\
[\![\text{case } e \text{ of } \{[\,] \to e_1';\; x \uparrow y \to e_2'\}]\!]_\kappa &= \begin{cases} [\![e_1']\!]_\kappa & \text{when } [\![e]\!]_\kappa = [\,] \\ [\![e_2']\!]_{x:\, v, y:\, w, \kappa} & \text{when } [\![e]\!]_\kappa = v \uparrow w \end{cases} \\
[\![\text{for } x \text{ in } e \text{ return } e']\!]_\kappa &= [\![e']\!]_{x:\, v, \kappa} \,\text{+\!\!+}\, \cdots \,\text{+\!\!+}\, [\![e']\!]_{x:\, w, \kappa} \\
&\qquad \text{where } [\![e]\!]_\kappa = [v, \ldots, w] \\
[\![\langle e \rangle \, e']\!]_\kappa &= \langle [\![e]\!]_\kappa \rangle \, [\![e']\!]_\kappa \\
[\![\text{case } e \text{ of } \{\langle x \rangle \, y \to e'\}]\!]_\kappa &= [\![e']\!]_{x:\, a, y:\, v, \kappa} \quad \text{where } [\![e]\!]_\kappa = \langle a \rangle \, v \\
[\![\lambda x^\sigma . e]\!]_\kappa &= f \quad \text{where } f \colon [\![\sigma]\!] \to [\![\tau]\!] \colon v \mapsto [\![e]\!]_{x:\, v, \kappa} \\
[\![f \, e]\!]_\kappa &= [\![f]\!]_\kappa([\![e]\!]_\kappa)
\end{aligned}
$$

by $name(e)$ and case e of $\{\langle x \rangle \, y \to y\}$ by $children(e)$. Also, we abbreviate the iteration for x in $children(e)$ return (if $name(x) = a$ then $[x]$ else $[\,]$) by e/a. Finally, we simulate general tuple construction by nested pairs. For example, we write (e_1, e_2, e_3) for $((e_1, e_2), e_3)$. General tuple inspection is defined similarly. For example, the expression case x of $\{(x_1, x_2, x_3) \to e\}$ is a shorthand for case x of $\{(y, x_3) \to \text{case } y \text{ of } \{(x_1, x_2) \to e\}\}$.

Example 1. Let *friends* be a variable of type $[\text{atom} \times \text{atom}]$ whose value is a set of friends, as a list of pairs of atoms. The following closed function expression generates a list of trees, each tree grouping the friends of a single person.

$\lambda friends.$ for x in *friends* return $[$
    $\langle \pi_1(x) \rangle$ for y in *friends* return if $\pi_1(x) = \pi_2(y)$ then $[\langle \pi_1(y) \rangle \,[\,]\,]$ else $[\,]$
$]$ □

3.2   Structural Recursion Operators

To $\mathcal{NTC}$ we add *structural recursion on lists* (*srl*) and *structural recursion on trees* (*srt*):

$$
\frac{e \colon \tau \quad f \colon \sigma \times \tau \to \tau}{srl(e, f) \colon [\sigma] \to \tau}
\qquad\qquad
\frac{f \colon \text{atom} \times [\tau] \to \tau}{srt(f) \colon \text{tree} \to \tau}
$$

Here, $[\![srl(e, f)]\!]_\kappa$ is the unique function that maps the empty list to $[\![e]\!]_\kappa$ and non-empty lists $u \uparrow v$ to $[\![f]\!]_\kappa(u, [\![srl(e, f)]\!]_\kappa(v))$. Similarly, $[\![srt(f)]\!]_\kappa$ is the unique function h defined by $h(\langle a \rangle [t_1, \ldots, t_n]) = [\![f]\!]_\kappa (a, [h(t_1), \ldots, h(t_n)])$. We denote by $\mathcal{NTC}(V)$ the language obtained by adding operators in $V \subseteq \{srl, srt\}$ to $\mathcal{NTC}$.

Definition 1. *Let $V \subseteq \{srl, srt\}$ and let σ, τ be types. A query $q \colon \sigma \to \tau$ is expressible in $\mathcal{NTC}(V)$ if there exists a closed function expression $f \colon \sigma \to \tau$ in $\mathcal{NTC}(V)$ such that $q = [\![f]\!]$.*

Example 2. We can compute the transitive closure of a graph in $\mathcal{NTC}(srl)$ as follows. Let a directed graph G be represented by a pair (V, E) with V a list containing the nodes in G (represented by atoms) and E a list containing the edges in G (represented by pairs of atoms). Transitive closure is then expressed in $\mathcal{NTC}(srl)$ by $\lambda(V, E). (V, srl(E, f)(V))$ with f the function expression

$\lambda(y, closure). closure \mathbin{+\!\!+}$
    for x in V return
      for z in V return
        if $(x, y) \in closure$ and $(y, z) \in closure$ then $[(x, z)]$ else $[\,]$

Here, $(x, y) \in closure$ checks whether the edge (x, y) occurs in $closure$. It is an abbreviation of $srl(false, g)(closure) = true$ with g the expression:

$\lambda(edge, res). \text{if } edge = (x, y) \text{ then } true \text{ else } res.$

Example 3. To express toc from the Introduction by means of srt we face a problem: in a computation of $srt(f)$ on a tree t the function expression f must compute the output based solely on the label of t and the recursive result on the children of t. To express toc, it is clear that f also needs to inspect the children of t themselves. This problem is solved by letting f return a pair of trees where the first component contains the actual table of contents (a list of trees) and the second component is t itself. Then toc is expressed in $\mathcal{NTC}(srt)$ by $\lambda t. \pi_1(srt(f)(t))$ where $f \colon \text{atom} \times [[\text{tree}] \times \text{tree}] \to ([\text{tree}] \times \text{tree})$ is $\lambda(lab, res). (e_1, e_2)$. Here, e_1 is:

for x in res return
    case x of $\{(stoc, s) \to$
      if $name(s) = \text{section}$ then $[\langle\text{section}\rangle (s/\text{title} \mathbin{+\!\!+} stoc)]$ else $[\,]\}$

and e_2 is $\langle lab \rangle$ for x in res return $[\pi_2(x)]$.   □

4   Expressive Power

4.1   Primitive Recursion

In this section we investigate the class of queries expressible in $\mathcal{NTC}(srl, srt)$. As a first result we have:

Theorem 1. *A query is expressible in $\mathcal{NTC}(srl, srt)$ if, and only if, it is computable in primitive recursive time.*

This result is slightly stronger than that of Immerman et al. [21]; Suciu and Wong [27]; and Libkin and Wong [24], who have shown that, in the presence of object invention, the class of functions $f\colon \mathbb{N} \times \cdots \times \mathbb{N} \to \mathbb{N}$ representable with structural recursion on (nested) sets and bags, coincides with the class of primitive recursive functions on natural numbers [6]. Indeed, if we fix a representation of natural numbers as values, then the theorem above implies that the class of functions $f\colon \mathbb{N} \times \cdots \times \mathbb{N} \to \mathbb{N}$ representable in $\mathcal{NTC}(srl, srt)$ coincides with the class of primitive recursive functions, as it is known that the primitive recursive functions are exactly those functions on the natural numbers that can be computed in primitive recursive time. Note, however, that their results do not necessarily imply that the class of expressible *queries* coincides with the class of primitive recursive time queries.

Theorem 1 shows that the combination of structural recursion on lists and trees taken together gives rise to a robust class of queries. Unfortunately, the expressiveness drops dramatically when we consider structural recursion on lists or trees separately. Indeed, let *lastlab*: tree → atom be the query that maps its input tree t to the label of the last node visited when traversing t in pre-order. This query is clearly computable in linear time. Nevertheless:

Theorem 2. *The query lastlab is inexpressible in both $\mathcal{NTC}(srl)$ and $\mathcal{NTC}(srt)$. Hence, structural recursion on lists or trees alone is not strong enough to express all linear time queries.*

Intuitively, this is because *srl* only provides "horizontal" recursion along lists, while *srt* only provides "vertical" recursion down trees. As such, $\mathcal{NTC}(srl)$ can only manipulate inputs up to bounded depth, while $\mathcal{NTC}(srt)$ can only manipulate inputs up to bounded width.

4.2   Taming Structural Recursion

From a complexity point of view, it follows from Theorem 1 that $\mathcal{NTC}(srl, srt)$ is too powerful a query language. In this section we investigate intrinsic restrictions on structural recursion that capture exactly the polynomial time queries. We start with a semantical restriction, from which we next derive a suitable syntactical restriction.

Let us refer to the function expressions g in $srl(e, g)$ or $srt(g)$ as *step expressions*. It is clear that, in order for the function expressed by a function expression f to be computable in polynomial time, f should never create intermediate results of more than polynomial size. This condition is trivially satisfied if f does not use structural recursion. To see how structural recursion can create results of exponential size or more, consider the function expression $explist := srl([a], \lambda(x, y). \, y +\!\!+ y)$. It is clear that, if v is a list of length k, then $[\![explist]\!](v)$ returns a list of length 2^k. As Caseiro [9] was the first to note, the problem here is that the step expression $\lambda(x, y). \, y +\!\!+ y$ *doubles* the size of the result at each recursive invocation. A similar problem arises with structural tree recursion. Indeed, consider $exptree := srt(\lambda(x, y). \, \langle x \rangle \, y +\!\!+ y)$. It is clear that, if v is a linear tree (i.e., a tree in which each node has at most one child) of depth k, then $[\![exptree]\!](v)$ returns a tree of size 2^k. Again, the problem is that the step expression $\lambda(x,y).\langle x \rangle\, y + y$ of $exptree$ doubles its result at each recursive invocation. This leads us to the following definitions.

Definition 2 (Tamed expressions). *A function expression* $f\colon \sigma \times \sigma' \to \tau$ *is non-multiplying (in its second argument) if there exists a polynomial P such that for all contexts κ; all $v\colon \sigma$; and all $w\colon \sigma'$, the size of $[\![f]\!]_\kappa(v,w)$ is bounded by*

$$
P\left(\mathbf{s}\,(v) + \sum_{x \in FV(f)} \mathbf{s}\,(\kappa(x))\right) + \mathbf{s}\,(w).
$$

An expression $e \in \mathcal{NTC}(srl, srt)$ is tamed *if every step expression occurring in it is non-multiplying.*

Clearly, *explist* and *exptree* are not tamed. The following proposition shows that being tamed is a strong enough restriction to ensure polynomial time computability.

Proposition 1. *Every tamed function expression in $\mathcal{NTC}(srl, srt)$ expresses a polynomial time query.*

Proof (Crux). The proof proceeds by induction on tamed expressions. We only illustrate the reasoning involved in showing that tamed *srl* and *srt* expressions can be computed in polynomial time, as these are the hard cases.

First, consider a closed function expression f of the form $srl(e, f')$ with e and f' also closed. Assume by induction that $[\![f']\!]$ is computable in polynomial time T'. Since $[\![f']\!]$ is non-multiplying, there exists a polynomial P such that $\mathbf{s}\,([\![f']\!](v,w)) \leq P(\mathbf{s}\,(v)) + \mathbf{s}\,(w)$ for all v and w of the correct type. We assume without loss of generality that T' and P are monotone increasing. To compute $[\![f]\!](v)$ for a given list $v = [w_1, \ldots, w_m]$ of size n we first compute $w = [\![e]\!]$. Since e is closed, this can be done in constant time. Next, we compute $[\![f']\!](w_1, [\![f']\!](w_2, \ldots [\![f']\!](w_m, w)\ldots))$. In order to do so, we need to evaluate $[\![f']\!]$ at most $m \leq n$ times. Every w_i has size at most n and the size of w is some constant c. Because $[\![f']\!]$ is non-multiplying, $[\![f']\!](w_m, w)$ then has size at most $P(n) + c$; $[\![f']\!](w_{m-1}, [\![f']\!](w_m, w))$ has size at most $P(n) + P(n) + c$; and so on. The maximum size of an input to f' is hence bounded by $n \times P(n) + c$. The total time needed to compute $[\![f]\!](v)$ is then bounded by $O(n \times T'(n \times P(n) + c))$, which is clearly a polynomial in n.

Next, consider a closed function expression f of the form $srt(f')$ with f' also closed. Assume that $[\![f']\!](v,w)$ can be computed in polynomial time T'. Since $[\![f']\!]$ is non-multiplying, there exists a polynomial P such that $\mathbf{s}\,([\![f']\!](v,w)) \leq P(\mathbf{s}\,(v)) + \mathbf{s}\,(w)$. Again, we assume without loss of generality that T' and P are monotone increasing. Using the fact that $[\![f']\!]$ is non-multiplying, it is straightforward to prove by induction on a tree t that $\mathbf{s}\,([\![f]\!](t)) \leq \mathbf{s}\,(t) \times (P(1) + 2)$. To compute $[\![f]\!](t)$ for a given input tree $t = \langle a \rangle\,[t_1, \ldots, t_m]$ of size n we must compute $[\![f']\!](a, [[\![f]\!](t_1), \ldots, [\![f]\!](t_m)])$. Hence, we first need to compute $[\![f]\!](t_i)$

for every i. This involves calling $[\![f']\!]$ again multiple times. Note, however, that the total number of times that $[\![f']\!]$ gets called is bounded by n. Furthermore, at each such call, the size of the input to $[\![f']\!]$ is bounded by $n \times (P(1)+2)$. The total time needed to compute $[\![f]\!](t)$ is hence bounded by $O(n \times T'(n \times (P(1)+2)))$, which is clearly a polynomial in n. $\qquad\square$

The converse is also true: every polynomial time query can be expressed by a tamed function expression, as we will show below. Note that "non-multiplying" and "tamed" are *semantical* notions. Using a standard reduction from the satisfiability problem of the relational algebra, it is straightforward to show that checking whether an expression satisfies one of these semantical properties is undecidable. We can, however, restrict the syntax of expressions in $\mathcal{NTC}(srl, srt)$ in such a way that all expressions are tamed, as we shown next.

To motivate our syntactical restriction, consider again the problematic step expression $\lambda(x, y). y \mathbin{+\!\!+} y$ from *explist*. Since this step expression is multiplying (and *explist* is hence not tamed), we want our syntactical restriction to exclude it. The first solution that comes to mind is to require that y occurs at most once in the body e of a step expression $\lambda(x, y).e$. This solution is defective in multiple ways. On the one hand it is too restrictive. Indeed, harmless, non-multiplying step expressions like $\lambda(x, y).$ if $e_1 = e_2$ then $x \uparrow y$ else y with y occurring in e_1 or e_2 are excluded. Clearly, there is a difference between testing a variable and actually using it to construct the output. On the other hand, the solution is not restrictive enough. Indeed, the step expression, $\lambda(x, y).$ for x in $[a, b]$ return y would be accepted, although it is equivalent to the problematic $\lambda(x, y). y \mathbin{+\!\!+} y$ above. For these reasons, a more fine-grained restriction is in order.

Definition 3 (Testing and outputting). *An expression e tests a variable x if every free occurrence of x as a subexpression in e is in e_1 or e_2 of a conditional test* if $e_1 = e_2$ then e_3 else e_4. *An expression e outputs x if x is free in e and e does not test x.*

Example 4. The expression if $x = y$ then (y, z) else (z, z) tests x and outputs y and z. $\qquad\square$

Next, we define linearity. Here, linearity should be understood in the sense of Caseiro [9] and Hofmann [18]: if e is linear in a variable x, then e uses x to compute its output at most once.

Definition 4 (Linearity). *A value expression in $\mathcal{NTC}(srl, srt)$ is linear in a variable x if either*

- *it is an expression of the form y, a, or $[\,]$;*
- *it is a conditional test* if $e_1 = e_2$ then e_3 else e_4 *with e_3 and e_4 linear in x;*
- *it is $[e]$ or $\langle e' \rangle e$ with e linear in x;*
- *it is (e, e') or $e \mathbin{+\!\!+} e'$ with e and e' linear in x and at most one of e and e' outputting x;*
- *it is a case expression of the form* case e' of $\{(y, z) \rightarrow e_2'\}$, case e' of $\{[\,] \rightarrow e_1'; y \uparrow z \rightarrow e_2'\}$, *or* case e' of $\{\langle y \rangle z \rightarrow e_2'\}$ *with (1) e', e_1', and e_2' linear in x; and (2) if e' outputs x, then e_2' tests x and e_2' is linear in y and z;*

- it is for y in e_1 return e_2 with e_1 and e_2 testing x;
- it is for y in e_1 return y with e_1 linear in x; or
- it is for y in e_1 return children(y) with e_1 linear in x.

We clarify this definition with some examples.

Example 5. The expression $y + y$ is not linear in y. The expression from Example 4 is linear in x and y, but not in z. The expression for y in x return (if $y = z$ then $[y]$ else $[]$) is linear in z, but not in x. The expression case x of $\{(y, z) \rightarrow (z, y)\}$ is linear in x. The expression e_1 from Example 3 is not linear in the variable *res* because the for-loop does not have the required form. Finally, the expression e from Example 2 is linear in x. □

Definition 5 (Safety). *An expression in $\mathcal{NTC}(srl, srt)$ is safe if every step expression occurring in it is of the form $\lambda(x, y).\, e$ with e linear in y.*

From Example 5 above, it follows that the function expression computing the transitive closure of a graph given in Example 2 is safe, whereas the function expression computing the table of contents of a book given in Example 3 is not.

Lemma 1. *If $e \in \mathcal{NTC}(srl, srt)$ is a value expression linear in x then there exists a polynomial $P\colon \mathbb{N} \rightarrow \mathbb{N}$ such that for all environments κ:*

$$\mathbf{s}\left(\llbracket e \rrbracket_\kappa\right) \leq P\left(\sum_{y \in FV(e) - \{x\}} \mathbf{s}\left(\kappa(y)\right)\right) + \mathbf{s}\left(\kappa(x)\right).$$

It immediately follows that safe expressions are tamed; they are hence computable in polynomial time by Proposition 1. Note, however, that some function expressions, like the one expressing *toc* from the Introduction in Example 3 denote polynomial time queries, but are not safe. This hence raises the question how powerful safe expressions are. Fortunately,

Proposition 2. *Every polynomial time query is expressible by a safe, closed function expression in $\mathcal{NTC}(srl, srt)$.*

In particular, *toc* from Example 3 can hence be expressed in a safe way. From Lemma 1 and Propositions 1 and 2 it immediately follows that safe expressions provide an effective syntax for the polynomial time queries.

Theorem 3. *A query is expressible in safe $\mathcal{NTC}(srl, srt)$ if, and only if, it is computable in polynomial time.*

5   Natural Sublanguages

Note that the results of Section 4 do not necessarily imply anything about the expressiveness of structural recursion in XQuery or about the expressiveness of structural recursion on list-based complex objects. Indeed, the expressions of $\mathcal{NTC}(srl, srt)$ can create and manipulate arbitrary values (including e.g., lists of lists and list of pairs) during their computation, while XQuery only manipulate XQuery values (i.e., values in some xq-type). Conversely, the expressions of $\mathcal{NTC}(srl, srt)$ can create and manipulate trees, while trees are not present in complex object data models. Nevertheless, the results for $\mathcal{NTC}(srl, srt)$ transfer cleanly to both structural recursion in XQuery and structural recursion on list-based complex objects, as we show in this section.

Let us define *structural recursive XQuery* to be the natural sublanguage of $\mathcal{NTC}(srl, srt)$ in which we restrict expressions to only manipulate XQuery values. Since we still want to be able to define and call multiple-argument functions however, we do allow to create and manipulate tuples of XQuery values, but only in function abstraction and application.

Definition 6 (Structural recursive XQuery). *If $V \subseteq \{srl, srt\}$ then $\mathcal{XQ}(V)$ is the set of expressions $e \in \mathcal{NTC}(V)$ in which every subexpression e' of e has type either $e' : \tau$ or $e' : \sigma \times \cdots \times \sigma' \to \tau$ with $\sigma, \ldots, \sigma', \tau$ xq-types, except when e' is a variable $x^{\sigma \times \cdots \times \sigma'}$ in a function abstraction $\lambda x.\, \mathsf{case}\ x\ \mathsf{of}\ \{(y, \ldots, y') \to e''\}$ or e' is a product $(e_1, \ldots, e_n)$ in a function application $f\, e'$.*

The function expression from Example 1 is not in $\mathcal{XQ}(srl, srt)$ as the subexpression *friends* has type $[\text{atom} \times \text{atom}]$, which is not an xq-type. The expression $\lambda x^{\text{tree} \times \text{tree}}.\, \mathsf{case}\ x\ \mathsf{of}\ \{(y, z) \to \langle name\ y \rangle\ children\ z\}$ which we would normally abbreviate by $\lambda(y^{\text{tree}}, z^{\text{tree}}).\, \langle name(y) \rangle\ children(z)$ does belong to $\mathcal{XQ}(srl, srt)$, however. Unfortunately, the function expression $\lambda(lab, res).\, (e_1, e_2)$ from Example 3 that is used to simulate *toc* from the Introduction is not in $\mathcal{XQ}(srl, srt)$. Indeed, the subexpression (e_1, e_2) creates a pair without directly giving it as argument to a function. Nevertheless, *toc* is expressible in $\mathcal{XQ}(srt)$, as Proposition 3 below shows.

The structural recursive complex object calculus is the natural sublanguage of $\mathcal{NTC}(srl, srt)$ in which we restrict expressions to only manipulate complex objects. Such expressions hence cannot create or manipulate trees. In particular, they cannot recur on trees.

Definition 7 (Complex object calculus). *If $V \subseteq \{srl\}$, then $\mathcal{COC}(V)$ is the subset of expressions e in $\mathcal{NTC}(V)$ in which every subexpression e' of e has type either $e' : \tau$ or $e' : \sigma \to \tau$ with σ and τ complex object types.*

The Nested Tree Calculus is a conservative extension of both XQuery and the complex object calculus, as the following proposition shows.

Proposition 3. *Let $V \subseteq \{srl, srt\}$.*

1. *An xquery is expressible in $\mathcal{NTC}(V)$ if, and only if, it is expressible in $\mathcal{XQ}(V)$.*
2. *An xquery is expressible by a safe expression in $\mathcal{NTC}(V)$ if, and only if, it is expressible by a safe expression in $\mathcal{XQ}(V)$.*
3. *A complex object query is expressible in $\mathcal{NTC}(srl, srt)$ if, and only if, it is expressible in $\mathcal{COC}(srl)$.*

4. A complex object query is expressible by a safe expression in $\mathcal{NTC}(srl, srt)$ if, and only if, it is expressible by a safe expression in $\mathcal{COC}(srl)$.

It follows that our results about the expressiveness of (safe) structural recursion in $\mathcal{NTC}$ as stated in Theorems 1,2, and 3 transfer to $\mathcal{XQ}$ and $\mathcal{COC}$.

In particular, a complex object query is hence expressible in $\mathcal{COC}(srl)$ if, and only if, it is primitive recursive. We note that this result may seem in contrast to that of Grumbach and Milo [17], who consider a language that includes structural recursion on pomsets (a datatype that generalizes sets, bags, and lists), which is claimed to capture the elementary queries on pomsets. It seems counter-intuitive that a language that generalizes $\mathcal{COC}(srl)$ has lower complexity. There is an error in their upper-bound proof, however; also non-elementary queries can be expressed [16].

We also note that the polynomial time queries on list-based complex objects have already been captured by means of the *list-trav* iteration construct of Colby et al. [13]. This iteration construct is rather awkward, however, and we think that safe structural recursion provides an elegant alternative.

Another such alternative in the restricted case of list of atomic values was given by Bonner and Mecca, in their work on *Sequence Datalog* [5]. Sequence Datalog is a query language that extends Datalog with functions on lists of atomic values. Using suitable syntactic restrictions, they give a query language sound and complete for the *flat* relational queries. In these relations, tuple components may either contain atomic values or lists of atomic values.

References

1. S. Abiteboul and C. Beeri. The power of languages for the manipulation of complex values. *VLDB Journal*, 4(4):727–794, 1995.
2. S. Abiteboul, R. Hull, and V. Vianu. *Foundations Of Databases*. Addison-Wesley, 1995.
3. S. Bellantoni and S. Cook. A new recursion-theoretic characterization of the poly-time functions (extended abstract). In *STOC 1992*, pages 283–293. ACM Press, 1992.
4. S. Boag, D. Chamberlin, M. F. Fernández, D. Florescu, J. Robie, and J. Siméon. *XQuery 1.0: An XML Query Language*. W3C Candidate Recommendation, November 2005.
5. A. J. Bonner and G. Mecca. Sequences, datalog, and transducers. *J. Comput. Syst. Sci.*, 57(3):234–259, 1998.
6. G. Boolos and R. Jeffrey. *Computability and Logic*. Cambridge University Press, third edition, 1989.
7. P. Buneman, M. Fernandez, and D. Suciu. UnQL: a query language and algebra for semistructured data based on structural recursion. *VLDB Journal*, 9(1):76–110, 2000.
8. P. Buneman, S. A. Naqvi, V. Tannen, and L. Wong. Principles of programming with complex objects and collection types. *Theoretical Comput. Sci.*, 149(1):3–48, 1995.
9. V. Caseiro. *Equations for Defining Poly-time Functions*. PhD thesis, University of Oslo, 1997.

10. A. K. Chandra and D. Harel. Computable queries for relational data bases. *J. Comput. Syst. Sci.*, 21(2):156–178, 1980.

11. A. Cobham. The intrinsic computational difficulty of functions. In *Logic, Methodology, and Philosophy of Science II*, pages 24–30. Springer Verlag, 1965.

12. L. S. Colby and L. Libkin. Tractable iteration mechanisms for bag languages. In *ICDT 1997*, volume 1186 of *LNCS*, pages 461–475. Springer, 1997.

13. L. S. Colby, E. L. Robertson, L. V. Saxton, and D. V. Gucht. A query language for list-based complex objects. In *PODS 1994*, pages 179–189. ACM Press, 1994.

14. D. Draper, P. Fankhauser, M. F. Fernández, A. Malhotra, K. Rose, M. Rys, J. Siméon, and P. Wadler. *XQuery 1.0 and XPath 2.0 Formal Semantics*. W3C Candidate Recommendation, June 2006.

15. M. F. Fernández, J. Siméon, and P. Wadler. A semi-monad for semi-structured data. In *ICDT 2001*, volume 1973 of *LNCS*, pages 263–300. Springer, 2001.

16. S. Grumbach and T. Milo. Personal communication.

17. S. Grumbach and T. Milo. An algebra for pomsets. *Inf. Comput.*, 150(2):268–306, 1999.

18. M. Hofmann. A mixed modal/linear lambda calculus with applications to Bellantoni-Cook safe recursion. In *CSL 1997*, volume 1414 of *LNCS*, pages 275–294. Springer, 1997.

19. M. Hofmann. Semantics of linear/modal lambda calculus. *Journal of Functional Programming*, 9(3):247–277, 1999.

20. R. Hull and J. Su. Algebraic and calculus query languages for recursively typed complex objects. *J. Comput. Syst. Sci.*, 47(1):121–156, 1993.

21. N. Immerman, S. Patnaik, and D. W. Stemple. The expressiveness of a family of finite set languages. *Theor. Comput. Sci.*, 155(1):111–140, 1996.

22. C. Koch. On the complexity of nonrecursive XQuery and functional query languages on complex values. In *PODS 2005*, pages 84–97. ACM, 2005.

23. D. Leivant. Stratified functional programs and computational complexity. In *POPL 1993*, pages 325–333. ACM Press, 1993.

24. L. Libkin and L. Wong. Query languages for bags and aggregate functions. *J. Comput. Syst. Sci.*, 55(2):241–272, 1997.

25. V. Y. Sazonov. Hereditarily-finite sets, data bases and polynomial-time computability. *Theor. Comput. Sci.*, 119(1):187–214, 1993.

26. D. Suciu. Bounded fixpoints for complex objects. *Theor. Comput. Sci.*, 176(1-2): 283–328, 1997.

27. D. Suciu and L. Wong. On two forms of structural recursion. In *ICDT 1995*, volume 893 of *LNCS*, pages 111–124. Springer, 1995.

28. H. S. Thompson, D. Beech, M. Maloney, and N. Mendelsohn. *XML Schema Part 1: Structures*. W3C Recommendation, May 2001.

29. J. Van den Bussche, D. Van Gucht, and S. Vansummeren. Well-definedness and semantic type-checking in the nested relational calculus and xquery. In *ICDT 2005*, volume 3363 of *LNCS*, pages 99–113. Springer, 2005.

Combining Temporal Logics for Querying XML Documents

Marcelo Arenas[1], Pablo Barceló[2], and Leonid Libkin[3]

[1] Pontificia Universidad Católica de Chile
[2] Universidad de Chile
[3] University of Edinburgh

Abstract. Close relationships between XML navigation and temporal logics have been discovered recently, in particular between logics LTL and CTL* and XPath navigation, and between the μ-calculus and navigation based on regular expressions. This opened up the possibility of bringing model-checking techniques into the field of XML, as documents are naturally represented as labeled transition systems. Most known results of this kind, however, are limited to Boolean or unary queries, which are not always sufficient for complex querying tasks.

Here we present a technique for combining temporal logics to capture n-ary XML queries expressible in two yardstick languages: FO and MSO. We show that by adding simple terms to the language, and combining a temporal logic for words together with a temporal logic for unary tree queries, one obtains logics that select arbitrary tuples of elements, and can thus be used as building blocks in complex query languages. We present general results on the expressiveness of such temporal logics, study their model-checking properties, and relate them to some common XML querying tasks.

1 Introduction

It has been observed many times that the basic settings of the fields of database querying and model checking are very similar: in both cases one needs to evaluate a logical formula on a finite relational structure. Both fields have invested heavily in developing logical formalisms and efficient algorithms for query evaluation and model checking, but despite this, there are very few direct connections between them, although there is certainly interest in bringing them closer together (see, e.g., an invited talk at the last ICDT [36]).

Our goal is to explore one possible connection between database querying and temporal-logic model-checking: we concentrate on the recently discovered connections between XML querying/navigation, and temporal and modal logics [1,3,6,25,15,27]. Since XML documents are modeled as labeled unranked trees with a sibling ordering [19,28], they can naturally be viewed as labeled transition systems. Furthermore, many common XML tasks involve navigation via paths in a document, reminiscent of temporal properties of paths in transition systems.

In terms of expressiveness, the yardstick logics for XML querying are FO (first-order) and MSO (monadic second-order). But from the point of view of

T. Schwentick and D. Suciu (Eds.): ICDT 2007, LNCS 4353, pp. 359–373, 2007.
© Springer-Verlag Berlin Heidelberg 2007

efficiency of query evaluation, they are not the best, as they cannot guarantee fast (linear-time) query-evaluation – which is often the goal for query evaluation on trees [20] – without a very high (nonelementary) price in terms of the size of the query [14]. However, many temporal logics overcome this problem [20,25,3], which makes them suitable for XML querying.

The connection between XML navigation and temporal logics was best demonstrated in the work of Marx [25] and his followers [7,1,2,15]. In particular, [25] gave an expressive completeness result for XPath: adding a temporal *until* operator (found in logics such as LTL, CTL) to the core of XPath gives it precisely the power of FO, one of the yardstick database query languages. FO sentences over both binary and unranked trees are also known [18,3] to have the power of a commonly used temporal logic CTL*, and MSO has the power of the modal μ-calculus over both binary [30] and unranked trees [3].

The main limitation of these results is that they only apply to Boolean (i.e., yes/no) queries, or unary queries, that select a set of nodes from a document (and the result of [25] also extends to queries with two free variables). While for problems such as validation, or for some information extraction tasks [16] this is sufficient, there are many cases where more expressiveness is needed than Boolean or unary queries provide. For example, the core of XQuery consists of expressions that essentially select arbitrary tuples of nodes, based on properties of paths leading to them, and then output them rearranged as a different tree. But while it is known that the usual MSO/automata connection extends to the case of n-ary queries [31], logical formalisms for n-ary queries and their model-checking properties have not been adequately explored.

In this paper, we show how standard temporal logics can define n-ary queries over XML documents, thus opening a possibility of using efficient model-checking algorithms [9] in XML querying. We begin with an easy observation that languages capturing binary FO (or MSO) queries can be extended with a simple binary term to capture arbitrary n-ary queries. While some languages for binary FO and MSO are known [25,15], there is an abundance of nice formalisms for unary and Boolean queries, and those logics tend to have very good model-checking properties. Thus, as our main contribution, we present a technique for *combining* temporal logics to obtain languages for n-ary XML queries. To characterize n-ary $\mathcal{L}$ queries, where $\mathcal{L}$ could be FO or MSO (and the result applies to several other logics lying between FO and MSO), one needs:

Ingredients: – a temporal logic $\mathcal{L}_0$ that captures Boolean $\mathcal{L}$ over words (e.g., LTL for FO, or μ-calculus for MSO);

– a temporal logic $\mathcal{L}_1$ that captures *unary* $\mathcal{L}$ queries over XML trees (quite a few are known [25,32,24,3]: for example, CTL* with the past for FO, or the full μ-calculus for MSO);

– some binary operations on trees, such as the largest common ancestor for two nodes.

Combination mechanism: This comes in the form of XPath's *node tests*: for each formula ψ of $\mathcal{L}_1$, we have a node test $[\psi]$ that becomes an atomic proposition of $\mathcal{L}_0$ and simply checks if ψ is true in a given node.

Let us add a few early comments on binary operations (exact sets of those will be defined later in Section 3). Consider the standard *document order* for XML documents: $s \leq_d s'$ if either s' is a descendant of s, or s occurs ahead of s' as one looks at the string representation of a document:

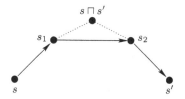

Fig. 1. Document ordering and binary terms

Then a path from s to s' witnessing $s \leq_d s'$ naturally defines two points, s_1 and s_2, where it changes direction. Note that s_1 is the successor of $s \sqcap s'$ in the direction of s, and s_2 is the successor of $s \sqcap s'$ in the direction of s', where $s \sqcap s'$ is the meet (largest common ancestor) of s and s'. This naturally suggests two terms: one of them is the meet $\sqcap$ of two nodes, and the other is the successor of one node in the direction of its descendant. This is the set of terms we use here.

In this paper we look at combined logics that capture n-ary FO and MSO queries. We give their precise definition, prove expressive completeness for n-ary queries, study their model-checking properties, and relate them to XPath queries and XML tree patterns.

2   Notation

Unranked trees as transition systems. A *tree domain* D is a finite prefix-closed subset of $\mathbb{N}^*$ (strings of natural numbers) such that $s \cdot i \in D$ and $j < i$ imply $s \cdot j \in D$. That is, if a node s has n children, they are $s \cdot 0, \ldots, s \cdot (n-1)$. Nodes of trees are labeled by letters from a finite alphabet Σ. A Σ-*tree* is viewed as a transition system

$$T = (D, \prec_{ch}, \prec_{sb}, (P_a)_{a \in \Sigma}),$$

where D is a tree domain, $\prec_{ch}$ is the child relation ($s \prec_{ch} s \cdot i$ for all $s, s \cdot i \in D$), $\prec_{sb}$ is the next-sibling relation ($s \cdot i \prec_{sb} s \cdot (i+1)$ for all $s \cdot (i+1) \in D$), and P_a's are labeling predicates ($s \in P_a$ iff s is labeled a). We shall write $\prec_{ch}^*$ and $\prec_{sb}^*$ for the transitive-reflexive closures of $\prec_{ch}$ and $\prec_{sb}$. The root of T is the empty string denoted by ε.

We also use the *document ordering* $s \leq_d s'$ which holds iff s appears before s' if the document is written as a string; i.e., either $s \prec_{ch}^* s'$, or there exist distinct s_0, s_1, s_2 such that $s_0 \prec_{ch} s_1 \prec_{ch}^* s$, $s_0 \prec_{ch} s_2 \prec_{ch}^* s'$, and $s_1 \prec_{sb}^* s_2$ (see Fig. 1).

We shall also view Σ-words as transition systems; the domain of a word w of length n is $\{0, \ldots, n-1\}$, with the successor relation $i \prec i+1$ on it, together with the labeling relations P_a's. We assume, as is common when one deals with temporal logics over words, that each position i can be labeled by more than one symbol from Σ.

FO and MSO over trees. First-order logic (FO) is the closure of atomic formulae under Boolean connectives and first-order quantification $\forall x, \exists x$. MSO in addition allows quantification over sets $\forall X, \exists X$ and new atomic formulae $X(x)$ (or $x \in X$). When we deal with FO which cannot define the transitive closure of a relation, we use $x \prec_{\mathrm{ch}}^* y$ and $x \prec_{\mathrm{sb}}^* y$, as well as $P_a(x)$, as atomic formulae for trees, and the ordering $<$ as well as $P_a(x)$'s for words. For MSO, one can use either $\prec_{\mathrm{ch}}^*$ and $\prec_{\mathrm{sb}}^*$, or $\prec_{\mathrm{ch}}$ and $\prec_{\mathrm{sb}}$, since transitive closure is MSO-definable. We shall only deal with MSO formulae with free first-order variables.

If $\varphi(x_1, \ldots, x_n)$ is an FO or MSO formula with n free variables, it defines an n-ary query on a tree T which produces the set $\{\bar{a} \in D^n \mid T \models \varphi(\bar{a})\}$. We let FO_n (resp., MSO_n) stand for the class of n-ary queries definable in FO (resp., MSO). Queries definable by sentences are *Boolean* queries (they produce yes/no answers) and queries definable in FO_1 and MSO_1 are *unary* queries.

Temporal logics. We shall use standard temporal logics such as LTL, CTL*, and the μ-calculus L_μ, cf. [9]. LTL is interpreted over Σ-words and its syntax is:

$$\varphi, \varphi' := a, \ a \in \Sigma \mid \varphi \vee \varphi' \mid \neg\varphi \mid \mathbf{X}\varphi \mid \varphi \mathbf{U}\varphi'.$$

(As usual, $\mathbf{X}$ stands for 'next' and $\mathbf{U}$ for 'until'.) If we have a word w with n positions $0, \ldots, n-1$ labeled by symbols from Σ, the semantics of $(w, i) \models \varphi$ (that is, φ is satisfied in the ith position) is defined by:

- $(w, i) \models a$ iff i labeled with a;
- $(w, i) \models \varphi \vee \varphi'$ iff $(w, i) \models \varphi$ or $(w, i) \models \varphi'$; $(w, i) \models \neg\varphi$ iff $(w, i) \not\models \varphi$;
- $(w, i) \models \mathbf{X}\varphi$ iff $(w, i+1) \models \varphi$;
- $(w, i) \models \varphi \mathbf{U}\varphi'$ iff there exists $k \geq i$ such that $(w, k) \models \varphi'$ and $(w, j) \models \varphi$ for every $i \leq j < k$.

Each LTL formula φ defines a Boolean query over words, that is, the set of words w such that $(w, 0) \models \varphi$. A theorem by Kamp says that this set of queries is precisely the set of Boolean FO queries over words, i.e. $\mathrm{LTL} = \mathrm{FO}_0$.

For other logics, we need their versions that can refer to the past. $\mathrm{CTL}^*_{\mathrm{past}}$, a version of CTL* with the past operators [21], is given below specifically for unranked trees. The grammars for *state* formulae α (satisfied by a node and thus defining unary queries) and *path* formulae β (satisfied by a path) are:

$$\alpha, \alpha' := a \ (a \in \Sigma) \mid \neg\alpha \mid \alpha \vee \alpha' \mid \mathbf{E}\beta$$
$$\beta, \beta' := \alpha \mid \neg\beta \mid \beta \vee \beta' \mid \mathbf{X}_{\mathrm{ch}}\beta \mid \mathbf{X}_{\mathrm{ch}}^-\beta \mid \mathbf{X}_{\mathrm{sb}}\beta \mid \mathbf{X}_{\mathrm{sb}}^-\beta \mid \beta \mathbf{U}\beta' \mid \beta \mathbf{S}\beta'$$

Here $\mathbf{X}^-$ is the 'previous' and $\mathbf{S}$ is the 'since' operator. A path π is a sequence $s_1 s_2 \ldots$ of nodes such that for every j, either $s_j \prec_{\mathrm{ch}} s_{j+1}$ or $s_j \prec_{\mathrm{sb}} s_{j+1}$. As usual with logics with the past, we require the paths to be maximal: that is, $s_1 = \varepsilon$, and all paths end in a leaf that is also the youngest child of its parent. We define the semantics of path formulae $(T, \pi, \ell) \models \beta$ with respect to a position ℓ in a path (where ℓ is an integer). The truth of state formulae is defined with respect to a node of a tree. The rules are as follows (omitting Boolean connectives):

- $(T, s) \models a$ for $a \in \Sigma$ iff s is labeled a.
- $(T, s) \models \mathbf{E}\beta$ iff there exists a path $\pi = s_1 s_2 \ldots$ and $\ell \geq 1$ such that $s = s_\ell$ and $(T, \pi, \ell) \models \beta$;
- $(T, \pi, \ell) \models \alpha$ iff $(T, s_\ell) \models \alpha$;
- $(T, \pi, \ell) \models \mathbf{X}_{\mathrm{ch}}\beta$ (or $\mathbf{X}_{\mathrm{ch}}^-\beta$) iff $(T, \pi, \ell + 1) \models \beta$ and $s_\ell \prec_{\mathrm{ch}} s_{\ell+1}$ (or if $(T, \pi, \ell - 1) \models \beta$ and $s_{\ell-1} \prec_{\mathrm{ch}} s_\ell$); the rules for $\mathbf{X}_{\mathrm{sb}}$ are analogous.
- $(T, \pi, \ell) \models \beta\mathbf{U}\beta'$ iff there exists $k \geq \ell$ such that $(T, \pi, k) \models \beta'$ and $(T, \pi, j) \models \beta$ whenever $\ell \leq j < k$.
- $(T, \pi, \ell) \models \beta\mathbf{S}\beta'$ iff there exists $k \leq \ell$ such that $(T, \pi, k) \models \beta'$ and $(T, \pi, j) \models \beta$ whenever $k < j \leq \ell$.

The version of the μ-calculus we consider here is the full μ-calculus L_μ^{full} [35] that also allows one to refer to the past. Its formulae are defined as

$$\varphi := \top \mid \bot \mid a \mid X \mid \neg\varphi \mid \varphi \vee \varphi \mid \Diamond(\prec)\varphi \mid \mu X.\varphi(X),$$

where $a \in \Sigma$, $\prec$ refers to either $\prec_{\mathrm{ch}}$ or $\prec_{\mathrm{sb}}$, or their inverses: parent ($\prec_{\mathrm{ch}}^-$), and previous sibling ($\prec_{\mathrm{sb}}^-$); X ranges over a collection $\mathcal{V}$ of variables, and in $\mu X.\varphi(X)$, the variable X occurs positively in $\varphi(X)$. The semantics, with respect to a valuation v that associates a set of nodes with each variable, is standard: $\top$ is *true*, $\bot$ is *false*, $\Diamond(\prec)\varphi$ is true in s if φ is true in some s' such that $s \prec s'$, X is true in s iff $s \in v(X)$, and $\mu X.\varphi(X)$ defines the least fixed point of the operator $S \mapsto \{s \mid (T, v[S/X], s) \models \varphi\}$, where $v[S/X]$ refers to a valuation that extends v by assigning S to X. Queries (unary or Boolean) are defined by formulae without free variables.

L_μ over words is defined by using one modality for the successor relation. Over words, L_μ formulae evaluated in the initial position have the power of MSO sentences: $L_\mu = \mathrm{MSO}_0$. For unary queries over unranked trees, we have:

Fact 1. ([3,25,32]) *Over unranked trees,* $\mathrm{CTL}^\star_{\mathrm{past}} = \mathrm{FO}_1$ *and* $L_\mu^{\mathrm{full}} = \mathrm{MSO}_1$.

3 Capturing n-Ary Queries

From binary to n-ary queries. As mentioned in the introduction, there is a simple technique for extending a logic capturing FO_2 or MSO_2 to a logic capturing FO_n or MSO_n. It is already implicit in [33], and we briefly outline it.

Let $\mathcal{Q}_2$ be a collection of binary queries given by formulae $\alpha(x, y)$ with two free variables. We then define $\mathcal{Q}_n$ to be the collection of n-ary queries $\psi(x_1, \ldots, x_n)$ which are Boolean combinations of $\alpha(t, t')$, with $\alpha \in \mathcal{Q}_2$ and t, t' being terms given by the grammar $t, t' := x_i, i \in [1, n] \mid t \sqcap t'$. The meaning of $t \sqcap t'$ is the largest common ancestor of t and t'.

Each $\psi(x_1, \ldots, x_n)$ in $\mathcal{Q}_n$ naturally defines a query that returns a set of n-tuples of nodes in a tree. Using the composition technique, and in particular the composition lemma from [33], one can easily show

Proposition 1. *If* $\mathcal{Q}_2$ *captures* FO_2 *(or* MSO_2*), then* $\mathcal{Q}_n$ *captures* FO_n *(or* MSO_n*, respectively) over unranked trees.*

For example, if $\mathcal{Q}_2$ is the set of binary conditional XPath queries [25], then $\mathcal{Q}_n$ captures FO_n over unranked trees.

However, characterizations of binary FO or MSO over XML trees are not nearly as common as characterizations of Boolean and unary queries (with the notable exceptions of conditional XPath in [25], which captures FO_2, and caterpillars expressions extended with unary MSO tests in [5], which capture MSO_2). Moreover, for Boolean and unary queries much has been invested into efficient query-evaluation and model-checking [9,24,20]. Thus, our goal is to find a way to get a language for n-ary queries out of languages for Boolean and unary queries.

From Boolean and unary queries to n-ary queries. We now show how to characterize n-ary FO and MSO queries by combining temporal logics. In what follows, we assume that:

- $\mathcal{L}_0$ is a temporal logic that, for an arbitrary finite alphabet, captures either Boolean FO or Boolean MSO queries over words over that alphabet;
- $\mathcal{L}_1$ is a logic that, for an arbitrary finite alphabet Σ, captures either unary FO or unary MSO queries over Σ-labeled unranked trees.

We then define a combined logic $\mathcal{I}^n(\mathcal{L}_0, \mathcal{L}_1)$ that will capture FO_n or MSO_n. For now, we use a fixed set of binary relations ($\prec_{\mathrm{ch}}^*$) and ($\prec_{\mathrm{sb}}^*$) and a fixed grammar generating terms, but we shall present alternatives at the end of the section.

Variables. Fix n variables $x_1, \ldots, x_n$. Given a tree T, a valuation v in T is a mapping that assigns to each x_i an element s_i of the domain of T.

Terms. These are given by the grammar:

$$(\mathbb{T}) \qquad t, t' := x_i, \; i \in [1, n] \mid \texttt{root} \mid t \sqcap t' \mid \mathrm{succ}(t, t')$$

Each valuation v on the variables extends to a valuation on terms: $v(\texttt{root}) = \varepsilon$, $v(t \sqcap t')$ is the longest common prefix of $v(t)$ and $v(t')$, and $v(\mathrm{succ}(t, t'))$ is defined as the child of $v(t)$ in the direction of $v(t')$. More precisely, if $v(t) \prec_{\mathrm{ch}}^* v(t')$, and s is such that $v(t) \prec_{\mathrm{ch}} s$ and $s \prec_{\mathrm{ch}}^* v(t')$, then $s = v(\mathrm{succ}(t, t'))$. Otherwise we set $v(\mathrm{succ}(t, t')) = v(t)$.

Node tests. We define an alphabet Δ that consists of symbols $[\psi]$ for each formula ψ of $\mathcal{L}_1$ (the notation comes from XPath's node tests, because this is precisely the role of $\mathcal{L}_1$ formulae). Notice that Δ is infinite but in all formulae we shall only use finitely many symbols $[\psi]$ and thus we can restrict ourselves to a finite sub-alphabet used in each particular formula.

Interval formulae. An interval formula is a formula of the form $\chi(t, t')$ where χ is an $\mathcal{L}_0$ formula over a finite subset of Δ, and t, t' are two terms.

The semantics is as follows. Let v be a valuation on x_i's. The *interval* between $s = v(t)$ and $s' = v(t')$ is defined as:

- if $s \prec_{\mathrm{ch}}^* s'$, then the interval is the sequence $s = s_0, s_1, \ldots, s_m = s'$ such that $s_i \prec_{\mathrm{ch}} s_{i+1}$ for each $0 \leq i < m$ (and the interval between s' and s is simply listed "backwards": $s' = s_m, \ldots, s_0 = s$);

- if $s \prec^*_{\text{sb}} s'$, then it is the sequence $s = s_0, s_1, \ldots, s_m = s'$ such that $s_i \prec_{\text{sb}} s_{i+1}$ for each $0 \leq i < m$ (listed backwards for the interval between s' and s);
- otherwise the interval is just $\{s\}$.

Let $[\psi_1], \ldots, [\psi_r]$ be all the Δ-symbols mentioned in χ. Then the interval between s and s' naturally defines a Δ-word in which s_i is labeled by all $[\psi_p]$'s such that $(T, s_i) \models \psi_p$. Then $(T, v) \models \chi(t, t')$ iff the interval between $v(t)$ and $v(t')$, viewed as a Δ-word, satisfies χ.

$\mathcal{I}^n(\mathcal{L}_0, \mathcal{L}_1)$ *formulae.* are finally defined as Boolean combinations of the following formulae:

$$t \prec^*_{\text{ch}} t', \quad t \prec^*_{\text{sb}} t', \quad \chi(t, t'),$$

where t, t' are terms, and $\chi(t, t')$ ranges over interval formulae. Given a valuation v, the semantics of $\chi(t, t')$ has already been defined, and $(T, v) \models t \prec^*_{\text{ch}} t'$ (or $t \prec^*_{\text{sb}} t'$) iff $v(t) \prec^*_{\text{ch}} v(t')$ (or $v(t) \prec^*_{\text{sb}} v(t')$, respectively). For $\bar{s} = (s_1, \ldots, s_n)$ and a formula φ we shall write $(T, \bar{s}) \models \varphi$ if $(T, v) \models \varphi$ under the valuation $v(x_i) = s_i, i \leq n$.

Each $\mathcal{I}^n(\mathcal{L}_0, \mathcal{L}_1)$ formula φ then defines an n-ary query which maps a tree T with domain D to $\{\bar{s} \in D^n \mid (T, \bar{s}) \models \varphi\}$.

Theorem 1. *If $\mathcal{L}_0$ captures Boolean FO (respectively, Boolean MSO) queries over words, and $\mathcal{L}_1$ captures unary FO (respectively, unary MSO) queries over unranked trees, then the queries definable by $\mathcal{I}^n(\mathcal{L}_0, \mathcal{L}_1)$ are precisely the n-ary FO (respectively, n-ary MSO) queries over unranked trees.*

The proof of Theorem 1 is based on the composition method, cf. [18,29,33]. We start with the (already mentioned) composition lemma from [33], which was used there to obtain n-ary languages that involved regular or star-free expressions over formulae of FO or MSO in one or two variables, and modify it to eliminate regular expressions and formulae referring to two variables by using temporal logics over words and trees.

Other binary relations and terms. Our choice of terms and binary relations $\prec^*_{\text{ch}}$ and $\prec^*_{\text{sb}}$ is not the only possible one. In general, if we have a grammar τ defining a set of terms and a collection ρ of binary relations, we can define a logic $\mathcal{I}^n[\tau, \rho](\mathcal{L}_0, \mathcal{L}_1)$ in exactly the same way as $\mathcal{I}^n(\mathcal{L}_0, \mathcal{L}_1)$ except:

1. τ-terms are used in place of the terms defined by the grammar ($\mathbb{T}$), and
2. in Boolean combinations only relations from ρ between terms are used.

Now define a new grammar $\mathbb{T}'$ for terms:

$$(\mathbb{T}') \qquad t, t' := x_i, \ i \in [1, n] \mid \texttt{root} \mid \texttt{gen\_succ}(t, t'),$$

where $\texttt{gen\_succ}(s, s')$ is the generalized successor of s in the direction of s'. Its meaning is as follows: look at the path from s to s' which is either a child/parent path (if $s \prec^*_{\text{ch}} s'$ or $s' \prec^*_{\text{ch}} s$), or next/previous-sibling path (if $s \prec^*_{\text{sb}} s'$ or $s' \prec^*_{\text{sb}} s$), or the path shown in the Fig. 1 (that witnesses either $s \leq_{\text{d}} s'$ or

$s' \leq_d s$). In the first two cases, gen_succ(s, s') is the successor of s on that path; in the third case, it is the first node where the direction of path changes between child/parent and next/previous sibling. For example, in Fig. 1, gen_succ(s, s') = s_1 and gen_succ(s', s) = s_2.

Theorem 2. *If $\mathcal{L}_0$ captures Boolean FO (respectively, Boolean MSO) queries over words, and $\mathcal{L}_1$ captures unary FO (respectively, unary MSO) queries over unranked trees, then the queries definable by $\mathcal{I}^n[\mathbb{T}', \leq_d](\mathcal{L}_0, \mathcal{L}_1)$ are precisely the n-ary FO (respectively, n-ary MSO) queries over unranked trees.*

That is, with the new set of terms based on just one binary operation, one can capture all n-ary queries by using only the document ordering.

4   Model-Checking for Combined Logics

We now deal with the complexity of the model-checking problem for $\mathcal{I}^n(\mathcal{L}_0, \mathcal{L}_1)$, that is, the complexity of checking, for an $\mathcal{I}^n(\mathcal{L}_0, \mathcal{L}_1)$ formula φ, a tree T and an n-tuple $\bar{s}$ of its nodes, whether $(T, \bar{s}) \models \varphi$. (The results will hold for the alternative system of terms and the document order $\leq_d$ as well.)

We first offer a general result that makes some mild assumptions on logics $\mathcal{L}_0$ and $\mathcal{L}_1$. We then consider specific cases of logics $\mathcal{L}_0$ and $\mathcal{L}_1$ so that $\mathcal{I}^n(\mathcal{L}_0, \mathcal{L}_1)$ captures FO_n or MSO_n and provide better complexity bounds.

Let $\mathcal{MC}^{\mathcal{L}} : \mathbb{N} \times \mathbb{N} \to \mathbb{N}$ be the complexity of model-checking for a logic $\mathcal{L}$; i.e., given a structure $\mathfrak{M}$ and an $\mathcal{L}$-formula γ, verifying $\mathfrak{M} \models \gamma$ can be done in $O(\mathcal{MC}^{\mathcal{L}}(\|\mathfrak{M}\|, \|\gamma\|))$, where $\|\cdot\|$ is the size of encoding of structures (formulae).

We make three very mild assumptions on model-checking algorithms for $\mathcal{L}_0$ and $\mathcal{L}_1$. First, we assume that formulae are given by their parse-trees; second, that labeling nodes by additional symbols not used in formulae does not change their truth values; and third, that $\mathcal{MC}^{\mathcal{L}}(\cdot, \cdot)$ is a nondecreasing function in both arguments such that $\mathcal{MC}^{\mathcal{L}}(n, m_1) + \mathcal{MC}^{\mathcal{L}}(n, m_2) \leq \mathcal{MC}^{\mathcal{L}}(n, m_1 + m_2)$. All logics considered here – FO, MSO, LTL, CTL^*, L_μ, etc. – easily satisfy these properties.

Proposition 2. *If logics $\mathcal{L}_0$ and $\mathcal{L}_1$ satisfy the three properties described above, then the complexity of model-checking for the combined logic $\mathcal{I}^n(\mathcal{L}_0, \mathcal{L}_1)$ is*
$$O\big(\|T\| \cdot \mathcal{MC}^{\mathcal{L}_1}(\|T\|, \|\varphi\|) + \mathcal{MC}^{\mathcal{L}_0}(\|T\|, \|\varphi\|)\big).$$

These bounds are produced by a naive model-checking algorithm. An $\mathcal{I}^n(\mathcal{L}_0, \mathcal{L}_1)$ formula is a Boolean combination of term comparisons and interval formulae $\chi(t, t')$. To evaluate $\chi(t, t')$ in $(T, \bar{s})$, we define a valuation $v(x_i) = s_i, i \leq n$, and do the following:

1. Compute $v(t)$ and $v(t')$ and the interval between them.
2. For each symbol $[\psi]$ for $\psi \in \mathcal{L}_1$ mentioned in φ, and each s in the interval between $v(t)$ and $v(t')$, mark s with $[\psi]$ if $(T, s) \models \psi$ (by using the model-checking algorithm for $\mathcal{L}_1$).
3. With all elements in the interval marked, use the model-checking algorithm for $\mathcal{L}_0$ to check if χ holds.

The bound easily follows from this and our assumptions on $\mathcal{L}_0$ and $\mathcal{L}_1$.

Even if we assume that $\mathcal{L}_0$ is a logic with very good model-checking complexity (say, $O(\|T\| \cdot \|\varphi\|)$), the bound of Proposition 2 still says that model-checking is quadratic in $\|T\|$, while in XML query processing, generally acceptable complexity is of the form $O(f(\|\varphi\|) \cdot \|T\|)$ for reasonable f [20,24], and ideally $O(\|T\| \cdot \|\varphi\|)$ (see, e.g., [16,25]).

However, the bound can be lowered if we make some assumptions (that will hold in cases of interest) not only on model-checking properties of $\mathcal{L}_1$, but also on the complexity of computing the set $\{s \mid (T, s) \models \psi\}$ for $\mathcal{L}_1$ formulae ψ (that is, on the complexity of unary query evaluation). Assume that there is a function $f : \mathbb{N} \to \mathbb{N}$ satisfying $f(m) + f(k) \leq f(m + k)$ (e.g., $f(m) = c \cdot m^p$ or $f(m) = 2^m$) and a number $\ell > 0$ such that unary query evaluation in $\mathcal{L}_1$ is done in time $f(\|\psi\|) \cdot \|T\|^\ell$. In this case, if an $\mathcal{I}^n(\mathcal{L}_0, \mathcal{L}_1)$ formula φ mentions $[\psi_1], \ldots, [\psi_r]$, we can in time $\sum_i f(\|\psi_i\|) \cdot \|T\|^\ell \leq f(\|\varphi\|) \cdot \|T\|^\ell$ label all nodes in which ψ_i holds with $[\psi_i]$, $1 \leq i \leq r$, and thus check φ in time $O(f(\|\varphi\|) \cdot \|T\|^\ell + \mathcal{MC}^{\mathcal{L}_0}(\|\varphi\|, \|T\|))$. We thus obtain the following:

Theorem 3. *If unary query evaluation in $\mathcal{L}_1$ is done in time $f(\|\psi\|) \cdot \|T\|^\ell$, and the complexity of model-checking for an $\mathcal{L}_0$ formula α on a word w is $g(\|\alpha\|) \cdot \|w\|^p$, then the complexity of model-checking of $\mathcal{I}^n(\mathcal{L}_0, \mathcal{L}_1)$ is*

$$O\big(\max\{f(\|\varphi\|), g(\|\varphi\|)\} \cdot \|T\|^{\max\{\ell, p\}}\big).$$

In particular, if both f and g are linear functions and $\ell = p = 1$, we get an $O(\|\varphi\| \cdot \|T\|)$ model-checking algorithm for $\mathcal{I}^n(\mathcal{L}_0, \mathcal{L}_1)$.

We now use known results on model-checking over words and trees to obtain good model-checking algorithms for combined logics over unranked trees.

MSO$_n$ queries. To get a logic $\mathcal{I}^n(\mathcal{L}_0, \mathcal{L}_1)$ that captures MSO$_n$ we need a logic for unary MSO on trees, and a logic for MSO sentences on words. The former is provided by L_μ^{full}, the full μ-calculus [3]. Over trees (in general, acyclic transition systems), L_μ is known to admit $O(\|\varphi\|^2 \cdot \|t\|)$ model-checking complexity [26], but this result does not extend to L_μ^{full} since introduction of the past modalities effectively transforms trees into cyclic transition systems. However, it can be shown by coding query automata [29] that a small fragment of L_μ^{full} suffices to capture MSO$_1$ over trees. We let $(L_\mu^{\text{full}})^+$ be the fragment of L_μ^{full} that contains no negation (and thus is alternation-free) but is allowed to use additional labels "root", "leaf", "first-sibling", and "last-sibling" [16] with their intuitive meanings.

Lemma 1. *Over unranked trees, $(L_\mu^{\text{full}})^+ = \text{MSO}_1$.*

Unary query evaluation in alternation-free μ-calculus L_μ^+ can be done in linear-time for arbitrary transition systems [10], and hence it is linear-time for $(L_\mu^{\text{full}})^+$ over trees. For words, alternation-free μ-calculus L_μ^0 captures MSO$_0$ (by coding automata), and again from [10], the complexity of model-checking is linear in both the formula and the word. Combining this with Theorem 3 we get:

Corollary 1. *The logic* $\mathcal{I}^n(L^0_\mu, (L^{\text{full}}_\mu)^+)$ *captures* MSO_n *over unranked trees, and the complexity of* $\mathcal{I}^n(L^0_\mu, (L^{\text{full}}_\mu)^+)$ *model-checking is* $O(\|T\| \cdot \|\varphi\|)$.

FO_n queries. We need logics for Boolean FO queries on words and unary FO on trees. The former is, by Kamp's theorem, LTL, which has linear-time complexity over words.

Among logics used in verification, $\text{CTL}^\star$ with the past is known to capture unary FO over trees (see Fact 1). However, even though it can be embedded in L^{full}_μ, the complexity of $\text{CTL}^\star$ does not match the linear complexity we had for $(L^{\text{full}}_\mu)^+$, being in general $2^{O(\|\varphi\|)} \cdot \|T\|$ (see [12]; also, [4] shows that translation into L^{full}_μ will exhibit exponential blowup).

In fact, we can show that it is highly unlikely that we can get linear time evaluation for $\text{CTL}^\star_{\text{past}}$ over trees. In general, $\text{CTL}^\star$ is known to be PSPACE-complete [34]. Here we show that over trees, the complexity of model-checking is lower, but still intractable, being in the second level of the polynomial hierarchy.

Theorem 4. *The model-checking problem for* $\text{CTL}^\star_{\text{past}}$ *over unranked trees is* Δ^p_2-*complete.*

Proof sketch. The usual algorithm for $\text{CTL}^\star$ model checking combines the state labeling technique for CTL model checking with LTL model checking. Its complexity mainly depends on the complexity of the LTL part. In particular, it runs in polynomial time if we have an oracle for verifying whether a formula $\mathbf{E}\,\varphi$ holds in a state s, where φ is an LTL formula. For unranked trees, it can be proved that the latter problem is NP-complete and, thus, the model-checking problem for $\text{CTL}^\star_{\text{past}}$ is in Δ^p_2. For hardness reduction, we use (as [23] for CTL^+) the problem of verifying whether the largest satisfying assignment (interpreted as a binary number) of a propositional formula is even.   □

Nonetheless, there is a temporal logic for trees that has the desired linear complexity. The logic, which we call TL^{tree} (for tree temporal logic), was first defined in [32] for the case of trees without a sibling order $\prec_{\text{sb}}$, and further used in XPath investigations [25]. Its syntax is given by:

$$\alpha, \alpha' := \top \mid \bot \mid a \; (a \in \Sigma) \mid \alpha \vee \alpha' \mid \neg\alpha \mid \mathbf{X}_*\alpha \mid \mathbf{X}^-_*\alpha \mid \alpha\mathbf{U}_*\alpha' \mid \alpha\mathbf{S}_*\alpha',$$

where $*$ is either 'ch' (child) or 'sb' (next sibling). We define the semantics with respect to a tree and a node in a tree:

- $(T, s) \models \top; \quad (T, s) \not\models \bot$;
- $(T, s) \models a$ iff s is labeled a;
- $(T, s) \models \mathbf{X}_{\text{ch}}\alpha$ if $(T, s \cdot i) \models \alpha$ for some i;
- $(T, s) \models \mathbf{X}^-_{\text{ch}}\alpha$ if $(T, s') \models \alpha$ where s' is the parent of s ($s' \prec_{\text{ch}} s$);
- $(T, s) \models \alpha\mathbf{U}_{\text{ch}}\alpha'$ if there is a node s' such that $s \prec^*_{\text{ch}} s'$, $(T, s') \models \alpha'$, and for all $s'' \neq s'$ satisfying $s \prec^*_{\text{ch}} s'' \prec^*_{\text{ch}} s'$ we have $(T, s'') \models \alpha$.

The semantics of $\mathbf{S}_{\text{ch}}$ is defined by reversing the order in the semantics of $\mathbf{U}_{\text{ch}}$, and the semantics of $\mathbf{X}_{\text{sb}}, \mathbf{X}^-_{\text{sb}}, \mathbf{U}_{\text{sb}}$, and $\mathbf{S}_{\text{sb}}$ is the same by replacing the child relation with the next sibling relation.

Whenever we deal with $\mathrm{TL}^{\mathrm{tree}}$, we assume (for the convenience of translations) that the *weak until* or *unless* operator [9] $\varphi \mathbf{W} \psi \equiv \neg(\neg\psi \mathbf{U} \neg(\varphi \vee \psi))$ is available for each of the until operators. This changes neither expressiveness nor the complexity of model-checking [9].

$\mathrm{TL}^{\mathrm{tree}}$ naturally defines unary queries on trees, and the results in [32] can be extended to show that $\mathrm{TL}^{\mathrm{tree}} = \mathrm{FO}_1$ (see, for instance, [25]). Furthermore, we can show:

Lemma 2. *Unary query evaluation in* $\mathrm{TL}^{\mathrm{tree}}$ *can be done in time* $O(\|T\| \cdot \|\varphi\|)$.

We thus have a logic for FO_n with linear model-checking:

Corollary 2. *The logic* $\mathcal{I}^n(\mathrm{LTL}, \mathrm{TL}^{\mathrm{tree}})$ *captures* FO_n *over unranked trees, and the complexity of* $\mathcal{I}^n(\mathrm{LTL}, \mathrm{TL}^{\mathrm{tree}})$ *model-checking is* $O(\|T\| \cdot \|\varphi\|)$.

5   Combined Temporal Logics and XML Querying

In this section we present two concrete translations from XML query languages into combined temporal logics. We start with XPath (or, more precisely, CX-Path, or conditional XPath [25]). As it captures FO_2, one immediately obtains from Corollary 2 that it can be translated into $\mathcal{I}^2(\mathrm{LTL}, \mathrm{TL}^{\mathrm{tree}})$. We present a translation which shows how the main features of combined temporal logics correspond naturally to navigation through XML documents. We then give an example of translating *tree patterns* – a common mechanism for expressing queries for selecting tuples of nodes in XML documents [8,22] – into $\mathcal{I}^n(\mathrm{LTL}, \mathrm{TL}^{\mathrm{tree}})$.

From Conditional XPath to $\mathcal{I}^2(\mathrm{LTL}, \mathrm{TL}^{\mathrm{tree}})$. Conditional XPath (CXPath) [25] is an extension of the logical core of XPath 1.0 that captures FO_2 queries over XML documents. The language contains basic expressions `step`, path expressions `path`, and node tests `test`, given by the grammar below:

$$\begin{aligned}
\texttt{step} &:= \texttt{child} \mid \texttt{parent} \mid \texttt{right} \mid \texttt{left}, \\
\texttt{path} &:= \texttt{step} \mid \texttt{?test} \mid (\texttt{step/?test})^+ \mid \texttt{path/path} \mid \texttt{path} \cup \texttt{path}, \\
\texttt{test} &:= a, a \in \Sigma \mid \langle \texttt{path} \rangle \mid \neg\texttt{test} \mid \texttt{test} \vee \texttt{test}.
\end{aligned}$$

Given a tree T, the semantics of a `step` or a `path` expression e is the set $[\![e]\!]_T$ of pairs of nodes, and for a `test` expression e, $[\![e]\!]_T$ is a set of nodes of T. The semantics is defined in Figure 2. Note that '/' is the concatenation of paths, and the $\langle \texttt{path} \rangle$ test corresponds to $\mathbf{E}\beta$ of CTL^*. We use the notation $\prec^+$ for the transitive closure, that is, $\prec \circ \prec^*$.

Translating FO_2 into CXPath is necessarily non-elementary (which easily follows from the fact that translation from FO to LTL over words is necessarily nonelementary [11]). For the combined logic, we can show:

Theorem 5. *For every CXPath path formula* φ *there exists an equivalent* $\mathcal{I}^2(\mathrm{LTL}, \mathrm{TL}^{\mathrm{tree}})$ *formula* φ°. *Moreover,* φ° *can be constructed in single-exponential time.*

$$[\![\text{child}]\!]_T = \{(s, s') \mid s \prec_{\text{ch}} s'\} \qquad\qquad [\![a]\!]_T = \{s \mid s \text{ is labeled } a\}$$
$$[\![\text{parent}]\!]_T = \{(s, s') \mid s' \prec_{\text{ch}} s\} \quad [\![\text{test} \vee \text{test}']\!]_T = [\![\text{test}]\!]_T \cup [\![\text{test}']\!]_T$$
$$[\![\text{right}]\!]_T = \{(s, s') \mid s \prec_{\text{sb}} s'\} \qquad\qquad [\![\neg\text{test}]\!]_T = D - [\![\text{test}]\!]_T$$
$$[\![\text{left}]\!]_T = \{(s, s') \mid s' \prec_{\text{sb}} s\} \qquad\qquad [\![\langle\text{path}\rangle]\!]_T = \{s \mid \exists s' : (s, s') \in [\![\text{path}]\!]_T\}$$
$$[\![?\text{test}]\!]_T = \{(s, s) \mid s \in [\![\text{test}]\!]_T\}$$
$$[\![\text{path}/\text{path}']\!]_T = [\![\text{path}]\!]_T \circ [\![\text{path}']\!]_T \quad [\![\text{path} \cup \text{path}']\!]_T = [\![\text{path}]\!]_T \cup [\![\text{path}']\!]_T$$
$$[\![(\text{child}/?\text{test})^+]\!]_T = \{(s, s') \mid s \prec_{\text{ch}}^+ s', \text{ and } \forall s'' : (s \prec_{\text{ch}}^+ s'' \prec_{\text{ch}}^* s' \to s'' \in [\![\text{test}]\!]_T)\}$$

Fig. 2. The semantics of CXPath

Below we sketch the translation and explain the reason for the exponential blowup (intuitively, it arises from putting CXPath expressions in a certain normal form [25] that fits in nicely with $\mathcal{I}^2(\text{LTL}, \text{TL}^{\text{tree}})$).

We start with path expressions. CXPath, as well as XPath 1.0, allows expressions containing any combination of the four axes `child`, `parent`, `right` and `left`, but [25] gave a normal form for paths: namely, every CXPath expression is equivalent to a union of simple paths defined by:

```
simple-path := ?test | dpath | upath | lpath | rpath |
               upath/rpath | rpath/dpath | upath/rpath/dpath |
               upath/lpath | lpath/dpath | upath/lpath/dpath,
```

where `dpath` (down-path) is a concatenation of paths `child`, `?test` and $(\text{child}/?\text{test})^+$ that mentions `child` or $(\text{child}/?\text{test})^+$ at least once; and `upath`, `rpath` and `lpath` (up-, right-, and left-paths) are defined in the same way but replacing `child` by `parent`, `right` and `left`, respectively. Thus, it suffices to provide translations for simple path expressions. As an example we show translations of `dpath` and `upath/rpath/dpath`, as the remaining translations are very similar. For a downpath π, we define an interval formula $\pi^\circ(x_1, x_2)$ such that for every Σ-tree T and a pair of nodes s_1, s_2 in it, $(s_1, s_2) \in [\![\pi]\!]_T$ iff $(T, s_1, s_2) \models x_1 \prec_{\text{ch}}^* x_2 \wedge (\pi^\circ)(x_1, x_2)$:

$$
\begin{aligned}
(\text{child})^\circ &:= \mathbf{X}\neg\mathbf{X}\top \\
(?\text{test})^\circ &:= [\text{test}^\circ] \wedge \neg\mathbf{X}\top \\
((\text{child}/?\text{test})^+)^\circ &:= \mathbf{X}\neg(\top\,\mathbf{U}\neg[\text{test}^\circ]) \\
(\text{child}/\text{dpath})^\circ &:= \mathbf{X}\,\text{dpath}^\circ \\
(?\text{test}/\text{dpath})^\circ &:= [\text{test}^\circ] \wedge \text{dpath}^\circ \\
((\text{child}/?\text{test})^+/\text{dpath})^\circ &:= \mathbf{X}\,([\text{test}^\circ]\,\mathbf{U}\,(\mathbf{X}^-\text{dpath}^\circ)),
\end{aligned}
$$

where `test`$^\circ$ is the translation of `test` expressions into TL^{tree} formulae.

As another example, consider a simple path `upath/rpath/dpath`. Assume that a node s' is reachable from a node s by following this path, as in Fig. 1, where $s_1 = \text{succ}(s \sqcap s', s)$ and $s_2 = \text{succ}(s \sqcap s', s')$. Then `upath/rpath/dpath` is expressed by an $\mathcal{I}^2(\text{LTL}, \text{TL}^{\text{tree}})$ formula $\varphi(x_1, x_2)$:

$$(\text{upath}^\circ)(x_1, \text{succ}(x_1 \sqcap x_2, x_1)) \wedge \text{succ}(x_1 \sqcap x_2, x_1) \prec_{\text{sb}}^* \text{succ}(x_1 \sqcap x_2, x_2) \wedge$$
$$(\text{rpath}^\circ)(\text{succ}(x_1 \sqcap x_2, x_1), \text{succ}(x_1 \sqcap x_2, x_2)) \wedge (\text{dpath}^\circ)(\text{succ}(x_1 \sqcap x_2, x_2), x_2).$$

Finally we must deal with node tests which will be translated into $\mathrm{TL}^{\mathrm{tree}}$. Had we used $\mathrm{CTL}^\star_{\mathrm{past}}$, the translation would have have been immediate as $\langle\mathrm{path}\rangle$ is simply $\mathbf{E}(\mathrm{path}^\circ)$. But $\mathrm{TL}^{\mathrm{tree}}$ is more restrictive, and thus our first step is to give an equivalent grammar for CXPath node tests:

$$
\begin{aligned}
\mathtt{test} &:= a, a \in \Sigma \mid \langle\mathtt{union}\rangle \mid \neg\mathtt{test} \mid \mathtt{test} \vee \mathtt{test} \\
\mathtt{union} &:= \mathtt{concat} \mid \mathtt{union} \cup \mathtt{union} \\
\mathtt{concat} &:= \mathtt{step} \mid \mathtt{?test} \mid (\mathtt{step/?test})^+ \mid \\
&\qquad \mathtt{step/concat} \mid \mathtt{?test/concat} \mid (\mathtt{step/?test})^+/\mathtt{concat}
\end{aligned}
$$

Here the semantics is existential: $\mathtt{test}$ is true in s if for some s' it is the case that (s, s') is in the semantics of the corresponding path expression. With the new grammar, the translation (given below for the 'child' axis) is quite straight-forward:

$$
\begin{aligned}
a^\circ &:= a & \langle\mathtt{union}\rangle^\circ &:= \mathtt{union}^\circ \\
(\neg\mathtt{test})^\circ &:= \neg\mathtt{test}^\circ & (\mathtt{test}_1 \vee \mathtt{test}_2)^\circ &:= \mathtt{test}_1^\circ \vee \mathtt{test}_2^\circ \\
(\mathtt{union}_1 \cup \mathtt{union}_2)^\circ &:= \mathtt{union}_1^\circ \vee \mathtt{union}_2^\circ & \mathtt{child}^\circ &:= \mathbf{X}_{\mathrm{ch}} \top \\
(\mathtt{?test})^\circ &:= \mathtt{test}^\circ & ((\mathtt{child/?test})^+)^\circ &:= \mathbf{X}_{\mathrm{ch}} \mathtt{test}^\circ \\
(\mathtt{child/concat})^\circ &:= \mathbf{X}_{\mathrm{ch}} \mathtt{concat}^\circ & (\mathtt{?test/concat})^\circ &:= \mathtt{test}^\circ \wedge \mathtt{concat}^\circ \\
((\mathtt{child/?test})^+/\mathtt{concat})^\circ &:= \mathbf{X}_{\mathrm{ch}} \neg(\neg\mathtt{concat}^\circ \, \mathbf{W}_{\mathrm{ch}} \, \neg\mathtt{test}^\circ)
\end{aligned}
$$

To conclude, we note that the translation of paths into the normal form is exponential [25] and the same is true for the translation for tests; for formulae in normal form, translations into both $\mathrm{TL}^{\mathrm{tree}}$ and $\mathcal{I}^2(\mathrm{LTL}, \mathrm{TL}^{\mathrm{tree}})$ are linear, which proves the theorem.

From tree-patterns to $\mathcal{I}^n(\mathrm{LTL}, \mathrm{TL}^{\mathrm{tree}})$. Tree-pattern queries are a popular way of navigating in XML documents and retrieving n-ary tuples of nodes [8,22]. Fix an alphabet Σ and n variables $x_1, \ldots, x_n$. Tree-pattern queries use a restricted language for paths (where a ranges over Σ):

$$
\begin{aligned}
\mathtt{step} &:= \mathtt{self} \mid \mathtt{child} \mid \mathtt{child}^+ \\
\mathtt{path} &:= \mathtt{step} \mid \mathtt{step/?a} \mid \mathtt{step}/x_i \mid \mathtt{step/?a}/x_i, \quad i \le n
\end{aligned}
$$

Variables retrieve nodes from documents: for example, $\mathtt{self}/x_i$ retrieves the node where the formula is evaluated, and $\mathtt{child}^+/\mathtt{?a}/x_i$ retrieves all the descendants of a node that are labeled a. Tree-pattern formulae are defined as follows:

$$
\varphi := \mathtt{path} \mid \mathtt{path}[\varphi, \ldots, \varphi],
$$

with the additional requirement that each variable x_i is mentioned at most once. In a tree-pattern formula, square brackets are used to indicate that a list of paths have a common starting point.

An n-ary tree-pattern formula φ is definable in FO and thus in $\mathcal{I}^n(\mathrm{LTL}, \mathrm{TL}^{\mathrm{tree}})$. In fact, one can prove a stronger result:

Proposition 3. *For every tree-pattern formula φ one can construct in linear-time an equivalent $\mathcal{I}^n(\mathrm{LTL}, \mathrm{TL}^{\mathrm{tree}})$ formula φ°.*

6   Conclusions

Connections between XML querying and temporal logics were discovered recently but familiar logics such as CTL^* or the μ-calculus were only suitable for Boolean or unary queries over XML documents. Here we have shown how to combine temporal logics to obtain query languages for selecting arbitrary tuples of nodes from XML trees, that capture the power of FO and MSO querying. The observation that composing monadic queries is sufficient to capture n-ary MSO was also made recently in [13].

One of the main goals of this work is to bring techniques developed in the model-checking community into the field of XML querying, where complexity of query evaluation for languages such as XPath and XQuery is a very recent and active topic of research [17,20]. We have shown that some of the combined logics achieve the best possible complexity of model-checking: linear in both the formula and the document. Two natural extensions of this work are: (1) an experimental evaluation of the combined temporal logics proposed here using existing model-checkers, and (2) further extension of the logics by allowing them to reshape tuples of nodes, thus making them closer to languages such as XQuery.

Acknowledgments. We thank anonymous referees for their comments. Arenas is supported by FONDECYT grant 1050701; Arenas and Barceló by Grant P04-067-F from the Millennium Nucleus Centre for Web Research; Libkin is on leave from the University of Toronto, supported by the European Commission Marie Curie Excellence grant MEXC-CT-2005-024502, EPSRC grant E005039, and a grant from NSERC.

References

1. L. Afanasiev, M. Franceschet, M. Marx, M. de Rijke. CTL model checking for processing simple XPath queries. In *TIME 2004*, pages 117–124.
2. L. Afanasiev, P. Blackburn, I. Dimitriou, B. Gaiffe, E. Goris, M. Marx, M. de Rijke: PDL for ordered trees. *J. Appl. Non-Classical Logics* 15 (2005), 115–135.
3. P. Barceló, L. Libkin. Temporal logics over unranked trees. *LICS'05*, pages 31–40.
4. G. Bhat, R. Cleaveland. Efficient model checking via the equational μ-calculus. In *LICS 1996*, pages 304–312.
5. R. Bloem, J. Engelfriet. Monadic second order logic and node relations on graphs and trees. *Struct. in Logic and Comp. Science*, 1997: 144-161.
6. L. Cardelli, G. Ghelli. A query language based on the ambient logic. In *ESOP 2001*, pages 1–22.
7. B. ten Cate. Expressivity of XPath with transitive closure. In *PODS'06*, pages 328–337.
8. Z. Chen, H.V.Jagadish, L. Lakshmanan, S. Paparizos. From tree patterns to generalized tree patterns: on efficient evaluation of XQuery. *VLDB'03*, pages 237–248.
9. E. Clarke, B.-H. Schlingloff. Model Checking. In *Handbook of Automated Reasoning*, Elsevier 2001, pages 1635–1790.
10. R. Cleaveland, B. Steffen. A linear-time model-checking algorithm for the alternation-free modal mu-calculus. *CAV'91*, pages 48–58.

11. K. Compton, C.W. Henson. A uniform method for proving lower bounds on the computational complexity of logical theories. *APAL* 48 (1990), 1–79.
12. E. A. Emerson, C.-L. Lei. Modalities for model checking: branching time logic strikes back. *Sci. Comput. Program.* 8 (1987), 275–306.
13. E. Filiot, J. Niehren, J-M. Talbot, S. Tison. Composing monadic queries in trees. In *PLAN-X* 2006: 61-70.
14. M. Frick, M. Grohe. The complexity of first-order and monadic second-order logic revisited. In *LICS 2002*, 215–224.
15. E. Goris, M. Marx. Looping caterpillars. In *LICS 2005*, pages 51–60.
16. G. Gottlob, C. Koch. Monadic datalog and the expressive power of languages for web information extraction. *J. ACM* 51 (2004), 74–113.
17. G. Gottlob, C. Koch, R. Pichler, L. Segoufin. The complexity of XPath query evaluation and XML typing. *J. ACM* 52 (2005), 284–335.
18. T. Hafer, W. Thomas. Computation tree logic CTL* and path quantifiers in the monadic theory of the binary tree. In *ICALP'87*, pages 269–279.
19. N. Klarlund, Th. Schwentick, D. Suciu. XML: model, schemas, types, logics, and queries. In *Logics for Emerging Applications of Databases*, Springer 2003.
20. C. Koch. Processing queries on tree-structured data efficiently. In *PODS'06*, pages 213–224.
21. O. Kupferman, A. Pnueli. Once and for all. In *LICS'95*, pages 25–35.
22. L. Lakshmanan, G. Ramesh, H. Wang and Z. Zhao. On testing satisfiability of tree pattern queries. In *VLDB'04*, pages 120–131.
23. F. Laroussinie, N. Markey and Ph. Schnoebelen. Model checking CTL$^+$ and FCTL is hard. In *FoSSaCS'01*, pages 318–331.
24. L. Libkin. Logics for unranked trees: an overview. In *ICALP'05*, pages 35–50.
25. M. Marx. Conditional XPath. *ACM TODS* 30(4) (2005).
26. R. Mateescu. Local model-checking of modal mu-calculus on acyclic labeled transition systems. In *TACAS'02*, pages 281–295.
27. G. Miklau and D. Suciu. Containment and equivalence for a fragment of XPath. *J. ACM* 51(1): 2–45 (2004).
28. F. Neven. Automata, logic, and XML. In *CSL 2002*, pages 2–26.
29. F. Neven, Th. Schwentick. Query automata over finite trees. *TCS*, 275 (2002), 633–674.
30. D. Niwinski. Fixed points vs. infinite generation. In *LICS 1988*, pages 402–409.
31. L. Planque, J. Niehren, J.M. Talbot, S. Tison. N-ary queries by tree automata. In *DBPL'05*, pages 217–231.
32. B.-H. Schlingloff. Expressive completeness of temporal logic of trees. *Journal of Applied Non-Classical Logics* 2 (1992), 157–180.
33. Th. Schwentick. On diving in trees. In *MFCS'00*, pages 660-669.
34. A. P. Sistla, E. Clarke. The complexity of propositional linear temporal logics. *J. ACM* 32 (1985), 733–749.
35. M. Y. Vardi. Reasoning about the past with two-way automata. In *ICALP'98*, pages 628–641.
36. M. Y. Vardi. Model checking for database theoreticians. In *ICDT'05*, pages 1–16.

Commutativity Analysis in XML Update Languages

Giorgio Ghelli[1], Kristoffer Rose[2], and Jérôme Siméon[2]

[1] Università di Pisa, Dipartimento di Informatica
Via Buonarroti 2, I-56127 Pisa, Italy
ghelli@di.unipi.it
[2] IBM T.J. Watson Research Center
P.O.Box 704, Yorktown Heights, NY 10598, U.S.A.
{krisrose,simeon}@us.ibm.com

Abstract. A common approach to XML updates is to extend XQuery with update operations. This approach results in very expressive languages which are convenient for users but are difficult to reason about. Deciding whether two expressions can commute has numerous applications from view maintenance to rewriting-based optimizations. Unfortunately, commutativity is undecidable in most recent XML update languages. In this paper, we propose a conservative analysis for an expressive XML update language that can be used to determine whether two expressions commute. The approach relies on a form of path analysis that computes upper bounds for the nodes that are accessed or modified in a given update expression. Our main result is a commutativity theorem that can be used to identify commuting expressions.

1 Introduction

Most of the proposed XML updates languages [1,2,3,4,5] extend a full-fledged query language such as XQuery [6] with update primitives. To simplify specification and reasoning, some of the first proposals [1,2,4] have opted for a so-called *snapshot semantics*, which delays update application until the end of the query. However, this leads to counter-intuitive results for some queries, and limits the expressiveness in a way that is not always acceptable for applications. For that reason, more recent proposals [5,7] give the ability to apply updates in the course of query evaluation. Such languages typically rely on a semantics with a strict evaluation order. For example, consider the following query, which first inserts a set of elements, then accesses those elements using a path expression.

```
for $x in $doc/country return insert {<new/>} into {$x},
count($doc/country/new)
```

Such an example cannot be written in a language based on a snapshot semantics, as the count would always return zero. However, it can be written in the XQuery! [5] or the XQueryP [7] proposals, which both rely on an explicit left-to-right evaluation order. Still, such a semantics severely restricts the optimizer's ability for rewritings, unless the optimizer is able to decide that some pairs of expressions commute.

T. Schwentick and D. Suciu (Eds.): ICDT 2007, LNCS 4353, pp. 374–388, 2007.

Deciding commutativity, or more generally whether an update and a query *interfere*, has numerous applications, including optimizations based on algebraic rewritings, detecting when an update needs to be propagated through a view (usually specified as a query), deciding whether sub-expressions of a given query can be executed in parallel, etc. Unfortunately, commutativity is undecidable for XQuery extended with updates. In this paper, we propose a conservative approach to detect whether two query/update expressions interfere, i.e., whether they can be safely commuted or not. Our technique relies on an extension of the path analysis proposed in [8] that infers upper bounds for the nodes accessed and modified by a given expression. Such upper bounds are specified as simple path expressions for which disjointness is decidable [9,10].

Our commutativity analysis serves a similar purpose to independence checking in the relational context [11,12]. To the best of our knowledge, our work is the first to study such issues in the XML context, where languages are typically much more expressive. A simpler form of static analysis is proposed in [4,13], suggesting that similar techniques can be used to optimize languages with a snapshot semantics. Finally, commutativity of tree operations is used in transactional models [14,15], but relies on run-time information while our purpose is static detection.

Problem and examples. In the rest of the paper, we focus on a simple XQuery extension with insertion and deletion operations. The syntax and semantics of that language is essentially that of [5], with updates applied immediately. This language is powerful enough to exhibit the main problems related to commutativity analysis, yet simple enough to allow a complete formal treatment within the space available for this paper. Here are some sample queries and updates in that language.

Q1 `count($doc/country/new)`   **U1** `delete {$doc/wines/california}`

Q2 `$doc/country[population > 20]`   **U2** `for $x in $doc/country return`
                                `insert {<new/>} into {$x}`

Q3 `for $x in $doc//country`
      `return ($x//name)`   **U3** `for $x in`
                                `$doc/country[population < 24]`
Q4 `for $x in $doc/country`   `return`
      `return $x/new/../very_new`   `delete {$x/city}`

Some of those examples obviously commute, for instance **U1** deletes nodes that are unrelated to the nodes accessed by **Q1** or **Q2**. This can be inferred easily by looking at the paths in the query used to access the corresponding nodes. On the contrary, **U2** does not commute with **Q1** since the query accesses nodes being inserted. Deciding whether the set of nodes accessed or modified are disjoint quickly becomes hard for any non-trivial update language. For instance, deciding whether **U3** and **Q2** interfere requires some analysis of the predicates, which can be arbitrarily complex in XQuery.

Approach. We rely on a form of abstract interpretation that approximates the set of nodes processed by a given expression. The analysis must satisfy the following properties. Firstly, since we are looking to check *disjointness*, we must infer an upper bound for the corresponding nodes. Secondly, the analysis must be precise enough to be useful in practical applications. Finally, the result of the analysis must make disjointness decidable. In the context of XML updates, *paths* are a natural choice for the approximation of the nodes being accessed or updated, and they satisfy the precision and decidability requirements.

Contributions. The path analysis itself is a relatively intuitive extension of [8] to handle update operations. However, coming up with a sound analysis turns out to be a hard problem for a number of reasons. First of all, we use paths to denote sets of accessed nodes, but the forthcoming updates will change the nodes denoted by the paths that are being accumulated. We need a way to associate a meaning to a path that is *stable* in the face of a changing data model instance. To address that issue, we introduce a store-based formalization of the XML data model and a notion of store history that allows us to talk about the effect of each single update and to solve the stability issue. Another challenge is to find a precise definition of which nodes are actually used or updated by a query. For instance, one may argue that **U3** only modifies nodes reached by the path *country/city*. However, one would then miss the fact that **U3** interferes with **Q3** because the *city* nodes may have a *country* or a *name* descendant, which is made unreachable by the deletion. In our analysis, this is kept into account by actually inserting into the updated paths of **U3** all the descendants of the deleted expression *country/city*, as detailed in the table below.

U3 accessed paths:	**Q3** accessed paths:
`$doc/country`	`$doc//country`
`$doc/country/population`	`$doc//country//name`
`$doc/country/city`	
updated paths:	updated paths:
`$doc/country/city/descendant-or-self::*`	

In **Q4**, if the returned expression *$x/new/../very_new* were just associated to the path *country/new/../very_new*, the interference with **U2** would not be observed, since the path *country/new/descendant-or-self::*::∗* updated by **U2** refers to a disjoint set of nodes. Hence, the analysis must also consider the nodes traversed by the evaluation of *$x/new/../very_new*, which correspond to the path *country|country/new|country/new/..*, whose second component intersects with *country/new/descendant-or-self::*.* The main contributions of the paper are as follows:

- We propose a form of static analysis that infers paths to the nodes that are *accessed* and *modified* by an expression in that language;
- We present a formal definition of when such an analysis is sound, based on a notion of *store history equivalence*; this formal definition provides a guide for the definition of the inference rules;
- We show the soundness of the proposed path analysis;
- We prove a commutativity theorem, that provides a sufficient condition for the commutativity of two expressions, based on the given path analysis.

Organization. The rest of the paper is organized as follows. Section 2 presents the XML data model and the notion of store history. Section 3 reviews the update language syntax and semantics. Section 4 presents the path analysis and the main soundness theorem. Section 5 presents the commutativity theorem. Section 6 reviews related work, and Section 7 concludes the paper. For space reasons, proofs for the analysis soundness and for the commutativity theorem are provided separately in the extended version of this paper [16].

2 A Store for Updates

We define here the notions of *store* and *store history*, which are used to represent the effect of XML updating expressions. Our store is a simplification of the XQuery Data Model [17] to the parts that are most relevant to our path analysis. In this formalization we ignore sibling order, since it has little impact on the approach and on the analysis precision.

2.1 The Store

We assume the existence of disjoint infinite sets of *node ids*, $\mathcal{N}$, the *node kinds*, $\mathcal{K} = \{\texttt{element}, \texttt{text}\}$, *names*, Q, and possible *textual content*, $\mathcal{T}$. A node *location* is used to identify where a document or an XML fragment originates from; it is either a URI or a unique code-location identifier: $loc ::= uri \mid code\text{-}loc$.

A *uri* typically corresponds to the URI associated to a document and a *code-loc* is used to identify document fragments generated during query evaluation by an element constructor. Now we are ready to define our basic notion of store.

Definition 1 (Store). *A store σ is a quadruple (N, E, R, F) where $N \subset \mathcal{N}$ contains the set of nodes in the document, $E \subset N \times N$ contains the set of edges, $R: N \to loc$ is a partial function mapping some nodes to their location, and the node description $F = (kind_F, name_F, content_F)$ is a triple of partial functions where $kind_F : N \to \mathcal{K}$ maps each node to its kind, $name_F : N \to Q$ maps nodes to their name (if any), and $content_F : N \to \mathcal{T}$ maps nodes to their text content (if any).*

We use N_σ, E_σ, R_σ, F_σ to denote the N, E, R, F component of σ. When $(m, n) \in E$, we say that m is a parent of n and n is a child of m. A "root" is a node that has no parent.

Finally a store must be "well-formed": (1) all nodes mapped by R must be root nodes, (2) every non-root node must be the child node of exactly one parent node, (3) the transitive closure E^+ of E must be irreflexive (4) element nodes must have a name and no content; and (5) text nodes must have no name and no children but do have content.

In what follows, every store operation preserves store well-formedness.

2.2 Accessing and Updating the Store

We assume the standard definitions for the usual accessors (parent, children, descendants, ancestors, name, text-content...), and focus on operations that modify the store (insert, delete, and node creation).[1] We define a notion of *atomic update record*, which captures the dynamic information necessary for each update, notably allowing the update to be re-executed on a store, using the *apply* operation defined below.

Definition 2 (Atomic update records). *Atomic update records are terms with the following syntax:*

$$\texttt{create}(\bar{n}, F) \mid \texttt{R-insert}(n, loc) \mid \texttt{insert}(E) \mid \texttt{delete}(\bar{n})$$

---

[1] Note that replace is trivial to add to the framework.

Definition 3 (Atomic update application). *The operation apply(σ, u) returns a new store as detailed below, but fails when the listed preconditions do not hold. $\bot$ denotes undefined.*

- *apply$(\sigma, \mathtt{create}(\bar{n}, F'))$ adds $\bar{n}$ to N and extends F with F'.*
  Preconditions: $\bar{n}$ disjoint from N. $(\bar{n}, (), (), F')$ is a well-formed store.
- *apply$(\sigma, \mathtt{R\text{-}insert}(n, loc))$ extends R with $n \to loc$.*
  Preconditions: n is a root node and $R(n_c) = \bot$.
- *apply$(\sigma, \mathtt{insert}(E'))$ extends E with E'.*
  Preconditions: for each $(n_p, n_c) \in E'$, n_c has no parent in $E \cup E' \setminus \{(n_p, n_c)\}$, and $R(n_c) = \bot$. The transitive closure of $E \cup E'$ is irreflexive.
- *apply$(\sigma, \mathtt{delete}(\bar{n}))$ deletes each edge $(n_p, n_c) \in E$ where $n_c \in \bar{n}$.*
  Preconditions: $\bar{n} \subseteq N$.

Definition 4 (Composite updates). *A composite update, Δ, is an ordered sequence of atomic updates: $\Delta \equiv (u_1, \ldots, u_n)$. apply$(\sigma, \Delta)$ denotes the result of applying $u_1 \ldots u_n$ on store σ, in this order.*

We use *created*(Δ) to denote the set of nodes created by Δ. A composite update Δ *respects creation time* iff, for any $\Delta_1, \Delta_2 = \Delta$, no node in *created*$(\Delta_2)$ appears in Δ_1. Hereafter we will always assume that we only work with such Δ's.

Finally, the notion of *updated*(Δ_1) gives a sufficient condition for non-interference (*S#T* means that S and T are disjoint).

Definition 5 (Update target). *The* update target *of each update operation is defined as*

$$
\begin{aligned}
updated(\mathtt{create}(\bar{n}, F)) &=_{def} \{\} \\
updated(\mathtt{R\text{-}insert}(n, loc)) &=_{def} \{\} \\
updated(\mathtt{insert}(E)) &=_{def} \{n_c \mid (n_p, n_c) \in E\} \\
updated(\mathtt{delete}(\bar{n})) &=_{def} \bar{n}
\end{aligned}
$$

Property 1. If Δ_1, Δ_2 and Δ_2, Δ_1 both respect creation time, then

$$updated(\Delta_1) \# updated(\Delta_2) \Rightarrow \mathrm{apply}(\sigma, (\Delta_1, \Delta_2)) = \mathrm{apply}(\sigma, (\Delta_2, \Delta_1))$$

Intuitively, provided that creation time is respected, the only two operations that do not commute are $\mathtt{insert}(n_p, n_c)$ and $\mathtt{delete}(n_c)$. Any other two operations either do not interfere at all or they fail in whichever order are applied, as happens for any conflicting $\mathtt{R\text{-}insert\text{-}R\text{-}insert}$, $\mathtt{R\text{-}insert\text{-}insert}$, or $\mathtt{insert\text{-}insert}$ pair.

2.3 Store History

Finally, we introduce a notion of store history, as a pair $(\sigma, (u_1, \ldots, u_n))$. In our semantics each expression, instead of modifying its input store, extends the input history with new updates. With this tool we will be able, for example, to discuss commutativity of two expressions $Expr_1, Expr_2$ by analysing the histories $(\sigma, (\Delta_1, \Delta_2))$ and $(\sigma, (\Delta_2', \Delta_1'))$ produced by their evaluations in different orders, and by proving that, under some conditions, $\Delta_1 = \Delta_1'$ and $\Delta_2 = \Delta_2'$.

Definition 6 (Store history). *A store history* $\eta = (\sigma_\eta, \Delta_\eta)$ *is a pair formed by a store and a composite update.*

A store history (σ, Δ) can be mapped to a plain store either by apply(σ, Δ) or by applying *no-delete*(Δ) only, which is the Δ without any deletion. The second mapping $(\text{mrg}((\sigma, \Delta)))$ will be crucial to capture the degree of approximation that store dynamicity imposes over our static analysis.

$$\text{apply}((\sigma, \Delta)) =_{\text{def}} \text{apply}(\sigma, \Delta)$$
$$\text{mrg}((\sigma, \Delta)) =_{\text{def}} \text{apply}(\sigma, \textit{no-delete}(\Delta))$$

By abuse of notation we shall (1) implicitly interpret σ as $(\sigma, ())$; (2) extend accessors to store histories using the convention that, for any function defined on stores, $f(\eta) =_{\text{def}} f(\text{apply}(\eta))$; (3) when $\eta = (\sigma, \Delta)$ then write $\eta, \Delta' =_{\text{def}} (\sigma, (\Delta, \Delta'))$. We define history difference $\eta \setminus \eta'$ as follows: $(\sigma, (\Delta, \Delta')) \setminus (\sigma, \Delta) =_{\text{def}} \Delta'$.

Definition 7 (Well-formed History). *A history η is well-formed (wf(η)), if mrg(η) and apply(η) are both defined.*

3   Update Language

The language we consider is a cut-down version of XQuery! [5] characterized by the fact that the evaluation order is fixed and each update operation is applied immediately. It is not difficult to extend our analysis to languages with snapshot semantics, but the machinery becomes heavier, while we are trying here to present the simplest incarnation of our approach. The language has the following syntax; we will use the usual abbreviations for the parent (**p**/..), child (**p**/*name*), and descendant (**p**//*name*) axes. We assume that *code-loc* (See Section 2) is generated beforehand by the compiler.

$Expr ::= \$x \mid Expr/axis::ntest \mid Expr, Expr \mid Expr = Expr$
$\qquad \mid$ let $\$x := Expr$ return $Expr \mid$ for $\$x$ in $Expr$ return $Expr$
$\qquad \mid$ if $(Expr)$ then $Expr$ else $Expr \mid$ delete $\{Expr\}$
$\qquad \mid$ insert $\{Expr_1\}$ into $\{Expr\} \mid$ element$_{code\text{-}loc}\{Expr\}\{Expr\}$
$axis ::= child \mid descendant \mid parent \mid ancestor$
$ntest ::= text() \mid node() \mid name \mid *$

The main semantic judgement "$dEnv \vdash \eta_0; Expr \Rightarrow \eta_1; \bar{n}$" specifies that the evaluation of an expression *Expr*, with respect to a store history η_0 and to a dynamic environment *dEnv* that associates a value to each variable free in *Expr*, produces a value $\bar{n}$ and extends η_0 to $\eta_1 = \eta_0, \Delta$. A value is just a node sequence $\bar{n}$; textual content may be accessed by a function f, but we otherwise ignore atomic values, since they are ignored by path analysis. In an implementation, we would not manipulate the history η_0 but the store apply(η_0), since the value of every expression only depends on that. However, store histories allow us to isolate the store effect of each single expression, both in our definition of soundness and in our proof of commutativity.

As an example, we present here the rule for insert expressions; the complete semantics can be found in [16]. Let $\bar{n}_d$ be the descendants-or-self of the nodes in $\bar{n}$. Insert-into uses *prepare-deep-copy* to identify a fresh node $m_i \in \bar{m}_d$ for each node in $\bar{n}_d$, while E_{copy} and F_{copy} reproduce for $E_{\text{apply}(\eta_2)}$ and $F_{\text{apply}(\eta_2)}$ for $\bar{m}_d$, and $\bar{m}$ is the subset of $\bar{m}_d$ that corresponds to $\bar{n}$. Hence, $\text{create}(\bar{m}_d, F_{\text{copy}}), \text{insert}(E_{\text{copy}})$ copy $\bar{n}$ and their descendants, while $\text{insert}(\{n\} \times \bar{m})$ links the copies of $\bar{n}$ to n. Notice how the rule only depends on apply(η_2), not on the internal structure of η_2.

$$dEnv \vdash \eta_0; Expr_1 \Rightarrow \eta_1; \bar{n}$$
$$dEnv \vdash \eta_1; Expr_2 \Rightarrow \eta_2; n$$
$$(\bar{m}, \bar{m}_d, E_{\text{copy}}, F_{\text{copy}}) = \textit{prepare-deep-copy}(\text{apply}(\eta_2), \bar{n})$$
$$\eta_3 = \eta_2, \text{create}(\bar{m}_d, F_{\text{copy}}), \text{insert}(E_{\text{copy}}), \text{insert}(\{n\} \times \bar{m})$$
$$\overline{dEnv \vdash \eta_0; \text{insert } \{Expr_1\} \text{ into } \{Expr_2\} \Rightarrow \eta_3; ()}$$

It is easy to prove that, whenever $dEnv \vdash \eta_0; Expr \Rightarrow \eta_1; \bar{n}$ holds and η_0 is well-formed, then η_1 is well-formed as well.

4   Path Analysis

4.1   Paths and Prefixes

We now define the notion of paths that is used in our static analysis. Observe that the paths used by the analysis are not the same as the paths in the target language. For example, they are rooted in a different way, and the steps need not coincide: if we added order to the store, we could add a following-sibling axis to the language, but approximate it with *parent::*/*child::* in the analysis.

Definition 8 (Static paths). *Static paths, or simply* paths, *are defined as follows.*

$$\mathbf{p} ::= () \mid loc \mid \mathbf{p}_0|\mathbf{p}_1 \mid \mathbf{p}/axis::ntest$$

where axis denotes any of the axes in the grammar.

Note that paths are always rooted at a given location. In addition, the particular fragment chosen here is such that important operations, notably intersection, can be checked using known algorithms [9,10].

Definition 9 (Path Semantics). *For a path* $\mathbf{p}$ *and store* σ, $[\![\mathbf{p}]\!]_\sigma$ *denotes the set of nodes selected from the store by the path with the standard semantics [18] except that order is ignored, and* R_σ *is used to interpret the locations loc. The following concepts are derived from the standard semantics:*

Inclusion. *A path* $\mathbf{p}_1$ *is included in* $\mathbf{p}_2$, *denoted* $\mathbf{p}_1 \subseteq \mathbf{p}_2$, *iff* $\forall \sigma: [\![\mathbf{p}_1]\!]_\sigma \subseteq [\![\mathbf{p}_2]\!]_\sigma$.

Disjointness. *Two paths* $\mathbf{p}_1, \mathbf{p}_2$ *are disjoint, denoted* $\mathbf{p}_1 \# \mathbf{p}_2$, *iff* $\forall \sigma: [\![\mathbf{p}_1]\!]_\sigma \cap [\![\mathbf{p}_2]\!]_\sigma = \emptyset$.

Prefixes. *For each path* $\mathbf{a}$ *we define pref($\mathbf{a}$) as follows.*

$\mathbf{a}$	loc	$\mathbf{p}/axis::ntest$	$\mathbf{p}\|\mathbf{q}$
$pref(\mathbf{a})$	$\{loc\}$	$\{\mathbf{p}/axis::ntest\} \cup pref(\mathbf{p})$	$\{\mathbf{p}\|\mathbf{q}\} \cup pref(\mathbf{p}) \cup pref(\mathbf{q})$

Prefix Closure. *For a path* **a** *we write prefclosed*(**a**) *iff* $\forall \mathbf{p}$: $\mathbf{p} \in pref(\mathbf{a}) \Rightarrow \mathbf{p} \subseteq \mathbf{a}$.

The *prefixes* of a path are all its initial subpaths, and a path is prefix-closed when it includes all of its prefixes. For example, the paths $/a//b | /a | /a//b/c$ and $/*| /a/b$ are both prefix-closed (the latter because $/a \subseteq /*$).

4.2 The Meaning of the Analysis

Definition 10 (Path analysis). *Given an expression Expr and a path environment* **pEnv** *which is a mapping from variables to paths, our path-analysis judgment*

$$\mathbf{pEnv} \vdash Expr \Rightarrow \mathbf{r}; \langle \mathbf{a}, \mathbf{u} \rangle$$

associates three paths to the expression: **r** *is an upper approximation of the nodes that are returned by the evaluation of Expr,* **a** *of those that are accessed, and* **u** *of those that are updated.*

The **r** path is not actually needed to check commutativity, but is used to infer **u** and **a** for those expression that update, or access, their argument.

There are many reasonable ways to interpret which nodes are "returned" and "accessed" by an expression. For example, a path $\$x//a$ only returns the $\$x$ descendants with an a name but, in a naive implementation, may access every descendant of $\$x$. Deciding what is "updated" is even trickier. This definition should be as natural as possible, should allow for an easy computation of a static approximation and, above all, should satisfy the following property: if what is accessed by $Expr_1$ is disjoint from what is accessed or updated by $Expr_2$, and vice-versa, then the two expressions commute.

In the following paragraphs we present our interpretation, which will guide the definition of the inference rules and is one of the basic technical contributions of this work.

The meaning of **r** seems the easiest to describe: an analysis is sound if $\mathbf{pEnv} \vdash Expr \Rightarrow \mathbf{r}; \langle \mathbf{a}, \mathbf{u} \rangle$ and $d\!Env \vdash \eta_0; Expr \Rightarrow \eta_1; \bar{n}$ imply that $\bar{n} \subseteq [\![\mathbf{r}]\!]_{\mathrm{apply}(\eta_1)}$. Unfortunately, this is simplistic. Consider the following example:

```
let $x := doc('u1')/a return (delete($x), $x/b)
```

Our rules bind a path $u1/a$ to $\$x$, and finally deduce a returned path $u1/a/b$ for the expression above. However, after *delete*($\$x$), the value of $\$x/b$ is not in $[\![\mathbf{p}]\!]_{\mathrm{apply}(\eta)}$ anymore; the best we can say it is that it is still in $[\![\mathbf{p}]\!]_{\mathrm{mrg}(\eta)}$. This is just an instance of a general "stability" problem: we infer something about a specific store history, but we need the same property to hold for the store in some future. We solve this problem by accepting that our analysis only satisfies $\bar{n} \subseteq [\![\mathbf{r}]\!]_{\mathrm{mrg}(\eta_1)}$, which is weaker than $\bar{n} \subseteq [\![\mathbf{r}]\!]_{\mathrm{apply}(\eta_1)}$ but is stable; we also generalize the notion to environments.

Definition 11 (Approximation). *A path* **p** *approximates a value* $\bar{n}$ *in the store history* η, *denoted* $\mathbf{p} \supseteq_\eta \bar{n}$, *iff* $\bar{n} \subseteq [\![\mathbf{p}]\!]_{\mathrm{mrg}(\eta)}$.

A path environment **pEnv** *approximates a dynamic environment* $d\!Env$ *in a store history* η, *denoted* $\mathbf{pEnv} \supseteq_\eta d\!Env$, *iff*

$$(\$x \mapsto \bar{n}) \in d\!Env \Rightarrow \exists \mathbf{b}. \ (\$x \mapsto \mathbf{b}) \in \mathbf{pEnv} \ and \ \mathbf{b} \supseteq_\eta \bar{n}$$

Thanks to this "merge" interpretation, a path denotes all nodes that are reached by that path, or were reached by the path in some past version of the current history. This approximation has little impact, because the merge interpretation of a history is still a well-formed store, where every node has just one parent and one name, hence the usual algorithms can be applied to decide path disjointness.

The approach would break if we had, for example, the possibility of moving a node from one parent to another. Formally, $mrg(\eta)$ may now contain nodes with two parents. In practice, one could not deduce, for example, that $(a/d)\#(b/c/d)$, because $\$x/a/d$ and $\$x/b/c/d$, if evaluated at different times, may actually return the same node, because its parent was moved from $\$x/a$ to $\$x/b/c$ in the meanwhile. Similarly, if nodes could be renamed, then node names would become useless in the process of checking path disjointness.

The commutativity theorem in Section 5 is based on the following idea: assume that $Expr_1$ transforms η_0 into (η_0, Δ) and only modifies nodes reachable through a path $\mathbf{u}$, while $Expr_2$ only depends on nodes reachable through $\mathbf{a}$, such that $\mathbf{u}\#\mathbf{a}$. Because $Expr_1$ only modifies nodes in $\mathbf{u}$, the histories η_0 and (η_0, Δ) are "the same" with respect to $\mathbf{a}$, hence we may evaluate $Expr_2$ either before or after $Expr_1$.

This is formalized by defining a notion of history equivalence wrt a path $\eta \sim_{\mathbf{p}} \eta'$, and by proving that the inferred $\mathbf{a}$ and $\mathbf{u}$ and the evaluation relation are related by the following soundness properties.

Parallel evolution from a-equivalent stores, first version:

$\eta_0' \sim_{\mathbf{a}} \eta_0$ and $dEnv \vdash \eta_0; Expr \Rightarrow (\eta_0, \Delta); \bar{n}$
imply $dEnv \vdash \eta_0'; Expr \Rightarrow (\eta_0', \Delta); \bar{n}$, i.e. the same $\bar{n}$ and Δ are produced.

Immutability out of u, first version:

$\forall \mathbf{c}: \mathbf{c}\#\mathbf{u}$ and $dEnv \vdash \eta_0; Expr \Rightarrow (\eta_0, \Delta); \bar{n}$
imply $\eta_0 \sim_{\mathbf{c}} (\eta_0, \Delta)$.

To define the right notion of path equivalence, consider the Comma rule

$$\frac{\mathbf{pEnv} \vdash Expr_1 \Rightarrow \mathbf{r}_1; \langle \mathbf{a}_1, \mathbf{u}_1 \rangle \qquad \mathbf{pEnv} \vdash Expr_2 \Rightarrow \mathbf{r}_2; \langle \mathbf{a}_2, \mathbf{u}_2 \rangle}{\mathbf{pEnv} \vdash Expr_1, Expr_2 \Rightarrow \mathbf{r}_1 | \mathbf{r}_2; \langle \mathbf{a}_1 | \mathbf{a}_2, \mathbf{u}_1 | \mathbf{u}_2 \rangle} \quad \text{(COMMA)}$$

The rule says that if $\eta_0' \sim_{\mathbf{a}_1 | \mathbf{a}_2} \eta_0$ then the evaluation of $Expr_1, Expr_2$ gives the same result in both η_0 and η_0'. Our equivalence over $\mathbf{p}$ will be defined as "$\forall \mathbf{p}' \in \text{pref}(\mathbf{p}). P(\mathbf{p}')$", so that $\eta_0' \sim_{\mathbf{a}_1 | \mathbf{a}_2} \eta_0$ implies $\eta_0' \sim_{\mathbf{a}_1} \eta_0$ and $\eta_0' \sim_{\mathbf{a}_2} \eta_0$. Hence, by induction, if we start the evaluation of $Expr_1, Expr_2$ from $\eta_0 \sim_{\mathbf{a}_1 | \mathbf{a}_2} \eta_0'$, then $Expr_2$ will be evaluated against (η_0, Δ) and (η_0', Δ), but we have still to prove that $\eta_0 \sim_{\mathbf{a}_2} \eta_0'$ implies $(\eta_0, \Delta) \sim_{\mathbf{a}_2} (\eta_0', \Delta)$. This is another instance of the "stability" problem. In this case, the simplest solution is the adoption of the following notion of path equivalence: two histories η_1 and η_2 are equivalent modulo a path $\mathbf{p}$, denoted $\eta_1 \sim_{\mathbf{p}} \eta_2$, iff:

$$\forall \mathbf{p}' \in \text{pref}(\mathbf{p}). \forall \Delta. \ [\![\mathbf{p}']\!]_{\text{apply}(\eta_1, \Delta)} = [\![\mathbf{p}']\!]_{\text{apply}(\eta_2, \Delta)}$$

The quantification on Δ makes this notion "stable" with respect to store evolution, which is extremely useful for our proofs, but the equality above actually implies that:

$$\forall \Delta. \ (wf(\eta_1, \Delta) \ \Rightarrow \ wf(\eta_2, \Delta)) \ \wedge \ (\forall \Delta. \ wf(\eta_2, \Delta) \ \Rightarrow \ wf(\eta_1, \Delta))$$

This is too strong, because, whenever two stores differ in one node, the Δ that creates the node can only be added to the store that is missing it. Similarly, it they differ in one edge, the Δ that inserts the edge can only be added to the store that is missing it. Hence, only identical stores can be extended with exactly the same set of Δ's.

So, we have to weaken the requirement. We first restrict the quantification to updates that only create nodes that are fresh in both stores. Moreover, we do not require that $wf(\eta_1, \Delta) \ \Rightarrow \ wf(\eta_2, \Delta)$, but only that, for every n of interest, a subset Δ' of Δ exists which can be used to extend η_1 and η_2 so to have n in both. The resulting notion of equivalence is preserved by every update in the language whose path does not intersect $pref(\mathbf{p})$; this notion is strong enough for our purposes ($\Delta' \subseteq^i \Delta$ means the Δ' creates and deletes the same edges as Δ, but the inserted edges are a subset).

Definition 12 (Store equivalence modulo a path). *Two stores σ_1 and σ_2 are equivalent modulo a path $\mathbf{p}$, denoted $\sigma_1 \sim_\mathbf{p} \sigma_2$, iff:*

$$\forall \mathbf{p}' \in pref(\mathbf{p}). \ \forall \Delta. \ created(\Delta) \# (N_{\sigma_1} \cup N_{\sigma_2}) \ \wedge \ n \in [\![\mathbf{p}']\!]_{apply(\sigma_1, \Delta)}$$
$$\Rightarrow \ \exists \Delta' \subseteq^i \Delta. \ n \in [\![\mathbf{p}']\!]_{apply(\sigma_1, \Delta')} \ \wedge \ n \in [\![\mathbf{p}']\!]_{apply(\sigma_2, \Delta')}$$
$$\forall \mathbf{p}' \in pref(\mathbf{p}). \ \forall \Delta. \ created(\Delta) \# (N_{\sigma_1} \cup N_{\sigma_2}) \ \wedge \ n \in [\![\mathbf{p}']\!]_{apply(\sigma_2, \Delta)}$$
$$\Rightarrow \ \exists \Delta' \subseteq^i \Delta. \ n \in [\![\mathbf{p}']\!]_{apply(\sigma_1, \Delta')} \ \wedge \ n \in [\![\mathbf{p}']\!]_{apply(\sigma_2, \Delta')}$$

Definition 13 (Store history equivalence modulo a path)

$$\eta_1 \sim_\mathbf{p} \eta_2 \ \Leftrightarrow_{def} \ apply(\eta_1) \sim_\mathbf{p} apply(\eta_2)$$

Since $[\![\mathbf{p}]\!]_{apply(\eta_1, \Delta)}$ is monotone wrt $\subseteq^i$, the above definition implies that:

$$\eta_1 \sim_\mathbf{p} \eta_2 \ \Rightarrow \ (\forall \Delta. \ wf(\eta_1, \Delta) \ \wedge \ wf(\eta_2, \Delta) \ \Rightarrow \ [\![\mathbf{p}]\!]_{apply(\eta_1, \Delta)} = [\![\mathbf{p}]\!]_{apply(\eta_2, \Delta)})$$

We are now ready for the formal definition of soundness.

Definition 14 (Soundness). *The static analysis $\mathbf{pEnv} \vdash Expr \Rightarrow \mathbf{r}; \langle \mathbf{a}, \mathbf{u} \rangle$ is sound for the semantic evaluation $dEnv \vdash \eta_0; Expr \Rightarrow \eta_1; \bar{n}$ iff for any well-formed $\eta_0, \eta_1, dEnv$, $\mathbf{pEnv}, Expr, \bar{n}, \mathbf{r}, \mathbf{a}, \mathbf{u}$, such that:*

$$\mathbf{pEnv} \vdash Expr \Rightarrow \mathbf{r}; \langle \mathbf{a}, \mathbf{u} \rangle$$
$$dEnv \vdash \eta_0; Expr \Rightarrow (\eta_0, \Delta); \bar{n}$$
$$\mathbf{pEnv} \supseteq_{\eta_0} dEnv$$

the following properties hold.

- **Approximation by $\mathbf{r}$:** $\mathbf{r}$ *is an approximation of the result:* $\mathbf{r} \supseteq_{\eta_1} \bar{n}$

- **Parallel evolution from $\mathbf{a}$-equivalent stores:** *For any store history η_0', if $\eta_0' \sim_\mathbf{a} \eta_0$ and $N_{\eta_0'} \# created(\Delta)$, then $dEnv \vdash \eta_0'; Expr \Rightarrow (\eta_0', \Delta); \bar{n}$*

– Immutability out of u: (1) $\mathbf{u} \supseteq_{\eta_1} updated(\Delta)$
    (2) $\forall prefclosed(\mathbf{c})$: $\mathbf{c}\#\mathbf{u} \;\Rightarrow\; \eta_0 \sim_{\mathbf{c}} (\eta_0, \Delta)$.

In the *Parallel evolution* property, the condition $N_{\eta_0'}\#created(\Delta)$ is needed because, if η_0' did already contain some of the nodes that are added by Δ, then it would be impossible to extend η_0' with Δ. This condition is not restrictive, and is needed because we identify nodes in different stores by the fact that they have the same identity. We could relate different store using a node morphism, rather that node identity, but that would make the proofs much heavier.

Immutability has two halves. The first, $\mathbf{u} \supseteq_{\eta_1} updated(\Delta)$, confines the set of edges that are updated to those that are in $\mathbf{u}$, and is important to prove that two updates commute if $\mathbf{u}_1\#\mathbf{u}_2$. The second half specifies that, for every $\mathbf{c}\#\mathbf{u}$, the store after the update is $\mathbf{c}$-equivalent to the store before. Together with *Parallel evolution*, it essentially says that after *Expr* is evaluated, the value returned by any expression *Expr*$_1$ that only accesses $\mathbf{c}$ is the same value returned by *Expr*$_1$ before *Expr* was evaluated, and is important to prove that an update and a query commute if $\mathbf{a}_1\#\mathbf{u}_2$. The path $\mathbf{c}$ must be prefix-closed for this property to hold. For example, according to our rules, $delete(/a/b)$ updates a path $\mathbf{u} = /a/b/descendant\text{-}ir\text{-}self::*$. It is disjoint from $\mathbf{c} = /a/b/..$, but still the value of $/a/b/..$ changes after $delete(/a/b)$. This apparent unsoundness arises because $\mathbf{c}$ is not prefix-closed. If we consider the prefix-closure $\mathbf{a} = /a|/a/b|/a/b/..$ of $/a/b/..$, we notice that $\mathbf{a}$ is *not* disjoint from $\mathbf{u}$.

4.3   Path Analysis Rules

We present the rules in two groups: selection and update rules.

Selection rules. These rules regard the querying fragment of our language. We extend the rules from [8] for the proper handling of updated paths.

The (Comma) rule has been presented above.

The (Var) rule specifies that variable access does not access the store. One may wonder whether $\mathbf{r}$ should not be regarded as "accessed" by the evaluation of $\$x$. The doubt is easily solved by referring to the definition of soundness: the value of $\$x$ is the same in two stores η_0 and η_0' independently of any equivalence among them, hence the accessed path should be empty. This rule also implicitly specifies that variable access commutes with any other expression. For example, $\$x, delete(\$x)$ is equivalent to $delete(\$x), \$x$.

$$\frac{(\$x \mapsto \mathbf{r}) \in \mathbf{pEnv}}{\mathbf{pEnv} \vdash \$x \;\Rightarrow\; \mathbf{r}; \, \langle (), () \rangle} \qquad \text{(VAR)}$$

The (Step) rule specifies that a step accesses the prefix closure of $\mathbf{r}$. Technically, the rule would still be sound if we only put $\mathbf{r}|(\mathbf{r}/axis::ntest)$ in the accessed set. However, the commutativity theorem relies on the fact that, for any expression, its inferred accessed path is prefix-closed, for the reasons discussed at the end of the previous section, and the addition of the prefix closure of $\mathbf{r}$ does not seem to seriously affect the analysis precision.

$$\frac{\mathbf{pEnv} \vdash Expr \;\Rightarrow\; \mathbf{r}; \, \langle \mathbf{a}, \mathbf{u} \rangle}{\mathbf{pEnv} \vdash Expr/axis::ntest \;\Rightarrow\; \mathbf{r}/axis::ntest; \, \langle pref(\mathbf{r}/axis::ntest)|\mathbf{a}, \mathbf{u} \rangle} \qquad \text{(STEP)}$$

Iteration binds the variable and analyses the body once. Observe that the analysis ignores the order and multiplicity of nodes.

$$\frac{\begin{array}{c} \mathbf{pEnv} \vdash \mathit{Expr}_1 \Rightarrow \mathbf{r}_1; \langle \mathbf{a}_1, \mathbf{u}_1 \rangle \\ (\mathbf{pEnv} + \$x \mapsto \mathbf{r}_1) \vdash \mathit{Expr}_2 \Rightarrow \mathbf{r}_2; \langle \mathbf{a}_2, \mathbf{u}_2 \rangle \end{array}}{\begin{array}{c} \mathbf{pEnv} \vdash \texttt{for } \$x \texttt{ in } \mathit{Expr}_1 \texttt{ return } \mathit{Expr}_2 \\ \Rightarrow \mathbf{r}_2; \langle \mathbf{a}_1 | \mathbf{a}_2, \mathbf{u}_1 | \mathbf{u}_2 \rangle \end{array}} \quad \text{(For)}$$

Element construction returns the unique constructor location, but there is no need to regard that location as accessed.

$$\frac{\begin{array}{c} \mathbf{pEnv} \vdash \mathit{Expr}_1 \Rightarrow \mathbf{r}_1; \langle \mathbf{a}_1, \mathbf{u}_1 \rangle \\ \mathbf{pEnv} \vdash \mathit{Expr}_2 \Rightarrow \mathbf{r}_2; \langle \mathbf{a}_2, \mathbf{u}_2 \rangle \end{array}}{\begin{array}{c} \mathbf{pEnv} \vdash \texttt{element}_{code\text{-}loc}\{\mathit{Expr}_1\}\{\mathit{Expr}_2\} \\ \Rightarrow code\text{-}loc; \langle \mathbf{a}_1 | \mathbf{a}_2, \mathbf{u}_1 | \mathbf{u}_2 \rangle \end{array}} \quad \text{(Elt)}$$

Local bindings just returns the result of evaluating the body, but the accesses and side effects of both subexpressions are both considered.

$$\frac{\begin{array}{c} \mathbf{pEnv} \vdash \mathit{Expr}_1 \Rightarrow \mathbf{r}_1; \langle \mathbf{a}_1, \mathbf{u}_1 \rangle \\ (\mathbf{pEnv} + \$x \mapsto \mathbf{r}_1) \vdash \mathit{Expr}_2 \Rightarrow \mathbf{r}_2; \langle \mathbf{a}_2, \mathbf{u}_2 \rangle \end{array}}{\mathbf{pEnv} \vdash \texttt{let } \$x := \mathit{Expr}_1 \texttt{ return } \mathit{Expr}_2 \Rightarrow \mathbf{r}_2; \langle \mathbf{a}_1 | \mathbf{a}_2, \mathbf{u}_1 | \mathbf{u}_2 \rangle} \quad \text{(Let)}$$

The conditional approximates the paths by merging the results of both branches.

$$\frac{\begin{array}{c} \mathbf{pEnv} \vdash \mathit{Expr} \Rightarrow \mathbf{r}_0; \langle \mathbf{a}_1, \mathbf{u}_1 \rangle \\ \mathbf{pEnv} \vdash \mathit{Expr}_1 \Rightarrow \mathbf{r}_1; \langle \mathbf{a}_2, \mathbf{u}_2 \rangle \\ \mathbf{pEnv} \vdash \mathit{Expr}_2 \Rightarrow \mathbf{r}_2; \langle \mathbf{a}_3, \mathbf{u}_3 \rangle \end{array}}{\begin{array}{c} \mathbf{pEnv} \vdash \texttt{if } (\mathit{Expr}) \texttt{ then } \mathit{Expr}_1 \texttt{ else } \mathit{Expr}_2 \\ \Rightarrow \mathbf{r}_1 | \mathbf{r}_2; \langle \mathbf{a}_1 | \mathbf{a}_2 | \mathbf{a}_3, \mathbf{u}_1 | \mathbf{u}_2 | \mathbf{u}_3 \rangle \end{array}} \quad \text{(If)}$$

Update rules. The second set of rules deals with update expressions.

The first rule is the one for delete. The "updated path" $\mathbf{u}$ is extended with all the descendants of $\mathbf{r}$ because $\mathbf{u}$ approximates those paths whose semantics may change after the expression is evaluated, and the semantics of each path in $\mathbf{r}/\mathit{descendant\text{-}or\text{-}self}::*$ is affected by the deletion. Assume, for example, that $(\$x \mapsto loc) \in \mathbf{pEnv}$, $(\$x \mapsto n) \in dEnv$, and n is the root of a tree of the form $\langle a \rangle \langle b \rangle \langle c/\rangle \langle b/\rangle \langle a/\rangle$.

The evaluation of `delete {$x/b}` would change the semantics of $\$x//c$, although this path does not explicitly traverse loc/b. This is correctly dealt with, since the presence of $loc/b/\mathit{descendant\text{-}or\text{-}self}::*$ in $\mathbf{u}$ means: every path that is not disjoint from $loc/b/\mathit{descendant\text{-}or\text{-}self}::*$ may be affected by this operation, and, by Definition 9, $loc//c$ is *not* disjoint from $loc/b/\mathit{descendant\text{-}or\text{-}self}::*$.

Observe that `delete {$x/b}` also affects expressions that do not end below $\$x/b$, such as "$\$x/b/..$". This is not a problem either, since the accessed path $\mathbf{a}$ computed for the expression $\$x/b/..$ is actually $loc|(loc/b)|(loc/b/..)$, and the second component is not disjoint from $loc/b/\mathit{descendant\text{-}or\text{-}self}::*$.

$$\frac{\mathbf{pEnv} \vdash \mathit{Expr} \Rightarrow \mathbf{r}; \langle \mathbf{a}, \mathbf{u} \rangle}{\mathbf{pEnv} \vdash \mathtt{delete}\ \{\mathit{Expr}\} \Rightarrow (); \langle \mathbf{a}, \mathbf{u} | (\mathbf{r}/\mathit{descendant\text{-}or\text{-}self}::*) \rangle}$$

(DELETE)

Similarly, $\mathtt{insert}\ \{\mathit{Expr}_1\}\ \mathtt{into}\ \{\mathit{Expr}_2\}$ may modify every path that ends with descendants of Expr_2. Moreover, it depends on all the descendants of Expr_1, since it copies all of them.

$$\frac{\mathbf{pEnv} \vdash \mathit{Expr}_1 \Rightarrow \mathbf{r}_1; \langle \mathbf{a}_1, \mathbf{u}_1 \rangle \qquad \mathbf{pEnv} \vdash \mathit{Expr}_2 \Rightarrow \mathbf{r}_2; \langle \mathbf{a}_2, \mathbf{u}_2 \rangle}{\begin{array}{c}\mathbf{pEnv} \vdash \mathtt{insert}\ \{\mathit{Expr}_1\}\ \mathtt{into}\ \{\mathit{Expr}_2\} \\ \Rightarrow (); \langle \mathbf{a}_1 | \mathbf{a}_2 | (\mathbf{r}_1/\mathit{descendant\text{-}or\text{-}self}::*), \mathbf{u}_1 | \mathbf{u}_2 | (\mathbf{r}_2//*) \rangle\end{array}}$$

(INSERTCHILD)

4.4 Soundness Theorem

Theorem 1 (Soundness of the analysis). *The static analysis rules presented in Section 4.3 are sound.*

Soundness is proved by induction, showing that the soundness properties are preserved by each rule. A detailed presentation of the soundness proof for the most important rules can be found in [16].

5 Commutativity Theorem

Our analysis is meant as a tool to prove for specific expressions whether they can be evaluated on a given store in any order or, put differently, whether they *commute*.

Definition 15 (Commutativity). *We shall use $[\![\mathit{Expr}]\!]_\eta^{dEnv}$ as a shorthand for the pair $(apply(\eta'), bag\text{-}of(\bar{n}))$ such that $dEnv \vdash \eta; \mathit{Expr} \Rightarrow \eta'; \bar{n}$, and where $bag\text{-}of(\bar{n})$ forgets the order of the nodes in $\bar{n}$.*

Two expressions Expr_1 and Expr_2 commute in $\mathbf{pEnv}$, written $\mathit{Expr}_1 \overset{\mathbf{pEnv}}{\longleftrightarrow} \mathit{Expr}_2$, iff, for all η and $dEnv$ such that $\mathbf{pEnv} \supseteq_\eta dEnv$, the following equality holds:

$$[\![\mathit{Expr}_1, \mathit{Expr}_2]\!]_\eta^{dEnv} = [\![\mathit{Expr}_2, \mathit{Expr}_1]\!]_\eta^{dEnv}$$

Hence, $\mathit{Expr}_1 \overset{\mathbf{pEnv}}{\longleftrightarrow} \mathit{Expr}_2$ means that the order of evaluation of Expr_1 and Expr_2 only affects the order of the result. We explicitly do not require that the order of the individual nodes updated by the expressions is preserved.

Theorem 2 (Commutativity). *Consider two expressions and their analyses in $\mathbf{pEnv}$:*

$$\mathbf{pEnv} \vdash \mathit{Expr}_1 \Rightarrow \mathbf{r}_1; \langle \mathbf{a}_1, \mathbf{u}_1 \rangle$$
$$\mathbf{pEnv} \vdash \mathit{Expr}_2 \Rightarrow \mathbf{r}_2; \langle \mathbf{a}_2, \mathbf{u}_2 \rangle$$

If the updates and accesses obtained by the analysis are independent then the expressions commute, in any environment that respects $\mathbf{pEnv}$:

$$\mathbf{u}_1 \# \mathbf{a}_2, \mathbf{a}_1 \# \mathbf{u}_2, \mathbf{u}_1 \# \mathbf{u}_2 \Rightarrow \mathit{Expr}_1 \overset{\mathbf{pEnv}}{\longleftrightarrow} \mathit{Expr}_2$$

Commutativity is our main result. The proof can be found in [16]. It follows the pattern sketched in Section 4, after Definition 11. The proof is far easier than the proof of soundness, and is essentially independent on the actual definition of the equivalence relation. It only relies on soundness plus the following five properties, where only *Stability* is non-trivial.

$$\mathbf{p} \supseteq_{\eta_0} \bar{n} \; \Rightarrow \; \mathbf{p} \supseteq_{\eta_0, \Delta} \bar{n} \qquad \text{(Stability)}$$

$$\text{for each } \mathbf{p}, \; \sim_{\mathbf{p}} \text{ is an equivalence relation} \qquad \text{(Equivalence)}$$

$$\mathbf{p}\#(\mathbf{q}_0|\mathbf{q}_1) \; \Leftrightarrow \; \mathbf{p}\#\mathbf{q}_0 \wedge \mathbf{p}\#\mathbf{q}_1 \qquad (|\#)$$

$$\eta_0 \sim_{(\mathbf{q}_0|\mathbf{q}_1)} \eta_1 \; \Rightarrow \; \eta_0 \sim_{\mathbf{q}_0} \eta_1 \qquad (|\sim)$$

$$\mathbf{q}_0 \subseteq \mathbf{q}_0|\mathbf{q}_1 \qquad (|\subseteq)$$

6 Related Work

Numerous update languages have been proposed in the last few years [1,2,3,4,5]. Some of the most recent proposals [5,7] are very expressive, as they provide the ability to observe the effect of updates during query evaluation. Although [7] limits the locations where updates occur, this has little impact on our static analysis which also works for a language where updates can occur anywhere in the query such as [5]. Very little work has been done so far on optimization or static analysis for such XML update languages, a significant exception being the work by Benedikt et al [4,13]. However, they focus on analysis techniques for a language based on snapshot semantics, while we consider a much more expressive language. A notion of path analysis was proposed in [8], which we extend here by considering side effects.

Independence between updates and queries has been studied in the relational context [11,12]. The problem becomes more difficult in the XML context because of the expressivity of existing XML query languages. In the relational case, the focus has been on trying to identify fragments of datalog for which the problem is decidable, usually by reducing the problem to deciding reachability. Instead, we propose a conservative approach using a technique based on paths analysis which works for arbitrary XML updates and queries. Finally, commutativity properties for tree operations are important in the context of transactions for tree models [14,15], but these papers rely on dynamic knowledge while we are interested in static commutativity properties, hence the technical tools involved are quite different.

7 Conclusion

In this paper, we have proposed a conservative approach to detect whether two expressions commute in an expressive XML update language with strict evaluation order and immediate update application. The approach relies on a form of path analysis which computes an upper bound for the nodes accessed or updated in an expression. As there is a growing need to extend XML languages with imperative features [7,5,19], we believe the kind of analysis we propose here will be essential for the long-term development of those languages. We are currently exploring the use of our commutativity analysis for the purpose of algebraic optimization of XML update languages.

References

1. Chamberlin, D., Florescu, D., Robie, J.: XQuery update facility. W3C Working Draft (2006)
2. Lehti, P.: Design and implementation of a data manipulation processor for an XML query processor, Technical University of Darmstadt, Germany, Diplomarbeit (2001)
3. Tatarinov, I., Ives, Z., Halevy, A., Weld, D.: Updating XML. In: SIGMOD. (2001)
4. Benedikt, M., Bonifati, A., Flesca, S., Vyas, A.: Adding updates to XQuery: Semantics, optimization, and static analysis. In: XIME-P'05. (2005)
5. Ghelli, G., Ré, C., Siméon, J.: XQuery!: An XML query language with side effects. In: DataX Workshop. Lecture Notes in Computer Science, Munich, Germany (2006)
6. Boag, S., Chamberlin, D., Fernandez, M.F., Florescu, D., Robie, J., Siméon, J.: XQuery 1.0: An XML query language (2006)
7. Carey, M., Chamberlin, D., Florescu, D., Robie, J.: Programming with XQuery. Draft submitted for publication (2006)
8. Marian, A., Simeon, J.: Projecting XML documents. In: Proceedings of International Conference on Very Large Databases (VLDB), Berlin, Germany (2003) 213–224
9. Benedikt, M., Fan, W., Kuper, G.M.: Structural properties of xpath fragments. Theor. Comput. Sci. 336(1) (2005) 3–31
10. Miklau, G., Suciu, D.: Containment and equivalence for a fragment of xpath. J. ACM 51(1) (2004) 2–45
11. Elkan, C.: Independence of logic database queries and updates. In: PODS. (1990) 154–160
12. Levy, A.Y., Sagiv, Y.: Queries independent of updates. In: 19th International Conference on Very Large Data Bases, August 24-27, 1993, Dublin, Ireland, Proceedings, Morgan Kaufmann (1993) 171–181
13. Benedikt, M., Bonifati, A., Flesca, S., Vyas, A.: Verification of tree updates for optimization. In: CAV. (2005) 379–393
14. Dekeyser, S., Hidders, J., Paredaens, J.: A transaction model for xml databases. World Wide Web 7(1) (2004) 29–57
15. Lanin, V., Shasha, D.: A symmetric concurrent b-tree algorithm. In: FJCC. (1986) 380–389
16. Ghelli, G., Rose, K., Siméon, J.: Commutativity analysis in XML update languages (2006) http://www.di.unipi.it/~ghelli/papers/UpdateAnalysis.pdf.
17. Fernández, M., Malhotra, A., Marsh, J., Nagy, M., Walsh, N.: XQuery 1.0 and XPath 2.0 data model (2006)
18. Wadler, P.: Two semantics of xpath. Discussion note for W3C XSLT Working Group (1999) http://homepages.inf.ed.ac.uk/wadler/papers/xpath-semantics/xpath-semantics.pdf.
19. Cooper, E., Lindley, S., Wadler, P., Yallop, J.: Links: Web programming without tiers (2006) Unpublished Manuscript.

Containment of Conjunctive Queries over Databases with Null Values⋆

Carles Farré[1], Werner Nutt[2], Ernest Teniente[1], and Toni Urpí[1]

[1] Departament de Llenguatges i Sistemes Informatics
Unversitat Politècnica de Catalunya, c/ Jordi Girona, 1–3
08034-Barcelona, Spain
{farre,teniente,urpi}@lsi.upc.edu
[2] Faculty of Computer Science, Free University of Bozen-Bolzano
Dominikanerplatz 3, I-39100 Bozen, Italy
nutt@inf.unibz.it

Abstract. We study containment of conjunctive queries that are evaluated over databases that may contain tuples with null values. We assume the semantics of SQL for single block queries with a SELECT DISTINCT clause. This problem ("null containment" for short) is different from containment over databases without null values and sometimes more difficult.

We show that null-containment for boolean conjunctive queries is NP-complete while it is Π_2^P-complete for queries with distinguished variables. However, if no relation symbol is allowed to appear more than twice, then null-containment is polynomial, as it is for databases without nulls. If we add a unary test predicate IS NULL, as it is available in SQL, then containment becomes Π_2^P-hard for boolean queries, while it remains in Π_2^P for arbitrary queries.

1 Introduction

Containment of queries is a key topic in database theory. The main motivation, which was already at the origin of containment studies, is query optimization. In their seminal paper, Chandra and Merlin developed a containment-based technique to minimize the number of joins in a query while retaining equivalence [3]. Other problems for which containment is relevant include transaction management [11], query rewriting [10], and verification of integrity constraints [6].

The study of query containment started off with conjunctive queries. Since then, the work has been extended to a wealth of query types, such as conjunctive queries with comparisons [8,18], queries with union and difference [15], datalog queries [16], conjunctive queries with negated atoms [11,17], aggregate queries [5], queries over semistructured data [1,2], and XPath queries [12].

Containment has been studied under several semantics. In most cases, authors assume that queries are evaluated under set semantics, that is, a query returns

---

⋆ This work was supported by the British EPSRC (Grant GR/SS44830/01 MAGIK-I) and the Spanish Ministerio de Educacion y Ciencia (Grant TIN 2005-05406).

T. Schwentick and D. Suciu (Eds.): ICDT 2007, LNCS 4353, pp. 389–403, 2007.

each answer item only once. Chaudhuri and Vardi considered containment under bag semantics, which allows tuples to occur more than once in an answer and is the semantics implemented in SQL database systems [4]. Another line of research considers the effect of integrity constraints such as functional dependencies or foreign key constraints on containment, which restrict the class of databases to consider [13].

All this work did not take into account null values, which are the means by which incomplete information is represented in SQL databases. In the presence of null values, SQL queries are evaluated in a way that makes the existing theory of containment inapplicable. The semantics of single block SELECT-FROM-WHERE queries is as follows [7]:

- a query returns values for those combinations of tuples for which the WHERE clause evaluates to *true*;
- an equality or a comparison involving null has the logical value *unknown*;
- a conjunction of conditions has the logical value *true* only if all conjuncts evaluate to *true*.

Example 1. As an example, consider the two queries Q, Q', which use a relation with the schema residence(loc, person):

Q: SELECT DISTINCT r1.loc
    FROM   residence r1, residence r2
    WHERE r1.loc = r2.loc

Q': SELECT DISTINCT r.loc
    FROM   residence r

According to the SQL semantics, the second query returns the projection of residence onto the attribute loc, which may include the value null. The first query, however, returns only loc-values of residence that pass the test "r1.loc = r2.loc". In other words, Q returns the non-null values in the projection of residence onto loc. As a consequence, Q and Q' are equivalent over databases that do not contain nulls. However, in the presence of nulls, Q is contained in Q', but not the other way round. □

In the present paper we study null containment of conjunctive queries, that is, containment under set semantics over databases that contain null values, where conditions involving nulls are evaluated as in SQL. Such queries can be equivalently expressed in SQL as single block queries with the keyword DISTINCT in the SELECT clause. Note that this is also the semantics of nested subqueries in EXISTS or IN clauses and of subqueries that are combined by the boolean operators UNION, INTERSECTION, or MINUS.

In Section 2, we fix our notation. Section 3 presents a general criterion for checking null-containment. In Section 4, we introduce J-homomorphisms, and show that the existence of a J-homomorphism is sufficient for null-containment while for boolean queries it is also necessary. We prove in Section 5 that null-containment is Π_2^P-complete in general, while we show in Section 6 that it is polynomial for queries with at most two occurrences of each predicate. Finally, in Section 7, we model SQL's built-in predicate IS NULL and show that in the presence of such null tests, null-containment becomes Π_2^P-hard for boolean queries while it remains in Π_2^P in the general case.

2 Preliminaries

A *term* (like s, t) is either a *constant* (like c, d) or a *variable* (like u, $v,\ldots, z$). A *predicate* symbol (like p, q, r) has an arity, which may be 0. An *atom* has the form $p(s_1,\ldots,s_n)$, where p is a predicate symbol with arity n. Denoting *tuples* of terms as $\bar{s}$ (and tuples of constants and variables as $\bar{c}$, $\bar{d}$, and $\bar{u}$, $\bar{v}$, etc.) we sometimes write atoms as $p(\bar{s})$. An atom is *ground* if it does not contain variables. If $a = p(s_1,\ldots,s_n)$ is an atom and $j \in [1,n]$, then $a[j]$ denotes the term occurring at position j in a, that is, $a[j] = s_j$.

A *condition* B is a list of atoms, written as $B = a_1, \ldots, a_n$, where $n \geq 0$. We sometimes view a condition as a set of atoms. In particular, if B' and B are conditions, we write $B' \subseteq B$ to express that each atom of B' occurs among the atoms of B.

A *conjunctive query* is a rule of the form $q(\bar{x}) \leftarrow B$, where $\bar{x}$ is a tuple of distinct variables. We often identify the query and the head predicate q, defined by the query. A conjunctive query is *boolean* if the head predicate has the arity 0. Distinguished and nondistinguished variables of q are defined as usual.

A *database* $\mathcal{D}$ is a finite set of ground atoms. The *carrier* of $\mathcal{D}$ is the set of constants occurring in the atoms of $\mathcal{D}$. An *assignment* over $\mathcal{D}$, say δ, for the query $q(\bar{x}) \leftarrow B$ is a mapping from the set of variables of q to the carrier of $\mathcal{D}$. For a constant c we define $\delta c := c$. Assignments are extended in the obvious way to complex syntactic objects such as tuples, atoms, conditions, etc. An atom a is *satisfied* by δ over $\mathcal{D}$ if $\delta a \in \mathcal{D}$ and a condition B is *satisfied* by δ if $\delta B \subseteq \mathcal{D}$. We say that B is satisfied over $\mathcal{D}$ if it is satisfied by some δ over $\mathcal{D}$. For a boolean query $q() \leftarrow B$, we say that q is satisfied over $\mathcal{D}$ if the body B is satisfied over $\mathcal{D}$.

A tuple of constants $\bar{d}$ is an *answer* over $\mathcal{D}$ to the query $q(\bar{x}) \leftarrow B$ if there exists an assignment δ such that (1) δ satisfies B, and (2) $\delta\bar{x} = \bar{d}$. The set of all answers to q over $\mathcal{D}$ is denoted as $q^{\mathcal{D}}$. Let q, q' be queries with the same arity. Then q is *contained* in q', written $q \subseteq q'$, if $q^{\mathcal{D}} \subseteq q'^{\mathcal{D}}$ for all databases $\mathcal{D}$.

A *substitution* is a mapping from a set of variables to a set of terms. Substitutions can be naturally extended to atoms and conditions. Let B, B' be conditions. A substitution γ for the variables of B' is a *condition homomorphism* from B' to B if $\gamma B' \subseteq B$. Suppose that q, q' are defined as $q(\bar{x}) \leftarrow B$, $q'(\bar{x}) \leftarrow B'$, respectively. Then γ is a *query homomorphism* from q' to q if γ is a condition homomorphism from B' to B and $\gamma\bar{x} = \bar{x}$. The Homomorphism Theorem for conjunctive queries says that q is contained in q' if and only if there exists a query homomorphism from q' to q [3].

3   Null-Containment

We adapt the framework of Section 2 to capture query evaluation over databases with nulls. We introduce a new constant $\bot$ to model the value `null` in SQL. The value $\bot$ may occur in databases, but not in queries.

Let B be a condition and y be a variable occurring in B. We say that y is a *join variable* of B if y has at least two occurrences in B and a *singleton variable* otherwise. An assignment δ *satisfies* B over $\mathcal{D}$ if (1) $\delta B \subseteq \mathcal{D}$ and (2) δ *respects join variables*, that is $\delta y \neq \bot$ for every join variable y of B. Note that this definition captures SQL's semantics of equalities involving `null`. A variable occurring at two positions in B corresponds in SQL notation to an equality between two (not necessarily distinct) attributes, which is only satisfied if the values of the attributes are identical and not `null`.

The set of answers to a query q over a database with nulls is defined as before and is denoted in the same way as $q^{\mathcal{D}}$. We say that q is *null-contained* in q' and write $q \subseteq_\bot q'$ if $q^{\mathcal{D}} \subseteq q'^{\mathcal{D}}$ for all databases $\mathcal{D}$, where $\mathcal{D}$ may contain the value $\bot$.

Example 2. The two rule-based queries

$$q(x) \leftarrow \texttt{residence}(x, y), \texttt{residence}(x, w)$$
$$q'(x) \leftarrow \texttt{residence}(x, y)$$

are translations of the SQL queries Q, Q' in Example 1. We see that the equality in the `WHERE` clause of Q is reflected by the join variable x in q. □

Clearly, null-containment implies containment. However, as seen in Example 1, the converse is not true. This raises the question in which way we can check null-containment and how difficult it is to decide this problem.

In the non-null case, a standard approach to checking whether q' contains q is to turn q into the *canonical database* $\mathcal{D}_q$, obtained from q by "freezing" the variables into constants (see for instance [17]). For instance, the canonical database for the query q in Example 2 is $\mathcal{D}_q = \{\texttt{residence}(x, y), \texttt{residence}(x, w)\}$ where for the sake of simplicity we have identified the variables of q with their frozen versions. We will do so also in the rest of the paper as long as no misunderstanding can arise. Clearly, q returns the tuple consisting of the frozen distinguished variables over $\mathcal{D}_q$. The test criterion says that q is contained in q' if also q' returns this tuple over $\mathcal{D}_q$. Note that for boolean queries this tuple is the empty tuple ().

Example 2 shows that this test cannot be used to decide null-containment because $x \in q^{\mathcal{D}_{q'}}$, although q is not null-contained in q'. Fortunately, we can modify the test so that it can be applied to the case of databases with nulls. A *null version* of $\mathcal{D}_q$ is a database $\mathcal{D}$ obtained from $\mathcal{D}_q$ by replacing some frozen variables of q with $\bot$. By some slight abuse of notation we represent null versions of $\mathcal{D}_q$ as instantiations $\theta \mathcal{D}_q$, where θ is a substitution that replaces some frozen non-join variables of q with $\bot$ and is the identity otherwise.

Theorem 1 (General Criterion). *Let $q(\bar{x})$, $q'(\bar{x})$ be conjunctive queries. Then q is null-contained in q' if and only if for every null version $\theta \mathcal{D}_q$ of $\mathcal{D}_q$, we have that q' returns the tuple $\theta \bar{x}$ over $\theta \mathcal{D}_q$.*

Proof. The proof of the theorem is straightforward. Clearly, if q is null-contained in q', then q' returns $\theta\bar{x}$ over $\theta\mathcal{D}_q$ because q returns $\theta\bar{x}$ over $\theta\mathcal{D}_q$.

Conversely, suppose $\mathcal{D}$ is an arbitrary database with nulls and q returns an answer $\bar{d}$ over $\mathcal{D}$. Let B, B' be the bodies of q, q', respectively. Then there is an assignment δ from the variables of B to the carrier of $\mathcal{D}$ such that δ respects join variables, $\delta B \subseteq \mathcal{D}$, and $\delta\bar{x} = \bar{d}$. We define a substitution θ such that $\theta y = \bot$ if $\delta y = \bot$ and θ is the identity otherwise. Thus, also θ respects join variables.

Due to our hypothesis, there is an assignment η for the variables of B' such that η respects join variables, $\eta B' \subseteq \theta\mathcal{D}_q$, and $\eta\bar{x} = \bar{x}$. We can view η also as a substitution if we identify variables and their frozen versions. Let $\delta' := \delta\eta$. Then it follows that δ' respects join variables because η does so and because δ maps no variable in θB to $\bot$. Moreover, $\delta' B' = \delta\eta B' \subseteq \delta B \subseteq \mathcal{D}$, and finally $\delta'\bar{x} = \delta\eta\bar{x} = \delta\bar{x} = \bar{d}$. This shows that δ' satisfies q' over $\mathcal{D}$ and $\delta'\bar{x} = \bar{d}$. $\square$

Corollary 1 (Upper Complexity Bound). *Null-containment of conjunctive queries is in Π_2^P.*

Proof. According to Theorem 1, we can check that q is *not* null-contained in q' by exhibiting a null-version $\theta\mathcal{D}_q$ of $\mathcal{D}_q$ where q' does not retrieve $\theta\bar{x}$. Deciding whether q' retrieves a specific tuple over a database with nulls is in NP. Thus, the complement of null-containment is in Σ_2^P. $\square$

Example 3. As a continuation of Example 2, consider the null-version $\mathcal{D}_0' := \{\text{residence}(\bot, \bot)\}$ of $\mathcal{D}_{q'}$. According to our definition of query answers, we have that $q^{\mathcal{D}_0'} = \emptyset$, hence q' is not null-contained in q.

4 Homomorphisms That Respect Join Variables

The general criterion of Theorem 1 is prohibitively complex. Therefore, we look for a simpler test, which may not completely characterize null-containment, but may serve as a sufficient criterion.

We say that a homomorphism γ from condition B' to B *respects join variables* if γ maps no join variable of B' to a singleton variable of B, that is, γ maps join variables to join variables or constants. A query homomorphism from q' to q is a *J-homomorphism* if it respects the join variables of the body of q'.

Proposition 1 (Sufficiency). *Let q, q' be conjunctive queries. If there exists a J-homomorphism from q' to q, then q is null-contained in q'.*

The proof resembles the one that existence of a homomorphism is a sufficient condition for containment.

Proposition 2 (NP-Completeness). *Existence of J-homomorphisms is NP-complete. This holds already for boolean conjunctive queries.*

The proof reduces containment to the existence of a J-homomorphism.

For the discussion of boolean queries we introduce some extra notation. For a query q, the substitution that maps every singleton variable of q to $\bot$ is denoted as $\theta_\bot$. The corresponding null version $\theta_\bot\mathcal{D}_q$ is denoted as $\mathcal{D}_q^\bot$.

Theorem 2 (Characterization for Boolean Queries). *Let q, q' be boolean conjunctive queries. Then q is null-contained in q' if and only if there exists a J-homomorphism from q' to q.*

Proof. We know by Proposition 1 that existence of a J-homomorphism is a sufficient condition. It remains to show the necessity.

Suppose that q, q' have the form $q() \leftarrow B$, $q'() \leftarrow B'$, respectively and that $q \subseteq_\perp q'$. By Theorem 1, there exists an assignment η for the variables of q' that satisfies q' over $\mathcal{D}_q^\perp$. We will use η to construct a J-homomorphism γ from q' to q.

We identify the substitution $\theta_\perp$ with the mapping that maps every atom $a \in B$ to the atom $\theta_\perp a \in \mathcal{D}_q^\perp$. Similarly, we identify η with the mapping that maps every atom $a' \in B'$ to $\eta a' \in \mathcal{D}_q^\perp$. The homomorphism γ will be defined in such a way that $\eta = \theta_\perp \gamma$.

We first define γ as a mapping from the atoms of B' to the atoms of B and then show that γ is induced by a substitution. We choose γ as an arbitrary mapping that maps an atom $a' \in B'$ to an atom $a \in B$ such that $\eta a' = \theta_\perp a$. In other words, γ has the property that $\gamma a' \in \theta_\perp^{-1}(\eta(a'))$ for every atom $a' \in B'$.

It follows from the definition that the relation symbols of a' and $\gamma(a')$ are identical. Moreover, if $a'[i] = c$ for some constant c, then $\eta(a')[i] = c$ and also $a[i] = c$ for every $a \in \theta_\perp^{-1}(\eta(a'))$, hence $\gamma(a')[i] = c$.

Now, consider two distinct atoms a', $b' \in B'$ such that $a'[i] = b'[j] = y$ for some variable y. It follows that $\eta(a')[i] = \eta(b')[j] = \eta y$. Since y is a join variable, we have $\eta y = s$ for some term $s \neq \perp$. Let $a := \gamma a'$ and $b := \gamma b'$. If s is a constant c, then $a[i] = b[j] = c$ by the definition of $\theta_\perp$. If $s = z$ for a (frozen) variable z, then z is a join variable of B and the definition of $\theta_\perp$ implies that $a[i] = b[j] = z$.

Thus, $a'[i] = b'[j]$ implies that $\gamma(a')[i] = \gamma(b')[j]$ for all atoms a', $b' \in B'$ and all positions i, j. Hence, γ is induced by a homomorphism, which we call γ, too. Also, since $\theta_\perp \gamma = \eta$ and η respects join variables, it follows that γ respects join variables. $\qquad\square$

Combining Proposition 2 and Theorem 2, we can precisely characterize the complexity of null-containment for boolean queries.

Corollary 2 (Complexity for Boolean Queries). *For boolean conjunctive queries null-containment is NP-complete.*

A closer inspection of the proof of Theorem 2 reveals that for boolean queries the general containment test of Theorem 1 can be simplified to one that uses only a single test database.

Proposition 3. *Let $q()$, $q'()$ be boolean conjunctive queries. Then q is null-contained in q' if and only if q' is satisfied by $\mathcal{D}_q^\perp$.*

5   Complexity of Null-Containment

The next example shows that the existence of a J-homomorphism is not a necessary condition for null-containment of general conjunctive queries.

Example 4. We consider the following two queries:

$$q(x) \leftarrow p(x, y_1, z_1), \ p(x_2, y_2, z_2), \ p(x_3, y_3, x_3),$$
$$r(y_1, z_1), \ r(y_1, z_2), \ r(y_2, x_3)$$
$$q'(x) \leftarrow p(x, v_1, w_1), \ p(u, v_2, w_2), \ p(u, v_3, w_3),$$
$$r(v_1, w_2).$$

To simplify our discussion we denote the atoms of q as $a_1, a_2, a_3, b_1, b_2, b_3$ and the atoms of q' as a_1', a_2', a_3', b', respectively. Thus, the two queries can be written as

$$q(x) \leftarrow a_1, a_2, a_3, b_1, b_2, b_3$$
$$q'(x) \leftarrow a_1', a_2', a_3', b'.$$

One easily checks that there exist exactly two query homomorphisms from q' to q. To see this, note that there is no choice in mapping a_1', since x has to be mapped to x. Then, there are two choices to map b', namely either to b_1 or to b_2. Depending on this choice, there is only one possibility to map a_2' and a_3'. In conclusion, the two mappings map the atoms of q' to the atoms of q as follows:

$$\gamma_1 = \{a_1' \mapsto a_1, \ a_2' \mapsto a_1, \ a_3' \mapsto a_1, \ b' \mapsto b_1\}$$
$$\gamma_2 = \{a_1' \mapsto a_1, \ a_2' \mapsto a_2, \ a_3' \mapsto a_2, \ b' \mapsto b_2\}.$$

None of the two mappings preserves the join variable u, since $\gamma_1 u = x$, and $\gamma_2 u = x_2$. There exists, however, a third substitution that is a homomorphism from the body of q' to the body of q, but which fails to be a query homomorphism, since it maps the distinguished variable x to x_2. This is the mapping

$$\gamma_3 = \{a_1' \mapsto a_2, \ a_2' \mapsto a_3, \ a_3' \mapsto a_3, \ b' \mapsto b_3\}.$$

Note that q' has three join variables, namely u, v_1, and w_2, and that all three substitutions map v_1 and w_2 to join variables of q. Moreover, γ_3 also maps u to the join variable x_3.

We will see in the following that q is null-contained in q'. Let $\mathcal{D}$ be a database and d an answer retrieved by q over $\mathcal{D}$. Then there is an assignment δ such that $\delta x = d$ and δ satisfies the body of q. We distinguish between three cases and show that in each case also q' retrieves d:

1. If $\delta x \neq \perp$, then $\delta \gamma_1$ satisfies the body of q' and $\delta \gamma_1 x = d$.
2. If $\delta x = \perp$ and $\delta x_2 \neq \perp$, then $\delta \gamma_2$ satisfies the body of q' and $\delta \gamma_2 x = d$.
3. If $\delta x = \perp$ and $\delta x_2 = \perp$, then $\delta \gamma_3$ satisfies the body of q' and $\delta \gamma_3 x = \delta x_2 = \perp = \delta x = d$.

Note that in the third case the reason why q' retrieves $\perp$ is that δ binds the non-distinguished variable x_2 to $\perp$ instead of binding x to $\perp$.   □

The queries of Example 4 will be a crucial ingredient for a reduction that proves Π_2^P-hardness of null-containment for conjunctive queries.

We reduce the problem of deciding the validity of quantified boolean formulas with a prefix of the form $\forall^*\exists^*$ to the null-containment problem. We note that the former problem is already Π_2^P-complete if the matrix is a conjunction of 3-clauses. Let

$$\Phi = \forall y_1 \ldots \forall y_l \exists z_1 \ldots \exists z_m \phi_1 \wedge \ldots \wedge \phi_n \tag{1}$$

be such a formula, where each ϕ_k is a 3-clause containing variables among the y_i and z_j.

We denote the values "true" and "false" as t and f and we identify the truth values with constants that are interpreted as "true" and "false", respectively.

The validity of Φ can be rephrased as the satisfiability of a set of formulas derived from Φ. Let $\alpha\colon \{y_1, \ldots, y_l\} \to \{\mathsf{t}, \mathsf{f}\}$ be a truth value assignment. If ψ is a propositional formula, we denote with ψ^α the formula obtained from ψ by replacing each variable y_i with the constant αy_i. Let us denote the matrix of Φ as $\phi := \phi_1 \wedge \ldots \wedge \phi_n$. Then Φ is valid if and only if for every $\alpha\colon \{y_1, \ldots, y_l\} \to \{\mathsf{t}, \mathsf{f}\}$ the formula ϕ^α is satisfiable.

We construct two conjunctive queries q, q' such that q is null-contained in q' if and only if Φ is valid. The two queries have the form

$$q(x_1, \ldots, x_l) \leftarrow G_1, \ldots, G_l, C_1, \ldots, C_n \tag{2}$$

$$q'(x_1, \ldots, x_l) \leftarrow G'_1, \ldots, G'_l, C'_1, \ldots, C'_n, \tag{3}$$

with conditions G_k, G'_k, C_j, C'_j. Intuitively, the pair of conditions C_j, C'_j encodes which bindings of the variables in the clause ϕ_j actually satisfy ϕ_j while the pair G_k, G'_k together with the distinguished variable x_i generates bindings of y_i to t and f.

We first define the C_k and C'_k. Let u_1, u_2, u_3 be the variables occurring in ϕ_k. We introduce a new ternary relation symbol cl_k and define

$$C'_k := cl_k(u_1, u_2, u_3). \tag{4}$$

Out of the eight possible truth value assignments for the three variables, there are seven, say $\beta_1, \ldots, \beta_7$, that satisfy the clause ϕ_k. We define

$$C_k := cl_k(\beta_1 u_1, \beta_1 u_2, \beta_1 u_3), \ldots, cl_k(\beta_7 u_1, \beta_7 u_2, \beta_7 u_3). \tag{5}$$

For instance, if

$$\phi_k = \neg y_2 \vee y_3 \vee \neg z_1,$$

then only the assignment $\{y_2 \mapsto \mathsf{t}, y_3 \mapsto \mathsf{f}, z_1 \mapsto \mathsf{t}\}$ does not satisfy ϕ_k. Hence,

$$C'_k = cl_k(y_2, y_3, z_1)$$
$$C_k = cl_k(\mathsf{f}, \mathsf{f}, \mathsf{f}),\; cl_k(\mathsf{f}, \mathsf{f}, \mathsf{t}),\; cl_k(\mathsf{f}, \mathsf{t}, \mathsf{f}),\; cl_k(\mathsf{f}, \mathsf{t}, \mathsf{t}),$$
$$cl_k(\mathsf{t}, \mathsf{f}, \mathsf{f}),\; cl_k(\mathsf{t}, \mathsf{t}, \mathsf{f}),\; cl_k(\mathsf{t}, \mathsf{t}, \mathsf{t}).$$

Consider a substitution θ for the variables y_i, z_j, where $i \in [1, l]$ and $j \in [1, m]$, such that θ maps every variable either to t or to f. Obviously, such a substitution can be viewed as a truth value assignment for the variables and vice versa. Moreover, by construction we have for each $k \in [1, n]$ that $\theta C'_k \subseteq C_k$ if and only if the corresponding assignment satisfies ϕ_k.

Next, consider a fixed index $i \in [1, l]$. We define the G_i and G'_i by modifying the bodies of the queries in Example 4. More specifically, the body of q will give rise to G_i and the body of q' to G'_i. To this end, we introduce a ternary relation p_i and a binary relation r_i and turn every atom for p and r into one for p_i and r_i, respectively. We do so by renaming the output variable x as x_i, instantiating y_1 and y_2 by t and f, respectively. and renaming v_1 as y_i. All other variables are renamed by adding the number i to their subscript. Thus, G_i and G'_i look as follows

$$G_i = p_i(\boxed{x_i}, \boxed{t}, z_{i1}), \; p_i(x_{i2}, \boxed{f}, z_{i2}), \; p_i(x_{i3}, y_{i3}, x_{i3}),$$
$$r_i(\boxed{t}, z_{i1}), \; r_i(\boxed{t}, z_{i2}), \; r_i(\boxed{f}, x_{i3})$$
$$G'_i = p_i(\boxed{x_i}, \boxed{y_i}, w_{i1}), \; p_i(u_i, v_{i2}, w_{i2}), \; p_i(u_i, v_{i3}, w_{i3}),$$
$$r_i(y_i, w_{i2}),$$

where we have highlighted the terms that have been introduced as replacements of x, y_1, y_2 and v_1. It follows from the discussion of Example 4, that any homomorphism from G'_i to G_i either maps y_i to t or to f and that the homomorphisms mapping y_i to t are exactly the ones that map x_i to x_i.

Lemma 1. *Let Φ be a quantified boolean formula as in Equation (1) and q, q' be a pair of conjunctive queries encoding Φ as in Equations (2) and (3). Then*

$$\Phi \text{ is valid} \quad \Longleftrightarrow \quad q \subseteq_{\perp} q'.$$

Theorem 3 (Complexity of Null-Containment). *Null-containment of conjunctive queries is Π_2^P-complete.*

6   Binary Queries

A conjunctive query that for every predicate contains at most two atoms with that predicate in its body is called *binary*. Sagiv and Saraiya have shown that containment of binary queries is polynomial [14]. We prove that this extends to null-containment.

We show first that for the class of binary queries the existence of a J-homomorphism is also a necessary condition for null-containment. This holds already if only the containee is binary.

Theorem 4. *Let q, q' be conjunctive queries such that $q \subseteq_{\perp} q'$. If q is binary, then there exists a J-homomorphism from q' to q.*

Proof. If q, q' are boolean queries, then the claim follows from Proposition 2. Suppose, therefore, that the queries have the form $q'(\bar{x}) \leftarrow B'$, $q(\bar{x}) \leftarrow B$, where the tuple $\bar{x}$ is nonempty.

Since $q \subseteq_\perp q'$, it follows that $q \subseteq q'$. Hence, there exists a homomorphism from q' to q. Let $\gamma_1, \ldots, \gamma_n$ be all the homomorphisms from q' to q. We want to show that one of the γ_i preserves join variables.

The proof is by contradiction. We assume that each γ_i maps some join variable of B' to a singleton variable in B. We say a null version $\theta \mathcal{D}_q$ of $\mathcal{D}_q$ is a *witness* for this fact if for every $i \in [1, n]$ there is a join variable y of B' such that $\theta \gamma_i y = \perp$, that is, if every γ_i maps some join variable of B' to a singleton variable of B that is mapped to $\perp$ by θ. There is at least one witness, namely the null version $\theta_\perp \mathcal{D}_q$ defined by the substitution $\theta_\perp$ that maps every singleton variable of B to $\perp$.

We introduce a partial order on null versions of $\mathcal{D}_q$ by defining $\theta_1 \mathcal{D}_q \preceq \theta_2 \mathcal{D}_q$ if $\theta_1 z = \perp$ implies $\theta_2 z = \perp$ for all variables z occurring in B. Let $\mathcal{D}_0 := \theta_0 \mathcal{D}_q$ be a witness that is minimal with respect to "$\preceq$". Note that, due to the minimality of $\mathcal{D}_0$, for every variable z with $\theta_0 z = \perp$, there is a homomorphism γ_i such that $\gamma_i y = z$ for some join variable y of B'. If there were a z without this property, then we could redefine $\theta_0 z := z$ while still retaining a witness, contrary to the minimality of $\mathcal{D}_0$.

Clearly, q retrieves $\theta_0 \bar{x}$ over $\mathcal{D}_0$. Since $q \subseteq_\perp q'$, there exists an assignment η for the variables in B' such that (1) η satisfies B' over $\mathcal{D}_0$ and (2) $\eta \bar{x} = \theta_0 \bar{x}$. Moreover, since $\mathcal{D}_0$ is a witness, we also have that (3) $\eta \neq \theta_0 \gamma_i$ for all $i \in [1, n]$.

The assignment η has the property that $\eta B' \subseteq \mathcal{D}_0$ and η maps some singleton variables of B' to $\perp$. The database $\mathcal{D}_0$ has been obtained from $\mathcal{D}_q$ by applying θ_0, which maps some frozen singleton variables in $\mathcal{D}_q$ to $\perp$. Thus, each $\perp$ in $\mathcal{D}_0$ replaces a singleton variable in $\mathcal{D}_q$. As a consequence, there is a substitution ρ such that $\rho B' \subseteq B$ and η can be factorized as $\eta = \theta_0 \rho$.

Thus, ρ satisfies B' over $\mathcal{D}_q$. However, ρ cannot map $\bar{x}$ to $\bar{x}$ because then it would be a query homomorphism. Note that, in general, ρ is not uniquely determined. In summary, the following facts hold for ρ: (1) ρ satisfies B' over $\mathcal{D}_q$, (2) $\theta_0 \rho$ satisfies B' over $\mathcal{D}_0$, (3) $\theta_0 \rho \bar{x} = \theta_0 \bar{x}$, and (4) $\rho \bar{x} \neq \bar{x}$.

The above implies that $\rho x \neq x$ for some x in $\bar{x}$. For this x we have that $\theta_0 x = \perp$, since otherwise $\theta_0 \rho x = \theta_0 x$ could not hold. Thus, $\theta_0 \bar{x}$ has at least one occurrence of $\perp$. Moreover, ρx is a variable, say v, since otherwise $\theta_0 \rho x = \theta_0 x = \perp$ could not hold. In summary, there are two singleton variables x, v occurring in B such that (1) x occurs in $\bar{x}$, (2) $\rho x = v$, and (3) $\theta_0 x = \theta_0 v = \perp$.

From $\eta x = \theta_0 \rho x = \perp$ we conclude that x is also a singleton variable in B'. Hence, there is a unique atom a' in B' containing x. Given that x is a distinguished variable, there is a unique atom a_1 in B such that $a_1 = \gamma_i a'$ for all $i \in [1, n]$, and given that $v \neq x$, there is a unique atom a_2 in B such that $a_2 = \rho a'$.

Suppose that a' has the predicate p and that x occurs in a' at position j, that is, $a'[j] = x$. Then a_1 and a_2 have the predicate p, too. Moreover, $a_1[j] = x$ and $a_2[j] = v$, which implies that $(\theta_0 a_1)[j] = (\theta_0 a_2)[j] = \perp$ in $\mathcal{D}_0$.

Since $\mathcal{D}_0$ is a minimal witness, B' contains a join variable, say y, such that $\gamma_i y = x$ for some $i \in [1, n]$. The variable x being a singleton, we conclude that in B' there is an atom b' such that $b'[j] = y$, and b' has the predicate p, too.

Given that q is binary, there are only two atoms in $\mathcal{D}_0$ to which b' can be mapped by the assignment η, namely $\theta_0 a_1$ and $\theta_0 a_2$. However, both atoms contain the value $\bot$ at position j, which contradicts the requirement that $\eta y \neq \bot$, since y is a join variable.   □

Next, we introduce a simple transformation of queries that will allow us to reduce the existence check for J-homomorphisms to the one for simple homomorphisms. For every relational query $q(\bar{x})$ we define a query $\hat{q}(\bar{x})$, the *J-transform* of q, as follows:

- for every predicate p occurring in the body of q we introduce a new predicate $\hat{p}$ of the same arity;
- for every atom $a = p(\bar{c}, \bar{y}, \bar{z})$ in the body of q, where $\bar{c}$ are the constants in a, $\bar{y}$ are the join variables in a, and $\bar{z}$ are the singleton variables in a, we construct the atom $\hat{a} := \hat{p}(\bar{c}, \bar{y}, \bar{w})$, where $\bar{w}$ are fresh variables;
- if q has the body B, then $\hat{q}$ has the body $B, \hat{B}$, where $\hat{B}$ contains for every $a \in B$ the corresponding $\hat{a}$.

Example 5. Consider the two queries

$$q(x) \leftarrow r(x, z_1)$$
$$q'(x) \leftarrow r(x, z_1), r(x, z_2).$$

The corresponding J-transforms are

$$\hat{q}(x) \leftarrow r(x, z_1), \hat{r}(w, w_1)$$
$$\hat{q}'(x) \leftarrow r(x, z_2), r(x, z_3), \hat{r}(x, w_2), \hat{r}(x, w_3).$$

Note that x is a singleton variable in q and therefore the variable w has been introduced as a duplicate of x in $\hat{q}$.   □

Lemma 2 (J-Transform). *Let q, q' be two relational conjunctive queries. There is a J-homomorphism from q' to q if and only if there is a query homomorphism from $\hat{q}'$ to $\hat{q}$.*

Theorem 5 (Polynomiality for Binary Queries). *For binary queries, null-containment can be decided in polynomial time.*

Proof. By Lemma 2, null-containment of conjunctive queries can be reduced to the containment of their J-transforms. Clearly, the J-transform of a binary query is again binary. As shown in [14], containment can be checked in polynomial time for binary queries.   □

7   Null Tests

Our SQL-like semantics of conjunctive queries allows us to enforce that a variable y be bound only to non-null values. To see this, suppose that $p(y, \bar{z})$ is an atom in a condition B. Let B' be obtained from B by adding an atom $p(y, \bar{w})$, where $\bar{w}$ is a tuple of fresh variables. If $\mathcal{D}$ is a database, then an assignment δ satisfies B' over $\mathcal{D}$ if and only if δ satisfies B over $\mathcal{D}$ and $\delta y \neq \bot$.

Also SQL allows one, by writing "att IS NULL", to test whether the value of an attribute att is null. We model this facility to test for null by introducing a unary built-in predicate *isNull*, which can appear in conditions, but not in databases. Atoms with a predicate other than *isNull* are *relational*. A condition B is *safe* if for every atom *isNull*(y) in B we have that (1) y occurs also in a relational atom of B and (2) y is a singleton variable of B. We only consider queries with safe bodies. An assignment δ *satisfies isNull*(y) if $\delta y = \bot$.

Null-containment of conjunctive queries with *isNull* can be decided using null versions of canonical databases as in Theorem 1. The difference is that (1) a canonical database $\mathcal{D}_q$ contains only the frozen *relational* atoms of q and (2) null versions $\theta \mathcal{D}_q$ can only be obtained from substitutions θ such that $\theta y = \bot$ whenever *isNull*(y) occurs in the body of q.

A substitution γ is a *homomorphism* or *J-homomorphism* between queries with null tests if γ is a homomorphism or J-homomorphism, respectively, when *isNull* is treated like a relational predicate. We say that γ is a *relational homomorphism* if γ is a homomorphism when we ignore all *isNull* atoms. It is straightforward to check that the existence of a J-homomorphism continues to be a sufficient condition for null-containment.

However, as the following example shows, the existence of a J-homomorphism is no longer a necessary condition for null-containment of boolean queries with null tests. The intuitive reason is that adding null tests allows us to express alternatively that a variable must be bound to null or that it must be bound to a non-null value. This is a form of negation, which forces us to make case analyses when checking containment.

The reader will verify that examples and proofs in this section can be amended in a straightforward way to yield results for other extensions of conjunctive queries that allow one to express the negation of specific atoms. Two examples for such extensions are negation of atoms and comparisons. While it is well-known that containment is Π_2^P-hard in the presence of comparisons [18], to the best of our knowledge this has not yet been proven for negated atoms.

Example 6. Consider the queries

$$q() \leftarrow p(c, v_1),\, p(c, v_2),\, p(v_1, v_2),\, p(v_2, v_3),$$
$$r(v_1, z_1),\, isNull(z_1),$$
$$r(v_2, z_2),$$
$$r(v_3, z_3),\, r(z_4, z_3)$$

$$q'() \leftarrow p(c, u_1),\, p(u_1, u_2),$$
$$r(u_1, w_1),\, isNull(w_1),$$
$$r(u_2, w_2),\, r(w_3, w_2).$$

Note that graphically, the first three p-atoms of q form a triangle, while the fourth p-atom extends the triangle at the variable v_2. Each variable v_i is connected to a variable z_i by the predicate r. The p-atoms in q' form a path of length 2. Analogously to the situation in q, each variable u_j is connected by the predicate r to a variable w_j. The conditions on w_1, w_2 in q' require that u_1 be connected by r to a null value and u_2 to a non-null value. The conditions on z_1, z_2, z_3 in q require that v_1 be connected to a null value, v_3 to a non-null value, and v_2 to a value that may be null, but need not.

Clearly, there is no J-homomorphism from q' to q. Such a substitution would have to contain the mappings $[u_1/v_1, w_1/z_1, u_2/v_2]$. This partial substitution cannot be extended to a J-homomorphism because w_2 is a join variable, which cannot be mapped to the singleton variable z_2.

Nonetheless, $q \subseteq_\perp q'$, which can be seen by considering the two substitutions

$$\gamma_1 = [u_1/v_1, w_1/z_1, u_2/v_2, w_2/z_2, w_3/v_2]$$
$$\gamma_2 = [u_1/v_2, w_1/z_2, u_2/v_3, w_2/z_3, w_3/v_3].$$

Clearly, γ_1 and γ_2 are relational homomorphisms. Let $\mathcal{D}$ be a database and δ be an assignment that satisfies q over $\mathcal{D}$. Then one checks that $\delta\gamma_1$ satisfies q' if $\delta z_2 \neq \perp$ and $\delta\gamma_2$ satisfies q' if $\delta z_2 = \perp$. □

The Π_2^P-hardness proof in this section is based on a similar idea as the one in Section 5. We translate a quantified boolean formula as in Equation 1 into two boolean queries

$$q() \leftarrow H_1, \ldots, H_l, C_1, \ldots, C_n \tag{6}$$
$$q'() \leftarrow H'_1, \ldots, H'_l, C'_1, \ldots, C'_n, \tag{7}$$

where the C_k and C'_k are defined as in Equations (5) and (4), respectively.

The conditions H_i, H'_i play the role of generators of assignments for the variables y_i and are defined as modifications of the bodies of the queries in Example 6, obtained by parameterising predicates and variables with the index i, and substituting variables v_2, v_3 in q by t and f, respectively, and by substituting u_2 with y_i. Thus, H_i and H'_i look as follows:

$$H_i = p_i(c, v_{i1}),\ p_i(c, \boxed{\mathsf{t}}),\ p_i(v_{i1}, \boxed{\mathsf{t}}),\ p_i(\boxed{\mathsf{t}}, \boxed{\mathsf{f}}),$$
$$\qquad r_i(v_{i1}, z_{i1}),\ isNull(z_{i1}),\ r_i(\boxed{\mathsf{t}}, z_{i2}),\ r_i(\boxed{\mathsf{f}}, z_{i3}),\ r_i(z_{i4}, z_{i3})$$
$$H'_i = p_i(c, u_{i1}),\ p_i(u_{i1}, \boxed{y_i}),$$
$$\qquad r_i(u_{i1}, w_{i1}),\ isNull(w_{i1}),\ r_i(\boxed{y_i}, w_{i2}),\ r_i(w_{i3}, w_{i2}).$$

Lemma 3. *Let Φ be a quantified boolean formula as in Equation (1) and q, q' be a pair of boolean queries encoding Φ as in Equations (6) and (7) Then*

$$\Phi \text{ is valid} \qquad \Longleftrightarrow \qquad q \subseteq_\perp q'.$$

Corollary 3. *The null-containment problem for boolean conjunctive queries with null tests is Π_2^P-complete.*

Corollary 4. *The containment problem for boolean conjunctive queries with negated atoms is Π_2^P-hard.*

Proof. We modify Example 6 by first dropping all r-atoms and all null tests. Then we add in q and in q' the atoms $p'(u_1)$ and $\neg p'(u_2)$. For the new queries, one shows $q \subseteq q'$ by a similar argument as above.

Based on the modified example, we encode a quantified boolean formula as in Equation (1) into a containment problem for conjunctive queries with negated atoms. The reduction and the proof of the corresponding lemma are analogous to the ones for queries with null tests. □

8   Conclusion

Query containment has been studied extensively for a variety of query types and semantics. However, the fact that real databases contain null values has been widely ignored by this work. We feel that it is important to understand the effect of null values on containment if one wants to apply containment based techniques in realistic scenarios. Moreover, containment plays a key role in information integration, where it is increasingly likely to encounter data sets with null values after merging heterogeneous data sources.

In the present paper, we have concentrated on relational conjunctive queries because it is in this basic setting that the most crucial differences to the classical non-null results become apparent. A characterization of null-containment in terms of homomorphisms, analogous to the classical case, is only possible for boolean queries, while for queries with distinguished variables null-containment is strictly more complex than containment. A similar characterization, using homomorphisms, exists for queries with at most two atoms per predicate, while an example shows that it no longer holds for queries with three atoms per predicate. Adding an SQL style IS NULL test creates a limited form of negation, which resembles the one introduced by comparisons like $y > 1$ and $y \leq 1$, or by the negation of relational atoms. These additional constructs raise complexity to Π_2^P-completeness, which was already known for comparisons [18].

Containment of conjunctive queries over databases with null values can be reduced to containment of conjunctive queries with disequations over regular databases. The fact that a join variable x cannot be bound to $\perp$ can be expressed by adding to the query body a disequation $x \neq \perp$. Since it is known that containment of conjunctive queries with disequations is Π_2^P-complete, this yields an alternative proof for Corollary 1 in the present paper. The Π_2^P lower bound for null-containment in Theorem 3 yields also the new result that containment of conjunctive queries with disequations is already Π_2^P-hard if all disequations are of the form $x \neq c$ with a single constant c, which complements the lower bounds in [9,18].

Acknowledgment

We would like to thank an anonymous referee for pointing out the relationship of our work and the one on queries with disequalities.

References

1. D. Calvanese, G. D. Giacomo, M. Lenzerini, and M. Y. Vardi. Containment of conjunctive regular path queries with inverse. In *Proc. 7th KR*, pages 176–185, 2000.
2. D. Calvanese, G. D. Giacomo, and M. Y. Vardi. Decidable containment of recursive queries. In *Proc. 9th ICDT*, pages 1–18, 2003.
3. A. Chandra and P. Merlin. Optimal implementation of conjunctive queries in relational databases. In *Proc. 9th STOC*, 1977.
4. S. Chaudhuri and M. Vardi. Optimization of real conjunctive queries. In *Proc. 12th PODS*, 1993.
5. S. Cohen, W. Nutt, and Y. Sagiv. Containment of aggregate queries. In *Proc. 9th ICDT*, 2003.
6. M. Fernandez, D. Florescu, A. Levy, and D. Suciu. Verifying integrity constraints on web-sites. In *Proc. 16th IJCAI*, pages 614–619, 1999.
7. H. Garcia-Molina, J. Ullman, and J. Widom. *Database Systems: The Complete Book*. Pearson Education International, 2002.
8. A. Klug. On conjunctive queries containing inequalities. *J. ACM*, 35(1):146–160, 1988.
9. P. Kolaitis, D. Martin, and M. Thakur. On the complexity of the containment problem for conjunctive queries with built-in predicates. In *Proc. 17th PODS*, pages 197–204, 1998.
10. A. Levy, A. Mendelzon, Y. Sagiv, and D. Srivastava. Answering queries using views. In *Proc. 14th PODS*, pages 95–104, 1995.
11. A. Levy and Y. Sagiv. Queries independent of updates. In *Proc. 19th VLDB*, pages 171–181, 1993.
12. G. Miklau and D. Suciu. Containment and equivalence for an XPath fragment. In *Proc. 21st PODS*, pages 65–76, 2002.
13. L. Popa and V. Tannen. An equational chase for path-conjunctive queries, constraints, and views. In *Proc. 7th ICDT*, pages 39–57, 1999.
14. Y. Sagiv and Y. Saraiya. Minimizing restricted-fanout queries. *Discrete Applied Mathematics*, 40:245–264, 1992.
15. Y. Sagiv and M. Yannakakis. Equivalence among relational expressions with the union and difference operators. *J. ACM*, 27(4):633–655, 1981.
16. O. Shmueli. Equivalence of datalog programs is undecidable. *Theoretical Computer Science*, 15(3):231–242, 1993.
17. J. Ullman. Information integration using logical views. In *Proc. 6th ICDT*, pages 19–40, 1997.
18. R. van der Meyden. The complexity of querying indefinite data about linearly ordered domains. *J. Computer and System Sciences*, 54(1):113–135, 1997.

Some Algorithmic Improvements for the Containment Problem of Conjunctive Queries with Negation

Michel Leclère and Marie-Laure Mugnier

LIRMM, Université de Montpellier,
161, rue Ada, F-34392 Montpellier cedex - France
{leclere,mugnier}@lirmm.fr

Abstract. Query containment is a fundamental problem of databases. Given two queries q_1 and q_2, it asks whether the set of answers to q_1 is included in the set of answers to q_2 for any database. In this paper, we investigate this problem for conjunctive queries with negated subgoals. We use graph homomorphism as the core notion, which leads us to extend the results presented in [Ull97] and [WL03]. First, we exhibit sufficient (but not necessary) conditions for query containment based on special subgraphs of q_2, which generalize that proposed in [WL03]. As a corollary, we obtain a case where the time complexity of the problem decreases. From a practical viewpoint, these properties can be exploited in algorithms, as shown in the paper. Second, we propose an algorithm based on the exploration of a space of graphs, which improves existing algorithms.

1 Introduction

In this paper, we investigate the problem of deciding on query containment for conjunctive queries with negated subgoals (but without inequalities). *Query containment checking* is one of the fundamental problems of databases. A query q_1 is said to be contained in a query q_2 (notation $q_1 \sqsubseteq q_2$) if for any database instance the set of answers to q_1 is included in the set of answers to q_2. Algorithms based on query containment can be used to solve various problems, such as query evaluation and optimization [CM77] [ASU79], rewriting queries using views [Hal01], detecting independance of queries from database updates [LS93], etc. However, the problem is undecidable for general queries expressed as Datalog programs.

Positive conjunctive queries are a class of frequently used queries which have been investigated since the early days of databases [CM77, Ull89]. Their expressive power is equivalent to the select-join-project queries of relational algebra. Checking containment of positive conjunctive queries is an NP-complete problem. It can be solved by testing the existence of a *query homomorphism* from q_2 to q_1, which maps q_2 to q_1 by substituting its variables by terms (constants or variables) in q_2.

Example 1. Let $q_1 = ans(x, y) \leftarrow r(x, y), r(y, x), p(x, x), s(y)$ and $q_2 = ans(u, v) \leftarrow r(u, v), r(v, w), p(u, w)$ be two conjunctive queries. There is one query homomorphism from q_2 to q_1, which is $h = \{u \rightarrow x, v \rightarrow y, w \rightarrow x\}$. Check that $h(q_2)$ has the same head as q_1 and its body is a part of q_1's body. This proves that $q_1 \sqsubseteq q_2$.

This problem can also be recast as a query evaluation problem by considering the *canonical database* associated with a query. Roughly, this database D^q is obtained from a query q by "freezing" its variables, that is considering them as new elements of the schema domain. Then query containment can be reformulated as evaluating q_2 on D^{q_1} and checking that the set of answers contains the head of q_1 [CM77].

When conjunctive queries are extended to negated subgoals, query containment becomes Π_P^2-complete (Π_P^2 is the class $(co\text{-}NP)^{NP}$). To our best knowledge, only two proposals about algorithms deciding on query containment for this class of queries can be found in the literature. We outline the main points of these proposals here, and will go into further detail later. In [Ull97], Ullman gives the scheme of an algorithm (adapted from a uniform equivalence checking method for Datalog programs [LS93]). This scheme involves generating an exponential number (in the size of q_1) of databases representative of q_1 and evaluating q_2 on these databases. This set of databases can be seen as a generalization of the canonical database of the positive case. A database that does not yield the head of q_1 as an answer to q_2 is a counter-example to the containment.

Example 2. Let $q_1 = ans() \leftarrow r(x, y), s(y, z), p(t), p(z), \neg r(z, t)$ and $q_2 = ans() \leftarrow r(u, v), p(w), \neg r(v, w)$. As $ans()$ has no argument, these queries represent boolean queries. It holds that $q_1 \sqsubseteq q_2$, as will be shown later. In a first step, Ullman's scheme builds the 15 partitions on $\{x, y, z, t\}$, which can be seen as all ways of mapping the variables in q_1 to database values. Each partition yields a database by substituting in q_1 the same value to each set of variables and taking the positive part of the query obtained. For instance, the partition $\{\{x, y\}, \{z, t\}\}$ yields the database $\{r(0, 0), s(0, 1), p(1)\}$. If a database does not make the body of q_1 true, as the database obtained from the partition $\{\{x, z\}, \{y, t\}\}$, it is eliminated. In a second step, for each database D, all its extensions obtained by adding tuples using the values and the relation symbols in D, and that still make the body of q_1 true, are considered and it is checked that they yield the substituted head of q_1 as an answer to q_2. For instance, for $D = \{r(0, 0), s(0, 1), p(1)\}$, all extensions with tuples $r(0, 1), r(1, 0), s(0, 0), s(1, 0), s(1, 1)$ and $p(0)$ are considered.

In the general case, if v is the number of variables in q_1, a number of databases exponential in v are generated in the first step, then, for each generated database D_i, $2^{((\sum_{r \in R} n_i^{arity(r)}) - t)}$ representative databases have to be checked, where R is the set of relation symbols appearing in q_1, n_i is the number of terms in D_i and t is the number of tuples in q_1.

In [WL03], Wei and Lausen exhibit a necessary but not sufficient condition for containment of *safe* queries (which are queries in which all variables appear in positive subgoals): if q_1 is contained in q_2 then there must be a query homomorphism (say h) from the positive part of q_2 (say q_2^+) to the positive part of q_1 (say q_1^+), that does not "contradict" the negative subgoals of q_2 (i.e. for all negative subgoals $\neg p(u)$ in q_2, q_1 does not contain the positive subgoal $p(h(u))$). This property is central to the proposed algorithm. It yields a heuristic for the generation of representative databases, with the aim of concluding sooner from partial representative databases. To check that $q_1 \sqsubseteq q_2$, the algorithm tries to find a query homomorphism (without contradiction) h from q_2^+ to q_1^+, such that for each negative literal $\neg p(u)$ in q_2, either $\neg p(h(u))$ is in q_1 or the query q_1' built from q_1 by adding $p(h(u))$ is such that $q_1' \sqsubseteq q_2$.

Let us outline this algorithm in example 2. There are 2 homomorphisms from $q_2^+ = ans() \leftarrow r(u,v), p(w)$ to q_1^+: $h_1 = \{u \rightarrow x, v \rightarrow y, w \rightarrow z\}$ and $h_2 = \{u \rightarrow x, v \rightarrow y, w \rightarrow t\}$. Both homomorphisms do not contradict any negative subgoal in q_2. Let us consider h_1 and the negative literal $\neg r(v, w)$ in q_2. The idea is that any database answering q_1 that does not contain $r(y, z)$ also answers q_2, thus databases containing $r(y, z)$ have to be checked. $r(y, z)$ is added to q_1, yielding q_1'. There are four query homomorphisms from q_2^+ to $q_1'^+$. If it can be concluded that $q_1' \sqsubseteq q_2$, then $q_1 \sqsubseteq q_2$. Otherwise, the homomorphism h_2 has to be considered.

Example 3. (ex. 1.2 in [WL03]) Let $q_1 = ans(x,y) \leftarrow r(x,y), r(y,z), \neg r(x,z)$ and $q_2 = ans(u,w) \leftarrow r(u,v), r(v,w), \neg s(w,w)$. There is one query homomorphism, $h = \{u \rightarrow x, v \rightarrow y, w \rightarrow z\}$, from $q_2^+ = ans(u,w) \leftarrow r(u,v), r(v,w)$ to q_1^+. h does not contradict the negative subgoal of q_2. Then, q_1' is generated from q_1 by adding $s(z, z)$. Again h is the sole homomorphism from q_2^+ to $q_1'^+$ but it contradicts $\neg s(w, w)$. Thus, $q_1' \not\sqsubseteq q_2$ and as there is no other homomorphism from q_2^+ to q_1^+ it is concluded that $q_1 \not\sqsubseteq q_2$.

Contribution. In this paper, we consider *homomorphism* as a core notion, where a homomorphism is not restricted to the positive parts of queries as in previous proposals, but extended to whole queries. For this, we propose to view the queries as labeled graphs, called *polarized graphs*. More specifically, a query is represented as a bipartite graph, with two kinds of nodes: relation nodes and terms nodes[1]. Each term of the query becomes a term node, labeled by $\star$ if it is a variable (it can be seen as a "blank node") otherwise by the constant itself. A positive (resp. negative) literal with relation symbol r becomes a relation node labeled by $+r$ (resp. $-r$) and it is linked to the nodes assigned to its terms. The numbers on edges correspond to the position of each term in the literal. See Figure 1, which displays the queries in example 2.

Basically, a homomorphism from an algebraic structure to another maps the elements of the first structure to elements of the second structure while preserving the relations between elements. A homomorphism h from a graph G_2 to a graph G_1 is a mapping from the nodes of G_2 to the nodes of G_1, which preserves edges, that is if xy is an edge of G_2 then $h(x)h(y)$ is an edge of G_1. Since our graphs are labeled, there are additional conditions on labels: a relation node is mapped to a node with the same label; a term node can be mapped to any term node if it is labeled by a $\star$, otherwise it is mapped to a node with the same constant. Numbers on edges are preserved.

Graph homomorphism yields another perspective on queries, as it naturally considers positive and negative occurrences of relations in the same way; moreover, it is defined on subgraphs that do not necessarily correspond to a query, which is convenient for our study. However, let us point out that all definitions and results in this paper can be expressed using the classical vocabulary on queries. In what follows, the term homomorphism can be understood as "query homomorphism extended to negative subgoals" or "graph homomorphism".

A first property, extending the central property in [WL03], is that the existence of a homomorphism from q_2 to q_1 is a sufficient condition for containment.

---

[1] Queries have often been considered as hypergraphs. The graphs we consider can be seen as the incidence bipartite graphs of these hypergraphs.

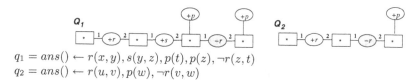

$q_1 = ans() \leftarrow r(x,y), s(y,z), p(t), p(z), \neg r(z,t)$
$q_2 = ans() \leftarrow r(u,v), p(w), \neg r(v,w)$

Fig. 1. Queries as graphs

Example 4. Let $q_1 = ans(y,z) \leftarrow r(x,z), r(y,z), \neg r(x,y)$ and $q_2 = ans(u,v) \leftarrow r(u,v), r(w,e)\neg r(w,u)$. There is a homomorphism, say h, from q_2 to q_1, thus $q_1 \sqsubseteq q_2$. $h = \{w \to x, u \to y, v \to z, e \to z\}$.

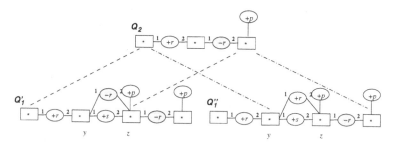

Fig. 2. Graph homomorphisms from Q_2 to Q'_1 and Q''_1

The existence of a homomorphism is not a necessary condition, as can be seen in example 2 (pictured in Figure 1): $q_1 \sqsubseteq q_2$ but there is no homomorphism from q_2 to q_1. However, q_1 can be equivalently rewritten as the union of two queries: one obtained by adding $\neg r(y,z)$, the other by adding $r(y,z)$. These queries are shown in Figure 2. As there is a homomorphism from q_2 to both queries, we conclude that $q_1 \sqsubseteq q_2$.

More generally, instead of considering representative databases, we rewrite q_1 into more and more specific queries. We are lead to consider a space of graphs (or queries) partially ordered by inclusion, with greatest element q_1 and least elements the "complete" graphs, obtained from q_1 by adding as many literals as possible. A brute-force algorithm generates all complete graphs and check that there is a homomorphism from q_2 to each of them.

Roughly, Ullman's scheme can be seen as generating all complete graphs from q_1. We should point out, however, that the first step in computing all partitions on q_1 terms is not necessary, *i.e.* the discrete partition is sufficient. The set of representative databases generated from the discrete partition is the set of complete graphs. Although it is not claimed in [Ull97], Ullman's algorithm is in fact able to process queries with inequalities (see section 2.4).

This framework being settled, we focus on two points. First, we search for cases where the problem is simpler. We study special subgraphs of q_2 that necessarily map to q_1 (theorem 2 and 3); q_2^+ is a specific case. As a corollary, when the whole q_2 satisfies one of these conditions, the containment problem becomes equivalent to homomorphism checking, thus its time complexity falls into NP (property 8). From a practical viewpoint, these properties can be exploited in algorithms, including Wei and Lausen's algorithm. They can be used in a preprocessing phase (to limit the number of representative databases or to conclude before entering the generation phase) or to guide the construction of representative databases. Second, we propose an algorithm based on exploration of the graph space. This algorithm is simple to describe and implement. Its correctness is directly given by the exhibited properties (theorem 4) and its complexity is analyzed (property 10). We compare this algorithm to Wei and Lausen's algorithm, which can be seen as exploring the same space of graphs but in a radically different way. In particular, our algorithm requires a space polynomial in the size of the initial queries (provided that the maximal arity of a relation is bounded by a constant), which is not the case for Wei and Lausen's algorithm.

The paper is organized as follows. The next section introduces the graph framework and reformulates the query containment problem in terms of graph homomorphism. It ends with a brute-force algorithm, whose complexity is compared to that of Ullman's scheme. Section 3 is devoted to necessary or sufficient conditions for containment. Section 4 presents our algorithm based on space exploration and compares it to Wei and Lausen's algorithm.

2   Preliminary Considerations

We first recall basic definitions and results on databases. Then we introduce the graph framework, which leads us to recast CQC as a conjunction of homomorphism tests. We end with a brute-force algorithm, that we compare with Ullman's scheme.

2.1   Basic Database Notions

A *database schema* $S = (R, dom)$ includes a finite set of relations R and a countably infinite set of constants dom. Each relation has an *arity* (not equal to zero) defining the number of its arguments. A *database instance* D (or simply a *database*) over S maps each k-ary relation r_i of R to a finite subset of dom^k (denoted $D(r_i)$). A *conjunctive query (with negation)* is of form:

$$q = ans(u) \leftarrow r_1(u_1), \dots r_n(u_n), \neg s_1(v_1), \dots \neg s_m(v_m) \quad n \geq 0, \ m \geq 0, \ n + m \geq 1$$

where $r_1 \dots r_n, s_1 \dots s_m$ are relations, ans is a special relation not belonging to R, u and $u_1 \dots u_n, v_1 \dots v_m$ are tuples of terms (variables or constants of dom), and each variable of u occurs at least once in the body of the rule. Without loss of generality, we assume that the same literal does not appear twice in the body of the rule. A *positive query* is a query without negative literals ($m = 0$, thus $n \geq 1$). A query is *safe* if each variable occurring in a negative literal also occurs in a positive one. A query is *inconsistent* if it contains two opposite literals (i.e. $\exists i, j \ 1 \leq i \leq n, \ 1 \leq j \leq m$ such that $r_i(u_i) = s_j(v_j)$), otherwise it is consistent.

Given a query $q = ans(u) \leftarrow r_1(u_1), \dots r_n(u_n), \neg s_1(v_1), \dots \neg s_m(v_m)$ and a database D on S, $q(D)$ denotes the *set of answers* to q in D; $q(D)$ is the set of tuples $\mu(u)$ where μ is a substitution of the variables in q by constants in dom such that for any i in $\{1, \dots, n\}$, $\mu(u_i) \in D(r_i)$ and for any j in $\{1, \dots, m\}$, $\mu(v_j) \notin D(s_j)$. We also call μ a substitution *from q to D*. When the arity of ans is 0, $q(D)$ is the set $\{()\}$ if there is such a substitution μ, otherwise it is $\emptyset$. If $q(D)$ is not empty, D is said to *answer* the query.

A query q_1 is said to be *contained* in a query q_2, noted $q_1 \sqsubseteq q_2$, if for any database D, $q_1(D) \subseteq q_2(D)$. The *conjunctive query containment problem* (CQC) takes as input two conjunctive queries q_1 and q_2 and asks whether $q_1 \sqsubseteq q_2$. When q_1 and q_2 are positive, it can be reformulated as a query homomorphism problem, where a homomorphism is defined as follows: a *query homomorphism* from $q = ans(u) \leftarrow r_1(u_1), \ldots r_n(u_n)$ to $q' = ans(u') \leftarrow r'_1(u'_1), \ldots r'_{n'}(u'_{n'})$ is a substitution θ of the variables in q by terms (variables or constants) in q' such that $\theta(u) = u'$ (thus u and u' have the same size) and for any i in $\{1, \ldots, n\}$, there is j in $\{1, \ldots, n'\}$ such that $\theta(r_i(u_i)) = r'_j(u'_j)$. The query homomorphism theorem proves that, given two positive queries q_1 and q_2, $q_1 \sqsubseteq q_2$ iff there is a query homomorphism from q_2 to q_1.

2.2   CQC and Homomorphism

As explained in the introduction, it is convenient to see a query as a bipartite labeled graph, that we call a polarized graph (PG)[2]. The mappings between graph and database notions used in this paper are immediate. To represent heads of queries, we use special relations ans_i for each possible arity i, possibly 0 (which corresponds to boolean queries). Then the head of a query (say $ans(t_1...t_k)$) is mapped to a positive relation node with label ans_k and with i-th neighbor the node assigned to t_i. We usually omit ans_0 in drawings (f.i. Figure 1: there is an implicit isolated relation node labeled ans_0 in each graph). It is easily checked that a graph homomorphism from a graph representing a query to another is equivalent to a query homomorphism extended to negative subgoals from the first query to the second (the above definition of a query homomorphism can be used without change if we consider that r_i and r'_j represent possibly negated relation). That is why we use the same term homomorphism for both notions. If there is a homomorphism from q_2 to q_1, we say that q_2 can be *mapped* to q_1. We will keep the term literal and its notation $p(u)$ or $\neg p(u)$, where u is a sequence of terms, to denote a subgraph induced by a relation node and its neighbors.

For positive conjunctive queries q_1 and q_2, $q_1 \sqsubseteq q_2$ iff there is a homomorphism from q_2 to q_1. For conjunctive queries with negation, one part of this property still holds:

Property 1. Given conjunctive queries q_1 and q_2, if there is a homomorphism from q_2 to q_1 then $q_1 \sqsubseteq q_2$.

For the other direction, we assume that q_1 and q_2 are consistent. This assumption will be made in the sequel of the paper. Even if q_1 and q_2 are consistent, we might have $q_1 \sqsubseteq q_2$ and no homomorphism from q_2 to q_1, as illustrated by Figures 1 and 2.

Definition 1. *A consistent query (or a PG) q is* complete *w.r.t. a set of relations R, if for each relation r in R with arity k, for each k-tuple of terms u in q, not necessarily distinct, q contains $r(u)$ or $\neg r(u)$.*

---

[2] For space limitation reasons, we do not provide here precise definitions concerning PGs. These graphs are a simplification of graphs used in a knowledge representation context, see [Ker01, ML06].

A complete query is obtained from a query q by repeatedly adding positive and negative literals (on terms already present in q), as long as it does not yield a redundancy or an inconsistency. CQC can be expressed as the conjunction of homomorphism checking problems: one for each complete query generated from q_1.

Property 2. Given two conjunctive queries q_1 and q_2 (with q_1 being consistent), $q_1 \sqsubseteq q_2$ iff for each complete query q_1^c generated from q_1, there is a homomorphism from q_2 to q_1^c.

Note that q_2 can be considered as a *connected* graph: indeed, if q_2 is not connected, a homomorphism from q_2 to q_1 is given by a set of homomorphisms from each connected component of q_2 to q_1, and reciprocally.

2.3   A Brute Force Algorithm for CQC

Property 2 yields a brute force algorithm (cf. algorithm 1) for CQC.

Algorithm 1. Brute force CQC Check

Data: consistent queries q_1 and q_2
Result: true if $q_1 \sqsubseteq q_2$, false otherwise
begin
    Let $\mathcal{B}$ be the set of complete queries obtained from q_1 w.r.t. $\mathcal{R}$;
    forall $q_1^c \in \mathcal{B}$ **do**
        if *there is no homomorphism from q_2 to q_1^c* **then**
            // q_1^c is a counter-example
            return *false*;
    return *true*;
end

Property 3. The time complexity of Algorithm 1 is in $\mathcal{O}(2^{(n_1)^k \times |\mathcal{R}|} \times hom(q_2, q_1^c))$, where n_1 is the number of terms in q_1, k is the maximum arity of a relation, $\mathcal{R}$ is the set of considered relations and $hom(q_2, q_1^c)$ is the complexity of checking the existence of a homomorphism from q_2 to q_1^c.

Its space complexity is in $\mathcal{O}(max(size(q_2), size(q_1), (n_1)^k \times |\mathcal{R}|))$.

Homomorphism checking is NP-complete (but polynomial as soon as q_2 has a tree-like structure). A brute force algorithm solving this problem for q_2 and q_1^c has a time complexity in $\mathcal{O}(min(n_1^{v_2}, r_1^{r_2}))$, where n_1 is the number of term nodes in q_1^c, v_2 is the number of variable nodes in q_2, r_1 and r_2 are the number of literals in q_1^c and q_2 resp. For comparison with other algorithms, it should be noted that the space complexity of Algorithm 1 is not exponential in the size of q_1 or q_2 but only in the maximum arity of a relation in $\mathcal{R}$. Indeed, as completions can be generated one by one, the space complexity corresponds to the size of one q_1^c.

2.4   Relationships with Ullman's Scheme

Ullman's scheme involves the two following steps:

1. Consider all partitions of the variables in q_1. Build a canonical database from each partition as follows: first assign a distinct constant to each set of the partition, then substitute in q_1 each variable by the constant assigned to its set; let q'_1 be the substituted query; the canonical database is composed of the positive literals of q'_1 body. We obtain $D_1 \ldots D_k$ canonical databases if k is the number of partitions. Eliminate the D_i which do not make the body of q_1 true, (i.e. the body of q'_1 is inconsistent).
2. For each remaining D_i, test whether for each database $D'i$ obtained from D_i by adding tuples on the same symbol set as D_i, and without contradicting negative subgoals of q_1, it holds that $q_2(D'_i)$ includes the head of q'_1. If all D_i satisfy the test, then $q_1 \sqsubseteq q_2$, otherwise not.

This scheme can be reformulated as follows in our framework:

1. *Build all consistent queries D_i obtainable from q_1 by merging some variables.*
2. *The test is satisfied iff q_2 can be mapped to all complete queries obtainable from these D_i.*

From property 2, it is clear that step 1 is useless. Indeed, there is a homomorphism from q_1 to each D_i, $1 \leq i \leq k$, q_1 being identical to the D_i obtained with the discrete partition, say D_1. For a given D'_i there is a D'_1 with a homomorphism from D'_1 to D'_i induced by the partition on the variables in q_1 yielding D_i. It is thus sufficient to test all D'_1, i.e. *all complete queries obtainable from q_1*. This observation leads to an important reduction in the number of tested databases/queries: if v is the number of variables in q_1, step 1 builds a number of databases D_i exponential in v (from which only consistent ones are kept) and each remaining D_i leads in turn to an exponential test (see Algorithm 1).

Step 1 would be necessary if the queries would contain inequalities as in [LS93]. However in [Ull97] and further papers dealing with queries without inequalities, it seems that the uselessness of step 1 had not be noticed.

3   Necessary/Sufficient Conditions for Containment

This section studies conditions that are necessary or sufficient for containment. These properties can be used as filtering properties leading to conclude before entering the generation phase. They can also be used to reduce the number of graphs generated either because they eliminate relations that are not needed in the completion or because they guide the incremental generation of complete graphs (see the next section). Besides their practical algorithmic interest, they also yield particular cases where the theoretical complexity of CQC decreases.

3.1   Immediate Properties on Labels

Let us begin by considering the node labels. An immediate observation is that if a constant or a relation label (that is a relation with a given polarity) in q_2 does not appear in q_1, then $q_1 \not\sqsubseteq q_2$. A second observation is that relations that do not appear in both q_1 and q_2 are not needed in the completion of q_1. The next property takes the polarity of their occurrences into account.

Property 4. If r is a relation that does not have both positive and negative occurrences in q_2, then r is not needed in the completion of q_1 (i.e. $q_1 \sqsubseteq q_2$ iff q_2 can be mapped to each completion of q_1 built without considering r).

Proof. ($\Leftarrow$) If q_2 can be mapped to each complete query without considering r then $q_1 \sqsubseteq q_2$. Indeed, let q_1^c be any complete query built from q_1. Let $q_1^{c-\{r\}}$ be obtained from q_1^c by removing all literals, occurrences of r, that do not belong to q_1. There is a natural homomorphism, say h_1 from $q_1^{c-\{r\}}$ to q_1^c. By hypothesis there is a homomorphism, say h, from q_2 to $q_1^{c-\{r\}}$. The composition of these homomorphisms $h_1 \circ h$ is a homomorphism from q_2 to q_1^c.

($\Rightarrow$) Let $q_1 \sqsubseteq q_2$. Assume that $q_1^{c-\{r\}}$ is a completion (without considering r) of q_1 such that there is no homomorphism from q_2 to $q_1^{c-\{r\}}$. We show that this assumption leads to contradict $q_1 \sqsubseteq q_2$. If all the occurrences of r in q_2 are positive (resp. negative), let q_1^{c-} (resp. q_1^{c+}) be the complete query obtained from $q_1^{c-\{r\}}$ by adding solely negative (resp. positive) literals with relation r. Since $q_1 \sqsubseteq q_2$ there is a homomorphism from q_2 to q_1^{c-} (resp. q_1^{c+}). This homomorphism necessarily maps all occurrences of r in q_2 into q_1; more generally, no literal of q_2 can be mapped to the added negative (resp. positive) occurrences of r. h is thus a homomorphism from q_2 to $q_1^{c-\{r\}}$, which contradicts the hypothesis. $\qquad\square$

As a corollary to the previous properties, we obtain:

Theorem 1. *$q_1 \sqsubseteq q_2$ iff q_2 can be mapped to each completion of q_1 w.r.t. relations occurring in both positive and negative forms in q_1 and q_2.*

Let us consider the queries in example 3: as $\neg s$ does not appear in q_1, it can be immediately concluded that $q_1 \not\sqsubseteq q_2$. Would $\neg s(w,w)$ not exist in q_2, as r does not appear positively and negatively both in q_1 and q_2, no relation can be used for completion, thus there is also immediate failure.

3.2 Special Subgraphs

As we have seen, a homomorphism from q_2 to q_1 is a sufficient but not necessary condition for containment. The objective here is to identify parts - or subgraphs - of q_2 (i.e. conjunctions of literals appearing in q_2) for which there must be a homomorphism to q_1. Moreover, such a homomorphism from a subgraph of q_2 to q_1 has to be potentially extensible to a homomorphism from the entire q_2 to a completion of q_1. We call it a *compatible* homomorphism. See Figure 3: there are three homomorphisms from q_2^- to q_1: $h_1 = \{x \to t, y \to u, z \to w\}$, $h_2 = \{x \to t, y \to w, z \to v\}$, $h_3 = \{x \to u, y \to w, z \to v\}$. To check the compatibility, we have to consider $s(y,x)$ and $r(x,z)$. h_1 is not compatible because it leads to map $r(x,z)$ to $\neg r(t,w)$.

Definition 2 (compatible homomorphism). *Given two queries q_2 and q_1, and q'_2 any subgraph of q_2 defining a well-formed PG (i.e. q'_2 is any conjunction of literals appearing in q_2), a homomorphism h from q'_2 to q_1 is said to be compatible (w.r.t. q_2) if for*

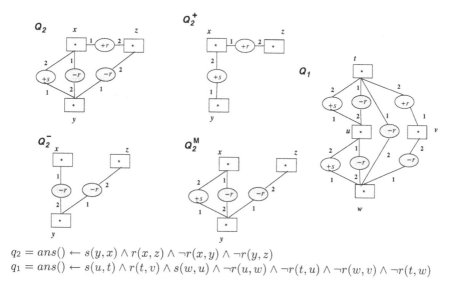

$q_2 = ans() \leftarrow s(y, x) \wedge r(x, z) \wedge \neg r(x, y) \wedge \neg r(y, z)$
$q_1 = ans() \leftarrow s(u, t) \wedge r(t, v) \wedge s(w, u) \wedge \neg r(u, w) \wedge \neg r(t, u) \wedge \neg r(w, v) \wedge \neg r(t, w)$

Fig. 3. Pure subgraphs of q_2 ($q_1 \sqsubseteq q_2$)

each literal of q_2 that does not appear in q'_2 but has all its terms in q'_2, say $t_1...t_k$, there is no literal with the same relation and the opposite polarity on $h(t_1)...h(t_k)$ in q_1.

Given a query q, the *positive subgraph* of q, denoted by q^+ is the subgraph obtained from q by selecting only the positive literals of q. The *negative subgraph* q^- of q is the dual notion, that is the subgraph obtained from q by selecting only the negative literals of q. See q_2^+ and q_2^- in Figure 3. The next property is the same as theorem 1 in [WL03] reformulated and proven in the graph framework, except that we extend the definition of q^+ to non-safe queries. Note that, when q is a safe query, q^+ contains all term nodes of q.

Property 5. [WL03] If there is no compatible homomorphism from q_2^+ to q_1 (or equivalently to q_1^+), then $q_1 \not\sqsubseteq q_2$.

Proof. Let q_1^{c-} be the negative completion of q_1. If $q_1 \sqsubseteq q_2$ then there is a homomorphism h from q_2 to q_1^{c-}, which necessarily maps q_2^+ to q_1^+. Let $l_i = \neg r(t_1...t_k)$ be any negative literal of q_2. Since h is a homomorphism, q_1^{c-} contains a literal $\neg r(h(t_1)...h(t_k))$. As q_1 is consistent, it cannot contain a literal $r(h(t_1)...h(t_k))$. We conclude that h with domain restricted to q_2^+ is a compatible homomorphism to q_1. □

A similar property is obtained by considering q_2^- instead of q_2^+.

Property 6. If there is no compatible homomorphism from q_2^- to q_1 (or equivalently to q_1^-), then $q_1 \not\sqsubseteq q_2$.

Proof. Consider q_1^{c+} the positive completion of q_1 instead of q_1^{c-}. □

Both q_2^+ and q_2^- notions can be generalized in the following way.

Definition 3 (q_2^{max} **pure subgraph**). *A pure subgraph of q_2 is a subgraph that does not contain opposite occurrences of the same relation. We note q_2^{max} a pure subgraph of q_2 that is maximal for inclusion.*

Observe that a q_2^{max} is obtained from q_2 by selecting, for each relation appearing in q_2, either all its positive occurrences or all its negative occurrences. See Figure 3: q_2 has two pure subgraphs maximal for inclusion; q_2^+ and q_2^M. q_2^+ (resp. q_2^-) is the particular case where positive (resp. negative) occurrences are chosen for all relations; but it is not necessarily maximal for inclusion as a relation may appear only negatively (res. positively). The ans_i relation is a particular case of such relation.

Theorem 2. *If there is a q_2^{max} that cannot be mapped by a compatible homomorphism to q_1, then $q_1 \not\sqsubseteq q_2$.*

Proof. Consider q_1^{-max} as the completion of q_1 built as follows: for each relation r, if r occurs positively (resp. negatively) in q_2^{max} then complete q_1 with negative (resp. positive) occurrences of r. If q_2^{max} cannot be mapped to q_1 by a compatible homomorphism, then it cannot be mapped by a compatible homomorphism to q_1^{-max} (since by construction no literal of q_2^{max} can be mapped to an added literal). Since q_2 cannot be mapped to q_1^{-max}, q_1^{-max} is a counter-example to the property $q_1 \sqsubseteq q_2$.   □

This theorem can be slightly extended by taking into account the occurrences of terms in the literals.

Definition 4. *Two literals are said to be dependant if (1) they have an opposite polarity, (2) they have the same relation and (3) their atoms are unifiable after a renaming of their common variables. Otherwise they are said to be independant.*

Two atoms are not unifiable after a renaming of their common variables if their unification would lead to unify different constants. For instance, let a and b be distinct constants; $r(x, a)$ and $\neg r(y, b)$ are independant literals; $p(x, x, a)$ and $\neg p(b, y, y)$ are independant literals as well, whereas $r(x, a)$ and $\neg r(b, y)$ are dependant literals.

Definition 5. *An independant subgraph of a query q_2 is a subgraph of q_2 composed of pairwise independant literals.*

More generally, let us say that two literals are "exchangeable" if they can have the same list of images for their arguments by homomorphisms to (necessarily distinct) completions of q_1. F.i. given the distinct constants a and b, the literals $r(x, a)$ and $\neg r(b, y)$ are dependant but, if q_1 contains $r(a, b)$, they are not exchangeable. Independant subgraphs, and a fortiori pure subgraphs, are only particular cases of subgraphs without exchangeable literals; the general notion of "exchangeability" remains to be studied. Exchangeable literals are responsible for the problem complexity, as shown by the next property.

Property 7. If $q_1 \sqsubseteq q_2$, then there is a compatible homomorphism from every subgraph of q_2 composed of pairwise non-exchangeable literals to q_1.

Sketch of proof. Consider such a subgraph q' of q_2. Let q_1^{c+} be the completion of q_1 with solely positive literals. If there is no homomorphism from q' to q_1, then for each homomorphism from q' to q_1^{c+}, there is at least one added literal, say $p(u)$, such that a literal $p(v)$ in q' is mapped to $p(u)$. Let us replace *all* such $p(u)$ by $\neg p(u)$. Let $q_1^{c'}$ be the graph obtained. Let h be a homomorphism from q' to $q_1^{c'}$ (there is such a homomorphism since $q_1 \sqsubseteq q_2$). h maps a literal $\neg p(w)$ in q' to a literal $\neg p(u)$, otherwise there would be a homomorphism from q' to q_1. By construction, there is a literal $p(v)$ mapped to $p(u)$ by a homomorphism from q' to q_1^{c+}, thus $p(v)$ and $\neg p(w)$ are exchangeable literals. $\square$

The following extension to the theorem 2 is a corollary of property 7.

Theorem 3. *[Extension to the theorem 2] If there is an independant subgraph of q_2 that cannot be mapped by a compatible homomorphism to q_1, then $q_1 \not\sqsubseteq q_2$.*

We thus obtain a case for which CQC has the same complexity as homomorphism checking:

Property 8. If q_2 is an independant subgraph, then $q_1 \sqsubseteq q_2$ iff there is a homomorphism from q_2 to q_1.

3.3   Filtering Implementation

Let us end this section with an implementation of some filtering properties (algorithm 2 that will be used next section).

Algorithm 2. Filtering

Data: consistent queries q_1 and q_2
Result: true, false or undetermined; if true then $q_1 \sqsubseteq q_2$; if false then $q_1 \not\sqsubseteq q_2$
begin

Test 1 | **if** *there is a label (r) or $(\neg r)$ or a constant occurring in q_2 but not in q_1* **then**
     ⌊ **return** *false*

Test 2 | **if** *there is a homomorphism from q_2 to q_1* **then**
     ⌊ **return** *true*

Test 3 | Let q_2^{Max} be an independant subgraph of q_2 with maximum cardinality;
  if *there is no compatible homomorphism from q_2^{Max} to q_1* **then**
     ⌊ **return** *false*

  return *undetermined*;
end

Roughly, Test 1 is in $\mathcal{O}(r \log_2(r))$ where r is the maximum number of relations in q_1 or q_2. Test 2 and Test 3 perform a homomorphism check. For Test 3, choosing a subgraph with maximum size is an obvious choice but there may be other criteria f.i. based on the structure of the obtained subgraph. Alternatively, one can choose to check several or all independant subgraphs instead of one.

4   Space Exploration Algorithm

The space of queries "leading" from q_1 to its completions is structured in a sup-semi-lattice by graph inclusion (given two queries q_1 and q_2 in this space, $q_1 \leq q_2$ if q_2 is a subgraph of q_1). The question "is there a homomorphism from q_2 to each q_1^c (completion of q_1)" can be reformulated as follows "is there a *covering set*, that is a subset of incomparable queries of this space $\{q_1, ..., q_k\}$ such that (1) there is a homomorphism from q_2 to each q_i ; (2) for each q_1^c there is a q_i with $q_1^c \leq q_i$.

The brute-force algorithm (Algorithm 1) takes the set of all completions of q_1 as covering set. The next algorithm (Algorithm 3 and recursive search Algorithm 4) searches the space in a top-down way starting from q_1 and tries to build a covering set with partial completions of q_1. Case-based reasoning is applied at each step: for a given relation r with arity k and a tuple $(t_1...t_k)$ such that neither $r(t_1...t_k)$ nor $\neg r(t_1...t_k)$ is present in the current partial completion, two queries are generated according to each case. The algorithm is justified by the following property:

Theorem 4. $q_1 \sqsubseteq q_2$ *if and only if:*
1. There is a homomorphism h from q_2 to q_1 **or**
2. $q' \sqsubseteq q_2$ and $q'' \sqsubseteq q_2$ where q' (resp. q'') is obtained from q_1 by adding the positive literal $r(t_1...t_k)$ (resp. the negative literal $\neg r(t_1...t_k)$) where r is a relation of arity k occurring in q_2 (both in positive and negative forms) and $t_1...t_k$ are terms of q_1 such that neither the literal $r(t_1...t_k)$ nor the literal $\neg r(t_1...t_k)$ is already present in q_1.

Proof (sketch). ($\Rightarrow$) By recurrence on the number of literals to add to q_1 to obtain a complete query. ($\Leftarrow$) Condition 1 corresponds to property 1. For condition 2, see that $\{q', q''\}$ is a covering set.   □

Subalgorithm 4 is supposed to have direct access to data available in the main algorithm 3. The choice of r and $t_1...t_k$, in Algorithm 4, can be guided by a compatible homomorphism from an independant graph.

Algorithm 3. Check by space exploration

Data: Consistent queries q_1 and q_2
Result: true if $q_1 \sqsubseteq q_2$, false otherwise
begin
    Result ← **Filtering**(); // *See Algorithm 2*
    if *(Result ≠ undetermined)* **then**
        └ **return** *Result*
    Let $\mathcal{R}^{+-}$ be the set of relation names occurring in both negative and positive forms in q_2;
    return RecCheck(q_1); // *See Algorithm 4*
end

The following property ensures that Algorithm 4 does not generate the same query several times, which is a crucial point for complexity. Otherwise the algorithm could be worse than the brute-force algorithm in the worse-case.

Algorithm 4. RecCheck(q)

Data: Consistent query q **Access:** $q_2, \mathcal{R}^{+-}$
Result: true if $q \sqsubseteq q_2$, false otherwise
begin

    if *there is a homomorphism from q_2 to q* **then**
        └ **return** *true*

    if *q is complete w.r.t. $\mathcal{R}^{+-}$* **then**
        └ **return** *false*

    `/* Test 3 of filtering can be reused in each call    */`
    $(r, t_1...t_k) \leftarrow$ **ChooseLiteralsToAdd**(q);
    `/* r is a relation of `$\mathcal{R}^{+-}$` and `$t_1...t_k$` are terms of q  */`
    Let q' be obtained from q by adding the literal $r(t_1...t_k)$;
    Let q'' be obtained from q by adding the literal $\neg r(t_1...t_k)$;
    return (**RecCheck**(q') AND **RecCheck**(q''))

end

Property 9. The subspace explored by Algorithm 4 is a (binary) tree.

Indeed, at each recursive call, $\{q', q''\}$ is a covering set inducing a bipartition of the covered space: each query in this space is below exactly one of these two queries.

Property 10. Algorithm 3 has the same time and space complexity as Algorithm 1.

Proof. Property 9 ensures that the number of queries generated is at most twice the number of completions of q_1 (in the worse case, the complete queries are the leaves of the generated tree of queries). Checking whether a query is complete can be done in constant time if the number of literals in the query is incrementally maintained. Thus time complexity is the same as Algorithm 1. For space complexity, see that the tree is explored in a depth-first way. □

Wei and Lausen's algorithm is based on the following theorem (theorem 2 of their paper reformulated in graph terms; moreover, in (1) "compatible" has been added, as well as step (2.1) to prevent inconsistent queries to be built[3]). This theorem considers *safe* queries (otherwise h could be undefined on some variables in q_2).

Theorem 5. *[WL03] With q_1 and q_2 being safe queries, $q_1 \sqsubseteq q_2$ if and only if:*
1. There is a compatible homomorphism h from q_2^+ to q_1^+, such that:
2. for each negative literal $l_i = \neg r(t_1...t_k)$ in q_2, (2.1) either h can be extended to include l_i or (2.2) $q_i' \sqsubseteq q_2$ holds, where q_i' is obtained from q_1 by adding the positive literal $r(h(t_1) ... h(t_k))$.

Note that if each negative literal l_i can be included in h then h is a homomorphism from q_2 in q_1. An important point is that this theorem induces a radically different way of searching the space than that of Algorithm 3. Indeed, whereas Algorithm 3 develops a tree, condition (2) leads to build a covering set that does not partition the space. An algorithm applying this property directly is thus likely to explore the same subspaces several times.

---

[3] Indeed, the theorem does not apply to inconsistent queries. If q_1 is inconsistent, it is by definition included in any q_2, but there might be no homomorphism from q_2^+ to q_1^+.

The algorithm proposed by Wei and Lausen (in the appendix of their paper) sketchily proceeds as follows. First, all homomorphisms from q_2^+ to q_1^+ are generated. Then for each compatible homomorphism, say h, and for each negative literal that cannot be mapped by extending h, a new query to test is generated from q_1 by adding a positive literal according to the previous theorem. This algorithm can be seen as developing a *and/or* tree: a homomorphism h leads to success if all queries q_i' directly generated from it lead to containment; a query q_i' leads to containment if there is a homomorphism from $q_i'^+$ leading to success. The and/or tree is traversed in a breadth-first manner.

This algorithm has a space complexity exponential in the size of the initial queries, at least because all homomorphisms from q_2^+ to q_1^+ are first generated and the and/or tree is traversed in a breadth-first manner. Concerning time complexity, the key question is whether the same query can be generated several times. The notion of "new" mapping is mentioned in the algorithm (when the homomorphisms from q_2^+ to q_1^+ are enumerated, only *new* mappings are retained) but without detail about how a "new" mapping is recognized. *A priori* one has to store all already generated mappings to recognize a new one. If so, the space complexity would be exponential in the size of q_2 even with the assumption that homomorphisms are generated one by one and the tree is traversed in a depth-first way. To summarize, the algorithm we propose in this paper (see Algorithms 3 and 4) has the following qualities compared to Wei and Lausen's algorithm:

- it is not restricted to safe queries;
- the space exploration is based on special subgraphs, which generalize the q_2^+ notion (and could be used instead of it in condition 1 of Wei and Lausen's theorem);
- it is polynomial in space (if the arity of relations is bound by a constant);
- it is simple to describe and implement.

Acknowledgments. We specially thank a referee for his/her valuable comments.

References

[ASU79]   A. V. Aho, Y. Sagiv, and J. D. Ullman. Equivalences among relational expressions. *SIAM J. Comput.*, 8(2):218–246, 1979.

[CM77]   A.K. Chandra and P.M. Merlin. Optimal implementation of conjunctive queries in relational databases. In *9th ACM Symposium on Theory of Computing*, pages 77–90, 1977.

[Hal01]   A. Y. Halevy. Answering queries using views: A survey. *VLDB Journal: Very Large Data Bases*, 10(4):270–294, 2001.

[Ker01]   G. Kerdiles. *Saying it with Pictures: a Logical Landscape of Conceptual Graphs.* PhD thesis, Univ. Montpellier II / Amsterdam, Nov. 2001.

[LS93]   A. Y. Levy and Y. Sagiv. Queries independent of updates. In *VLDB*, pages 171–181, 1993.

[ML06]   M.L. Mugnier and M. Leclère.   On querying simple conceptual graphs with negation.   *Data and Knowledge Engineering (DKE)*, 2006.   In press, doi:10.1016/j.datak.2006.03.008.

[Ull89]   J. D. Ullman. *Principles of Database and Knowledge-Base Systems, Volume II*. Computer Science Press, 1989.

[Ull97]   J. D. Ullman. Information Integration using Logical Views. In *International Conference on Database Theory (ICDT)*, 1997.

[WL03]   F. Wei and G. Lausen. Containment of Conjunctive Queries with Safe Negation. In *International Conference on Database Theory (ICDT)*, 2003.

Author Index

Lecture Notes in Computer Science

For information about Vols. 1–4257

please contact your bookseller or Springer

Vol. 4296: M.S. Rhee, B. Lee (Eds.), Information Security and Cryptology – ICISC 2006. XIII, 358 pages. 2006.

Vol. 4295: J.D. Carswell, T. Tezuka (Eds.), Web and Wireless Geographical Information Systems. XI, 269 pages. 2006.

Vol. 4294: A. Dan, W. Lamersdorf (Eds.), Service-Oriented Computing – ICSOC 2006. XIX, 653 pages. 2006.

Vol. 4293: A. Gelbukh, C.A. Reyes-Garcia (Eds.), MICAI 2006: Advances in Artificial Intelligence. XXVIII, 1232 pages. 2006. (Sublibrary LNAI).

Vol. 4292: G. Bebis, R. Boyle, B. Parvin, D. Koracin, P. Remagnino, A. Nefian, G. Meenakshisundaram, V. Pascucci, J. Zara, J. Molineros, H. Theisel, T. Malzbender (Eds.), Advances in Visual Computing, Part II. XXXII, 906 pages. 2006.

Vol. 4291: G. Bebis, R. Boyle, B. Parvin, D. Koracin, P. Remagnino, A. Nefian, G. Meenakshisundaram, V. Pascucci, J. Zara, J. Molineros, H. Theisel, T. Malzbender (Eds.), Advances in Visual Computing, Part I. XXXI, 916 pages. 2006.

Vol. 4290: M. van Steen, M. Henning (Eds.), Middleware 2006. XIII, 425 pages. 2006.

Vol. 4289: M. Ackermann, B. Berendt, M. Grobelnik, A. Hotho, D. Mladenič, G. Semeraro, M. Spiliopoulou, G. Stumme, V. Svatek, M. van Someren (Eds.), Semantics, Web and Mining. X, 197 pages. 2006. (Sublibrary LNAI).

Vol. 4288: T. Asano (Ed.), Algorithms and Computation. XX, 766 pages. 2006.

Vol. 4287: C. Mao, T. Yokomori (Eds.), DNA Computing. XII, 440 pages. 2006.

Vol. 4286: P. Spirakis, M. Mavronicolas, S. Kontogiannis (Eds.), Internet and Network Economics. XI, 401 pages. 2006.

Vol. 4285: Y. Matsumoto, R. Sproat, K.-F. Wong, M. Zhang (Eds.), Computer Processing of Oriental Languages. XVII, 544 pages. 2006. (Sublibrary LNAI).

Vol. 4284: X. Lai, K. Chen (Eds.), Advances in Cryptology – ASIACRYPT 2006. XIV, 468 pages. 2006.

Vol. 4283: Y.Q. Shi, B. Jeon (Eds.), Digital Watermarking. XII, 474 pages. 2006.

Vol. 4282: Z. Pan, A. Cheok, M. Haller, R.W.H. Lau, H. Saito, R. Liang (Eds.), Advances in Artificial Reality and Tele-Existence. XXIII, 1347 pages. 2006.

Vol. 4281: K. Barkaoui, A. Cavalcanti, A. Cerone (Eds.), Theoretical Aspects of Computing - ICTAC 2006. XV, 371 pages. 2006.

Vol. 4280: A.K. Datta, M. Gradinariu (Eds.), Stabilization, Safety, and Security of Distributed Systems. XVII, 590 pages. 2006.

Vol. 4279: N. Kobayashi (Ed.), Programming Languages and Systems. XI, 423 pages. 2006.

Vol. 4278: R. Meersman, Z. Tari, P. Herrero (Eds.), On the Move to Meaningful Internet Systems 2006: OTM 2006 Workshops, Part II. XLV, 1004 pages. 2006.

Vol. 4277: R. Meersman, Z. Tari, P. Herrero (Eds.), On the Move to Meaningful Internet Systems 2006: OTM 2006 Workshops, Part I. XLV, 1009 pages. 2006.

Vol. 4276: R. Meersman, Z. Tari (Eds.), On the Move to Meaningful Internet Systems 2006: CoopIS, DOA, GADA, and ODBASE, Part II. XXXII, 752 pages. 2006.

Vol. 4275: R. Meersman, Z. Tari (Eds.), On the Move to Meaningful Internet Systems 2006: CoopIS, DOA, GADA, and ODBASE, Part I. XXXI, 1115 pages. 2006.

Vol. 4274: Q. Huo, B. Ma, E.-S. Chng, H. Li (Eds.), Chinese Spoken Language Processing. XXIV, 805 pages. 2006. (Sublibrary LNAI).

Vol. 4273: I. Cruz, S. Decker, D. Allemang, C. Preist, D. Schwabe, P. Mika, M. Uschold, L. Aroyo (Eds.), The Semantic Web - ISWC 2006. XXIV, 1001 pages. 2006.

Vol. 4272: P. Havinga, M. Lijding, N. Meratnia, M. Wegdam (Eds.), Smart Sensing and Context. XI, 267 pages. 2006.

Vol. 4271: F.V. Fomin (Ed.), Graph-Theoretic Concepts in Computer Science. XIII, 358 pages. 2006.

Vol. 4270: H. Zha, Z. Pan, H. Thwaites, A.C. Addison, M. Forte (Eds.), Interactive Technologies and Sociotechnical Systems. XVI, 547 pages. 2006.

Vol. 4269: R. State, S. van der Meer, D. O'Sullivan, T. Pfeifer (Eds.), Large Scale Management of Distributed Systems. XIII, 282 pages. 2006.

Vol. 4268: G. Parr, D. Malone, M. Ó Foghlú (Eds.), Autonomic Principles of IP Operations and Management. XIII, 237 pages. 2006.

Vol. 4267: A. Helmy, B. Jennings, L. Murphy, T. Pfeifer (Eds.), Autonomic Management of Mobile Multimedia Services. XIII, 257 pages. 2006.

Vol. 4266: H. Yoshiura, K. Sakurai, K. Rannenberg, Y. Murayama, S. Kawamura (Eds.), Advances in Information and Computer Security. XIII, 438 pages. 2006.

Vol. 4265: L. Todorovski, N. Lavrač, K.P. Jantke (Eds.), Discovery Science. XIV, 384 pages. 2006. (Sublibrary LNAI).

Vol. 4264: J.L. Balcázar, P.M. Long, F. Stephan (Eds.), Algorithmic Learning Theory. XIII, 393 pages. 2006. (Sublibrary LNAI).

Vol. 4263: A. Levi, E. Savaş, H. Yenigün, S. Balcısoy, Y. Saygın (Eds.), Computer and Information Sciences – ISCIS 2006. XXIII, 1084 pages. 2006.

Vol. 4262: K. Havelund, M. Núñez, G. Roşu, B. Wolff (Eds.), Formal Approaches to Software Testing and Runtime Verification. VIII, 255 pages. 2006.

Vol. 4261: Y. Zhuang, S. Yang, Y. Rui, Q. He (Eds.), Advances in Multimedia Information Processing - PCM 2006. XXII, 1040 pages. 2006.

Vol. 4260: Z. Liu, J. He (Eds.), Formal Methods and Software Engineering. XII, 778 pages. 2006.

Vol. 4259: S. Greco, Y. Hata, S. Hirano, M. Inuiguchi, S. Miyamoto, H.S. Nguyen, R. Słowiński (Eds.), Rough Sets and Current Trends in Computing. XXII, 951 pages. 2006. (Sublibrary LNAI).

Vol. 4258: G. Danezis, P. Golle (Eds.), Privacy Enhancing Technologies. VIII, 431 pages. 2006.